Marketing | An Introduction

7/e

Gary Armstrong
University of North Carolina

Philip Kotler
Northwestern University

PEARSON

Prentice
Hall

Upper Saddle River, New Jersey 07458

Library of Congress Cataloging-in-Publication Data

Armstrong, Gary.

   Marketing : an introduction / Gary Armstrong, Philip Kotler.--7th ed.
         p.   cm.
   Kotler's name appears first on the earlier ed.
   Includes bibliographical references and indexes.
   ISBN 0-13-142410-6
 1. Marketing.   I. Kotler, Philip.   II. Title.
   HF5415.K625 2004
   658.8--dc22

                                          2003060906

Acquisitions Editor: Katie Stevens
VP/Editorial Director: Jeff Shelstad
Editorial Assistant: Rebecca Cummings
Assistant Editor: Melissa Pellerano
AVP/Executive Marketing Manager: Michelle O'Brien
Marketing Assistant: Amanda Fisher
Senior Managing Editor (Production): Judy Leale
Production Editor: Cindy Durand
Production Assistant: Joe DeProspero
Manufacturing Buyer: Diane Peirano
Design Manager: Maria Lange
Designer: Jill Little
Cover Illustration/Photo: N. Gleis/Raw Talent Photo
Image Manager: Keri Jean Miksza
Photo Researcher: Sheila Norman
Image Permission Coordinator: Charles Morris
Manager, Print Production: Christy Mahon
Composition/Full-Service Project Management: Lynn Steines, Carlisle Communications
Printer/Binder: Courier/Kendallville

Credits and acknowledgments borrowed from other sources and reproduced,with permission,
in this textbook appear on the appropriate page within text; photo credits appear on page CR1.

Pearson Education LTD.
Pearson Education Singapore, Pte., Ltd
Pearson Education, Canada, Ltd
Pearson Education-Japan

Pearson Education Australia PTY, Limited
Pearson Education North Asia Ltd
Pearson Educaión de Mexico, S.A. de C.V.
Pearson Education Malaysia, Pte. Ltd

10 9 8 7 6 5 4 3 2
ISBN 0-13-142410-6

To Kathy, Betty, Mandy, Matt, K.C., Keri, and Delaney;
Nancy, Amy, Melissa, and Jessica

About the Authors

As a team, Gary Armstrong and Philip Kotler provide a blend of skills uniquely suited to writing an introductory marketing text. Professor Armstrong is an award-winning teacher of undergraduate business students. Professor Kotler is one of the world's leading authorities on marketing. Together they make the complex world of marketing practical, approachable, and enjoyable.

Gary Armstrong is Crist W. Blackwell Distinguished Professor of Undergraduate Education in the Kenan-Flagler Business School at the University of North Carolina at Chapel Hill. He holds undergraduate and masters degrees in business from Wayne State University in Detroit, and he received his Ph.D. in marketing from Northwestern University. Dr. Armstrong has contributed numerous articles to leading business journals. As a consultant and researcher, he has worked with many companies on marketing research, sales management, and marketing strategy. But Professor Armstrong's first love is teaching. His Blackwell Distinguished Professorship is the only permanent endowed professorship for distinguished undergraduate teaching at the University of North Carolina at Chapel Hill. He has been very active in the teaching and administration of Kenan-Flagler's undergraduate program. His recent administrative posts include Chair of the Marketing Faculty, Associate Director of the Undergraduate Business Program, Director of the Business Honors Program, and others. He works closely with business student groups and has received several campus-wide and business school teaching awards. He is the only repeat recipient of the school's highly regarded Award for Excellence in Undergraduate Teaching, which he won three times. In 2004, Professor Armstrong received the UNC Board of Governors Award for Excellence in Teaching, the highest teaching honor bestowed at the University of North Carolina at Chapel Hill.

Philip Kotler is the S. C. Johnson & Son Distinguished Professor of International Marketing at the Kellogg Graduate School of Management, Northwestern University. He received his master's degree at the University of Chicago and his Ph.D. at M.I.T., both in economics. Dr. Kotler is author of *Marketing Management: Analysis, Planning, Implementation, and Control* (Prentice Hall), now in its eleventh edition and the most widely used marketing textbook in graduate schools of business. He has authored several successful books and has written over 100 articles for leading journals. He is the only three-time winner of the coveted Alpha Kappa Psi award for the best annual article in the *Journal of Marketing*. Dr. Kotler's numerous major honors include the Paul D. Converse Award given by the American Marketing Association to honor "outstanding contributions to science in marketing" and the Stuart Henderson Britt Award as Marketer of the Year. He was named the first recipient of two major awards: the Distinguished Marketing Educator of the Year Award given by the American Marketing Association and the Philip Kotler Award for Excellence in Health Care Marketing presented by the Academy for Health Care Services Marketing. He has also received the Charles Coolidge Parlin Award which each year honors an outstanding leader in the field of marketing. In 1995, he received the Marketing Educator of the Year Award from Sales and Marketing Executives International. Dr. Kotler has served as chairman of the College on Marketing of the Institute of Management Sciences (TIMS) and a director of the American Marketing Association. He has received honorary doctorate degrees from DePaul University, the University of Zurich, and the Athens University of Economics and Business. He has consulted with many major U.S. and foreign companies on marketing strategy.

Brief Contents

Contents

PART FOUR | Extending Marketing 478

Welcome to the Seventh Edition of
Marketing: An Introduction!

As we present this new edition, we want to take a moment to thank you and the millions of other marketing students and professors who have used our texts over the years. You've helped to make this text an international best seller and Prentice Hall Business Publishing's book of the year! Thank you.

Our goal with the seventh edition is to create an even more effective text from which to learn about and teach marketing. Most students learning marketing, whether majors or non-majors, want a complete picture of basic marketing principles and practices. However, they don't want to drown in a sea of details or to be overwhelmed by marketing's complexities. They want a text that's complete yet easy to manage and master.

The seventh edition of *Marketing: An Introduction* strikes a careful balance between depth of coverage and ease of learning. The seventh edition presents the latest marketing thinking. It builds upon a marketing framework which positions marketing simply as the art and science of creating value *for* customers in order to capture value *from* customers in return. It explains how marketing works with other company departments—such as accounting, information technology, finance, operations, and human resources—and with marketing partners outside the company to jointly bring value to customers.

Finally, the seventh edition takes a practical approach—concepts are applied through examples in which well-known and lesser-known companies assess and solve marketing challenges. An entirely new and comprehensive set of teaching resources, both print and digital, has been developed to support this edition. Our goal is this: offer innovative supplements that simplify—that are easier to find, access, manage, and use. You won't have to sift through boxes and books to find what you need.

In all, we think that this edition of *Marketing: An Introduction* is the best edition yet. We hope that you'll enjoy your journey down the road to learning marketing. So buckle up, and let's get rolling!

Gary Armstrong
University of North Carolina at Chapel Hill

Philip Kotler
Northwestern University

Preface

The seventh edition of *Marketing: An Introduction* presents an innovative framework for understanding and learning about marketing. Today's marketing is all about building profitable customer relationships. It starts with understanding consumer needs and wants, deciding which target markets the organization can serve best, and developing a compelling value proposition by which the organization can attract, keep, and grow targeted consumers. If the organization does these things well, it will reap the rewards in terms of market share, profits, and customer equity. Simply put, marketing is the art and science of creating value *for* customers in order to capture value *from* customers in return. From beginning to end, the seventh edition of *Marketing: An Introduction* presents and develops this customer-relationships/customer-equity framework.

What's New: Customer Value Is the Key

Marketing: An Introduction has been thoroughly revised to reflect the major trends and forces that are changing marketing in this new age of customer relationships. It offers important new thinking and expanded coverage on:

1. A "customer-relationships/customer-equity" framework:

■ *The customer relationship management/customer equity framework* is established from the start of the text, in the completely revised Chapter 1, *Marketing: Managing Profitable Customer Relationships*, and carried forward throughout the text.

■ The framework is presented in a five-step model of the marketing process, a model that details how marketing creates customer value and captures value in return. This model can be found in simplified form on page 7 and expanded form on page 33.

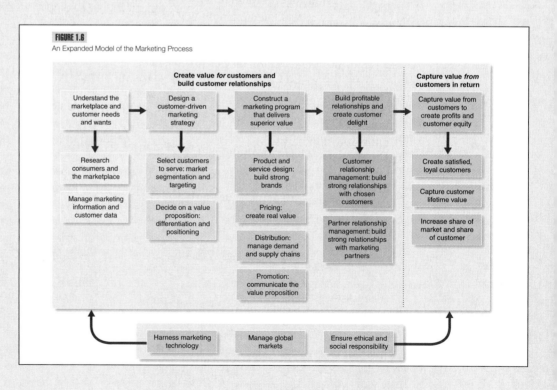

FIGURE 1.6
An Expanded Model of the Marketing Process

- The greatly revised opening chapter includes a major new section on *Building Customer Relationships,* which covers customer relationship management, the changing nature of customer relationships, and partner relationship management. The chapter also features a major new section on *Capturing Value from Customers,* which addresses topics such as building customer loyalty and retention, growing "share of customer," identifying customer relationship groups, and managing customer equity.

- The managing-customer-relationships theme continues in Chapter 2, *Company and Marketing Strategy: Partnering to Build Customer Relationships.* This revised chapter places profitable customer relationships at the center of marketing strategy and the marketing mix. This chapter also extends the corollary concept of *partner relationship* management, working closely with marketing partners inside and outside the company to build strong customer relationships.

2. Brand strategy and managing brand equity:

- Chapter 6, *Segmentation, Targeting, and Positioning: Building the Right Relationships with the Right Customers,* presents new discussions on developing brand positioning statements and brand positioning maps.

- Chapter 7, *Product, Services, and Branding Strategies*, now includes a separate and expanded section—*Branding Strategy: Building Strong Brands.* The new section includes new material on brand equity and brand value, brand positioning, managing brands, and re-branding.

3. Marketing technology and marketing in a socially responsible way around the globe:

- *Marketing technologies in the digital age.* Technological advances have created a digital age, which continues to have a dramatic impact on both buyers and the marketers who serve them. New coverage is integrated chapter-by-chapter. In addition, Chapter 14, *Marketing in the New Digital Age,* explores the exciting strategies and tactics that firms are applying in order to prosper in today's high-tech environment.

- *Global marketing.* Coverage is integrated chapter-by-chapter. Plus, Chapter 15, *Global Marketing,* focuses on global marketing considerations. The globalization versus Americanization issue is highlighted in this chapter.

- *Marketing ethics, environmentalism, and social responsibility.* Chapter 16 focuses on *Marketing and Society: Social Marketing and Marketing Ethics* and new coverage is integrated chapter-by-chapter. Chapter 16, *Marketing and Society: Social Responsibility and Marketing Ethics,* highlights Nike's approach to social responsibility and how some companies maximize profits while helping to save the planet.

Additional Major Themes Include:

- value propositions
- supplier development
- database marketing
- dynamic pricing
- buzz marketing
- environmental sustainability

- supply chain management
- direct marketing
- value pricing
- integrated marketing communications
- Web selling
- marketing and diversity

Marketing In The Real World

Marketing: An Introduction tells the stories that reveal the excitement behind these and other modern marketing successes:

- How NASCAR creates avidly loyal fans by selling not just stock car racing but a high-octane, totally involving experience

- How Southwest Airlines flies high on the wings of its classic "less-for-much-less" value proposition

- How Kmart's BlueLight strategy started a price war only Wal-Mart could win

- How MTV moved into the global brand elite by making music the universal language

- How Wal-Mart became the world's largest company by delivery on a simple promise— "Always Low Prices, *Always*"

- How Pottery Barn succeeded in selling not just home furnishings but an entire lifestyle

- How Office Depot transformed itself from a traditional "brick-and-mortar" marketer to a full-fledged "click-and-mortar" marketer

- How Microsoft develops a passion for innovation and its quest for "the Next Big Thing"

- How Google flourished despite the dot-com meltdown

- How Wholesaler Grainger became the biggest market leader you have never heard of

- How Loreal's skillful use of cultural nuances helped it become "the United Nations of Beauty."

Marketing at Work 6.1

Pottery Barn: Oh, What a Lifestyle!

Shortly after Hadley MacLean got married, she and her husband, Doug, agreed that their old bed had had to go. It was a mattress and box spring on a cheap metal frame, a relic of Doug's Harvard days. But Hadley never anticipated how tough it would be to find a new bed. "We couldn't find anything we liked, even though we were willing to spend the money," says Hadley, a 31-year-old marketing director. It turned out to be much more than just finding a piece of furniture at the right price. It was a matter of emotion: They needed a bed that meshed with their lifestyle—with who they are and where they are going.

The couple finally ended up at the Pottery Barn on Boston's upscale Newbury Street, where Doug fell in love with a mahogany sleigh bed that Hadley had spotted in the store's catalog. The couple was so pleased with how great it looked in their Dutch Colonial home that they hurried back to the store for a set of end tables. And then they bought a quilt. And a mirror for the living room. And some stools for the dining room. "We got kind of addicted," Hadley confesses.

The MacLeans aren't alone. Pottery Barn's smart yet accessible product mix, seductive merchandising, and first-rate customer service have made it the front-runner in the fragmented home furnishings and housewares industry—not just because of the products that it sells, but also because of the connections that it makes with customers. Pottery Barn does more than just sell home furnishings. It sells an entire lifestyle.

Three thousand miles away from Hadley MacLean's home in Massachusetts, Laura Alber is obsessed with a towel. A tall, slim blond with pale-blue eyes and no m... ...could

be the poster child for the Pottery Barn lifestyle. The 34-year-old California mother of two says that she enjoys entertaining, describes herself as living "holistically," and has just bought the company's Westport sectional sofa, with its kid-resistant twill slipcovers. She also happens to be Pottery Barn's president. "Feel how great this is," says Alber, pulling a large white bath towel from a stack. "It's thick, it's got a beautiful dobby [the woven band a few inches from the towel's edge], it's highly absorbent, and it's $24. I can say with great confidence that you can't top this." To some merchants, a towel is just a towel. But to Alber, the towel is a fluffy icon of the lifestyle to which Pottery Barn customers aspire: upscale but casual, active but laid back, family-

Pottery Barn sells more than just home furnishings; it sells all that its customers aspire to be. ... offers idyllic scenes of the perfect childhood at Pottery Barn Kids; trendy, fashion... expression at PB Teen; and an upscale yet casual, family- and frien... ...flashy Pottery Barn.

Many in-text elements help link the classroom to the real-world of marketing:

Chapter-opening vignettes. Each chapter starts with an exciting, real-world marketing story that introduces the chapter material.

Marketing at Work exhibits. Additional examples demonstrating marketing in action are highlighted in Marketing at Work exhibits throughout the text.

Video cases. Every chapter is supplemented with a written case that also has a video component to bring the material to life. These cases are located in Appendix 1 and are correlated by chapter subject. Teaching notes are available for instructors in the instructor edition of the text, in the instructor's manual, and online at www.prenhall.com/marketing.

Keys To Success: Our Learning Approach

Learning the aids located throughout each chapter help students review, link, and apply marketing concepts:

Road Map: Previewing the Concepts. A section at the beginning of each chapter briefly previews chapter concepts, links them with previous chapter concepts, outlines chapter-learning objectives, and introduces the chapter-opening vignette.

Speed Bump: Linking the Concepts. "Concept checks" are inserted at key points in each chapter as "speed bumps" to slow students down to be certain they are grasping and applying key concepts and links. Each speed bump consists of a brief statement and a few concept and application questions. By utilizing the Study Guide optional supplement, students can review feedback on the Speed Bump concept checks for reinforcement.

> **SPEED BUMP**
>
> ### Linking the Concepts
>
> Stop here for a moment and stretch your legs. What have you learned so far about marketing? For the moment, set aside the more formal definitions we've examined and try to develop your own understanding of marketing.
>
> - In your own words, what is marketing? Write down your definition. Does your definition include key concepts such as customer value and relationships?
> - What does marketing mean to you? How does it affect your daily life?
> - What marketing management philosophy appears to guide NASCAR? How does this compare with the marketing philosophy that guides Johnson & Johnson? Can you think of another company guided by a very different philosophy? Is there one marketing management philosophy that's best for all companies?

Rest Stop: Reviewing the Concepts. A summary of key concepts at the end of each chapter reviews chapter concepts and summarizes each chapter objective.

Navigating the Key Terms. A list of the chapter's key terms.

Travel Log. "Discussing the Issues" and "Applications Questions" help students keep track of and apply what they've studied in the chapter.

✳ **NEW Under the Hood: Focus on Technology.** Application exercises and questions focus attention and discussion on important marketing technologies in this digital age.

✳ **NEW Focus on Ethics.** Situation descriptions and questions highlight important issues in marketing ethics. This feature can be used to begin classroom discussions or as a basis for group projects.

✳ **NEW Marketing Plan.** New to this edition—a sample marketing plan with annotations of key highlights is now included as Appendix 2.

Glossary and Indexes. At the end of the book, an extensive glossary provides quick reference to the key terms found in the book. Subject, company, and author indexes reference all information and examples in the book.

APPENDIX 2 Marketing Plan

▰▰ The Marketing Plan: An Introduction

As a marketer, you'll need a good marketing plan to provide direction and focus for your brand, product, or company. With a detailed plan, any business will be better prepared to launch a new product or build sales for existing products. Nonprofit organizations also use marketing plans to guide their fundraising and outreach efforts. Even government agencies put together marketing plans for initiatives such as building public awareness of proper nutrition and stimulating area tourism.

The Purpose and Content of a Marketing Plan

Unlike a business plan, which offers a broad overview of the entire organization's mission, objectives, strategy, and resource allocation, a marketing plan has a more limited scope. It serves to document how the organization's strategic objectives will be achieved through specific marketing strategies and tactics, with the customer as the starting point. It is also linked to the plans of other departments within the organization. Suppose a marketing plan calls for selling 200,000 units annually. The production department must gear up to make that many units, the finance department must have funding available to cover the expenses, the human resources department must be ready to hire and train staff, and so on. Without the appropriate level of organizational support and resources, no marketing plan can succeed.

Although the exact length and layout will vary from company to company, a marketing plan usually contains the sections described in Table X on page Y. Smaller businesses may create shorter or less formal marketing plans, whereas corporations frequently require highly structured marketing plans. To guide implementation effectively, every part of the plan must be described in considerable detail. Sometimes a company will post its marketing plan on an internal Web site, which allows managers and employees in different locations to consult specific [...] and collaborate [...] tions or changes.

toward objectives and identify areas for improvement if results fall short of projections. Finally, marketers use marketing research to learn more about their customers' requirements, expectations, perceptions, and satisfaction levels. This deeper understanding provides a foundation for building competitive advantage through well-informed segmenting, targeting, and positioning decisions. Thus, the marketing plan should outline what marketing research will be conducted and how the findings will be applied.

The Role of Relationships

The marketing plan shows how the company will establish and maintain profitable customer relationships. In the process, however, it also shapes a number of internal and external relationships. First, it affects how marketing personnel work with each other and with other departments to deliver value and satisfy customers. Second, it affects how the company works with suppliers, distributors, and strategic alliance partners to achieve the objectives listed in the plan. Third, it influences the company's dealings with other stakeholders, including government regulators, the media, and the community at large. All of these relationships are important to the organization's success, so they should be considered when a marketing plan is being developed.

From Marketing Plan to Marketing Action

Companies generally create yearly marketing plans, although some plans cover a longer period. Marketers start planning well in advance of the implementation date to allow time for marketing research, thorough analysis, management review, and coordination between departments. Then, after each action program begins, marketers monitor ongoing results, compare them with projections, analyze any differences, and take corrective steps as needed. Some marketers design contingency plans, as in the sample plan below, for implementation if certain conditions emerge. Because of inevitable and sometimes unpredictable environmental changes, marketers must be ready to update and adapt marketing plans at any time.

Teaching and Learning Support

A successful marketing course requires more than a well-written book. Today's classroom requires a dedicated teacher and a fully-integrated teaching package. A total package of teaching and learning supplements extends this edition's emphasis on effective teaching and learning. The following aids support *Marketing: An Introduction*:

For Instructors

What's new? Easier access to more innovative resources!

What's Online?

✳ **NEW Instructor's Resource Center** (www.prenhall.com/marketing)—This password protected site is accessible from the catalog page for *Marketing: An Introduction*, 7e and hosts the following resources:

- ▪ **Instructor's Manual**—View this rich resource chapter-by-chapter or download the entire manual as a .zip file.
- ▪ **Test Item File**—View questions chapter-by-chapter or download the entire test item file as a .zip file.
- ▪ **TestGen EQ for PC/MAC**—Download the test-generating software preloaded with seventh edition test questions and a user's manual.
- ▪ **Image bank**—Access most of the images and illustrations featured in the text. Animated figures are also provided. Ideal for PowerPoint customization.

✳ **NEW Three sets of PowerPoints**—Basic, Image/Media Rich, and PRS.

- ▪ **Basic** is ideal for users who prefer a manageable file size for printing, posting online and customization. These slides won't require the time-intensive activity of 'stripping out' preloaded animation and images. The slides are provided via our Instructor's Resource Center (online and CD-ROM).
- ▪ **Image/Media Rich** is ideal for users that want a 'turnkey' solution that includes photos, ads, and figures from in and out of the text. Links to video and Web sites are embedded throughout. NOTE: Due to its higher file size and video clips, the Image/Media Rich set is provided only on the Instructor's Resource CD-ROM.
- ▪ **Personal Response System (PRS)** is ideal for professors that want to activate the classroom. These PowerPoints are designed for in-class use with EduCue's Personal Response Transmitter system.

✳ **NEW OneKey (ISBN: 0-13-142606-0)—A student access code can be shrink-wrapped FREE with new copies of this textbook.** Prentice Hall's OneKey site is all you and your students need for anytime online access to interactive materials that enhance this text. Resources hosted on OneKey are listed in the *Student Resources* section of this Preface. Request Value Pack ISBN: 0-13-161585-8 on your book order.

What's on CD-ROM or DVD?

- ▪ **Instructor's Resource CD-ROM (ISBN: 0-13-142596-X)**—With a new interface and searchable database, sorting through and locating specific resources has never been easier. Includes all of the supplements that are hosted on our online Instructor's Resource Center; however, the Image/Media Rich PowerPoint set is provided only on this CD-ROM due to its larger file size and embedded video clips.

- **Test Gen EQ for PC/MAC (ISBN: 0-13-142598-6)**—This PC and Mac compatible test generating software, new for the seventh edition, is more powerful and easier to use. It's preloaded with all of the questions from the new Test Item File and allows users to manually or randomly view test bank questions and drag-and-drop them to create a test. Add or modify testbank questions using the built in Question Editor, print up to twenty five variations of a single test, deliver the test on a local area network using the built-in QuizMaster feature, and much more. Technical support is available at media.support@pearsoned.com or 1-800-6-PROFESSOR between 8:00 a.m.–5:00 p.m. (C.S.T.)

- ✳ NEW **Videos on DVD (ISBN: 0-13-147203-8)**—Every video in the new video library was filmed in 2002 or 2003. Professionally produced with the help of BusinessNOW. This is the most current video library available. These segments correlate with the *all new* chapter video cases at the end of the text. Segments are also available on VHS (ISBN: 0-13-142603-6) and Video teaching notes are bound in the Instructor's Edition of this text, within the Instructor's Manual and online as part of the Instructor's Resource Center. The 16 companies featured are:

Subaru	Dunkin' Donuts
Nike	Burke
Sony (Metreon)	Marriott
Accenture	eGo Bikes
Nextel	Snapple
Federated Department Stores	AFLAC
Motorola	IWON
Starbucks	Honest Tea

What's in Print:

- **Test Item File (ISBN: 0-13-142594-3)**—Features over two thousand questions written specifically for the seventh edition. Multiple choice, true/false, and essay questions are organized by level of difficulty and include page references.

- **Instructor's Manual (ISBN: 0-13-142593-5)**—Your handbook for this text includes suggestions for using features and elements of the text, and a new *Great Ideas* section extends the text resources to provide a springboard for innovative learning experiences in the classroom.

- **Video Notes**—Now bound in the special Instructor's Edition (ISBN: 0-13-161536-X) for easy access and within the Instructor's Manual.

- ✳ NEW **Study Guide (ISBN: 0-13-147028-0)**—See *Student Resources* for information about this learning aid for students. Available FREE when ordered shrink-wrapped with this text. Request VALUE PACK ISBN: 0-13-132153-6 on your book order.

For Students

What's Online?

- ✳ NEW **OneKey—A student access code is available FREE when shrink-wrapped with this text.** Prentice Hall's new OneKey site is all you need for anytime access to supplemental materials that enhance this text. Your instructor must specify this special offer when placing his/her book order. Codes may be purchased separately at **www.prenhall.com/ marketing**. OneKey for *Marketing: An Introduction,* 7e, includes:

  - **Marketing ToolKit**—Created by Scott Follows, a marketing professor at Acadia University, these innovative self-review modules allow you to interact with and apply 18 specific marketing concepts, including pricing, B2B, retailing, and services.

- **ADventure exercises**—Features exercises that can be used with our online database of print ads.

- **Interactive and animated figures and tables**—Many of the illustrations that appear in this book are interactive or animated when viewed within OneKey.

- **MarketingUpdates powered by Research Navigator**—Now you have easy access to current marketing news and articles from leading periodicals and journals. What's more is the news feeds are mapped to the text's chapters, and every month twenty new articles are added per chapter. Also includes access to **www.researchnavigator.com**, which features *New York Times* and *Financial Times* archives, EBSCO database, and more.

- **Self Study Quizzes**—OneKey hosts a wealth of self-study quizzes so you can test yourself along the way. These quizzes are in addition to the review material posted on the FREE companion website: **www.prenhall.com/kotler.**

What's on CD-ROM or DVD?

- **Marketing Plan Handbook with Marketing PlanPro™ (ISBN: 0-13-175947-7)**—Instructor's can choose to have this handbook that includes the popular Marketing PlanPro software shrink-wrapped with this text at a deep discount.

- **Student Videos on DVD (ISBN: 0-13-147203-8)**—Contains the 16 new video segments that support the video cases within the text. Instructors can have this DVD shrink-wrapped FREE with new copies of this text. Not available for stand-alone sales.

What's in Print:

- ✳ NEW **Study Guide (ISBN: 0-13-147028-0)**—This new study guide with flashcards is delivered in one compact binder and can be packaged FREE with new copies of this text. Your instructor must specify this special offer when placing his/her book order. This item can also be purchased separately at **www.prenhall.com/marketing.**

- **DK Essential Manager Series**—These compact, full color reference guides by award winning publisher Dorling Kindersley are being offered for a limited time with Prentice Hall Marketing textbooks. Topics include *Making Presentations* and *Marketing Effectively.* Your instructor must specify this special offer when placing his/her book-order.

ACKNOWLEDGMENTS

No book is the work only of its authors. We owe much to the pioneers of marketing who first identified its major issues and developed its concepts and techniques. Our thanks also goes to our colleagues at the Kenan-Flagler Business School, University of North Carolina at Chapel Hill, and at the J. L. Kellogg Graduate School of Management, Northwestern University, for ideas and suggestions. We owe special thanks to Mandy Roylance for her constant and invaluable advice, assistance, and involvement throughout every phase of the project. Thanks also go to Dawn Iacobucci, Northwestern University, for her great work in preparing high-quality video cases; to Andrea Meyer for her able development assistance; and to Kevin Gwinner, Kansas State University, for his skillful development of end-of-chapter material. In addition, we thank Marian Wood for help in creating the marketing plan for this edition.

Many reviewers at other colleges and universities provided valuable comments and suggestions for this and previous editions. We are indebted to the following colleagues: Ron Lennon, Barry University; Alan Brokaw, Michigan Technological University; Mernoush Banton, University of Miami; Gordon Snider, California Poly-Technical School of San Luis Obispo; Karen Stone, Southern New Hampshire University; Martha Leham, Diablo Valley College; Thomas Drake, University of Miami; Rebecca Ratner, University of North Carolina—Chapel Hill; and Steve Hoeffler, University of North Carolina–Chapel Hill.

Seventh Edition Reviewers:

Rajshri Agarwal, Iowa State University

S. Allen Broyles, University of Tennessee

Mee-Shew Cheung, University of Tennessee

Renee Florsheim, Loyola Marymount University

Charles Goeldner, University of Colorado, Boulder

Carol Gwin, Baylor University

Richard Hansen, Ferris State University

Kathy Illing, Greenville Technical College

Jerry L. Thomas, San Jose State University

Merv Yeagle, University of Maryland

Robert Jones, California State University, Fullerton

Ann Kuzma, Minnesota State University, Mankato

Mark Mitchell, University of South Carolina, Spartanburg

William Rodgers, St. Cloud State University

Jeff Schmidt, U. Illinois, Champaign-Urbana

Roberta Schultz, Western Michigan University

Donald Self, Auburn University, Montgomery

Steve Taylor, Illinois State University

Ron Young, Kalamazoo Valley Community College

Former Reviewers:

Gemmy Allen, Mountain View College

Abi Almeer, Nova University

Arvid Anderson, University of North Carolina, Wilmington

Mernoush Banton, University of Miami

Arnold Bornfriend, Worcester State College

Alan Brokaw, Michigan Technological University

Donald Boyer, Jefferson College

Alejandro Camacho, University of Georgia

William Carner, University of Texas, Austin

Gerald Cavallo, Fairfield University

Lucette Comer, Florida International University

Ron Cooley, South Suburban College

Michael Conard, Teikyo Post University

June Cotte, University of Connecticut

Ronald Cutter, Southwest Missouri State University

John de Young, Cumberland County College

Lee Dickson, Florida International University

Mike Dotson, Appalachian State University

Peter Doukas, Westchester Community College

Thomas Drake, University of Miami

David Forlani, University of North Florida

Jack Forrest, Middle Tennessee State University

John Gauthier, Gateway Technical Institute

Eugene Gilbert, California State University, Sacramento

Diana Grewel, University of Miami

Esther Headley, Wichita State University

Sandra Heusinkveld, Normandale Community College

Steve Hoeffler, University of North Carolina, Chapel Hill

James Jeck, North Carolina State University

Eileen Keller, Kent State University

James Kennedy, Navarro College

Eric Kulp, Middlesex Community College

Ed Laube, Macomb Community College

Martha Leham, Diablo Valley College

Ron Lennon, Barry University

Gregory Lincoln, Westchester Community College

John Lloyd, Monroe Community College

Dorothy Maas, Delaware County Community College

Ajay Manrai, University of Delaware

Lalita Manrai, University of Delaware

James McAlexander, Oregon State University

Donald McBane, Clemson University

Debbora Meflin-Bullock, California State Polytechnic University

Randall Mertz, Mesa Community College

Herbert Miller, University of Texas, Austin

Veronica Miller, Mt. St. Mary's College

Joan Mizis, St. Louis Community College

Melissa Moore, University of Connecticut

Robert Moore, University of Connecticut

William Morgenroth, University of South Carolina, Columbia

Linda Moroble, Dallas County Community College

Sandra Moulton, Technical College of Alamance

Jim Muney, Valdosta State

Lee Neuman, Bucks County Community College

Dave Olsen, North Hennepin Community College

Thomas Paczkowski, Cayuga Community College

George Paltz, Erie Community College

Tammy Pappas, Eastern Michigan University

Alison Pittman, Brevard Community College

Lana Podolak, Community College of Beaver County

Joel Porrish, Springfield College

Robert L. Powell, Gloucester County College

Eric Pratt, New Mexico State University

Rebecca Ratner, University of North Carolina, Chapel Hill

Robert Ross, Wichita State University

Andre San Augustine, University of Arizona

Dwight Scherban, Central Connecticut College

Eberhard Scheuing, St. John's University

Pamela Schindler, Wittenburg University

Raymond Schwartz, Montclair State University

Raj Sethuraman, University of Iowa

Reshima H. Shah, University of Pittsburgh

Jack Sheeks, Broward Community College

Herbert Sherman, Long Island University, Southhampton

Dee Smith, Lansing Community College

Gordon Snider, California Poly-Technical School of San Luis Obispo

Jim Spiers, Arizona State University

Karen Stone, Southern New Hampshire University

Peter Stone, Spartanburg Technical College

Ira Teich, Long Island University

Donna Tillman, California State Polytechnic University

Andrea Weeks, Fashion Institute of Design and Merchandising

Summer White, Massachusetts Bay Community College

Bill Worley, Allan Hancock College

We also owe a great deal to the people at Prentice Hall who helped develop this book. Marketing Editors Katie Stevens and Bruce Kaplan provided caring and valuable advice and assistance through several phases of this revision. To Michelle O'Brien, we thank you for your energy and creative efforts in marketing our text. We also thank the members of our outstanding production team at Prentice Hall for their expertise in taking a rough manuscript and creating a beautiful, living text: Judy Leale, Senior Managing Editor; Cindy Durand and Virginia Somma, Production Editors; Jill Little, Designer; and Keri Miksza, Image Manager.

Finally, we owe many thanks to our families for all of their support and encouragement — Kathy, Betty, Mandy, Matt, KC, Keri, and Delaney from the Armstrong family and Nancy, Amy, Melissa, and Jessica from the Kotler family. To them, we dedicate this book.

Gary Armstrong
Philip Kotler

Marketing: An Introduction
7/e

amazon.com.

Dear Customers,

The American Customer Satisfaction Index is, by far, the most authoritative and widely followed survey of customer satisfaction. Last year, Amazon.com received an ACSI score of 84, the highest ever recorded -- not just online, not just in retailing -- but the highest score ever recorded in any service industry. This year, Amazon.com scored an 88 -- again the highest score ever recorded in any service industry.

In ACSI's words:

"Amazon.com continues to show remarkably high levels of customer satisfaction. With a score of 88 (up 5%), it is generating satisfaction at a level unheard of in the service industry...Can customer satisfaction for Amazon climb more? The latest ACSI data suggest that it is indeed possible. Both service and the value proposition offered by Amazon have increased at a steep rate".

Thank you very much for being a customer, and we'll work even harder for you in the future. (We already have lots of customer experience improvements planned for 2003.)

On behalf of everyone at Amazon.com,

Sincerely,

Jeff Bezos
Founder & CEO

■ *After studying this chapter, you should be able to*

1. *Define* marketing and outline the steps in the marketing process **2.** *Explain* the importance of understanding customers and the marketplace, and identify the five core marketplace concepts **3.** *Identify* the key elements of a customer-driven marketing strategy, and discuss the marketing management orientations that guide marketing strategy **4.** *Discuss* customer relationship management, and identify strategies for creating value *for* customers and capturing value *from* customers in return **5.** *Describe* the major trends and forces that are changing the marketing landscape in this new age of relationships

Marketing: Managing Profitable Customer Relationships

1

ROAD MAP | Previewing the Concepts

Welcome to the exciting world of marketing! In this chapter, to start you off, we will introduce you to the basic concepts. We'll start with a simple question: What *is* marketing? Simply put, marketing is building profitable customer relationships. The aim of marketing is to create value for customers and to capture value in return. Chapter 1 is organized around five steps in the marketing process—from understanding customer needs, to designing customer-driven marketing strategies and constructing marketing programs, to building customer relationships and capturing value for the firm. Throughout the chapter, we focus on the most important concept of modern marketing—managing customer relationships. Understanding these basic concepts, and forming your own ideas about what they really mean to you, will give you a solid foundation for all that follows.

To set the stage, let's look first at Amazon.com. In only a few years, Amazon.com has blossomed from an obscure dot-com upstart into one of the best-known names on the Internet. In the process, it has forever changed the practice of marketing. It pioneered the use of Web technology to build strong, one-to-one customer relationships based on creating genuine customer value. The only problem: This seemingly successful company has yet to prove that it can turn long-term profits. As you read on, ask yourself: Will Amazon.com eventually become the Wal-Mart of the Internet? Or will it become just another interactive catalog company?

Chances are, when you think of shopping on the Web, you think of Amazon.com. Amazon.com first opened its virtual doors in mid-July 1995, selling books out of founder Jeff Bezos's garage in suburban Seattle. It still sells books—by the millions. But it now sells products in a dozen other categories as well: from music, videos, consumer electronics, and computers to tools and hardware, kitchen and housewares, apparel, and toys and baby products. "We have the Earth's Biggest Selection," declares the company's Web site.

In less than a decade, Amazon.com has become one of the best-known names on the Net. In perfecting the art of online selling, it has also rewritten the rules of marketing. Its most ardent fans view Amazon.com as *the* model for New Economy businesses of the twenty-first century. If any dot-com can make it big, they believe, Amazon.com can.

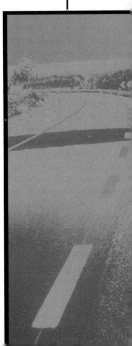

But not everything has clicked smoothly for Amazon.com. If you believe the skeptics, the company will never become a workable business. Attracting customers and sales hasn't been a problem. Over the past six years, Amazon.com's customer base has grown more than 23-fold, to 35 million customers in more than 220 countries. Sales have rocketed from a modest $15 million a year in 1996 to more than $4 billion today, and they are growing by more than 20 percent per year. Some analysts confidently predict that sales will reach $8 billion by 2007. So, what's the problem? Profits—or a lack thereof. Although its losses continue to shrink, and although it made first-quarter profits in 2002 and 2003, Amazon.com has yet to experience a profitable year. Doubters say that Amazon.com's Web-only model can never be truly profitable.

No matter what your view on its future, there's little doubt that Amazon.com is an outstanding marketing company. To its core, the company is relentlessly customer driven. "The thing that drives everything is creating genuine value for customers," says founder Jeff Bezos. "Nothing happens without that." A few years back, when asked when Amazon.com would start putting profits first rather than growth, Bezos replied, "Customers come first. If you focus on what customers want and build a relationship, they will allow you to make money."

The relationship with customers is the key to the company's future. Anyone at Amazon.com will tell you that the company wants to do much more than just sell books or DVDs or digital cameras. It wants to deliver a special *experience* to every customer. "The customer experience really matters," says Bezos. "We've focused on just having a better store, where it's easier to shop, where you can learn more about the products, where you have a bigger selection, and where you have the lowest prices. You combine all of that stuff together and people say, 'Hey, these guys really get it.'"

And they do get it. Most Amazon.com regulars feel a surprisingly strong and personal relationship with the company, especially given the almost complete lack of actual human interaction. For each of the last two years, the American Customer Satisfaction Index has rated Amazon the highest ever in customer satisfaction for a service company, regardless of industry. Analyst Geoffrey Colvin comments:

> I travel a lot and talk with all kinds of people, and I'm struck by how many of them speak passionately about their retail experience with Amazon.com. . . . How can people get so cranked up about an experience in which they don't see, touch, or hear another soul? The answer is that Amazon.com creates a more human relationship than most people realize. . . . The experience has been crafted so carefully that most of us actually enjoy it.

Amazon.com obsesses over making each customer's experience uniquely personal. For example, the site's "Your Recommendations" feature prepares personalized product recommendations, and its "New for You" feature links customers through to their own personalized home pages. Amazon.com was the first to use "collaborative filtering" technology, which sifts through each customer's past purchases and the purchasing patterns of customers with similar profiles to come up with personalized site content. "We want Amazon.com to be the right store for you as an individual," says Bezos. "If we have 35 million customers, we should have 35 million stores."

Visitors to Amazon.com's Web site receive a unique blend of benefits: huge selection, good value, convenience, and what Amazon vice president Jason Kilar calls "discovery." In books alone, for example, Amazon.com offers an easily searchable virtual selection of more than 3 million titles, 15 times more than in any physical bookstore. Good value comes in the form of reasonable prices. And at Amazon.com, it's irresistibly convenient to buy. You can log on, find what you want, and order with a single mouse click, all in less time than it takes to find a parking space at the local mall.

But it's the "discovery" factor that makes the Amazon.com experience really special. Once on the Web site, you're compelled to stay for a while—looking, learning, and discovering. Amazon.com has become a kind of online community, in which customers can browse for products, research purchase alternatives, share opinions and reviews with other visitors, and chat online with authors and experts. In this way, Amazon.com does much more than just sell goods on the Web. It creates customer relationships and satisfying online experiences.

In fact, Amazon.com has become so good at managing online relationships that many traditional "brick-and-mortar" retailers are turning to Amazon for help in adding more "clicks" to their "bricks." For example, Amazon.com now partners with well-known retailers such as Target, Toys "*R*" Us, Circuit City, and Borders to help them run their Web interfaces. The brick-and-mortar partners handle purchasing and inventory; Amazon.com oversees the customer experience—maintaining the Web site, attracting customers, and managing customer service. Amazon.com has also formed alliances with dozens, even hundreds, of retailers who sell their wares through the Amazon site. For example, Amazon's "apparel store" is more of a mall, featuring the products of partners such as Gap, Old Navy, Eddie Bauer, Spiegel, Foot Locker, Nordstrom, and Sears-owned Lands' End.

So, what do you think? Will Amazon eventually become the Wal-Mart of the Web? Or will it end up as just another interactive catalog company? Despite its successes and improving financials, until Amazon proves that it can be profitable, the debate will continue. But here's one analyst's conclusion:

> I'm betting on Amazon.com. . . . In the old days, only small outfits could keep track of customers: your local tailor, the local barber, the butcher at the grocery store. [Lately,] we've bemoaned the loss of that personal touch. [Amazon.com can bring it back. It] understands that the real opportunity is in using the technology to build long-term relationships. . . . What Amazon.com has done is invent and implement a model for interacting with millions of customers, one at a time. Old-line companies can't do that. . . . Amazon.com's technology gives me exactly what I want, in an extraordinarily responsive way.

Whatever its fate, Amazon.com has forever changed the face of marketing. "No matter what becomes of Amazon," says the analyst, "it has taught us something new."[1]

Today's successful companies at all levels have one thing in common: Like Amazon.com, they are strongly customer focused and heavily committed to marketing. These companies share a passion for understanding and satisfying customer needs in well-defined target markets. They motivate everyone in the organization to help build lasting customer relationships through superior customer value and satisfaction. As cofounder Bernie Marcus of Home Depot asserted, "All of our people understand what the Holy Grail is. It's not the bottom line. It's an almost blind, passionate commitment to taking care of customers."

▪▌ What Is Marketing?

Marketing, more than any other business function, deals with customers. Building customer relationships based on customer value and satisfaction is at the very heart of modern marketing. Although we will soon explore more-detailed definitions of marketing, perhaps the simplest definition is this one: Marketing is managing profitable customer relationships.

The twofold goal of marketing is to attract new customers by promising superior value and to keep and grow current customers by delivering satisfaction.

Wal-Mart has become the world's largest retailer, and the world's largest company, by delivering on its promise, "Always low prices. Always!" Ritz-Carlton promises—and delivers—truly "memorable experiences" for its hotel guests. At Disney theme parks, "imagineers" work wonders in their quest to "make a dream come true today." Dell Computer leads the personal computer industry by consistently making good on its promise to "be direct." Dell makes it easy for customers to custom-design their own computers and have them delivered quickly to their doorsteps or desktops. These and other highly successful companies know that if they take care of their customers, market share and profits will follow.

Sound marketing is critical to the success of every organization—large or small, for-profit or not-for-profit, domestic or global. Large for-profit firms such as Procter & Gamble, Microsoft, Sony, Wal-Mart, IBM, and Marriott use marketing. But so do not-for-profit organizations such as colleges, hospitals, museums, symphony orchestras, and even churches. Moreover, marketing is practiced not only in the United States but also in the rest of the world.

You already know a lot about marketing—it's all around you. You see the results of marketing in the abundance of products in your nearby shopping mall. You see marketing in the advertisements that fill your TV screen, spice up your magazines, stuff your mailbox, or enliven your Web pages. At home, at school, where you work, and where you play, you see marketing in almost everything you do. Yet, there is much more to marketing than meets the consumer's casual eye. Behind it all is a massive network of people and activities competing for your attention and purchases.

This book will give you a more complete and formal introduction to the basic concepts and practices of today's marketing. In this chapter, we begin by defining marketing and the marketing process.

Marketing Defined

What does the term *marketing* mean? Many people think of marketing only as selling and advertising. And no wonder—every day we are bombarded with television commercials, newspaper ads, direct-mail offers, sales calls, and Internet pitches. However, selling and advertising are only the tip of the marketing iceberg.

Today, marketing must be understood not in the old sense of making a sale—"telling and selling"—but in the new sense of *satisfying customer needs.* If the marketer does a good job of understanding consumer needs; develops products that provide superior value; and prices, distributes, and promotes them effectively, these products will sell very easily. Thus, selling and advertising are only part of a larger "marketing mix"—a set of marketing tools that work together to affect the marketplace.

Marketing
A social and managerial process by which individuals and groups obtain what they need and want through creating and exchanging value with others.

We define **marketing** as a social and managerial process by which individuals and groups obtain what they need and want through creating and exchanging value with others.[2] In a business setting, marketing involves building and managing profitable exchange relationships with customers.

The Marketing Process

Figure 1.1 presents a simple five-step model of the marketing process. In the first four steps, companies work to understand consumers, create customer value, and build strong customer relationships. In the final step, companies reap the rewards of creating superior customer value. By creating value *for* consumers, they in turn capture value *from* consumers in the form of sales, profits, and long-term customer equity.[3]

In this and the next chapter, we will examine the steps of this simple model of marketing. In this chapter, we'll review each step but focus more on the customer relationship steps—understanding consumers, building customer relationships, and capturing value from customers. In Chapter 2, we'll look more deeply into the second and third steps—designing marketing strategies and constructing marketing programs.

FIGURE 1.1
A Simple Model of the Marketing Process

■ Understanding the Marketplace and Consumer Needs

The marketing process begins, continues, and ends with consumers. As a first step, marketers need to understand customer needs and wants and the marketplace within which they operate. We now examine five core marketplace concepts: needs, wants, and demands; marketing offers (products, services, and experiences); value and satisfaction; exchanges, transactions, and relationships; and markets.

Needs, Wants, and Demands

The most basic concept underlying marketing is that of human needs. Human **needs** are states of felt deprivation. They include basic *physical* needs for food, clothing, warmth, and safety; *social* needs for belonging and affection; and *individual* needs for knowledge and self-expression. These needs were not created by marketers; they are a basic part of the human makeup.

    Wants are the form human needs take as they are shaped by culture and individual personality. An American *needs* food but *wants* a Big Mac, french fries, and a soft drink. A person in Mauritius *needs* food but *wants* a mango, rice, lentils, and beans. Wants are shaped by one's society and are described in terms of objects that will satisfy needs. When backed by buying power, wants become **demands**. Given their wants and resources, people demand products with benefits that add up to the most value and satisfaction.

    Outstanding marketing companies go to great lengths to learn about and understand their customers' needs, wants, and demands. They conduct consumer research and analyze mountains of customer data. Their people at all levels—including top management—stay close to customers. For example, top executives from Wal-Mart spend two days each week visiting stores and mingling with customers. At Disney World, at least once in his or her career, each manager spends a day touring the park in a Mickey, Minnie, Goofy, or other character costume.

    At consumer products giant Procter & Gamble, top executives even visit with ordinary consumers in their homes and on shopping trips. "We read the data and look at the charts," says one P&G executive, "but to shop [with consumers] and see how the woman is changing retailers to save 10 cents on a loaf of bread [so she can] spend it on things that are more important—that's important to us to keep front and center."[4]

Needs
States of felt deprivation.

Wants
The form human needs take as shaped by culture and individual personality.

Demands
Human wants that are backed by buying power.

Marketing Offers—Products, Services, and Experiences

Consumers' needs and wants are fulfilled through a **marketing offer**—some combination of products, services, information, or experiences offered to a market to satisfy a need or want. Marketing offers are not limited to physical *products*. Marketing offers also include *services*, activities or benefits offered for sale that are essentially intangible and do not result in the ownership of anything. Examples include banking, airline, hotel, tax preparation, and home repair services. More broadly, marketing offers also include other entities, such as *persons*, *places*, *organizations*, *information*, and *ideas*.

    Many sellers make the mistake of paying more attention to the specific products they offer than to the benefits and experiences produced by these products. These sellers suffer

Marketing offer
Some combination of products, services, information, or experiences offered to a market to satisfy a need or want.

■ Products do not have to be physical objects. Here the "product" is an idea—protecting animals.

from "*marketing myopia.*" They are so taken with their products that they focus only on existing wants and lose sight of underlying customer needs.[5] They forget that a product is only a tool to solve a consumer problem. A manufacturer of quarter-inch drill bits may think that the customer needs a drill bit. But what the customer *really* needs is a quarter-inch hole. These sellers will have trouble if a new product comes along that serves the customer's need better or less expensively. The customer with the same *need* will *want* the new product.

Smart marketers look beyond the attributes of the products and services they sell. They create *brand meaning* and *brand experiences* for consumers. For example, Coca-Cola means much more to consumers than just something to drink—it has become an American icon with a rich tradition and meaning. And Nike is more than just shoes, it's what the shoes do for you and where they take you.

By orchestrating several services and products, companies can create, stage, and market brand experiences. Disney World is an experience; so is a ride on a Harley-Davidson motorcycle. You experience a visit to Barnes & Noble or surfing Sony's playstation.com Web site. And you don't just watch a NASCAR race, you immerse yourself in the NASCAR experience (see Marketing at Work 1.1). In fact, experiences have emerged for many firms as the next step in differentiating the company's offer. "What consumers really want [are offers] that dazzle their senses, touch their hearts, and stimulate their minds," declares one expert. "They want [offers] that deliver an experience."[6]

Value and Satisfaction

Consumers usually face a broad array of products and services that might satisfy a given need. How do they choose among these many marketing offers? Consumers make choices based on their perceptions of the value and satisfaction that various products and services deliver. Customers form expectations about the value of various marketing offers and buy accordingly. Satisfied customers buy again and tell others about their good experiences. Dissatisfied customers often switch to competitors and disparage the product to others.

Marketers must be careful to set the right level of expectations. If they set expectations too low, they may satisfy those who buy but fail to attract enough buyers. If they raise expectations too high, buyers will be disappointed. Customer value and customer satisfaction are key building blocks for developing and managing customer relationships. We will revisit these core concepts later in the chapter.

Exchange, Transactions, and Relationships

Marketing occurs when people decide to satisfy needs and wants through exchange. **Exchange** is the act of obtaining a desired object from someone by offering something in return. Whereas exchange is the core concept of marketing, a transaction, in turn, is marketing's unit of measurement. A **transaction** consists of a trade of values between two parties: One party gives X to another party and gets Y in return. For example, you pay Sears $350 and receive a television set.

In the broadest sense, the marketer tries to bring about a response to some marketing offer. The response may be more than simply buying or trading products and services. A political candidate, for instance, wants votes, a church wants membership, and a social action group wants idea acceptance.

Exchange
The act of obtaining a desired object from someone by offering something in return.

Transaction
A trade of values between two parties.

Marketing at Work | 1.1

NASCAR: Creating Customer Experiences

When you think of NASCAR, do you think of tobacco-spitting rednecks and run-down race tracks? Think again! These days, NASCAR (the National Association for Stock Car Auto Racing) is much, much more. In fact, it's one great marketing organization. And for fans, NASCAR is a lot more than a stock car race. It's a high-octane, totally involving experience.

As for the stereotypes, throw them away. NASCAR is now the second-highest-rated regular season sport on TV—only the NFL draws more viewers. NASCAR fans are young (58 percent are between the ages of 18 and 34). They are affluent (42 percent earn in excess of $50,000 a year). And they are decidedly family oriented (40 percent are women). What's more, they are 75 million strong—4 of every 10 people in the United States regularly watch or attend NASCAR events. Most important, they are passionate about NASCAR. An ardent NASCAR fan experiences almost 9 hours of NASCAR media coverage per week and spends nearly $700 a year on NASCAR-related clothing, collectibles, and other items.

What's NASCAR's secret? Its incredible success results from a single-minded focus: creating memorable experiences that translate into lasting customer relationships. The NASCAR experience consists of a careful blend of live racing events, abundant media coverage, and compelling Web sites.

Each year, fans experience the adrenaline-charged, heart-stopping excitement of NASCAR racing first-hand by attending national tours to some two dozen tracks around the country. NASCAR races attract the largest crowds of any U.S. sporting event. About 140,000 people attended the recent Daytona 500, twice as many as attended the Super Bowl. At these events, fans hold tailgate parties, camp and cook out, watch the cars roar around the track, meet the drivers, and swap stories with other NASCAR enthusiasts. To get fans even closer to the action, in addition to grandstands and skyboxes, track facilities include RV parks next to and right inside the racing oval.

NASCAR really cares about its customers and goes out of its way to show them a good time. For example, rather than fleecing fans with overpriced food and beer, NASCAR tracks encourage fans to bring their own. Marvels one sponsor, "[In] what other sport can you drive your beat-up RV or camper into the stadium and sit on it to watch the race? . . . How many NFL stadiums go so far as to print the allowable cooler dimensions on the back of the ticket?" Such actions mean that NASCAR might lose a sale today, but it will keep the customer tomorrow.

To further the experience, NASCAR makes the sport a wholesome family affair. Tracks feature professionally landscaped grounds, with manicured flower beds, no litter, and ample restrooms. The environment is safe for kids—uniformed security guards patrol the track to keep things in line. The family atmosphere extends to the drivers, too. Unlike the aloof and often distant athletes in other sports, NASCAR drivers seem like regular guys. They are approachable, friendly, and readily available to mingle with fans and sign autographs. Many drivers have children, brothers, sisters, or parents who work for NASCAR as drivers or pit crew. As a result, fans view drivers as good role models, and the long NASCAR tradition of family involvement creates the next generation of loyal fans.

Can't make it to the track? No problem. NASCAR TV coverage reaches 20 million viewers weekly. Well-orchestrated coverage and in-car cameras put fans in the middle of the action, giving them vicarious thrills that keep them glued to the

NASCAR's incredible success results from creating memorable experiences that translate into lasting customer relationships. The resulting fan loyalty attracts hundreds of marketers, who pay to sponsor cars and get their corporate logos emblazoned on team uniforms and on the hoods or side panels of cars.

(continued)

screen. "When the network gets it right, my surround-sound bothers my neighbors but makes my ears happy," says Angela Kotula, a 35-year-old human resources professional.

NASCAR also delivers the NASCAR experience through its engaging Web sites. NASCAR.com serves up a glut of news and entertainment to more than 2 million fans each month—in-depth news, driver bios, background information, online games, community discussions, and merchandise. True die-hard fans can subscribe to TrackPass for $4.95 a month (or $29.95 for the year) to get up-to-the-minute standings, race video, streaming audio from the cars, and access to a host of archived audio and video highlights. For another $3 per month, TrackPass with PitCommand delivers a real-time data feed, complete with the GPS locations of cars and data from drivers' dashboards.

Ready access to NASCAR races, drivers, and information makes fans feel more a part of the sport. But a big part of the NASCAR experience is the feeling that the sport itself is personally accessible. Anyone who knows how to drive feels that he or she, too, could be a champion NASCAR driver. As 48-year police officer Ed Sweat puts it: "Genetics did not bless me with the height of a basketball player, nor was I born to have the bulk of a lineman in the NFL. But . . . on any given Sunday, with a rich sponsor, the right car, and some practice, I could be draftin' and passin', zooming to the finish line, trad-

ing paint with Tony Stewart. . . . Yup, despite my advancing age and waistline, taking Zocor, and driving by a gym . . . I could be Dale Jarrett!" Some NASCAR tracks even have driving schools and let the public test their driving skills on the track.

Ultimately, all of this fan enthusiasm translates into financial success for NASCAR, and for its sponsors. Television networks pay some $2.4 billion per year for the rights to broadcast NASCAR events. And the sport is third in licensed merchandise sales, behind only the NFL and the NCAA. It rings up more than $1.3 billion in sales of NASCAR-branded retail merchandise every year.

Marketing studies show that NASCAR's fans are more loyal to the sport's sponsors than fans of any other sport. They are three times as likely to purchase a sponsor's product rather than a nonsponsor's product. Indeed, 71 percent always buy sponsors' products, and 42 percent will switch to support a sponsor. Just ask dental hygienist Jenny German, an ardent fan of NASCAR driver Jeff Gordon. According to one account: "She actively seeks out any product he endorses. She drinks Pepsi instead off Coke, eats Edy's ice cream for desert, and owns a pair of Ray-Ban sunglasses. 'If they sold underwear with the number 24 on it, I'd have it on,' German says."

Because of such loyal fan relationships, NASCAR has attracted more than 250 big-name sponsors, from Wal-Mart, Home Depot, and AT&T to Procter & Gamble, M&Ms, Wrangler, and the U.S.

Army. Sponsors eagerly pay up to $10 million per year to sponsor a top car and to get their corporate colors and logos emblazoned on team uniforms and on the hoods or side panels of team cars. Or they pay $3 million to $5 million a year to become the "official (fill-in-the-blank)" of NASCAR racing. They also invest in their own NASCAR promotions, which can produce amazing results. For example, in a recent Coca-Cola "Racing Family" promotion, 175 million NASCAR commemorative bottles flew off retailers' shelves in a matter of weeks.

So if you're still thinking of NASCAR as rednecks and moonshine, you'd better think again. NASCAR is a premier marketing organization that knows how to create customer experiences that translate into deep and lasting customer relationships. "Better than any other sport," says a leading sports marketing executive, "NASCAR listens to its fans and gives them what they want."

Sources: Quotes and other information from Mark Woods, "Readers Try to Explain Why Racin' Rocks," *The Florida Times Union,* February 16, 2003, p. C1; Tina Grady, "NASCAR Fan Base More Than Just Blue Collar," *Aftermarket Business,* May 2002, p. 11; George Pyne, "In His Own Words: NASCAR Sharpens Winning Strategy," *Advertising Age,* October 28, 2002, p. S6; Peter Spiegel, "Heir Gordon," *Forbes,* December 14, 1998, pp. 42–46; Tony Kontzer, "Backseat Drivers—NASCAR Puts You in the Race," *InformationWeek,* March 25, 2002, p. 83; Lisa Matte, "The Race Is On: Marketing Partnerships with Racing Teams Increase Awareness of, Loyalty to Hotel Brands," *Hotel & Motel Management,* August 2002, p. 127; Matthew Futterman, "What Fuels NASCAR," *The Star-Ledger,* February 16, 2003, p. 1; and www.NASCAR.com, July 2003.

Marketing consists of actions taken to build and maintain desirable *exchange relationships* with target audiences involving a product, service, idea, or other object. Beyond simply attracting new customers and creating transactions, the goal is to retain customers and grow their business with the company. Marketers want to build strong economic and social relationships by consistently delivering superior value. We will expand on the important concept of customer relationship management later in the chapter.

Markets

Market

The set of all actual and potential buyers of a product or service.

The concepts of exchange and relationships lead to the concept of a market. A **market** is the set of actual and potential buyers of a product. These buyers share a particular need or want that can be satisfied through exchange relationships. The size of a market depends on the number of people who exhibit the need, have resources to engage in exchange, and are willing to exchange these resources for what they want.

Marketers are keenly interested in markets. Marketing means managing markets to bring about profitable exchange relationships. However, creating exchange relationships

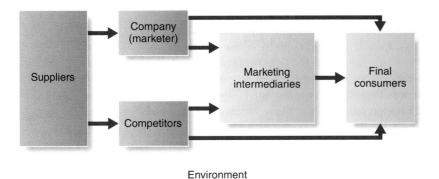

FIGURE 1.2

Elements of a Modern
Marketing System

takes work. Sellers must search for buyers, identify their needs, design good marketing offers, set prices for them, promote them, and store and deliver them. Activities such as product development, research, communication, distribution, pricing, and service are core marketing activities.

Although we normally think of marketing as being carried out by sellers, buyers also carry out marketing. Consumers do marketing when they search for the goods they need at prices they can afford. Company purchasing agents do marketing when they track down sellers and bargain for good terms.

Figure 1.2 shows the main elements in a modern marketing system. In the usual situation, marketing involves serving a market of final consumers in the face of competitors. The company and the competitors send their respective offers and messages to consumers, either directly or through marketing intermediaries. All of the actors in the system are affected by major environmental forces (demographic, economic, physical, technological, political/legal, social/cultural).

Each party in the system adds value for the next level. Thus, a company's success at building profitable relationships depends not only on its own actions but also on how well the entire system serves the needs of final consumers. Wal-Mart cannot fulfill its promise of low prices unless its suppliers provide merchandise at low costs. And Ford cannot deliver high quality to car buyers unless its dealers provide outstanding service.

Designing a Customer-Driven Marketing Strategy

Once it fully understands consumers and the marketplace, marketing management can design a customer-driven marketing strategy. We define **marketing management** as the art and science of choosing target markets and building profitable relationships with them. The marketing manager's aim is to get, keep, and grow target customers by creating, delivering, and communicating superior customer value. To design a winning marketing strategy, the marketing manager must answer two important questions: What customers will we serve (what's our target market)? and How can we serve these customers best (what's our value proposition)? We will discuss these marketing strategy concepts briefly here, then look at them in more detail in the next chapter.

Marketing management
The art and science of choosing target markets and building profitable relationships with them.

Selecting Customers to Serve

The company must first decide *who* it will serve. It does this by dividing the market into segments of customers (*market segmentation*) and selecting which segments it will cultivate (*target marketing*). Some people think of marketing management as finding as many customers as possible and increasing demand. But marketing managers know that they cannot serve all customers in every way. Trying to serve all customers may result in not serving any customers well. Instead, the company wants to select customers that it can serve well and profitably. For example, Porsche profitably targets affluent professionals; Family Dollar stores profitably target families with more modest means.

Some marketers may seek *fewer* customers and reduced demand. For example, Yosemite National Park is badly overcrowded in the summer. And power companies sometimes have trouble meeting demand during peak usage periods. In these and other cases of excess demand, **demarketing** may be required to reduce the number of customers or to shift their demand temporarily or permanently. For instance, to reduce demand for space on congested expressways in Washington, D.C., the Metropolitan Washington Council of Governments has set up a Web site encouraging commuters to carpool and use mass transit.[7]

Demarketing
Marketing to reduce demand temporarily or permanently; the aim is not to destroy demand but only to reduce or shift it.

Thus, marketing managers must decide which customers they want to target, and on the level, timing, and nature of their demand. Simply put, marketing management is *customer management* and *demand management.*

**What a dog feels
when the leash breaks.**

Instant freedom, courtesy of the Boxster S. The 250 horsepower boxer engine launches you forward with its distinctive growl. Any memory of life on a leash evaporates in the wind rushing overhead. It's time to run free. Contact us at 1·800·PORSCHE or porsche.com.

■ Value propositions: Porsche targets affluent buyers with promises of driving excitement: "What a dog feels like when the leash breaks."

Deciding on a Value Proposition

The company must also decide *how* it will serve targeted customers—how it will *differentiate and position* itself in the marketplace. A company's *value proposition* is the set of benefits or values it promises to deliver to consumers to satisfy their needs. Porsche promises driving performance and excitement: "What a dog feels when the leash breaks." Tide laundry detergent promises powerful, all-purpose cleaning, whereas Gain "cleans and freshens like sunshine." Altoids positions itself as "the curiously strong mint."

Such value propositions differentiate one brand from another. They answer the customer's question "Why should I buy your brand rather than a competitor's?" Companies must design strong value propositions that give them the greatest advantage in their target markets.

■■ Marketing Management Orientations

Marketing management wants to design strategies that will build profitable relationships with target consumers. But what *philosophy* should guide these marketing strategies? What weight should be given to the interests of customers, the organization, and society? Very often these interests conflict.

There are five alternative concepts under which organizations design and carry out their marketing strategies: the production, product, selling, marketing, and societal marketing concepts.

Production concept
The idea that consumers will favor products that are available and highly affordable.

The Production Concept The **production concept** holds that consumers will favor products that are available and highly affordable. Therefore, management should focus on improving production and distribution efficiency. This concept is one of the oldest orientations that guides sellers.

The production concept is still a useful philosophy in two types of situations. The first occurs when the demand for a product exceeds the supply. Here, management should look for ways to increase production. The second situation occurs when the product's cost is too high and improved productivity is needed to bring it down. For example, Henry Ford's philosophy was to perfect the production of the Model T so that its cost could be reduced and more people could afford it. He joked about offering people a car of any color as long as it was black.

Although useful in some situations, the production concept can lead to marketing myopia. Companies adopting this orientation run a major risk of focusing too narrowly on their own operations and losing sight of the real objective—building customer relationships by satisfying customers' needs.

The Product Concept The **product concept** holds that consumers will favor products that offer the most in quality, performance, and innovative features. Under this concept, marketing strategy should focus on making continuous product improvements. Some manufacturers believe that if they can build a better mousetrap, the world will beat a path to their door.[8] But they are often rudely shocked. Buyers may well be looking for a better solution to a mouse problem but not necessarily for a better mousetrap. The solution might be a chemical spray, an exterminating service, or something that works better than a mousetrap. Furthermore, a better mousetrap will not sell unless the manufacturer designs, packages, and prices it attractively; places it in convenient distribution channels; brings it to the attention of people who need it; and convinces buyers that it is a better product.

Thus, the product concept also can lead to marketing myopia. For instance, railroad management once thought that users wanted *trains* rather than *transportation* and overlooked the growing challenge of airlines, buses, trucks, and automobiles. Kodak assumed that consumers wanted photographic film rather than a way to capture and share memories and at first overlooked the challenge of digital cameras. Although it now leads the digital camera market in sales, it has yet to make significant profits from this business.[9]

The Selling Concept Many companies follow the **selling concept**, which holds that consumers will not buy enough of the firm's products unless it undertakes a large-scale selling and promotion effort. The concept is typically practiced with unsought goods—those that buyers do not normally think of buying, such as insurance or blood donations. These industries must be good at tracking down prospects and selling them on product benefits.

Most firms practice the selling concept when they face overcapacity. Their aim is to sell what they make rather than make what the market wants. Such a marketing strategy carries high risks. It focuses on creating sales transactions rather than on building long-term, profitable customer relationships. It assumes that customers who are coaxed into buying the product will like it. Or, if they don't like it, they will possibly forget their disappointment and buy it again later. These are usually poor assumptions. Most studies show that dissatisfied customers do not buy again. Worse yet, whereas the average satisfied customer may tell four or five others about good experiences, the average dissatisfied customer tells twice as many others about his or her bad experiences.[10]

The Marketing Concept The **marketing concept** holds that achieving organizational goals depends on knowing the needs and wants of target markets and delivering the desired satisfactions better than competitors do. Under the marketing concept, customer focus and value are the *paths* to sales and profits.

Instead of a product-centered "make and sell" philosophy, the marketing concept is a customer-centered "sense and respond" philosophy. It views marketing not as "hunting," but as "gardening." The job is not to find the right customers for your product, but the right products for your customers. As stated by famed direct marketer Lester Wunderman, "The chant of the Industrial Revolution was that of the manufacturer who said, 'This is what I make, won't you please buy it.' The call of the Information Age is the consumer asking, 'This is what I want, won't you please make it.' "[11]

Figure 1.3 contrasts the selling concept and the marketing concept. The selling concept takes an *inside-out* perspective. It starts with the factory, focuses on the company's existing products, and calls for heavy selling and promotion to obtain profitable sales. It focuses primarily on customer conquest—getting short-term sales with little concern about who buys or why.

In contrast, the marketing concept takes an *outside-in* perspective. As Herb Kelleher, Southwest Airlines's colorful CEO, puts it, "We don't have a Marketing Department; we have a Customer Department." And in the words of one Ford executive, "If we're not customer driven, our cars won't be either." The marketing concept starts with a well-defined

Product concept
The idea that consumers will favor products that offer the most quality, performance, and features and that the organization should therefore devote its energy to making continuous product improvements.

Selling concept
The idea that that consumers will not buy enough of the firm's products unless it undertakes a large-scale selling and promotion effort.

Marketing concept
The marketing management philosophy that holds that achieving organizational goals depends on knowing the needs and wants of target markets and delivering the desired satisfactions better than competitors do.

FIGURE 1.3

The Selling and Marketing
Concepts Contrasted

Starting point	Focus	Means	Ends
Factory	Existing products	Selling and promoting	Profits through sales volume

The selling concept

Market	Customer needs	Integrated marketing	Profits through customer satisfaction

The marketing concept

market, focuses on customer needs, and integrates all the marketing activities that affect customers. In turn, it yields profits by creating long-term customer relationships with the right customers based on customer value and satisfaction. Many successful and well-known companies have adopted the marketing concept. Procter & Gamble, Disney, Wal-Mart, Marriott, Nordstrom, Dell Computer, and Southwest Airlines follow it faithfully.

Implementing the marketing concept often means more than simply responding to customers' stated desires and obvious needs. *Customer-driven* companies research current customers deeply to learn about their desires, gather new product and service ideas, and test proposed product improvements. Such customer-driven marketing usually works well when a clear need exists and when customers know what they want.

In many cases, however, customers *don't* know what they want or even what is possible. For example, 20 years ago, how many consumers would have thought to ask for cell phones, fax machines, home copiers, 24-hour Internet brokerage accounts, DVD players, handheld global satellite positioning systems, or wearable PCs? Such situations call for *customer-driving* marketing—understanding customer needs even better than customers themselves do and creating products and services that will meet existing and latent needs, now and in the future.

Societal marketing concept

A principle of enlightened marketing that holds that a company should make good marketing decisions by considering consumers' wants, the company's requirements, consumers' long-run interests, and society's long-run interests.

As Sony's visionary leader, Akio Morita, puts it: "Our plan is to lead the public with new products rather than ask them what kinds of products they want. The public does not know what is possible, but we do." And according to an executive at 3M, "Our goal is to lead customers where they want to go before *they* know where they want to go."[12]

The Societal Marketing Concept The **societal marketing concept** questions whether the pure marketing concept overlooks possible conflicts between consumer *short-run wants* and consumer *long-run welfare*. Is a firm that senses, serves, and satisfies immediate needs, wants, and interests of target markets always doing what's best for consumers and society in the long run? The societal marketing concept holds that marketing strategy should deliver value to customers in a way that maintains or improves both the consumer's *and the society's* well-being.

Consider the fast-food industry. You may see today's giant fast-food chains as offering tasty and convenient food at reasonable prices. Yet many consumer and environmental groups have voiced concerns. Critics point out that hamburgers, fried chicken, french fries, and most other foods sold by fast-food restaurants are high in fat and salt. Meals are now "super-sized," leading consumers to overeat and contributing to a national obesity epidemic. The products are wrapped in convenient packaging, but this leads to waste and pollution. Thus, in satisfying short-term consumer wants, the highly successful fast-food chains may be harming consumer health and causing environmental problems in the long run.[13]

As Figure 1.4 shows, the societal marketing concept calls on marketers to balance three considerations in setting their marketing strategies:

■ Customer-driving marketing: How many of us would have thought to ask for a "wearable PC." Marketers must often understand customer needs even better than customers themselves do.

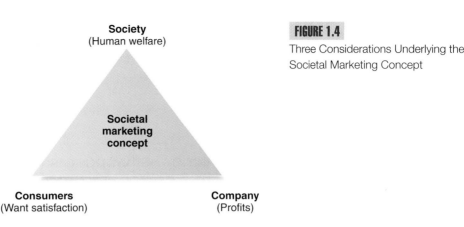

company profits, consumer wants, *and* society's interests. Originally, most companies based their marketing decisions largely on short-run company profit. Eventually, they recognized the long-run importance of satisfying consumer wants, and the marketing concept emerged. Now most companies consider society's interests when making their marketing decisions.

One such company is Johnson & Johnson, which has been rated each year in a *Fortune* magazine poll as one of America's most admired companies. Johnson & Johnson's concern for societal interests is summarized in a company document called "Our Credo," which stresses honesty, integrity, and putting people before profits. Under this credo, Johnson & Johnson would rather take a big loss than ship a bad batch of one of its products.

Consider the tragic tampering case in which eight people died from swallowing cyanide-laced capsules of Tylenol, a Johnson & Johnson brand. Although Johnson & Johnson believed that the pills had been altered in only a few stores, not in the factory, it quickly recalled all of its product. The recall cost the company $240 million in earnings. In the long run, however, the company's swift recall of Tylenol strengthened consumer confidence and loyalty, and Tylenol remains one of the nation's leading brands of pain reliever.

In this and other cases, Johnson & Johnson management has found that doing what's right benefits both consumers and the company. Says Johnson & Johnson's chief executive, "The Credo should not be viewed as some kind of social welfare program . . . it's just plain good business. If we keep trying to do what's right, at the end of the day we believe the marketplace will reward us." Thus, over the years, Johnson & Johnson's dedication to consumers and community service has made it one of America's most-admired companies *and* one of the most profitable.[14]

■ Preparing a Marketing Plan and Program

The company's marketing strategy outlines which customers the company will serve and how it will create value for these customers. Next, guided by the marketing strategy, the marketer constructs a marketing program that will actually deliver the intended value to its target customers. The marketing program builds customer relationships by transforming the strategy into action. It consists of the firm's *marketing mix*, the set of marketing tools the firm uses to implement its marketing strategy.

The major marketing tools are classified into four broad groups, called the *four Ps* of marketing: product, price, place, and promotion. To deliver on its value proposition, the firm must first create a need-satisfying marketing offer (product). It must decide

Our Credo

We believe our first responsibility is to the doctors, nurses and patients,
to mothers and fathers and all others who use our products and services.
In meeting their needs everything we do must be of high quality.
We must constantly strive to reduce our costs
in order to maintain reasonable prices.
Customers' orders must be serviced promptly and accurately.
Our suppliers and distributors must have an opportunity
to make a fair profit.

We are responsible to our employees,
the men and women who work with us throughout the world.
Everyone must be considered as an individual.
We must respect their dignity and recognize their merit.
They must have a sense of security in their jobs.
Compensation must be fair and adequate,
and working conditions clean, orderly and safe.
We must be mindful of ways to help our employees fulfill
their family responsibilities.
Employees must feel free to make suggestions and complaints.
There must be equal opportunity for employment, development
and advancement for those qualified.
We must provide competent management,
and their actions must be just and ethical.

We are responsible to the communities in which we live and work
and to the world community as well.
We must be good citizens — support good works and charities
and bear our fair share of taxes.
We must encourage civic improvements and better health and education.
We must maintain in good order
the property we are privileged to use,
protecting the environment and natural resources.

Our final responsibility is to our stockholders.
Business must make a sound profit.
We must experiment with new ideas.
Research must be carried on, innovative programs developed
and mistakes paid for.
New equipment must be purchased, new facilities provided
and new products launched.
Reserves must be created to provide for adverse times.
When we operate according to these principles,
the stockholders should realize a fair return.

Johnson & Johnson

■ Johnson & Johnson's concern for society is summarized in its credo and in the company's actions over the years.

how much it will charge for the offer (price) and how it will make the offer available to target consumers (place). Finally, it must communicate with target customers about the offer and persuade them of its merits (promotion).

We will explore marketing programs and the marketing mix in much more detail in Chapter 2. Then, in later chapters, we'll look more deeply into each element of the marketing mix.

SPEED BUMP

Linking the Concepts

Stop here for a moment and stretch your legs. What have you learned so far about marketing? For the moment, set aside the more formal definitions we've examined and try to develop your own understanding of marketing.

- In *your own words*, what *is* marketing? Write down *your* definition. Does your definition include key concepts such as customer value and relationships?
- What does marketing *mean* to you? How does it affect your daily life?
- What marketing management philosophy appears to guide NASCAR? How does this compare with the marketing philosophy that guides Johnson & Johnson? Can you think of another company guided by a very different philosophy? Is there one marketing management philosophy that's best for all companies?

■ Building Customer Relationships

The first three steps in the marketing process—understanding the marketplace and customer needs, designing a customer-driven marketing strategy, and constructing marketing programs—all lead up to the fourth and most important step: building profitable customer relationships.

Customer Relationship Management

Customer relationship management (CRM) is perhaps the most important concept of modern marketing. Until recently, CRM has been defined narrowly as a customer data management activity. By this definition, it involves managing detailed information about individual customers and carefully managing customer "touchpoints" in order to maximize customer loyalty. We will discuss this narrower CRM activity later in a chapter dealing with marketing information.

More recently, however, customer relationship management has taken on a broader meaning. In this broader sense, **customer relationship management** is the overall process of building and maintaining profitable customer relationships by delivering superior customer value and satisfaction. It deals with all aspects of acquiring, keeping, and growing customers.

Customer relationship management
The overall process of building and maintaining profitable customer relationships by delivering superior customer value and satisfaction.

Relationship Building Blocks: Customer Value and Satisfaction The key to building lasting customer relationships is to create superior customer value and satisfaction. Satisfied customers are more likely to be loyal customers and to give the company a larger share of their business.

Customer Value. Attracting and retaining customers can be a difficult task. Customers often face a bewildering array of products and services from which to choose. A customer buys from the firm that offers the highest **customer perceived value**—the customer's evaluation of the difference between all the benefits and all the costs of a marketing offer relative to those of competing offers.

Customer perceived value
The difference between total customer value and total customer cost.

For example, FedEx customers gain a number of benefits. The most obvious is fast and reliable package delivery. However, by using FedEx, customers also may receive some status and image values. Using FedEx usually makes both the package sender and the receiver feel more important. When deciding whether to send a package via FedEx, customers will weigh these and other perceived values against the money, effort, and psychological costs of using the service. Moreover, they will compare the value of using FedEx against the value of using other shippers—UPS, Airborne, the U.S. Postal Service. They will select the service that gives them the greatest perceived value.

Customers often do not judge product values and costs accurately or objectively. They act on *perceived* value. For example, does FedEx really provide faster, more reliable delivery? If so, is this better service worth the higher prices FedEx charges? The U.S. Postal Service argues that its express service is comparable, and its prices are much lower. However, judging by market share, most consumers perceive otherwise. Each day, they entrust FedEx with a 46 percent share of their next-day air shipping business, compared with the Postal Service's 6 percent share. The Postal Service's challenge is to change these customer value perceptions.[15]

■ Is FedEx's service worth the higher price? FedEx thinks so. It promises reliability, speed, and piece of mind. FedEx ads say "Need to get it there or else? Don't worry. There's a FedEx for that."

Customer Satisfaction. Customer satisfaction depends on the product's perceived performance relative to a buyer's expectations. If the product's performance falls short of expectations, the customer is dissatisfied. If performance matches expectations, the customer is satisfied. If performance exceeds expectations, the customer is highly satisfied or delighted.

Outstanding marketing companies go out of their way to keep important customers satisfied. Highly satisfied customers make repeat purchases and tell others about their good experiences with the product. The key is to match customer expectations with company performance. Smart companies aim to *delight* customers by promising only what they can deliver, then delivering *more* than they promise (see Marketing at Work 1.2).[16]

The American Customer Satisfaction Index, which tracks customer satisfaction in more than two dozen U.S. manufacturing and service industries, shows that overall customer satisfaction has been declining slightly in recent years.[17] It is unclear whether this has resulted from a decrease in product and service quality or from an increase in customer expectations. In either case, it presents an opportunity for companies that can consistently deliver superior customer value and satisfaction.

However, although the customer-centered firm seeks to deliver high customer satisfaction compared with its competitors, it does not attempt to *maximize* customer satisfaction. A company can always increase customer satisfaction by lowering its price or increasing its services. But this may result in lower profits. Thus, the purpose of marketing is to generate customer value profitably. This requires a very delicate balance: The marketer must continue to generate more customer value and satisfaction but not "give away the house."

Customer satisfaction
The extent to which a product's perceived performance matches a buyer's expectations.

Customer Relationship Levels and Tools

Companies can build customer relationships at many levels, depending on the nature of the target market. At one extreme, a company with many low-margin customers may seek to develop *basic relationships* with them. For example, Procter & Gamble does not phone or call on all of its Tide customers to get to know them personally. Instead, P&G creates relationships through brand-building advertising, sales promotions, a 1-800 customer response number, and its Tide Fabric Care Network Web site (www.Tide.com).

At the other extreme, in markets with few customers and high margins, sellers want to create *full partnerships* with key customers. For example, P&G customer teams work closely with Wal-Mart, Safeway, and other large retailers. And Boeing partners with American Airlines, Delta, and other airlines in designing airplanes that fully satisfy their requirements. In between these two extreme situations, other levels of customer relationships are appropriate.

Marketing at Work | 1.2

Customer Relationships: Delighting Customers

Top-notch marketing companies know that delighting customers involves more than simply opening a complaint department, smiling a lot, and being nice. These companies set very high standards for customer satisfaction and often make seemingly outlandish efforts to achieve them. Consider the following examples:

■ A man bought his first new Lexus—a $45,000 piece of machinery. He could afford a Mercedes, a Jaguar, or a Cadillac, but he bought the Lexus. He took delivery of his new honey and started to drive it home, luxuriating in the smell of the leather interior and the glorious handling. On the interstate, he put the pedal to the metal and felt the Gs in the pit of his stomach. The lights, the windshield washer, the cup holder that popped out of the dashboard, the seat heater that warmed his bottom on a cold winter morning—he tried all of these with mounting pleasure. On a whim, he turned on the radio. His favorite classical music station came on in splendid quadraphonic sound that ricocheted around the interior. He pushed the second button; it was his favorite news station. The third button brought his favorite talk station that kept him awake on long trips. The fourth button was set to his daughter's favorite rock station. In fact, every button was set to his specific tastes. The customer knew the car was smart, but was it psychic? No. The mechanic at Lexus had noted the radio settings on his trade-in and duplicated them on the new Lexus. The customer was delighted. This was his car now—through and through! No one told the mechanic to do it. It's just

part of the Lexus philosophy: Delight a customer and continue to delight that customer, and you will have a customer for life. What the mechanic did cost Lexus nothing. Not one red cent. Yet it solidified the relationship that could be worth high six figures to Lexus in customer lifetime value.

■ Don and Betts Jackson are two of the most fun and outgoing people around. And Betts is one of the great chefs of the world. Their holiday party at their farmhouse in Delaware—usually filled to overflowing with friends, relatives, neighbors, and members of the local chamber of commerce—is a stunner, with an array of foods, drinks, and wines that would shame a Michelin four-star restaurant in Lyons. Several years ago, the Jacksons gave each other $1,500 worth of kitchen gear

from Williams-Sonoma as their main gifts to go under the Christmas tree. Don placed the order in plenty of time for Christmas delivery. The order never arrived. It was a bleak sight under the tree, made bleaker by the knowledge that Betts needed the new implements for the upcoming holiday party. The next day, Jackson got a Williams-Sonoma sales rep on the phone and told him the sad story. A combination of factors was involved: a FedEx slowdown, a computer glitch in Williams-Sonoma's eastern distribution center, and unexpected snow all conspired to delay the order. The rep took instant action. "Here's what I'm going to do for you," he said. "First, I'm going to reassemble the order and get it out to you by FedEx overnight, so you'll have it tomorrow morning. Second, I'm

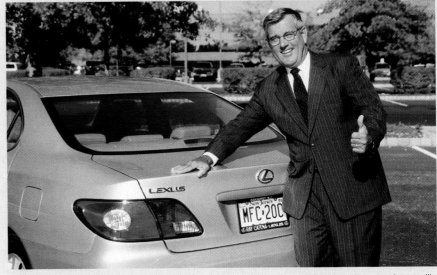

The Lexus philosophy: Delight a customer and continue to delight that customer, and you will have a customer for life.

Today, most leading companies are developing customer loyalty and retention programs. Beyond offering consistently high value and satisfaction, marketers can use specific marketing tools to develop stronger bonds with consumers.[18] First, a company might build value and satisfaction by adding financial benefits to the customer relationship. For example, many companies now offer frequency marketing programs that reward customers who buy frequently or in large amounts. Airlines offer frequent-flier programs, hotels give room upgrades to their frequent guests, and supermarkets give patronage discounts to "very important customers."

going to enclose merchandise return labels, so when the old order arrives, you can slap the labels on the packages and call FedEx to take them away. Third, I'm going to forgive all shipping costs for the original order, for the returns, and for this new order that you'll get tomorrow morning. And fourth, I'm going to send you a present—a thank-you for your patience and for being a customer of Williams-Sonoma." Jackson hung up the phone feeling better. The next day, the merchandise arrived as promised, together with the return labels and a giant, top-of-the-line, blue-glass turkey baster as the free gift. Despite the original goof, the Jacksons were delighted.

■ When a customer arrived early one winter morning at an Enterprise Rent-A-Car office in Cambridge, Massachusetts, to pick up an SUV to drive on a ski vacation to the Sugarbush resort in Vermont (a three-hour-plus drive away), there was no vehicle and no record of his reservation. Cambridge's customer service representative apologized profusely and called nearby branches until he found the car the customer wanted, a Chevy Trailblazer at a location several miles away. So far, so good. But then the customer service rep drove the customer back to his house to pick up his ski gear, and to the other branch to retrieve the Trailblazer. He knocked 20 percent off the rental price, provided the customer the two-dollar toll he would have to pay to get on the highway (which he wouldn't have had to pay leaving from Cambridge) and gave him a half-tank of gas. Within a month, the delighted customer had rented twice more from Enterprise and "will probably rent more," he says.

Studies show that going to extremes to keep customers happy, although sometimes costly, goes hand in hand with good financial performance. Delighted customers come back again and again. Thus, in today's highly competitive marketplace, companies can well afford to lose money on one transaction if it helps to cement a profitable long-term customer relationship.

For companies interested in delighting customers, exceptional value and service are more than a set of policies or actions—they are a companywide attitude, an important part of the overall company culture. American Express loves to tell stories about how its people have rescued customers from disasters ranging from civil wars to earthquakes, no matter what the cost. The company gives cash rewards of up to $1,000 to "Great Performers," such as Barbara Weber, who moved mountains of U.S. State Department and Treasury Department bureaucracy to refund $980 in stolen traveler's checks to a customer stranded in Cuba.

Southwest Airlines is well known for its low fares and prompt arrivals. But its friendly and often funny flight staff goes to great lengths to delight customers. In one instance, after pushing away from the departure gate, a Southwest pilot spied an anguished passenger, sweat streaming from her face, racing down the jetway only to find that that she'd arrived too late. He returned to the gate to pick her up. Says Southwest's executive vice president for customers, "It broke every rule in the book, but we congratulated the pilot on a job well done."

Four Seasons Hotels, long known for its outstanding service, tells its employees the story of Ron Dyment, a doorman in Toronto, who forgot to load a depart-

ing guest's briefcase into his taxi. The doorman called the guest, a lawyer in Washington, D.C., and learned that he desperately needed the briefcase for a meeting the following morning. Without first asking for approval from management, Dyment hopped on a plane and returned the briefcase. The company named Dyment Employee of the Year.

Similarly, the Nordstrom department store chain thrives on stories about its service heroics, such as employees dropping off orders at customers' homes or warming up cars while customers spend a little more time shopping. In one case, a salesclerk reportedly gave a customer a refund on a tire—Nordstrom doesn't carry tires, but the store prides itself on a no-questions-asked return policy. There's even a story about a man whose wife, a loyal Nordstrom customer, died with her Nordstrom account $1,000 in arrears. Not only did Nordstrom settle the account, it also sent flowers to the funeral.

There's no simple formula for taking care of customers, but neither is it a mystery. According to the president of L.L. Bean, "A lot of people have fancy things to say about customer service . . . but it's just a day-in, day-out, ongoing, never-ending, unremitting, persevering, compassionate type of activity." For the companies that do it well, it's also very rewarding.

Sources: The Lexus and Williams-Sonoma examples are adapted from Denny Hatch and Ernie Schell, "Delight Your Customers," *Target Marketing,* April 2002, pp. 32–39. The Enterprise example is from Dana James, "Lighting the Way," *Marketing News,* April 1, 2002, pp. 1, 11. Also see Patricia Sellers, "Companies That Serve You Best," *Fortune,* May 31, 1993, pp. 74-88; Len Ellis, "Customer Loyalty," *Executive Excellence,* July 2001, pp. 13–14; "Toyota [Lexus] Tops Rankings," *The Washington Post,* May 7, 2003, p. E02; and "Lexus Awards and Accolades," accessed online at www.lexus.com, May 2003.

A second approach is to add *social benefits* as well as financial benefits. Many companies sponsor *club marketing programs* that offer members special discounts and create member communities. For example[19]:

Swiss watchmaker, Swatch, uses its club to cater to collectors, who on average buy nine of the company's quirky watches every year. "Swatch: The Club" members get additional chances to buy limited edition Swatch specials.

■ Building customer relationships: Harley-Davidson sponsors the Harley Owners Group (H.O.G.), which gives Harley owners "an organized way to share their passion and show their pride." The worldwide club now numbers more than 1,300 local chapters and 700,000 members.

They also receive the *Swatch World Journal*, a magazine filled with Swatch-centric news from the four corners of the globe. And the club's Web site is the ultimate meeting place for Swatch enthusiasts. Swatch counts on enthusiastic word of mouth from club members as a boost to business. "Our members are like walking billboards," says the manager of Swatch's club, Trish O'Callaghan. "They love, live, and breathe our product. They are ambassadors for Swatch."

Harley-Davidson sponsors the Harley Owners Group (H.O.G.), which gives Harley riders "an organized way to share their passion and show their pride." H.O.G. membership benefits include two magazines (*Hog Tales* and *Enthusiast*), a *H.O.G. Touring Handbook,* a roadside assistance program, a specially designed insurance program, theft reward service, a travel center, and a "Fly & Ride" program that enables members to rent Harleys while on vacation. The company also maintains an extensive H.O.G. Web site, which offers information on H.O.G. chapters, rallies, events, and benefits. The worldwide club now numbers more than 1,300 local chapters and 700,000 members.

A third approach to building customer relationships is to add *structural ties* as well as financial and social benefits. For example, a business marketer might supply customers with special equipment or computer links that help them manage their orders, payroll, or inventory. McKesson Corporation, a leading pharmaceutical wholesaler, has invested millions of dollars in such linkages. It has set up direct computer links with drug manufacturers and an online system to help small pharmacies manage their inventories, their order entry, and their shelf space. FedEx offers Web links to its customers to keep them from defecting to competitors such as UPS. Customers can use the Web site to arrange shipments and track the status of their FedEx packages anywhere in the world.

The Changing Nature of Customer Relationships

Dramatic changes are occurring in the ways in which companies are relating to their customers. Yesterday's companies focused on mass marketing to all customers at arm's length. Today's companies are building more direct and lasting relationships with more carefully selected customers. Here are some important trends in the way companies are relating to their customers.

Relating with More Carefully Selected Customers Few firms today still practice true mass marketing—selling in a standardized way to any customer who comes along. Today, most marketers realize that they don't want relationships with every customer. Instead, companies are now targeting fewer, more profitable customers.

At the same time that companies are finding new ways to deliver more value *to* customers, they are also beginning to assess carefully the value *of* customers to the firm. Called *selective relationship management*, many companies now use customer profitability analysis to weed out losing customers and target winning ones for pampering. Once they identify profitable customers, firms can create attractive offers and special handling to capture these customers and earn their loyalty.

But what should the company do with unprofitable customers? If it can't turn them into profitable ones, it may even want to "fire" customers that are too unreasonable or that cost more to serve than they are worth. For example, the banking industry has led the way in assessing customer profitability. After decades of casting a wide net to lure as many customers as possible, many banks are now mining their vast databases to identify winning customers and cut out losing ones.

> Banks now routinely calculate customer value based on such factors as an account's average balances, account activity, services usage, branch visits, and other variables. A bank's customer service reps use such customer ratings when deciding how much—or how little—leeway to give a customer who wants, say, a lower credit-card interest rate or to escape the bank's bounced-check fee. Profitable customers often get what they want; for customers whose accounts lose money for the bank, the reps rarely budge.

This sorting-out process, of course, has many risks. For one, future profits are hard to predict. A high school student on his or her way to a Harvard MBA and a plum job on Wall Street might be unprofitable now but worth courting for the future. Or that shabby-looking guy might actually be or become an eccentric billionaire—so you may not want to give him the bum's rush.

Still, most banks believe that the benefits outweigh the risks. For example, after First Chicago imposed a three-dollar teller fee in 1995 on some of its money-losing customers, 30,000 of them—or close to 3 percent of the bank's customers—closed their accounts. However, many marginal customers became profitable by boosting their account balances high enough to avoid the fee or by visiting ATMs instead of tellers. On balance, imposing the fee improved the profitability of the bank's customer base.[20]

Relating for the Long Term Just as companies are being more selective about which customers they choose to serve, they are serving those they choose in a deeper, more lasting way. Today's companies are going beyond designing strategies to *attract* new customers and create *transactions* with them. They are using customer relationship management to *retain* current customers and build profitable, long-term *relationships* with them. The new view is that marketing is the science and art of finding, retaining, *and* growing profitable customers.

Why the new emphasis on retaining and growing customers? In the past, many companies took their customers for granted. Facing an expanding economy and rapidly growing markets, companies could practice a "leaky bucket" approach to marketing. Growing markets meant a plentiful supply of new customers. Companies could keep filling the marketing bucket with new customers without worrying about losing old customers through holes in the bottom of the bucket.

However, companies today face some new marketing realities. Changing demographics, more sophisticated competitors, and overcapacity in many industries mean that there are fewer customers to go around. Many companies are now fighting for shares of flat or fading markets. As a result, the costs of attracting new consumers are rising. In fact, on average, it costs 5 to 10 times as much to attract a new customer as it does to

■ Selective relationship management: BankOne in Louisiana lets its "Premier One" customers know that they are "special, exclusive, privileged, and valued." For example, after presenting a special gold card to the "concierge" near the front door, they are whisked away to a special teller window with no line or to the desk of a specially trained bank officer.

keep a current customer satisfied. Sears found that it costs 12 times more to attract a customer than to keep an existing one.[21] Given these new realities, companies now go all out to keep profitable customers.

Relating Directly   Beyond connecting more deeply with their customers, many companies are also connecting more *directly*. In fact, direct marketing is booming. Consumers can now buy virtually any product without going to a store—by telephone, mail-order catalogs, kiosks, and online. Business purchasing agents routinely shop on the Web for items ranging from standard office supplies to high-priced, high-tech computer equipment.

Some companies sell *only* via direct channels—firms such as Dell Computer, Expedia, 1-800-Flowers, and Amazon.com, to name only a few. Other companies use direct connections to supplement their other communications and distribution channels. For example, Sony sells Playstation consoles and game cartridges through retailers, supported by millions of dollars of mass-media advertising. However, Sony uses its www.PlayStation.com Web site to build relationships with game players of all ages. The site offers information about the latest games, news about events and promotions, game guides and support, and even online forums in which game players can swap tips and stories.

Some marketers have hailed direct marketing as the "marketing model of the next century." They envision a day when all buying and selling will involve direct connections between companies and their customers. Others, although agreeing that direct marketing will play a growing and important role, see it as just one more way to approach the marketplace. We will take a closer look at world of direct marketing in Chapter 13.

Partner Relationship Marketing

When it comes to creating customer value and building strong customer relationships, today's marketers know that they can't go it alone. They must work closely with a variety of marketing partners. In addition to being good at *customer relationship management*, marketers must also be good at **partner relationship management**. Major changes are occurring in how marketers partner with others inside and outside the company to jointly bring more value to customers.

Partner relationship management
Working closely with partners in other company departments and outside the company to jointly bring greater value to customers.

Partners Inside the Company   Traditionally, marketers have been charged with understanding customers and representing customer needs to different company departments. The old thinking was that marketing is done only by marketing, sales, and customer support people. However, in today's more connected world, marketing no longer has sole ownership of customer interactions. Every functional area can interact with customers, especially electronically. The new thinking is that every employee must be customer focused. David Packard, co-founder of Hewlett-Packard, wisely said, "Marketing is far too important to be left only to the marketing department."[22]

Today, rather than letting each department go its own way, firms are linking all departments in the cause of creating customer value. Rather than assigning only sales and marketing people to customers, they are forming cross-functional customer teams. For example, Procter & Gamble assigns "customer development teams" to each of its major retailer accounts. These teams—consisting of sales and marketing people, operations specialists, market and financial analysts, and others—coordinate the efforts of many P&G departments toward helping the retailer be more successful.

Marketing Partners Outside the Firm   Changes are also occurring in how marketers connect with their suppliers, channel partners, and even competitors. Most companies today are networked companies, relying heavily on partnerships with other firms.

Marketing channels consist of distributors, retailers, and others who connect the company to its buyers. The *supply chain* describes a longer channel, stretching from raw materials to components to final products that are carried to final buyers. For example, the supply chain for personal computers consists of suppliers of computer chips and other components, the computer manufacturer, and the distributors, retailers, and others who sell the computers.

Through *supply chain management*, many companies today are strengthening their connections with partners all along the supply chain. They know that their fortunes rest not just on how well they perform. Success at building customer relationships also rests on how well their entire supply chain performs compared with competitors' supply chains. These companies don't treat suppliers just as vendors and distributors just as customers. They treat both as partners in delivering customer value. On the one hand, for example, Lexus works closely with carefully selected suppliers to improve quality and operations efficiency. On the other hand, it works with its franchise dealers to provide top-grade sales and service support that will bring customers in the door and keep them coming back.

Beyond managing the supply chain, today's companies are also discovering that they need *strategic* partners if they hope to be effective. In the new, more competitive global environment, going it alone is going out of style. *Strategic alliances* are booming across almost all industries and services. For example, Dell Computer recently ran advertisements telling how it partners with Microsoft and Intel to provide customized e-business solutions. The ads ask: "Why do many corporations choose Windows running on Dell PowerEdge servers with Intel Pentium processors to power their e-business solutions?" The answer: "At Dell, Microsoft, and Intel, we specialize in solving the impossible." As Jim Kelly, former CEO at UPS, puts it, "The old adage 'If you can't beat 'em, join 'em,' is to being replaced by 'Join 'em and you can't be beat.' "[23]

■■ Capturing Value from Customers

The first four steps in the marketing process involve building customer relationships by creating and delivering superior customer value. The final step involves capturing value in return, in the form of current and future sales, market share, and profits. By creating superior customer value, the firm creates highly satisfied customers who stay loyal and buy more. This, in turn, means greater long-term returns for the firm. Here, we discuss the outcomes of creating customer value: customer loyalty and retention, share of market and share of customer, and customer equity.

Creating Customer Loyalty and Retention

Good customer relationship management creates customer delight. In turn, delighted customers remain loyal and talk favorably to others about the company and its products. Studies show big differences in the loyalty of customers who are less satisfied, somewhat satisfied, and completely satisfied. Even a slight drop from complete satisfaction can create an enormous drop in loyalty. Thus, the aim of customer relationship management is to create not just customer satisfaction, but customer delight.[24]

Companies are realizing that losing a customer means losing more than a single sale. It means losing the entire stream of purchases that the customer would make over a lifetime of patronage. For example, here is a dramatic illustration of **customer lifetime value**:

> Stew Leonard, who operates a highly profitable three-store supermarket chain, says that he sees $50,000 flying out of his store every time he sees a sulking customer. Why? Because his average customer spends about $100 a week, shops 50 weeks a year, and remains in the area for about 10 years. If this customer has an unhappy experience and switches to another supermarket, Stew Leonard's has lost $50,000 in revenue. The loss can be much greater if the disappointed customer shares the bad experience with other customers and causes them to defect. To keep customers coming back, Stew Leonard's has created what the *New York Times* has dubbed the "Disneyland of Dairy Stores," complete with costumed characters, scheduled entertainment, a petting zoo, and animatronics throughout the store. From its humble beginnings as a small dairy store in 1969, Stew Leonard's has grown at an amazing pace. It has built 29 additions onto the original store, which now serves more that 250,000 customers each week. This legion of loyal shoppers is largely a result of the store's passionate approach to customer service. Rule #1 at Stew Leonard's—The customer is always right. Rule #2—If the customer is ever wrong, reread rule #1![25]

Stew Leonard is not alone in assessing customer lifetime value. Lexus estimates that a single satisfied and loyal customer is worth $600,000 in lifetime sales. The customer lifetime

Customer lifetime value
The value of the entire stream of purchases that the customer would make over a lifetime of patronage.

■ Customer lifetime value: To keep customers coming back, Stew Leonard's has created the "Disneyland of dairy stores," Rule #1—the customer is always right. Rule #2—if the customer is ever wrong, reread rule #1!

Share of customer

The portion of the customer's purchasing in its product categories that a company gets.

Customer equity

The total combined customer lifetime values of all of the company's customers.

value of a Taco Bell customer exceeds $12,000.[26] Thus, working to retain and grow customers makes good economic sense. In fact, a company can lose money on a specific transaction but still benefit greatly from a long-term relationship.

This means that companies must aim high in building customer relationships. Customer delight creates an emotional relationship with a product or service, not just a rational preference. Hanging on to customers is "so basic, it's scary," claims one marketing executive. "We find out what our customers' needs and wants are, and then we overdeliver."[27]

Growing Share of Customer

Beyond simply retaining good customers to capture customer lifetime value, good customer relationship management can help marketers to increase their **share of customer**—the share they get of the customer's purchasing in their product categories. Many marketers are now spending less time figuring out how to increase share of market and more time trying to grow share of customer. Thus, banks want to increase "share of wallet." Supermarkets and restaurants want to get a greater "share of stomach." Car companies want to increase "share of garage" and airlines want greater "share of travel."

To increase share of customer, firms can leverage customer relationships by offering greater variety to current customers. Or they can train employees to cross-sell and up-sell in order to market more products and services to existing customers. For example, Amazon.com is highly skilled at leveraging relationships with its 35 million customers to increase its share of each customer's purchases. Originally an online bookseller, Amazon now offers customers music, videos, gifts, toys, consumer electronics, office products, home improvement items, lawn and garden products, apparel and accessories, and an online auction. In addition, based on each customer's purchase history, the company recommends related books, CDs, or videos that might be of interest. In this way, Amazon.com captures a greater share of each customer's leisure and entertainment budget.

Building Customer Equity

We can now see the importance of not just acquiring customers, but of keeping and growing them as well. Customer relationship management is oriented toward the long term. Today's smart companies not only want to create profitable customers, they want to "own" them for life, capture their customer lifetime value, and earn a greater share of their purchases.

What Is Customer Equity?   The ultimate aim of customer relationship management is to produce high **customer equity**.[28] Customer equity is the total combined customer lifetime values of all of the company's customers. Clearly, the more loyal the firm's profitable customers, the higher the firm's customer equity. Customer equity may be a better measure of a firm's performance than current sales or market share. Whereas sales and market share reflect the past, customer equity suggests the future. Consider Cadillac:

In the 1970s and 1980s, Cadillac had some of the most loyal customers in the industry. To an entire generation of car buyers, the name "Cadillac" defined American luxury. Cadillac's share of the luxury car market reached a whopping 51 percent in 1976. Based on market share and sales, the brand's future looked rosy. However, measures of customer equity would have painted a bleaker picture. Cadillac customers were getting older (average age, 60), and average customer lifetime value was falling. Many Cadillac buyers were on their last car. Thus, although

Cadillac's market share was good, its customer equity was not. Compare this with BMW. Its more youthful and vigorous image didn't win BMW the early market share war. However, it did win BMW younger customers with higher customer lifetime values. The result: Cadillac now captures only about a 15 percent market share, lower than BMW's. And BMW's customer equity remains much higher—it has more customers with a higher average customer lifetime value. Thus, market share is not the answer. We should care not just about current sales but also about future sales. Customer lifetime value and customer equity are the name of the game.[29]

Building the Right Relationships with the Right Customers Companies should manage customer equity carefully. They should view customers as assets that need to be managed and maximized. But not all customers, not even all loyal ones, are good investments. Surprisingly, some loyal customers can be unprofitable, and some disloyal customers can be profitable. Which customers should the company acquire and retain? "Up to a point, the choice is obvious: Keep the consistent big spenders and lose the erratic small spenders," says one expert. "But what about the erratic big spenders and the consistent small spenders? It's often unclear whether they should be acquired or retained, and at what cost."[30]

The company can classify customers according to their potential profitability and manage its relationships with them accordingly. Figure 1.5 classifies customers into one of four relationship groups, according to their profitability and projected loyalty.[31] Each group requires a different relationship management strategy. "Strangers" show low profitability and little projected loyalty. There is little fit between the company's offerings and their needs. The relationship management strategy for these customers is simple: don't invest anything in them.

"Butterflies" are profitable but not loyal. There is a good fit between the company's offerings and their needs. However, like real butterflies, we can enjoy them for only a short while and then they're gone. An example is stock market investors who trade shares often and in large amounts, but who enjoy hunting out the best deals without building a regular relationship with any single brokerage company. Efforts to convert butterflies into loyal customers are rarely successful. Instead, the company should enjoy the butterflies for the moment. It should use promotional blitzes to attract them, create satisfying and profitable transactions with them, and then cease investing in them until the next time around.

"True friends" are both profitable and loyal. There is a strong fit between their needs and the company's offerings. The firm wants to make continuous relationship investments to delight these customers and nurture, retain, and grow them. It wants to turn true friends into "true believers," who come back regularly and tell others about their good experiences with the company.

"Barnacles" are highly loyal but not very profitable. There is a limited fit between their needs and the company's offerings. An example is smaller bank customers who bank regularly but do not generate enough returns to cover the costs of maintaining their accounts. Like barnacles on the hull of a ship, they create drag. Barnacles are perhaps the most problematic customers. The company might be able to improve their profitability by selling them more, raising their fees, or reducing service to them. However, if they cannot be made profitable, they should be "fired."

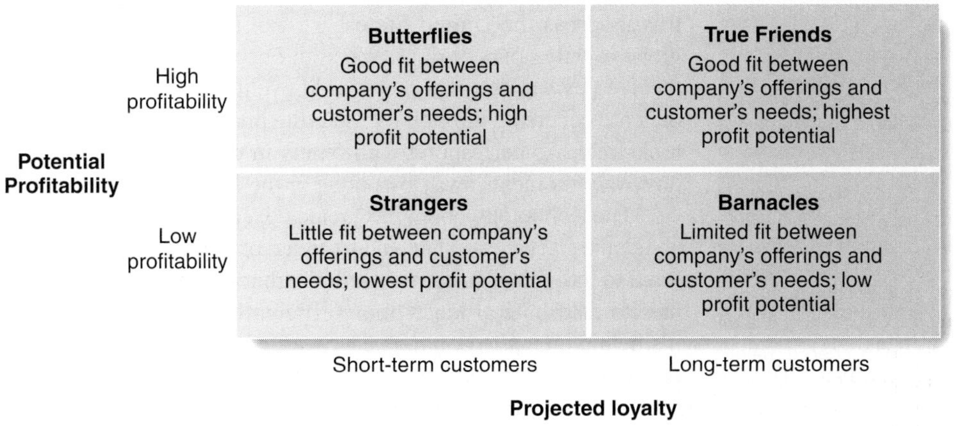

Potential Profitability		Short-term customers	Long-term customers
	High profitability	**Butterflies** Good fit between company's offerings and customer's needs; high profit potential	**True Friends** Good fit between company's offerings and customer's needs; highest profit potential
	Low profitability	**Strangers** Little fit between company's offerings and customer's needs; lowest profit potential	**Barnacles** Limited fit between company's offerings and customer's needs; low profit potential

Projected loyalty

FIGURE 1.5

Customer Relationship Groups

The point here is an important one: different types of customer require different relationship management strategies. The goal is to build the *right relationships* with the *right customers*.

Linking the Concepts

We've covered a lot of territory. Again, slow down for a moment and develop *your own* thoughts about marketing.

■ In *your own words*, what *is* marketing and what does it seek to accomplish?
■ How well does Lexus manage its relationships with customers? What customer relationship management strategy does it use? What relationship management strategy does Wal-Mart use?
■ Think of a company for which you are a "true friend." What strategy does this company use to manage its relationship with you?

■■ The New Marketing Landscape

As the world spins into the first decade of the twenty-first century, dramatic changes are occurring in the marketing arena. Richard Love of Hewlett-Packard observes, "The pace of change is so rapid that the ability to change has now become a competitive advantage." Yogi Berra, the legendary New York Yankees catcher, summed it up more simply when he said, "The future ain't what it used to be." Technological advances, rapid globalization, and continuing social and economic shifts—all are causing profound changes in the marketplace. As the marketplace changes, so must those who serve it.

In this section, we examine the major trends and forces that are changing the marketing landscape and challenging marketing strategy. We look at five major developments: the new digital age, rapid globalization, the call for more ethics and social responsibility, the growth in not-for-profit marketing, and the new world of marketing relationships.

The New Digital Age

The recent technology boom has created a new digital age. The explosive growth in computer, telecommunications, information, transportation, and other technologies has had a major impact on the ways companies bring value to their customers. Now, more than ever before, we are all connected to each other and to things near and far in the world around us. Moreover, we are relating in new and different ways. Where it once took weeks or months to travel across the United States, we can now travel around the globe in only hours or days. Where it once took days or weeks to receive news about important world events, we now see them as they are occurring through live satellite broadcasts. Where it once took weeks to correspond with others in distant places, they are now only moments away by phone or the Internet.

The technology boom has created exciting new ways to learn about and track customers, and to create products and services tailored to individual customer needs. Technology is helping companies to distribute products more efficiently and effectively. And it's helping them to communicate with customers in large groups or one-to-one. For example, through videoconferencing, marketing researchers at a company's headquarters in New York can look

■ The New Digital Age: The recent technology boom has had a major impact on the ways marketers connect with and bring value to their customers.

in on focus groups in Chicago or Paris without ever stepping onto a plane. With only a few clicks of a mouse button, a direct marketer can tap into online data services to learn anything from what car you drive to what you read to what flavor of ice cream you prefer.

Using today's vastly more powerful computers, marketers create detailed databases and use them to target individual customers with offers designed to meet their specific needs and buying patterns. Technology has also brought a new wave of communication and advertising tools—ranging from cell phones, fax machines, CD-ROMs, and interactive TVs to video kiosks at airports and shopping malls. Marketers can use these tools to zero in on selected customers with carefully targeted messages. Through e-commerce, customers can learn about, design, order, and pay for products and services—without ever leaving home. Then, through the marvels of express delivery, they can receive their purchases in less than 24 hours. From virtual reality displays that test new products to online virtual stores that sell them, the technology boom is affecting every aspect of marketing.

The Internet Perhaps the most dramatic new technology is the **Internet**. Today, the Internet links individuals and businesses of all types to each other and to information around the world. The Internet has been hailed as the technology behind a New Economy. It allows anytime, anywhere connections to information, entertainment, and communication. Companies are using the Internet to build closer relationships with customers and marketing partners. Beyond competing in traditional marketplaces, they now have access to exciting new market*spaces*.

Internet usage surged in the 1990s with the development of the user-friendly World Wide Web. Entering the twenty-first century, Internet penetration in the United States has reached 67 percent, with some 160 million people accessing the Web in any given month. The Internet is truly a global phenomenon—the number of Internet users worldwide reached 655 million last year and is expected to approach 1.5 billion by 2007.[32] This growing and diverse Internet population means that all kinds of people are now going to the Web for information and to buy products and services.

These days, it's hard to find a company that doesn't use the Web in a significant way. Most traditional "brick-and-mortar" companies have now become "click-and-mortar" companies. They have ventured online to attract new customers and build stronger relationships with existing ones. The Internet also spawned an entirely new breed of "click-only" companies—the so-called dot-coms. During the Web frenzy of the late 1990s, dot-coms popped up everywhere, selling anything from books, toys, and CDs to furniture, home mortgages, and 100-pound bags of dog food via the Internet. The frenzy cooled during the "dot-com meltdown" of 2000, when many poorly conceived e-tailers and other Web start-ups went out of business. Today, despite its turbulent start, online consumer buying is growing at a healthy rate, and many of the dot-com survivors face promising futures. More than half of the companies that survived the meltdown are now profitable.[33]

If consumer e-commerce looks promising, business-to-business e-commerce is just plain booming. Business-to-business transactions online amounted to $3.9 trillion last year and are expected to reach $4.3 trillion in 2005, compared with only $107 billion in consumer purchases. By 2005, more than 500,000 businesses will engage in e-commerce as buyers, sellers, or both. It seems that almost every major business has set up shop on the Web. Giants such as GE, IBM, Dell, Cisco Systems, Microsoft, and many others have moved quickly to exploit the power of the Internet.[34]

Thus, the technology boom is providing exciting new opportunities for marketers. We will explore the impact of the new digital age in more detail in Chapter 14.

Rapid Globalization

As they are redefining their relationships with customers and partners, marketers are also taking a fresh look at the ways in which they connect with the broader world around them. In an increasingly smaller world, many marketers are now connected *globally* with their customers and marketing partners.

The world economy has undergone radical change during the past two decades. Geographical and cultural distances have shrunk with the advent of jet planes, fax

Internet
A vast public web of computer networks, which connects users of all types all around the world to each other and to an amazingly large information repository.

■ Many U.S. companies have developed truly global operations. Coca-Cola offers more than 300 different brands in more than 200 countries including BPM Energy drink in Ireland, Mare Rosso Bitter in Spain, Sprite Ice Cube in Belgium, Fanta in Chile, and NaturAqua in Hungary.

machines, world satellite television broadcasts, global Internet hookups, and other technical advances. This has allowed companies to greatly expand their geographical market coverage, purchasing, and manufacturing. The result is a vastly more complex marketing environment for both companies and consumers.

Today, almost every company, large or small, is touched in some way by global competition. A neighborhood florist buys its flowers from Mexican nurseries, while a large U.S. electronics manufacturer competes in its home markets with giant Japanese rivals. A fledgling Internet retailer finds itself receiving orders from all over the world at the same time that an American consumer-goods producer introduces new products into emerging markets abroad.

American firms have been challenged at home by the skillful marketing of European and Asian multinationals. Companies such as Toyota, Siemens, Nestlé, Sony, and Samsung have often outperformed their U.S. competitors in American markets. Similarly, U.S. companies in a wide range of industries have found new opportunities abroad. General Motors, ExxonMobil, IBM, General Electric, DuPont, Motorola, and dozens of other American companies have developed truly global operations, making and selling their products worldwide. Coca-Cola offers a mind-boggling 300 different brands in more than 200 countries. Even MTV has joined the elite of global brands, delivering localized versions of its pulse-thumping fare to teens in 140 countries around the globe (see Marketing at Work 1.3).

Today, companies are not only trying to sell more of their locally produced goods in international markets, they also are buying more supplies and components abroad. For example, Bill Blass, one of America's top fashion designers, may choose cloth woven from Australian wool with designs printed in Italy. He will design a dress and e-mail the drawing to a Hong Kong agent, who will place the order with a Chinese factory. Finished dresses will be air-freighted to New York, where they will be redistributed to department and specialty stores around the country.

Thus, managers in countries around the world are increasingly taking a global, not just local, view of the company's industry, competitors, and opportunities. They are asking: What is global marketing? How does it differ from domestic marketing? How do global

Marketing at Work | 1.3

MTV Global: Music Is the Universal Language

Some say love is the universal language. But for MTV, the universal language is *music*. In 1981, MTV began offering its unique brand of programming for young music lovers across the United States. The channel's quirky but pulse-thumping lineup of shows soon attracted a large audience in its targeted 12-to-34 age group. MTV quickly established itself as the nation's youth-culture network, offering up "everything young people care about." With success in the United States secured, MTV went global in 1986, selling a few hours of programming to Japan's Asahi network. A short time later, in 1987, it launched MTV Europe, and the network has experienced phenomenal global growth ever since.

MTV now offers programming in 140 countries, including Brazil, Canada, France, Holland, India, Italy, Japan, Korea, Latin America, Poland, Russia, Southeast Asia, Spain, Taiwan, Hong Kong, the United Kingdom, and Germany. It recently became the first U.S. cable network to provide round-the-clock programming in China. The result of this global expansion? Today, MTV reaches twice as many people around the world as CNN, and 8 of 10 MTV viewers live outside the United States. Altogether, MTV reaches into an astounding 384 million households in 19 different languages on 31 different channels and 17 Web sites.

What is the secret to MTV's roaring international success? Of course, it offers viewers around the globe plenty of what made it so popular in the United States. Tune in to the network in Paris, or Beijing, or Moscow, or Tierra del Fuego, or anywhere else and you'll see all of the elements that make it uniquely MTV anywhere in the world—the global MTV brand symbols, fast-paced format, veejays, rockumentaries, and music, music, music. But rather than just offering a carbon copy of its U.S. programming to international viewers, MTV carefully localizes its fare. Each channel serves up a mix that includes 70 percent local programming tailored to the specific tastes of viewers in local markets. A *Business Week* analyst notes:

[MTV is] shrewd enough to realize that while the world's teens want American music, they really want the local stuff, too. So, MTV's producers and veejays scour their local markets for the top talent. The result is an endless stream of overnight sensations that keep MTV's global offerings fresh. Just over a year ago, for example, Lena Katina and Yulia Volkova were no different than most Moscow schoolgirls. Today, Katina, 16, and Volkova, 15, make up Tatu, one of the hottest bands ever to come out of Russia.

Tatu is just one of a slew of emerging local music groups gaining international exposure through MTV and a wider audience in the United States, too. Colombian rock singer Shakira, unknown outside Latin America until 1999 when she recorded an MTV Unplugged CD—the acoustic live concerts recorded by MTV—is now the winner of one U.S. Grammy and two Latin Grammy awards. Her CD has gone platinum, selling more than 2 million copies worldwide.

[MTV's] policy of 70 percent local content has resulted in some of the network's most creative shows, such as MTV Brazil's month-long *Rockgol*, a soccer championship that pits Brazilian musicians against record industry executives. In Russia, the locally produced *Twelve Angry Viewers* was voted one of Russia's top three talk programs. In a colorful studio amid bright blue steps and large green cushions, a dozen teens watch and discuss the latest videos. Periodically, they break into spontaneous dance or pop one another over the head with inflatable lollipops. Okay, it's not Chekhov. But Russian groups beg to be featured on it.

Ceding so much control to local channels does result in the occasional misstep. While watching MTV in Taiwan, [MTV executives were] aghast to see nude wrestling. That was one time

MTV has joined the ranks of the global brand elite. It reaches into an astounding 384 million households in 19 different languages on 33 different channels and 17 Web sites. From Germany to China, "MTV's version of globalization rocks."

(continued)

[they] had to intervene. And when MTV first entered the Indian market in 1996, Hindi film music—the romantic soundtracks of Bollywood movies—was wildly popular, but [MTV's] locally hired programmers disdained it as uncool. Viewers abandoned the channel, forcing it to [relent and] air Bollywood music. Since then its ratings have soared by some 700 percent.

At the center of MTV's global growth machine is Bill Roedy, president of MTV Networks International. He's a nonstop ambassador on a mission to make MTV available in every last global nook and cranny.

To give kids their dose of rock, [Roedy] has breakfasted with former Israeli Prime Minister Shimon Peres, dined with Singapore founder Lee Kuan Yew, and chewed the fat with Chinese leader Jiang Zemin. [He] even met with El Caudillo himself—

Cuban leader Fidel Castro—who wondered if MTV could teach Cuban kids English. Says Roedy: "We've had very little resistance once we explain that we're not in the business of exporting American culture."

MTV's unique blend of international and local programming is not only popular, it's also highly profitable. The network's hold on a young, increasingly wealthy population makes its programming especially popular with advertisers. Altogether, its mix of local and international content, combined with early entry in international markets, makes it tough to beat. "MTV Networks International makes buckets of money year after year from a potent combination of cable subscriber fees, advertising, and, increasingly, new media," concludes the analyst. "Revenues at MTV Networks International increased 19 percent [last year] . . . while operating

profits grew a hefty 50 percent. They are expected to more than double by 2004." Meanwhile, the competition struggles just to break even. VIVA, MTV's strongest competitor in Europe, has yet to turn a profit.

Thus, in only two decades, MTV has joined the ranks of the global brand elite, alongside such icons as Coke, Levi's, and Sony. Concludes the analyst: "MTV's version of globalization rocks."

Sources: Excerpts from Kerry Capell, "MTV's World: Mando-Pop. Mexican Hip Hop. Russian Rap. It's All Fueling the Biggest Global Channel," *Business Week*, February 18, 2002, pp. 81–84. Also see Lynn Elber, "U.S. TV Networks Expand Interests Overseas," *Marketing News*, November 7, 1994, p. 7; Alkman Granitsas, "MTV Is Launching a 24-Hour Network in Indonesian Cities," *Wall Street Journal*, March 13, 2002, p. B7; "MTV to Begin 24-Hour Service in Part of China," *New York Times*, March 27, 2003, p. C.13; the MTV Worldwide Web site, www.mtv.com/mtvinternational; and "MTV: Music Television: The Facts," accessed online at www.viacom.com/prodbyunit1.tin?ixBusUnit=19, May 2003.

competitors and forces affect our business? To what extent should we "go global"? Many companies are forming strategic alliances with foreign companies, even competitors, who serve as suppliers or marketing partners. Winning companies in the next century may well be those that have built the best global networks. We will discuss the global marketplace in more detail in Chapter 15.

The Call for More Ethics and Social Responsibility

Marketers are reexamining their relationships with social values and responsibilities and with the very Earth that sustains us. As the worldwide consumerism and environmentalism movements mature, today's marketers are being called upon to take greater responsibility for the social and environmental impacts of their actions. Corporate ethics and social responsibility have become hot topics for almost every business. And few companies can ignore the renewed and very demanding environmental movement.

The social-responsibility and environmental movements will place even stricter demands on companies in the future. Some companies resist these movements, budging only when forced to by legislation or organized consumer outcries. More forward-looking companies, however, readily accept their responsibilities to the world around them. They view socially responsible actions as an opportunity to do well by doing good. They seek ways to profit by serving the best long-run interests of their customers and communities.

Some companies—such as Ben & Jerry's, Saturn, Honest Tea, and others—are practicing "caring capitalism" and distinguishing themselves by being more civic-minded and caring. They are building social responsibility and action into their company value and mission statements. For example, consider Ben & Jerry's, a division of Unilever. Its mission statement challenges all employees, from top management to ice cream scoopers in each store, to include concern for individual and community welfare in their day-to-day decisions. We will revisit the relationship between marketing and social responsibility in greater detail in Chapter 16.[35]

The Growth of Not-for-Profit Marketing

In the past, marketing has been most widely applied in the for-profit business sector. In recent years, however, marketing also has become a major part of the strategies of many not-for-profit organizations, such as colleges, hospitals, museums, symphony orchestras, and even churches. Consider the following example:

"Want to feed your soul?" implores a subway ad for Marble Collegiate Church in New York City. "We've got a great menu." Indeed, Marble Collegiate has something on its plate for almost every type of hungering spiritual consumer. It has ministries targeting senior citizens; young singles; older singles; gays and lesbians; entrepreneurs; artists, actors, and writers; men; women; children; and people who love singing gospel music, to name a few. The church is now at work on yet another program. Called the New Spirit Café, it's a hip kind of spiritual eatery designed to feed the souls—and stomachs—of those who may be disillusioned by organized religion. The New Spirit Café aims to establish Marble Collegiate's "brand" with spiritually minded people in their twenties and thirties who may be wary of conventional religious organizations. It is purposely located several blocks from the sanctuary and offers its fare of hot food, snacks, and seminars six days a week.

Marble Collegiate is not alone in turning to marketing. To maintain their shrinking flocks, religious institutions have increasingly borrowed marketing tools and tactics from companies selling more worldly goods. Many are tailoring their core product—religion itself—to the needs of specific demographic groups. To get its message out, Marble Collegiate anointed a Madison Avenue advertising agency as its missionary. The agency produced a slick marketing campaign with hip, youth-oriented messages. One ad urges potential parishioners to "Make a friend in a very high place." Exhorts another: "Our product really does perform miracles." All the marketing seems to be working. Marble Collegiate's Web site traffic has increased by 30 percent since its ad campaign launched, and the church has had its highest attendance in more than 30 years.[36]

Similarly, private colleges, facing declining enrollments and rising costs, are using marketing to compete for students and funds. Many performing arts groups—even the Lyric Opera Company of Chicago, which has seasonal sellouts—face huge operating deficits that they must cover by more aggressive donor marketing. Finally, many

■ Broadening connections: Marble Collegiate Church's advertising agency has produced ads with hip, youth-oriented messages.

long-standing not-for-profit organizations—the YMCA, the Salvation Army, the Girl Scouts—have lost members and are now modernizing their missions and "products" to attract more members and donors.[37]

Government agencies have also shown an increased interest in marketing. For example, the U.S. Army has a marketing plan to attract recruits, and various government agencies are now designing *social marketing campaigns* to encourage energy conservation and concern for the environment or to discourage smoking, excessive drinking, and drug use. Even the once-stodgy U.S. Postal Service has developed innovative marketing to sell commemorative stamps, promote its priority mail services against those of its competitors, and lift its image. It invests some $100 million annually in advertising.[38]

Every type of organization—for-profit, not-for-profit, governmental—can connect through marketing. The continued growth of not-for-profit and public-sector marketing presents new and exciting challenges for marketing managers.

The New World of Marketing Relationships

As our discussion of the marketing process suggests, the major new developments in marketing can be summed up in a single word: *relationships*. Today, smart marketers of all kinds are taking advantage of new opportunities for building relationships with their customers, their marketing partners, and the world around them. Table 1.1 compares the old marketing thinking with the new. The old marketing thinking saw marketing as little more than selling or advertising. It viewed marketing as customer acquisition rather than customer care. It emphasized trying to make a profit on each sale rather than trying to profit by managing long-term customer equity. And it concerned itself with trying to sell products rather than to understand, create, communicate, and deliver real value to customers.

Fortunately, this old marketing thinking is now giving way to newer ways of thinking. Modern marketing companies are improving their customer knowledge and customer relationships. They are targeting profitable customers, then finding innovative ways to capture

TABLE 1.1   Marketing Relationships in Transition

The Old Marketing Thinking	The New Marketing Thinking
Relationships with Customers	
Be sales and product centered	Be market and customer centered
Practice mass marketing	Target selected market segments or individuals
Focus on products and sales	Focus on customer satisfaction and value
Make sales to customers	Develop customer relationships
Get new customers	Keep old customers
Grow share of market	Grow share of customer
Serve any customer	Serve profitable customers, "fire" losing ones
Communicate through mass media	Connect with customers directly
Make standardized products	Develop customized products
Relationships with Marketing Partners	
Leave customer satisfaction and value to sales and marketing	Enlist all departments in the cause of customer satisfaction and value
Go it alone	Partner with other firms
Relationships with the World Around Us	
Market locally	Market locally *and* globally
Assume profit responsibility	Assume social and environmental responsibility
Market for profits	Market for nonprofits
Conduct commerce in market*places*	Conduct e-commerce in market*spaces*

and keep these customers. They are forming more-direct connections with customers and building lasting customer relationships. Using more-targeted media and integrating their marketing communications, they are delivering meaningful and consistent messages through every customer contact. They are employing more technologies such as videoconferencing, sales automation software, and the Internet, intranets, and extranets. They view their suppliers and distributors as partners, not adversaries. In sum, today's companies are connecting in new ways to deliver superior value to and build relationships with their customers.

■■ So, What Is Marketing? Pulling It All Together

At the start of this chapter, Figure 1.1 presented a simple model of the marketing process. Now that we've discussed all of the steps in the model, Figure 1.6 presents an expanded model that will help you pull it all together. What is marketing? Simply put, marketing is the process of building profitable customer relationships by creating value for customers and capturing value in return.

The first four steps of the marketing process focus on creating value for customers. The company starts by researching consumer needs and wants and managing marketing information to gain a full understanding of the marketplace. It then designs a customer-driven marketing strategy based on the answers to two simple questions. The first question is "What consumers will we serve?" (market segmentation and targeting). Good marketing companies know that they cannot serve all customers in every way. They need to focus their resources on the customers they can serve best and most profitably. The

FIGURE 1.6

An Expanded Model of the Marketing Process

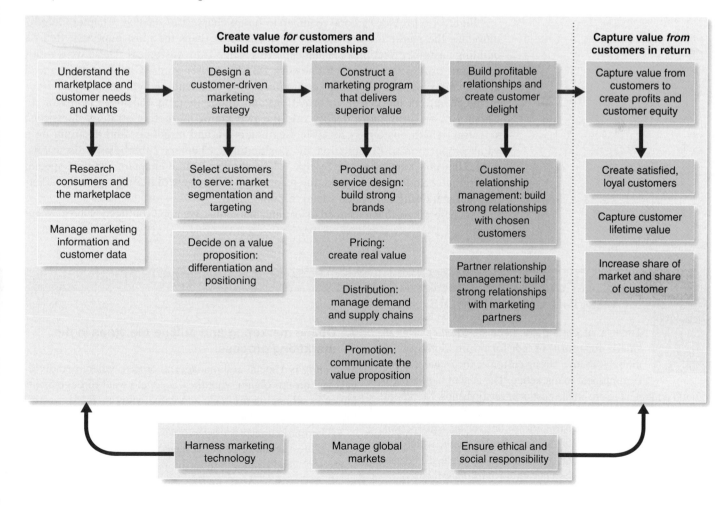

second marketing strategy question is "How can we best serve targeted customers?" (differentiation and positioning). Here, the marketer outlines a value proposition that spells out what benefits and values the company will deliver in order to win target customers.

With its marketing strategy decided, the company now constructs a marketing program—consisting of the four marketing mix elements, or the four Ps—that transforms the marketing strategy into real value for customers. The company develops product offers and creates strong brand identities for them. It prices these offers to create real customer value and distributes the offers to make them available to target consumers. Finally, the company develops promotion programs that communicate the value proposition to target consumers and persuade them to act on the marketing offer.

Perhaps the most important step in the marketing process involves building value-laden, profitable relationships with target customers. Throughout the process, marketers practice customer relationship management to create customer satisfaction and delight. In creating customer value and relationships, however, today's outstanding marketing companies know that they cannot go it alone. They must work closely with marketing partners inside the company and throughout the marketing system. Thus, in addition to practicing good customer relationship management, firms must also practice good partner relationship management.

The first four steps in the marketing process create value *for* customers. In the final step, the company reaps the rewards of the strong customer relationships by capturing value *from* customers. Delivering superior customer value creates highly satisfied customers who will buy more and will buy again. This helps the company to capture customer lifetime value and a greater share of customer. The result is increased long-term customer equity for the firm.

Finally, in the face of today's changing marketing landscape, companies must take into account three additional factors. In building customer and partner relationships, they must harness marketing technology, take advantage of global opportunities, and ensure that they act in an ethical and socially responsible way.

Figure 1.6 provides a good roadmap to future chapters of the text. Chapters 1 and 2 introduce the marketing process, with a focus on perhaps the most important steps—building customer relationships and capturing value from customers. These steps result from and provide a guiding framework for the earlier steps. Chapters 3, 4, and 5 address the first step of the marketing process—understanding the marketing environment, managing marketing information, and understanding consumer behavior. In Chapter 6, we look more deeply into the two major marketing strategy decisions: selecting which customers to serve (segmentation and targeting) and deciding on a value proposition (differentiation and positioning). Chapters 7 through 13 discuss the marketing mix variables, one by one. Then, the final three chapters examine special marketing considerations: marketing technology in this new digital age, global marketing, and marketing ethics and social responsibility.

So, here we go, down the road to learning marketing. We hope you'll enjoy the journey!

REST STOP:
Reviewing the Concepts

Today's successful companies—whether large or small, for-profit or not-for-profit, domestic or global—share a strong customer focus and a heavy commitment to marketing. The goal of marketing is to build and manage profitable customer relationships. Marketing seeks to attract new customers by promising superior value and to keep and grow current customers by delivering satisfaction. Marketing operates within a dynamic environment, which can quickly make yesterday's winning strategies obsolete. To be successful, companies will have to be strongly customer focused.

1. Define marketing and outline the steps in the marketing process.

Marketing is a social and managerial process whereby individuals and groups obtain what they need and want through creating and exchanging products and value with others. More simply, it's managing profitable customer relationships.

The marketing process involves five steps. The first four steps in the marketing process create value *for* customers. First, marketers need to understand the marketplace and customer needs and wants. Next, marketers design a customer-driven marketing strategy with the goal of getting, keeping, and growing target customers. In the third step, marketers construct a marketing program that actually delivers superior value. All of these steps form the basis for the fourth step, building profitable customer relationships and create customer delight. In the final step, the company reaps the rewards of the strong customer relationships by capturing value *from* customers.

2. Explain the importance of understanding customers and the marketplace, and identify the five core marketplace concepts.

Outstanding marketing companies go to great lengths to learn about and understand their customers' needs, wants, and demands. This understanding helps them to design want-satisfying marketing offers and build value-laden customer relationships by which they can capture customer lifetime value and greater share of customer. The result is increased long-term customer equity for the firm.

The core marketplace concepts are *needs, wants,* and *demands; marketing offers (products, services, and experiences); value* and *satisfaction; exchange, transactions,* and *relationships;* and *markets. Wants* are the form taken by human needs when shaped by culture and individual personality. When backed by buying power, wants become *demands.* Companies address needs by putting forth a *value proposition,* a set of benefits that they promise to consumers to satisfy their needs. The value proposition is fulfilled through a *marketing offer,* which delivers customer value and satisfaction, resulting in long-term exchange relationships with customers.

3. Identify the key elements of a customer-driven marketing strategy, and discuss marketing management orientations that guide marketing strategy.

To design a winning marketing strategy, the company must first decide *who* it will serve. It does this by dividing the market into segments of customers (*market segmentation*) and selecting which segments it will cultivate (*target marketing*). Next, the company must decide *how* it will serve targeted customers (how it will *differentiate and position* itself in the marketplace).

Marketing management can adopt one of five competing market orientations. The *production concept* holds that management's task is to improve production efficiency and bring down prices. The *product concept* holds that consumers favor products that offer the most in quality, performance, and innovative features; thus, little promotional effort is required. The *selling concept* holds that consumers will not buy enough of the organization's products unless it undertakes a large-scale selling and promotion effort. The *marketing concept* holds that achieving organizational goals depends on determining the needs and wants of target markets and delivering the desired satisfactions more effectively and efficiently than competitors do. The *societal marketing concept* holds that generating customer satisfaction *and* long-run societal well-being are the keys to both achieving the company's goals and fulfilling its responsibilities.

4. Discuss customer relationship management, and identify strategies for creating value *for* customers and capturing value *from* customers in return.

Broadly defined, *customer relationship management* is the overall process of building and maintaining profitable customer relationships by delivering superior customer value and satisfaction. The aim of customer relationship management is to produce high *customer equity,* the total combined customer lifetime values of all of the company's customers.

The key to building lasting relationships is the creation of superior *customer value* and *satisfaction,* and companies need to understand the determinants of these important elements. *Customer perceived value* is the difference between total customer value and total customer cost. Customers will usually choose the offer that maximizes their perceived value. *Customer satisfaction* results when a company's performance has fulfilled a buyer's expectations. Customers are dissatisfied if performance is below expectations, satisfied if performance equals expectations, and delighted if performance exceeds expectations. Highly satisfied customers buy more, are less price sensitive, talk favorably about the company, and remain loyal longer.

Companies want not only to acquire profitable customers, but to build relationships that will keep them and grow "share of customer." Companies must decide the level at which they want to build relationships with different market segments and individual customers, ranging from basic relationships to full partnerships. Today's marketers use a number of specific marketing tools to develop stronger bonds with customers by adding *financial* and *social benefits* or *structural ties.* Different types of customers require different customer relationship management strategies. The marketer's aim is to build the *right relationships* with the *right customers.* In return for creating value *for* targeted customers, the company captures value *from* customers in the form of profits and customer equity.

In building customer relationships, good marketers realize that they cannot go it alone. They must work closely with marketing partners inside and outside the company. In addition to being good at customer relationship management, they must also be good at *partner relationship management.*

5. Describe the major trends and forces that are changing the marketing landscape in this new age of relationships.

As the world spins into the twenty-first century, dramatic changes are occurring in the marketing arena. The explosive growth in computer, telecommunications, information, transportation, and other technologies has had a major impact on marketing. The technology boom has created exciting new ways to learn about and track customers, and to create products and services tailored to individual customer needs.

In an increasingly smaller world, many marketers are now connected *globally* with their customers and marketing partners. Today, almost every company, large or small, is touched in some way by global competition. Thus, managers in countries around the world are increasingly taking a global, not just local, view of the company's industry, competitors, and opportunities.

Today's marketers are also reexamining their social values and societal responsibilities. As the worldwide consumerism and environmentalism movements mature, marketers are being called upon to take greater responsibility for the social and environmental impacts of their actions. Corporate ethics and social responsibility have become hot topics for almost every business. And few companies can ignore the renewed and very demanding environmental movement.

In the past, marketing has been most widely applied in the for-profit business sector. In recent years, however, marketing also has become a major part of the strategies of many not-for-profit organizations, such as colleges, hospitals, museums, symphony orchestras, and even churches. Finally, as discussed throughout the chapter, the major new developments in marketing can be summed up in a single word: *relationships*. Today, smart marketers of all kinds are taking advantage of new opportunities for building relationships with their customers, their marketing partners, and the world around them.

Navigating the Key Terms

Customer equity
Customer lifetime value
Customer perceived value
Customer relationship
   management
Customer satisfaction
Demands
Demarketing
Exchange

Internet
Market
Marketing
Marketing concept
Marketing management
Marketing offer
Needs
Partner relationship
   management

Product concept
Production concept
Share of customer
Selling concept
Societal marketing concept
Transaction
Wants

Travel Log

Discussing the Issues

1. Why is understanding customer wants so critical for marketers? How are the concepts of value and satisfaction related to each other? Explain the difference between transactions and relationships.

2. Why is target-market selection important for a customer-driven marketing strategy? Discuss some of the negative consequences a company might incur from not paying enough attention to selecting its target market.

3. Discuss the differences between the production, product, selling, marketing, and societal marketing concepts. Identify circumstances where each one may be appropriate.

4. What are the advantages for a company in building relationships with its customers? What are some ways in which a company can build customer relationships?

5. Discuss the potential for technological advances and globalization to change the manner in which companies interact with their customers and business partners.

6. Think of a company in your town with which you have a relationship. What value do you get from that relationship and how does that company capture value from you in return?

Application Questions

1. Human *needs* are a basic desire for things one does not have (e.g., clothing). These needs are transformed into specific *wants* by one's individual personality and the culture in which one lives. Consider the basic need of self-expression. This need can be transformed into a variety of "wants." For example, clothing, hairstyles, tattoos, and body piercing could satisfy this need. Discuss the degree to which a company offering clothing should consider other companies offering hairstyles, tattoos, and body piercing as competitors for consumers motivated by self-expression.

2. Specific marketing tools to develop stronger bonds with consumers include financial benefits, social benefits, and structural ties. Identify three companies you feel exemplify each of these tools. Explain how each company uses the tool to build customer relationships. Among the three companies you identified, consider if it would be advisable for those using the financial or social benefits approach to also include structural ties.

3. Companies using the concept of customer lifetime value consider the potential profit from customers over their entire life with the company, not just their profit from a single transaction. When banks began tracking the profitability of individual customers, some found that a large percentage of them actually cost them more to do business with than the revenue they produced. Considering the lifetime value of a customer concept, should companies "fire" their unprofitable customers? What are the consequences of such an action? What factors should a company consider before taking steps to eliminate their unprofitable customers?

Under the Hood: Focus on Technology

While the Internet has provided a medium for companies to develop relationships with customers, it has also created a means by which customers can share consumption experiences with other customers. Some companies, such as amazon.com, allow customers to post product reviews directly on the company's Web site. In addition, dedicated consumer opinion Web sites (e.g., epinions.com, consumerreview.com, and rateitall.com) provide consumers with the opportunity to read other consumers' consumption opinions and experiences, as well as to write their own on just about any product or service sold.

Visit the rating Web sites listed above and read some of the reviews for a product in one of the following categories: digital cameras, video game systems, or athletic shoes. Next respond to the following questions with this product in mind.

1. How much influence do you think consumer-to-consumer ratings have on the purchase decision for this product? What factors may make this influence stronger or weaker?

2. Discuss whether the ability of a consumer to receive product performance information directly from other consumers helps or harms this company's promotional efforts?

3. What might this company do to use consumer rating Web sites to its advantage?

Focus on Ethics

The marketing concept focuses on satisfying consumers' needs, but what if doing so places the consumer at risk? A variety of legal products are sold that may have harmful effects on consumers. The health impact of tobacco and alcohol are well known. More recently, many individuals and the Food and Drug Administration have become concerned about the level of trans-fatty acids present in some food products. Companies such as McDonald's, Kraft Foods, and Frito-lay have recently been reevaluating their offerings and have begun to initiate changes to make their food healthier. For example, McDonald's will soon test a Happy Meal that will allow the option of replacing french fries with a bag of sliced fruit.

1. What ethical responsibility do companies producing products that have potentially adverse health effects have to consumers?

2. Are the goals of increasing profits and of the societal marketing concept at odds with one another?

3. Break into groups of four to six students. Within each group, half of the students should consider reasons for why marketing potentially unhealthy products, like McDonald's french fries, is ethical. The other half of the group should consider reasons for why such actions are unethical. Debate the issue.

4. What ethical concerns exist behind a McDonald's order taker asking *all* customers if they want to supersize their meal? Is this giving consumers what they want, or is this inducing many overweight people to eat more than necessary? Debate the issue.

Videos

The Subaru video case that accompanies this chapter is located in Appendix 1 at the back of the book.

Student Materials

Need a tune-up? A study guide and OneKey access code are available to aid in your review of chapter material. Your instructor may choose to have these items shrink-wrapped with your text or you may purchase them separately at www.prenhall.com/marketing.

■ *After studying this chapter, you should be able to*

1. Explain companywide strategic planning and its four steps   *2. Discuss* how to design business portfolios and develop growth strategies   *3. Explain* marketing's role in strategic planning and how marketing works with its partners to create and deliver customer value   *4. Describe* the elements of a customer-driven marketing strategy and mix, and the forces that influence it   *5. List* the marketing management functions, including the elements of a marketing plan

Company and Marketing Strategy:
Partnering to Build Customer Relationships

2

ROAD MAP | Previewing the Concepts

Ready to travel on? In the first chapter, we explored the marketing process by which companies create value for consumers in order to capture value in return. On this leg of our journey, we'll dig more deeply into steps two and three of the marketing process—designing customer-driven marketing strategies and constructing marketing programs. But first we'll examine marketing's role in the broader organization. We start with the companywide strategic planning process. Marketing contributes to and is guided by the company's overall strategic plan. First, marketing urges a whole-company philosophy that puts customers at the center. Then, under the overall strategic plan, marketers work with other company functions to design marketing strategies for delivering value to carefully targeted customers. Finally, marketers develop "marketing mixes"—consisting of product, price, distribution, and promotion tactics—to carry out these strategies profitably. These first two chapters will give you a full introduction to the basics of marketing, the decisions marketing managers make, and where marketing fits into an organization. After that, we'll take a look at the external environments in which marketing operates.

First stop: The Walt Disney Company. When you hear the name Disney, you probably think of wholesome family entertainment. Most people do. With its theme parks and family films, Disney long ago mastered the concepts of customer relationship building and customer delight that we examined in Chapter 1. For generations, it has woven its special "Disney magic" to create and fulfill fantasies for people around the world. But what you may not know is that The Walt Disney Company has now grown to include much, much more than just theme parks and family films. As you read on, think about all the strategic planning challenges facing Disney's modern-day Magic Kingdom.

W hen you think of The Walt Disney Company, you probably think first of theme parks and animated films. And no wonder. Since the release of its first Mickey Mouse cartoon 75 years ago, Disney has grown to become the undisputed master of family entertainment. It perfected the art of movie animation. From pioneering films such as *Snow White and the Seven Dwarfs, Fantasia, Pinocchio,* and *Song of the South* to more recent features such as *The Lion King, Toy Story,* and *Monsters, Inc.,* Disney has brought pure magic to the theaters, living rooms, and hearts and minds of audiences around the world.

But perhaps nowhere is the Disney magic more apparent than at the company's premier theme parks. Each year, nearly 40 million people flock to the Walt Disney World Resort alone—15 times more than visit Yellowstone National Park—making it the world's number one tourist attraction. What brings so many people to Walt Disney World Resort? Part of the answer lies in its many attractions. The resort's four major theme parks—Magic Kingdom, Epcot, Disney-MGM Studios, and Disney's Animal Kingdom—brim with attractions such as Cinderella's Castle, Space Mountain, The Twilight Zone Tower of Terror, Body Wars, the Kilimanjaro Safaris, Big Thunder Mountain Railroad, Typhoon Lagoon, Buzz Lightyear's Space Ranger Spin, and Honey I Shrunk the Audience.

But these attractions reveal only part of the Walt Disney World Resort value proposition. In fact, what visitors like even more, they say, is the park's sparkling cleanliness and the friendliness of Walt Disney World Resort employees. In an increasingly rude, dirty, and mismanaged world, Disney offers warmth, cleanliness, and order. As one observer notes, "In the Magic Kingdom, America still works the way it is supposed to. Everything is clean and safe, quality and service still matter, and the customer is always right."

Thus, the real "Disney Magic" lies in the company's obsessive dedication to its mission to "make people happy" and to "make a dream come true." The company orients all of its people—from the executive in the corner office, to the monorail driver, to the ticket seller at the gate—around the customer's experience. On their first day, all new Walt Disney World Resort employees report for a three-day motivational course at Disney University in Orlando, where they learn about the hard work of making fantasies come true. They learn that they are in the entertainment business—"cast members" in the Walt Disney World Resort "show." The job of each cast member is to enthusiastically serve Disney's "guests."

Before they receive their "theme costumes" and go "on stage," employees take courses titled Traditions I and Traditions II, in which they learn the Disney language, history, and culture. They are taught to be enthusiastic, helpful, and *always* friendly. They learn to do good deeds, such as volunteering to take pictures of guests, so that the whole family can be in the picture. Rumor has it that Disney is so confident that its cast members will charm guests that it forces contact. For example, many items in the park's gift shops bear no price tags, requiring shoppers to ask the price.

Cast members are taught never to say, "It's not my job." When a guest asks a question—whether it's "Where's the nearest restroom?" or "What are the names of Snow White's Seven Dwarfs?"—they need to know the answer. If they see a piece of trash on the ground, they pick it up. They go to extremes to fulfill guests' expectations and dreams. For example, to keep the Magic Kingdom feeling fresh and clean, five times a year the Main Street painters strip every painted rail in the park down to bare metal and apply a new coat of paint. Disney's customer-delight mission and marketing have become legendary. Its theme parks are so highly regarded for outstanding customer service that many of America's leading corporations send managers to Disney University to learn how Disney does it.

As it turns out, however, theme parks are only a small part of a much bigger Disney story. These units make up only a small part of today's Walt Disney Company empire. In recent years, Disney has become a real study in strategic planning. Throughout the 1990s, seeking growth, Disney diversified rapidly, transforming itself into a $25 billion international media and entertainment conglomerate. You might be surprised to learn that, beyond its theme parks, The Walt Disney Company now owns or has a major stake in all of the following:

- A major television and radio network—ABC—along with 10 company-owned television stations, 29 radio stations, and 13 international broadcast channels
- Sixteen cable networks (including the Disney Channel, Toon Disney, SoapNet, ESPN, A&E, the History Channel, Lifetime Television, E! Entertainment, and the ABC Family Channel)

- Four television production companies and eight movie production and distribution companies (including Walt Disney Pictures, Touchstone Pictures, Hollywood Pictures, Miramax Films, and Buena Vista Productions)
- Five book and magazine publishing groups (including Hyperion Books and Miramax Books)
- Five music labels (including Hollywood Records and Mammoth Records)
- Nineteen Internet groups (including Disney Online, Disney's Blast, ABC.com, ESPN.com, FamilyFun.com, NASCAR.com, NBA.com, and NFL.com)
- Disney Interactive (which develops and markets computer software, video games, and CD-ROMS)
- The Disney Store—660 retail store locations carrying Disney-related merchandise
- Disney Cruise Line

It's an impressive list. However, for Disney, managing this diverse portfolio of businesses has become a real *Monsters, Inc.* Although hurting recently because of the travel slump caused by a down economy and increased fears of terrorism, Disney's theme park and family movie operations have been wonderfully successful over the years. During the last half of the 1980s, the smaller, more focused Disney experienced soaring sales and profits. Revenues grew at an average rate of 23 percent annually; net income grew at 50 percent a year. In contrast, the new and more complex Disney has struggled for growth and profitability. During the most recent five years, the more diversified Disney's sales have grown at an average rate of only 3 percent annually; net income has *fallen* 23 percent a year.

Thus, for Disney, bigger isn't necessarily better. Many critics assert that Disney has grown too large, too diverse, and too distant from the core strengths that made it so successful over the years. Others, however, believe that such diversification is essential for profitable long-term growth. One thing seems certain—creating just the right blend of businesses to make up the new Magic Kingdom won't be easy. It will take masterful strategic planning—along with some big doses of the famed "Disney magic"—to give the modern Disney story a happy-ever-after ending.[1]

Marketing strategies and programs operate within the context of broader, companywide strategic plans. Thus, to understand the role of marketing within an organization, we must first understand the organization's overall strategic planning process. Like Disney, all companies must look ahead and develop long-term strategies to meet the changing conditions in their industries and ensure long-term survival.

In this chapter, we look first at the organization's overall strategic planning. Next, we discuss how marketers, guided by the strategic plan, work closely with others inside and outside the firm to serve customers. Finally, we examine marketing strategy and planning—how marketers choose target markets, position their marketing offers, and develop marketing mix programs.

■ Companywide Strategic Planning: Defining Marketing's Role

Strategic planning

The process of developing and maintaining a strategic fit between the organization's goals and capabilities and its changing marketing opportunities. It involves defining a clear company mission, setting supporting objectives, designing a sound business portfolio, and coordinating functional strategies.

The hard task of selecting an overall company strategy for long-run survival and growth is called *strategic planning*. Each company must find the game plan that makes the most sense given its specific situation, opportunities, objectives, and resources. This is the focus of **strategic planning**—the process of developing and maintaining a strategic fit between the organization's goals and capabilities and its changing marketing opportunities.

Strategic planning sets the stage for the rest of the planning in the firm. Companies usually prepare annual plans, long-range plans, and strategic plans. The annual and long-

FIGURE 2.1

Steps in Strategic Planning

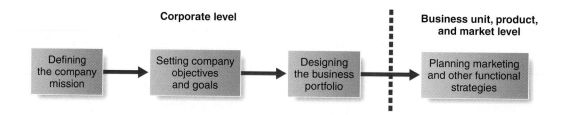

range plans deal with the company's current businesses and how to keep them going. In contrast, the strategic plan involves adapting the firm to take advantage of opportunities in its constantly changing environment.

At the corporate level, the company starts the strategic planning process by defining its overall purpose and mission (see Figure 2.1). This mission then is turned into detailed supporting objectives that guide the whole company. Next, headquarters decides what portfolio of businesses and products is best for the company and how much support to give each one. In turn, each business and product develops detailed marketing and other departmental plans that support the companywide plan. Thus, marketing planning occurs at the business-unit, product, and market levels. It supports company strategic planning with more detailed plans for specific marketing opportunities.[2]

Defining a Market-Oriented Mission

An organization exists to accomplish something. At first, it has a clear purpose or mission, but over time its mission may become unclear as the organization grows, adds new products and markets, or faces new conditions in the environment. When management senses that the organization is drifting, it must renew its search for purpose. It is time to ask: What is our business? Who is the customer? What do consumers value? What should our business be? These simple-sounding questions are among the most difficult the company will ever have to answer. Successful companies continuously raise these questions and answer them carefully and completely.

Many organizations develop formal mission statements that answer these questions. A **mission statement** is a statement of the organization's purpose—what it wants to accomplish in the larger environment. A clear mission statement acts as an "invisible hand" that guides people in the organization.

Some companies define their missions myopically in product or technology terms ("We make and sell furniture" or "We are a chemical-processing firm"). But mission statements should be *market oriented* and defined in terms of customer needs. Products and technologies eventually become outdated, but basic market needs may last forever.

A market-oriented mission statement defines the business in terms of satisfying basic customer needs. For example, Charles Schwab isn't just a brokerage firm—it sees itself as the "guardian of our customers' financial dreams." At Hill's Pet Nutrition, "Our mission is to enrich and lengthen the special relationship between people and their pets." Likewise, eBay's mission isn't simply to hold online auctions. Instead, it connects individual buyers and sellers in "the world's online marketplace." Its mission is to be a unique Web community in which people can shop around, have fun, and get to know each other, for example, by chatting at the eBay Cafe. Table 2.1 provides several other examples of product-oriented versus market-oriented business definitions.

Management should avoid making its mission too narrow or too broad. A pencil manufacturer that says it is in the communication equipment business is stating its mission too broadly. Missions should be *realistic*. Singapore Airlines would be deluding itself if it adopted the mission to become the world's largest airline. Missions should also be *specific*. Many mission statements are written for public relations purposes and lack specific, workable guidelines. Too often, companies develop mission statements that look much like this tongue-in-cheek version:

> We are committed to serving the quality of life of cultures and communities everywhere, regardless of sex, age, sexual preference, religion, or disability, whether

Mission statement

A statement of the organization's purpose—what it wants to accomplish in the larger environment.

TABLE 2.1 Market-Oriented Business Definitions

Company	Product-Oriented Definition	Market-Oriented Definition
Amazon.com	We sell books, videos, CDs, toys, consumer electronics, hardware, housewares, and other products.	We make the Internet buying experience fast, easy, and enjoyable—we're the place where you can find and discover anything you want to buy online.
America Online	We provide online services.	We create customer connectivity, anytime, anywhere.
Disney	We run theme parks.	We create fantasies—a place where America still works the way it's supposed to.
eBay	We hold online auctions.	We connect individual buyers and sellers in the world's online marketplace, a unique Web community in which they can shop around, have fun, and get to know each other.
Home Depot	We sell tools and home repair and improvement items.	We provide advice and solutions that transform ham-handed homeowners into Mr. and Mrs. Fixits.
Nike	We sell shoes.	We help people experience the emotion of competition, winning, and crushing competitors.
Revlon	We make cosmetics.	We sell lifestyle and self-expression; success and status; memories, hopes, and dreams.
Ritz-Carlton Hotels	We rent rooms.	We create the Ritz-Carlton experience—one that enlivens the senses, instills well-being, and fulfills even the unexpressed wishes and needs of our guests.
Wal-Mart	We run discount stores.	We deliver low prices, every day.

they be customers, suppliers, employees, or shareholders—we serve the planet—to the highest ethical standards of integrity, best practice, and sustainability, through policies of openness and transparency vetted by our participation in the International Quality Business Global Audit forum, to ensure measurable outcomes worldwide. . . .[3]

Such generic statements sound good but provide little real guidance or inspiration.

Missions should fit the *market environment*. The Girl Scouts of America would not recruit successfully in today's environment with its former mission: "to prepare young girls for motherhood and wifely duties." Today, its mission is to be the place "where girls grow strong." The organization should base its mission on its *distinctive competencies*. McDonald's could probably enter the solar energy business, but that would not take advantage of its core competence—providing low-cost food and fast service to large groups of customers.

Finally, mission statements should be *motivating*. A company's mission should not be stated as making more sales or profits—profits are only a reward for undertaking a useful activity. A company's employees need to feel that their work is significant and that it contributes to people's lives. For example, Walt Disney Company's aim is to "make people happy." Celestial Seasonings' pursues this mission: "To create and sell healthful, naturally oriented products that nurture people's bodies and uplift their souls."[4]

Setting Company Objectives and Goals

The company's mission needs to be turned into detailed supporting objectives for each level of management. Each manager should have objectives and be responsible for reaching them. For example, Monsanto operates in many businesses, including agriculture, pharmaceuticals, and food products. The company defines its mission as creating "abundant food and a healthy environment." It seeks to help feed the world's exploding population while at the same time sustaining the environment.

This mission leads to a hierarchy of objectives, including business objectives and marketing objectives. Monsanto's overall objective is to build profitable customer relationships by creating environmentally better products and getting them to market faster at lower costs. For

■ Mission statements: The Girl Scouts' mission is to be a place "Where Girls Grow Strong."

its part, the agricultural division's objective is to increase agricultural productivity and reduce chemical pollution. It does this by researching new pest- and disease-resistant crops that produce higher yields without chemical spraying. But research is expensive and requires improved profits to plow back into research programs. So improving profits becomes another major Monsanto objective. Profits can be improved by increasing sales or reducing costs. Sales can be increased by improving the company's share of the U.S. market, by entering new foreign markets, or both. These goals then become the company's current marketing objectives.

Marketing strategies and programs must be developed to support these marketing objectives. To increase its U.S. market share, Monsanto might increase its products' availability and promotion. To enter new foreign markets, the company may cut prices and target large farms abroad. These are its broad marketing strategies. Each broad marketing strategy must then be defined in greater detail. For example, increasing the product's promotion may require more salespeople and more advertising; if so, both requirements will have to be spelled out. In this way, the firm's mission is translated into a set of objectives for the current period.

Designing the Business Portfolio

Business portfolio
The collection of businesses and products that make up the company.

Guided by the company's mission statement and objectives, management now must plan its **business portfolio**—the collection of businesses and products that make up the company. The best business portfolio is the one that best fits the company's strengths and weaknesses to opportunities in the environment. Business portfolio planning involves two steps. First, the company must analyze its *current* business portfolio and decide which businesses should receive more, less, or no investment. Second, it must shape the *future* portfolio by developing strategies for growth and downsizing.

Portfolio analysis
A tool by which management identifies and evaluates the various businesses making up the company.

Analyzing the Current Business Portfolio The major activity in strategic planning is business **portfolio analysis**, whereby management evaluates the products and businesses making up the company. The company will want to put strong resources into its more profitable businesses and phase down or drop its weaker ones.

Management's first step is to identify the key businesses making up the company. These can be called the strategic business units. A *strategic business unit* (SBU) is a unit of the company that has a separate mission and objectives and that can be planned independently from other company businesses. An SBU can be a company division, a product line within a division, or sometimes a single product or brand.

The next step in business portfolio analysis calls for management to assess the attractiveness of its various SBUs and decide how much support each deserves. Most companies are well advised to "stick to their knitting" when designing their business portfolios. It's usually a good idea to focus on adding products and businesses that fit closely with the firm's core philosophy and competencies.

The purpose of strategic planning is to find ways in which the company can best use its strengths to take advantage of attractive opportunities in the environment. So most standard portfolio-analysis methods evaluate SBUs on two important dimensions—the attractiveness of the SBU's market or industry and the strength of the SBU's position in that market or industry. The best-known portfolio-planning method was developed by the Boston Consulting Group, a leading management consulting firm.

The Boston Consulting Group Approach. Using the Boston Consulting Group (BCG) approach, a company classifies all its SBUs according to the **growth-share matrix** shown in Figure 2.2. On the vertical axis, *market growth rate* provides a measure of market attractiveness. On the horizontal axis, *relative market share* serves as a measure of company strength in the market. The growth–share matrix defines four types of SBUs:

> **Stars.** Stars are high-growth, high-share businesses or products. They often need heavy investment to finance their rapid growth. Eventually their growth will slow down, and they will turn into cash cows.
>
> **Cash cows.** Cash cows are low-growth, high-share businesses or products. These established and successful SBUs need less investment to hold their market share. Thus, they produce a lot of cash that the company uses to pay its bills and to support other SBUs that need investment.
>
> **Question marks.** Question marks are low-share business units in high-growth markets. They require a lot of cash to hold their share, let alone increase it. Management has to think hard about which question marks it should try to build into stars and which should be phased out.
>
> **Dogs.** Dogs are low-growth, low-share businesses and products. They may generate enough cash to maintain themselves but do not promise to be large sources of cash.

The 10 circles in the growth-share matrix represent a company's 10 current SBUs. The company has two stars, two cash cows, three question marks, and three dogs. The areas of the circles are proportional to the SBU's dollar sales. This company is in fair shape, although not in good shape. It wants to invest in the more promising question marks to make them stars and to maintain the stars so that they will become cash cows as their markets mature. Fortunately, it has two good-sized cash cows. Income from these cash cows will help finance the company's question marks, stars, and dogs. The company should take some decisive action concerning its dogs and its question marks. The picture

Growth–share matrix

A portfolio-planning method that evaluates a company's strategic business units in terms of their market growth rate and relative market share. SBUs are classified as stars, cash cows, question marks, or dogs.

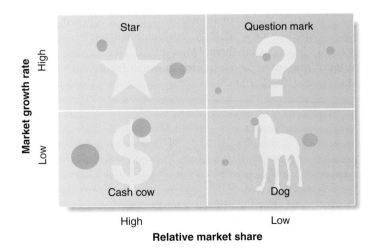

FIGURE 2.2

The BCG Growth-Share Matrix

would be worse if the company had no stars, if it had too many dogs, or if it had only one weak cash cow.

Once it has classified its SBUs, the company must determine what role each will play in the future. One of four strategies can be pursued for each SBU. The company can invest more in the business unit in order to *build* its share. Or it can invest just enough to *hold* the SBU's share at the current level. It can *harvest* the SBU, milking its short-term cash flow regardless of the long-term effect. Finally, the company can *divest* the SBU by selling it or phasing it out and using the resources elsewhere.

As time passes, SBUs change their positions in the growth-share matrix. Each SBU has a life cycle. Many SBUs start out as question marks and move into the star category if they succeed. They later become cash cows as market growth falls, then finally die off or turn into dogs toward the end of their life cycles. The company needs to add new products and units continuously so that some of them will become stars and, eventually, cash cows that will help finance other SBUs.

Problems with Matrix Approaches.   The BCG and other formal methods revolutionized strategic planning. However, such approaches have limitations. They can be difficult, time-consuming, and costly to implement. Management may find it difficult to define SBUs and measure market share and growth. In addition, these approaches focus on classifying *current* businesses but provide little advice for *future* planning.

Formal planning approaches can also place too much emphasis on market-share growth or growth through entry into attractive new markets. Using these approaches, many companies plunged into unrelated and new high-growth businesses that they did not know how to manage—with very bad results. At the same time, these companies were often too quick to abandon, sell, or milk to death their healthy mature businesses. As a result, many companies that diversified too broadly in the past now are narrowing their focus and getting back to the basics of serving one or a few of the industries that they know best.

Because of such problems, many companies have dropped formal matrix methods in favor of more customized approaches that are better suited to their specific situations. Unlike former strategic-planning efforts, which rested mostly in the hands of senior managers at company headquarters, today's strategic planning has been decentralized. Increasingly, companies are placing responsibility for strategic planning in the hands of cross-functional teams of managers who are close to their markets. Some teams even include customers and suppliers in their strategic-planning processes.[5]

Developing Strategies for Growth and Downsizing

Beyond evaluating current businesses, designing the business portfolio involves finding businesses and products the company should consider in the future. Companies need growth if they are to compete more effectively, satisfy their stakeholders, and attract top talent. "Growth is pure oxygen," states one executive. "It creates a vital, enthusiastic corporation where people see genuine opportunity." At the same time, a firm must be careful not to make growth itself an objective. The company's objective must be "profitable growth."

Marketing has the main responsibility for achieving profitable growth for the company. Marketing must identify, evaluate, and select market opportunities and lay down strategies for capturing them. One useful device for identifying growth opportunities is the **product/market expansion grid**, shown in Figure 2.3.[6] We apply it here to Starbucks (see Marketing at Work 2.1).

Product/market expansion grid
A portfolio-planning tool for identifying company growth opportunities through market penetration, market development, product development, or diversification.

FIGURE 2.3

The Product/Market Expansion Grid

	Existing products	New products
Existing markets	Market penetration	Product development
New markets	Market development	Diversification

Marketing at Work | *2.1*

Starbucks Coffee: Where Things Are Really Perking

Back in 1983, Howard Schultz hit on the idea of bringing a European-style coffeehouse to America. People needed to slow down, he believed—to "smell the coffee" and enjoy life a little more. The result was Starbucks, the coffeehouse chain that started the trend in America of enjoying coffee to its fullest. Starbucks doesn't sell just coffee, it sells *The Starbucks Experience*. As one Starbucks executive puts it, "We're not in the business of filling bellies, we're in the business of filling souls." Says another, "We changed the way people live their lives, what they do when they get up in the morning, how they reward themselves, and where they meet."

Starbucks is now a powerhouse premium brand in a category in which only cheaper commodity products once existed. As the brand has perked, Starbucks's sales and profits have risen like steam off a mug of hot java. Some 20 million customers visit the company's more than 5,900 stores worldwide each week. During just the past 5 years, Starbucks's sales and earnings have both more than tripled. Over the past decade, its stock has soared more than 2,200 percent, outperforming such superstars as Wal-Mart, General Electric, Coca-Cola, Microsoft, and IBM in total return.

Starbucks's success, however, has drawn a full litter of copycats, ranging from direct competitors such as Caribou Coffee to fast-food merchants. These days it seems that everyone is peddling its own brand of premium coffee. In the early 1990s, there were only 200 coffee houses in the United States. Today there are more than 14,000. To maintain its phenomenal growth in an increasingly overcaffeinated marketplace, Starbucks has brewed up an ambitious, multipronged growth strategy. Let's examine the key elements of this strategy:

More store growth: *Almost 85 percent of Starbucks's sales comes from*

its stores. So, not surprisingly, Starbucks is opening new stores at a breakneck pace. Seven years ago, Starbucks had just 1,015 stores, total—that's 200 fewer than it built last year alone. Starbucks's strategy is to put stores everywhere. In Seattle, there's a Starbucks for every 9,400 people; in Manhattan, there's one for every 12,000. One three-block stretch in Chicago contains six of the trendy coffee bars. In fact, cramming so many stores close together caused one satirical publication to run this headline: "A New Starbucks Opens in the Restroom of Existing Starbucks." Although it may seem that there aren't many places left without a Starbucks, there's still plenty of room to expand. Amazingly, there are still eight U.S. states with no Starbucks at all. Worldwide, Starbucks claims that it will grow to at least 10,000 stores worldwide by 2005, and to 25,000 stores ultimately.

Beyond opening new shops, Starbucks is adding in-store products

and features that get customers to stop in more often, stay longer, and buy more. Its beefed-up menu now includes hot breakfast sandwiches plus lunch and dinner items, increasing the average customer sales ticket. The chain has tested everything from Krispy Kreme doughnuts and Fresh Fields gourmet sandwiches to Greek pasta salads and assorted chips. To get customers to hang around longer, Starbucks now offers high-speed wireless Internet access in many of its stores. Out of cash? No problem— just swipe your prepaid Starbucks card on the way out ("a Starbucks store in your wallet," according to the company's Web site). And while you're at it, pick up the latest Starbucks compilation music CD, a board game, and a Starbucks coffee mug for home.

New retail channels: The vast majority of coffee in America is bought in retail stores and brewed at home. To capture this demand,

To maintain its phenomenal growth in an increasingly overcaffeinated marketplace, Starbucks has brewed up an ambitious, multipronged growth strategy.

(continued)

Starbucks is also pushing into America's supermarket aisles. However, rather than going head-to-head in this new channel, Starbucks struck a co-branding deal with Kraft. Under this deal, Starbucks will continue to roast and package its coffee while Kraft will market and distribute it. The deal gave Starbucks quick entry into 18,000 U.S. supermarkets, supported by the marketing muscle of 3,500 Kraft salespeople.

Beyond supermarkets, Starbucks has forged an impressive set of new ways to bring its brand to market. Some examples: Host Marriott operates Starbucks kiosks in America's airports and several airlines serve Starbucks coffee to their passengers. Westin and Sheraton hotels offer packets of Starbucks brew in their rooms. Starbucks recently signed deals to install coffee shops in all Borders Books and Target stores. Starbucks also sells gourmet coffee, tea, gifts, and related goods through business and consumer catalogs. And its Web site, Starbucks.com, has become a kind of "lifestyle portal" on which it sells coffee, tea, coffee-making equipment, compact discs, gifts, and collectibles.

New products and store concepts: Starbucks has partnered with several firms to extend its brand into new categories. For example, it joined with PepsiCo to stamp the Starbucks brand on bottled Frappuccino drinks and its DoubleShot espresso drink. Starbucks ice cream, marketed in a joint venture with Dreyer's, is now the leading brand of coffee ice cream. Starbucks has also examined a number of new store concepts. In San Francisco, for example, it's testing Circadia—a kind of bohemian coffeehouse concept with tattered rugs, high-speed Internet access, and live music as well as coffee specialties.

International growth: Finally, Starbucks has taken its American-brewed concept global. In 1996, the company had only 11 coffeehouses outside North America. By 2003, the number had grow to more than 1,300 stores in 30 international markets, including more than 440 in Japan, 300 in the UK, 102 in Taiwan, and 90 in China. Last year, Starbucks opened close to 400 international stores, entering nine new international markets, from Austria, Spain, and Greece to Indonesia and Oman. And it's now moving rapidly into Latin and South America, where it plans to build 900 stores by 2005.

Although Starbucks's growth strategy so far has met with great success, some analysts express strong concerns. What's wrong with Starbucks's rapid expansion? Some critics worry that the company may be overextending the Starbucks brand name. "People pay [up to $5.00] for a caffe latte because it's supposed to be a premium product," asserts one such critic. "When you see the Starbucks name on what an airline is pouring, you wonder." Others fear that, by pursuing such a broad-based growth strategy, Starbucks will stretch its resources too thin or lose its focus.

Still others, however, remain true believers. Some even see similarities between Starbucks and a young McDonald's, which rode the humble hamburger to such incredible success. "The similar focus on one product, the overseas opportunities, the rapid emergence as the dominant player in a new niche," says Goldman Sachs analyst Steve Kent, "this all applies to Starbucks, too." Only time will tell whether Starbucks turns out to be the next McDonald's—it all depends how well the company manages growth. For now, things are really perking. But Starbucks has to be careful that it doesn't boil over.

Sources: Quotes and other information from Cora Daniels, "Mr. Coffee," *Fortune,* April 14, 2003, pp. 139–140; Nelson D. Schwartz, "Still Perking after All These Years," *Fortune,* May 24, 1999, pp. 203–210; Stephane Fitch, "Latte Grande, Extra Froth," *Forbes,* March 19, 2001, p. 58; Jacqueline Doherty, "Make It Decaf," *Barrons,* May 20, 2002, pp. 20–21; Stanley Holmes, "Planet Starbucks: To Keep Up the Growth, It Must Go Global Quickly," *Business Week,* September 9, 2002, pp. 100–110; "Starbucks Corporation," *Hoover's Company Profiles,* Austin, May 1, 2003; and information accessed online at www.starbucks.com, July 2003.

Market penetration
A strategy for company growth by increasing sales of current products to current market segments without changing the product.

Market development
A strategy for company growth by identifying and developing new market segments for current company products.

First, Starbucks management might consider whether the company can achieve deeper **market penetration**—making more sales to current customers without changing its products. It might add new stores in current market areas to make it easier for more customers to visit. In fact, Starbucks is adding an average of 23 stores a week, 52 weeks a year. Improvements in advertising, prices, service, menu selection, or store design might encourage customers to stop by more often, stay longer, or to buy more during each visit. For example, Starbucks now features high-speed wireless Internet access in many of its stores. And it recently introduced a company debit card, which lets customers prepay for coffee and snacks or give the gift of Starbucks to family and friends. Customers using the card move through stores faster and return more often.[7] Basically, Starbucks would like to increase patronage by current customers and attract competitors' customers to Starbucks shops.

Second, Starbucks management might consider possibilities for **market development**—identifying and developing new markets for its current products. For instance, managers could review new *demographic markets.* Perhaps new groups—such as seniors or ethnic groups—could be encouraged to visit Starbucks coffee shops for the first time or to buy more from them. Managers also could review new *geographical markets.* Starbucks is now expanding swiftly into new U.S. markets, especially in the Southeast and Southwest. It is also developing its international markets, with stores popping up rapidly in Asia, Europe, Australia, and Latin and South America.

Third, management could consider **product development**—offering modified or new products to current markets. For example, Starbucks recently added hot breakfast sandwiches to its menu to steal some early-morning business from McDonald's and Burger King. It also increased its midday and evening food offerings to attract more business during the lunch and dinner hours. Finally, Starbucks has partnered with other firms to sell coffee in supermarkets and to extend its brand to new products, such as coffee ice cream (with Dreyers) and bottled coffee drinks (with PepsiCo).

Fourth, Starbucks might consider **diversification**. It could start up or buy businesses outside of its current products and markets. For example, in 1999, Starbucks purchased Hear Music and began making compilation music CDs to play and sell in its stores. And it has also tested new restaurant concepts—such as Circadia in San Francisco—in an effort to offer new formats to related but new markets. In a more extreme diversification, Starbucks might consider leveraging its strong brand name by making and marketing a line of branded casual clothing consistent with the "Starbucks Experience." However, this would probably be unwise. Companies that diversify too broadly into unfamiliar products or industries can lose their market focus, something that some critics are already concerned about with Starbucks.

Companies must not only develop strategies for *growing* their business portfolios but also strategies for **downsizing** them. There are many reasons that a firm might want to abandon products or markets. The market environment might change, making some of the company's products or markets less profitable. This might happen during an economic recession or when a strong competitor opens next door. The firm may have grown too fast or entered areas where it lacks experience. This can occur when a firm enters too many foreign markets without the proper research or when a company introduces new products that do not offer superior customer value. Finally, some products or business units just age and die.

When a firm finds products or businesses that no longer fit its overall strategy, it must carefully prune, harvest, or divest them. Weak businesses usually require a disproportionate amount of management attention. Managers should focus on promising growth opportunities, not fritter away energy trying to salvage fading ones.

Product development
A strategy for company growth by offering modified or new products to current market segments.

Diversification
A strategy for company growth through starting up or acquiring businesses outside the company's current products and markets.

Downsizing
Reducing the business portfolio by eliminating products or business units that are not profitable or that no longer fit the company's overall strategy.

Strategic Planning and Small Businesses

Many discussions of strategic planning focus on large corporations with many divisions and products. However, small businesses can also benefit from sound strategic planning. Whereas most small ventures start out with extensive business and marketing plans used to attract potential investors, strategic planning often falls by the wayside once the business gets going.

Entrepreneurs and presidents of small companies are more likely to spend their time "putting out fires" than planning. But what does a small firm do when it finds that it has taken on too much debt, or when its growth is exceeding production capacity. What does it do when it's losing market share to a competitor with lower prices? Strategic planning can help small business managers to anticipate such situations and determine how to prevent or handle them.

King's Medical Company of Hudson, Ohio, provides an example of how one small company has used very simple strategic-planning tools to chart its course every three years. King's Medical owns and manages magnetic-resonance-imaging (MRI) equipment—million-dollar-plus machines that produce X-ray-type pictures. Several years ago, William Patton, then a consultant and the company's "planning guru," pointed to strategic planning as the key to this small company's very rapid growth and high profit margins. Patton claimed, "A lot of literature says there are three critical issues to a small company: cash flow, cash flow, cash flow. I agree those issues are critical, but so are three more: planning, planning, planning."

King's Medical's planning process, which hinges on an assessment of the company, its place in the market, and its goals, includes the following steps.[8]

1. Identify the major elements of the business environment in which the organization has operated over the past few years.
2. Describe the mission of the organization in terms of its nature and function for the next two years.
3. Explain the internal and external forces that will have an impact on the mission of the organization.
4. Identify the basic driving force that will direct the organization in the future.
5. Develop a set of long-term objectives that will identify what the organization will become in the future.
6. Outline a general plan of action that defines the logistical, financial, and personnel factors needed to integrate the long-term objectives into the total organization.

Clearly, strategic planning is crucial to a small company's future. Thom Wellington, president of Wellington Environmental Consulting and Construction, Inc., says that it's important to do strategic planning at a site away from the office. An off-site location offers neutral ground where employees can be "much more candid." And it takes entrepreneurs away from the scene of the fires they spend so much time stamping out.[9]

■▌ Planning Marketing: Partnering to Build Customer Relationships

The company's strategic plan establishes what kinds of businesses the company will be in and its objectives for each. Then, within each business unit, more detailed planning takes place. The major functional departments in each unit—marketing, finance, accounting, purchasing, operations, information systems, human resources, and others—must work together to accomplish strategic objectives.

Marketing plays a key role in the company's strategic planning in several ways. First, marketing provides a guiding *philosophy*—the marketing concept—that suggests that company strategy should revolve around building profitable relationships with important consumer groups. Second, marketing provides *inputs* to strategic planners by helping to identify attractive market opportunities and by assessing the firm's potential to take advantage of them. Finally, within individual business units, marketing designs *strategies* for reaching the unit's objectives. Once the unit's objectives are set, marketing's task is to help carry them out profitably.

Customer value and satisfaction are important ingredients in the marketer's formula for success. However, as we noted in Chapter 1, marketers alone cannot produce superior value for customers. Although it plays a leading role, marketing can be only a partner in attracting, keeping, and growing customers. In addition to *customer relationship management*, marketers must also practice *partner relationship management*. They must work closely with partners in other company departments to form an effective *value chain* that serves the customer. Moreover, they must partner effectively with other companies in the marketing system to form a competitively superior *value-delivery network*. We now take a closer look at the concepts of a company value chain and value-delivery network.

Partnering with Other Company Departments

Value chain

The series of departments that carry out value-creating activities to design, produce, market, deliver, and support a firm's products.

Each company department can be thought of as a link in the company's **value chain**.[10] That is, each department carries out value-creating activities to design, produce, market, deliver, and support the firm's products. The firm's success depends not only on how well each department performs its work but also on how well the activities of various departments are coordinated.

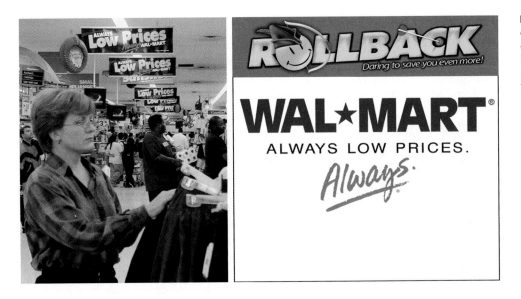

■ The value chain: Wal-Mart's ability to offer the right products at low prices depends on the contributions of people in all of the company's departments—marketing, purchasing, information systems, and operations.

For example, Wal-Mart's goal is to create customer value and satisfaction by providing shoppers with the products they want at the lowest possible prices. Marketers at Wal-Mart play an important role. They learn what customers need and want and stock the store's shelves with the desired products at unbeatable low prices. They prepare advertising and merchandising programs and assist shoppers with customer service. Through these and other activities, Wal-Mart's marketers help deliver value to customers. However, the marketing department needs help from the company's other departments. Wal-Mart's ability to offer the right products at low prices depends on the purchasing department's skill in tracking down the needed suppliers and buying from them at low cost. Similarly, Wal-Mart's information technology department must provide fast and accurate information about which products are selling in each store. And its operations people must provide effective, low-cost merchandise handling.

A company's value chain is only as strong as its weakest link. Success depends on how well each department performs its work of adding value for customers and on how well the activities of various departments are coordinated. At Wal-Mart, if purchasing can't wring the lowest prices from suppliers, or if operations can't distribute merchandise at the lowest costs, then marketing can't deliver on its promise of having the lowest prices.

Ideally, then, a company's different functions should work in harmony to produce value for consumers. But, in practice, departmental relations are full of conflicts and misunderstandings. The marketing department takes the consumer's point of view. But when marketing tries to develop customer satisfaction, it can cause other departments to do a poorer job *in their terms*. Marketing department actions can increase purchasing costs, disrupt production schedules, increase inventories, and create budget headaches. Thus, the other departments may resist the marketing department's efforts.

Yet marketers must find ways to get all departments to "think consumer" and to develop a smoothly functioning value chain. Marketing management can best gain support for its goal of customer satisfaction by working to understand the company's other departments. Marketing managers need to work closely with managers of other functions to develop a system of functional plans under which the different departments can work together to accomplish the company's overall strategic objectives.

Jack Welch, General Electric's highly regarded former CEO, told his employees: "Companies can't give job security. Only customers can!" He emphasized that all General Electric people, regardless of their department, have an impact on customer satisfaction and retention. His message: "If you are not thinking customer, you are not thinking."[11]

Value-delivery network
The network made up of the company, suppliers, distributors, and ultimately customers who "partner" with each other to improve the performance of the entire system.

Partnering with Others in the Marketing System

In its quest to create customer value, the firm needs to look beyond its own value chain and into the value chains of its suppliers, distributors, and, ultimately, customers. Consider McDonald's. McDonald's 30,000 restaurants worldwide serve more than 46 million customers daily, capturing a 43 percent share of the burger market.[12] People do not swarm to McDonald's only because they love the chain's hamburgers. In fact, consumers typically rank McDonald's behind Burger King and Wendy's in taste. Consumers flock to the McDonald's *system*, not just to its food products. Throughout the world, McDonald's finely tuned system delivers a high standard of what the company calls QSCV—quality, service, cleanliness, and value. McDonald's is effective only to the extent that it successfully partners with its franchisees, suppliers, and others to jointly deliver exceptionally high customer value.

More companies today are partnering with the other members of the supply chain to improve the performance of the customer **value-delivery network**. For example, Honda has designed a program for working closely with its suppliers to help them reduce their costs and improve quality. When Honda chose Donnelly Corporation to supply all of the mirrors for its U.S.-made cars, it sent engineers swarming over Donnelly's plants, looking for ways to improve its products and operations. This helped Donnelly reduce its costs by 2 percent in the first year. As a result of its improved performance, Donnelly's sales to Honda grew from $5 million annually to more than $60 million in less than 10 years. In turn, Honda gained an efficient, low-cost supplier of quality components. And Honda customers received greater value in the form of lower-cost, higher-quality cars.[13]

Increasingly in today's marketplace, competition no longer takes place between individual competitors. Rather, it takes place between the entire value-delivery networks created by these competitors. Thus, Honda's performance against Toyota depends on the quality of Honda's overall value-delivery network versus Toyota's. Even if Honda makes the best cars, it might lose in the marketplace if Toyota's dealer network provides more customer-satisfying sales and service.

■ The value-delivery network: Toyota and its dealers must work together to sell cars. Toyota makes good cars and builds the brand; dealerships like Modern Toyota bring value to customers and communities.

SPEED BUMP

Linking the Concepts

Here's a good place to pause for a moment to think about and apply what you've read in the first part of this chapter.

- Why are we talking about companywide strategic planning in a marketing textbook? What *does* strategic planning have to do with marketing?
- What are Starbucks's mission and strategy? What role does marketing play in helping Starbucks to accomplish this mission and strategy?
- What roles do other Starbucks functional departments play, and how can Starbucks's marketers partner with these others to maximize overall customer value?

■■ Marketing Strategy and the Marketing Mix

The strategic plan defines the company's overall mission and objectives. Marketing's role and activities are shown in Figure 2.4, which summarizes the major activities involved in managing marketing strategy and the marketing mix.

Consumers stand in the center. The goal is to build strong and profitable customer relationships. Next comes **marketing strategy**—the marketing logic by which the company hopes to achieve these profitable relationships. Through market segmentation, targeting, and positioning, the company decides which customers it will serve and how. It identifies the total market, then divides it into smaller segments, selects the most promising segments, and focuses on serving and satisfying these segments.

Guided by marketing strategy, the company designs a marketing mix made up of factors under its control—product, price, place, and promotion. To find the best marketing strategy and mix, the company engages in marketing analysis, planning, implementation, and control. Through these activities, the company watches and adapts to the actors and forces in the marketing environment. We will now look briefly at each activity. Then, in later chapters, we will discuss each one in more depth.

Customer-Centered Marketing Strategy

As we emphasized throughout Chapter 1, to succeed in today's competitive marketplace, companies need to be customer centered. They must win customers from competitors, then keep and grow them by delivering greater value. But before it can satisfy consumers, a company must first understand their needs and wants. Thus, sound marketing requires a careful customer analysis.

Companies know that they cannot profitably serve all consumers in a given market— at least not all consumers in the same way. There are too many different kinds of consumers with too many different kinds of needs. And most companies are in a position to serve some segments better than others. Thus, each company must divide up the total market, choose the best segments, and design strategies for profitably serving chosen segments. This process involves three steps: *market segmentation*, *target marketing*, and *market positioning*.

Marketing strategy
The marketing logic by which the company hopes to achieve strong and profitable customer relationships. It involves deciding which customers to serve (segmentation and targeting) and with what value proposition (differentiation and positioning).

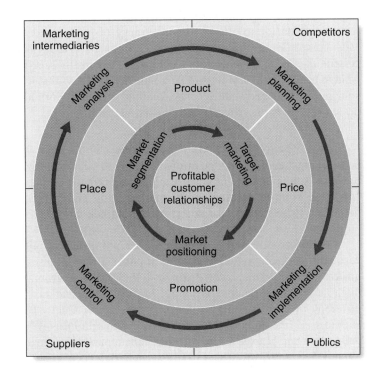

FIGURE 2.4
Managing Marketing Strategy and the Marketing Mix

Market segmentation

Dividing a market into distinct groups of buyers who have distinct needs, characteristics, or behavior and who might require separate products or marketing mixes.

Market Segmentation The market consists of many types of customers, products, and needs. The marketer has to determine which segments offer the best opportunity for achieving company objectives. Consumers can be grouped and served in various ways based on geographic, demographic, psychographic, and behavioral factors. The process of dividing a market into distinct groups of buyers with different needs, characteristics, or behavior who might require separate products or marketing programs is called **market segmentation**.

Every market has segments, but not all ways of segmenting a market are equally useful. For example, Tylenol would gain little by distinguishing between male and female users of pain relievers if both respond the same way to marketing efforts. A **market segment** consists of consumers who respond in a similar way to a given set of marketing efforts. In the car market, for example, consumers who choose the biggest, most comfortable car regardless of price make up one market segment. Customers who care mainly about price and operating economy make up another segment. It would be difficult to make one car model that was the first choice of consumers in both segments. Companies are wise to focus their efforts on meeting the distinct needs of individual market segments.

Market segment

A group of consumers who respond in a similar way to a given set of marketing efforts.

Target marketing

The process of evaluating each market segment's attractiveness and selecting one or more segments to enter.

Target Marketing After a company has defined market segments, it can enter one or many segments of a given market. **Target marketing** involves evaluating each market segment's attractiveness and selecting one or more segments to enter. A company should target segments in which it can profitably generate the greatest customer value and sustain it over time.

A company with limited resources might decide to serve only one or a few special segments or "market niches." Such "nichers" specialize in serving market segments that major competitors overlook or ignore. For example, Arm & Hammer has a lock on the baking soda corner of most consumer goods categories, including toothpaste, deodorizers, and others. Oshkosh Truck has found its niche as the world's largest producer of airport rescue trucks and front-loading concrete mixers. And Veterinary Pet Insurance provides 82 percent of all health insurance policies for our furry—or feathery—friends (see Marketing at Work 2.2).

Alternatively, a company might choose to serve several related segments—perhaps those with different kinds of customers but with the same basic wants. Pottery Barn, for example, targets kids, teens, and adults with the same lifestyle-themed merchandise in different outlets: the original Pottery Barn, Pottery Barn Kids, and PB Teen. Or a large company might decide to offer a complete range of products to serve all market segments. Most companies enter a new market by serving a single segment, and if this proves successful, they add segments. Large companies eventually seek full market coverage. They want to be the General Motors of their industry. GM says that it makes a car for every "person, purse, and personality." The leading company normally has different products designed to meet the special needs of each segment.

Market positioning

Arranging for a product to occupy a clear, distinctive, and desirable place relative to competing products in the minds of target consumers.

Market Positioning After a company has decided which market segments to enter, it must decide what positions it wants to occupy in those segments. A product's *position* is the place the product occupies relative to competitors in consumers' minds. Marketers want to develop unique market positions for their products. If a product is perceived to be exactly like others on the market, consumers would have no reason to buy it.

Market positioning is arranging for a product to occupy a clear, distinctive, and desirable place relative to competing products in the minds of target consumers. Thus, marketers plan positions that distinguish their products from competing brands and give them the greatest strategic advantage in their target markets. For example, Saturn is "a different kind of company, different kind of car"; Chevy Blazer is "like a rock"; the Hummer is "like nothing else"; and Toyota's hybrid Prius is "a revelation brilliantly disguised as a car." Lexus avows "the passionate pursuit of excellence" and Mercedes says, "In a perfect world, everyone would drive a Mercedes." The luxurious Bentley promises

Marketing at Work | 2.2

Niching: Health Insurance for Our Furry—or Feathery—Friends

Health insurance for pets? MetLife, Prudential, Northwestern Mutual, and most other large insurance companies haven't paid much attention to it. But that leaves plenty of room for more-focused nichers, for whom pet health insurance has become a lucrative business. The largest of the small competitors is Veterinary Pet Insurance (VPI). VPI's mission is to "make the miracles of veterinary medicine affordable to all pet owners."

VPI was founded in 1980 by veterinarian Jack Stephens. He never intended to leave his practice, but his life took a dramatic turn when he visited a local grocery store and was identified by a client's daughter as "the man who killed Buffy." Stephens had euthanized the family dog 2 weeks earlier. He immediately began researching the possibility of creating medical pet insurance. "There is nothing more frustrating for a veterinarian than knowing that you can heal a sick patient, but the owner lacks the financial resources and instructs you to put the pet down," says Stephens. "I wanted to change that."

Pet insurance is a still-small but fast-growing segment of the insurance business. Insiders think the industry offers huge potential. Currently, there are more than 60 million dogs and 68 million cats in the United States—more than 60 percent of all U.S. households own one or the other or both. Another 4.6 million U.S. households own one or more of about 300 species of birds; 2 million more own pet rabbits. Many people treat their pets as family members—and they buy accordingly. In fact, Americans now spend a whopping $28.5 billion a year on their pets.

Unlike in Sweden and Britain, where more than half of all pets owners carry pet health insurance, only 1 percent of pet owners in the United States carry such coverage. However, a recent study of pet owners found that nearly 75 per-

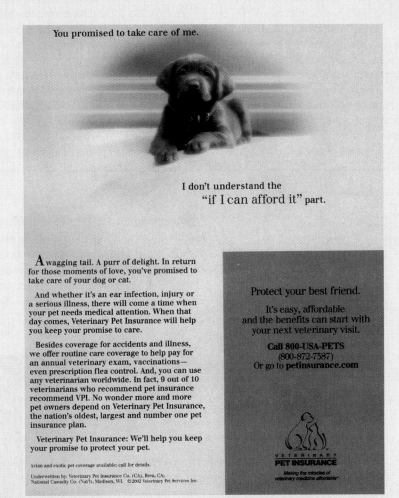

Nichers: Market nicher VPI is growing faster than a new-born puppy. Its mission is to "make the miracles of veterinary medicine affordable to all pet owners."

cent are willing to go into debt to pay for veterinary care for their furry—or feathery—companions. And for many pet medical procedures, they'd have to! If not diagnosed quickly, even a mundane ear infection in a dog can result in $1,000 worth of medical treatment. A more complicated feline kidney transplant can run as much as $6,500. Cancer treatments, including radiation and chemotherapy, could cost a pet owner more than $10,000. All of this adds up to a lot of potential growth for pet health insurers.

VPI's plans cover more than 6,400 pet medical problems and conditions. The insurance helps pay for office calls, prescriptions, treatments, lab fees, x-rays, surgery, and hospitalization. Like its handful of competitors, VPI issues health insurance policies for dogs and cats. Unlike its competitors, VPI recently expanded its coverage to a menagerie of exotic pets as well. Among other critters, the new Avian and Exotic Pet Plan covers birds, rabbits, ferrets, rats, guinea pigs, snakes (except extra large

(continued)

ones) and other reptiles, iguanas, possums, turtles, hedgehogs, and pot belly pigs. "There's such a vast array of pets," says a VPI executive, "and people love them. We have to respect that."

How's VPI doing in its niche? It's growing like a newborn puppy. VPI is by far the largest of the handful of companies that offer pet insurance, providing more than 85 percent of all U.S. pet insurance policies. Since its inception, VPI has issued more than 1 million policies, and it now serves more than 350,000 policyholders. Sales have grown 40 percent in each of the past seven years, reaching nearly $72 million last

year. That might not amount to much for the likes of Prudential or Northwestern Mutual, which rack up tens of billions of dollars in yearly revenues. But it's profitable business for nichers like VPI.

"Pet health insurance is no longer deemed so outlandish in a world where acupuncture for cats, hospice of dogs, and Prozac for ferrets are part of a veterinarian's routine," says one analyst. Such insurance is a real godsend for VPI's policyholders. Just ask Joe and Paula Sena, whose cocker spaniel, Elvis, is receiving radiation treatments for cancer. "He is not like our kids—he is our kid," says Ms. Pena. "He is a kid in a dog's body." VPI is

making Elvis's treatments possible by picking up a lion's share of the costs. "Cost often becomes the deciding factor in the level of care owners can provide," says VPI founder Stephens. "We [always will] strive to make the miracles of modern medicine affordable."

Sources: **AD:** As advertised in *Time,* Inc. MAGAZINE; Michelle Desai, "VPI—Twenty Years and Still Going Strong," VPI press release, January 13, 2002; Michelle Leder, "How Much Is That $100 Deductible in the Window?" *New York Times,* Jul 22, 2001, p. 3.10; Jane Bennett Clark, "Cover Your Tail," *Kiplinger's Personal Finance,* Jan 2002, pp. 108–112; Yilu Zhao, "Break a Leg, Fluffy, If You Have Insurance," *New York Times,* June 30, 2002, p. 9.11; and information from the Veterinary Health Insurance Web site at www.petinsurance.com, June 2003.

"18 handcrafted feet of shameless luxury." Such deceptively simple statements form the backbone of a product's marketing strategy.

In positioning its product, the company first identifies possible competitive advantages upon which to build the position. To gain competitive advantage, the company must offer greater value to target consumers. It can do this either by charging lower prices than competitors do or by offering more benefits to justify higher prices. But if

■ Positioning: Toyota's hybrid Prius is "a revelation brilliantly disguised as a car." The Hummer is "like nothing else—Sport utility? Define Sport!"

the company positions the product as *offering* greater value, it must then *deliver* that greater value. Thus, effective positioning begins with actually *differentiating* the company's marketing offer so that it gives consumers more value. Once the company has chosen a desired position, it must take strong steps to deliver and communicate that position to target consumers. The company's entire marketing program should support the chosen positioning strategy.

Developing the Marketing Mix

Once the company has decided on its overall marketing strategy, it is ready to begin planning the details of the marketing mix, one of the major concepts in modern marketing. The **marketing mix** is the set of controllable, tactical marketing tools that the firm blends to produce the response it wants in the target market. The marketing mix consists of everything the firm can do to influence the demand for its product. The many possibilities can be collected into four groups of variables known as the "four *P*s": *product*, *price*, *place*, and *promotion*. Figure 2.5 shows the particular marketing tools under each *P*.

Product means the goods-and-services combination the company offers to the target market. Thus, a Ford Taurus product consists of nuts and bolts, spark plugs, pistons, headlights, and thousands of other parts. Ford offers several Taurus styles and dozens of optional features. The car comes fully serviced and with a comprehensive warranty that is as much a part of the product as the tailpipe.

Price is the amount of money customers have to pay to obtain the product. Ford calculates suggested retail prices that its dealers might charge for each Taurus. But Ford dealers rarely charge the full sticker price. Instead, they negotiate the price with each customer, offering discounts, trade-in allowances, and credit terms. These actions adjust prices for the current competitive situation and bring them into line with the buyer's perception of the car's value.

Place includes company activities that make the product available to target consumers. Ford partners with a large body of independently owned dealerships that sell the company's many different models. Ford selects its dealers carefully and supports them strongly. The dealers keep an inventory of Ford automobiles, demonstrate them to potential buyers, negotiate prices, close sales, and service the cars after the sale.

Promotion means activities that communicate the merits of the product and persuade target customers to buy it. Ford spends more than $2.4 billion each year on advertising to

Marketing mix
The set of controllable tactical marketing tools—product, price, place, and promotion—that the firm blends to produce the response it wants in the target market.

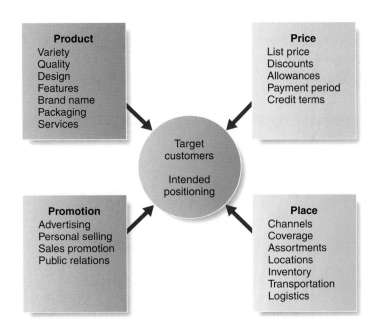

FIGURE 2.5

The Four *P*s of the Marketing Mix

tell consumers about the company and its many products.[14] Dealership salespeople assist potential buyers and persuade them that Ford is the best car for them. Ford and its dealers offer special promotions—sales, cash rebates, low financing rates—as added purchase incentives.

An effective marketing program blends all of the marketing mix elements into a coordinated program designed to achieve the company's marketing objectives by delivering value to consumers. The marketing mix constitutes the company's tactical tool kit for establishing strong positioning in target markets.

Some critics feel that the four Ps may omit or underemphasize certain important activities. For example, they ask, "Where are services?" Just because they don't start with a P doesn't justify omitting them. The answer is that services, such as banking, airline, and retailing services, are products too. We might call them *service products*. "Where is packaging?" the critics might ask. Marketers would answer that they include packaging as just one of many product decisions. All said, as Figure 2.5 suggests, many marketing activities that might appear to be left out of the marketing mix are subsumed under one of the four Ps. The issue is not whether there should be four, six, or ten Ps so much as what framework is most helpful in designing marketing programs.

There is another concern, however, that is valid. It holds that the four Ps concept takes the seller's view of the market, not the buyer's view. From the buyer's viewpoint, in this age of customer relationships, the four Ps might be better described as the four Cs[15]:

Four *Ps*	Four *Cs*
Product	Customer solution
Price	Customer cost
Place	Convenience
Promotion	Communication

Thus, while marketers see themselves as selling products, customers see themselves as buying value or solutions to their problems. And customers are interested in more than just the price; they are interested in the total costs of obtaining, using, and disposing of a product. Customers want the product and service to be as conveniently available as possible. Finally, they want two-way communication. Marketers would do well to think through the four Cs first and then build the four Ps on that platform.

■ Managing the Marketing Effort

In addition to being good at the *marketing* in marketing management, companies also need to pay attention to the *management* in marketing management. Managing the marketing process requires the four marketing management functions shown in Figure 2.6—*analysis*, *planning*, *implementation*, and *control*. The company first develops companywide strategic plans, then translates them into marketing and other plans for each division, product,

FIGURE 2.6

Marketing Analysis, Planning, Implementation, and Control

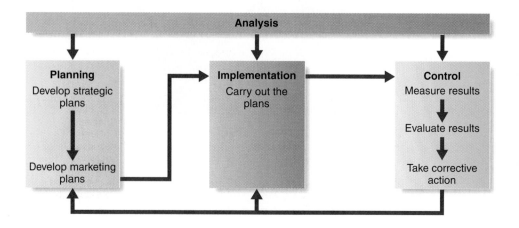

and brand. Through implementation, the company turns the plans into actions. Control consists of measuring and evaluating the results of marketing activities and taking corrective action where needed. Finally, marketing analysis provides information and evaluations needed for all of the other marketing activities.

Marketing Analysis

Managing the marketing function begins with a complete analysis of the company's situation. The company must analyze its markets and marketing environment to find attractive opportunities and avoid environmental threats. It must analyze company strengths and weaknesses as well as current and possible marketing actions to determine which opportunities it can best pursue. Marketing provides input to each of the other marketing management functions. We discuss marketing analysis more fully in Chapter 4.

■ Marketers must continually plan their analysis, implementation, and control activities.

Marketing Planning

Through strategic planning, the company decides what it wants to do with each business unit. Marketing planning involves deciding on marketing strategies that will help the company attain its overall strategic objectives. A detailed **marketing plan** is needed for each business, product, or brand. What does a marketing plan look like? Our discussion focuses on product or brand plans.

Table 2.2 outlines the major sections of a typical product or brand plan. The plan begins with an executive summary, which forms a quick overview of major assessments, goals, and recommendations. The main section of the plan presents a detailed analysis of the current marketing situation as well as potential threats and opportunities. It next states major objectives for the brand and outlines the specifics of a marketing strategy for achieving them.

A *marketing strategy* consists of specific strategies for target markets, positioning, the marketing mix, and marketing expenditure levels. In this section, the planner explains how each strategy responds to the threats, opportunities, and critical issues spelled out earlier in the plan. Additional sections of the marketing plan lay out an action program for implementing the marketing strategy along with the details of a supporting *marketing budget*. The last section outlines the controls that will be used to monitor progress and take corrective action.

Marketing plan
A detailed plan for a product or brand that assesses the current marketing situation and outlines marketing objectives, a marketing strategy, action programs, budgets, and controls.

Marketing Implementation

Planning good strategies is only a start toward successful marketing. A brilliant marketing strategy counts for little if the company fails to implement it properly. **Marketing implementation** is the process that turns marketing *plans* into marketing *actions* in order to accomplish strategic marketing objectives. Implementation involves day-to-day, month-to-month activities that effectively put the marketing plan to work. Whereas marketing planning addresses the *what* and *why* of marketing activities, implementation addresses the *who, where, when,* and *how.*

Many managers think that "doing things right" (implementation) is as important as, or even more important than, "doing the right things" (strategy). The fact is that both are critical to success, and companies can gain competitive advantages through effective implementation.[16] One firm can have essentially the same strategy as another, yet win in the marketplace through faster or better execution. Still, implementation is difficult—it is often easier to think up good marketing strategies than it is to carry them out.

Marketing implementation
The process that turns marketing strategies and plans into marketing actions in order to accomplish strategic marketing objectives.

TABLE 2.2 Contents of a Marketing Plan

Section	Purpose
Executive summary	Presents a brief summary of the main goals and recommendations of the plan for management review, helping top management to find the plan's major points quickly. A table of contents should follow the executive summary.
Current marketing situation	Describes the target market and company's position in it, including information about the market, product performance, competition, and distribution. This section includes: • A *market description* that defines the market and major segments, then reviews customer needs and factors in the marketing environment that may affect customer purchasing. • A *product review,* that shows sales, prices, and gross margins of the major products in the product line. • A review of *competition*, which identifies major competitors and assesses their market positions and strategies for product quality, pricing, distribution, and promotion. • A review of *distribution*, which evaluates recent sales trends and other developments in major distribution channels.
Threats and opportunity analysis	Assesses major threats and opportunities that the product might face, helping management to anticipate important positive or negative developments that might have an impact on the firm and its strategies.
Objectives and issues	States the marketing objectives that the company would like to attain during the plan's term and discusses key issues that will affect their attainment. For example, if the goal is to achieve a 15 percent market share, this section looks at how this goal might be achieved.
Marketing strategy	Outline the broad marketing logic by which the business unit hopes to achieve its marketing objectives and the specifics of target markets, positioning, and marketing expenditure levels. It outlines specific strategies for each marketing-mix element and explains how each responds to the threats, opportunities, and critical issues spelled out earlier in the plan.
Action programs	Spells out how marketing strategies will be turned into specific action programs that answer the following questions: *What* will be done? *When* will it be done? *Who* is responsible for doing it? *How* much will it cost?
Budgets	Details a supporting marketing budget that is essentially a projected profit-and-loss statement. It shows expected revenues (forecasted number of units sold and the average net price) and expected costs (of production, distribution, and marketing). The difference is the projected profit. Once approved by higher management, the budget becomes the basis for materials buying, production scheduling, personnel planning, and marketing operations.
Controls	Outlines the control that will be used to monitor progress and allow higher management to review implementation results and spot products that are not meeting their goals.

In an increasingly connected world, people at all levels of the marketing system must work together to implement marketing strategies and plans. At Black &Decker, for example, marketing implementation for the company's power tool products requires day-to-day decisions and actions by thousands of people both inside and outside the organization. Marketing managers make decisions about target segments, branding, packaging, pricing, promoting, and distributing. They connect with people elsewhere in the company to get support for their products and programs. They talk with engineering about product design, with manufacturing about production and inventory levels, and with finance about funding and cash flows. They also connect with outside people, such as advertising agencies to plan ad campaigns and the media to obtain publicity support. The sales force urges Home Depot, Wal-Mart, and other retailers to advertise Black & Decker products, provide ample shelf space, and use company displays.

Successful marketing implementation depends on how well the company blends its people, organizational structure, decision and reward systems, and company culture into a cohesive action program that supports its strategies. At all levels, the company must be staffed by people who have the needed skills, motivation, and personal characteristics. The company's formal organization structure plays an important role in implementing marketing strategy; so do its decision and reward systems. For example, if a company's compensation system rewards managers for short-term profit results, they will have little incentive to work toward long-term market-building objectives.

Finally, to be successfully implemented, the firm's marketing strategies must fit with its company culture, the system of values and beliefs shared by people in the organization. A study of America's most successful companies found that these companies have almost cultlike cultures built around strong, market-oriented missions. At companies such as Wal-Mart, Dell, Microsoft, Nordstrom, Citicorp, Procter &Gamble, and Walt Disney, "employees share such a strong vision that they know in their hearts what's right for their company."[17]

Marketing Department Organization

The company must design a marketing organization that can carry out marketing strategies and plans. If the company is very small, one person might do all of the research, selling, advertising, customer service, and other marketing work. As the company expands, a marketing department emerges to plan and carry out marketing activities. In large companies, this department contains many specialists. Thus, General Electric and Microsoft have product and market managers, sales managers and salespeople, market researchers, advertising experts, and other specialists.

Modern marketing departments can be arranged in several ways. The most common form of marketing organization is the *functional organization*. Under this organization, different marketing activities are headed by a functional specialist—a sales manager, advertising manager, marketing research manager, customer service manager, or new-product manager. A company that sells across the country or internationally often uses a *geographic organization*. Its sales and marketing people are assigned to specific countries, regions, and districts. Geographic organization allows salespeople to settle into a territory, get to know their customers, and work with a minimum of travel time and cost.

Companies with many very different products or brands often create a *product management organization*. Using this approach, a product manager develops and implements a complete strategy and marketing program for a specific product or brand. Product management first appeared at Procter & Gamble in 1929. A new company soap, Camay, was not doing well, and a young P&G executive was assigned to give his exclusive attention to developing and promoting this product. He was successful, and the company soon added other product managers.[18] Since then, many firms, especially consumer products companies, have set up product management organizations.

For companies that sell one product line to many different types of markets and customers that have different needs and preferences, a *market* or *customer management organization* might be best. A market management organization is similar to the product management organization. Market managers are responsible for developing marketing strategies and plans for their specific markets or customers. This system's main advantage is that the company is organized around the needs of specific customer segments.

Large companies that produce many different products flowing into many different geographic and customer markets usually employ some *combination* of the functional, geographic, product, and market organization forms. This ensures that each function, product, and market receives its share of management attention. However, it can also add costly layers of management and reduce organizational flexibility. Still, the benefits of organizational specialization usually outweigh the drawbacks.

Marketing organization has become an increasingly important issue in recent years. As we discussed in Chapter 1, many companies are finding that today's marketing environment calls for less focus on products, brands, and territories and more focus on customers and customer relationships. More and more companies are shifting their brand management focus toward *customer relationship management*—moving away from managing just product or brand profitability and toward managing customer profitability and customer equity.[19] And many companies now organize their marketing operations around major customers. For example, companies such as Procter & Gamble, Black & Decker,

FIGURE 2.7

The Marketing Control Process

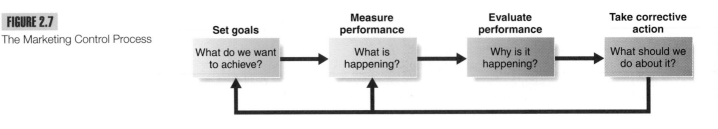

and Newell Rubbermaid have large teams, or even whole divisions, set up to serve large customers like Wal-Mart, Target, or Home Depot.

Marketing Control

Marketing control

The process of measuring and evaluating the results of marketing strategies and plans, and taking corrective action to ensure that objectives are achieved.

Because many surprises occur during the implementation of marketing plans, the marketing department must practice constant marketing control. **Marketing control** involves evaluating the results of marketing strategies and plans and taking corrective action to ensure that objectives are attained. Figure 2.7 shows that marketing control involves four steps. Management first sets specific marketing goals. It then measures its performance in the marketplace and evaluates the causes of any differences between expected and actual performance. Finally, management takes corrective action to close the gaps between its goals and its performance. This may require changing the action programs or even changing the goals.

Operating control involves checking ongoing performance against the annual plan and taking corrective action when necessary. Its purpose is to ensure that the company achieves the sales, profits, and other goals set out in its annual plan. It also involves determining the profitability of different products, territories, markets, and channels.

Strategic control involves looking at whether the company's basic strategies are well matched to its opportunities. Marketing strategies and programs can quickly become outdated, and each company should periodically reassess its overall approach to the marketplace. A major tool for such strategic control is a **marketing audit**. The marketing audit is a comprehensive, systematic, independent, and periodic examination of a company's environment, objectives, strategies, and activities to determine problem areas and opportunities. The audit provides good input for a plan of action to improve the company's marketing performance.[20]

Marketing audit

A comprehensive, systematic, independent, and periodic examination of a company's environment, objectives, strategies, and activities to determine problem areas and opportunities and to recommend a plan of action to improve the company's marketing performance.

The marketing audit covers *all* major marketing areas of a business, not just a few trouble spots. It assesses the marketing environment, marketing strategy, marketing organization, marketing systems, marketing mix, and marketing productivity and profitability. The audit is normally conducted by an objective and experienced outside party. The findings may come as a surprise—and sometimes as a shock—to management. Management then decides which actions make sense and how and when to implement them.

■■ The Marketing Environment

Managing the marketing function would be hard enough if the marketer had to deal with only the controllable marketing mix variables. But the company operates in a complex marketing environment, consisting of uncontrollable forces to which the company must adapt. The environment produces both threats and opportunities. The company must carefully analyze its environment so that it can avoid the threats and take advantage of the opportunities.

The company's marketing environment includes forces close to the company that affect its ability to serve consumers, such as other company departments, channel members, suppliers, competitors, and publics. It also includes broader demographic and economic forces, political and legal forces, technological and ecological forces, and social and cultural forces. Marketers need to consider all of these forces in the process of building and maintaining profitable relationships with customers and marketing partners. We will examine the marketing environment more fully in Chapter 3.

REST STOP:
Reviewing the Concepts

What have you learned so far on your journey through marketing? In Chapter 1, we defined marketing and outlined the steps in the marketing process. We learned that the aim of marketing is to create value for customers in order to capture value in return. In this chapter, we examined companywide strategic planning and marketing's role in the organization. Then, we looked more deeply into marketing strategy and the marketing mix, and reviewed the major marketing management functions. So you've had a pretty good overview of the fundamentals of modern marketing. In future chapters, we'll expand on these fundamentals.

1. Explain companywide strategic planning and its four steps.

Strategic planning sets the stage for the rest of the company's planning. Marketing contributes to strategic planning, and the overall plan defines marketing's role in the company. Although formal planning offers a variety of benefits to companies, not all companies use it or use it well. Although many discussions of strategic planning focus on large corporations, small business also can benefit greatly from sound strategic planning.

Strategic planning involves developing a strategy for long-term survival and growth. It consists of four steps: defining the company's mission, setting objectives and goals, designing a business portfolio, and developing functional plans. *Defining a clear company mission* begins with drafting a formal mission statement, which should be market oriented, realistic, specific, motivating, and consistent with the market environment. The mission is then transformed into detailed *supporting goals and objectives* to guide the entire company. Based on those goals and objectives, headquarters designs a *business portfolio*, deciding which businesses and products should receive more or fewer resources. In turn, each business and product unit must develop *detailed marketing plans* in line with the companywide plan. Comprehensive and sound marketing plans support company strategic planning by detailing specific opportunities.

2. Discuss how to design business portfolios and develop strategies for growth and downsizing.

Guided by the company's mission statement and objectives, management plans its *business portfolio*, or the collection of businesses and products that make up the company. The firm wants to produce a business portfolio that best fits its strengths and weaknesses to opportunities in the environment. To do this, it must analyze and adjust its *current* business portfolio and develop growth and downsizing strategies for adjusting the *future* portfolio. The company might use a formal portfolio-planning method. But many companies are now designing more-customized portfolio-planning approaches that better suit their unique situations. The *product/market expansion grid* suggests four possible growth paths: market penetration, market development, product development, and diversification.

3. Assess marketing's role in strategic planning and explain how marketers partner with others inside and outside the firm to build profitable customer relationships.

Under the strategic plan, the major functional departments—marketing, finance, accounting, purchasing, operations, information systems, human resources, and others—must work together to accomplish strategic objectives. Marketing plays a key role in the company's strategic planning by providing a *marketing-concept philosophy* and *inputs* regarding attractive market opportunities. Within individual business units, marketing designs *strategies* for reaching the unit's objectives and helps to carry them out profitably.

Marketers alone cannot produce superior value for customers. It can be only a partner in attracting, keeping, and growing customers. A company's success depends on how well each department performs its customer value-adding activities and how well the departments work together to serve the customer. Thus, marketers must practice *partner relationship management*. They must work closely with partners in other company departments to form an effective *value chain* that serves the customer. And they must partner effectively with other companies in the marketing system to form a competitively superior *value-delivery network*.

4. Describe the elements of a customer-driven marketing strategy and mix, and the forces that influence it.

Consumer relationships are at the center of marketing strategy and programs. Through market segmentation, target marketing, and market positioning, the company divides the total market into smaller segments, selects the segments it can best serve, and decides how it wants to bring value to target consumers. It then designs a *marketing mix* to produce the response it wants in the target market. The marketing mix consists of product, price, place, and promotion decisions.

5. List the marketing management functions, including the elements of a marketing plan.

To find the best strategy and mix and to put them into action, the company engages in marketing analysis, planning, implementation, and control. The main components of a *marketing plan* are the executive summary, current marketing situation, threats and opportunities, objectives and issues, marketing strategies, action programs, budgets, and controls. To plan good strategies is often easier than to carry them out. To be successful, companies must also be effective at *implementation*—turning marketing strategies into marketing actions.

Much of the responsibility for implementation goes to the company's marketing department. Modern marketing departments can be organized in one or a combination of ways: *functional marketing organization, geographic organization, product management organization*, or *market management organization*. In this age of customer relationships, more and more companies are now changing their organizational focus from product or territory management to customer relationship management. Marketing organizations carry out *marketing control*, both operating control and strategic control. They use *marketing audits* to determine marketing opportunities and problems and to recommend short-run and long-run actions to improve overall marketing performance. Through these activities, the company watches and adapts to the marketing environment.

Navigating the Key Terms

Business portfolio
Diversification
Downsizing
Growth-share matrix
Market development
Market penetration
Market positioning
Market segment

Market segmentation
Marketing audit
Marketing control
Marketing implementation
Marketing mix
Marketing planning
Marketing strategy
Mission statement

Portfolio analysis
Product development
Product/market expansion grid
Strategic planning
Target marketing
Value chain
Value-delivery network

Travel Log

Discussing the Issues

1. Four steps are identified in the strategic planning process. Why are they arranged in this order? What consequences might a company experience if one of the steps was performed out of order? What should be the role of marketing in the strategic planning process?

2. How can the BCG growth-share matrix be used to assess the current product portfolio and to plan for the future? What limitations does portfolio analysis have? Discuss how a product/market expansion grid can aid companies in identifying profitable growth opportunities.

3. Discuss the concept of the value chain. Is it true that the value chain is only as strong as its weakest link? Explain why or why not. How can partnering with other organizations to form a value delivery network further strengthen a firm's performance?

4. Discuss the differences between the following terms: market segmentation, target marketing, and market positioning.

5. Discuss the various activities encompassed by each of the four Ps. What insight might a firm develop by considering the four Cs, instead of the four Ps?

6. What role do analysis, planning, implementation, and control play in managing the marketing process? How are these four marketing management functions related to one another?

Application Questions

1. The product/market expansion grid can be useful in identifying growth opportunities for companies through market penetration, product development, market development, and diversification. Consider a food retailer like Subway, which makes sandwiches and offers chips and drinks. Think creatively to describe four growth opportunities for Subway that fit into each of the four product/market expansion grid cells.

2. Propel is a new lightly flavored, vitamin-enhanced "fitness" water from the maker of Gatorade. It comes in flavors such as berry, black cherry, and kiwi-strawberry. Describe the likely target market for this beverage. How should this beverage be positioned relative to competitive products such as sports drinks, bottled water, orange juice, and milk?

3. Nike has recently entered the golf market with a line of clubs, balls, bags, footwear, and clothing. Most visibly, Nike has enlisted the services of Tiger Woods to promote its golf products. Discuss the four-step marketing control process as it would apply to Nike's evaluation of Tiger Woods as its celebrity endorser.

Under the Hood: Focus on Technology

In order to improve 911 emergency services, the FCC has put forth guidelines that require cell phone carriers to be able to establish subscribers' locations within 100 meters by the end of 2005.

Two different approaches are being considered by wireless carriers. One uses phones with built-in GPS chips, while the other uses triangulation between three or more cell towers to pinpoint a caller's location. This technology, already in use in Hong

Kong, Tokyo, and Helsinki, has drawn the interest of marketers who envision other uses such as sending promotional offers to customers as they walk past their stores. In the beginning, the technology will likely be used to give subscribers directions to particular stores.

1. In a small group, brainstorm potential marketing uses for this technology other than those discussed above.

2. Assume you are a member of a cell phone carrier's marketing team selling this technology to retailers. Develop both a product-oriented and a market-oriented mission statement for the company.

3. What limitations does the product-oriented mission statement have that the market-oriented statement overcomes?

Focus on Ethics

High-profile scandals involving companies such as Enron and WorldCom have renewed interest in understanding how such debacles might be avoided. Corporate accountability is the new theme for concerned investors and politicians. Many agree that the culture of an organization influences the ethical and socially responsible behavior of its employees.

1. Discuss the role that a company's mission statement can play in encouraging ethical corporate behavior.

2. As more firms partner with suppliers, distributors, and even customers to improve their value delivery network, what challenges exist for monitoring and encouraging responsible decision making across the entire value delivery network? What can be done to address these challenges?

3. What function does a marketing audit play in avoiding scandals?

Videos

The Dunkin' Donuts video case that accompanies this chapter is located in Appendix 1 at the back of the book.

Student Materials

Need a tune-up? A study guide and OneKey access code are available to aid in your review of chapter material. Your instructor may choose to have these items shrink-wrapped with your text or you may purchase them separately at www.prenhall.com/marketing.

■ *After studying this chapter, you should be able to*

    1. *Describe* the environmental forces that affect the company's ability to serve its customers   ***2.*** *Explain* how changes in the demographic and economic environments affect marketing decisions   ***3.*** *Identify* the major trends in the firm's natural and technological environments   ***4.*** *Explain* the key changes in the political and cultural environments   ***5.*** *Discuss* how companies can react to the marketing environment

The Marketing
Environment

3

In Part 1 (Chapters 1 and 2), you learned about the basic concepts of marketing and the steps in the marketing process for building profitable relationships with targeted consumers. In Part 2, we'll look more deeply into the first step of the marketing process—understanding the marketplace and customer needs and wants. In this chapter, you'll discover that marketing does not operate in a vacuum, but rather in a complex and changing marketplace environment. Other *actors* in this environment—suppliers, intermediaries, customers, competitors, publics, and others—may work with or against the company. Major environmental *forces*—demographic, economic, natural, technological, political, and cultural—shape marketing opportunities, pose threats, and affect the company's ability to serve customers and develop profitable relationships with them. To understand marketing, and to develop effective marketing strategies, you must first understand the context in which marketing operates.

At our first stop, we'll check out a major development in the marketing environment, millennial fever, and the nostalgia boom that it has produced. Volkswagen responded with the introduction of a born-again New Beetle. As you read on, ask yourself: What has made this little car so right for the times?

A s we hurtle into the new millennium, social experts are busier than ever assessing the impact of a host of environmental forces on consumers and the marketers who serve them. "An old year turns into a new one," reflects one such expert, "and the world itself, at least for a moment, seems to turn also. Images of death and rebirth, things ending and beginning, populate . . . and haunt the mind. Multiply this a thousand-fold, and you get 'millennial fever' . . . driving consumer behavior in all sorts of interesting ways."

Such millennial fever has hit the nation's baby boomers, the most commercially influential demographic group in history, especially hard. The oldest boomers, now in their mid- to late 50s, are resisting the aging process with the vigor they once reserved for antiwar protests. Other factors are also at work. Today, people of all ages seem to feel a bit overworked, overstimulated, overloaded, and technostressed. "Americans are overwhelmed . . . by the breathtaking onrush of the Information Age, with its high-speed modems, cell phones, and pagers," suggests the expert. "While we hail the benefits of these wired [times], at the same time we are buffeted by the rapid pace of change."

The result of this millennial fever is a yearning to turn back the clock, to return to simpler times. This yearning has in turn produced a massive nostalgia wave. Marketers of all kinds have responded to these nostalgia pangs by recreating products and images that help take consumers back to the good old days. "In these tough times," says another expert, "nostalgia for rosier days seems to be driving a consumer appetite for retro products and design."

Examples are plentiful: Kellogg has revived old Corn Flakes packaging and car makers have created retro roadsters such as the Porsche Boxter and Chrysler's PT Cruiser. A Pepsi commercial rocks to the Rolling Stones's "Brown Sugar," James Brown's "I Feel Good" helps sell Senokot laxatives, and Janis Joplin's raspy voice crows, "Oh Lord, won't you buy me a Mercedes-Benz?" Heinz reintroduced its classic glass ketchup bottle, supported by nostalgic "Heinz was there" ads showing two 1950s-era boys eating hot dogs at a ballpark. And the television networks launched what one analyst calls a "retro feeding frenzy" of reunion programs "that revisit the good (*M*A*S*H*, *L.A. Law*, *The Cosby Show*, *The Mary Tyler Moore Show*), the bad (*That's Incredible!*, *Laverne & Shirley*), and the truly ancient (*American Bandstand*, *The Honeymooners*).

Perhaps no company has been more successful in riding the nostalgia wave than Volkswagen. The original Volkswagen Beetle first sputtered into America in 1949. With its simple, buglike design, no-frills engineering, and economical operation, the Beetle was the antithesis of Detroit's chrome-laden gas guzzlers. Although most owners would readily admit that their Beetles were underpowered, noisy, cramped, and freezing in the winter, they saw these as endearing qualities. Overriding these minor inconveniences, the Beetle was cheap to buy and own, dependable, easy to fix, fun to drive, and anything but flashy.

During the 1960s, as young baby boomers by the thousands were buying their first cars, demand exploded and the Beetle blossomed into an unlikely icon. Bursting with personality, the understated Bug came to personify an era of rebellion against conventions. It became the most popular car in American history, with sales peaking at 423,000 in 1968. By the late 1970s, however, the boomers had moved on, Bug mania had faded, and Volkswagen had dropped Beetle production for the United States. Still, decades later, the mere mention of these chugging oddities evokes smiles and strong emotions. Almost everyone over the age of 30, it seems, has a "feel-good" Beetle story to tell.

In an attempt to surf the nostalgia wave, Volkswagen introduced a New Beetle in 1998. Outwardly, the reborn Beetle resembles the original, tapping the strong emotions and memories of times gone by. Beneath the skin, however, the New Beetle is packed with modern features. According to an industry analyst, "The Beetle comeback is . . . based on a combination of romance and reason. . . . Built into the dashboard is a bud vase perfect for a daisy plucked straight from the 1960s. But right next to it is a high-tech multi-speaker stereo—and options like power windows, cruise control, and a power sunroof make it a very different car than the rattly old Bug. The new version . . . comes with all the modern features car buyers demand, such as four air bags and power outlets for cell phones. But that's not why . . . folks buy it. With a familiar bubble shape that still makes people smile as it skitters by, the new Beetle offers a pull that is purely emotional."

Initial advertising for the New Beetle played strongly on the nostalgia theme, while at the same time refreshing the old Beetle heritage. "If you sold your soul in the '80s," tweaked one ad, "here's your chance to buy it back." Other ads read, "Less flower, more power," and "Comes with wonderful new features. Like heat." Still another ad declared "0 to 60? Yes."

Volkswagen invested $560 million to bring the New Beetle to market. The investment paid big dividends as demand quickly outstripped supply. Even before the first cars reached VW showrooms, dealers across the country had long waiting lists of people who'd paid for the car without ever seeing it, let alone driving it. The New Beetle turned out to be a cross-generational hit, appealing to more than just Woodstock-recovered baby boomers. Even kids too young to remember the original Bug loved this new one.

Volkswagen's first-year sales projections of 50,000 New Beetles in North America proved pessimistic. After only nine months, the company had sold more than 64,000 of the new Bugs in the United States and Canada. Sales are still sizzling—the New Beetle now accounts for more than a quarter of Volkswagen's U.S. sales and has helped win VW a fivefold increase in sales during the past decade.

To follow up, Volkswagen launched the spunky little New Beetle convertible in early 2003. By the time they were introduced, more than half of the convertibles arriving at dealerships had already been sold. "It's just a nice, happy ride," notes one delighted owner. Upbeat ads for the new model evoke images of simpler, gentler times. One ad shows a chain reaction of smiles, as one person walking on a city sidewalk stops to help someone else, who in turn helps another, and so on. At the end, the ad rewinds to show what sparked the first smile: a VW convertible.

For an encore, Volkswagen plans to introduce a reincarnation of its old cult-classic flower-power Microbus in 2005. Although most younger buyers won't remember much about the original Microbus unless they encountered one at a Grateful Dead concert, test models have received rave reviews at auto shows in Japan and Europe.

"Millennial fever" results from the convergence of a wide range of forces in the marketing environment—from technological, economic, and demographic forces to cultural, social, and political ones. Most trend analysts believe that the nostalgia craze will only grow as the population ages and as times get more complex. If so, the New Beetle, so full of the past, has a very bright future. "The Beetle is not just empty nostalgia," says Gerald Celente, publisher of *Trend Journal*. "It is a practical car that is also tied closely to the emotions of a generation." Says another trend analyst, the New Beetle "is our romantic past, reinvented for our hectic here-and-now. Different, yet deeply familiar—a car for the times."[1]

As noted in previous chapters, marketers need to be good at building relationships with customers, others in the company, and external partners. To do this effectively, marketers must understand the major environmental forces that surround all of these relationships. A company's **marketing environment** consists of the actors and forces outside marketing that affect marketing management's ability to build and maintain successful relationships with target customers. The marketing environment offers both opportunities and threats. Successful companies know the vital importance of constantly watching and adapting to the changing environment.

As we move into the twenty-first century, both consumers and marketers wonder what the future will bring. The environment continues to change rapidly. More than any other group in the company, marketers must be the trend trackers and opportunity seekers. Although every manager in an organization needs to observe the outside environment, marketers have two special aptitudes. They have disciplined methods—marketing intelligence and marketing research—for collecting information about the marketing environment. They also spend more time in the customer and competitor environments. By carefully studying the environment, marketers can adapt their strategies to meet new marketplace challenges and opportunities.

The marketing environment is made up of a *microenvironment* and a *macroenvironment*. The **microenvironment** consists of the actors close to the company that affect its ability to serve its customers—the company, suppliers, marketing intermediaries, customer markets, competitors, and publics. The **macroenvironment** consists of the larger societal forces that affect the microenvironment—demographic, economic, natural, technological, political, and cultural forces. We look first at the company's microenvironment.

Marketing environment
The actors and forces outside marketing that affect marketing management's ability to build and maintain successful relationships with target customers.

Microenvironment
The actors close to the company that affect its ability to serve its customers—the company, suppliers, marketing intermediaries, customer markets, competitors, and publics.

Macroenvironment
The larger societal forces that affect the microenvironment—demographic, economic, natural, technological, political, and cultural forces.

▪▪ The Company's Microenvironment

Marketing management's job is to build relationships with customers by creating customer value and satisfaction. However, marketing managers cannot do this alone. Figure 3.1 shows the major actors in the marketer's microenvironment. Marketing success will require building relationships with other company departments, suppliers, marketing intermediaries, customers, competitors, and various publics, which combine to make up the company's value delivery network.

The Company

In designing marketing plans, marketing management takes other company groups into account—groups such as top management, finance, research and development (R&D), purchasing, operations, and accounting. All these interrelated groups form the internal environment. Top management sets the company's mission, objectives, broad strategies, and policies. Marketing managers make decisions within the strategies and plans made by top management.

Marketing managers must also work closely with other company departments. Finance is concerned with finding and using funds to carry out the marketing plan. The R&D department focuses on designing safe and attractive products. Purchasing worries about getting supplies and materials, whereas operations is responsible for producing and distributing the desired quality and quantity of products. Accounting has to measure revenues and costs to help marketing know how well it is achieving its objectives. Together, all of these departments have an impact on the marketing department's plans and actions. Under the marketing concept, all of these functions must "think consumer." They should work in harmony to provide superior customer value and satisfaction.

Suppliers

Suppliers form an important link in the company's overall customer value delivery system. They provide the resources needed by the company to produce its goods and services. Supplier problems can seriously affect marketing. Marketing managers must watch supply availability—supply shortages or delays, labor strikes, and other events can cost sales in the short run and damage customer satisfaction in the long run. Marketing managers also monitor the price trends of their key inputs. Rising supply costs may force price increases that can harm the company's sales volume.

Most marketers today treat their suppliers as partners in creating and delivering customer value. Wal-Mart goes to great lengths to work with its suppliers. For example, it helps them to test new products in its stores. And its Supplier Development Department publishes a Supplier Proposal Guide and maintains a supplier Web site, both of which help suppliers to navigate the complex Wal-Mart buying process. It knows that good partnership relationship management results in success for Wal-Mart, suppliers, and, ultimately, its customers.

FIGURE 3.1

Actors in the Microenvironment

Marketing Intermediaries

Marketing intermediaries help the company to promote, sell, and distribute its goods to final buyers. They include *resellers, physical distribution firms*, *marketing services agencies*, and *financial intermediaries. Resellers* are distribution channel firms that help the company find customers or make sales to them. These include wholesalers and retailers, who buy and resell merchandise. Selecting and partnering with resellers is not easy. No longer do manufacturers have many small, independent resellers from which to choose. They now face large and growing reseller organizations such as Wal-Mart, Target, Home Depot, Costco, and Best Buy. These organizations frequently have enough power to dictate terms or even to shut the manufacturer out of large markets.

Physical distribution firms help the company to stock and move goods from their points of origin to their destinations. Working with warehouse and transportation firms, a company must determine the best ways to store and ship goods, balancing factors such as cost, delivery, speed, and safety. *Marketing services agencies* are the marketing research firms, advertising agencies, media firms, and marketing consulting firms that help the company target and promote its products to the right markets. When the company decides to use one of these agencies, it must choose carefully because these firms vary in creativity, quality, service, and price. *Financial intermediaries* include banks, credit companies, insurance companies, and other businesses that help finance transactions or insure against the risks associated with the buying and selling of goods. Most firms and customers depend on financial intermediaries to finance their transactions.

Like suppliers, marketing intermediaries form an important component of the company's overall value delivery system. In its quest to create satisfying customer relationships, the company must do more than just optimize its own performance. It must partner effectively with marketing intermediaries to optimize the performance of the entire system.

Thus, today's marketers recognize the importance of working with their intermediaries as partners rather than simply as channels through which they sell their products. For example, Coca-Cola has a 10-year deal with Wendy's that makes it the fast-food chain's exclusive soft drink provider. In the deal, Coca-Cola provides Wendy's much more than just soft drinks. It also pledges powerful marketing support.

> Along with the soft drinks, Wendy's gets a cross-functional team of 50 Coke employees who are dedicated to understanding the finer points of Wendy's business. It also benefits from Coke dollars spent in joint marketing campaigns. Bigger still is the staggering amount of consumer research that Coca-Cola provides its partners. Coke . . . goes to great lengths to understand beverage drinkers—and to make sure its partners can use those insights. The company has also analyzed the demographics of every zip code in the country and used the information to create a software program called Solver. By answering questions about their target audience, Wendy's franchise owners can determine which Coke brands are preferred by the customers in their area. Coca-Cola also has even studied the design of drive-through menu boards to better understand which layouts, fonts, letter sizes, colors, and visuals induce consumers to order more food and drink. Such intense partnering efforts have earned Coca-Cola a 65 percent share of the U.S. fountain soft drink market, compared with a 24 percent share for Pepsi.[2]

Marketing intermediaries
Firms that help the company to promote, sell, and distribute its goods to final buyers; they include resellers, physical distribution firms, marketing service agencies, and financial intermediaries.

■ Partnering with marketing intermediaries: Coca-Cola provides Wendy's with much more than just soft drinks. It also pledges powerful marketing support.

Customers

The company needs to study five types of customer markets closely. *Consumer markets* consist of individuals and households that buy goods and services for personal consumption. *Business markets* buy goods and services for further processing or for use in their production process, whereas *reseller markets* buy goods and services to resell at a profit. *Government markets* are made up of government agencies that buy goods and services to produce public services or transfer the goods and services to others who need them. Finally, *international markets* consist of these buyers in other countries, including consumers, producers, resellers, and governments. Each market type has special characteristics that call for careful study by the seller.

Competitors

The marketing concept states that to be successful, a company must provide greater customer value and satisfaction than its competitors do. Thus, marketers must do more than simply adapt to the needs of target consumers. They also must gain strategic advantage by positioning their offerings strongly against competitors' offerings in the minds of consumers.

No single competitive marketing strategy is best for all companies. Each firm should consider its own size and industry position compared to those of its competitors. Large firms with dominant positions in an industry can use certain strategies that smaller firms cannot afford. But being large is not enough. There are winning strategies for large firms, but there are also losing ones. And small firms can develop strategies that give them better rates of return than large firms enjoy.

Public

Any group that has an actual or potential interest in or impact on an organization's ability to achieve its objectives.

■ Publics: In this ad, Wal-Mart recognizes the importance of both its local and employee publics. Its Good Works scholarship program "is just one of the reasons Wal-Mart associates in Mississippi (such as Tiffany, at lower right), and all over the country, are proud to get involved in the communities they serve."

Publics

The company's marketing environment also includes various publics. A **public** is any group that has an actual or potential interest in or impact on an organization's ability to achieve its objectives. We can identify seven types of publics.

■ *Financial publics* influence the company's ability to obtain funds. Banks, investment houses, and stockholders are the major financial publics.

■ *Media publics* carry news, features, and editorial opinion. They include newspapers, magazines, and radio and television stations.

■ *Government publics.* Management must take government developments into account. Marketers must often consult the company's lawyers on issues of product safety, truth in advertising, and other matters.

■ *Citizen-action publics.* A company's marketing decisions may be questioned by consumer organizations, environmental groups, minority groups, and others. Its public relations department can help it stay in touch with consumer and citizen groups.

■ *Local publics* include neighborhood residents and community organizations. Large companies usually appoint a community relations officer to deal with the community, attend meetings, answer questions, and contribute to worthwhile causes.

■ *General public.* A company needs to be concerned about the general public's attitude toward its products and activities. The public's image of the company affects its buying.

■ *Internal publics* include workers, managers, volunteers, and the board of directors. Large companies use newsletters and other means to inform and motivate their internal publics. When employees feel good about their company, this positive attitude spills over to external publics.

A company can prepare marketing plans for these major publics as well as for its customer markets. Suppose the company wants a specific response from a particular public, such as goodwill, favorable word of mouth, or donations of time or money. The company would have to design an offer to this public that is attractive enough to produce the desired response.

■■ The Company's Macroenvironment

The company and all of the other actors operate in a larger macroenvironment of forces that shape opportunities and pose threats to the company. Figure 3.2 shows the six major forces in the company's macroenvironment. In the remaining sections of this chapter, we examine these forces and show how they affect marketing plans.

Demographic Environment

Demography is the study of human populations in terms of size, density, location, age, gender, race, occupation, and other statistics. The demographic environment is of major interest to marketers because it involves people, and people make up markets.

The world population is growing at an explosive rate. It now totals more than 6.3 billion and will exceed 8.2 billion by the year 2030.[3] The world's large and highly diverse population poses both opportunities and challenges. Think for a few minutes about the world and your place in it. If we reduced the world to a village of 1,000 people representative of the world's population, this would be our reality[4]:

■ Our village would have 520 females and 480 males including 330 children and 60 people over age 65, 10 college graduates, and 335 illiterate adults.

■ We'd have 52 North Americans, 55 Russians, 84 Latin Americans, 95 Europeans, 124 Africans, and 584 Asians.

■ Communication would be difficult: 165 of us would speak Mandarin, 85 English, 83 Hindi, 64 Spanish, 58 Russian, and 37 Arabic. The other half of us would speak one of more than 5,000 other languages.

■ Among us we'd have 329 Christians, 178 Moslems, 32 Hindus, 60 Buddhists, 3 Jews, 167 nonreligious, 45 atheists, and 86 others.

■ About one-third of our people would have access to clean, safe drinking water. About half of our children would be immunized against infections.

Demography

The study of human populations in terms of size, density, location, age, gender, race, occupation, and other statistics.

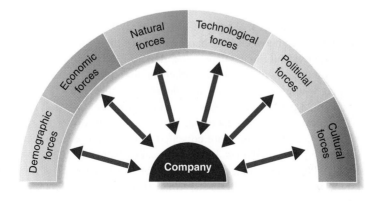

FIGURE 3.2

Major Forces in the Company's Macroenvironment

■ The world population is growing at an explosive rate, presenting both opportunities and challenges for marketers. Think for a few minutes about the world and your place in it.

■ The woodlands in our village would be decreasing rapidly and wasteland would be growing. Forty percent of the village's cropland, nourished by 83 percent of our fertilizer, would produce 72 percent of the food to feed its 270 well-fed owners. The remaining 60 percent of the land and 17 percent of the fertilizer would produce 28 percent of the food to feed the other 730 people. Five hundred people in the village would suffer from malnutrition.

■ Only 200 of the 1,000 people would control 75 percent of our village's wealth. Another 200 would receive only 2 percent of the wealth. Seventy people would own cars. One would have a computer, and that computer probably would not be connected to the Internet. Only 70 of us would own a car.

The explosive world population growth has major implications for business. A growing population means growing human needs to satisfy. Depending on purchasing power, it may also mean growing market opportunities. For example, to curb its skyrocketing population, the Chinese government has passed regulations limiting families to one child each. As a result, Chinese children are spoiled and fussed over as never before. Known in China as "little emperors and empresses," Chinese children are being showered with everything from candy to computers as a result of what's known as the "six-pocket syndrome." As many as six adults—including parents and two sets of doting grandparents—may be indulging the whims of each child. Parents in the average Beijing household now spend about 40 percent of their income on their cherished only child. This trend has encouraged toy companies such as Japan's Bandai Company (known for its Mighty Morphin Power Rangers), Denmark's Lego Group, and Mattel to enter the Chinese market. And McDonald's has triumphed in China in part because it has catered successfully to this pampered generation.[5]

Thus, marketers keep close track of demographic trends and developments in their markets, both at home and abroad. They track changing age and family structures, geographic population shifts, educational characteristics, and population diversity. Here, we discuss the most important demographic trends in the United States.

Changing Age Structure of the Population   The U.S. population stood at more than 291 million in 2003 and may reach 350 million by the year 2025.[6] The single most important demographic trend in the United States is the changing age structure of the population. As shown in Figure 3.3, the U.S. population contains seven generational groups. Here, we discuss the three largest age groups—the baby boomers, Generation X, and Generation Y—and their impact on today's marketing strategies.

Baby boomers
The 78 million people born during the baby boom following World War II and lasting until the early 1960s.

The Baby Boomers.   The post–World War II baby boom produced 78 million **baby boomers**, born between 1946 and 1964. Since then, the baby boomers have become one of the most powerful forces shaping the marketing environment. The boomers have presented a moving target, creating new markets as they grew from infancy to their preadolescent, teenage, young adult, and now middle-age to mature years. Today's baby boomers account for about 28 percent of the population but earn more than half of all personal income.

Marketers typically have paid the most attention to the smaller upper crust of the boomer generation—its more educated, mobile, and wealthy segments. These segments have gone by many names. In the 1980s, they were called "yuppies" (young urban professionals), "bumpies" (black upwardly mobile professionals), "yummies" (young upwardly mobile mommies), and "DINKs" (dual-income, no-kids couples). In the 1990s, yuppies

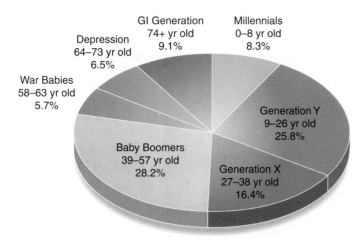

FIGURE 3.3

The Seven U.S. Generations

Source: Adapted from Alison Stein Wellner, "Generational Divide," *American Demographics*, October 2000, pp. 53-58.

and DINKs gave way to a new breed, with names such as "DEWKs" (dual-earners with kids) and "MOBYs" (mother older, baby younger). Now, to the chagrin of many in this generation, they are acquiring such titles as "WOOFs" (well-off older folks) or even "GRUMPIES" (just what the name suggests).

Although the more affluent boomers have grabbed most of the headlines, baby boomers cut across all walks of life, creating a diverse set of target segments for businesses. There are wealthy boomers but also boomers with more modest means. Boomers span a 20-year age range, and almost 25 percent of boomers belong to a racial or ethnic minority.[7]

The youngest boomers are now in their late 30s; the oldest are in their mid- to late 50s. In fact, somewhere in America, seven boomers will turn 50 every minute from now until 2014. By 2025, there will be 64 million baby boomers aged 61 to 79, a 90 percent increase in the size of this population from today. Thus, the boomers have evolved from the "youthquake generation" to the "backache generation." The maturing boomers are experiencing the pangs of midlife and rethinking the purpose and value of their work, responsibilities, and relationships. They are approaching life with a new stability and reasonableness in the way they live, think, eat, and spend. As they continue to age, they will create a large and important seniors market.

As they mature, the boomers are also reaching their peak earning and spending years. Thus, they constitute a lucrative market for new housing and home remodeling, financial services, travel and entertainment, eating out, health and fitness products, and high-priced cars and other luxuries. For example, more than half of all U.S. home remodeling expenditures last year were made by baby boomers.[8]

It would be a mistake to think of the boomers as aging and staid. In fact, the boomers are spending $30 billion a year on *anti*-aging products and services. Consider the following example[9]:

> Dave Conrath walked into the Grooming Lounge in downtown Washington D.C., with one thought in mind: turning back the clock. The 43-year-old commercial builder, who describes himself as "follically challenged," received a cut that puffed up the strands of his thinning blonde hair. He stretched out for a hot shave that seemed to take years off his sun-leathered skin. After a quick massage to loosen the knots in his neck, he headed to the display case for bottles of skin toner, moisturizer, and shaving oil. The trip cost him $100, but he left with a smile. "I feel like I'm 28 again," said Conrath, scrutinizing his reflection in the storefront window. "I work hard and feel that it's okay to drop 100 bucks to look young. . . . I deserve it."

Unlike previous generations, boomers are likely to postpone retirement. Many boomers are rediscovering the excitement of life and have the means to play it out. For

■ The baby boomers: It would be a mistake to think of the boomers as aging and staid. The personal watercraft industry has now virtually abandoned young adult consumers in favor of targeting middle-aged boomers.

example, according to the Travel Industry Association of America, one-half of all U.S. adults took adventure vacations within the past five years. Some 56 percent of these travelers were boomers. The median age of a Harley-Davidson buyer is 46 years old, squarely in the middle of the boomer age range. And the personal watercraft industry has now virtually abandoned young adult consumers in favor of targeting middle-aged boomers and their kids.[10]

Those one-man, stand-up Jet Skis that used to terrorize beachgoers, with ab-ribbed guys in shell necklaces vaulting over waves on their water hogs, now represent only about 1 percent of the market. New models have wider seats and room for three or even four people, with storage space for coolers and spray shields to keep legs dry. They're practically minivans. . . . The boomers want youthful lifestyle forever.

Generation X

The 45 million people born between 1965 and 1976 in the "birth dearth" following the baby boom.

Generation X. The baby boom was followed by a "birth dearth," creating another generation of 45 million people born between 1965 and 1976. Author Douglas Coupland calls them **Generation X**, because they lie in the shadow of the boomers and lack obvious distinguishing characteristics. Others call them the "baby busters," the "shadow generation," or the "yiffies"—young, individualistic, freedom-minded few.

The Generation Xers are defined as much by their shared experiences as by their age. Increasing divorce rates and higher employment for their mothers made them the first generation of latchkey kids. Having grown up during times of recession and corporate downsizing, they have developed a more cautious economic outlook.

As a result, the GenXers are a more skeptical bunch, cynical of frivolous marketing pitches that promise easy success. They share new cultural concerns. They care about the environment and respond favorably to socially responsible companies. Although they seek success, they are less materialistic; they prize experience, not acquisition. They are cautious romantics who want a better quality of life and are more interested in job satisfaction than in sacrificing personal happiness and growth for promotion.

Once labeled as "the MTV generation" and as body-piercing slackers who whined about "McJobs," the GenXers have now grown up and are beginning to take over. They do surf the Internet more than other groups, but with serious intent. The GenXers are poised to displace the lifestyles, culture, and materialistic values of the baby boomers. They represent close to $736 billion in annual purchasing power. By the year 2010, they will have overtaken the baby boomers as a primary market for almost every product category.[11]

With so much potential, many companies are focusing on GenXers. Consider the following example:

In a gritty Northside Chicago neighborhood, in a former grocery store here, under an L-train and next to a Trader Joe's, percolates CB2, the store where the definition of home for the next generation of consumers is being refined. Inside, the store pulses with techno-jazz and high-impact displays. The "CB" stands for Crate & Barrel, the "2" signals that the store is a spin-off, a cheekier cousin geared to price-and-design conscious customers in their twenties and thirties. Who are CB2's core consumers? GenXers. They're urban professionals, age 25 to 40, who are more likely to live in a loft, apartment, or townhouse than a house in the suburbs. They are skeptical, impatient, and highly mobile. They like trends but not gimmicks, and they gravitate to the cool and casual. At CB2, it's taken three years to get the mix right. For example, while Crate & Barrel attracts cooks, CB2 discovered that its core customers spend more time at their computers than at the stove. So gourmet was scaled down and home office beefed up.[12]

Generation Y. Both the baby boomers and GenXers will one day be passing the reins to the latest demographic group, **Generation Y** (also called echo boomers). Born between 1977 and 1994, these children of the baby boomers now number 72 million, dwarfing the GenXers and almost equal in size to the baby boomer segment. Ranging from preteens to mid-20s, the echo boomer generation is still forming its buying preferences and behaviors.

The echo boom has created large kid and teen markets (see Marketing at Work 3.1). With an average disposable income of $100 a week, echo boomers already spend $150 billion a year and influence another $50 billion in family spending. After years of bust, markets for kids' and teen's toys and games, clothes, furniture, and food have enjoyed a boom. Designers and retailers have created new lines, new products, and even new stores devoted to children and teens—Tommy Hilfiger, DKNY, Gap, Toys "*R*" Us, Guess, Talbots, Pottery Barn, and Eddie Bauer, to name just a few. New media appeared that cater specifically to this market: *Time*, *Sports Illustrated*, and *People* have all started new editions for kids and teens. Banks have offered banking and investment services for young people, including investment camps.[13]

Generation Y oldsters are now graduating from college and beginning careers. Like the trailing edge of the Generation Xers ahead of them, one distinguishing characteristic of Generation Y is their utter fluency and comfort with computer, digital, and Internet technology. About 9 of 10 teens have a home computer, half have Internet access, and more than 50 percent of teens 12 to 17 own a mobile phone. In all, they are an impatient, now-oriented bunch. "Blame it on the relentless and dizzying pace of the Internet, 24-hour cable news cycles, cell phones, and TiVo for creating the on-demand, gotta-get-it-now universe in which we live," says one observer. "Perhaps nowhere is the trend more pronounced than among the Gen Y set."[14]

Generation Y represents a complex target for marketers. On average, Gen Ys have access to 62 TV channels, not to mention mobile phones, personal digital assistants (PDAs), and the Internet, offering broad media access. Studies have shown that Gen Y consumers are smart, aware, and fair-minded. They like to be entertained in ads directed at them but don't like ads that make fun of people. They love things that are "green" and they relate well to causes. Making connections now with Gen Ys will pay dividends to

■ Targeting GenXers: Crate & Barrel's spin-off, CB2, sells edgy products aimed at price-and-design conscious customers aged 25 to 40.

Generation Y

The 72 million children of the baby boomers, born between 1977 and 1994.

Marketing at Work | 3.1

The Teen Market: Youth Will Be Served

Gone are the days when kids saved up their pennies for candy and ice cream at the corner soda fountain. Today's teens are big spenders. The average U.S. teen spends $101 each week; combined, the nation's 32 million 12-to-19-year-olds spend more than $170 billion a year. What's more, teens influence another $30 billion annually of their parents' spending. With so much cash to spend, teens represent a lucrative market for companies willing to cater to their often fickle, trend-driven tastes.

To tap into this vast market of potential new customers, all kinds of companies are targeting teens with new or modified products. Some of these products are naturals for the teen market, such as action movies, acne creams, teen magazines, cell phones, and N Sync. Others are less expected, such as Avon products, cars, and hotels. Here are just a few examples of companies attempting to cash in on the hot teen market:

■ *Wildseed:* Cell phone manufacturer Wildseed has spent years conducting research to develop cell phones for teens. For the past two years, the company has regularly summoned teenagers to focus groups, where it pays them $20 to lounge around, eat pizza, play Xbox video games, and give their thumbs up or thumbs down on various proposals. The research shows that for teenagers, a desirable cell phone is not about smaller, lighter, sleeker. What teens want from a cell phone ranges from the concrete (music, messaging, and games) to the abstract (style, personality, and individ-

uality). As a result, Wildseed phones have "smart skins"—replaceable faceplates with computer chips that allow teens to individualize the phone's functions and appearance to match their personalities. For example, skateboarders can choose graffiti-splattered

faceplates that come with edgy urban ringer tones and gritty icons.
■ *Teen Vogue:* After years of preliminary market testing, *Vogue* launched the first issue of the teen version of its popular women's magazine in early 2003. The publisher, Condé Nast,

Marketing to teens: Based on focus group research, Wildseed developed cell phones with "smart skins"—replaceable faceplates with computer chips that let teens individualize the phone's functions and appearance to match their personalities.

marketers beyond capturing their current spending. In future years, as they begin working and their buying power increases, this segment will more than rival the baby boomers in spending and market influence.[15]

Generational Marketing. Do marketers have to create separate products and marketing programs for each generation? Some experts caution that each generation spans decades

built an initial subscription base of more than 450,000 teens and expects the readership to expand to more than 750,000. In addition to including articles on fashion and stunning pictures, Condé Nast has decreased the size of the magazine, measuring only 6 3/4 inches by 9 1/8 inches, perfect for hiding in class.

■ *Hot Topic:* Clothing retailer Hot Topic targets the 17 percent of American high school students who consider themselves "alternative teens." Hot Topic's buyers go to rock concerts and raves to check out what performers and fashion-forward fans are wearing. The store carries an assortment of items you just won't find at Abercrombie & Fitch. Rather than khakis and tank tops, the store stocks pinstripe fishnet stockings, pink fur pants, feather boas, blue hair dye, black nail polish, and Morbid Makeup. Teens can buy T-shirts from TV shows such as "SpongeBob SquarePants," Kermit the Frog underwear, and licensed concert apparel from rockers such as Eminem, Marilyn Manson, Tool, and Linkin Park. Whereas Gap, American Eagle, and other teen retailers have recently reported flat or declining sales, Hot Topic's sales are, well, a hot topic. Sales have increased an average of 37 percent annually for the last three years.

■ *Avon:* Avon will soon roll out a Teen Business unit to target teenage buyers. The new department will employ teens as sales associates who sell to other teens through catalogs, the Internet, and slumber parties and other informal gatherings. Can a company known for its appeal to 25-to-55-year-old middle American-women sell successfully to teens and young women? Avon thinks so. The new brand is dis-

tinctly more upscale and trendier than Avon's traditional look. "This is very much not just another brand," says Avon's chief executive, Andrea Jung.

■ *Rockport:* When you think of Rockport, you probably think of casual shoes and clothing for the older set. However, in an attempt to build relationships with 12-to-19-year-olds, Rockport recently teamed up with Dubit, a youth-focused company in the United Kingdom, to produce a 3D online store targeting teens (www.dubit.co.uk). Teens roaming Dubit's virtual mall can enter the Rockport store and check out shoes with real youth appeal—such as the Copepoda Crustacean, a sleek "performance sandal with a rubber outsole," or the Tactonic Open Road, a "retro bowling style trainer with a contrast stitching." In the corner of the store, a deejay takes requests and spins digital tracks onto a personalized MP3 player.

■ *The Gorham Hotel:* Hotels and resorts are becoming more and more aware of the impact teens have on family vacation decisions. According to one study, 82 percent of parents said they choose vacations based on their kids' input. As a result, many hotels are catering to teens by offering family packages that include access to teen nightclubs, special teen-oriented outings, and computer rooms with unlimited Internet access. At the Gorham Hotel in New York, catering to teens means giving them a little space—in their parents' rooms. Special suites have denlike rooms with their own doors, pull-out sofas, televisions, phones, even Nintendo. Downstairs, in the lobby, the Gorham offers 24-hour access to the Internet.

■ *The National Cattlemen's Beef Association:* It's hard to imagine Robert Mitchum or Sam Elliott (the two men who have gruffly voiced the "Beef. It's what's for dinner" tagline) dominating discussion at a slumber party. . . . Yet the National Cattlemen's Beef Association is plenty interested in this young teen female cohort. It has been using Sasha Cohen, the 4-foot-11, 19-year-old figure skater, as a spokeswoman for the past several years. And now it has launched a girl-power-themed Web site, Cool-2B-Real.com, aimed at 8-to-12-year-olds (many of whom, the NCBA is well aware, are already vegetarians). Outfitted in pastel pinks, blues and yellows, the site looks a lot like Barbie.com, if you ignore the hamburger in the middle of the page. It offers games like "Burger Boggle" and "Grillin' & Chillin'," as well as polls, quizzes, chat rooms, message boards and, of course, recipes (almost all of which include beef).

Sources: Examples adapted from those found in Frand Washington, "Aim Young; No, Younger," *Advertising Age,* April 9, 2001; Nancy Keates, "Family Travel: Catering to Kids," *Wall Street Journal,* May 3, 2002, p. W-1; Jennifer Lee, "Youth Will Be Served, Wirelessly," *New York Times,* May 30, 2002, p. G1; Sally Beatty, "Avon Set to Sell to Teens," *Wall Street Journal,* October 17, 2002, p. B1; and Tim Nudd, "Beef. It's, Like, What's for Dinner," *Adweek,* March 17, 2003, p. 46. Also see "Hot Topic, Inc.," *Hoover Company Profiles,* Austin, May 15, 2003; Leslie Earnest, "California: Hot Topic Results Suit It to a Tee," *The Los Angeles Times,* March 5, 2003, p. C2; "Rockport Opens 3D Shop on Teen Web Site," *Marketing Week,* May 23, 2002, p. 39; Jon Fine, "Teen Vogue Takes Sophisticate Route," *Advertising Age,* January 13, 2003, p. 45; "Teens Spent $170 Billion in 2002," press release, Teenage Research Unlimited, February 17, 2003, accessed online at www.teenresearch.com/PRview.cfm?edit_id=152; and Arlene Weintraub, "Hotter Than a Pair of Vinyl Jeans," *Business Week,* June 9, 2003, pp. 84–85.

of time and many socioeconomic levels. For example, marketers often split the baby boomers into three smaller groups—leading boomers, core boomers, and trailing boomers—each with its own beliefs and behaviors. Similarly, they split Generation Y into Gen Y adults, Gen Y teens, and Gen Y kids. Thus, marketers need to form more precise age-specific segments within each group. More important, defining people by their birth date may be less effective than segmenting them by their lifestyle or life stage.

Others warn that marketers have to be careful about turning off one generation each time they craft a product or message that appeals effectively to another. "The idea is to try to be broadly inclusive and at the same time offer each generation something specifically designed for it," notes one expert. "Tommy Hilfiger has big brand logos on his clothes for teenagers and little pocket polo logos on his shirts for baby boomers. It's a brand that has a more inclusive than exclusive strategy."[16]

The Changing American Family The "traditional household" consists of a husband, wife, and children (and sometimes grandparents). Yet, the once American ideal of the two-child, two-car suburban family has lately been losing some of its luster. "Ward and June Cleaver used to represent the typical American household," says one demographer. "Today, marketers would be remiss in not incorporating the likes of Murphy Brown, Ally McBeal, and Will and Grace into their business plans."[17]

In the United States today, married couples with children now make up only about 34 percent of the nation's 105 million households, and this percentage is falling. Married couples and people living with other relatives make up 22 percent; single parents comprise another 12 percent. A full 32 percent are nonfamily households—single live-alones or adult live-togethers of one or both sexes.[18] More people are divorcing or separating, choosing not to marry, marrying later, or marrying without intending to have children. Marketers must increasingly consider the special needs of nontraditional households, because they are now growing more rapidly than traditional households. Each group has distinctive needs and buying habits.

The number of working women has also increased greatly, growing from under 30 percent of the U.S. workforce in 1950 to just over 60 percent today.[19] However, that trend may be slowing. After increasing steadily for 25 years, the percentage of women with children under age 1 in the workforce has fallen during the past few years. Meanwhile, men are staying home with their children in record numbers. Last year, more than 1.7 million stay-at-home dads managed the household while their wives went to work.

The significant number of women in the workforce has spawned the child-day-care business and increased consumption of convenience foods and services, career-oriented women's clothing, financial services, and many other business opportunities. For example, new niche malls feature customized mixes of specialty shops with extended hours for working women who can find time to shop only before or after work. Stores in these malls feature targeted promotions and phone-in shopping. Busy shoppers can phone ahead with color choices and other preferences while store employees perform a "wardrobe consulting" service.[20]

Geographic Shifts in Population This is a period of great migratory movements between and within countries. Americans, for example, are a mobile people, with about 16 percent of all U.S. residents moving each year.[21] Over the past two decades, the U.S. population has shifted toward the Sunbelt states. The West and South have grown, while the Midwest and Northeast states have lost population. Such population shifts interest marketers because people in different regions buy differently. For example, research shows that people in Seattle buy more

■ The changing American family: Non-family households—single live-alones or adult live-togethers of one or both sexes—make up a full 32 percent of U.S. households. Today's marketers must incorporate "the likes of Murphy Brown, Ally McBeal, and Will and Grace into their business plans."

toothbrushes per capita than people in any other U.S. city; people in Salt Lake City eat more candy bars; people from New Orleans use more ketchup; and people in Miami drink more prune juice.

Also, for more than a century, Americans have been moving from rural to metropolitan areas. In the 1950s, they made a massive exit from the cities to the suburbs. Today, the migration to the suburbs continues. And more and more Americans are moving to "micropolitan areas," small cities located beyond congested metropolitan areas. These smaller micros offer many of the advantages of metro areas—jobs, restaurants, diversions, community organizations—but without the population crush, traffic jams, high crime rates, and high property taxes often associated with heavily urbanized areas.[22]

The shift in where people live has also caused a shift in where they work. For example, the migration toward micropolitan and suburban areas has resulted in a rapid increase in the number of people who "telecommute"—work at home or in a remote office and conduct their business by phone, fax, modem, or the Internet. This trend, in turn, has created a booming SOHO (small office/home office) market. One in every five Americans are now working out of their homes with the help of electronic conveniences such as personal computers, cell phones, fax machines, and handheld organizers. Many marketers are actively courting the home office segment of this lucrative SOHO market. One example is Kinko's:

> Founded in the 1970s as a campus photocopying business, Kinko's is now reinventing itself as a document solutions provider for businesses, ranging from small offices to Fortune 500 companies. For the SOHO segment, Kinko's has become a well-appointed office outside the home. Where once there were copy machines, Kinko's 1,100 stores in this country and abroad now feature a uniform mixture of fax machines, ultrafast color printers, and networks of computers equipped with popular software programs and high-speed Internet connections. People can come to a Kinko's store to do all their office jobs: They can copy, send and receive faxes, use various programs on the computer, go on the Internet, order stationery and other printed supplies, rent a conference room, and even teleconference. As more and more people join the work-at-home trend, Kinko's offers an escape from the isolation of the home office. Besides adding state-of-the-art equipment, the company is talking to Starbucks about opening up coffee shops adjacent to some Kinko's.[23]

A Better-Educated and More White-Collar Population The U.S. population is becoming better educated. For example, in 2002, 84 percent of the U.S. population over age 25 had completed high school and 27 percent had completed college, compared with 69 percent and 17 percent in 1980. Moreover, nearly two-thirds of high school graduates now enroll in college within 12 months of graduating.[24] The rising number of educated people will increase the demand for quality products, books, magazines, travel, personal computers, and Internet services.

The workforce also is becoming more white collar. Between 1950 and 1985, the proportion of white-collar workers rose from 41 percent to 54 percent, that of blue-collar workers declined from 47 percent to 33 percent, and that of service workers increased from 12 percent to 14 percent. Between 1983 and 1999, the proportion of managers and professionals in the work force increased from 23 percent to more than 30 percent. These trends have continued into the new century.[25]

Increasing Diversity Countries vary in their ethnic and racial makeup. At one extreme is Japan, where almost everyone is Japanese. At the other extreme is the United States, with people from virtually all nations. The United States has often been called a melting pot—diverse groups from many nations and cultures have melted into a single, more homogeneous whole. Instead, the United States seems to have become more of a "salad bowl," in which various groups have mixed together but have maintained their diversity by retaining and valuing important ethnic and cultural differences.

Marketers are facing increasingly diverse markets, both at home and abroad as their operations become more international in scope. The U.S. population is 71 percent white, with African Americans and Hispanics each making up another 12 percent. Asian Americans now totals about 4 percent of the U.S. population, with the remaining 1 percent made up of American Indian, Eskimo, and Aleut. These ethnic populations are expected to explode during the next 20 years. During that time, the number of African Americans will increase 25 percent, and the numbers of Hispanics and Asian Americans will double. Moreover, nearly 26 million people living in the United States—more than 9 percent of the population—were born in another country.[26]

Most large companies, from Sears, Wal-Mart, and Bank of America to Levi Strauss, Procter & Gamble, and General Mills, now target specially designed products and promotions to one or more of these groups. General Mills targets the African American market with separate campaigns for its Big G cereals—Cheerios, Trix, Honey Nut Cheerios, and Cinnamon Toast Crunch. The campaigns consist of advertising, sponsorships, sampling, and community-based promotions that feature a strong family emphasis. For example, for the past several years, Honey Nut Cheerios has been the title sponsor of the Universal Circus and for a "Soul Fest" music event that travels to 30 urban markets.

Similarly, Bank of America is quadrupling its multicultural budget this year, to $40 million. Based on customer research and careful study of cultural differences, it has developed different advertising messages for Hispanic, Asian, and African American markets.

For Asians, the brand platform is "tangibly committed to the success and growth of all Americans." One commercial shot in China, Korea, and Vietnam—

■ Based on careful study of cultural differences, Bank of America has developed targeted advertising messages for different cultural subgroups, here Asians and Hispanics.

the beginning of an immigrant's journey—flashes back to a boy teaching his younger brother to ride a bike in his homeland. It then draws parallels with the helping hand today of Bank of America with a mortgage. The bike used in the ad is the exact kind an Asian child would learn to ride, not an American kids' bicycle. In contrast, one of the Hispanic spots opens on an exaggerated stack of mortgage-related paperwork the size of a house, and details how Bank of America can reduce it by 80 percent. The ads will run in the appropriate language—Spanish, Chinese, Korean, or Vietnamese—to target consumers who prefer to communicate in their native tongue.[27]

Diversity goes beyond ethnic heritage. For example, many major companies have recently begun to target gay and lesbian consumers explicitly. A Simmons Research study of readers of the National Gay Newspaper Guild's 12 publications found that, compared to the average American, respondents are 12 times more likely to be in professional jobs, almost twice as likely to own a vacation home, 8 times more likely to own a notebook computer, and twice as likely to own individual stocks. They are twice as likely as the general population to have a household income between $60,000 and $250,000. More than two-thirds have graduated from college, and 20 percent hold a master's degree. In addition, gays and lesbians tend to be early adopters, with word-of-mouth clout in their communities, making them a very attractive market segment.

Although measuring the size and impact of the gay market can be difficult, some experts estimate that 5 to 6 percent of the U.S. population—some 14 to 15 million people—freely identify as gay. Others estimate that gays account for as much as 10 percent of the U.S. population, with buying power of $450 billion. As a result, many large companies now target their products and services directly to gay consumers. For example, ad spending to reach gay and lesbian consumers is booming. Gay.com, a Web site that attracts more than 2 million unique visitors each month, has attracted a diverse set of well-known advertisers, from IBM, eBay, Quicken Mortgage, Saturn, and AT&T to American Airlines and Neiman Marcus. Other companies that target gays directly include American Express, Ford, Miller Brewing Company, Absolut Vodka, Johnson & Johnson, and John Hancock Financial Services. Here are examples of gay and lesbian marketing efforts[28]:

American Express Financial Advisors launched print ads that depict same-sex couples planning their financial futures. The ads ran in *Out* and *The Advocate*, the two highest-circulation national gay publications. The company's director of segment marketing, Margaret Vergeyle, said: "We're targeting gay audiences with targeted ads and promotions that are relevant to them and say that we understand their specific needs. Often, gay couples are very concerned about issues like Social Security benefits and estate planning, since same-sex marriages often are not recognized under the law."

The sleek jaguar whizzes past a curve, with the advertising tag line: "Life is full of twists and turns. Care for a partner?" It's Ford's latest commercial pitch—one where the word "partner" has a double meaning. Gays and lesbians are the target market here. The Jaguar ads are noteworthy because they come from one of America's biggest corporations and are gay-specific, rather than simply a general-interest ad running in a gay publication. "We believe in messaging that connects with the consumer," says Jan Valentic, vice president of global marketing for Ford.

Avis, the rental car company, dedicated about 5 percent of its advertising and marketing budget to the gay community in 2003. Its ad campaign highlights its policy for domestic partners to automatically be included as additional drivers. "It's a loyal group and an affluent group, and one that our research shows will respond to marketing that speaks directly to their consumer needs, says an Avis spokesperson. Avis' strategy includes the sponsorship of gay pride festivals and the placement of coupons noting that for every rental, Avis will donate a dollar to the nonprofit Gay and Lesbian Alliance Against Defamation.

Miller Brewing Company recently ran an ad which featured two women trying to attract a man in a bar by buying him a Miller Lite. When a second man enters, the women grow even bubblier. Then the two men lock hands. The humor of the ad, via the disappointment of the women was "a real home run," say Howard Buford, of Prime Access, Inc., the multicultural ad agency that created the Miller and Jaguar ads. "Women enjoyed it and gay men really liked it. Straight men really enjoyed it."

Another attractive segment is the more than 54 million people with disabilities in the United States—a market larger than African Americans or Hispanics—representing almost $1 trillion in annual spending power. People with mobility challenges are an ideal target market for companies such as Peapod (www.peapod.com), which teams up with large supermarket chains in many heavily populated areas to offer online grocery shopping and home delivery. They also represent a growing market for travel, sports, and other leisure-oriented products and services. Consider the following examples[29]:

Julie Perez sees the difference when she goes to the Divi Hotels resort at Flamingo Beach on the Caribbean island of Bonaire. "It's famous for being totally accessible," she says. "The hotel brochures show the wheelchair access. The dive staff are trained and aware, and they really want to take disabled people diving. They're not afraid." Perez, 35, of Ventura, California, is an experienced scuba diver, a travel agent—and a quadriplegic. Before she had children, she made five trips a year to the Caribbean; these days, she gets there only once or twice a year.

Volkswagen targets people with disabilities who want to travel. For example, it recently launched a special marketing campaign for its EuroVan. The campaign touted the EuroVan's extra-wide doors, high ceilings, and overall roominess as features that accommodate most wheelchair lifts and make driving more fun for those traditionally ignored by mainstream automakers. To make the EuroVan even more accessible, Volkswagen offers its Mobility Access Program. Drivers with disabilities who purchase or lease any VW can take advantage of $1,500 in purchase assistance for modifications such as hand controls and wheelchair lifts. Volkswagen even modified its catchy tag line "Drivers Wanted" to appeal to motorists with disabilities, coining the new slogan "All Drivers Wanted." The VW Web site sums up, "We build cars for people who love to drive. Some just happen to use wheelchairs."

■ Volkswagon targets people with disabilities who want to travel. It offers a Mobility Access Program and has even modified its catchy "Drivers Wanted" tag line to appeal to motorists with disabilities: "All Drivers Wanted."

All drivers wanted.

We build cars for people who love to drive. Some of them happen to use wheelchairs. For these drivers, and for families who transport someone in a wheelchair, we present the Volkswagen Mobility Access Program. This is our way of lending a hand to anyone who needs to make a new Volkswagen* more accessible. If you need to add hand controls, we'll refund up to $500! If you need to add a lift, we'll refund up to $1000! After all, when we say "Drivers wanted," we mean every one of them.

As the population in the United States grows more diverse, successful marketers will continue to diversify their marketing programs to take advantage of opportunities in fast-growing segments. Says one expert, "diversity will be more than a buzzword—diversity will be the key to economic survival."[30]

Linking the Concepts

SPEED BUMP

Pull over here for a moment and think about how deep an impact these demographic factors have on all of us and, as a result, on marketers' strategies.

- Apply these demographic developments to your own life. Think of some specific examples of how the changing demographic factors affect you and your buying behavior.
- Identify a specific company that has done a good job of reacting to the shifting demographic environment—generational segments (baby boomers, GenXers, or Generation Y), the changing American family, and increased diversity. Compare this company to one that's done a poor job.

Economic Environment

Markets require buying power as well as people. The **economic environment** consists of factors that affect consumer purchasing power and spending patterns. Nations vary greatly in their levels and distribution of income. Some countries have *subsistence economies*—they consume most of their own agricultural and industrial output. These countries offer few market opportunities. At the other extreme are *industrial economies*, which constitute rich markets for many different kinds of goods. Marketers must pay close attention to major trends and consumer spending patterns both across and within their world markets. Following are some of the major economic trends in the United States.

Economic environment
Factors that affect consumer buying power and spending patterns.

Changes in Income During the 1980s—tabbed the "roaring 80s" by some—American consumers fell into a consumption frenzy, fueled by income growth, federal tax reductions, rapid increases in housing values, and a boom in borrowing. They bought and bought, seemingly without caution, amassing record levels of debt. "It was fashionable to describe yourself as 'born to shop.' When the going gets tough, it was said, the tough go shopping."[31] Entering the 1990s, the baby boom generation moved into its prime wage-earning years, and the number of small families headed by dual-career couples continued to increase. Thus, many consumers continued to demand quality products and better service, and they were able to pay for them.

However, the free spending and high expectations of the 1980s were dashed by a recession in the early 1990s. In fact, the 1990s become the decade of the "squeezed consumer." Along with rising incomes in some segments came increased financial burdens. Consumers faced repaying debts acquired during earlier spending splurges, increased household and family expenses, and saving ahead for college tuition payments and retirement. These financially squeezed consumers sobered up, pulled back, and adjusted to their changing financial situations. They spent more carefully and sought greater value in the products and services they bought. *Value marketing* became the watchword for many marketers.

Now, in the 2000s, consumers continue to spend carefully.[32] Hence, the trend toward value marketing continues. Rather than offering high quality at a high price, or lesser quality at very low prices, marketers are looking for ways to offer today's more financially cautious buyers greater value—just the right combination of product quality and good service at a fair price.

Marketers should pay attention to *income distribution* as well as to average income. Income distribution in the United States is still very skewed. At the top are *upper-class* consumers, whose spending patterns are not affected by current economic events and who are a major market for luxury goods. There is a comfortable *middle class* that is somewhat careful about its spending but can still afford the good life some of the time. The *working class* must stick close to the basics of food, clothing, and shelter and must try hard to save. Finally, the *underclass* (persons on welfare and many retirees) must count their pennies when making even the most basic purchases.

Over the past three decades, the rich have grown richer, the middle class has shrunk, and the poor have remained poor. In 1998, the top 5 percent of income-earning households in the United States captured more than 21 percent of the aggregate income, up from 17.5 percent in 1967. Last year, 12 percent of American households had an annual income of $100,000 or more, compared to just 4 percent in the early 1990s. Meanwhile, the share of income captured by the bottom 20 percent of income-earning households decreased from 4 percent to 3.6 percent.[33] This distribution of income has created a two-tiered market. Many companies are aggressively targeting the affluent:

> Driven by [growing wealth in the affluent segment,] marketers have responded with a ceaseless array of pricey, upscale products aimed at satisfying wealthy Americans' appetite for "the very best": leather-lined SUVs as big as tanks, $1,300 sheets, restaurant-quality appliances, and vast cruise ships offering every form of luxurious coddling. . . . Huge increases in wealth among the very rich have fueled the sales of $17,500 Patek Philippe watches that are sold as family heirlooms (thus justifying the price tag), created the clamor for a $48,000 Lexus (options extra), and resulted in a two-year waiting list for $14,000 Hermes Kelly bags.[34]

Other companies are now tailoring their marketing offers to two different markets—the affluent and the less affluent. For example, Walt Disney Company markets two distinct Winnie-the-Pooh bears:

> The original line-drawn figure appears on fine china, pewter spoons, and pricey kids' stationery found in upscale specialty and department stores such as

■ Income distribution: Walt Disney markets two distinct Pooh bears to match its two-tiered market.

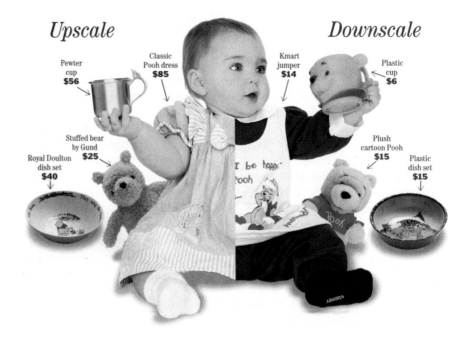

Nordstrom and Bloomingdale's. The plump, cartoonlike Pooh, clad in a red shirt and a goofy smile, adorns plastic key chains, polyester bed sheets, and animated videos. It sells in Wal-Mart stores and five-and-dime shops. Except at Disney's own stores, the two Poohs do not share the same retail shelf. [Thus, Disney offers both] upstairs [upscale?] and downstairs [downscale?] Poohs, hoping to land customers on both sides of the [income] divide.[35]

Changing Consumer Spending Patterns   Table 3.1 shows the proportion of total expenditures made by U.S. households at different income levels for major categories of goods and services. Food, housing, and transportation use up most household income. However, consumers at different income levels have different spending patterns. Some of these differences were noted over a century ago by Ernst Engel, who studied how people shifted their spending as their income rose (see Table 3.1). He found that as family income rises, the percentage spent on food declines, the percentage spent on housing remains about constant (except for utilities such as gas, electricity, and public services, which decrease), and both the percentage spent on most other categories and that devoted to savings increase. **Engel's laws** generally have been supported by later studies.

Changes in major economic variables such as income, cost of living, interest rates, and savings and borrowing patterns have a large impact on the marketplace. Companies watch these variables by using economic forecasting. Businesses do not have to be wiped out by an economic downturn or caught short in a boom. With adequate warning, they can take advantage of changes in the economic environment.

Engel's laws
Differences noted over a century ago by Ernst Engel in how people shift their spending across food, housing, transportation, health care, and other goods and services categories as family income rises.

Natural Environment

The **natural environment** involves the natural resources that are needed as inputs by marketers or that are affected by marketing activities. Environmental concerns have grown steadily during the past three decades. In many cities around the world, air and water pollution have reached dangerous levels. World concern continues to mount about the possibilities of global warming, and many environmentalists fear that we soon will be buried in our own trash.

Natural environment
Natural resources that are needed as inputs by marketers or that are affected by marketing activities.

TABLE 3.1   Consumer Spending at Different Income Levels

Expenditure	Percent of Spending at Different Income Levels			
	$10–15,000	$20–30,000	$30–40,000	$70,000 and Over
Food	16.5	15.7	14.3	11.9
Housing	26.5	24.7	23.6	26.0
Utilities	9.7	8.6	7.5	5.0
Clothing	4.2	3.7	4.6	4.6
Transportation	17.1	19.7	21.3	18.2
Health care	8.7	7.3	6.2	3.8
Entertainment	3.8	4.1	4.6	5.2
Contributions	2.9	3.1	3.0	3.6
Insurance	3.4	6.2	8.5	15.2

Source: Consumer Expenditure Survey, 2001, U.S. Department of Labor, Bureau of Labor Statistics, accessed online at www.bls.gov/cex/csxann01.pdf, April 2003.

Marketers should be aware of several trends in the natural environment. The first involves growing *shortages of raw materials*. Air and water may seem to be infinite resources, but some groups see long-run dangers. Air pollution chokes many of the world's large cities, and water shortages are already a big problem in some parts of the United States and the world. Renewable resources, such as forests and food, also have to be used wisely. Nonrenewable resources, such as oil, coal, and various minerals, pose a serious problem. Firms making products that require these scarce resources face large cost increases, even if the materials do remain available.

A second environmental trend is *increased pollution*. Industry will almost always damage the quality of the natural environment. Consider the disposal of chemical and nuclear wastes; the dangerous mercury levels in the ocean; the quantity of chemical pollutants in the soil and food supply; and the littering of the environment with nonbiodegradable bottles, plastics, and other packaging materials.

A third trend is *increased government intervention* in natural resource management. The governments of different countries vary in their concern and efforts to promote a clean environment. Some, like the German government, vigorously pursue environmental quality. Others, especially many poorer nations, do little about pollution, largely because they lack the needed funds or political will. Even the richer nations lack the vast funds and political accord needed to mount a worldwide environmental effort. The general hope is that companies around the world will accept more social responsibility, and that less expensive devices can be found to control and reduce pollution.

In the United States, the Environmental Protection Agency (EPA) was created in 1970 to set and enforce pollution standards and to conduct pollution research. In the future, companies doing business in the United States can expect continued strong controls from government and pressure groups. Instead of opposing regulation, marketers should help develop solutions to the material and energy problems facing the world.

Concern for the natural environment has spawned the so-called green movement. Today, enlightened companies go beyond what government regulations dictate. They are developing *environmentally sustainable* strategies and practices in an effort to create a world economy that the planet can support indefinitely. They are responding to consumer demands with ecologically safer products, recyclable or biodegradable packaging, recycled materials and components, better pollution controls, and more energy-efficient operations.

■ Environmental responsibility: McDonald's has made a substantial commitment to the so-called "green movement."

3M runs a Pollution Prevention Pays program that helps prevent pollution at the source—in products and manufacturing processes. Between 1975 and 2001, the program prevented 821,344 tons of pollutants and saved $857 million. AT&T uses a special software package to choose the least harmful materials, cut hazardous waste, reduce energy use, and improve product recycling in its operations. McDonald's eliminated polystyrene cartons years ago and now uses paper-based packaging and napkins that contain recycled content. Beyond this, the company has a long-standing rainforest policy and a commitment to purchasing recycled products and energy-efficient restaurant construction techniques. UPS's fleet now includes 1,800 energy-efficient, low-polluting alternative-fuel vehicles. And Starbucks is buying more organic and shade-grown coffee, a move that minimizes damage to rain forests. More and more, companies are recognizing the link between a healthy economy and a healthy ecology.[36]

Technological Environment

The **technological environment** is perhaps the most dramatic force now shaping our destiny. Technology has released such wonders as antibiotics, organ transplants, notebook computers, and the Internet. It also has released such horrors as nuclear missiles, chemical weapons, and assault rifles. It has released such mixed blessings as the automobile, television, and credit cards. Our attitude toward technology depends on whether we are more impressed with its wonders or its blunders. For example, what would you think about having tiny little transmitters implanted in all of the products you buy that would allow tracking products from their point of production though use and disposal? On the one hand, it would provide many advantages. On the other hand, it could be a bit scary. Either way, it probably won't be long before it happens (see Marketing at Work 3.2).

Technological environment
Forces that create new technologies, creating new product and market opportunities.

The technological environment changes rapidly. Think of all of today's common products that were not available 100 years ago or even 30 years ago. Abraham Lincoln did not know about automobiles, airplanes, radios, or the electric light. Woodrow Wilson did not know about television, aerosol cans, automatic dishwashers, air conditioners, antibiotics, or computers. Franklin Delano Roosevelt did not know about xerography, synthetic detergents, tape recorders, birth control pills, or earth satellites. John F. Kennedy did not know about personal computers, DVD players, or the World Wide Web.

New technologies create new markets and opportunities. However, every new technology replaces an older technology. Transistors hurt the vacuum-tube industry, xerography hurt the carbon-paper business, the auto hurt the railroads, and compact disks hurt phonograph records. When old industries fought or ignored

■ Technological environment: Technology is perhaps the most dramatic force shaping the marketing environment. Here, a herder makes a call on his cell phone.

new technologies, their businesses declined. Thus, marketers should watch the technological environment closely. Companies that do not keep up with technological change soon will find their products outdated. And they will miss new product and market opportunities.

The United States leads the world in research and development spending. Total U.S. R&D spending reached an estimated $302 billion in 2003. The federal government was the largest R&D spender, at $108 billion.[37] Scientists today are researching a wide range of promising new products and services, ranging from practical solar energy, electric cars, and cancer cures to voice-controlled computers and genetically engineered food crops. Today's research usually is carried out by research teams rather than by lone inventors such as Thomas Edison, Samuel Morse, or Alexander Graham Bell. Many companies are adding marketing people to R&D teams to try to obtain a stronger marketing orientation. Scientists also speculate about fantasy products, such as flying cars, three-dimensional televisions, and space colonies. The challenge in each case is not only technical but also commercial—to make *practical*, *affordable* versions of these products.

As products and technology become more complex, the public needs to know that these are safe. Thus, government agencies investigate and ban potentially unsafe products. In the United States, the Food and Drug Administration (FDA) has set up complex regulations for testing new drugs. The Consumer Product Safety Commission sets safety standards for consumer products and penalizes companies that fail to meet them. Such regulations have resulted in much higher research costs and in longer times between new-product ideas and their introduction. Marketers should be aware of these regulations when applying new technologies and developing new products.

Marketing at Work | 3.2

Tiny Transmitters in Every Product: Is This Great Technology, or What?

Envision a world in which every product contains a tiny transmitter, loaded with information. Imagine a time when we could track every item electronically—anywhere in the world, at any time, automatically. Producers could track the precise flow of goods up and down the supply chain, ensuring timely deliveries and lowering inventory and distribution costs. Retailers could track real-time merchandise movements in their stores, helping them manage inventories, keep shelves full, and automatically reorder goods.

And think about the whole new world that such technology would create for consumers. Picture this futuristic scenario:

As you stroll through the aisles of your supermarket, you pluck a six-pack of your favorite beverage from the shelf. Shelf sensors detect your selection and beam an ad to the screen on your shopping cart. The ad offers special deals on salty snacks that might go great with your beverage. When you reach the shampoo section, electronic readers scan your cart and note that you haven't made the usual monthly purchase of your favorite brand. "Did you forget the shampoo?" asks the screen. As your shopping cart fills, scanners detect that you might be buying for a dinner party. The screen suggests a wine that complements the meal you've planned. After shopping, you bag your groceries and

head for home. Exit scanners automatically total up your purchases and charge them to your credit card. At home, readers track what goes into and out of your pantry, automatically updating your shopping list when stocks run low. To plan your Sunday dinner, you scan the Butterball turkey you just purchased. An embedded transmitter chip yields serving instructions and recipes for several side dishes. You pop the bird into your "smart oven," which follows instructions coded on the chip and cooks the Turkey to perfection. Is this great technology, or what?

Seem far-fetched? Not according to the Auto-ID Center. Founded in 1999,

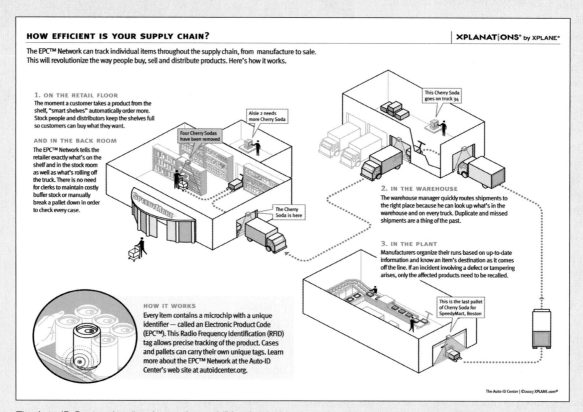

HOW EFFICIENT IS YOUR SUPPLY CHAIN?   **XPLANATiONS® by XPLANE®**

The EPC™ Network can track individual items throughout the supply chain, from manufacture to sale. This will revolutionize the way people buy, sell and distribute products. Here's how it works.

1. ON THE RETAIL FLOOR
The moment a customer takes a product from the shelf, "smart shelves" automatically order more. Stock people and distributors keep the shelves full so customers can buy what they want.

AND IN THE BACK ROOM
The EPC™ Network tells the retailer exactly what's on the shelf and in the stock room as well as what's rolling off the truck. There is no need for clerks to maintain costly buffer stock or manually break a pallet down in order to check every case.

Aisle 2 needs more Cherry Soda

Four Cherry Sodas have been removed

The Cherry Soda is here

This Cherry Soda goes on truck 34

2. IN THE WAREHOUSE
The warehouse manager quickly routes shipments to the right place because he can look up what's in the warehouse and on every truck. Duplicate and missed shipments are a thing of the past.

3. IN THE PLANT
Manufacturers organize their runs based on up-to-date information and know an item's destination as it comes off the line. If an incident involving a defect or tampering arises, only the affected products need to be recalled.

This is the last pallet of Cherry Soda for SpeedyMart, Boston

HOW IT WORKS
Every item contains a microchip with a unique identifier — called an Electronic Product Code (EPC™). This Radio Frequency Identification (RFID) tag allows precise tracking of the product. Cases and pallets can carry their own unique tags. Learn more about the EPC™ Network at the Auto-ID Center's web site at autoidcenter.org.

The Auto-ID Center | ©2003 XPLANE.com®

The Auto-ID Center aims "to change the world" by developing tiny transmitters that can be imbedded in products, benefiting both sellers and consumers.

the Center formed a unique partnership among almost 100 global companies and five of the world's leading research universities. The Auto-ID Center's aim was "to change the world . . . to give companies something that, until now, they have only dreamed of: near-perfect supply chain visibility." This seems like a lofty mission. But it might soon become a reality with the backing of such marketing heavyweights as Wal-Mart, Home Depot, Target, Best Buy, Procter & Gamble, Coca-Cola, IBM, Gillette, Michelin, and the U.S. Post Office.

The Auto-ID Center developed tiny, affordable radio-frequency identification (RFID) transmitters—or smart chips—that can be embedded in all of the products you buy. The transmitters are so small that several would fit on the head of a pin. Yet they can be packed with coded information and can be read and rewritten at any point in the supply chain. Auto-ID technology provides producers and retailers with amazing new ways to track inventories, trends, and sales. They can use embedded chips to follow products—everything from ice cream and cat food to tires, insulation, and jet engines—step by step from factories, to warehouses, to retail shelves, to recycling centers.

The smart chips make today's bar code systems seem badly outmoded. Whereas bar codes must be visible to be read, embedded RFID chips can be read in any location. Bar codes identify only a product's manufacturer. In contrast, the chips can identify each individual product item and can carry codes that, when paired with a database containing the details, reveal an almost endless supply of information. Thus, beyond identifying an item as a gallon of Borden 2% skim milk, an embedded smart chip can identify that *specific* gallon of milk—its manufacture date, expiration date, location in the supply chain, and a storehouse of other product-specific information.

Although it may seem futuristic, Auto-ID technology is already being tested at several sites across the United States and the United Kingdom. Recently, Gillette ordered a half-billion chips and launched two RFID pilot projects. The first project uses embedded transmitters to track products from the factory to grocery store shelves. Gillette hopes that the technology will improve service to its retail customers while at the same time reducing its inventories from 5 percent to 25 percent. In the second project, Gillette has installed readers on shelves in selected Wal-Mart and Tesco stores. It claims that retailers lose more than $30 billion a year in sales because shelves aren't fully stocked. The shelf readers track Gillette's razors as they come and go, and prompt store staff to restock when quantities dwindle. "We'll have a world where shelves are always full," says Gillette's vice president for global business management. The readers also alert staff when unusually large quantities of razors leave a shelf in a short time, helping to reduce theft.

Michelin is also testing the chips, in this case to help it comply with federal regulations that govern tracing products in the event of a recall. The tire maker plans to embed the chips in tires installed on passenger cars and light trucks for the 2005 model year. At the factory, it will include information such as time and date of manufacture, tire size and dimensions, plant location, and vehicle identification numbers.

In addition to mega-marketers like Gillette, Michelin, and Wal-Mart, smaller retailers are putting smart chips to work. Fashion retailer Prada recently installed the chips in its store in New York City. Based on scans of items in customers hands, video screens show personalized product demonstrations and designer sketches. In dressing rooms, readers identify each item of clothing a customer tries on and offers additional size, color, and design information through interactive touch screens.

With innovations like these, you'd think most consumers would welcome the tiny transmitters. But some consumers and many consumer advocates worry about invasion-of-privacy issues. If companies can link products to specific consumers and track consumer buying and usage, they fear, marketers would gain access to too much personal information. Says one analyst, "backers of the technology appear torn between the urge to hype its huge potential and fear that consumers will get spooked."

To counter these concerns, Auto-ID technology proponents point out that the transmitters have limited range, most under 20 feet. So reading chips inside consumers' homes or tracking them on the move would be nearly impossible. The Auto-ID industry is also working to address consumer privacy concerns. Among other things, it is drafting a privacy policy that includes giving customers the option of permanently disabling the chips at checkout. And according to an Auto-ID consultant, the basic mission is not to spy on consumers. It's to serve them better. "It's not Orwellian. That is absolutely, positively not the vision of Auto-ID," she says. "The vision is for . . . brand manufacturers and retailers to be able to have right-time, right-promotion, real-time eye-to-eye [contact] with the consumer."

Last year the Auto-ID Center transferred responsibility for the administration and development of its technology to EPC Global, ushering in a new phase of RFID research and application. In coming years, as smart chips appear on more and more products, Auto-ID technology will no doubt bring significant benefits to both marketers and the customers they serve. "The idea of someone using tiny radio transmitters to influence consumer purchase behavior was once only the stuff of paranoid delusions," says the analyst. "But in the not-so-distant future, it could become the basis of a new generation of marketing."

Sources: Jack Neff, "A Chip over Your Shoulder?" *Advertising Age,* April 22, 2002, p. 4; Kimberly Hill, "Prada Uses Smart Tags to Personalize Shopping," April 24, 2002, accessed online at www.crmdaily.com; "Business: The Best Thing Since the Bar-Code: The IT Revolution," *The Economist,* February 8, 2003, pp. 57–58; "Gillette, Michelin Begin RFID Pilots," *Frontline Solutions,* March 2003, p. 8; "RFID Benefits Apparent," *Chain Store Age,* March 2003, p. 63; Faith Keenan, "If Supermarket Shelves Could Talk," *Business Week,* March 31, 2003, pp. 66–67; and information accessed online at www.autoidcenter.org, July 2003, and information accessed online at www.autoidlabs.org, November 2003.

Political Environment

Political environment
Laws, government agencies, and pressure groups that influence and limit various organizations and individuals in a given society.

Marketing decisions are strongly affected by developments in the political environment. The **political environment** consists of laws, government agencies, and pressure groups that influence or limit various organizations and individuals in a given society.

Legislation Regulating Business Even the most liberal advocates of free-market economies agree that the system works best with at least some regulation. Well-conceived regulation can encourage competition and ensure fair markets for goods and services. Thus, governments develop *public policy* to guide commerce—sets of laws and regulations that limit business for the good of society as a whole. Almost every marketing activity is subject to a wide range of laws and regulations.

Increasing Legislation. Legislation affecting business around the world has increased steadily over the years. The United States has many laws covering issues such as competition, fair trade practices, environmental protection, product safety, truth in advertising, consumer privacy, packaging and labeling, pricing, and other important areas (see Table 3.2). The European Commission has been active in establishing a new framework of laws covering competitive behavior, product standards, product liability, and commercial transactions for the nations of the European Union.

Several countries have gone further than the United States in passing strong consumerism legislation. For example, Norway bans several forms of sales promotion—trading stamps, contests, premiums—as being inappropriate or unfair ways of promoting products. Thailand requires food processors selling national brands to market low-price brands also, so that low-income consumers can find economy brands on the shelves. In India, food companies must obtain special approval to launch brands that duplicate those already existing on the market, such as additional cola drinks or new brands of rice.

Understanding the public policy implications of a particular marketing activity is not a simple matter. For example, in the United States, there are many laws created at the national, state, and local levels, and these regulations often overlap. Aspirins sold in Dallas are governed both by federal labeling laws and by Texas state advertising laws. Moreover, regulations are constantly changing—what was allowed last year may now be prohibited, and what was prohibited may now be allowed. Marketers must work hard to keep up with changes in regulations and their interpretations.

Business legislation has been enacted for a number of reasons. The first is to *protect companies* from each other. Although business executives may praise competition, they sometimes try to neutralize it when it threatens them. So laws are passed to define and prevent unfair competition. In the United States, such laws are enforced by the Federal Trade Commission and the Antitrust Division of the Attorney General's office.

The second purpose of government regulation is to *protect consumers* from unfair business practices. Some firms, if left alone, would make shoddy products, tell lies in their advertising, and deceive consumers through their packaging and pricing. Unfair business practices have been defined and are enforced by various agencies.

The third purpose of government regulation is to *protect the interests of society* against unrestrained business behavior. Profitable business activity does not always create a better quality of life. Regulation arises to ensure that firms take responsibility for the societal costs of their production or products.

Changing Government Agency Enforcement. International marketers will encounter dozens, or even hundreds, of agencies set up to enforce trade policies and regulations. In the United States, Congress has established federal regulatory agencies such as the Federal Trade Commission, the Food and Drug Administration, the Federal Communications Commission, the Federal Energy Regulatory Commission, the Civil Aeronautics Board, the Consumer Product Safety Commission, and the Environmental Protection Agency. Because such government agencies have some discretion in enforcing the laws, they can have a major impact on a company's marketing performance. At times, the staffs of these

TABLE 3.2   Major U.S. Legislation Affecting Marketing

Legislation	Purpose
Sherman Antitrust Act (1890)	Prohibits monopolies and activities (price fixing, predatory pricing) that restrain trade or competition in interstate commerce.
Federal Food and Drug Act (1906)	Forbids the manufacture or sale of adulterated or fraudulently labeled foods and drugs. Created the Food and Drug Administration.
Clayton Act (1914)	Supplements the Sherman Act by prohibiting certain types of price discrimination, exclusive dealing, and tying clauses (which require a dealer to take additional products in a seller's line).
Federal Trade Commission Act (1914)	Establishes a commission to monitor and remedy unfair trade methods.
Robinson–Patman Act (1936)	Amends Clayton Act to define price discrimination as unlawful. Empowers FTC to establish limits on quantity discounts, forbid some brokerage allowances, and prohibit promotional allowances except when made available on proportionately equal terms.
Wheeler–Lea Act (1938)	Makes deceptive, misleading, and unfair practices illegal regardless of injury to competition. Places advertising of food and drugs under FTC jurisdiction.
Lanham Trademark Act (1946)	Protects and regulates distinctive brand names and trademarks.
National Traffic and Safety Act (1958)	Provides for the creation of compulsory safety standards for automobiles and tires.
Fair Packaging and Labeling Act (1966)	Provides for the regulation of packaging and labeling of consumer goods. Requires that manufacturers state what the package contains, who made it, and how much it contains.
Child Protection Act (1966)	Bans sale of hazardous toys and articles. Sets standards for child-resistant packaging.
Federal Cigarette Labeling and Advertising Act (1967)	Requires that cigarette packages contain the following statement: "Warning: The Surgeon General Has Determined That Cigarette Smoking Is Dangerous to Your Health."
National Environmental Policy Act (1969)	Establishes a national policy on the environment. The 1970 Reorganization Plan established the Environmental Protection Agency.
Consumer Product Safety Act (1972)	Establishes the Consumer Product Safety Commission and authorizes it to set safety standards for consumer products as well as exact penalties for failure to uphold those standards.
Magnuson–Moss Warranty Act (1975)	Authorizes the FTC to determine rules and regulations for consumer warranties and provides consumer access to redress, such as the class-action suit.
Children's Television Act (1990)	Limits number of commercials aired during children's programs.
Nutrition Labeling and Education Act (1990)	Requires that food product labels provide detailed nutritional information.
Telephone Consumer Protection Act (1991)	Establishes procedures to avoid unwanted telephone solicitations. Limits marketers' use of automatic telephone dialing systems and artificial or prerecorded voices.
Americans with Disabilities Act (1991)	Makes discrimination against people with disabilities illegal in public accommodations, transportation, and telecommunications.
Children's Online Privacy Protection Act (2000)	Prohibits Web sites or online services operators from collecting personal information from children without obtaining consent from a parent and allowing parents to review information collected from their children.

agencies have appeared to be overly eager and unpredictable. Some of the agencies sometimes have been dominated by lawyers and economists who lacked a practical sense of how business and marketing work. In recent years, the Federal Trade Commission has added staff marketing experts, who can better understand complex business issues.

New laws and their enforcement will continue to increase. Business executives must watch these developments when planning their products and marketing programs. Marketers need to know about the major laws protecting competition, consumers, and society. They need to understand these laws at the local, state, national, and international levels.

Increased Emphasis on Ethics and Socially Responsible Actions

Written regulations cannot possibly cover all potential marketing abuses, and existing laws are often difficult to enforce. However, beyond written laws and regulations, business is also governed by social codes and rules of professional ethics.

Socially Responsible Behavior. Enlightened companies encourage their managers to look beyond what the regulatory system allows and simply "do the right thing." These socially responsible firms actively seek out ways to protect the long-run interests of their consumers and the environment.

The recent rash of business scandals and increased concerns about the environment have created fresh interest in the issues of ethics and social responsibility. Almost every aspect of marketing involves such issues. Unfortunately, because these issues usually involve conflicting interests, well-meaning people can honestly disagree about the right course of action in a given situation. Thus, many industrial and professional trade associations have suggested codes of ethics. And more companies are now developing policies, guidelines, and other responses to complex social responsibility issues. For example, 45 percent of Fortune 250 companies issued environmental, social, or sustainability reports in 2001, up from 35 percent in 1998.[38]

The boom in e-commerce and Internet marketing has created a new set of social and ethical issues. Online privacy issues are the primary concern. For example, Web site visitors often provide extensive personal information that might leave them open to abuse by unscrupulous marketers. Moreover, both Intel and Microsoft have been accused of covert, high-tech computer chip and software invasions of customers' personal computers to obtain information for marketing purposes.[39]

Throughout this book, we present Marketing at Work exhibits that summarize the main public policy and social responsibility issues surrounding major marketing decisions. These exhibits discuss the legal issues that marketers should understand and the common ethical and societal concerns that marketers face. In Chapter 16, we discuss a broad range of societal marketing issues in greater depth.

Cause-Related Marketing. To exercise their social responsibility and build more positive images, many companies are now linking themselves to worthwhile causes. These days, every product seems to be tied to some cause. Buy Purina cat food and help the American Association of Zoological Parks and Aquariums save endangered big cat species. Drink Tang and earn money for Mothers Against Drunk Driving. Drive a Dollar rental car and help support the Special Olympics. Buy from EddieBauer.com and have a percentage of your purchase go to support your local grade school. Buy a pink mixer from Kitchenaid and support breast cancer research. Or if you want to help the Leukemia Society of America, buy Helping Hand trash bags or toilet paper. Pay for these purchases with the right charge card and you can support a local cultural arts group or help fight cancer or heart disease.

Cause-related marketing has become a primary form of corporate giving. It lets companies "do well by doing good" by linking purchases of the company's products or services with fund-raising for worthwhile causes or charitable organizations. Companies now sponsor dozens of cause-related marketing campaigns each year. Many are backed by large budgets and a full complement of marketing activities. Consider these examples:

■ Cause-related marketing: KitchenAid donates $50 to breast cancer research for every pink mixer it sells and encourages consumers to host a "Cook for the Cure" dinner party.

In 1987, Johnson & Johnson teamed with the Children's National Medical Center and the National Safety Council to sponsor the National SAFE KIDS Campaign. Designed to reduce preventable children's injuries, the leading killer of children, the campaign offered consumers a free SAFE KIDS safety kit for children in exchange for proofs of purchase. Consumers could also buy a Child's Safety Video for $9.95. To promote the campaign, Johnson & Johnson distributed almost 50 million advertising inserts in daily newspapers. It also developed a special information kit for retailers containing posters, floor displays, and other in-store promotion materials. Started as a program of the Children's National Medical Center, the National SAFE KIDS Campaign has now grown into an independent organization, SAFE KIDS, made up of 300 state and local coalitions across America. Each May the organization teams with Johnson & Johnson to present National SAFE KIDS Week. J&J continues to support the organization with millions of dollars in annual grants, public awareness campaigns, corporate advertising, and retail promotions.

In 1996, General Mills launched its Box Tops for Education program. The program offers schools nationwide a chance to earn cash to pay for everything from field trips, to computers, to playground equipment. Box Tops for Education has really caught on. Today, more than 60 percent of the nation's elementary schools are enrolled. To participate, students and parents clip box tops and labels from any of more than 330 eligible products, including brands like Yoplait, Big G, Lloyd's, and Betty Crocker. General Mills then pays the school 10 cents for every box top redeemed. To date, the company has given nearly $70 million to local public, private, and parochial schools. Based on that success, General Mills has now teamed up with Visa to offer a Box Tops for Education credit card. Visa donates 1 percent of every purchase made to the cardholder's designated school. In addition, consumers who link to Web sites such as Amazon.com and EddieBauer.com from the Box Tops for Education Web site are guaranteed a donation to their schools amounting up to 10 percent of every purchase.

Cause-related marketing has stirred some controversy. Critics worry that cause-related marketing is more a strategy for selling than a strategy for giving—that "cause-related" marketing is really "cause-exploitative" marketing. Thus, companies using cause-related marketing might find themselves walking a fine line between increased sales and an improved image, and facing charges of exploitation.

However, if handled well, cause-related marketing can greatly benefit both the company and the cause. The company gains an effective marketing tool while building a more positive public image. The charitable organization or cause gains greater visibility and important new sources of funding. Cause-related marketing programs generate more than $700 million from U.S. corporations each year for various causes.[40] Thus, when cause marketing works, everyone wins.

Cultural Environment

The **cultural environment** is made up of institutions and other forces that affect a society's basic values, perceptions, preferences, and behaviors. People grow up in a particular society that shapes their basic beliefs and values. They absorb a world view that defines their relationships with others. The following cultural characteristics can affect marketing decision making.

Cultural environment
Institutions and other forces that affect society's basic values, perceptions, preferences, and behaviors.

Persistence of Cultural Values People in a given society hold many beliefs and values. Their core beliefs and values have a high degree of persistence. For example, most Americans believe in working, getting married, giving to charity, and being honest. These beliefs shape more specific attitudes and behaviors found in everyday life. *Core* beliefs and values are passed on from parents to children and are reinforced by schools, churches, businesses, and government.

Secondary beliefs and values are more open to change. Believing in marriage is a core belief; believing that people should get married early in life is a secondary belief. Marketers have some chance of changing secondary values but little chance of changing core values. For example, family-planning marketers could argue more effectively that people should get married later than that they should not get married at all.

Shifts in Secondary Cultural Values   Although core values are fairly persistent, cultural swings do take place. Consider the impact of popular music groups, movie person-alities, and other celebrities on young people's hairstyling, clothing, and sexual norms. Marketers want to predict cultural shifts in order to spot new opportunities or threats. Several firms offer "futures" forecasts in this connection, such as the Yankelovich Monitor, Market Facts' BrainWaves Group, and the Trends Research Institute.

The Yankelovich Monitor has tracked consumer value trends for years. At the dawn of the twenty-first century, it looked back to capture lessons from the past decade that might offer insight into the 2000s. It identified the following eight major consumer themes[41]:

1. **Paradox:**   People agree that "life is getting better and worse at the same time."
2. **Trust not:**   Confidence in doctors, public schools, TV news, newspapers, federal gov-ernment, and corporations drops sharply.
3. **Go it alone:**   More people agree with the statement "I rely more on my own instincts than on experts."
4. **Smarts really count:**   For example, fewer people agree with "It's risky to buy a brand you are not familiar with."
5. **No sacrifices:**   For example, many people claim that looks are important but not at any price, that keeping house for show instead of comfort is over, and that giving up taste for nutrition is no longer acceptable.
6. **Stress hard to beat:**   For example, more people claim that they are "concerned about getting enough rest."
7. **Reciprocity is the way to go:**   More people agree that "Everybody should feel free to do his or her own thing."
8. **Me 2:**   For example, people express the need to live in a world that is built by "me," not by you.

Yankelovich maintains that the decade drivers for the 2000s will primarily come from the baby boomers and Generation Xers. The baby boomers will be driven by four factors in the 2000s: "adventure" (fueled by a sense of youthfulness), "smarts" (fueled by a sense of empowerment and willingness to accept change), "intergenerational support" (caring for younger and older people, often in nontraditional arrangements), and "retreading" (embracing early retirement with second career or phase of their work life). GenXers will be driven by three factors: "redefining the good life" (being highly motivated to improve their economic well-being and remain in control), "new rituals" (returning to traditional values but with a tolerant mind-set and active lifestyle), and "cutting and pasting" (bal-ancing work, play, sleep, family, and other aspects of their lives).

The major cultural values of a society are expressed in people's views of themselves and others, as well as in their views of organizations, society, nature, and the universe.

People's Views of Themselves.   People vary in their emphasis on serving themselves versus serving others. Some people seek personal pleasure, wanting fun, change, and escape. Others seek self-realization through religion, recreation, or the avid pursuit of careers or other life goals. People use products, brands, and services as a means of self-expression, and they buy products and services that match their views of themselves.

In the 1980s, personal ambition and materialism increased dramatically, with signifi-cant marketing implications. In a "me society," people buy their "dream cars" and take their "dream vacations." They tended to spend to the limit on self-indulgent goods and ser-vices. Today, in contrast, people are adopting more conservative behaviors and ambitions. As we move into the new millennium, materialism, flashy spending, and self-indulgence have been replaced by more sensible spending, saving, family concerns, and helping others. The maturing baby boomers are limiting their spending to products and services that improve their lives instead of boosting their images. This suggests a bright future for products and services that serve basic needs and provide real value rather than those relying on glitz and hype.

People's Views of Others. Recently, observers have noted a shift from a "me society" to a "we society," in which more people want to be with and serve others.[42]

> After years of serious "nesting"—staying close to the security and creature comforts of home and hearth—Americans are finally starting to tiptoe out of their homes to hang out in the real world. The nesting instinct has gone in and out of fashion before. When the first big wave hit in the early '80s, trend watchers coined the term "cocooning" to describe the surge of boomers buying their first homes and filling them up with oversized furniture and fancy gadgets. The dot-com boom set off another round, partly fueled by cool home gizmos like plasma TVs and PlayStations. Though many expected 9/11 to send people even deeper into nesting mode, sociologists say it actually got people out looking for companionship. After being hunkered down through terror alerts and the war in Iraq, many people were naturally itching to get out. "You can only cocoon with your family for so long," says one sociologist. "Even if they don't drive you nuts, they bore you."

Marketers are beginning to notice the shift. In Las Vegas, the Saks Fifth Avenue store is trying to ease folks back out of the house with a simulated living room, complete with sofas where shoppers can sit and mingle, or munch from bowls of candy and watch a giant TV. The Applebee's restaurant chain has dropped ads that focus on food in favor of feel-good spots with a community theme. The latest: a "Neighborhood Hero" contest in which diners nominate a local figure to be honored. And as people move away from the confines of their snug dens and out into the fresh air and sunshine, nesting icon Home Depot is expanding its gardening business, testing out landscape-supply stores.

More and more, people are wanting to get out of the house and be with others. This trend suggests a greater demand for "social support" products and services that improve direct communication between people, such as health clubs and family vacations.

People's Views of Organizations. People vary in their attitudes toward corporations, government agencies, trade unions, universities, and other organizations. By and large, people are willing to work for major organizations and expect them, in turn, to carry out society's work. The late 1980s saw a sharp decrease in confidence in and loyalty toward America's business and political organizations and institutions. In the workplace, there has been an overall decline in organizational loyalty. During the 1990s, waves of company downsizings bred cynicism and distrust. Recent corporate scandals at Enron, WorldCom, Tyco International, and other large companies resulted in a further loss of confidence in big business. Many people today see work not as a source of satisfaction but as a required chore to earn money to enjoy their nonwork hours. This trend suggests that organizations need to find new ways to win consumer and employee confidence.

People's Views of Society. People vary in their attitudes toward their society; patriots defend it, reformers want to change it, malcontents want to leave it. People's orientation to their society influences their consumption patterns and attitudes toward the marketplace. American patriotism has been increasing gradually for the past two decades. It surged, however, following the September 11 terrorist attacks and the Iraq war. For example, before the 9/11 attacks, Americans spent some $200 million a year on flags of all sizes and shapes. But in 2001, American flag sales quadrupled. Within the two weeks following the September 11 attacks, K-Mart alone sold more than 662,000 handheld flags nationwide. The summer following the Iraq war saw a surge of pumped-up

■ American patriotism has been increasing gradually for the past two decades but surged following the September 11 terrorist attacks. Marketers such as Mars, Inc. (the maker of M&Ms) responded with patriotic products and promotions.

Americans visiting U.S. historic sites, ranging from the Washington, D.C., monuments, Mount Rushmore, the Gettysburg battlefield, and the USS Constitution ("Old Ironsides") to Pearl Harbor and the Alamo.[43]

Marketers have responded with patriotic products and promotions, offering everything from floral bouquets to clothing with patriotic themes. For example, following the September 11 attacks, Mars introduced a new limited-edition patriotic package for its M&M brand, featuring red, white, and blue candy pieces. It donated 100 percent of the profits from the sale of those special packages to the American Red Cross. For Christmas, Hallmark offered a card showing a snowman bearing the American flag and reading "God Bless America!" Wal-Mart sold "Little Patriots Diapers" with tiny blue stars. The Heartland Brewery in Times Square even came out with a new beer, DetermiNation Ale. And a heart-rending Budweiser Super Bowl ad featured the venerable Budweiser Clydesdales bowing to honor the forever changed Manhattan skyline.[44]

Although most of these marketing efforts were tasteful and well received, waving the red, white, and blue proved tricky for some marketers. Following September 11, consumers quickly became wary of patriotic products and ads. Except in cases in which companies tied product sales to charitable contributions, "patriotism as a marketing program was largely unwelcome," says one analyst. They were often "seen by consumers as attempts to cash in on the tragedy." Another expert advises that marketers must take care when responding to such national emotions. Whatever their intentions, they must "be careful not to come across as saying 'Wasn't it awful, now go spend money on our product.'"[45]

It's not just for health nuts.
Regular nuts like it, too.

All natural, lactose free, high in protein, with a surprisingly good taste. Don't be so stubb...

■ Marketers are responding to changes in people's view of the natural environment by offering more natural and organic products. White Wave's Silk soymilk has found success in the $25 billion industry.

People's Views of Nature. People vary in their attitudes toward the natural world. Some feel ruled by it, others feel in harmony with it, and still others seek to master it. A long-term trend has been people's growing mastery over nature through technology and the belief that nature is bountiful. More recently, however, people have recognized that nature is finite and fragile, that it can be destroyed or spoiled by human activities.

Love of nature is leading to more camping, hiking, fishing, bird-watching, and other outdoor activities. Business has responded by offering more products and services catering to these interests. Tour operators are offering more wilderness adventures, and retailers are offering more fitness gear and apparel. Marketing communicators are using appealing natural backgrounds in advertising their products. And food producers have found growing markets for natural and organic foods. Natural and organic products are now a $25 billion industry, growing at a rate of 20 percent annually. Niche marketers, such as Whole Foods Markets, have sprung up to serve this market, and traditional food chains such as Kroger and Safeway have added separate natural and organic food sections. Sales of White Wave's Silk soymilk, for example, have jumped from $10 million to $200 million in just two years. Even McDonald's has joined the movement, recently replacing its milk offering with cartons of organic milk.[46]

People's Views of the Universe. Finally, people vary in their beliefs about the origin of the universe and their place in it. Although most Americans practice religion, religious conviction and practice have been dropping off gradually through the years. Some futurists, however, have noted a renewed interest in spirituality, perhaps as a part of a broader search for a new inner purpose. People have been moving away from materialism and dog-eat-dog ambition to seek more permanent values—family, community, earth, faith— and a more certain grasp of right and wrong.

"Americans are on a spiritual journey," observes one expert, "increasingly concerned with the meaning of life and issues of the soul and spirit. The journey can encompass religion, but it is much more likely to take the form of . . . 'spiritual individualism'." This new spiritualism affects consumers in everything from the television shows they watch and the books they read to the products and services they buy. "Since consumers don't park their beliefs and values on the bench outside the marketplace," adds the expert, "they are bringing this awareness to the brands they buy. Tapping into this heightened sensitivity presents a unique marketing opportunity for brands."[47]

Linking the Concepts

SPEED BUMP

Slow down and cool your engine. You've now read about a large number of environmental forces. How are all of these environments *linked* with each other? With company marketing strategy?

- How are major demographic forces linked with economic changes? With major cultural trends? How are the natural and technological environments linked? Think of an example of a company that has recognized one of these links and turned it into a marketing opportunity.
- Is the marketing environment uncontrollable—something that the company can only prepare for and react to? Or can companies be proactive in changing environmental factors? Think of a good example that makes your point, then read on.

Responding to the Marketing Environment

Someone once observed, "There are three kinds of companies: those who make things happen, those who watch things happen, and those who wonder what's happened."[48] Many companies view the marketing environment as an uncontrollable element to which they must adapt. They passively accept the marketing environment and do not try to change it. They analyze the environmental forces and design strategies that will help the company avoid the threats and take advantage of the opportunities the environment provides.

Other companies take an **environmental management perspective.**[49] Rather than simply watching and reacting, these firms take aggressive actions to affect the publics and forces in their marketing environment. Such companies hire lobbyists to influence legislation affecting their industries and stage media events to gain favorable press coverage. They run advertorials (ads expressing editorial points of view) to shape public opinion. They press lawsuits and file complaints with regulators to keep competitors in line, and they form contractual agreements to better control their distribution channels.

Environmental management perspective
A management perspective in which the firm takes aggressive actions to affect the publics and forces in its marketing environment rather than simply watching and reacting to them.

Marketing at Work | 3.3

YourCompanySucks.com

Richard Hatch is one of the few people in this world with a passion for both Harley-Davidson motorcycles and collecting dolls and cute little toys. One day a few years ago, the tattooed, 210-pound Hatch got into a shouting match with an employee in his local Wal-Mart and was banned from the store. Hatch claims that his actions didn't warrant his ousting. He says he'd complained to store managers for months that employees were snapping up the best Hot Wheels and NASCAR collectible toy cars before they hit the shelves.

Wal-Mart didn't budge and the angry Hatch retaliated. He hired a Web designer and created the Wal-Mart Sucks Web site (www.walmartsucks.com). In only a few years, according to one account, the Web site "sprouted beyond Hatch's wildest dreams of revenge. [Thousands] of customers have written in to attack rude store managers, complain about alleged insects in the aisles, offer shoplifting tips, and, from time to time, write romantic odes to cashiers." Hatch, who had amassed some 5,000 Beanie Babies, also had a dispute with employees at his local Toys 'R' Us store about similar complaints. He was banished from there as well. His response? You guessed it: another sucks.com Web site (www.toysrussucks.com).

An extreme event? Not anymore. As more and more well-intentioned grassroots organizations, consumer watchdog groups, or just plain angry consumers take their gripes to the Web, such "sucks.com" sites are becoming almost commonplace. According to one source, more than half of the Fortune 1000 companies have encountered some type of Web site critical of their businesses. The sites target some highly respected companies with some highly *dis*respectful labels: Microsucks; Gapsucks.org; NonAmazon; Starbucked; BestBuy-sucks; The I Hate McDonald's Page; Just Do Not Do It (Nike); America Offline; NorthWorst Air; Untied Airlines: The Most Unfriendly Skies; The Unofficial BMW Lemon Site; AllStateInsurancesucks ("Their hands in your pockets"); and Dunkindonuts.org (featuring "unhappy tales about coffee, crullers, and cinnamon buns") to name only a few. Some of these attack sites are little more than a nuisance. Others, however, can draw serious attention and create real headaches. "The same people who used to stand on [the] corner and rail against things to 20 people now can put up a Web site and rail in front of 2 million people," says William Comcowich, whose firm helps companies monitor what's said about them on the Internet.

How should companies react to these attack sites? The real quandary

Environmental management: The best strategy for dealing with consumer hate sites is to address complaints directly. "If a company solves my problem, why would I keep up the Web site?"

Often, companies can find positive ways to overcome seemingly uncontrollable environmental constraints. For example:

Cathay Pacific Airlines . . . determined that many travelers were avoiding Hong Kong because of lengthy delays at immigration. Rather than assuming that this was a problem they could not solve, Cathay's senior staff asked the Hong Kong government how to avoid these immigration delays. After lengthy discussions, the airline agreed to make an annual grant-in-aid to the government to hire more immigration inspectors—but these reinforcements would service primarily

for targeted companies is figuring out how far they can go to protect their image without fueling the fire already raging at the sites. One point upon which all experts seem to agree: Don't try to retaliate in kind. "Avoid 'testosterosis'—or the urge to hit someone in the face because they are doing something you don't like," advises one consultant. "It's a free country, and the Web is completely unregulated. Don't get angry and think about doing foolish things."

Some companies have tried to silence the critics through lawsuits, but few have succeeded. For example, McDonald's sued one such site for libel; it spent $16 million on the case and won the suit but received only $94,000 in damages. Wal-Mart's attorneys threatened Hatch with legal action unless he shut down his Wal-Mart sucks Web site. However, Hatch stood up to the $250 billion retailer, and Wal-Mart eventually backed down. As it turns out, a company has legal recourse only when the unauthorized use of its trademarks, brand names, or other intellectual property is apt to be confusing to the public. And no reasonable person is likely to be confused that Wal-Mart maintains and supports a site tagged Walmartsucks.com.

Beyond the finer legal points, Wal-Mart also feared that a lawsuit would draw only more attention to the consumer hate site. An industry analyst comments: "Those who operate hate sites adore posting cease-and-desist letters they receive from corporate attorneys. Such letters also validate their fight for the cause, whatever they perceive that to be, and they can use them to cast yet another negative spotlight on the company. They revel in the attention."

Given the difficulties of trying to sue consumer hate sites out of existence, some companies have tried other strategies. For example, most big companies now routinely buy up Web addresses for their firm names preceded by the words "Ihate" or followed by "sucks.com." In general, however, attempts to block, counterattack, or shut down consumer hate sites may be shortsighted. Such sites are often based on real consumer concerns. Hence, the best strategy might be to proactively monitor these sites and respond positively to the concerns they express.

Some targeted companies actively listen to concerns posted on hate sites and develop Web presentations to tell their own side of the story. For example, Nike is the target of at least eight different attack sites, mostly criticizing it for alleged unfair labor practices in Southeast Asia. In response, Nike commissioned an independent investigation of labor practices in its Indonesian factories and presented the results on its own Web site (www.Nikebiz.com/social/labor).

Monitoring consumer hate sites can yield additional benefits. For example, some sites can actually provide the targeted company with useful information. "Most sites are full of genuine, free market research . . . on what is going wrong in customer service and product terms," advises an expert. "Rather than closing down such sites, companies should encourage them as a healthy outlet for unresolved anger."

According to James Alexander, president of EWatch, an Internet monitoring service, the best strategy for dealing with consumer hate sites is to address their complaints directly. "If a company solves my problem," he says, "why would I keep up the Web site?" Take Dunkin' Donuts, for example:

After a disgruntled customer established dunkindonuts.org, an attack site that appeared on many Internet search engines ahead of the company's own Web page, the company contacted about 25 people who had written in with complaints and offered them coupons for free donuts. "If this was where customers were going to post their comments, we thought it was important for us to go ahead and address them," says spokesperson Jennifer Rosenberg. Now, the company is in negotiations to buy the site from its founder, 25-year-old David Felton, who says he'll sell because "they have been taking complaints and responding."

By proactively responding to a seemingly uncontrollable event in its environment, Dunkin' Donuts has been able to turn a negative into a positive. Dunkinsucks.com is now all smiles.com.

Sources: Quotes and excerpts from Leslie Goff, "<YourCompanyNameHere>sucks.com," *Computerworld,* July 20, 1998, pp. 57–58; Mike France, "A Site for Soreheads," *Business Week,* April 12, 1999, pp. 86–90; and Wanda Goldwag, "Complaint Sites Can Focus Firms on Issues to Fix," *Marketing,* September 5, 2002, p. 16. Also see Oscar S. Cisneros, "Legal Tips for Your 'Sucks' Site," accessed online at www.wired.com, August 14, 2000; Hilary Appelman, "I Scream, You Scream: Consumers Vent over the Net," *New York Times,* March 4, 2001, p. 3.13; Eric J. Sinrod, " 'Suck' Sites Live in the Eyes of the Courts," November 29, 2002, accessed online at www.USAToday.com; and Ronald F. Lopez, "Corporate Strategies for Addressing Internet "Complaint" Sites," accessed online at www.constructionweblinks.com, June 2003.

the Cathay Pacific gates. The reduced waiting period increased customer value and thus strengthened [Cathay's competitive advantage].[50]

Marketing management cannot always control environmental forces. In many cases, it must settle for simply watching and reacting to the environment. For example, a company would have little success trying to influence geographic population shifts, the economic environment, or major cultural values. But whenever possible, smart marketing managers will take a *proactive* rather than *reactive* approach to the marketing environment (see Marketing at Work 3.3).

REST STOP:
Reviewing the Concepts

In this chapter and the next two chapters, you'll examine the environments of marketing and how companies analyze these environments to discover marketplace opportunities and create effective marketing strategies. Companies must constantly watch and adapt to the *marketing environment* in order to seek opportunities and ward off threats. The marketing environment comprises all the actors and forces influencing the company's ability to transact business effectively with its target market.

1. Describe the environmental forces that affect the company's ability to serve its customers.

The company's *microenvironment* consists of other actors close to the company that combine to form the company's value delivery network or that affect its ability to serve its customers. It includes the company's *internal environment*—its several departments and management levels—as it influences marketing decision making. *Marketing-channel firms*—suppliers and marketing intermediaries, including resellers, physical distribution firms, marketing services agencies, and financial intermediaries—cooperate to create customer value. Five types of customer *markets* include consumer, business, reseller, government, and international markets. *Competitors* vie with the company in an effort to serve customers better. Finally, various *publics* have an actual or potential interest in or impact on the company's ability to meet its objectives.

The *macroenvironment* consists of larger societal forces that affect the entire microenvironment. The six forces making up the company's macroenvironment include demographic, economic, natural, technological, political, and cultural forces. These forces shape opportunities and pose threats to the company.

2. Explain how changes in the demographic and economic environments affect marketing decisions.

Demography is the study of the characteristics of human populations. Today's *demographic environment* shows a changing age structure, shifting family profiles, geographic population shifts, a better-educated and more white-collar population, and increasing diversity. The *economic environment* consists of factors that affect buying power and patterns. The economic environment is characterized by more consumer concern for value and shifting consumer spending patterns. Today's squeezed consumers are seeking greater value—just the right combination of good quality and service at a fair price. The distribution of income also is shifting. The rich have grown richer, the middle class has shrunk, and the poor have remained poor, leading to a two-tiered market. Many companies now tailor their marketing offers to two different markets—the affluent and the less affluent.

3. Identify the major trends in the firm's natural and technological environments.

The *natural environment* shows three major trends: shortages of certain raw materials, higher pollution levels, and more government intervention in natural resource management. Environmental concerns create marketing opportunities for alert companies. The marketer should watch for four major trends in the *technological environment*: the rapid pace of technological change, high R&D budgets, the concentration by companies on minor product improvements, and increased government regulation. Companies that fail to keep up with technological change will miss out on new product and marketing opportunities.

4. Explain the key changes in the political and cultural environments.

The *political environment* consists of laws, agencies, and groups that influence or limit marketing actions. The political environment has undergone three changes that affect marketing worldwide: increasing legislation regulating business, strong government agency enforcement, and greater emphasis on ethics and socially responsible actions. The *cultural environment* is made up of institutions and forces that affect a society's values, perceptions, preferences, and behaviors. The environment shows long-term trends toward a "we society," a lessening trust of institutions, increasing patriotism, greater appreciation for nature, a new spiritualism, and the search for more meaningful and enduring values.

5. Discuss how companies can react to the marketing environment.

Companies can passively accept the marketing environment as an uncontrollable element to which they must adapt, avoiding threats and taking advantage of opportunities as they arise. Or they can take an *environmental management perspective*, proactively working to change the environment rather than simply reacting to it. Whenever possible, companies should try to be proactive rather than reactive.

Navigating the Key Terms

Baby boomers
Cultural environment
Demography
Economic environment
Engel's laws
Environmental management
 perspective

Generation X
Generation Y
Macroenvironment
Marketing environment
Marketing intermediaries

Microenvironment
Natural environment
Political environment
Public
Technological environment

Travel Log

Discussing the Issues

1. The microenvironment includes a variety of publics that have an interest in the company or can have an impact on its operations. Discuss how the goals of some of these publics may be opposed to one another. How would opposing goals among a company's relevant publics have an impact on its strategy?

2. The changing structure of the American family was identified as an important demographic force shaping the opportunities and threats to the company. Explain how a grocery store could change its positioning to appeal to each of the following segments: married couples with children, single parents, and adults living alone.

3. Value marketing—the right combination of product quality and good service at a fair price—has increased in popularity. Pick an industry and identify two competing companies, one that is good at value marketing and one that is poor at value marketing. For the company that is poor at value marketing, discuss why consumers purchase from that company. What need is it fulfilling better than the firm that is good at value marketing?

4. The 2002 Sarbanes–Oxley Act, among other things, has made high-level corporate executives personally accountable for the accuracy of their company's earnings statements, requires public companies to improve their financial control systems, and calls for some board members to be from outside the company. What impact might this legislation have on business operations?

5. An environmental management perspective advocates taking a proactive, rather than reactive, approach to dealing with the marketing environment. Identify a company you feel characterizes this approach. What specific actions do they take to proactively influence their environment?

Application Questions

1. For an educational institution, the number, quality, and characteristics of its student body are heavily impacted by changes in the size and structure of the general population. Discuss how your school is likely to be impacted by the following trends: an aging population, a growing population, a changing definition of the family, geographic shifts in population, a more white-collar workforce, and increasing ethnic and cultural diversity. For the trends that have a negative impact, what strategy would you recommend for reducing the negative influence?

2. The text argues that major cultural values in society are defined by individuals' views of themselves and others, as well as their views of organizations, society, nature, and the universe. Break into groups of four to five students, with each group focusing on one of these six views. Noting the shift discussed in the text for your group's assigned area, identify a company that has benefited from the shift and one whose position has worsened. For those organizations that have not fared as well under the shift, what must they do to better adjust to this trend?

3. The Federal Trade Commission estimates that its national do-not-call registry will contain more than 60 million phone numbers by July 2004. In response, a telemarketing trade association has challenged the legality of this consumer telemarketing call-blocking service in federal court. Describe what activities might have been engaged in if the telemarketing industry had taken a more proactive environmental management perspective toward this issue. What is your opinion on balancing the privacy of consumers with the rights of legitimate telemarketing firms to conduct business?

Under the Hood: Focus on Technology

Customer loyalty for online travel companies is low, with the average consumer checking three travel websites for the best prices on airlines, hotels, and rental cars. Today, approximately 15 percent of all travel is purchased online, with airline ticket sales accounting for about half of that amount. Three online travel companies, Expedia (36 percent of the market), Travelocity (24 percent), and Orbitz (13 percent) account for the majority of online travel sales. While consumers have been focused on where to get the best deals, many online travel companies have been investing in new technology that will allow them to differentiate themselves with regard to the services they provide rather than the prices they offer.

1. What macroenvironmental forces do you feel will have the largest positive and largest negative impact on online travel companies? Why?

2. Discuss how online travel companies should address these negative impacts.

3. What do you think is the long-run future of the online travel industry?

4. What do you feel are the most significant environmental issues facing the online travel industry in the next 5 years?

Focus on Ethics

How many times have you or your parents purchased a new computer in the past 5 years? As computers become more and more powerful, regular updating of computer equipment has become common. Have you ever wondered where all of the old computers and monitors go? Are they sitting in your house somewhere, in the garage maybe?

Concerns over decreasing raw materials, increasing pollution levels, and global warming have gained momentum over the past several years. While many companies have been accused of polluting the environment, some have used society's concern over the natural environment to differentiate themselves from competitors. One such company is Dell Computer, which recently initiated a recycling program for businesses and consumers that includes computers, monitors, keyboards, and mice—all those items that may be hanging around in your house.

How does this work? You pay a fee of $15.00 per 50 pounds of weight, and Dell has someone pick up your computers and monitors. The average computer and monitor weigh more than 50 pounds but less than 100 pounds, so the cost is likely to be $30.00 to the customer. Dell then will either recycle or resell the old computer equipment, thus sparing landfills from the hazardous materials contained in much of today's existing computer equipment.

1. Assume that the price paid by the owners of the old computer equipment does not cover Dell's cost of recycling. What benefits might Dell gain that would be worth this expense?

2. What actions might the government take if it became concerned about the disposal of unwanted computer equipment? How can Dell's recycling efforts be considered similar to an environmental management perspective?

3. Might Dell's computer recycling program help to differentiate it from other computer manufacturers? How much influence would a recycling program like the one described above for Dell computer have on your decision to buy a computer from a particular company?

Videos

The Nike video case that accompanies this chapter is located in Appendix 1 at the back of the book.

Student Materials

Need a tune-up? A study guide and OneKey access code are available to aid in your review of chapter material. Your instructor may choose to have these items shrink-wrapped with your text or you may purchase them separately at www.prenhall.com/marketing.

Managing Marketing Information

4

ROAD MAP | Previewing the Concepts

In the last chapter, you learned about the complex and changing marketing environment. In this chapter, we'll continue our exploration of how marketers go about understanding the marketplace and consumers. We'll look at how companies develop and manage information about important marketplace elements—information about customers, competitors, products, and marketing programs. We'll examine marketing information systems designed to give managers the right information, in the right form, at the right time to help them make better marketing decisions. We'll also take a close look at the marketing research process and at some special marketing research considerations. To succeed in today's marketplace, companies must know how to manage mountains of marketing information effectively.

We'll start the chapter with a look at a classic marketing blunder—Coca-Cola's ill-considered decision some years ago to introduce New Coke. The company based its decision on substantial marketing research, yet the new product fizzled badly. As you read on, ask yourself how a large and resourceful marketing company such as Coca-Cola could make such a huge research mistake. The moral: If it can happen to Coca-Cola, it can happen to any company.

I n 1985, in what has now become an all-time classic marketing tale, the Coca-Cola Company made a major marketing blunder. After 99 successful years, it set aside its long-standing rule—"Don't mess with Mother Coke"—and dropped its original-formula Coke! In its place came *New* Coke with a sweeter, smoother taste.

At first, amid the introductory flurry of advertising and publicity, New Coke sold well. But sales soon went flat, as a stunned public reacted. Coke began receiving sacks of mail and more than 1,500 phone calls each day from angry consumers. One angry consumer addressed his concerns in a letter sent to "Chief Dodo, The Coca-Cola Company." (Coke's CEO claimed that he was less concerned about the letter than about the fact that it was actually delivered to him!) Other consumers panicked, filling their basements with cases of the old tried-and-true. One man in Texas drove to a local bottler and bought $1,000 worth of the old Coca-Cola. A group called "Old Cola Drinkers" staged protests, handed out T-shirts, and threatened a class-action suit

unless Coca-Cola brought back the old formula. Meanwhile, Pepsi was so delighted that it declared April 23, 1985, New Coke's debut day, a corporate holiday.

After only three months, the Coca-Cola Company brought old Coke back. That July day, virtually every major newspaper featured the return of the "old Coke" on the front page. Now called "Coke Classic," the old formula sold side-by-side with New Coke on supermarket shelves. The company said that New Coke would remain its flagship brand, but consumers had a different idea. By the end of that year, Classic was outselling New Coke in supermarkets by two to one.

Quick reaction saved Coca-Cola from potential disaster. The company stepped up efforts for Coke Classic and slotted New Coke into a supporting role. Coke Classic again became the company's main brand and the country's leading soft drink. New Coke became the company's "attack brand"—its Pepsi stopper—and ads boldly compared New Coke's taste with Pepsi's. Still, New Coke managed only a 2 percent market share. In the spring of 1990, the company repackaged New Coke and relaunched it as a brand extension with a new name, Coke II. Today, Coke Classic captures more than 19 percent of the U.S. soft drink market; Coke II sells in only a few selected markets.

Why was New Coke introduced in the first place? What went wrong? Many analysts blame the blunder on poor marketing research.

In the early 1980s, although Coke was still the leading soft drink, it was slowly losing market share to Pepsi. For almost 15 years, Pepsi had successfully mounted the "Pepsi Challenge," a series of televised taste tests showing that consumers preferred the sweeter taste of Pepsi. By early 1985, although Coke led in the overall market, Pepsi led in share of supermarket sales by 2 percent. (That doesn't sound like much, but 2 percent of today's huge U.S. soft drink market amounts to almost $1.2 billion in retail sales!) Coca-Cola had to do something to stop the loss of its market share, and the solution appeared to be a change in Coke's taste.

Coca-Cola began the largest new-product research project in the company's history. It spent more than two years and $4 million on research before settling on a new formula. It conducted some 200,000 taste tests—30,000 on the final formula alone. In blind tests, 60 percent of consumers chose the new Coke over the old, and 52 percent chose it over Pepsi. Research showed that New Coke would be a winner, and the company introduced it with confidence. So what happened?

Looking back, we can see that Coke defined its marketing research problem too narrowly. The research looked only at taste; it did not explore consumers' feelings about dropping the old Coke and replacing it with a new version. It took no account of the *intangibles*—Coke's name, history, packaging, cultural heritage, and image. However, to many people, Coke stands alongside baseball, hot dogs, and apple pie as an American institution; it represents the very fabric of America. Coke's symbolic meaning turned out to be more important to many consumers than its taste. Research addressing a broader set of issues would have detected these strong emotions.

Coke's managers may also have used poor judgment in interpreting the research and planning strategies around it. For example, they took the finding that 60 percent of consumers preferred New Coke's taste to mean that the new product would win in the marketplace, as when a political candidate wins with 60 percent of the vote. But it also meant that 40 percent still liked the original formula. By dropping the old Coke, the company trampled the taste buds of the large core of loyal Coke drinkers who didn't want a change. The company might have been wiser to leave the old Coke alone and introduce New Coke as a brand extension, as it later did successfully with Cherry Coke.

The Coca-Cola Company has one of the largest, best-managed, and most advanced marketing research operations in America. Good marketing research has kept the company atop the rough-and-tumble soft drink market for decades. But marketing research is far from an exact science. Consumers are full of surprises, and figuring them out can be awfully tough. If Coca-Cola can make a large marketing research mistake, any company can.[1]

In order to produce superior value and satisfaction for customers, companies need information at almost every turn. As the New Coke story highlights, good products and marketing programs begin with a thorough understanding of consumer needs and wants. Companies also need an abundance of information on competitors, resellers, and other actors and forces in the marketplace.

Increasingly, marketers are viewing information not only as an input for making better decisions but also as an important strategic asset and marketing tool. A company's information may prove to be its chief competitive advantage. Competitors can copy each other's equipment, products, and procedures, but they cannot duplicate the company's information and intellectual capital. Several companies have recently recognized this by appointing vice presidents of knowledge, learning, or intellectual capital.

In today's more rapidly changing environments, managers need up-to-date information to make timely, high-quality decisions. In turn, with the recent explosion of information technologies, companies can now generate information in great quantities. In fact, today's managers often receive too much information.

One study found that with all the companies offering data, and with all the information now available through supermarket scanners, a packaged-goods brand manager is bombarded with 1 million to 1 *billion* new numbers each week. Another study found that large retailers typically now have the equivalent of 320 miles of bookshelves of information on their products. Wal-Mart, the largest retailer of all, has more than three and a half times that much information in it's data warehouse. Thus, running out of information is not a problem, but seeing through the "data smog" is. "In this oh-so-overwhelming Information age," comments one observer, "it's all too easy to be buried, burdened, and burned out by data overload.[2]

Despite this data glut, marketers frequently complain that they lack enough information of the *right* kind. One recent study found that managers lose as much as three hours a day looking for the right information, costing U.S. companies more than $2.5 billion annually. Another study found that although half of the managers surveyed said they couldn't cope with the volume of information coming at them, two-thirds wanted even more. The researcher concluded that, "despite the volume, they're still not getting what they want."[3] Thus, most marketing managers don't need *more* information, they need *better* information.

A former CEO at Unilever once said that if Unilever only knew what it knows, it would double its profits. The meaning is clear: Many companies sit on rich information but fail to manage and use it well.[4] Companies must design effective marketing information systems that give managers the right information, in the right form, at the right time to help them make better marketing decisions.

■ Information overload: "In this oh so overwhelming Information age, it's all too easy to be buried, burdened, and burned out by data overload."

A **marketing information system (MIS)** consists of people, equipment, and procedures to gather, sort, analyze, evaluate, and distribute needed, timely, and accurate information to marketing decision makers. Figure 4.1 shows that the MIS begins and ends with information users—marketing managers, internal and external partners, and others who need marketing information. First, it interacts with these information users to *assess information needs*. Next, it *develops needed information* from internal company databases, marketing intelligence activities, and marketing research. Then it helps users to analyze information to put it in the right form for making marketing decisions and managing customer relationships. Finally, the MIS *distributes* the marketing information and helps managers *use* it in their decision making.

Marketing information system (MIS)

People, equipment, and procedures to gather, sort, analyze, evaluate, and distribute needed, timely, and accurate information to marketing decision makers.

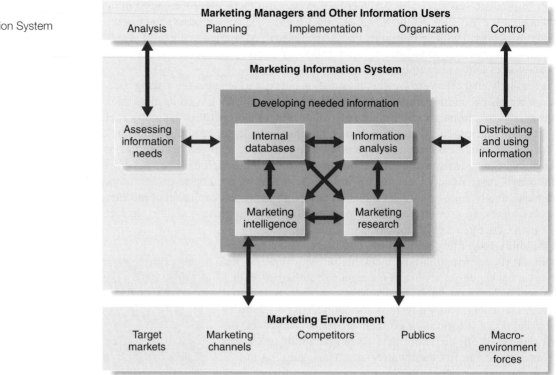

▪▪ Assessing Marketing Information Needs

The marketing information system primarily serves the company's marketing and other managers. However, it may also provide information to external partners, such as suppliers, resellers, or marketing services agencies. For example, Wal-Mart might give Procter & Gamble and other key suppliers access to information on customer buying patterns and inventory levels. In addition, important customers may be given limited access to the information system. Dell Computer creates tailored Premium Pages for large customers, giving them access to product design, order status, and product support and service information. FedEx lets customers into its information system to schedule and track shipments. In designing an information system, the company must consider the needs of all of these users.

A good marketing information system balances the information users would *like* to have against what they really *need* and what is *feasible* to offer. The company begins by interviewing managers to find out what information they would like. Some managers will ask for whatever information they can get without thinking carefully about what they really need. Too much information can be as harmful as too little. Other managers may omit things they ought to know, or they may not know to ask for some types of information they should have. For example, managers might need to know that a competitor plans to introduce a new product during the coming year. Because they do not know about the new product, they do not think to ask about it. The MIS must monitor the marketing environment in order to provide decision makers with information they should have to make key marketing decisions.

Sometimes the company cannot provide the needed information, either because it is not available or because of MIS limitations. For example, a brand manager might want to know how competitors will change their advertising budgets next year and how these changes will affect industry market shares. The information on planned budgets probably is not available. Even if it is, the company's MIS may not be advanced enough to forecast resulting changes in market shares.

Finally, the costs of obtaining, processing, storing, and delivering information can mount quickly. The company must decide whether the benefits of having additional information are worth the costs of providing it, and both value and cost are often hard to assess.

By itself, information has no worth; its value comes from its *use*. In many cases, additional information will do little to change or improve a manager's decision, or the costs of the information may exceed the returns from the improved decision. Marketers should not assume that additional information will always be worth obtaining. Rather, they should weigh carefully the costs of getting more information against the benefits resulting from it.

Developing Marketing Information

Marketers can obtain the needed information from *internal data, marketing intelligence,* and *marketing research.*

Internal Data

Many companies build extensive **internal databases**, electronic collections of information obtained from data sources within the company. Marketing managers can readily access and work with information in the database to identify marketing opportunities and problems, plan programs, and evaluate performance.

Information in the database can come from many sources. The accounting department prepares financial statements and keeps detailed records of sales, costs, and cash flows. Operations reports on production schedules, shipments, and inventories. The sales force reports on reseller reactions and competitor activities. The marketing department furnishes information on customer demographics, psychographics, and buying behavior. And the customer service department keeps records of customer satisfaction or service problems. Research studies done for one department may provide useful information for several others.

Here is an example of how one company uses its internal database to make better marketing decisions:

Internal databases
Electronic collections of information obtained from data sources within the company.

USAA, which provides financial services to U.S. military personnel and their families, maintains a customer database built from customer purchasing histories and from information collected directly from customers. To keep the database fresh, the organization regularly surveys its 5 million customers worldwide to learn things such as whether they have children (and if so, how old they are), if they have moved recently, and when they plan to retire. USAA uses the database to tailor marketing offers to the specific needs of individual customers. For example, if the family has college-age children, the USAA sends those children information on how to manage their credit cards. If the family has younger children, it sends booklets on things like financing a child's education. Or, for customers looking toward retirement, it sends information on estate planning. Through skillful use of its database, USAA serves each customer uniquely, resulting in high levels of customer loyalty—the roughly $8.6 billion company retains 97 percent of its customers.[5]

Internal databases usually can be accessed more quickly and cheaply than other information sources, but they also present some problems. Because internal information was collected for other purposes, it may be incomplete or in the wrong form for making marketing decisions. For example, sales and cost data used by the accounting department for preparing financial statements must be adapted for use in evaluating the value of specific

■ Financial services provider USAA uses its extensive database to tailor marketing offers to the specific needs of individual customers, resulting in greater than 96 percent customer retention.

customers or segments or product, sales force, or channel performance. Data ages quickly; keeping the database current requires a major effort. In addition, a large company produces mountains of information, and keeping track of it all is difficult. The database information must be well integrated and readily accessible so that managers can find it easily and use it effectively.

Marketing Intelligence

Marketing intelligence
The systematic collection and analysis of publicly available information about competitors and developments in the marketing environment.

Marketing intelligence is the systematic collection and analysis of publicly available information about competitors and developments in the marketplace. The goal of marketing intelligence is to improve strategic decision making, assess and track competitors' actions, and provide early warning of opportunities and threats.

Competitive intelligence gathering has grown dramatically as more and more companies are now busily snooping on their competitors. Techniques range from quizzing the company's own employees and benchmarking competitors' products to researching the Internet, lurking around industry trade shows, and rooting through rivals' trash bins.

Much intelligence can be collected from people inside the rival companies—executives, engineers and scientists, purchasing agents, and the sales force. Consider the following example:

> Spies don't always enter a rival's lair through the back door. Sometimes they stride in, and are even welcomed by their hosts. Bob Ayling, ex-chief executive of British Airways, accomplished such a mission when he visited the offices of the recently launched EasyJet. . . . Ayling approached the company's founder, Stelios Haji-Ioannou, to ask whether he could visit, claiming to be fascinated as to how the Greek entrepreneur had made the budget airline formula work. Haji-Ioannou not only agreed, but allegedly showed Ayling his business plan. [A year later, British Air] announced the launch of Go. "It was a carbon copy of EasyJet," says . . . EasyGroup's director of corporate affairs. "Same planes, same direct ticket sales, same use of a secondary airport, and same idea to sell on-board refreshments. They succeeded in stealing our business model—it was a highly effective spying job."[6]

The company can also obtain important intelligence information from suppliers, resellers, and key customers. Or it can get good information by observing competitors. It can buy and analyze competitors' products, monitor their sales, check for new patents, and examine various types of physical evidence. For example, one company regularly checks out competitors' parking lots—full lots might indicate plenty of work and prosperity; half-full lots might suggest hard times.

Some companies have even rifled their competitors' garbage, which is legally considered abandoned property once it leaves the premises. In one garbage-snatching incident, Oracle was caught rifling through rival Microsoft's dumpsters. Microsoft objected loudly. But a later investigation of the incident was closed because, technically, no crime had been committed. In another case, Procter & Gamble admitted to "dumpster diving" at rival Unilever's headquarters. The target was Unilever's hair-care products—including Salon Selectives, Finesse, Thermasilk, and Helen Curtis—which competed with P&G's own Pantene, Head & Shoulders, and Pert brands. "Apparently, the operation was a big success," notes an analyst. "P&G got its mitts on just about every iota of info there was to be had about Unilever's brands." However, when news of the questionable tactics reached top P&G managers, they were shocked. They immediately stopped the project, vol-

■ Marketing intelligence: Procter & Gamble admitted to "dumpster diving" at rival Unilever's Helene Curtis headquarters. When P&G's top management learned of the questionable practice, it stopped the project, voluntarily informed Unilever, and set up talks to right whatever competitive wrongs had been done.

untarily informed Unilever, and set up negotiations to right whatever competitive wrongs had been done. Although P&G claims it broke no laws, the company reported that the dumpster raids "violated our strict guidelines regarding our business policies."[7]

Competitors may reveal intelligence information through their annual reports, business publications, trade show exhibits, press releases, advertisements, and Web pages. The Internet is proving to be a vast new source of competitor-supplied information. Most companies now place volumes of information on their Web sites, providing details to attract customers, partners, suppliers, or franchisees. Using Internet search engines, marketers can search specific competitor names, events, or trends and see what turns up.[8]

> Even companies with the most basic technology can use it to gather intelligence, advises a competitive intelligence consultant. Keep tabs on your rivals' Web sites, and check to see if they have updated or altered their copy on any product lines. Have they redesigned the site or shifted its focus? What do search engines turn up on rivals? How is the press covering them? Your industry? Often, publicly accessible bulletin boards offer additional clues: Investors may log on to discuss rumors and tidbits of information. And keep watch for off-duty employees. They post, too. "Clients are often surprised that there's so much out there to know," says the consultant. "They're busy with their day-to-day operations and they don't realize how much information can be obtained with a few strategic keystrokes."

Intelligence seekers can also pore through any of thousands of online databases. Some are free. For example, the U.S. Security and Exchange Commission's database provides a huge stockpile of financial information on public competitors, and the U.S. Patent Office database reveals patents competitors have filed. And for a fee, companies can subscribe to any of more than 3,000 online databases and information search services such as Dialog, DataStar, LEXIS-NEXIS, Dow Jones News Retrieval, UMI ProQuest, and Dun & Bradstreet's Online Access.

Facing determined marketing intelligence efforts by competitors, most companies are now taking countermeasures. For example, Unilever has begun widespread competitive intelligence training. According to a former Unilever staffer, "We were told how to protect information, as well as how to get it from competitors. We were warned to always keep our mouths shut when traveling. . . . We were even warned that spies from competitors could be posing as drivers at the mini-cab company we used." Unilever even performs random checks on internal security. Says the former staffer, "At one [internal marketing] conference, we were set up when an actor was employed to infiltrate the group. The idea was to see who spoke to him, how much they told him, and how long it took to realize that no one knew him. He ended up being there for a long time."[9]

The growing use of marketing intelligence raises a number of ethical issues. Although most of the preceding techniques are legal, and some are considered to be shrewdly competitive, some may involve questionable ethics. Clearly, companies should take advantage of publicly available information. However, they should not stoop to snoop. With all the legitimate intelligence sources now available, a company does not have to break the law or accepted codes of ethics to get good intelligence.

Marketing Research

In addition to information about competitor and marketplace happenings, marketers often need formal studies of specific situations. For example, Sears wants to know what appeals will be most effective in its corporate advertising campaign. Or Toshiba wants to know how many and what kinds of people or companies will buy its new superfast notebook computer. In such situations, marketing intelligence will not provide the detailed information needed. Managers will need marketing research.

Marketing research is the systematic design, collection, analysis, and reporting of data relevant to a specific marketing situation facing an organization. Companies use marketing research in a wide variety of situations. For example, marketing research can help marketers understand customer satisfaction and purchase behavior. It can help them assess

Marketing research
The systematic design, collection, analysis, and reporting of data relevant to a specific marketing situation facing an organization.

market potential and market share or to measure the effectiveness of pricing, product, distribution, and promotion activities.

Some large companies have their own research departments that work with marketing managers on marketing research projects. This is how Kraft, Citigroup, and many other corporate giants handle marketing research. In addition, these companies—like their smaller counterparts—frequently hire outside research specialists to consult with management on specific marketing problems and conduct marketing research studies. Sometimes firms simply purchase data collected by outside firms to aid in their decision making.

The marketing research process has four steps (see Figure 4.2): *defining the problem and research objectives*, *developing the research plan*, *implementing the research plan*, and *interpreting and reporting the findings*.

Defining the Problem and Research Objectives

Marketing managers and researchers must work closely together to define the problem and agree on research objectives. The manager best understands the decision for which information is needed; the researcher best understands marketing research and how to obtain the information.

Defining the problem and research objectives is often the hardest step in the research process. The manager may know that something is wrong, without knowing the specific causes. For example, in the New Coke case, Coca-Cola defined its research problem too narrowly, with disastrous results. In another example, managers of a large discount retail store chain hastily decided that falling sales were caused by poor advertising. As a result, they ordered research to test the company's advertising. When this research showed that current advertising was reaching the right people with the right message, the managers were puzzled. It turned out that the real problem was that the chain was not delivering the prices, products, and service promised in the advertising. Careful problem definition would have avoided the cost and delay of doing advertising research.

After the problem has been defined carefully, the manager and researcher must set the research objectives. A marketing research project might have one of three types of objectives. The objective of **exploratory research** is to gather preliminary information that will help define the problem and suggest hypotheses. The objective of **descriptive research** is to describe things, such as the market potential for a product or the demographics and attitudes of consumers who buy the product. The objective of **causal research** is to test hypotheses about cause-and-effect relationships. For example, would a 10 percent decrease in tuition at a private college result in an enrollment increase sufficient to offset the reduced tuition? Managers often start with exploratory research and later follow with descriptive or causal research.

The statement of the problem and research objectives guides the entire research process. The manager and researcher should put the statement in writing to be certain that they agree on the purpose and expected results of the research.

Developing the Research Plan

Once the research problems and objectives have been defined, researchers must determine the exact information needed, develop a plan for gathering it efficiently, and present the plan to management. The research plan outlines sources of existing data and spells out the specific research approaches, contact methods, sampling plans, and instruments that researchers will use to gather new data.

Research objectives must be translated into specific information needs. For example, suppose Campbell decides to conduct research on how soup consumers would react to the introduction of new bowl-shaped plastic containers that it has used successfully for a number of its other products. The containers would cost more but would allow consumers to

Exploratory research
Marketing research to gather preliminary information that will help define problems and suggest hypotheses.

Descriptive research
Marketing research to better describe marketing problems, situations, or markets, such as the market potential for a product or the demographics and attitudes of consumers.

Causal research
Marketing research to test hypotheses about cause-and-effect relationships.

FIGURE 4.2
The Marketing Research Process

| Defining the problem and research objectives | → | Developing the research plan for collecting information | → | Implementing the research plan—collecting and analyzing the data | → | Interpreting and reporting the findings |

heat the soup in a microwave oven without adding water or milk and to eat it without using dishes. This research might call for the following specific information:

- The demographic, economic, and lifestyle characteristics of current soup users. (Busy working couples might find the convenience of the new packaging worth the price; families with children might want to pay less and wash the bowls.)

- Consumer-usage patterns for soup: how much soup they eat, where, and when. (The new packaging might be ideal for adults eating lunch on the go, but less convenient for parents feeding lunch to several children.)

- Retailer reactions to the new packaging. (Failure to get retailer support could hurt sales of the new package.)

- Consumer attitudes toward the new packaging. (The red-and-white Campbell can has become an American institution—will consumers accept the new packaging?)

- Forecasts of sales of both new and current packages. (Will the new packaging increase Campbell's profits?)

Campbell managers will need these and many other types of information to decide whether to introduce the new packaging.

The research plan should be presented in a *written proposal*. A written proposal is especially important when the research project is large and complex or when an outside firm carries it out. The proposal should cover the management problems addressed and the research objectives, the information to be obtained, and the way the results will help management decision making. The proposal also should include research costs.

To meet the manager's information needs, the research plan can call for gathering secondary data, primary data, or both. **Secondary data** consist of information that already exists somewhere, having been collected for another purpose. **Primary data** consist of information collected for the specific purpose at hand.

Secondary data
Information that already exists somewhere, having been collected for another purpose.

Primary data
Information collected for the specific purpose at hand.

Online databases
Computerized collections of information available from online commercial sources or via the Internet.

Gathering Secondary Data Researchers usually start by gathering secondary data. The company's internal database provides a good starting point. However, the company can also tap a wide assortment of external information sources, including commercial data services and government sources (see Table 4.1).

Companies can buy secondary data reports from outside suppliers.[10] For example, Information Resources, Inc., sells supermarket scanner purchase data from a panel of 55,000 households nationally, with measures of trial and repeat purchasing, brand loyalty, and buyer demographics. The *Monitor* service by Yankelovich and Partners sells information on important social and lifestyle trends. These and other firms supply high-quality data to suit a wide variety of marketing information needs.

Using commercial **online databases**, marketing researchers can conduct their own searches of secondary data sources. General database services such as CompuServe, Dialog, and LEXIS-NEXIS put an incredible wealth of information at the keyboards of marketing decision makers. Beyond commercial Web sites offering information for a fee, almost every industry association, government agency, business publication, and news medium offers free information to those tenacious enough to find their Web sites. There are so many Web sites offering data that finding the right ones can become an almost overwhelming task.

Secondary data can usually be obtained more quickly and at a lower cost than primary data. For example, an Internet or online

■ Online database services such as Dialog put an incredible wealth of information at the keyboards of marketing decision makers. Dialog puts "information to change the world, or your corner of it," at your fingertips.

TABLE 4.1 Selected External Information Sources

For business data:

AC Nielsen Corporation (www.acnielsen.com) provides supermarket scanner data on sales, market share, and retail prices; data on household purchasing; and data on television audiences.

Information Resources, Inc. (www.infores.com) provides supermarket scanner data for tracking grocery product movement and new product purchasing data.

Arbitron (www.arbitron.com) provides local-market and Internet radio audience and advertising expenditure information, among other media and ad spending data.

NDC Health Information Services (www.ndchealth.com) reports on the movement of drugs, laboratory supplies, animal health products, and personal care products.

Simmons Market Research Bureau (www.smrb.com) provides detailed analysis of consumer patterns in 400 product categories in selected markets.

Dun & Bradstreet (www.dnb.com) maintains a database containing information on more than 50 million individual companies around the globe.

Media Metrix (www.mediametrix.com) provides audience measurement and geodemographic analysis of Internet and digital media users around the world.

Dialog (http://library.dialog.com) offers access to ABI/INFORM, a database of articles from 800+ publications and to reports, newsletters, and directories covering dozens of industries.

LEXIS-NEXIS (www.lexis-nexis.com) features articles from business, consumer, and marketing publications plus tracking of firms, industries, trends, and promotion techniques.

CompuServe (www.compuserve.com) provides access to databases of business and consumer demographics, government reports, and patent records, plus articles from newspapers, and research reports.

Dow Jones Interactive (www.djinteractive.com) specializes in in-depth financial, historical, and operational information on public and private companies.

Hoover's Online (www.hoovers.com) provides business descriptions, financial overviews, and news about major companies around the world.

CNN (www.cnn.com) reports U.S. and global news and covers the markets and news-making companies in detail.

American Demographics (www.americandemographics.com) reports on demographic trends and their significance for businesses.

For government data:

Securities and Exchange Commission Edgar database (www.sec.gov) provides financial data on U.S. public corporations.

Small Business Administration (www.sba.gov) features information and links for small business owners.

Federal Trade Commission (www.ftc.gov) shows regulations and decisions related to consumer protection and antitrust laws.

Stat-USA (www.stat-usa.gov) a Department of Commerce site, highlights statistics on U.S. business and international trade.

U.S. Census (www.census.gov) provides detailed statistics and trends about the U.S. population.

U.S. Patent and Trademark Office (www.uspto.gov) allows searches to determine who has filed for trademarks and patents.

For Internet data:

Cyber Atlas (http://cyberatlas.internet.com) brings together a wealth of information about the Internet and its users, from consumers to e-commerce.

Interactive Advertising Bureau (www.iab.net) covers statistics about advertising on the Internet.

Jupiter Research (www.jupiterresearch.com) monitors Web traffic and ranks the most popular sites.

database search might provide all the information Campbell needs on soup usage, quickly and at low cost. A study to collect primary information might take weeks or months and cost thousands of dollars. Also, secondary sources sometimes can provide data an individual company cannot collect on its own—information that either is not directly available or would be too expensive to collect. For example, it would be too expensive for Campbell to conduct a continuing retail store audit to find out about the market shares, prices, and displays of competitors' brands. But it can buy the InfoScan service from Information

TABLE 4.2   Planning Primary Data Collection

Research Approaches	Contact Methods	Sampling Plan	Research Instruments
Observation	Mail	Sampling unit	Questionnaire
Survey	Telephone	Sample size	Mechanical instruments
Experiment	Personal	Sampling procedure	
	Online		

Resources, Inc., which provides this information from thousands of scanner-equipped supermarkets in dozens of U.S. markets.

Secondary data can also present problems. The needed information may not exist—researchers can rarely obtain all the data they need from secondary sources. For example, Campbell will not find existing information about consumer reactions to new packaging that it has not yet placed on the market. Even when data can be found, they might not be very usable. The researcher must evaluate secondary information carefully to make certain it is *relevant* (fits research project needs), *accurate* (reliably collected and reported), *current* (up-to-date enough for current decisions), and *impartial* (objectively collected and reported).

Primary Data Collection   Secondary data provide a good starting point for research and often help to define problems and research objectives. In most cases, however, the company must also collect primary data. Just as researchers must carefully evaluate the quality of secondary information, they also must take great care when collecting primary data. They need to make sure that it will be relevant, accurate, current, and unbiased. Table 4.2 shows that designing a plan for primary data collection calls for a number of decisions on *research approaches*, *contact methods*, *sampling plan*, and *research instruments*.

Research Approaches.   Research approaches for gathering primary data include observation, surveys, and experiments. **Observational research** involves gathering primary data by observing relevant people, actions, and situations. For example, a consumer packaged-goods marketer might visit supermarkets and observe shoppers as they browse the store, pick up products and examine packages, and make actual buying decisions. Or a bank might evaluate possible new branch locations by checking traffic patterns, neighborhood conditions, and the location of competing branches. Fisher-Price even set up an observation lab in which it could observe the reactions of little tots to new toys:

> The Fisher-Price Play Lab is a sunny, toy-strewn space where, since 1961, lucky kids have tested Fisher-Price prototypes. Today three boys and three girls,

Observational research
The gathering of primary data by observing relevant people, actions, and situations.

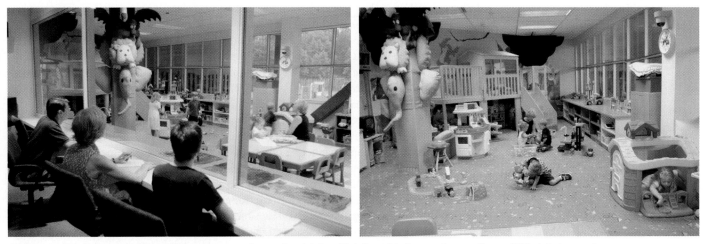

■ Observational research: Fisher-Price set up an observation lab in which it could observe the reactions of little tots to new toys.

all four-year-olds, speed through the front door. Two boys tug quietly, but firmly, for the wheel of a new radio-controlled race set—a brand-new offering. The girls skid to a stop near a small subdevelopment of dollhouses. And from behind the one-way glass, toy designers study the action intently, occasionally stepping out to join the play. At the Play Lab, creation and (attempted) destruction happily coexist. Over an eight week session with these kids, designers will test dozens of toy concepts, sending out crude models, then increasingly sophisticated revisions, to figure out what gets kids worked up into a new-toy frenzy.[11]

A wide range of companies now use *ethnographic research.* Ethnographic research involves sending trained observers to watch consumers in their "natural environments." Researchers observe consumers up close to learn how they use and feel about products and services. Consider the following example:

> Four years ago, Sunbeam wanted to extend its Coleman brand—known for its distinctive forest green encased lanterns and its red coolers—into gas barbecue grills. But company execs couldn't decide how to design and position the new line. Even after hours of focus groups and reams of quantitative data, the outdoor cooking team felt like it had a whole lot of information but little insight. "We were hearing a lot of passion about grilling, particularly among men," says a Sunbeam marketer, "but they couldn't really describe *why* they had the passion." Sunbeam execs turned to ethnography for help. Researchers hoisted video cameras onto shoulders and headed to their consumers' native habitat: the backyard. By hanging out with the guys around the grill and listening in on the gab, the team eventually gathered a key insight: A gas grill isn't really a tool that cooks hamburgers and hot dogs. Rather, it's the centerpiece of warm family moments worthy of a summer highlights reel. So, rather than create and promote the new Coleman Grill in terms of BTUs, rotisserie options, and cooking square inches, Sunbeam designed the grill to evoke nostalgia for the camping experience with friends and family. The company positioned the product and grilling experience as "a relaxing ritual where the grilling area is the stage," an event that takes place in a "backyard oasis." The result: The Coleman Grill did a scorching $50 million in sales in its first year, making the product line one of the most successful launches in Sunbeam history.[12]

Ethnographic research often yields the kinds of intimate details that just don't emerge from traditional focus groups. For example, by videotaping consumers in the shower, plumbing fixture maker Moen uncovered safety risks that consumers didn't recognize—such as the habit some women have of shaving their legs while holding on to one unit's temperature control. Moen would find it almost impossible to discover such design flaws simply by asking questions.[13] To glean greater insights into buying behavior, one company even went so far as to set up an actual retail store that serves as an ethnographic lab (see Marketing at Work 4.1).

Many companies collect data through *mechanical* observation via machine or computer. For example, Nielsen Media Research attaches *people meters* to television sets in selected homes to record who watches which programs. Other companies use *checkout scanners* to record shoppers' purchases so that manufacturers and retailers can assess product sales and store performance. MediaMetrix places special software on consumers' PCs to monitor Web surfing patterns and produce ratings for top Web sites.

Observational research can obtain information that people are unwilling or unable to provide. In some cases, observation may be the only way to obtain the needed information. In contrast, some things simply cannot be observed, such as feelings, attitudes and motives, or private behavior. Long-term or infrequent behavior is also difficult to observe. Because of these limitations, researchers often use observation along with other data collection methods.

Survey research, the most widely used method for primary data collection, is the approach best suited for gathering *descriptive* information. A company that wants to know about people's knowledge, attitudes, preferences, or buying behavior can often find out by asking them directly.

Survey research

The gathering of primary data by asking people questions about their knowledge, attitudes, preferences, and buying behavior.

Some firms provide marketers with a more comprehensive look at buying patterns through **single-source data systems**. These systems start with surveys of huge consumer panels—carefully selected groups of consumers who agree to participate in ongoing research. Then, they electronically monitor survey respondents' purchases and exposure to various marketing activities. Combining the survey and monitoring information gives a better understanding of the link between consumer characteristics, attitudes, and purchase behavior.

The major advantage of survey research is its flexibility—it can be used to obtain many different kinds of information in many different situations. However, survey research also presents some problems. Sometimes people are unable to answer survey questions because they cannot remember or have never thought about what they do and why. People may be unwilling to respond to unknown interviewers or about things they consider private. Respondents may answer survey questions even when they do not know the answer in order to appear smarter or more informed. Or they may try to help the interviewer by giving pleasing answers. Finally, busy people may not take the time, or they might resent the intrusion into their privacy.

Whereas observation is best suited for exploratory research and surveys for descriptive research, **experimental research** is best suited for gathering *causal* information. Experiments involve selecting matched groups of subjects, giving them different treatments, controlling unrelated factors, and checking for differences in group responses. Thus, experimental research tries to explain cause-and-effect relationships.

For example, before adding a new sandwich to its menu, McDonald's might use experiments to test the effects on sales of two different prices it might charge. It could introduce the new sandwich at one price in one city and at another price in another city. If the cities are similar, and if all other marketing efforts for the sandwich are the same, then differences in sales in the two cities could be related to the price charged.

Contact Methods. Information can be collected by mail, telephone, personal interview, or online. Table 4.3 shows the strengths and weaknesses of each of these contact methods.

Mail questionnaires can be used to collect large amounts of information at a low cost per respondent. Respondents may give more honest answers to more personal questions on a mail questionnaire than to an unknown interviewer in person or over the phone. Also, no interviewer is involved to bias the respondent's answers. However, mail questionnaires are not very flexible—all respondents answer the same questions in a fixed order. Mail surveys usually take longer to complete, and the response rate—the number of people returning completed questionnaires—is often very low. Finally, the researcher often has little control over the mail questionnaire sample. Even with a good mailing list, it is hard to control *who* at the mailing address fills out the questionnaire.

Telephone interviewing is the one of the best methods for gathering information quickly, and it provides greater flexibility than mail questionnaires. Interviewers can explain difficult questions and, depending on the answers they receive, skip some questions or probe

---

Single-source data systems

Electronic monitoring systems that link consumers' exposure to television advertising and promotion (measured using television meters) with what they buy in stores (measured using store checkout scanners).

Experimental research

The gathering of primary data by selecting matched groups of subjects, giving them different treatments, controlling related factors, and checking for differences in group responses.

TABLE 4.3   Strengths and Weaknesses of Contact Methods

	Mail	Telephone	Personal	Online
Flexibility	Poor	Good	Excellent	Good
Quantity of data that can be collected	Good	Fair	Excellent	Good
Control of interviewer effects	Excellent	Fair	Poor	Fair
Control of sample	Fair	Excellent	Fair	Poor
Speed of data collection	Poor	Excellent	Good	Excellent
Response rate	Fair	Good	Good	Good
Cost	Good	Fair	Poor	Excellent

Source: Adapted with permission from *Marketing Research: Measurement and Method*, 7th ed., by Donald S. Tull and Dell Hawkins. Copyright 1993 by Macmillan Publishing Company.

Marketing at Work | 4.1

OnceFamous: Watching Consumers in Their Natural Settings

Microphones capture every word while cameras record the action. Observers, posted everywhere, document each move. The runway at the Academy Awards? Or the paparazzi shadowing the royal family in London? No, it's all happening at a retail store called OnceFamous, and the observers and microphones aren't focused on celebrities, they're scrutinizing consumers.

OnceFamous is a unique ethnographic laboratory for studying consumer behavior in a natural setting. Although designed to look and feel like an ordinary retail store, this boutique is anything but ordinary. For starters, surveillance is everywhere at OnceFamous. Ethnographers watch from behind mirrored glass, while salespeople interview would-be buyers. Store employees—both on the floor and hidden behind glass—study the meanderings, whims,

and buying behaviors of those who wander in. Five cameras track consumers as they prowl the store—documenting both the smiles and scowls of browsers. Sensitive hidden microphones catch every utterance, from shoppers' questions to salespeople to snide comments between friends. Later, researchers pore over the tapes and analyze each shopper's behavior, looking for clues.

Although it all sounds like a massive invasion of consumer privacy, there's no need to fear Big Brother here. The store posts a prominent sign, complete with flashing lights, to alert shoppers that the store is in "Testing Mode." Additional signs invite shoppers who don't wish to be observed to "kindly visit us when this sign has been removed."

This 2300-sq-ft retail store is the work of FAME, a retail brand advertising agency located in Minneapolis. In late

2001, FAME opened the unique observational research lab in a heavily trafficked downtown skyway. Stocked with fancy pillows, knickknacks, and hand-made arts and crafts, the store attracts a variety of shoppers. Mingled with the store's regular inventory is an ever-changing assortment of clients' test products, including everything from ornaments to a new line of funny infant T-shirts.

When it comes to consumer research, OnceFamous beats the sterile, artificial cubicles used in many opinion survey research situations. Rather than interrogate test subjects in an artificial environment, researchers at OnceFamous watch shoppers in their natural surroundings. In fact, much of the time OnceFamous is just a store like any other store—it doesn't stay in "test mode" all of the time and it even turns a profit on sales. Such ethnographic

Watching consumers in their natural settings: OnceFamous is an actual retail store that serves as an ethnographic lab to yield greater insights into buying behavior.

on others. Response rates tend to be higher than with mail questionnaires, and interviewers can ask to speak to respondents with the desired characteristics or even by name.

However, with telephone interviewing, the cost per respondent is higher than with mail questionnaires. Also, people may not want to discuss personal questions with an interviewer. The method also introduces interviewer bias—the way interviewers talk, how they

research often yields insights that just don't emerge from traditional survey or focus group studies.

For FAME and its clients, the store helps fill a big gap in everyone's understanding of that elusive species, the shopper. Retailers know from inventory records what is on the shelf, and they know from point-of-sale data what ends up in shopper's baskets. But they lack a true understanding of the mysterious, often fickle buying process that connects the shelf to the checkout counter. What causes a consumer to skip past one aisle but spend a half hour strolling down another? Why does a shopper peer at one shelf but not even glance at the next one? What leads a person to pick up a product, examine it, put it back, walk away, come back later, pick it up again, and then finally buy it? How do the off-hand or pointed comments of friends, spouses, or sales staff have an impact on the buying decision?

The video and audio data FAME collects at OnceFamous help marketers understand a bit more about consumers and how they interact with the wealth of sensory and social cues in a retail store. "Ninety percent of all purchases are made on impulse," says Jeri Quest, FAME's executive vice president for strategic development. "We can get really close to customers at the point of decision making."

To gain these valuable insights into consumer preferences, manufacturers and retailers pay anywhere from $40,000 to $200,000 to have their products stocked at OnceFamous. In addition to product tests, FAME uses the lab as a testing ground for a variety of retailing decisions, such as product placement and traffic flow. Although OnceFamous is usually outfitted as an eclectic home furnishings and gift bou-

tique, FAME can strip it to the walls and reconfigure it for other product categories in a matter of days.

OnceFamous experiments have yielded interesting details on how people shop, including differences in the shopping approaches of men and women. "Women find an object they like and visit it," Quest says. "Men look at how it's made, what's the construction." Men stand back and study things, but women can't wait to get their hands on merchandise. Such differences may go as far back as childhood shopping experiences. Mothers are more likely to tell their sons to keep their hands to themselves while shopping. As a result, as adults, men are much less likely to pick up a product to get a closer look unless explicitly invited to. In contrast, daughters who shop with mom are more likely to learn her approach to evaluating a product by experiencing it. As adults, women evaluate products based on the stories the products tell and what the products may say about their owners.

Based on results like these, many stores tailor their displays to appeal differently to men and women. Stores like Brookstone and Sharper Image, which target mostly men, provide details about design and construction. They post signs urging shoppers to push buttons, test out massage chairs, and ask questions. In contrast, Pottery Barn, with its largely female audience, displays products in quaint groupings, allowing shoppers to visualize merchandise in their own homes, experience the products more intimately, and discover what those products might say about them.

Other in-store research has revealed that consumers react strongly to colors. Researchers at OnceFamous conducted an experiment by launching three separate sales, all on the same merchandise and with the same signs and promo-

tions. The researchers varied only the colors of the signs. The sales promoted with signs colored blue and green failed, whereas the event with red signs enticed shoppers to buy. The conclusion? Consumers associate cool colors, including blue and green, with higher prices. They associate warm colors, such as red and yellow, with low prices. Consumers are so drawn to the warm colors that red and yellow signs posted toward the rear of a store will draw shoppers in and through the aisles.

In another case, a retailer was desperate to get customers to turn left instead of right when entering its store. But research shows that 9 of 10 customers turn right. OnceFamous tested a video fireplace placed to the left of its entrance and found that this made 8 in 10 customers turn left instead.

OnceFamous may be the first research lab of its kind, but it won't be the last. Analysts predict a rise in the number of such detailed, "retail ethnography" labs as the retail world grows more and more competitive. To keep up with demand for consumer behavior insights, FAME plans to open a second retail shop at the ultimate retailing venue, the Mall of America. We'll be watching.

Sources: Keyla Kokmen, "The Company Store," *City Pages Media*, June 5, 2002, accessed at www.citypages.com/databank/23/1122/article10444.asp; Erik Baard, "Going Retail with Market Research," *Wired News*, August 8, 2002, p.1; Bruce Horovitz, "Shop, You're on Candid Camera," *USA Today*, November 5, 2002, p. 1B; Timothy Henderson, "Shopping Guinea Pigs," *Stores*, December 2002, accessed at www.stores.org/archives/archives02.html; "Little Shop of Habits," *NACS (National Association of Convenience Stores) Online*, November 8, 2002; Stephanie Simon, "Shopping with Big Brother," *Los Angeles Times*, May 2, 2002, accessed at www.chicagotribune.com/technology/chi-020502shopping.story; information gathered from www.fameretail.com, August 2003; and interviews with Tina Wilcox, President and Chief Creative Officer, FAME, June 2003.

ask questions, and other differences may affect respondents' answers. Finally, different interviewers may interpret and record responses differently, and under time pressures some interviewers might even cheat by recording answers without asking questions.

Personal interviewing takes two forms—individual and group interviewing. *Individual interviewing* involves talking with people in their homes or offices, on the street, or in shopping malls. Such interviewing is flexible. Trained interviewers can guide interviews, explain difficult questions, and explore issues as the situation requires. They can show subjects actual products, advertisements, or packages and observe reactions and behavior. However, individual personal interviews may cost three to four times as much as telephone interviews.

Group interviewing consists of inviting 6 to 10 people to talk with a trained moderator about a product, service, or organization. Participants normally are paid a small sum for attending. The moderator encourages free and easy discussion, hoping that group interactions will bring out actual feelings and thoughts. At the same time, the moderator "focuses" the discussion—hence the name **focus group interviewing**. Researchers and marketers watch the focus group discussions from behind one-way glass, and comments are recorded in writing or on videotape for later study.

Focus group interviewing has become one of the major marketing research tools for gaining insight into consumer thoughts and feelings. However, focus group studies usually employ small sample sizes to keep time and costs down, and it may be hard to generalize from the results. Because interviewers have more freedom in personal interviews, the problem of interviewer bias is greater.

Today, many researchers are changing the way they conduct focus groups. Some are employing videoconferencing technology to connect marketers in distant locations with live focus group action. Using cameras and two-way sound systems, marketing executives in a far-off boardroom can look in and listen, even using remote controls to zoom in on faces and pan the focus group at will. Other researchers are changing the environments in which they conduct focus groups. To help consumers relax and to elicit more authentic responses, they are using settings that are more comfortable and more relevant to the products being researched. For example, they might conduct focus groups for cooking products in a kitchen setting, or focus groups for home furnishings in a living room setting. One research firm offers facilities that look just like anything from a living room or play room to a bar or even a courtroom.

Some firms are now going on-site to conduct focus group sessions. Target did this before designing a new line of products for students entering college:

> To hear firsthand from college-bound students about their concerns when shopping for their dorm rooms, and to get a sense from college students of what life in a dorm is like, Target hired research firm Jump Associates to conduct focus groups. But rather than inviting respondents to a research facility, Jump put a different spin on the traditional focus group. It sponsored a series of "game nights" at high school grads' homes, inviting incoming college freshman as well as students with a year of dorm living under their belts. To get teens talking about dorm life, Jump devised a board game that involved issues associated with going to college. The game naturally led to informal conversations—and questions—about college life. Jump researchers were on the sidelines to observe, while a video camera recorded the proceedings. The research paid off. Last year, Target launched the Todd Oldham Dorm Room product line designed for college freshman. Among the new offerings: Kitchen in a Box, which provides basic accessories for a budding college cook; Bath in a Box, which includes an extra-large bath towel to preserve modesty on the trek to and from the shower; and a laundry bag with instructions printed on the bag about how to actually do the laundry.[14]

Advances in communication technologies have resulted in a number of new high-tech contact methods. One is *computer-assisted telephone interviewing (CATI)*, in which interviewers sit at computers, read questions on the screen, and type in respondents' answers. Another is *completely automated telephone surveys (CATS)*, in which respondents are dialed by computer and asked prerecorded questions. They enter responses by voice

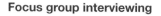

Focus group interviewing
Personal interviewing that involves inviting 6 to 10 people to gather for a few hours with a trained interviewer to talk about a product, service, or organization. The interviewer "focuses" the group discussion on important issues.

■ A new spin on focus groups: Before designing a new line of products for students entering college, Target sponsored "game nights" at high school grads' homes, inviting incoming college freshmen as well as students with a year of dorm living under their belts. To get teens talking, Target devised a board game that involved issues associated with going to college.

or through the phone's touchpad. Other high-tech contact methods include disks-by-mail, e-mail surveys, and computer-based fax surveys.[15]

The latest technology to hit marketing research is the Internet. Increasingly, marketing researchers are collecting primary data through **online (Internet) marketing research**— *Internet surveys, experiments,* and *online focus groups.* Online focus groups offer advantages over traditional methods in terms of low cost, access to respondents, and speed. However, although online research offers much promise, and some analysts predict that the Internet will soon be the primary marketing research tool, others are much more cautious. Marketing at Work 4.2 summarizes the advantages, drawbacks, and prospects for conducting marketing research on the Internet.

Sampling Plan. Marketing researchers usually draw conclusions about large groups of consumers by studying a small sample of the total consumer population. A **sample** is a segment of the population selected to represent the population as a whole. Ideally, the sample should be representative so that the researcher can make accurate estimates of the thoughts and behaviors of the larger population.

Designing the sample requires three decisions. First, *who* is to be surveyed (what *sampling unit*)? The answer to this question is not always obvious. For example, to study the decision-making process for a family automobile purchase, should the researcher interview the husband, wife, other family members, dealership salespeople, or all of these? The researcher must determine what information is needed and who is most likely to have it.

Second, *how many* people should be surveyed (what *sample size*)? Large samples give more reliable results than small samples. It is not necessary to sample the entire target market or even a large portion to get reliable results, however. If well chosen, samples of less than 1 percent of a population can often give good reliability.

Third, *how* should the people in the sample be *chosen* (what *sampling procedure*)? Table 4.4 describes different kinds of samples. Using *probability samples,* each population member has a known chance of being included in the sample, and researchers can calculate confidence limits for sampling error. But when probability sampling costs too much or takes too much time, marketing researchers often take *nonprobability samples,* even though their sampling error cannot be measured. These varied ways of drawing samples have different costs and time limitations as well as different accuracy and statistical properties. Which method is best depends on the needs of the research project.

Research Instruments. In collecting primary data, marketing researchers have a choice of two main research instruments—the *questionnaire* and *mechanical devices.* The *questionnaire* is by far the most common instrument, whether administered in person, by phone, or online.

Online (Internet) marketing research

Collecting primary data through Internet surveys and online focus groups.

Sample

A segment of the population selected for marketing research to represent the population as a whole.

TABLE 4.4   Types of Samples

Probability Sample	
Simple random sample	Every member of the population has a known and equal chance of selection.
Stratified random sample	The population is divided into mutually exclusive groups (such as age groups), and random samples are drawn from each group.
Cluster (area) sample	The population is divided into mutually exclusive groups (such as blocks), and the researcher draws a sample of the groups to interview.

Nonprobability Sample	
Convenience sample	The researcher selects the easiest population members from which to obtain information.
Judgment sample	The researcher uses his or her judgment to select population members who are good prospects for accurate information.
Quota sample	The researcher finds and interviews a prescribed number of people in each of several categories.

Marketing at Work | 4.2

Online Marketing Research

As more and more consumers have connected with the Internet, an increasing number of marketers have begun conducting marketing research on the Web. Online research now accounts for 8 percent of all spending on quantitative marketing research, and most industry insiders predict healthy growth.

Web research offers some real advantages over traditional surveys and focus groups. The most obvious advantages are speed and low costs. Online focus groups require some advance scheduling, but results are practically instantaneous. Survey researchers routinely complete their online studies in a matter of only days or weeks. For example, consider a recent online survey by a soft drink company to test teenagers' opinions of new packaging ideas. The 10- to 15-minute Internet survey included dozens of questions, along with 765 different images of labels, bottle shapes, and such. Some 600 teenagers participated over a three- to four-day period. Detailed analysis from the survey was available just five days after all the responses had come in—lightning quick compared with offline efforts. Similarly, Hershey Foods now does all of its new product testing research online. Whereas the old system of mail testing took six weeks or more to complete, online results can be garnered in two weeks or less.

Internet research is also relatively low in cost. Participants can dial in for a focus group from anywhere in the world, eliminating travel, lodging, and facility costs. For surveys, the Internet eliminates most of the postage, phone, labor, and printing costs associated with other approaches. "The cost [of Web research] can be anywhere from 10 percent to 80 percent less," says

Tod Johnson, head of NPD Group, a firm that conducts online research. Moreover, sample size has little influence on costs. "There's not a huge difference between 10 and 10,000 on the Web," says Johnson.

Online surveys and focus groups are also excellent for reaching the hard-to-reach—the often-elusive teen, single, affluent, and well-educated audiences. "It's very solid for reaching . . . doctors, lawyers, professionals—people you might have difficulty reaching because they are not interested in taking part in surveys," says Paul Jacobson, an executive of Greenfield Online. "It's also a

good medium for reaching working mothers and others who lead busy lives. They can do it in their own space and at their own convenience." The Internet also works well for bringing together people from different parts of the country, especially those in higher-income groups who can't spare the time to travel to a central site.

However, using the Internet to conduct marketing research does have some drawbacks. For one, many consumers still don't have access to the Internet. That makes it difficult to construct research samples that represent a broad cross section of Americans.

Brand manager eliminates pilot costs, becomes hero

Testing new package designs online with rotating 3-D images not only saved the client expensive tooling costs but also saved time. Now manufacturers can design today and test tomorrow. Eliminating pilot costs and shortening "time to market" are just some of the many ways that Greenfield Online quantitative research beats the old-fashioned kind. Put our expert consultants and advanced technology to work for you.
www.greenfield.com
888.291.9997

Greenfield Online
Leading the Research Revolution

• Quantitative Studies
• Qualitative Studies
• Media Research
• Self-Directed Research
• Syndicated Studies
• Website Evaluations

HERO

More and more companies are moving their research onto the Web. According to this Greenfield Online ad, in many ways, it "beats the old-fashioned kind."

Still, as Internet usage broadens, many mainstream marketers are now using Web research. General Mills, for example, conducts 60 percent of its consumer research online, reducing costs by 50 percent. And UPS uses online research extensively. "Between 40 percent and 50 percent of our customers are online, so it makes sense," says John Gilbert, UPS marketing research manager. He finds little difference in the results of traditional and online studies, and the online studies are much cheaper and faster.

Another major problem of online research is controlling who's in the sample. Tom Greenbaum, president of Groups Plus, recalls a cartoon in *The New Yorker* in which two dogs are seated at a computer: "On the Internet, nobody knows you are a dog," one says to the other. "If you can't see a person with whom you are communicating, how do know who they really are?" he says. To overcome such sample and response problems, many online research firms use opt-in communities and respondent panels. For example, Greenfield Online maintains a 1.3-million-member Internet-based respondent panel, recruited through cooperative marketing arrangements with other sites. Because such respondents opt in and can answer questions whenever they are ready, they yield high response rates. Whereas response rates for telephone surveys have plummeted to less than 14 percent in recent years, online response rates typically reach 40 percent or higher.

Even when you reach the right respondents, online surveys and focus groups can lack the dynamics of more personal approaches. "You're missing all of the key things that make a focus group a viable method," says Greenbaum. "You may get people online to talk to each other and play off each other, but it's very different to

watch people get excited about a concept." The online world is devoid of the eye contact, body language, and direct personal interactions found in traditional focus group research. And the Internet format—running, typed commentary and online "emoticons" (punctuation marks that express emotion, such as :-) to signify happiness)—greatly restricts respondent expressiveness.

Increasingly, however, advances in technology—such as the integration of animation, streaming audio and video, and virtual environments—will help to overcome these limitations. "In the online survey of the not-so-distant-future," notes an online researcher, "respondents will be able to rotate, zoom in on, and manipulate (like change the color or size of) three-dimensional products. They'll be able to peruse virtual stores, take items off shelves, and see how they function."

Just as the impersonal nature of the Web hinders two-way interactions, it can also provide anonymity. This often yields less guarded, more honest responses, especially when discussing topics such as income, medical conditions, lifestyle, or other sensitive issues. "People hiding behind a keyboard get pretty brave," says one researcher. Adds another:

From those questions that may simply make you squirm a little ("How much money did you lose in the stock market last month?"), to those you most probably don't want to answer to another human being, even if you don't know the person on the other end of the line ("How often do you have sex each week?"), Internet-based surveys tend to draw more honest responses. I once conducted the same survey in a mall and via the Internet. The question was, "How often do you bathe or shower each week?" The average answer, via the

mall interview, was 6.2 times per week. The average via the Internet interview was 4.8 times per week, probably a more logical—and honest—response.

Perhaps the most explosive issue facing online researchers concerns consumer privacy. Critics worry that online researchers will spam our e-mail boxes with unsolicited e-mails to recruit respondents. They fear that unethical researchers will use the e-mail addresses and confidential responses gathered through surveys to sell products after the research is completed. They are concerned about the use of electronic agents (called Spambots or Spiders) that collect personal information without the respondents' consent. Failure to address such privacy issues could result in angry, less cooperative consumers and increased government intervention.

Although most researchers agree that online research will never completely replace traditional research, some are wildly optimistic about its prospects. Others, however, are more cautious. "Ten years from now, national telephone surveys will be the subject of research methodology folklore," proclaims one expert. "That's a little too soon," cautions another. "But in 20 years, yes."

Sources: "Market Trends: Online Research Growing," accessed at www.greenfieldcentral.com/research_solutions/rsrch_solns_main.htm, June 2003; Ian P. Murphy, "Interactive Research," *Marketing News,* January 20, 1997, pp. 1, 17; "NFO Executive Sees Most Research Going to Internet," *Advertising Age,* May 19, 1997, p. 50; Noah Shachtman, "Web Enhanced Market Research," *Advertising Age,* June 18, 2001, p. T18; Thomas W. Miller, "Make the Call: Online Results Are a Mixed Bag," *Marketing News,* September 24, 2001, pp. 30–35; Catherine Arnold, "Hershey Research Sees Net Gain," *Marketing News,* November 25, 2003, p. 17; Beth Mack, "Online Privacy Critical to Research Success," *Marketing News,* November 25, 2002, p. 21; and Nina M. Ray and Sharon W. Tabor, "Cybersurveys Come of Age," *Marketing Research,* Spring 2003, pp. 32–37.

TABLE 4.5   A Questionable Questionnaire

Suppose that a summer camp director had prepared the following questionnaire to use in interviewing the parents of prospective campers. How would you assess each question?

1. What is your income to the nearest hundred dollars? *People don't usually know their income to the nearest hundred dollars, nor do they want to reveal their income that closely. Moreover, a researcher should never open a questionnaire with such a personal question.*

2. Are you a strong or weak supporter of overnight summer camping for your children? *What do "strong" and "weak" mean?*

3. Do your children behave themselves well at a summer camp? Yes ( ) No ( ) *"Behave" is a relative term. Furthermore, are yes and no the best response options for this question? Besides, will people answer this honestly and objectively? Why ask the question in the first place?*

4. How many camps mailed literature to you last year? This year? *Who can remember this?*

5. What are the most salient and determinant attributes in your evaluation of summer camps? *What are salient and determinant attributes? Don't use big words on me!*

6. Do you think it is right to deprive your child of the opportunity to grow into a mature person through the experience of summer camping? *A loaded question. Given the bias, how can any parent answer yes?*

Questionnaires are very flexible—there are many ways to ask questions. *Closed-end questions* include all the possible answers, and subjects make choices among them. Examples include multiple-choice questions and scale questions. *Open-end questions* allow respondents to answer in their own words. In a survey of airline users, Southwest might ask simply, "What is your opinion of Southwest Airlines?" Or it might ask people to complete a sentence: "When I choose an airline, the most important consideration is. . . ." These and other kinds of open-end questions often reveal more than closed-end questions because respondents are not limited in their answers. Open-end questions are especially useful in exploratory research, when the researcher is trying to find out *what* people think but not measuring *how many* people think in a certain way. Closed-end questions, on the other hand, provide answers that are easier to interpret and tabulate.

Researchers should also use care in the *wording* and *ordering* of questions. They should use simple, direct, unbiased wording. Questions should be arranged in a logical order. The first question should create interest if possible, and difficult or personal questions should be asked last so that respondents do not become defensive. A carelessly prepared questionnaire usually contains many errors (see Table 4.5).

Although questionnaires are the most common research instrument, researchers also use *mechanical instruments* to monitor consumer behavior, such as supermarket scanners and people meters. Other mechanical devices measure subjects' physical responses. For example, a galvanometer detects the minute degree of sweating that accompanies emotional arousal. It can be used to measure the strength of interest or emotions aroused by a subject's exposure to marketing stimuli such as an ad or product. Eye cameras are used to study respondents' eye movements to determine at what points their eyes focus first and how long they linger on a given item. Here are examples of new technologies that capture information on consumers' emotional and physical responses[16]:

Machine response to facial expressions that indicate emotions will soon be a commercial reality. The technology discovers underlying emotions by capturing an image of a user's facial features and movements—especially around the eyes and mouth—and comparing the image against facial feature templates in a database. Hence, an elderly man squints at an ATM screen and the font size doubles almost instantly. A woman at a shopping center kiosk smiles at a travel ad, prompting the device to print out a travel discount coupon. Several users at another kiosk frown at a racy ad, leading a store to pull it.

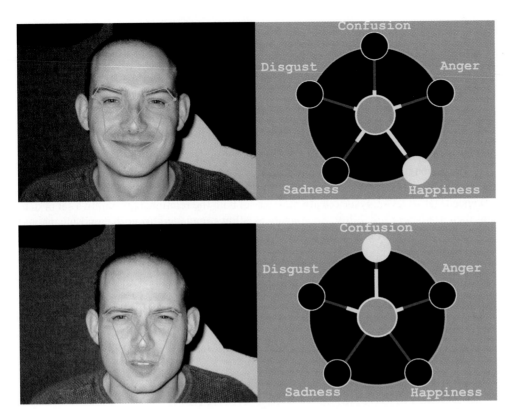

■ Mechanical measures of consumer response: devices are in the works that will allow marketers to measure facial expressions and adjust their offers or communications accordingly.

IBM is perfecting an "emotion mouse" that will figure out users' emotional states by measuring pulse, temperature, movement, and galvanic skin response. The company has mapped those measurements for anger, fear, sadness, disgust, happiness, and surprise. The idea is to create a style that fits a user's personality. An Internet marketer, for example, might offer to present a different kind of display if it senses that the user is frustrated.

Implementing the Research Plan The researcher next puts the marketing research plan into action. This involves collecting, processing, and analyzing the information. Data collection can be carried out by the company's marketing research staff or by outside firms. The data collection phase of the marketing research process is generally the most expensive and the most subject to error. Researchers should watch closely to make sure that the plan is implemented correctly. They must guard against problems with contacting respondents, with respondents who refuse to cooperate or who give biased answers, and with interviewers who make mistakes or take shortcuts.

Researchers must process and analyze the collected data to isolate important information and findings. They need to check data for accuracy and completeness and code it for analysis. The researchers then tabulate the results and compute averages and other statistical measures.

Interpreting and Reporting the Findings The market researcher must now interpret the findings, draw conclusions, and report them to management. The researcher should not try to overwhelm managers with numbers and fancy statistical techniques. Rather, the researcher should present important findings that are useful in the major decisions faced by management.

However, interpretation should not be left only to the researchers. They are often experts in research design and statistics, but the marketing manager knows more about the problem and the decisions that must be made. The best research is meaningless if the manager blindly accepts faulty interpretations from the researcher. Similarly, managers may be biased—they might tend to accept research results that show what they expected and to reject those that they did not expect or hope for. In many cases, findings can be interpreted in different ways, and discussions between researchers and managers will help point to the best interpretations. Thus, managers and researchers must work together closely when interpreting research results, and both must share responsibility for the research process and resulting decisions.

◼◼ Analyzing Marketing Information

Information gathered in internal databases and through marketing intelligence and marketing research usually requires more analysis. And managers may need help in applying the information to their marketing problems and decisions. This help may include advanced statistical analysis to learn more about both the relationships within a set of data and their statistical reliability. Such analysis allows managers to go beyond means and standard deviations in the data and to answer questions about markets, marketing activities, and outcomes.

Information analysis might also involve a collection of analytical models that will help marketers make better decisions. Each model represents some real system, process, or outcome. These models can help answer the questions of *What if?* and *Which is best?* Marketing scientists have developed numerous models to help marketing managers make better marketing mix decisions, design sales territories and sales call plans, select sites for retail outlets, develop optimal advertising mixes, and forecast new-product sales.

Customer Relationship Management (CRM)

The question of how best to analyze and use individual customer data presents special problems. Most companies are awash in information about their customers. In fact, smart companies capture information at every possible customer *touch point*. These touch points include customer purchases, sales force contacts, service and support calls, Web site visits, satisfaction surveys, credit and payment interactions, market research studies—every contact between the customer and the company.

The trouble is that this information is usually scattered widely across the organization. It is buried deep in the separate databases, plans, and records of different company functions and departments. To overcome such problems, many companies are now turning to **customer relationship management (CRM)** to manage detailed information about individual customers and carefully manage customer "touchpoints" in order to maximize customer loyalty. In recent years, there has been an explosion in the number of companies using CRM. In fact, one research firm found that 97 percent of all U.S. businesses plan to boost spending on CRM technology within the next two years.[17]

CRM consists of sophisticated software and analytical tools that integrate customer information from all sources, analyze it in depth, and apply the results to build stronger customer relationships. CRM integrates everything that a company's sales, service, and marketing teams know about individual customers to provide a 360-degree view of the customer relationship. It pulls together, analyzes, and provides easy access to customer information from all of the various touch points. Companies use CRM analysis to assess the value of individual customers, identify the best ones to target, and customize the company's products and interactions to each customer.

CRM analysts develop *data warehouses* and use sophisticated *data mining* techniques to unearth the riches hidden in customer data. A data warehouse is a company-wide electronic storehouse of customer information—a centralized database of finely detailed customer data that needs to be sifted through for gems. The purpose of a data warehouse is not to gather information—many companies have already amassed endless stores of information about their customers. Rather, the purpose is to allow managers to integrate the information the company already has. Then, once the data warehouse brings the data together for analysis, the company uses high-powered data mining techniques to sift through the mounds of data and dig out interesting relationships and findings about customers.

Customer relationship management (CRM)
Managing detailed information about individual customers and carefully managing customer "touch points" in order to maximize customer loyalty.

Companies can gain many benefits from customer relationship management. By understanding customers better, they can provide higher levels of customer service and develop deeper customer relationships. They can use CRM to pinpoint high-value customers, target them more effectively, cross-sell the company's products, and create offers tailored to specific customer requirements. Consider the following examples[18]:

■ FedEx recently launched a multimillion-dollar CRM system in an effort to cut costs, improve its customer support, and use its existing customer data to cross-sell and up-sell services to potential or existing customers. The new system gives every member of FedEx's 3,300-person sales force a comprehensive view of every customer, detailing each one's needs and suggesting services that might meet those needs. For instance, if a customer who does a lot of international shipping calls to arrange a delivery, a sales rep will see a detailed customer history on his or her computer screen, assess the customer's needs, and determine the most appropriate offering on the spot. Beleaguered sales reps can use such high-tech help. FedEx offers 220 different services—from logistics to transportation to customs brokerage—often making it difficult for salespeople to identify the best fit for customers. The new CRM system will also help FedEx conduct promotions and qualify potential sales leads. The CRM software analyzes market segments, points out market "sweet spots," and calculates how profitable those segments will be to the company and to individual salespeople.

■ At Marks & Spencer—Britain's "most trusted retailer"—CRM plays an important role in helping achieve the company's mission "to focus on our customers and be driven by their needs." M&S has one of the richest customer databases of any retailer in the world. The database contains demographic and purchasing information on more than 3 million M&S charge account customers, point-of-sale information from 10 million store transactions per week, and a wealth of data from external sources such as the census. "We have at least 80 explanatory variables for every household in the UK, rising to more than 300 for any customer holding a charge card," says Steven Bond, head of the retailer's Customer Insight Unit (CIU). The CRM system organizes this wealth of data and analyzes it to tell Marks & Spencer a great deal about its customers. The result is better decisions on everything from corporate branding to targeted communications and sales promotions. "We have a much better idea of what kinds of offers to put in front of different customers and when, and what tone of voice to use, based on their individual tastes, preferences, and behavior," says Bond. For example, by identifying who shops and when—older customers tend to shop early to avoid the crowds, while younger male shoppers leave things until the last minute, for instance—M&S can align its product availability and marketing activity accordingly. Or a regular customer checking out of the store's food section might be enticed into the menswear department with a promotion personalized according to whether he or she is an "Egyptian cotton and silk tie" purchaser or has a lifestyle that demands non-iron shirts. CRM has put Marks & Spencer at the leading edge of customer analysis. The improved customer insights help Marks & Spenser make better marketing decisions. This, in turn, creates more satisfied customers and more profitable customer relationships.

Most experts believe that good customer data, by itself, can give companies a substantial competitive advantage. Just ask American Express. At a secret location in Phoenix, security guards watch over American Express's 500 billion bytes of data on how customers have used its 35 million green, gold, and platinum charge cards. Amex uses the database to design carefully targeted offers in its monthly mailing of millions of customer bills.

CRM benefits don't come without cost or risk, not only in collecting the original customer data but also in maintaining and mining it. U.S. companies will spend an estimated $10 billion to $20 billion this year on CRM software alone from companies such as Siebel Systems, Oracle, SAS, and SPSS. Yet more than half of all CRM efforts fail to meet their objectives. The most common cause of CRM failures is that companies mistakenly view CRM only as a technology and software solution.[19] But technology alone cannot build profitable customer relationships. "CRM is not a technology solution—you can't achieve . . . improved customer relationships by simply slapping in some software," says a CRM expert. Instead, CRM is just one part of an effective overall *customer relationship management strategy*. "Focus on the *R*," advises the expert. "Remember, a relationship is what CRM is all about."[20]

Identify and keep your most valuable customers.

SAS® provides you with a complete view of your customers. So you'll understand their needs, enhance their lifetime value and achieve greater competitive advantage. To find out how leading companies are reaping the rewards of SAS customer intelligence software, call **1 866 270 5723** or visit our Web site.

www.sas.com/customer

The Power to Know. | **§sas**

■ CRM: SAS offers CRM software that provides "a complete view of your customers." So you'll understand their needs, enhance their lifetime value, and achieve greater competitive advantage.

When it works, the benefits of CRM can far outweigh the costs and risks. Based on regular polls of its customers, Siebel Systems claims that customers using its CRM software report an average 16 percent increase in revenues and 21 percent increase in customer loyalty and staff efficiency. "No question that companies are getting tremendous value out of this," says a CRM consultant. "Companies [are] looking for ways to bring disparate sources of customer information together, then get it to all the customer touch points." The powerful new CRM techniques can unearth "a wealth of information to target that customer, to hit their hot button."[21]

◼ Distributing and Using Marketing Information

Marketing information has no value until it is used to make better marketing decisions. Thus, the marketing information system must make the information available to the managers and others who make marketing decisions or deal with customers on a day-to-day basis. In some cases, this means providing managers with regular performance reports, intelligence updates, and reports on the results of research studies.

But marketing managers may also need nonroutine information for special situations and on-the-spot decisions. For example, a sales manager having trouble with a large customer may want a summary of the account's sales and profitability over the past year. Or a retail store manager who has run out of a best-selling product may want to know the current inventory levels in the chain's other stores. Increasingly, therefore, information distribution involves entering information into databases and making these available in a user-friendly and timely way.

Many firms use a company *intranet* to facilitate this process. The intranet provides ready access to research information, stored reports, shared work documents, contact information for employees and other stakeholders, and more. For example, iGo, a catalog and Web retailer, integrates incoming customer service calls with up-to-date database information about customers' Web purchases and e-mail inquiries. By accessing this information on the intranet while speaking with the customer, iGo's service representatives can get a well-rounded picture of each customer's purchasing history and previous contacts with the company.

In addition, companies are increasingly allowing key customers and value-network members to access account and product information and other data on demand on *extranets*. Suppliers, customers, and select other network members may access a company's extranet to update their accounts, arrange purchases, and check orders against inventories to improve customer service. For example, one insurance firm allows its 200 independent agents access to a Web-based database of claim information covering 1 million customers. This allows the agents to avoid high-risk customers and to compare claim data with their own customer databases. And Wal-Mart's Retail Link system provides suppliers with up to two years worth of data on how their products have sold in Wal-Mart stores.[22]

Thanks to modern technology, today's marketing managers can gain direct access to the information system at any time and from virtually any location. They can tap into the system while working at a home office, in a hotel room, at an airport—anyplace where they can turn on a laptop computer and link up. Such systems allow managers to get the information they need directly and quickly and to tailor it to their own needs. From just about anywhere, they can obtain information from company or outside data bases, analyze it using statistical software, prepare reports and presentations, and communicate directly with others in the network.

■ Other Marketing Information Considerations

This section discusses marketing information in two special contexts: marketing research in small businesses and nonprofit organizations, and international marketing research. Finally, we look at public policy and ethics issues in marketing research.

Marketing Research in Small Businesses and Nonprofit Organizations

Just like larger firms, small organizations need market information. Start-up businesses need information about their industries, competitors, potential customers, and reactions to new market offers. Existing small businesses must track changes in customer needs and wants, reactions to new products, and changes in the competitive environment.

Managers of small businesses and nonprofit organizations often think that marketing research can be done only by experts in large companies with big research budgets. True, large-scale research studies are beyond the budgets of most small businesses. However, many of the marketing research techniques discussed in this chapter also can be used by smaller organizations in a less formal manner and at little or no expense.

Managers of small businesses and nonprofit organizations can obtain good marketing information simply by *observing* things around them. For example, retailers can evaluate new locations by observing vehicle and pedestrian traffic. They can monitor competitor advertising by collecting ads from local media. They can evaluate their customer mix by recording how many and what kinds of customers shop in the store at different times. In addition, many small business managers routinely visit their rivals and socialize with competitors to gain insights. Tom Coohill, a chef who owns two Atlanta restaurants, gives managers a food allowance to dine out and bring back ideas. Atlanta jeweler Frank Maier Jr., who often visits out-of-town rivals, spotted and copied a dramatic way of lighting displays.[23]

Managers can conduct informal *surveys* using small convenience samples. The director of an art museum can learn what patrons think about new exhibits by conducting informal focus groups—inviting small groups to lunch and having discussions on topics of interest. Retail salespeople can talk with customers visiting the store; hospital officials can interview patients. Restaurant managers might make random phone calls during slack hours to interview consumers about where they eat out and what they think of various restaurants in the area. Bissell, a nicher in the carpet-cleaning industry, used a small convenience sample to quickly and cheaply test the market for its Steam Gun—a newly developed home-cleaning device that resembled a hand-held vacuum cleaner.

> Bissell had only four weeks and a tight budget to get a feel for how consumers would respond to the new product. Aware that women with children often purchase such products, Bissell made a $1,500 donation to a local Parent Teacher Association (PTA) for the opportunity to make a presentation. After the presentation, it gave 20 interested women the Steam Gun to take home, along with journals to record their experiences. Following a two-week trial period, Bissell's marketing research director visited the mothers in their homes to watch them use the product. This "research on a shoestring" yielded several interesting discoveries. First, Bissell learned that the women weren't sold on the cleaning ability of hot water used without chemicals. Second, it would have to change the name of the product. When roped into chores, children would arm themselves with the Steam Gun and take aim at their siblings. One child was quoted as saying, "Freeze, or I'll melt your face off!" Finally, Bissell found that the product had special appeal to those who were serious about cleaning. They used it to get into hard to reach places and blast off tough grime. Based on these findings, Bissell changed the name of the product to the Steam 'n Clean and focused on the cleaning power of super hot steam when promoting the product. The Steam 'n Clean was successfully launched through infomercials and in nationwide retail chains.[24]

Managers also can conduct their own simple *experiments*. For example, by changing the themes in regular fund-raising mailings and watching the results, a nonprofit manager can learn much about which marketing strategies work best. By varying newspaper advertisements, a store manager can learn the effects of things such as ad size and position, price coupons, and media used.

Small organizations can obtain most of the secondary data available to large businesses. In addition, many associations, local media, chambers of commerce, and government agencies provide special help to small organizations. The U.S. Small Business Administration offers dozens of free publications and a Web site (www.sbaonline.sba.gov) that give advice on topics ranging from starting, financing, and expanding a small business to ordering business cards. Other excellent Web resources for small businesses include the U.S. Census Bureau (www.census.gov) and the Bureau of Economic Analysis (www.bea.doc.gov).

The business sections at local libraries can also be a good source of information. Local newspapers often provide information on local shoppers and their buying patterns. Finally, small businesses can collect a considerable amount of information at very little cost on the Internet. They can scour competitor and customer Web sites and use Internet search engines to research specific companies and issues.

In summary, secondary data collection, observation, surveys, and experiments can all be used effectively by small organizations with small budgets. Although these informal research methods are less complex and less costly, they still must be conducted carefully. Managers must think carefully about the objectives of the research, formulate questions in advance, recognize the biases introduced by smaller samples and less skilled researchers, and conduct the research systematically.[25]

International Marketing Research

International marketing researchers follow the same steps as domestic researchers, from defining the research problem and developing a research plan to interpreting and reporting the results. However, these researchers often face more and different problems. Whereas domestic researchers deal with fairly homogeneous markets within a single country, international researchers deal with differing markets in many different countries. These markets often vary greatly in their levels of economic development, cultures and customs, and buying patterns.

■ Many associations, media, and government agencies provide special help to small organizations. Here the U.S. Small Business Administration offers a Web site that gives advice on topics ranging from starting, financing, and expanding a small business to ordering business cards.

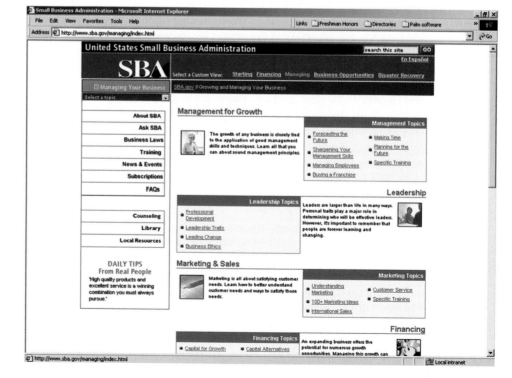

In many foreign markets, the international researcher sometimes has a difficult time finding good secondary data. Whereas U.S. marketing researchers can obtain reliable secondary data from dozens of domestic research services, many countries have almost no research services at all. Some of the largest international research services do operate in many countries. For example, AC Nielsen Corporation, the world's largest marketing research company, has offices in more than 100 countries. And 63 percent of the revenues of the world's 25 largest marketing research firms comes from outside their home countries.[26] However, most research firms operate in only a relative handful of countries. Thus, even when secondary information is available, it usually must be obtained from many different sources on a country-by-country basis, making the information difficult to combine or compare.

Because of the scarcity of good secondary data, international researchers often must collect their own primary data. Here again, researchers face problems not found domestically. For example, they may find it difficult simply to develop good samples. U.S. researchers can use current telephone directories, census tract data, and any of several sources of socioeconomic data to construct samples. However, such information is largely lacking in many countries.

Once the sample is drawn, the U.S. researcher usually can reach most respondents easily by telephone, by mail, on the Internet, or in person. Reaching respondents is often not so easy in other parts of the world. Researchers in Mexico cannot rely on telephone and mail data collection—most data collection is door to door and concentrated in three or four of the largest cities. In some countries, few people have phones; for example, there are only 32 phones per thousand people in Argentina. In other countries, the postal system is notoriously unreliable. In Brazil, for instance, an estimated 30 percent of the mail is never delivered. In many developing countries, poor roads and transportation systems make certain areas hard to reach, making personal interviews difficult and expensive. Finally, few people in developing countries are connected to the Internet.[27]

If knowledge is power, then knowledge applied is power realized. Roper Starch Worldwide provides you with the intelligence you need to move your global business plan forward—critical analysis for today's international marketplace. We identify opportunities, giving you the ability to anticipate change; and the power to conquer the world. From Brazil to Eastern Europe; from Cape Town to Beijing; if you are there, Roper Starch Worldwide is there.

As the company that pioneered international market research over 50 years ago, we have the knowledge and the expertise that comes from continually proving our leadership. You can profit from unparalleled resources, such as the *Roper Reports Worldwide* global consumer database

service, featuring proprietary segmentations based on personal values, lifestage, and nationality—the three drivers of consumer behavior worldwide. Powerful brand management tools, such as Roper Starch's *Brand Architect* program, help you align your brand's values with those of your target market. Or choose from an array of sophisticated custom research approaches, where valuable insight leads to action that impacts your bottom line.

Roper Starch Worldwide,
strategic intelligence in the battle
for global market share.

Contact us for more information or to schedule an appointment with one of our representatives.
globalstrategy@roper.com   www.roper.com

■ Some of the largest research services operate in many countries: Roper ASW, Inc. provides companies with information resources "from Brazil to Eastern Europe; from Cape Town to Beijing—if you are there, Roper is there."

Cultural differences from country to country cause additional problems for international researchers. Language is the most obvious obstacle. For example, questionnaires must be prepared in one language and then translated into the languages of each country researched. Responses then must be translated back into the original language for analysis and interpretation. This adds to research costs and increases the risk of errors.

Translating a questionnaire from one language to another is anything but easy. Many idioms, phrases, and statements mean different things in different cultures. For example, a Danish executive noted, "Check this out by having a different translator put back into English what you've translated from English. You'll get the shock of your life. I remember [an example in which] 'out of sight, out of mind' had become 'invisible things are insane'."[28]

Consumers in different countries also vary in their attitudes toward marketing research. People in one country may be very willing to respond; in other countries, nonresponse can be a major problem. Customs in some countries may prohibit people from talking with strangers. In certain cultures, research questions often are considered too personal. For example, in many Latin American countries, people may feel embarrassed to talk with researchers about their choices of shampoo, deodorant, or other personal care products. Similarly, in most Muslim countries, mixed-gender focus groups are taboo, as is videotaping female-only focus groups.[29]

Even when respondents are *willing* to respond, they may not be *able* to because of high functional illiteracy rates. And middle-class people in developing countries often make false claims in order to appear well off. For example, in a study of tea consumption in India, over 70 percent of middle-income respondents claimed that they used one of several national brands. However, the researchers had good reason to doubt these results—more than 60 percent of the tea sold in India is unbranded generic tea.

Despite these problems, the recent growth of international marketing has resulted in a rapid increase in the use of international marketing research. Global companies have little choice but to conduct such research. Although the costs and problems associated with international research may be high, the costs of not doing it—in terms of missed opportunities and mistakes—might be even higher. Once recognized, many of the problems associated with international marketing research can be overcome or avoided.

Public Policy and Ethics in Marketing Research

Most marketing research benefits both the sponsoring company and its consumers. Through marketing research, companies learn more about consumers' needs, resulting in more satisfying products and services and stronger customer relationships. However, the misuse of marketing research can also harm or annoy consumers. Two major public policy and ethics issues in marketing research are intrusions on consumer privacy and the misuse of research findings.

Intrusions on Consumer Privacy Many consumers feel positively about marketing research and believe that it serves a useful purpose. Some actually enjoy being interviewed and giving their opinions. However, others strongly resent or even mistrust marketing research. A few consumers fear that researchers might use sophisticated techniques to probe our deepest feelings and then use this knowledge to manipulate our buying. Or they worry that marketers are building huge databases full of personal information about customers.

For example, DoubleClick has profiles on 100 million Web users. Privacy groups have worried that such huge profiling databases could be merged with offline databases and threaten individual privacy. In fact, DoubleClick did integrate its online data with that collected by a consumer panel firm to construct frighteningly accurate consumer profiles. It stirred up much controversy when it announced that it would sell about 100,000 of these Web-user profiles to businesses, complete with names and contact information. However, in response to a Federal Trade Commission investigation and to settle federal and state class-action suits, DoubleClick recently adopted sweeping privacy standards.[30]

Others consumers may have been taken in by previous "research surveys" that actually turned out to be attempts to sell them something. Still other consumers confuse legitimate marketing research studies with telemarketing efforts and say "no" before the interviewer can even begin. Most, however, simply resent the intrusion. They dislike mail or telephone surveys that are too long or too personal or that interrupt them at inconvenient times.

Increasing consumer resentment has become a major problem for the research industry. One recent poll found that 82 percent of Americans worry that they lack control over how businesses use their personal information, and 41 percent said that businesses had invaded their privacy. These concerns have led to lower survey response rates in recent years. One study found that 45 percent of Americans had refused to participate in a survey over the past year, up from 24 percent 15 years ago. Another study found that 59 percent of consumers had refused to give information to a company because they thought it was not really needed or too personal, up from 42 percent five years earlier.[31]

The research industry is considering several options for responding to this problem. One example is the Council for Marketing and Opinion Research's "Your Opinion Counts" program to educate consumers about the benefits of marketing research and to distinguish it from telephone selling and database building. Another is the industry's effort to provide a toll-free number that people can call to verify that a survey is legitimate. The industry also has considered adopting broad standards, perhaps based on The International Chamber of Commerce's International Code of Marketing and Social Research Practice. This code outlines researchers' responsibilities to respondents and to the general public.

For example, it says that researchers should make their names and addresses available to participants, and it bans companies from representing activities such as database compilation or sales and promotional pitches as research.[32]

Many companies—including IBM, AT&T, American Express, DoubleClick, and Microsoft—are now appointing a "chief privacy officer (CPO)," whose job is to safeguard the privacy of consumers who do business with the company. The chief privacy officer for Microsoft says that his job is to come up with data policies for the company to follow, make certain that every program the company creates enhances customer privacy, and inform and educate company employees about privacy issues and concerns. At least 100 U.S. companies now employ such privacy chiefs and the number is expected to grow rapidly. In fact, one expert estimates that laws requiring companies to protect consumer privacy will create 30,000 CPO jobs by 2006.[33]

According to Sally Cowan, who runs the privacy operations of American Express, any business that deals with consumers' information has to take privacy issues seriously. "Privacy is not the new hot issue at American Express," she says. The company developed a set of formal privacy principles in 1991, and in 1998 it became one of the first companies to post privacy policies on its Web site. This penchant for customer privacy led American Express to introduce new services that protect consumers' privacy when they use an American Express card to buy items online. American Express views privacy as way to gain competitive advantage—as something that leads consumers to choose one company over another.[34]

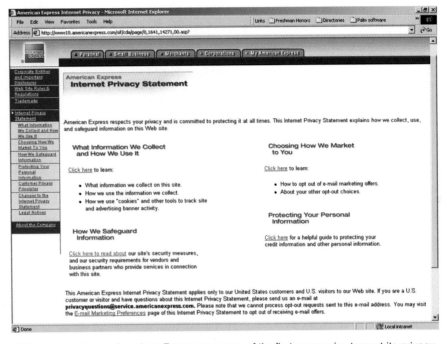

■ Consumer privacy: American Express was one of the first companies to post its privacy policies on the Web. "American Express respects your privacy and is committed to protecting it at all times."

In the end, if researchers provide value in exchange for information, customers will gladly provide it. For example, Amazon.com's customers do not mind if the firm builds a database of products they buy in order to provide future product recommendations. This saves time and provides value. Similarly, Bizrate users gladly complete surveys rating e-tail sites because they can view the overall ratings of others when making purchase decisions. The best approach is for researchers to ask only for the information they need, to use it responsibly to provide value, and to avoid sharing information without the customer's permission.

Misuse of Research Findings   Research studies can be powerful persuasion tools; companies often use study results as claims in their advertising and promotion. Today, however, many research studies appear to be little more than vehicles for pitching the sponsor's products. In fact, in some cases, the research surveys appear to have been designed just to produce the intended effect. Few advertisers openly rig their research designs or blatantly misrepresent the findings; most abuses tend to be subtle "stretches." Consider the following examples:[35]

A study by Chrysler contends that Americans overwhelmingly prefer Chrysler to Toyota after test-driving both. However, the study included just 100 people in each of two tests. More importantly, none of the people surveyed owned a foreign car, so they appear to be favorably predisposed to U.S. cars.

A Black Flag survey asked: "A roach disk . . . poisons a roach slowly. The dying roach returns to the nest and after it dies is eaten by other roaches. In turn these roaches become poisoned and die. How effective do you think this type of product would be in killing roaches?" Not surprisingly, 79 percent said effective.

A poll sponsored by the disposable diaper industry asked: "It is estimated that disposable diapers account for less than 2 percent of the trash in today's landfills. In contrast, beverage containers, third-class mail, and yard waste are estimated to account for about 21 percent of the trash in landfills. Given this, in your opinion, would it be fair to ban disposable diapers?" Again, not surprisingly, 84 percent said no.

Thus, subtle manipulations of the study's sample or the choice or wording of questions can greatly affect the conclusions reached.

In others cases, so-called independent research studies are actually paid for by companies with an interest in the outcome. Small changes in study assumptions or in how results are interpreted can subtly affect the direction of the results. For example, at least four widely quoted studies compare the environmental effects of using disposable diapers to those of using cloth diapers. The two studies sponsored by the cloth diaper industry conclude that cloth diapers are more environmentally friendly. Not surprisingly, the other two studies, sponsored by the paper diaper industry, conclude just the opposite. Yet both appear to be correct *given* the underlying assumptions used.

Recognizing that surveys can be abused, several associations—including the American Marketing Association, the Council of American Survey Research Organizations, and the Marketing Research Association—have developed codes of research ethics and standards of conduct. In the end, however, unethical or inappropriate actions cannot simply be regulated away. Each company must accept responsibility for policing the conduct and reporting of its own marketing research to protect consumers' best interests and its own.

REST STOP:
Reviewing the Concepts

In the previous chapter, we discussed the marketing environment. In this chapter, we've continued our exploration of how marketers go about understanding the marketplace and consumers. We've studied tools used to gather and manage information that marketing managers and others can use to assess opportunities in the marketplace and the impact of a firm's marketing efforts. After this brief pause for rest and reflection, we'll head out again in the next chapter to take a closer look at the object of all of this activity—consumers and their buying behavior.

In today's complex and rapidly changing marketplace, marketing managers need more and better information to make effective and timely decisions. This greater need for information has been matched by the explosion of information technologies for supplying information. Using today's new technologies, companies can now handle great quantities of information, sometimes even too much. Yet marketers often complain that they lack enough of the *right* kind of information or have an excess of the *wrong* kind. In response, many companies are now studying their managers' information needs and designing information systems to help managers develop and manage market and customer information.

1. Explain the importance of information to the company and its understanding of the marketplace.

The marketing process starts with a complete understanding of the marketplace and consumer needs and wants. Thus, the company needs sound information in order to produce superior value and satisfaction for customers. The company also requires information on competitors, resellers, and other actors and forces in the marketplace. Increasingly, marketers are viewing information not only as an input for making better decisions but also as an important strategic asset and marketing tool.

2. Define the marketing information system and discuss its parts.

The *marketing information system (MIS)* consists of people, equipment, and procedures to gather, sort, analyze, evaluate, and distribute needed, timely, and accurate information to marketing decision makers. A well-designed information system begins and ends with users. The MIS first *assesses information needs*. The marketing information system primarily serves the company's marketing and other managers. However, it may also provide information to external partners, such as suppliers or marketing services agencies. Then, the MIS *develops information* from internal databases, marketing intelligence activities, and marketing research. *Internal databases* provide information on the company's own sales, costs, inventories, cash flows, and accounts receivable and payable. Such data can be obtained quickly and cheaply but often needs to be adapted for marketing decisions. *Marketing intelligence* activities supply everyday information about developments in the external marketing environment. *Market research* consists of collecting information relevant to a specific marketing problem faced by the company. Lastly, the MIS *distributes information* gathered from these sources to the right managers in the right form and at the right time to help them make better marketing decisions.

3. Outline the steps in the marketing research process.

The first step in the marketing research process involves *defining the problem and setting the research objectives,* which may be exploratory, descriptive, or causal research. The second step consists of *developing a research plan* for collecting data from primary and secondary sources. The third step calls for *implementing the marketing research plan* by gathering, processing, and analyzing the information. The fourth step consists of *interpreting and reporting the findings.* Additional information analysis helps marketing managers apply the information and provides them with sophisticated statistical procedures and models from which to develop more rigorous findings.

Both *internal* and *external* secondary data sources often provide information more quickly and at a lower cost than primary data sources, and they can sometimes yield information that a company cannot collect by itself. However, needed information might not exist in secondary sources, and even if data can be found, they might be largely unusable. Researchers must also evaluate secondary information to ensure that it is *relevant, accurate, current,* and *impartial.* Primary research must also be evaluated for these features. Each primary data collection method—*observational, survey,* and *experimental*—has its own advantages and disadvantages.

Each of the various primary research contact methods—mail, telephone, personal interview, and online—also has its own advantages and drawbacks. Similarly, each contact method has its pluses and minuses.

4. Explain how companies analyze and distribute marketing information.

Information gathered in internal databases and through marketing intelligence and marketing research usually requires more analysis. This may include advanced statistical analysis or the application of analytical models that will help marketers make better decisions. In recent years, marketers have paid special attention to the analysis of individual customer data. Many companies have now acquired or developed special software and analysis techniques—called *customer relationship management (CRM)*—that integrate, analyze, and apply the mountains of individual customer data contained in their databases.

Marketing information has no value until it is used to make better marketing decisions. Thus, the marketing information system must make the information available to the managers and others who make marketing decisions or deal with customers. In some cases, this means providing regular reports and updates; in other cases it means making nonroutine information available for special situations and on-the-spot decisions. Many firms use company intranets and extranets to facilitate this process. Thanks to modern technology, today's marketing managers can gain direct access to the information system at any time and from virtually any location.

5. Discuss the special issues some marketing researchers face, including public policy and ethics issues.

Some marketers face special marketing research situations, such as those conducting research in small business, nonprofit, or international situations. Marketing research can be conducted effectively by small businesses and nonprofit organizations with limited budgets. International marketing researchers follow the same steps as domestic researchers but often face more and different problems. All organizations need to respond responsibly to major public policy and ethical issues surrounding marketing research, including issues of intrusions on consumer privacy and misuse of research findings.

Navigating the Key Terms

Causal research
Customer relationship
  management (CRM)
Descriptive research
Experimental research
Exploratory research
Focus group interviewing

Internal databases
Marketing information system
  (MIS)
Marketing intelligence
Marketing research
Observational research
Online databases

Online (Internet) marketing
  research
Primary data
Sample
Secondary data
Single-source data systems
Survey research

Travel Log

Discussing the Issues

1. Distinguish between internal databases, marketing intelligence, and marketing research as methods for developing marketing information. How does each of these three sources assist an organization differently in meeting its information needs?

2. Taking the role of a brand manager for Hawaiian Tropic suntan lotion, create an exploratory research objective, a descriptive research objective, and a causal research objective. How does the nature of each research objective guide data collection?

3. Small businesses face budget constraints that can limit the type and scope of research conducted. In a small group, brainstorm what a small furniture retailer might be able to do to gain competitor and consumer information on a limited budget.

4. Discuss some of the unique challenges U.S. researchers may encounter in conducting research in other countries. How might these obstacles be overcome?

5. What advantages do secondary data have over primary data? What advantages do primary data have over secondary data? Why is secondary data typically the starting point for marketing researchers?

6. How might observational research be used to understand a consumer's decision process in selecting greeting cards? What other information that is not observable might you want to know about the consumer's greeting card choices and how would you get it?

Application Questions

1. It has been reported that more than 7 million people have discontinued their regular home phone lines in favor of using cell phones at home to place and receive calls. Assume you work for one of the land-based telephone companies that is losing customers to cell phones. Describe both an experiment and a survey that would aid your company in understanding how to reverse this trend. Which approach makes the most sense for this research question?

2. You and three other students work for United Airlines and serve on a committee making decisions about an upcoming customer satisfaction questionnaire. Each team member is to be an advocate for one of the following contact methods: mail, telephone, personal, and online. Debate the pros and cons of the different contact methods and then have the group vote for using one of the four methods.

3. Browse through the list of external information sources provided in Table 4.1. Pick one Web site to visit from the business data section, government data section, and Internet data section of Table 4.1. What types of data can be found that would be useful to a Toyota car dealer interested in finding a location for a new dealership?

Under the Hood: Focus on Technology

SAP is the leading enterprise software company, claiming the majority of Fortune 500 companies among its clients. Its products are used to manage sales and distribution, production, inventory, and accounting, among other things. One of its products is a customer relationship management module that is designed to help companies manage the vast amounts of data associated with individual customers. Visit the SAP Web site (www.sap.com) and read about the customer relationship management tools under the "solutions" link.

1. Based on information available at the SAP Web site, describe some of the capabilities of CRM.

2. If you were creating a customer database to use individual customer data for CRM in a hotel chain, what types of information would you capture about the customer?

3. How would you collect information about the hotel customer and how could a marketing manager use it to improve the relationship with that customer?

Focus on Ethics

Survey research, either by phone or on the Internet, has become more difficult because even legitimate survey efforts are often viewed by suspicious consumers, who have been burned once too often, as thinly veiled sales calls. Furthermore, consumers are concerned with privacy and do not want their personal information misused. In addition, given the volume of unsolicited e-mail (SPAM) received (some estimates suggest that SPAM will account for over half of all e-mail in the near future), many people don't have time to try to separate legitimate research

requests from unsolicited product advertisements, and end up deleting them all.

1. What ways might legitimate survey researchers overcome growing public resistance to online surveys and telephone surveys?

2. How have you responded in the past when asked to participate in a survey on the phone or Internet? Did you participate? Why or why not?

3. What methods might a company conducting an online survey use to distinguish its e-mail from SPAM?

Videos

The Burke, Inc. video case that accompanies this chapter is located in Appendix 1 at the back of the book.

Student Materials

Need a tune-up? A study guide and OneKey access code are available to aid in your review of chapter material. Your instructor may choose to have these items shrink-wrapped with your text or you may purchase them separately at www.prenhall. com/marketing.

■ *After studying this chapter, you should be able to*

1. Understand the consumer market and the major factors that influence consumer buyer behavior   *2. Identify* and discuss the stages in the buyer decision process   *3. Describe* the adoption and diffusion process for new products   *4. Define* the business market and identify the major factors that influence business buyer behavior   *5. List* and define the steps in the business buying decision process

Consumer and Business Buyer Behavior

5

In the previous chapter, you studied how marketers obtain, analyze, and use information to understand the marketplace and to assess marketing programs. In this chapter, you'll continue your marketing journey with a closer look at the most important element of the marketplace—customers. The aim of marketing is to affect how customers think about and behave toward the organization and its marketing offers. To affect the whats, whens, and hows of buying behavior, marketers must first understand the *whys*. We look first at *final consumer* buying influences and processes and then at the buying behavior of *business customers*. You'll see that understanding buying behavior is an essential but very difficult task.

Our first point of interest: Harley-Davidson, maker of the nation's top-selling heavyweight motorcycles. Who rides these big Harley "Hogs"? What moves them to tattoo their bodies with the Harley emblem, abandon home and hearth for the open road, and flock to Harley rallies by the hundreds of thousands? *You* might be surprised, but Harley-Davidson knows *very* well.

---

ew brands engender such intense loyalty as that found in the hearts of Harley-Davidson owners. Harley buyers are granitelike in their devotion to the brand. Observes the publisher of *American Iron*, an industry publication, "You don't see people tattooing Yamaha on their bodies." And according to the president of a motorcycle research company, "For a lot of people, it's not that they want a motorcycle; it's that they want a Harley—the brand is that strong."

Each year, in early March, more than 400,000 Harley bikers rumble through the streets of Daytona Beach, Florida, to attend Harley-Davidson's Bike Week celebration. Bikers from across the nation lounge on their low-slung Harleys, swap biker tales, and sport T-shirts proclaiming "I'd rather push a Harley than drive a Honda."

Riding such intense emotions, Harley-Davidson has rumbled its way to the top of the fast-growing heavyweight motorcycle market. Harley's "Hogs" capture more than one-fifth of all U.S. bike sales and more than half of the heavyweight segment. Both the segment and Harley's sales are growing rapidly. In fact, for several years running, sales have far outstripped supply, with customer waiting lists of up to two years for popular models and street prices running well above suggested list prices. "We've seen people buy a new Harley and then sell it in the parking

lot for $4,000 to $5,000 more," says one dealer. During just the past 5 years, Harley sales have quadrupled, and earnings have increased sixfold. By 2003, the company had experienced 17 straight years of record sales and income.

Harley-Davidson's marketers spend a great deal of time thinking about customers and their buying behavior. They want to know who their customers are, what they think and how they feel, and why they buy a Harley rather than a Yamaha or a Kawasaki or a big Honda American Classic. What is it that makes Harley buyers so fiercely loyal? These are difficult questions; even Harley owners themselves don't know exactly what motivates their buying. But Harley management puts top priority on understanding customers and what makes them tick.

Who rides a Harley? You might be surprised. It's no longer the Hell's Angels crowd—the burly, black-leather-jacketed rebels and biker chicks who once made up Harley's core clientele. Motorcycles are attracting a new breed of riders—older, more affluent, and better educated. Harley now appeals more to "rubbies" (rich urban bikers) than to rebels. The average Harley customer is a 46-year-old husband with a median household income of $78,300. "In case you haven't noticed," notes one observer, "the young motorcycle tough of American mythology has matured a bit. Less Easy Rider and more easy-fit Dockers."

Harley-Davidson makes good bikes, and to keep up with its shifting market, the company has upgraded its showrooms and sales approaches. But Harley customers are buying a lot more than just a quality bike and a smooth sales pitch. To gain a better understanding of customers' deeper motivations, Harley-Davidson conducted focus groups in which it invited bikers to make cut-and-paste collages of pictures that expressed their feelings about Harley-Davidsons. (Can't you just see a bunch of hard-core bikers doing this?) It then mailed out 16,000 surveys containing a typical battery of psychological, sociological, and demographic questions as well as subjective questions such as "Is Harley more typified by a brown bear or a lion?"

The research revealed seven core customer types: adventure-loving traditionalists, sensitive pragmatists, stylish status seekers, laid-back campers, classy capitalists, cool-headed loners, and cocky misfits. However, all owners appreciated their Harleys for the same basic reasons. "It didn't matter if you were the guy who swept the floors of the factory or if you were the CEO at that factory, the attraction to Harley was very similar," says a Harley executive. "Independence, freedom, and power were the universal Harley appeals."

These studies confirm that Harley customers are doing more than just buying motorcycles. "It's much more than a machine," says one analyst. "It is part of their own self expression and lifestyle." Another analyst suggests that owning a Harley makes you "the toughest, baddest guy on the block. Never mind that [you're] a dentist or an accountant. You [feel] wicked astride all that power." Your Harley renews your spirits and announces your independence. As the Harley Web site's home page announces, "Thumbing the starter of a Harley-Davidson does a lot more than fire the engine. It fires the imagination." Adds a Harley dealer: "We sell a dream here."

The classic look, the throaty sound, the very idea of a Harley—all contribute to its mystique. Owning this "American legend" makes you a part of something bigger, a member of the Harley family. The fact that you have to wait to get a Harley makes it all that much more satisfying to have one. In fact, the company deliberately restricts its output. "Our goal is to eventually run production at a level that's always one motorcycle short of demand," says Harley-Davidson's chief executive.

Such strong emotions and motivations are captured in a classic Harley-Davidson advertisement. The ad shows a close-up of an arm, the bicep adorned with a Harley-Davidson tattoo. The headline asks, "When was the last time you felt this strongly about anything?" The ad copy outlines the problem and suggests a solution: "Wake up in the morning and life picks up where it left off. You do what has to be done. Use what it takes to get there. And what once seemed exciting has now become part of the numbing routine. It all begins to feel the same. Except when you've got a Harley-Davidson. Something strikes a nerve. The heartfelt thunder rises up, refusing to become part of the background. Suddenly things are different. Clearer. More real. As they should have been all along. The feeling is personal. For some, owning a Harley is a statement of individuality. For others, owning a Harley means being a part of a homegrown legacy that was born in a tiny Milwaukee shed in 1903. . . . To the uninitiated, a Harley-Davidson motorcycle is associated with a certain look, a certain sound. Anyone who owns one will tell you it's much more than that. Riding a Harley changes you from within. The effect is permanent. Maybe it's time you started feeling this strongly. Things are different on a Harley."[1]

The Harley-Davidson example shows that many different factors affect consumer buying behavior. Buying behavior is never simple, yet understanding it is the essential task of marketing management. First we explore the dynamics of the consumer market and final-consumer buyer behavior. We then examine business markets and the business buying process.

■■ Consumer Markets and Consumer Buyer Behavior

Consumer buyer behavior refers to the buying behavior of final consumers—individuals and households who buy goods and services for personal consumption. All of these final consumers combine to make up the **consumer market**. The American consumer market consists of more than 290 million people who consume many trillions of dollars' worth of goods and services each year, making it one of the most attractive consumer markets in the world. The world consumer market consists of almost 6.3 *billion* people.[2]

Consumers around the world vary tremendously in age, income, education level, and tastes. They also buy an incredible variety of goods and services. How these diverse consumers connect with each other and with other elements of the world around them impacts their choices among various products, services, and companies. Here we examine the fascinating array of factors that affect consumer behavior.

Consumer buyer behavior
The buying behavior of final consumers—individuals and households who buy goods and services for personal consumption.

Consumer market
All the individuals and households who buy or acquire goods and services for personal consumption.

Model of Consumer Behavior

Consumers make many buying decisions every day. Most large companies research consumer buying decisions in great detail to answer questions about what consumers buy, where they buy, and how much they buy, when they buy, and why they buy. Marketers can study actual consumer purchases to find out what they buy, where, and how much. But learning about the *whys* of consumer buying behavior is not so easy—the answers are often locked deep within the consumer's head.

Penetrating the dark recesses of the consumer's mind is no easy task. Often, consumers themselves don't know exactly what influences their purchases. "Ninety-five percent of the thought, emotion, and learning [that drive our purchases] occur in the unconscious mind—that is, without our awareness," notes one consumer behavior expert.[3]

The central question for marketers is: How do consumers respond to various marketing efforts the company might use? The starting point is the stimulus–response model of buyer behavior shown in Figure 5.1. This figure shows that marketing and other stimuli enter the consumer's "black box" and produce certain responses. Marketers must figure out what is in the buyer's black box.

Marketing stimuli consist of the four *P*s: product, price, place, and promotion. Other stimuli include major forces and events in the buyer's environment: economic, technological, political, and cultural. All these inputs enter the buyer's black box, where they are turned into a set of observable buyer responses: product choice, brand choice, dealer choice, purchase timing, and purchase amount.

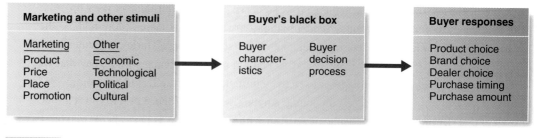

FIGURE 5.1

Model of Buyer Behavior

The marketer wants to understand how the stimuli are changed into responses inside the consumer's black box, which has two parts. First, the buyer's characteristics influence how he or she perceives and reacts to the stimuli. Second, the buyer's decision process itself affects the buyer's behavior. We look first at buyer characteristics as they affect buying behavior and then discuss the buyer decision process.

Characteristics Affecting Consumer Behavior

Consumer purchases are influenced strongly by cultural, social, personal, and psychological characteristics, as shown in Figure 5.2. For the most part, marketers cannot control such factors, but they must take them into account. We illustrate these characteristics for the case of a hypothetical consumer named Anna Flores. Anna is a married college graduate who works as a brand manager in a leading consumer packaged-goods company. She wants to find a new leisure-time activity that will provide some contrast to her working day. This need has led her to consider buying a camera and taking up photography. Many characteristics in her background will affect the way she evaluates cameras and chooses a brand.

Cultural Factors   Cultural factors exert a broad and deep influence on consumer behavior. The marketer needs to understand the role played by the buyer's *culture*, *subculture*, and *social class*.

Culture

The set of basic values, perceptions, wants, and behaviors learned by a member of society from family and other important institutions.

Culture. **Culture** is the most basic cause of a person's wants and behavior. Human behavior is largely learned. Growing up in a society, a child learns basic values, perceptions, wants, and behaviors from the family and other important institutions. A child in the United States normally learns or is exposed to the following values: achievement and success, activity and involvement, efficiency and practicality, progress, material comfort, individualism, freedom, humanitarianism, youthfulness, and fitness and health. Every group or society has a culture, and cultural influences on buying behavior may vary greatly from country to country. Failure to adjust to these differences can result in ineffective marketing or embarrassing mistakes.

FIGURE 5.2

Factors Influencing Consumer Behavior

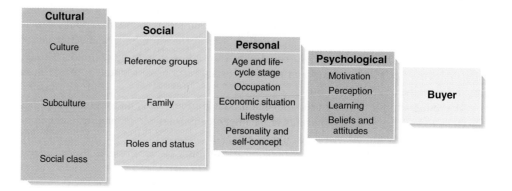

Anna Flores's cultural background will affect her camera buying decision. Anna's desire to own a camera may result from her being raised in a modern society that has developed camera technology and a whole set of consumer learnings and values.

Marketers are always trying to spot *cultural shifts* in order to discover new products that might be wanted. For example, the cultural shift toward greater concern about health and fitness has created a huge industry for health and fitness services, exercise equipment and clothing, and lower-fat and more-natural foods. The shift toward informality has resulted in more demand for casual clothing and simpler home furnishings.

Subculture. Each culture contains smaller **subcultures**, or groups of people with shared value systems based on common life experiences and situations. Subcultures include nationalities, religions, racial groups, and geographic regions. Many subcultures make up important market segments, and marketers often design products and marketing programs tailored to their needs. Examples of four such important subculture groups include Hispanic, African American, Asian, and mature consumers.

Subculture

A group of people with shared value systems based on common life experiences and situations.

The U.S. *Hispanic market*—Americans of Cuban, Mexican, Central American, South American, and Puerto Rican descent—consists of almost 35 million consumers. Last year, Hispanic consumers bought more than $425 billion worth of goods and services, up 25 percent from just two years earlier. Expected to almost double in the next 20 years, this group will make up more than 19 percent of the total U.S. population by 2025.[4]

Hispanic consumers tend to buy more branded, higher-quality products—generics don't sell well to this group. And they tend to make shopping a family affair, and children have a big say in what brands they buy. Perhaps more important, Hispanics are brand loyal, and they favor companies who show special interest in them.[5]

Most marketers now produce products tailored to the Hispanic market and promote them using Spanish-language ads and media. For example, General Mills offers a line of Para su Familia (for your family) cereals for Hispanics, and Mattel has opened a Spanish-language site for its Barbie dolls—BarbieLatina.com—targeting U.S. Hispanic girls. Blockbuster recently set aside space in nearly 1,000 of its stores for videos dubbed in Spanish. Kmart launched an apparel line named after Mexican pop star Thalia.

Sears makes a special effort to market to Hispanic American consumers, especially for the 20 percent of its stores that are located in heavily Hispanic neighborhoods:

> Sears is widely considered one of the most successful marketers to the U.S. Hispanic population. Last year, it spent some $25 million on advertising to Hispanics—more than any other retailer. Sears neighborhoods receive regular visits from a Fiesta Mobile, a colorful Winnebago that plays music, gives out prizes, and promotes the Sears credit card. Sears also sponsors major Hispanic cultural festivals and concerts. The retailer's Spanish-language Web site—Sears En Espanol (Sears in Spanish)—features content and events carefully tailored to Hispanic consumers. One of Sears's most successful marketing efforts is its magazine *Nuestra Gente*—which means Our People—the nation's largest Spanish-language magazine. The magazine features articles about Hispanic celebrities alongside glossy spreads of Sears fashions. As a result of this careful cultivation of Hispanic consumers, although Sears has lost sales in recent years to discount retailers, the Hispanic segment has remained steadfastly loyal.[6]

■ Sears is widely considered one of the most successful marketers to the U.S. Hispanic population. Its Spanish-language Web site features content and events carefully tailored to Hispanic consumers.

If the U.S. population of 35 million *African Americans* were a separate nation, its buying power of $646 billion annually would rank among the top 15 in the world. The black population in the United States is growing in affluence and sophistication. Although more price conscious than other segments, blacks are also strongly motivated by quality and selection. Brands are important. So is shopping—black consumers seem to enjoy shopping more than other groups, even for something as mundane as groceries. Black consumers are also the most fashion-conscious of the ethnic groups.[7]

In recent years, many companies have developed special products and services, packaging, and appeals to meet the needs of African Americans. For example, Hallmark launched its Afrocentric brand, Mahogany, with only 16 cards in 1987. Today the brand features more than 900 cards designed to celebrate African American culture, heritage, and traditions.

A wide variety of magazines, television channels, and other media now target African American consumers. Marketers are also reaching out to the African American virtual community. Per capita, black consumers spend twice as much as white consumers for online services. African Americans are increasingly turning to Web sites such as BlackPlanet.com, an African American community site with 5.8 million registered users. BlackPlanet.com's mission is to enable members to "cultivate meaningful personal and professional relationships, stay informed about the world, and gain access to goods and services that allow members to do more in life." Other popular sites include Afronet and Black Voices.[8]

Asian Americans, the fastest-growing and most affluent U.S. demographic segment, now number more than 12 million, with disposable income of $296 billion annually. Chinese Americans constitute the largest group, followed by Filipinos, Japanese Americans, Asian Indians, and Korean Americans. The U.S. Asian American population is estimated to reach 24 million by 2025. Asian consumers may be the most tech-savvy segment—more than a third made an Internet purchase last year. As a group, Asian consumers shop frequently and are the most brand-conscious of all the ethnic groups. Interestingly, they are also the least brand loyal—they change brands more often compared with the other groups.[9]

Because of the segment's rapidly growing buying power, many firms now target the Asian American market. For example, consider Wal-Mart. Today, in one Seattle store, where the Asian American population represents over 13 percent of the population, Wal-Mart stocks a large selection of CDs and videos from Asian artists, Asian-favored health and beauty products, and children's learning videos that feature multiple language tracks. Financial services provider Charles Schwab goes all out to court the large and particularly lucrative Chinese American market:

Schwab estimates that there are over 3 million in the U.S. Asian community, half of whom are foreign-born and learned English as a second language. To cater to this audience, Schwab's Asia Pacific Services (APS) division has opened 14 Chinese American offices in hub locations such as New York's Chinatown and LA's Koreatown (many of which are open on Saturdays, when Asians tend to handle money matters). In addition, APS employs more than 200 people who speak Chinese, Korean, or Vietnamese at call centers serving Asian customers who prefer to speak their own languages. Schwab's Chinese-language Web site racks up millions of hits per month, including visits to an online Chinese-language news service, where customers can check real-time market activity, news headlines, and earnings estimates on their U.S. investments. Schwab's marketing to this segment focuses on educating clients on how to invest sensibly, whether they are short-term investors who trade frequently or long-term investors who are seeking investment or portfolio management advice. As a result, Schwab's APS' clients tend to be very loyal.[10]

As the U.S. population ages, *mature consumers* are becoming a very attractive market. Now 75 million strong, the population of U.S. seniors will more than double during in the next 25 years. The 65-and-over crowd alone numbers 35 million, more than 12 percent of the population. Mature consumers are better off financially than are younger consumer groups.[11] Because mature consumers have more time and money, they are an ideal market for exotic travel, restaurants, high-tech home entertainment products, leisure goods and services, designer furniture and fashions, financial services, and health care services.

Their desire to look as young as they feel also makes more-mature consumers good candidates for cosmetics and personal care products, health foods, fitness products, and

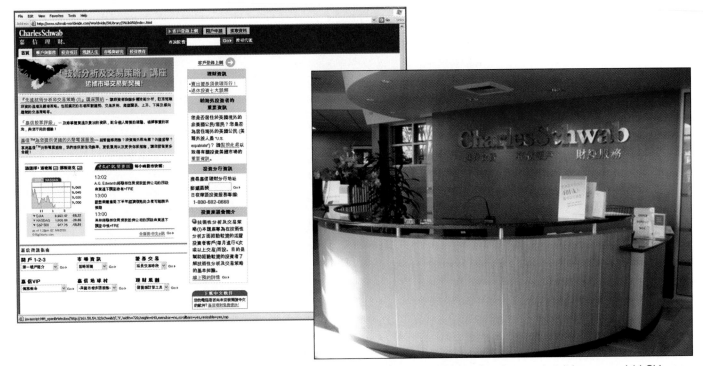

■ Financial services provider Charles Schwab goes all out to court the large and lucrative Chinese American market. It has opened 14 Chinese-language offices and its Chinese-language Web site racks up more than 5 million hits per month.

other items that combat the effects of aging. The best strategy is to appeal to their active, multidimensional lives. For example, Kellogg aired a TV spot for All-Bran cereal in which individuals ranging in age from 53 to 81 are featured playing ice hockey, water skiing, running hurdles, and playing baseball, all to the tune of "Wild Thing." A recent Pepsi ad features a young man in the middle of a mosh pit at a rock concert who turns around to see his father rocking out nearby. And an Aetna commercial portrays a senior who, after retiring from a career as a lawyer, fulfills a lifelong dream of becoming an archeologist.[12]

Anna Flores's buying behavior will be influenced by her subculture identification. These factors will affect her food preferences, clothing choices, recreation activities, and career goals. Subcultures attach different meanings to picture taking, and this could affect both Anna's interest in cameras and the brand she buys.

Social Class. Almost every society has some form of social class structure. **Social classes** are society's relatively permanent and ordered divisions whose members share similar values, interests, and behaviors. Social scientists have identified the seven American social classes shown in Figure 5.3.

Social class is not determined by a single factor, such as income, but is measured as a combination of occupation, income, education, wealth, and other variables. In some social systems, members of different classes are reared for certain roles and cannot change their social positions. In the United States, however, the lines between social classes are not fixed and rigid; people can move to a higher social class or drop into a lower one. Marketers are interested in social class because people within a given social class tend to exhibit similar buying behavior.[13]

Social classes show distinct product and brand preferences in areas such as clothing, home furnishings, leisure activity, and automobiles. Anna Flores's social class may affect her camera decision. If she comes from a higher social class background, her family probably owned an expensive camera and she may have dabbled in photography.

Social Factors A consumer's behavior also is influenced by social factors, such as the consumer's *small groups, family,* and *social roles* and *status.*

Social class

Relatively permanent and ordered divisions in a society whose members share similar values, interests, and behaviors.

FIGURE 5.3

The Major American Social Classes

Upper Class

Upper Uppers (1 percent) The social elite who live on inherited wealth. They give large sums to charity, own more than one home, and send their children to the finest schools.

Lower Uppers (2 percent) Americans who have earned high income or wealth through exceptional ability. They are active in social and civic affairs and buy expensive homes, educations, and cars.

Middle Class

Upper Middles (12 percent) Professionals, independent businesspersons, and corporate managers who possess neither family status nor unusual wealth. They believe in education, are joiners and highly civic minded, and want the "better things in life."

Middle Class (32 percent) Average-pay white- and blue-collar workers who live on "the better side of town." They buy popular products to keep up with trends. Better living means owning a nice home in a nice neighborhood with good schools.

Working Class

Working Class (38 percent) Those who lead a "working-class lifestyle," whatever their income, school background, or job. They depend heavily on relatives for economic and emotional support, for advice on purchases, and for assistance in times of trouble.

Lower Class

Upper Lowers (9 percent) The working poor. Although their living standard is just above poverty, they strive toward a higher class. However, they often lack education and are poorly paid for unskilled work.

Lower Lowers (7 percent) Visibly poor, often poorly educated unskilled laborers. They are often out of work and some depend on public assistance. They tend to live a day-to-day existence.

Group

Two or more people who interact to accomplish individual or mutual goals.

Opinion leader

Person within a reference group who, because of special skills, knowledge, personality, or other characteristics, exerts influence on others.

Groups. A person's behavior is influenced by many small **groups**. Groups that have a direct influence and to which a person belongs are called *membership groups*. In contrast, *reference groups* serve as direct (face-to-face) or indirect points of comparison or reference in forming a person's attitudes or behavior. People often are influenced by reference groups to which they do not belong. For example, an *aspirational group* is one to which the individual wishes to belong, as when a teenage basketball player hopes to play someday for the Los Angeles Lakers. Marketers try to identify the reference groups of their target markets. Reference groups expose a person to new behaviors and lifestyles, influence the person's attitudes and self-concept, and create pressures to conform that may affect the person's product and brand choices.

The importance of group influence varies across products and brands. It tends to be strongest when the product is visible to others whom the buyer respects. Manufacturers of products and brands subjected to strong group influence must figure out how to reach **opinion leaders**—people within a reference group who, because of special skills, knowledge, personality, or other characteristics, exert influence on others. According to one recent study:

> One American in ten tells the other nine how to vote, where to eat, and what to buy. They are the influentials. They drive trends, influence mass opinion and, most importantly, sell a great many products. These are the early adopters who had a digital camera before everyone else and who were the first to fly again after September 11. They are the 10 percent of Americans who determine how the rest consume and live by chatting about their likes and dislikes.[14]

Many marketers try to identify opinion leaders for their products and direct marketing efforts toward them. They use *buzz marketing* by enlisting or even creating opinion leaders to spread the word about their brands. For example, one New York marketing firm, Big Fat Promotions, hires bar "leaners" to talk casually with tavern patrons about merits of certain liquors, doormen to stack packages from a particular online catalog company in their building lobbies, mothers to chat up new laundry products at their kids' little-league games, and commuters to play with new PDAs during the ride home.[15] Here's another buzz marketing example:

■ Opinion leaders: Marketers use *buzz marketing* by enlisting or even creating opinion leaders to spread the word about their brands. For example, scooter riding models on the Vespa payroll generate favorable word of mouth for the company's products.

> Frequent the right cafes . . . in and around Los Angeles this summer, and you're likely to encounter a gang of sleek, impossibly attractive motorbike riders who seem genuinely interested in getting to know you over an iced latte. Compliment them on their Vespa scooters glinting in the brilliant curbside sunlight, and they'll happily pull out a pad and scribble down an address and phone number—not theirs, but that of the local "boutique" where you can buy your own Vespa, just as (they'll confide) the rap artist Sisqo and the movie queen Sandra Bullock recently did. And that's when the truth hits you: This isn't any spontaneous encounter. Those scooter-riding models are on the Vespa payroll, and they've been hired to generate some favorable word of mouth for the recently reissued European bikes. Welcome to the new world of buzz marketing. Buzz marketers are now taking to the streets, as well as cafes, nightclubs, and the Internet, in record numbers. Vespa . . . has its biker gang. Hebrew National is dispatching "mom squads" to grill up its hot dogs in backyard barbecues, while Hasbro Games has deputized hundreds of fourth- and fifth-graders as "secret agents" to tantalize their peers with Hasbro's POX electronic game. Their goal: to seek out the trendsetters in each community and subtly push them into talking up their brand to their friends and admirers.[16]

Family. Family members can strongly influence buyer behavior. The family is the most important consumer buying organization in society, and it has been researched extensively. Marketers are interested in the roles and influence of the husband, wife, and children on the purchase of different products and services.

Husband–wife involvement varies widely by product category and by stage in the buying process. Buying roles change with evolving consumer lifestyles. In the United States, the wife traditionally has been the main purchasing agent for the family in the areas of food, household products, and clothing. But with 70 percent of women holding jobs outside the home and the willingness of husbands to do more of the family's purchasing, all this is changing. Whereas women make up just 40 percent of drivers, they now influence more than 80 percent of car-buying decisions. Men now account for about 40 percent of all food-shopping dollars. In all, women now make almost 85 percent of all purchases, spending $6 trillion each year.[17]

Such changes suggest that marketers who've typically sold their products to only men or only women are now courting the opposite sex. For example, consider home improvement retailer Lowe's:

> War has broken out over your home-improvement dollar, and Lowe's has superpower Home Depot on the defensive. Its not-so-secret ploy: Lure women, because they'll drag their Tim Allen tool-guy husbands behind them. According to Lowe's research, women initiate 80 percent of all home-improvement purchase decisions, especially the big-ticket orders like kitchen cabinets, flooring,

■ Family buying influences: To attract women shoppers, Lowe's focuses on aesthetics—bright and airy stores with wide, uncluttered aisles and supermarket-like signs. "Lure women, and they'll drag their Tim Allen tool-guy husbands behind them."

and bathrooms. And women appreciate Lowe's obsession with store aesthetics. Lowe's stores are bright and airy with wide, uncluttered aisles and supermarket-like signs that list what is in each aisle. Managers patrol every new store with light meters to make sure aisles are lit to the company standard of 90 foot-candles. Stack-outs, those pallets of merchandise set out on the floor in front of the main shelves, are banned. They add to revenue per square foot, but they also obstruct the aisles, triggering the dreaded "butt-brush" phenomenon: Female shoppers don't like to be touched by passersby. Pam and Shawn Panuline, a young North Carolina couple who just bought a three-bedroom home, have shopped the nearby Home Depot and Lowe's stores. For Pam, Lowe's felt friendlier and had far more choices in home decor, and she liked that it wasn't as contractor-oriented. "But it's not too froofy," says her husband. Lowe's focus on women has paid off handsomely. Over the past 10 years, Lowe's has earned a 30 percent annual return, compared with 10 percent for Home Depot.[18]

Children may also have a strong influence on family buying decisions. For example, children as young as age six may influence the family car purchase decision. Recognizing this fact, Toyota recently launched a new kid-focused ad campaign for its Sienna minivan. Whereas most other minivan ads have focused on soccer moms, the new Sienna ads show kids expressing what they want out of a minivan. In one spot, for example, engineers in Sienna's design center anxiously await what looks to be a shakedown by company big shots. Instead, in rush three little girls on bicycles who begin demanding certain features and offering other advice, "I want a hundred cup holders," says one. "Is 14 all right?" asks the engineer. In another ad, a sales-kid in a Toyota dealership makes a sales pitch to a kid-customer as the two bounce on a mini trampoline. "It's got a 230hpV6," says the sales-kid. "What's that?" asks the customer. "I'm not sure," he responds. The ad concludes: "Everything kids want. Everything you need."[19]

Roles and Status. A person belongs to many groups—family, clubs, organizations. The person's position in each group can be defined in terms of both role and status. With her parents, Anna Flores plays the role of daughter; in her family, she plays the role of wife; in her company, she plays the role of brand manager. A *role* consists of the activities people are expected to perform according to the people around them. Each of Anna's roles will influence some of her buying behavior. Each role carries a *status* reflecting the general esteem given to it by society. People often choose products that show their status in society. For example, the role of brand manager has more status in our society than does the role of daughter. As a brand manager, Anna will buy the kind of clothing that reflects her role and status.

Personal Factors A buyer's decisions also are influenced by personal characteristics such as the buyer's *age* and *life-cycle stage, occupation, economic situation, lifestyle,* and *personality* and *self-concept.*

Age and Life-Cycle Stage. People change the goods and services they buy over their lifetimes. Tastes in food, clothes, furniture, and recreation are often age related. Buying is also shaped by the stage of the *family life cycle*—the stages through which families might pass as they mature over time. Marketers often define their target markets in terms of life-cycle stage and develop appropriate products and marketing plans for each stage.

Traditional family life-cycle stages include young singles and married couples with children. Today, however, marketers are increasingly catering to a growing number of alternative, nontraditional stages such as unmarried couples, singles marrying later in life, childless couples, same-sex couples, single parents, extended parents (those with young adult children returning home), and others. For example, more and more companies are now reaching out to serve the fast-growing corps of the recently divorced (see Marketing at Work 5.1).

Sony recently overhauled its marketing approach in order to target products and services to consumers based on their life stages. It created a new unit called the Consumer Segment Marketing Division, which has identified seven life-stage segments. They include, among others, Gen Y (under 25), Young Professionals/DINKs (double income, no kids, 25 to 34), Families (35 to 54), and Zoomers (55 and over). A recent Sony ad aimed at Zoomers, people who have just retired or are close to doing so, shows a man living his dream by going into outer space. The ad deals not just with going into retirement, but with the psychological life-stage changes that go with it. "The goal is to get closer to consumers," says a Sony segment marketing executive.[20]

Occupation. A person's occupation affects the goods and services bought. Blue-collar workers tend to buy more rugged work clothes, whereas executives buy more business suits. Marketers try to identify the occupational groups that have an above-average interest in their products and services. A company can even specialize in making products needed by a given occupational group. Thus, computer software companies will design different products for brand managers, accountants, engineers, lawyers, and doctors.

Economic Situation. A person's economic situation will affect product choice. Anna Flores can consider buying an expensive Nikon if she has enough spendable income, savings, or borrowing power. Marketers of income-sensitive goods watch trends in personal income, savings, and interest rates. If economic indicators point to a recession, marketers can take steps to redesign, reposition, and reprice their products closely.

Lifestyle. People coming from the same subculture, social class, and occupation may have quite different lifestyles. **Lifestyle** is a person's pattern of living as expressed in his or her *psychographics*. It involves measuring consumers' major *AIO dimensions—activities* (work, hobbies, shopping, sports, social events), *interests* (food, fashion, family, recreation), and *opinions* (about themselves, social issues, business, products). Lifestyle captures something more than the person's social class or personality. It profiles a person's whole pattern of acting and interacting in the world.

Several research firms have developed lifestyle classifications. The most widely used is SRI Consulting's *Values and Lifestyles (VALS)* typology. VALS classifies people according to how they spend their time and money. It divides consumers into eight groups based on two major dimensions: primary motivation and resources. *Primary motivations* include ideals, achievement, and self-expression. According to SRI Consulting, consumers who are primarily motivated by ideals are guided by knowledge and principles. Consumers who are primarily motivated by *achievement* look for products and services that demonstrate success to their peers. Consumers who are primarily motivated by *self-expression* desire social or physical activity, variety, and risk.

Consumers within each orientation are further classified into those with *high resources* and those with *low resources*, depending on whether they have high or low levels of income, education, health, self-confidence, energy, and other factors. Consumers with either very high or very low levels of resources are classified without regard to their primary motivations (Innovators, Survivors). Innovators are people with so many resources that they exhibit all three primary motivations in varying degrees. In contrast,

Lifestyle
A person's pattern of living as expressed in his or her activities, interests, and opinions.

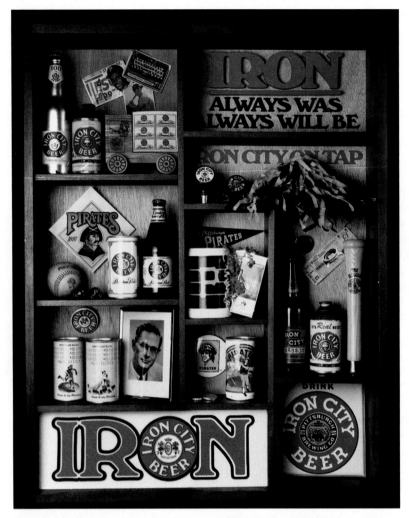

■ Lifestyles: To promote a new image, Iron City beer ads mingled images of the old Pittsburgh with those of the new, dynamic city and scenes of young Experiencers and Strivers having fun and working hard.

Survivors are people with so few resources that they do not show a strong primary motivation. They must focus on meeting needs rather than fulfilling desires.

Iron City beer, a well-known brand in Pittsburgh, used VALS to update its image and improve sales. Iron City was losing sales—its aging core users were drinking less beer, and younger men weren't buying the brand. VALS research showed that one VALS segment, Experiencers, drink the most beer, followed by Strivers. To assess Iron City's image problems, the company interviewed men in these categories. It gave the men stacks of pictures of different kinds of people and asked them to identify first Iron City brand users and then people most like themselves. The men pictured Iron City drinkers as blue-collar steelworkers stopping off at the local bar. However, they saw themselves as more modern, hardworking, and fun loving. They strongly rejected the outmoded, heavy-industry image of Pittsburgh. Based on this research, Iron City created ads linking its beer to the new self-image of target consumers. The ads mingled images of the old Pittsburgh with those of the new, dynamic city and scenes of young Experiencers and Strivers having fun and working hard. Within just one month of the start of the campaign, Iron City sales shot up by 26 percent.[21]

Lifestyle segmentation can also be used to understand how consumers use the Internet, computers, and other technology. Forrester developed its "Technographics" scheme, which segments consumers according to motivation, desire, and ability to invest in technology. The framework splits people into 10 categories, such as[22]:

■ *Fast Forwards:* the biggest spenders on computer technology. Fast Forwards are career focused, time-strapped, driven, and top users of technology.

■ *New Age Nurturers:* also big spenders. However, they are focused on technology for home uses, such as a family education and entertainment.

■ *Mouse Potatoes:* consumers who are dedicated to interactive entertainment and willing to spend for the latest in "technotainment."

■ *Techno-Strivers:* consumers who are up-and-coming believers in technology for career advancement.

■ *Traditionalists:* small-town folks, suspicious of technology beyond the basics.

Delta Airlines used Technographics to better target online ticket sales. It created marketing campaigns for time-strapped Fast Forwards and New Age Nurturers, and eliminated Technology Pessimists from its list of targets.

When used carefully, the lifestyle concept can help marketers understand changing consumer values and how they affect buying behavior. Anna Flores, for example, can choose to live the role of a capable homemaker, a career professional, or a free spirit—or all three. She plays several roles, and the way she blends them expresses her lifestyle. If she becomes a professional photographer, this would change her lifestyle, in turn changing what and how she buys.

Marketing at Work | 5.1

Targeting Nontraditional Life Stages: Just Divorced, Gone Shopping

When Los Angeles psychologist Leila Mesghali walked out of her marriage of three years, she didn't look back. She took only her clothes and some heirloom dishes. A few months later, however, the decorating urge kicked in. Even on a limited budget, she spent $6,000 on a dark teak armoire, sofa, and bedroom set. "I had a lot of motivation to fill my apartment up quickly," she said. "It was an opportunity to do my own thing."

Kim Lombard, a television producer in Toronto, also refurnished from scratch after splitting two years ago—although not of his own will. "When my wife left me, she took everything," he says. He quickly spent about $25,000 on a sofa, a good mattress, and a 50-inch television. Consider, too, the suddenly single Wall Street banker who spent $3,000 in an afternoon to outfit a bedroom for his 17-month-old twins just like the one they already knew. Or the newly separated publisher who visited an Arts and Crafts furniture store to buy a Gustav Stickley headboard and walked out with a recliner, a table, and an armoire as well.

The number of divorced people in the United States has quintupled over the past 30 years, from 4 million in 1970 to almost 20 million in 2000. With about half of all first marriages ending in divorce, marketers are beginning to recognize that divorcees represent a distinct consumer segment in a not so nontraditional life-cycle stage. When two people untie the knot, there's rarely an equitable split of their possessions. One person usually keeps the belongings; the other goes shopping.

"The divorce rate is keeping the furniture business alive," says a consultant who advises furniture retailers and manufacturers. "There's no doubt that life stages are driving consumers. They buy when they get married; they buy when

they get divorced." Like newlyweds, the newly separated need to stock their homes with everything from dish towels to four-poster beds (for her), from recliners to flat-screen televisions (for him). "Next year, at least half of the 2.4 million people who will get divorced in the United States and Canada are going to buy new beds," says Dan Couvrette, publisher of *Divorce Magazine.* "That's over a million people. You can't find a bigger niche."

Divorcees don't just buy out of necessity; the shopping cure can ease the pain. People going through a divorce, Couvrette says, "represent a tremendous market potential because they'll spend money to get stuff that makes them feel better." He adds that even those who suffer financial setbacks—often the case with women leaving long-term marriages—try to

treat themselves to the best they can afford. A survey of the magazine's readers found that 78 percent of the men bought new entertainment systems, while 69 percent of the women opted for new bedroom furniture.

Retail stores, such as Crate & Barrel, Sears, and Ikea, are learning to recognize and take care of the shopper who may be dazed and alone, trailing a long list of household needs. "Our salespeople say they sometimes feel like therapists," says a Crate & Barrel spokesperson. "They know they can't be all bubbly around someone who might be upset. It's clearly a situation that demands their most sensitive approach." One North Carolina furniture maker has trained its salespeople to keep an eye out for customers with such special needs. "We teach our sales associates to look out for that

Life-stage marketing: Marketers are discovering that when couples split, someone goes shopping. Divorcees, much like newly-weds, restock their homes with everything from pots and pans to televisions.

(continued)

man wandering around. He may have just been kicked out of the house," says a company's owner.

One Ikea spokeswoman estimates that as many as one-third of the customers she worked with over five years as a design consultant at the Ikea store in Elizabeth, New Jersey, were ex-husbands. Sometimes saleswomen find themselves playing surrogate wife. As a home furnishings consultant at Ikea in Chicago, Sharon Klein provides design advice to customers as they shop. She said she is frequently approached by "gentlemen who want help from someone with a woman's touch in buying just about everything. They come right up to you and say, 'Help!'" She adds that when it came to outfitting rooms for children, those same shoppers have bottomless wallets. "They always want a lot of extras to make their kid's new bedroom more exciting than the one at the other parent's house," she says.

In response to the growing market, advertisers are tentatively reaching out. Sears tested the waters with a coy tele-vision ad about divorce. A once-loving couple, having split their washer and dryer, are each shown while shopping at Sears for replacement appliances. They smile awkwardly at each other. "It was a humorous look at a real-life situation," says a Sears marketer.

Some years ago, Ikea ran a television ad that put a positive spin on shopping one's way to a fresh start. It showed a woman driving at night with her daughter asleep in the back seat. She muses aloud about her divorce and starting a new life. Flashbacks show her shopping up a storm in the aisles of Ikea. The campaign was well received by the press and the public.

Many marketers have shunned the divorcee segment as too downbeat. "Divorce is still a niche market with negative connotations," says one analyst. "Historically, advertisers go with more positive images. But that's going to change in keeping with the whole trend to go after more targeted groups."

Montauk Sofas was among the first to run an upbeat breakup ad. A smiling woman cozies up in the embrace of a $1,900 extra-plush armchair. The text begins in bold type: "He left me. Good Riddance," and ends: "Who cares . . . I kept the sofa." The ad has generated such good feelings for Montauk, a Montreal-based furniture manufacturer with seven stores in the United States and Canada, that it has kept running it for five years. "We've gotten an excellent reaction from all walks of life and ages," said Tim Zyto, the owner of Montauk. "Women especially like it. They find it empowering."

It may be only a matter of time before the once taboo D-word comes to stand for "divorce registry." Mr. Couvrette at *Divorce Magazine* is confident that that day is not far off. "It's not going to be called a divorce registry," he predicted, "but everyone's going to know what it's for."

Source: Adapted from Julie V. Iovine, "Just Divorced, Gone Shopping," *New York Times*, July 12, 2001, p. F1. Also see Pamela Sebastian Ridge, "Tool Sellers Tap Their Feminine Side," *Wall Street Journal*, March 29, 2002, p. B1; and David Anderson and Rosemary Clandos, "Dating after Divorce," *Psychology Today*, January/February 2003, pp. 46–56.

Personality

The unique psychological characteristics that lead to relatively consistent and lasting responses to one's own environment.

Personality and Self-Concept. Each person's distinct personality influences his or her buying behavior. **Personality** refers to the unique psychological characteristics that lead to relatively consistent and lasting responses to one's own environment. Personality is usually described in terms of traits such as self-confidence, dominance, sociability, autonomy, defensiveness, adaptability, and aggressiveness. Personality can be useful in analyzing consumer behavior for certain product or brand choices. For example, coffee marketers have discovered that heavy coffee drinkers tend to be high on sociability. Thus, to attract customers, Starbucks and other coffeehouses create environments in which people can relax and socialize over a cup of steaming coffee.

The idea is that brands also have personalities, and that consumers are likely to choose brands whose personalities match their own. A *brand personality* is the specific mix of human traits that may be attributed to a particular brand. One researcher identified five brand personality traits[23]:

1. Sincerity (down-to-earth, honest, wholesome, and cheerful)
2. Excitement (daring, spirited, imaginative, and up-to-date)
3. Competence (reliable, intelligent, and successful)
4. Sophistication (upper class and charming)
5. Ruggedness (outdoorsy and tough)

The researcher found that a number of well-known brands tended to be strongly associated with one particular trait: Levi's with "ruggedness," MTV with "excitement," CNN with "competence," and Campbell's with "sincerity." Hence, these brands will attract persons who are high on the same personality traits.

Many marketers use a concept related to personality—a person's *self-concept* (also called *self-image*). The basic self-concept premise is that people's possessions contribute to and reflect their identities; that is, "we are what we have." Thus, in order to understand consumer behavior, the marketer must first understand the relationship between consumer self-concept and possessions.

Psychological Factors A person's buying choices are further influenced by four major psychological factors: *motivation, perception, learning,* and *beliefs* and *attitudes.*

Motivation. We know that Anna Flores became interested in buying a camera. Why? What is she *really* seeking? What *needs* is she trying to satisfy? A person has many needs at any given time. Some are *biological,* arising from states of tension such as hunger, thirst, or discomfort. Others are *psychological,* arising from the need for recognition, esteem, or belonging. A need becomes a *motive* when it is aroused to a sufficient level of intensity. A **motive** (or *drive*) is a need that is sufficiently

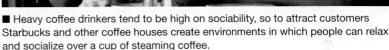

■ Heavy coffee drinkers tend to be high on sociability, so to attract customers Starbucks and other coffee houses create environments in which people can relax and socialize over a cup of steaming coffee.

pressing to direct the person to seek satisfaction. Psychologists have developed theories of human motivation. Two of the most popular—the theories of Sigmund Freud and Abraham Maslow—have quite different meanings for consumer analysis and marketing.

Sigmund Freud assumed that people are largely unconscious about the real psychological forces shaping their behavior. He saw the person as growing up and repressing many urges. These urges are never eliminated or under perfect control; they emerge in dreams, in slips of the tongue, in neurotic and obsessive behavior, or ultimately in psychoses. Thus, Freud suggested that a person does not fully understand his or her motivation. If Anna Flores wants to purchase an expensive camera, she may describe her motive as wanting a hobby or career. At a deeper level, she may be purchasing the camera to impress others with her creative talent. At a still deeper level, she may be buying the camera to feel young and independent again.

The term *motivation research* refers to qualitative research designed to probe consumers' hidden, subconscious motivations. Motivation researchers collect in-depth information from small samples of consumers to uncover the deeper motives for their product choices. The techniques range from sentence completion, word association, and inkblot or cartoon interpretation tests, to having consumers describe typical brand users or form daydreams and fantasies about brands or buying situations (see Marketing at Work 5.2).

Abraham Maslow sought to explain why people are driven by particular needs at particular times. Why does one person spend much time and energy on personal safety and another on gaining the esteem of others? Maslow's answer is that human needs are arranged in a hierarchy, as shown in Figure 5.4 on page 158, from the most pressing at the bottom to the least pressing at the top. They include *physiological* needs, *safety* needs, *social* needs, *esteem* needs, and *self-actualization* needs.

A person tries to satisfy the most important need first. When that need is satisfied, it will stop being a motivator and the person will then try to satisfy the next most important need. For example, starving people (physiological need) will not take an interest in the latest happenings in the art world (self-actualization needs), nor in how they are seen or esteemed by others (social or esteem needs), nor even in whether they are breathing clean air (safety needs). But as each important need is satisfied, the next most important need will come into play.

What light does Maslow's theory throw on Anna Flores's interest in buying a camera? We can guess that Anna has satisfied her physiological, safety, and social needs; they do not motivate her interest in cameras. Her camera interest might come from a strong need for more esteem. Or it might come from a need for self-actualization—she might want to be a creative person and express herself through photography.

Motive (drive)
A need that is sufficiently pressing to direct the person to seek satisfaction of the need.

Marketing at Work | 5.2

"Touchy-Feely" Research: Psyching Out Consumers

Consumers often don't know or can't describe just why they act as they do. Thus, motivation researchers use a variety of probing techniques to uncover underlying emotions and attitudes toward brands and buying situations. These sometimes bizarre techniques range from free association and inkblot interpretation tests to having consumers form daydreams and fantasies about brands or buying situations. One writer offers the following tongue-in-cheek summary of a motivation research session:

Good morning, ladies and gentlemen. We've called you here today for a little consumer research. Now, lie down on the couch, toss your inhibitions out the window, and let's try a little free association. First, think about brands as if they were your friends. Imagine you could talk to your TV dinner. What would he say? And what would you say to him? . . . Now, think of your shampoo as an animal. Go on, don't be shy. Would it be a panda or a lion? A snake or a wooly worm? For our final exercise, let's all sit up and pull out our magic markers. Draw a picture of a typical cake-mix user. Would she wear an apron or a negligee? A business suit or a can-can dress?

Such projective techniques seem pretty goofy. But more and more, marketers are using such touchy-feely approaches to dig deeply into consumer psyches and develop better marketing strategies. For example, Shell Oil used motivation research in an attempt to uncover the real reasons behind a decade-long sales slump:

The manager of corporate advertising for Shell Oil, Sixtus Oeschle, was at his wits' end. For months, he and his team of researchers had pumped the consumer psyche. For months, they'd come up empty. "We tried psychographic memory triggers," he recalls. "We tried dream therapy." All to no avail. At one point, respondents were even given mounds of wet clay and urged to mold figures that expressed their inner feelings about Shell.

It was time, Oeschle decided, to try something radical. To craft a more

potent appeal for its brand of gasoline, Shell would have to go deeper—much deeper. Oeschle called in a consumer researcher who specializes in focus groups conducted under hypnosis. The results, Oeschle says, wowed even the skeptics. "I've got to tell you, it was fascinating, fascinating stuff," he says. After dimming the lights, the researcher took respondents back, back—back all the way to their infancy. "He just kept taking them back and back," Oeschle says, "until . . . he's saying, 'Tell me about your first experience in a gas station.' And people were actually having memory flash-

The PT Cruiser: The phenomenally successful retro style car that's "part 1920s gangster car, part 1950s hot rod, and part London taxicab"—an actual chrome-and-sheet-metal incarnation of the popular will.

backs. I mean, they were going there. They were saying, 'I was three-and-a half years old. I was in the back of my dad's brand new Chevy.' It was like it was yesterday to them. I was stunned."

The real breakthrough, however, came after the respondents awoke out of their trance. "When he brought them all back out, he asked them who'd they prefer as a gasoline purveyor," Oeschle says. "What staggered me was that, to a person, it was always linked to that experience in their youth." One woman volunteered that she always made a point of filling up at Texaco. "We asked her why," Oeschle recalls. "And she said, 'I don't know, I guess I just feel good about Texaco.' Well, this was the little three-and-a-half-year-old in the back of her daddy's car speaking."

Shell is now designing new marketing approaches based on the insights gleaned from the groups of mesmerized motorists. Where Shell had gone wrong, it seems, was in reasoning that, since people don't start buying gas until at least age 16, there was no need to target the tiniest consumers. "They weren't even on Shell's radar," Oeschle laments. "It dawned on us . . . that we'd better figure out how to favorably impact people from an early age."

Similarly, DaimlerChrysler used a dose of deep motivation research to create a successful new concept car.

A few years back, DaimlerChrysler set out to find the next "wow car," the "segment buster" that would reach across age and income lines, into the subconscious. That meant doing more than the usual focus group research. So DaimlerChrysler hired psychologist Clothaire Rapaille to probe consumers' innermost feelings. The underlying premise: the products we buy mean something; they form

part of a greater whole. "The more we learn about American culture, the more we see how our vehicles fit into our psyche—the more we see how it is that we fit into the overall scheme of living," says David Bostwick, director of market research at DaimlerChrysler.

Rather than convening traditional focus groups, Rapaille used a method known as "archetype research." He had participants lie on soft mats, listen to mood music, and free-associate in the dark. According to Bostwick, this recreates the same brain activity you have when you first wake up from a dream. "It's a very special brain activity," he says. "It allows us to actually access some of those unconscious thoughts."

When the lights came back up, Rapaille had learned that Americans are entrepreneurial, individualistic, freedom loving, and inventive—but also juvenile and self-indulgent. More important, he discovered that many suffered nostalgia pangs. In these complex and often unsettling times, car buyers yearned for the good old days—for a time when things seemed simpler and more secure, and when people felt good about themselves. "What that said to us is that people are looking for something that offers protection on the outside, and comfort on the inside," says Bostwick. "We communicated that to our design team."

The result: the PT Cruiser, DaimlerChrysler's phenomenally successful retro style car. Described by the Wall Street Journal as "part 1920s gangster car, part 1950s hot rod, and part London taxicab," the PT Cruiser is what one analyst calls "a focus group on wheels—an actual chrome-and-sheet-metal incarnation of the popular will." Its nostalgic look and

protective exterior, combined with a well-appointed and highly functional interior, inspires an emotional reaction from almost everyone. In just two years following its introduction, U.S. consumers snapped up more than 225,000 PT Cruisers. "We didn't set out to create a market," Bostwick says earnestly. "We just tapped into what people had in their heads in the first place. . . . The vehicle takes you back, but not to a particular time in the century. It just takes you back to a time you felt cool." Says a PT Cruiser designer, "it's a celebration of automotive heritage . . . with a twist of rebellion."

Some marketers dismiss such motivation research as mumbo jumbo. However, like Shell and DaimlerChrysler, many companies are now delving into the murky depths of the consumer unconscious. "Such tactics have been worshipfully embraced by even the no-nonsense, jut-jawed captains of industry," claims an analyst. "At companies like Kraft, Coca-Cola, Proctor & Gamble, and DaimlerChrysler, the most sought-after consultants hail not from [traditional consulting firms like McKinsey. They come] from brand consultancies with names like Archetype Discoveries, PsychoLogics and Semiotic Solutions."

Sources: Examples adapted from Ruth Shalit, "The Return of the Hidden Persuaders," Salon Media, September 27, 1999, accessed online at www.salon.com. Also see Annetta Miller and Dody Tsiantar, "Psyching Out Consumers," *Newsweek*, February 27, 1989, pp. 46–47; Alison Stein Wellner, "Research on a Shoestring," *American Demographics,* April 2001, pp. 38–39; Phil Patton, "Car Shrinks," *Fortune*, March 18, 2002, pp. 187–190; "PT Cruiser," *Journal of Business and Design,* accessed online at the Corporate Design Foundation Web site, www.cdf.org, June 2003; "Taste—Review & Outlook: Sweet 16," *Wall Street Journal*, January 24, 2003, p. W13; and information found at www.ptcruiserclub.com, August 2003.

FIGURE 5.4

Maslow's Hierarchy of Needs

Sources: From *Motivation and Personality* by Abraham H. Maslow. Copyright © 1970 by Abraham H. Maslow. Copyright 1954, 1987 by Harper & Row Publishers, Inc. Reprinted by permission of Addison Wesley Educational Publishers, Inc. Also see Barbara Marx Hubbard, "Seeking Our Future Potentials," *The Futurist,* May 1998, pp. 29–32.

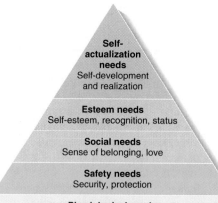

Perception

The process by which people select, organize, and interpret information to form a meaningful picture of the world.

Perception. A motivated person is ready to act. How the person acts is influenced by his or her own perception of the situation. All of us learn by the flow of information through our five senses: sight, hearing, smell, touch, and taste. However, each of us receives, organizes, and interprets this sensory information in an individual way. **Perception** is the process by which people select, organize, and interpret information to form a meaningful picture of the world.

People can form different perceptions of the same stimulus because of three perceptual processes: selective attention, selective distortion, and selective retention. People are exposed to a great amount of stimuli every day. For example, one analyst estimates that people are exposed to about 5,000 ads every day.[24] It is impossible for a person to pay attention to all these stimuli. *Selective attention*—the tendency for people to screen out most of the information to which they are exposed—means that marketers have to work especially hard to attract the consumer's attention.

Even noted stimuli do not always come across in the intended way. Each person fits incoming information into an existing mind-set. *Selective distortion* describes the tendency of people to interpret information in a way that will support what they already believe. Anna Flores may hear a salesperson mention some good and bad points about a competing camera brand. Because she already has a strong leaning toward Nikon, she is likely to distort those points in order to conclude that Nikon is the better camera. Selective distortion means that marketers must try to understand the mind-sets of consumers and how these will affect interpretations of advertising and sales information.

People also will forget much that they learn. They tend to retain information that supports their attitudes and beliefs. Because of *selective retention,* Anna is likely to remember good points made about the Nikon and to forget good points made about competing cameras. Because of selective exposure, distortion, and retention, marketers have to work hard to get their messages through. This fact explains why marketers use so much drama and repetition in sending messages to their market.

Interestingly, although most marketers worry about whether their offers will be perceived at all, some consumers worry that they will be affected by marketing messages without even knowing it—through *subliminal advertising*. In 1957, a researcher announced that he had flashed the phrases "Eat popcorn" and "Drink Coca-Cola" on a screen in a New Jersey movie theater every five seconds for 1/300 of a second. He reported that although viewers did not consciously recognize these messages, they absorbed them subconsciously and bought 58 percent more popcorn and 18 percent more Coke. Suddenly, advertisers and consumer-protection groups became intensely interested in subliminal perception. People voiced fears of being brainwashed, and California and Canada declared the practice illegal. Although the researcher later admitted to making up the data, the issue has not died. Some consumers still fear that they are being manipulated by subliminal messages.

Numerous studies by psychologists and consumer researchers have found no link between subliminal messages and consumer behavior. It appears that subliminal advertising simply doesn't have the power attributed to it by its critics. Most advertisers scoff at the notion of an industry conspiracy to manipulate consumers through "invisible" messages. Says one industry insider: "[Some consumers believe we are] wizards who can manipulate them at will. Ha! Snort! Oh my sides! As we know, just between us, most of [us] have difficulty getting a 2 percent increase in sales with the help of $50 million in media and extremely liminal images of sex, money, power, and other [motivators] of human emotion. The very idea of [us] as puppeteers, cruelly pulling the strings of consumer marionettes, is almost too much to bear."[25]

Learning. When people act, they learn. **Learning** describes changes in an individual's behavior arising from experience. Learning theorists say that most human behavior is learned. Learning occurs through the interplay of *drives, stimuli, cues, responses,* and *reinforcement.*

We have seen that Anna Flores has a drive for self-actualization. A *drive* is a strong internal stimulus that calls for action. Her drive becomes a motive when it is directed toward a particular *stimulus object,* in this case a camera. Anna's response to the idea of buying a camera is conditioned by the surrounding cues. *Cues* are minor stimuli that determine when, where, and how the person responds. Seeing cameras in a shop window, hearing of a special sale price, and receiving her husband's support are all cues that can influence Anna's *response* to her interest in buying a camera.

Suppose Anna buys the Nikon. If the experience is rewarding, she will probably use the camera more and more. Her response to cameras will be *reinforced.* Then the next time she shops for a camera, binoculars, or some similar product, the probability is greater that she will buy a Nikon product. The practical significance of learning theory for marketers is that they can build up demand for a product by associating it with strong drives, using motivating cues, and providing positive reinforcement.

Beliefs and Attitudes. Through doing and learning, people acquire beliefs and attitudes. These, in turn, influence their buying behavior. A **belief** is a descriptive thought that a person has about something. Anna Flores may believe that a Nikon camera takes great pictures, stands up well under hard use, and costs $450. These beliefs may be based on real knowledge, opinion, or faith, and may or may not carry an emotional charge. For example, Anna Flores's belief that a Nikon camera is heavy may or may not matter to her decision.

Marketers are interested in the beliefs that people formulate about specific products and services, because these beliefs make up product and brand images that affect buying behavior. If some of the beliefs are wrong and prevent purchase, the marketer will want to launch a campaign to correct them.

People have attitudes regarding religion, politics, clothes, music, food, and almost everything else. **Attitude** describes a person's relatively consistent evaluations, feelings, and tendencies toward an object or idea. Attitudes put people into a frame of mind of liking or disliking things, of moving toward or away from them. Thus, Anna Flores may hold attitudes such as "Buy the best," "The Japanese make the best products in the world," and "Creativity and self-expression are among the most important things in life." If so, the Nikon camera would fit well into Anna's existing attitudes.

Attitudes are difficult to change. A person's attitudes fit into a pattern, and to change one attitude may require difficult adjustments in many others. Thus, a company should usually try to fit its products into existing attitudes rather than attempt to change attitudes. Of course, there are exceptions in which the great cost of trying to change attitudes may pay off handsomely:

> By 1994, milk consumption had been in decline for 20 years. The general perception was that milk was unhealthy, outdated, just for kids, or good only with cookies and cake. To counter these notions, the National Fluid Milk Processors Education Program (MilkPEP) began an ad campaign featuring milk be-

Learning
Changes in an individual's behavior arising from experience.

Belief
A descriptive thought that a person holds about something.

Attitude
A person's consistently favorable or unfavorable evaluations, feelings, and tendencies toward an object or idea.

got milk?

Try this at home.*

*We mean the drinking milk part.
Lowfat milk helps prevent osteoporosis
and keeps your bones supple.

■ Attitudes are difficult to change, but the National Fluid Milk Processors' wildly popular milk mustache campaign succeeded in changing attitudes toward milk.

mustached celebrities and the tag line "Got Milk?" The campaign has not only been wildly popular, it has been successful as well—not only did it stop the decline, milk consumption actually increased. The campaign is still running. Although initially the target market was women in their twenties, the campaign has been expanded to other target markets and has gained cult status with teens, much to their parents' delight. Teens collect the print ads featuring celebrities ranging from music stars Hanson and LeAnn Rimes, supermodel Tyra Banks, Kermit the Frog, and Garfield to sports idols such as Jeff Gordon, Mia Hamm, and Venus and Serena Williams. Building on this popularity with teens, the industry set up a Web site (www.whymilk.com) where young folks can make their own mustache, check out the latest Got Milk? ads, or get facts about "everything you every need to know about milk." The industry also promotes milk to them through grass-roots marketing efforts. It recently sponsored a traveling promotion event featuring a 28-foot truck that turns into a backdrop that looks like Manhattan's Times Square. Once recruited, teens can listen to music and do a 15-second "audition" on an artificial set of MTV's "Total Request Live." They can also enter a contest to make an appearance in *Rolling Stone* magazine with a milk mustache of their own. While there, teens are encouraged to drink milk rather than soda. Each is invited to sign a pledge to reduce the national "calcium debt."[26]

We can now appreciate the many forces acting on consumer behavior. The consumer's choice results from the complex interplay of cultural, social, personal, and psychological factors.

The Buyer Decision Process

Now that we have looked at the influences that affect buyers, we are ready to look at how consumers make buying decisions. Figure 5.5 shows that the buyer decision process consists of five stages: *need recognition, information search, evaluation of alternatives, purchase decision,* and *postpurchase behavior.* Clearly, the buying process starts long before actual purchase and continues long after. Marketers need to focus on the entire buying process rather than on just the purchase decision.

The figure implies that consumers pass through all five stages with every purchase. But in more routine purchases, consumers often skip or reverse some of these stages. A woman buying her regular brand of toothpaste would recognize the need and go right to the purchase decision, skipping information search and evaluation. However, we use the model in Figure 5.5 because it shows all the considerations that arise when a consumer faces a new and complex purchase situation.

Need Recognition The buying process starts with need recognition—the buyer recognizes a problem or need. The need can be triggered by *internal stimuli* when one of the

FIGURE 5.5
Buyer Decision Process

Need recognition → Information search → Evaluation of alternatives → Purchase decision → Postpurchase behavior

person's normal needs—hunger, thirst, sex—rises to a level high enough to become a drive. A need can also be triggered by *external stimuli*. Anna Flores might have felt the need for a new hobby when her busy season at work slowed down, and she thought of cameras after talking to a friend about photography or seeing a camera ad. At this stage, the marketer should research consumers to find out what kinds of needs or problems arise, what brought them about, and how they led the consumer to this particular product.

Information Search An interested consumer may or may not search for more information. If the consumer's drive is strong and a satisfying product is near at hand, the consumer is likely to buy it then. If not, the consumer may store the need in memory or undertake an information search related to the need. At the least, Anna Flores will probably pay more attention to camera ads, cameras used by friends, and camera conversations. Or Anna may actively look for reading material, phone friends, and gather information in other ways. The amount of searching she does will depend on the strength of her drive, the amount of information she starts with, the ease of obtaining more information, the value she places on additional information, and the satisfaction she gets from searching.

The consumer can obtain information from any of several sources. These include *personal sources* (family, friends, neighbors, acquaintances), *commercial sources* (advertising, salespeople, dealers, packaging, displays), *public sources* (mass media, consumer-rating organizations), and *experiential sources* (handling, examining, using the product). The relative influence of these information sources varies with the product and the buyer. Generally, the consumer receives the most information about a product from commercial sources—those controlled by the marketer. The most effective sources, however, tend to be personal. Commercial sources normally *inform* the buyer, but personal sources *legitimize* or *evaluate* products for the buyer.

■ Need recognition can be triggered by advertising. This ad from America's Dairy Farmers alerts consumers of their need for more dairy products to build strong bones.

As more information is obtained, the consumer's awareness and knowledge of the available brands and features increases. In her information search, Anna Flores learned about the many camera brands available. The information also helped her drop certain brands from consideration. A company must design its marketing mix to make prospects aware of and knowledgeable about its brand. It should carefully identify consumers' sources of information and the importance of each source.

Evaluation of Alternatives We have seen how the consumer uses information to arrive at a set of final brand choices. How does the consumer choose among the alternative brands? The marketer needs to know about alternative evaluation—that is, how the consumer processes information to arrive at brand choices. Unfortunately, consumers do not use a simple and single evaluation process in all buying situations. Instead, several evaluation processes are at work.

The consumer arrives at attitudes toward different brands through some evaluation procedure. How consumers go about evaluating purchase alternatives depends on the individual consumer and the specific buying situation. In some cases, consumers use careful calculations and logical thinking. At other times, the same consumers do little or no evaluating; instead they buy on impulse and rely on intuition. Sometimes consumers make buying decisions on their own; sometimes they turn to friends, consumer guides, or salespeople for buying advice.

Suppose Anna Flores has narrowed her choices to four cameras. And suppose that she is primarily interested in four attributes—picture quality, ease of use, camera size, and price. Anna has formed beliefs about how each brand rates on each attribute. Clearly, if one camera rated best on all the attributes, we could predict that Anna would choose it. However, the brands vary in appeal. Anna might base her buying decision on only one attribute, and her choice would be easy to predict. If she wants picture quality above everything, she will buy the camera that she thinks has the best picture quality. But most buyers consider several attributes, each with different importance. If we knew the importance weights that Anna assigns to each of the four attributes, we could predict her camera choice more reliably.

Marketers should study buyers to find out how they actually evaluate brand alternatives. If they know what evaluative processes go on, marketers can take steps to influence the buyer's decision.

Purchase Decision   In the evaluation stage, the consumer ranks brands and forms purchase intentions. Generally, the consumer's purchase decision will be to buy the most preferred brand, but two factors can come between the purchase *intention* and the purchase *decision*. The first factor is the *attitudes of others*. If Anna Flores's husband feels strongly that Anna should buy the lowest-priced camera, then the chances of Anna's buying a more expensive camera will be reduced.

The second factor is *unexpected situational factors*. The consumer may form a purchase intention based on factors such as expected income, expected price, and expected product benefits. However, unexpected events may change the purchase intention. Anna Flores may lose her job, some other purchase may become more urgent, or a friend may report being disappointed in her preferred camera. Or a close competitor may drop its price. Thus, preferences and even purchase intentions do not always result in actual purchase choice.

Postpurchase Behavior   The marketer's job does not end when the product is bought. After purchasing the product, the consumer will be satisfied or dissatisfied and will engage in postpurchase behavior of interest to the marketer. What determines whether the buyer is satisfied or dissatisfied with a purchase? The answer lies in the relationship between the *consumer's expectations* and the product's *perceived performance*. If the product falls short of expectations, the consumer is disappointed; if it meets expectations, the consumer is satisfied; if it exceeds expectations, the consumer is delighted.

The larger the gap between expectations and performance, the greater the consumer's dissatisfaction. This suggests that sellers should make product claims that faithfully represent the product's performance so that buyers are satisfied. Some sellers might even understate performance levels to boost consumer satisfaction with the product. For example, Boeing's salespeople tend to be conservative when they estimate the potential benefits of their aircraft. They almost always underestimate fuel efficiency—they promise a 5 percent savings that turns out to be 8 percent. Customers are delighted with better-than-expected performance; they buy again and tell other potential customers that Boeing lives up to its promises.

Cognitive dissonance
Buyer discomfort caused by post-purchase conflict.

Almost all major purchases result in **cognitive dissonance**, or discomfort caused by postpurchase conflict. After the purchase, consumers are satisfied with the benefits of the chosen brand and are glad to avoid the drawbacks of the brands not bought. However, every purchase involves compromise. Consumers feel uneasy about acquiring the drawbacks of the chosen brand and about losing the benefits of the brands not purchased. Thus, consumers feel at least some postpurchase dissonance for every purchase.[27]

Why is it so important to satisfy the customer? Such satisfaction is important because a company's sales come from two basic groups—*new customers* and *retained customers*. It usually costs more to attract new customers than to retain current ones. And the best way to retain current customers is to keep them satisfied. Customer satisfaction is a key to building profitable relationships with consumers—to keeping and growing consumers and reaping their customer lifetime value. Satisfied customers buy a product again, talk favorably to others about the product, pay less attention to competing brands and advertising, and buy other products from the company. Many marketers go beyond merely *meeting* the expectations of customers—they aim to *delight* the customer.

A dissatisfied consumer responds differently. Bad word of mouth often travels farther and faster than good word of mouth. It can quickly damage consumer attitudes about a company and its products. But companies cannot simply rely on dissatisfied customers to volunteer their complaints when they are dissatisfied. Most unhappy customers never tell the company about their problem. Therefore, a company would be wise to measure customer satisfaction regularly. It should set up systems that *encourage* customers to complain. In this way, the company can learn how well it is doing and how it can improve.

But what should companies do about dissatisfied customers? At a minimum, most companies offer toll-free numbers and Web sites to handle complaints and inquiries. For example, over the past two decades, the Gerber help line (1-800-4-GERBER) has received more than 5 million calls. Help-line staffers, most of them mothers or grandmothers themselves, handle customer concerns and provide baby care advice 24 hours a day, 365 days a year to more than 2,400 callers a day. General Electric offers an online GE Answer Center. At this Web site, customers can find a wealth of information on GE's thousands of appliance products—from answers to frequently asked postpurchase questions to do-it-yourself installation and repair tips. Customers who can't find answers at the Web site can call GE's telephone Answer Center and talk directly with a GE customer service representative.

By studying the overall buyer decision, marketers may be able to find ways to help consumers move through it. For example, if consumers are not buying a new product because they do not perceive a need for it, marketing might launch advertising messages that trigger the need and show how the product solves customers' problems. If customers know about the product but are not buying because they hold unfavorable attitudes toward it, the marketer must find ways either to change the product or change consumer perceptions.

■ The adoption process: This ad encourages trial by offering a coupon.

The Buyer Decision Process for New Products

We have looked at the stages buyers go through in trying to satisfy a need. Buyers may pass quickly or slowly through these stages, and some of the stages may even be reversed. Much depends on the nature of the buyer, the product, and the buying situation.

We now look at how buyers approach the purchase of new products. A **new product** is a good, service, or idea that is perceived by some potential customers as new. It may have been around for a while, but our interest is in how consumers learn about products for the first time and make decisions about whether to adopt them. We define the **adoption process** as "the mental process through which an individual passes from first learning about an innovation to final adoption," and *adoption* as the decision by an individual to become a regular user of the product.[28]

New product
A good, service, or idea that is perceived by some potential customers as new.

Adoption process
The mental process through which an individual passes from first hearing about an innovation to final adoption.

Stages in the Adoption Process Consumers go through five stages in the process of adopting a new product:

■ *Awareness:* The consumer becomes aware of the new product, but lacks information about it.

■ *Interest:* The consumer seeks information about the new product.

■ *Evaluation:* The consumer considers whether trying the new product makes sense.

■ *Trial:* The consumer tries the new product on a small scale to improve his or her estimate of its value.

■ *Adoption:* The consumer decides to make full and regular use of the new product.

FIGURE 5.6

Adopter Categorization on the Basis of Relative Time of Adoption of Innovations

Source: Reprinted with the permission of The Free Press, a Division of Simon & Schuster, from *Diffusion of Innovations*, Fifth Edition, by Everett M. Rogers. Copyright © 2003 by The Free Press.

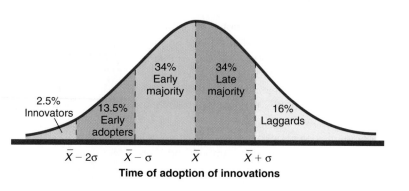

This model suggests that the new-product marketer should think about how to help consumers move through these stages. A manufacturer of large-screen televisions may discover that many consumers in the interest stage do not move to the trial stage because of uncertainty and the large investment. If these same consumers were willing to use a large-screen television on a trial basis for a small fee, the manufacturer should consider offering a trial-use plan with an option to buy.

Individual Differences in Innovativeness People differ greatly in their readiness to try new products. In each product area, there are "consumption pioneers" and early adopters. Other individuals adopt new products much later. People can be classified into the adopter categories shown in Figure 5.6. After a slow start, an increasing number of people adopt the new product. The number of adopters reaches a peak and then drops off as fewer nonadopters remain. Innovators are defined as the first 2.5 percent of the buyers to adopt a new idea (those beyond two standard deviations from mean adoption time); the early adopters are the next 13.5 percent (between one and two standard deviations); and so forth.

The five adopter groups have differing values. *Innovators* are venturesome—they try new ideas at some risk. *Early adopters* are guided by respect—they are opinion leaders in their communities and adopt new ideas early but carefully. The *early majority* are deliberate—although they rarely are leaders, they adopt new ideas before the average person. The *late majority* are skeptical—they adopt an innovation only after a majority of people have tried it. Finally, *laggards* are tradition bound—they are suspicious of changes and adopt the innovation only when it has become something of a tradition itself.

This adopter classification suggests that an innovating firm should research the characteristics of innovators and early adopters and should direct marketing efforts toward them. In general, innovators tend to be relatively younger, better educated, and have a higher income than later adopters and nonadopters. They are more receptive to unfamiliar things, rely more on their own values and judgment, and are more willing to take risks. They are less brand-loyal and more likely to take advantage of special promotions such as discounts, coupons, and samples.

Influence of Product Characteristics on Rate of Adoption The characteristics of the new product affect its rate of adoption. Some products catch on almost overnight (Beanie Babies), whereas others take a long time to gain acceptance (high-density television, or HDTV). Five characteristics are especially important in influencing an innovation's rate of adoption. For example, consider the characteristics of HDTV in relation to the rate of adoption:

■ *Relative advantage:* the degree to which the innovation appears superior to existing products. The greater the perceived relative advantage of using HDTV—say, in picture quality and ease of viewing—the sooner HDTVs will be adopted.

■ *Compatibility:* the degree to which the innovation fits the values and experiences of potential consumers. HDTV, for example, is highly compatible with the lifestyles found in upper-middle-class homes. However, it is not very compatible with the programming and broadcasting systems currently available to consumers.

■ *Complexity:* the degree to which the innovation is difficult to understand or use. HDTVs are not very complex and, therefore, once programming is available and prices come down, it will take less time to penetrate U.S. homes than more complex innovations.

■ *Divisibility:* the degree to which the innovation may be tried on a limited basis. HDTVs are still very expensive. To the extent that people can lease them with an option to buy, their rate of adoption will increase.

■ *Communicability:* the degree to which the results of using the innovation can be observed or described to others. Because HDTV lends itself to demonstration and description, its use will spread faster among consumers.

Other characteristics influence the rate of adoption, such as initial and ongoing costs, risk and uncertainty, and social approval. The new-product marketer has to research all these factors when developing the new product and its marketing program.

Consumer Behavior Across International Borders

Understanding consumer behavior is difficult enough for companies marketing within the borders of a single country. For companies operating in many countries, however, understanding and serving the needs of consumers can be daunting. Although consumers in different countries may have some things in common, their values, attitudes, and behaviors often vary greatly. International marketers must understand such differences and adjust their products and marketing programs accordingly.

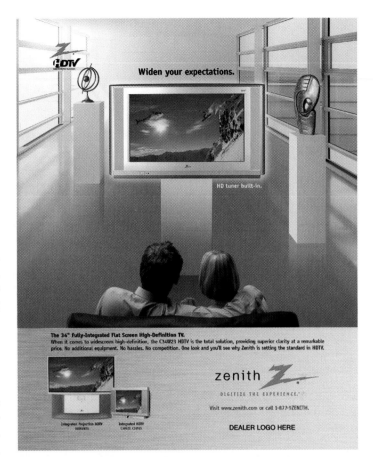

Widen your expectations.

HD tuner built-in.

The 34" Fully-Integrated Flat Screen High-Definition TV.
When it comes to widescreen high-definition, the C34W23 HDTV is the total solution, providing superior clarity at a remarkable price. No additional equipment. No hassles. No competition. One look and you'll see why Zenith is setting the standard in HDTV.

zenith
DIGITIZE THE EXPERIENCE.
Visit www.zenith.com or call 1-877-9ZENITH.

DEALER LOGO HERE

Integrated Projection HDTV
H30W23S

Integrated HDTV
C34W23 C32V23

■ New-product adoption rate: Some products catch on almost overnight. Others, such as HDTV, take a long time to gain acceptance.

Sometimes the differences are obvious. For example, in the United States, where most people eat cereal regularly for breakfast, Kellogg focuses its marketing on persuading consumers to select a Kellogg brand rather than a competitor's brand. In France, however, where most people prefer croissants and coffee or no breakfast at all, Kellogg advertising simply attempts to convince people that they should eat cereal for breakfast. Its packaging includes step-by-step instructions on how to prepare cereal. In India, where many consumers eat heavy, fried breakfasts and many consumers skip the meal altogether, Kellogg's advertising attempts to convince buyers to switch to a lighter, more nutritious breakfast diet.

Often, differences across international markets are more subtle. They may result from physical differences in consumers and their environments. For example, Remington makes smaller electric shavers to fit the smaller hands of Japanese consumers and battery-powered shavers for the British market, where few bathrooms have electrical outlets. Other differences result from varying customs. In Japan, for example, where humility and deference are considered great virtues, pushy, hard-hitting sales approaches are considered offensive. Failing to understand such differences in customs and behaviors from one country to another can spell disaster for a marketer's international products and programs.

Marketers must decide on the degree to which they will adapt their products and marketing programs to meet the unique cultures and needs of consumers in various markets. On the one hand, they want to standardize their offerings in order to simplify operations and take advantage of cost economies. On the other hand, adapting marketing efforts within each country results in products and programs that better satisfy the needs of local consumers. The question of whether to adapt or standardize the marketing mix across international markets has created a lively debate in recent years.

Linking the Concepts

Here's a good place to pull over and apply the concepts you've examined in the first part of this chapter.

- Think about a specific major purchase you've made recently. What buying process did you follow? What major factors influenced your decision?
- Pick a company that we've discussed in a previous chapter—Coca-Cola, Starbucks, NASCAR, Disney, Wal-Mart, MTV, Volkswagen, Amazon.com, or another. How does the company you chose use its understanding of customers and their buying behavior to build better customer relationships?
- Think about a company like Intel, which sells its products to computer makers and other businesses rather than to final consumers. How would Intel's marketing to business customers differ from Starbucks's marketing to final consumers? The second part of the chapter deals with this issue.

■■ Business Markets and Business Buyer Behavior

In one way or another, most large companies sell to other organizations. Many companies, such as DuPont, Boeing, Cisco Systems, Caterpillar, and countless other firms, sell *most* of their products to other businesses. Even large consumer-products companies, which make products used by final consumers, must first sell their products to other businesses. For example, General Mills makes many familiar consumer products—Cheerios, Betty Crocker cake mixes, Gold Medal flour, and others. But to sell these products to consumers, General Mills must first sell them to the wholesalers and retailers that serve the consumer market.

Business buyer behavior

The buying behavior of the organizations that buy goods and services for use in the production of other products and services or for the purpose of reselling or renting them to others at a profit.

Business buyer behavior refers to the buying behavior of the organizations that buy goods and services for use in the production of other products and services that are sold, rented, or supplied to others. It also includes the behavior of retailing and wholesaling firms that acquire goods for the purpose of reselling or renting them to others at a profit. In the *business buying process*, business buyers determine which products and services their organizations need to purchase, and then find, evaluate, and choose among alternative suppliers and brands. Companies that sell to other business organizations must do their best to understand business markets and business buyer behavior.

Business Markets

The business market is *huge*. In fact, business markets involve far more dollars and items than do consumer markets. For example, think about the large number of business transactions involved in the production and sale of a single set of Goodyear tires. Various suppliers sell Goodyear the rubber, steel, equipment, and other goods that it needs to produce the tires. Goodyear then sells the finished tires to retailers, who in turn sell them to consumers. Thus, many sets of *business* purchases were made for only one set of *consumer* purchases. In addition, Goodyear sells tires as original equipment to manufacturers, who install them on new vehicles, and as replacement tires to companies that maintain their own fleets of company cars, trucks, buses, or other vehicles.

Characteristics of Business Markets In some ways, business markets are similar to consumer markets. Both involve people who assume buying roles and make purchase decisions to satisfy needs. However, business markets differ in many ways from consumer markets. The main differences are in *market structure and demand*, the *nature of the buying unit*, and the *types of decisions and the decision process* involved.

Market Structure and Demand   The business marketer normally deals with *far fewer but far larger buyers* than the consumer marketer does. For example, when Goodyear sells replacement tires to final consumers, its potential market includes the owners of the millions of cars currently in use in the United States and around the world. But Goodyear's fate in the business market depends on getting orders from one of only a handful of large auto makers. Even in large business markets, a few buyers often account for most of the purchasing. Similarly, Black & Decker sells its power tools and outdoor equipment to tens of millions of consumers worldwide. However, it must sell these products through three huge retail customers—Home Depot, Lowe's, and Wal-Mart—which combined account for more than half its sales.

Business markets are also *more geographically concentrated.* More than half the nation's business buyers are concentrated in eight states: California, New York, Ohio, Illinois, Michigan, Texas, Pennsylvania, and New Jersey. Furthermore, business demand is **derived demand**—it ultimately derives from the demand for consumer goods. General Motors buys steel because consumers buy cars. If consumer demand for cars drops, so will the demand for steel and all the other products used to make cars. Therefore, business marketers sometimes promote their products directly to final consumers to increase business demand.

For example, Intel's long-running "Intel Inside" advertising campaign sells personal computer buyers on the virtues of Intel microprocessors. The increased demand for Intel chips boosts demand for the PCs containing them, and both Intel and its business partners win. Similarly, DuPont promotes Teflon directly to final consumers as a key ingredient in many products—from nonstick cookware to stain-repellent, wrinkle-free clothing. You see Teflon Fabric Protector hangtags on clothing lines such as Levi's Dockers, Donna Karan's menswear, and Ralph Lauren denim.[29] By making Teflon familiar and attractive to final buyers, DuPont also makes the products containing it more attractive.

Nature of the Buying Unit   Compared with consumer purchases, a business purchase usually involves *more decision participants* and a *more professional purchasing effort.* Often, business buying is done by trained purchasing agents, who spend their working lives learning how to buy better. The more complex the purchase, the more likely that several people will participate in the decision-making process. Buying committees made up of technical experts and top management are common in the buying of major goods. Beyond this, many companies are now upgrading their purchasing functions to "supply management" or "supplier development" functions. As one observer notes, "It's a scary thought:

Derived demand
Business demand that ultimately comes from (derives from) the demand for consumer goods.

■ Business markets: B2B marketers often role up their sleeves and partner with customers to jointly create solutions. Here, Fujitsu promises, "Our technology helps keep you moving upward. And our people won't let you down."

THE HIGHER THE TECHNOLOGY, THE MORE IMPORTANT THE SUPPORT.

FUJITSU

COMPUTERS, COMMUNICATIONS, MICROELECTRONICS

Your customers may know more about your company and products than you do. . . . Companies are putting their best and brightest people on procurement patrol."[30] Therefore, business marketers must have well-trained salespeople to deal with well-trained buyers.

Types of Decisions and the Decision Process Business buyers usually face *more complex* buying decisions than do consumer buyers. Purchases often involve large sums of money, complex technical and economic considerations, and interactions among many people at many levels of the buyer's organization. Because the purchases are more complex, business buyers may take longer to make their decisions. The business buying process also tends to be *more formalized* than the consumer buying process. Large business purchases usually call for detailed product specifications, written purchase orders, careful supplier searches, and formal approval.

Finally, in the business buying process, buyer and seller are often much *more dependent* on each other. Consumer marketers are often at a distance from their customers. In contrast, B2B marketers may roll up their sleeves and work closely with their customers during all stages of the buying process—partnering to jointly create solutions to the customer's problems and to support customer operations.

Business Buyer Behavior

At the most basic level, marketers want to know how business buyers will respond to various marketing stimuli. Figure 5.7 shows a model of business buyer behavior. In this model, marketing and other stimuli affect the buying organization and produce certain buyer responses. As with consumer buying, the marketing stimuli for business buying consist of the four *P*s: product, price, place, and promotion. Other stimuli include major forces in the environment: economic, technological, political, cultural, and competitive. These stimuli enter the organization and are turned into buyer responses: product or service choice; supplier choice; order quantities; and delivery, service, and payment terms. In order to design good marketing mix strategies, the marketer must understand what happens within the organization to turn stimuli into purchase responses.

Within the organization, buying activity consists of two major parts: the buying center, made up of all the people involved in the buying decision, and the buying-decision process. The model shows that the buying center and the buying decision process are influenced by internal organizational, interpersonal, and individual factors as well as by external environmental factors.

The model in Figure 5.7 suggests four questions about business buyer behavior: What buying decisions do business buyers make? Who participates in the buying process? What are the major influences on buyers? How do business buyers make their buying decisions?

FIGURE 5.7

A Model of Business Buyer Behavior

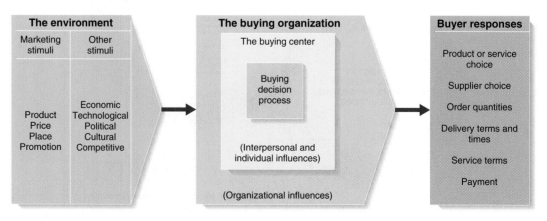

Major Types of Buying Situations There are three major types of buying situations.[31] At one extreme is the *straight rebuy*, which is a fairly routine decision. At the other extreme is the *new task*, which may call for thorough research. In the middle is the *modified rebuy*, which requires some research.

In a **straight rebuy**, the buyer reorders something without any modifications. It is usually handled on a routine basis by the purchasing department. Based on past buying satisfaction, the buyer simply chooses from the various suppliers on its list. "In" suppliers try to maintain product and service quality. They often propose automatic reordering systems so that the purchasing agent will save reordering time. "Out" suppliers try to offer something new or exploit dissatisfaction with other suppliers so that the buyer will consider them.

In a **modified rebuy**, the buyer wants to modify product specifications, prices, terms, or suppliers. The modified rebuy usually involves more decision participants than does the straight rebuy. The in suppliers may become nervous and feel pressured to put their best foot forward to protect an account. Out suppliers may see the modified rebuy situation as an opportunity to make a better offer and gain new business.

A company buying a product or service for the first time faces a **new-task** situation. In such cases, the greater the cost or risk, the larger the number of decision participants and the greater their efforts to collect information will be. The new-task situation is the marketer's greatest opportunity and challenge. The marketer not only tries to reach as many key buying influences as possible but also provides help and information.

The buyer makes the fewest decisions in the straight rebuy and the most in the new-task decision. In the new-task situation, the buyer must decide on product specifications, suppliers, price limits, payment terms, order quantities, delivery times, and service terms. The order of these decisions varies with each situation, and different decision participants influence each choice.

Many business buyers prefer to buy a packaged solution to a problem from a single seller. Instead of buying and putting all the components together, the buyer may ask sellers to supply the components *and* assemble the package or system. The sale often goes to the firm that provides the most complete system meeting the customer's needs. Thus, **systems selling** is often a key business marketing strategy for winning and holding accounts. For example, ChemStation provides a complete solution for its customers' industrial cleaning problems:

ChemStation sells industrial cleaning chemicals to a wide range of business customers, ranging from car washes to the U.S. Air Force. Whether a customer is washing down a fleet or a factory, a store or a restaurant, a distillery or an Army base, ChemStation comes up with the right cleaning solution every time. It supplies thousands of products in hundreds of industries. But ChemStation does more than just sell chemicals. First, ChemStation works closely with each individual customer to concoct a soap formula specially designed for that customer. It has brewed special formulas for cleaning hands, feathers, mufflers, flutes, perfume vats, cosmetic eye makeup containers, yacht-making molds, concrete trucks, ocean-going trawlers, and about anything else you can imagine. Next, ChemStation delivers the custom-made mixture to a tank installed at the customer's site. Finally, it maintains the tank by monitoring usage and automatically refilling the tank when supplies run low. Thus, ChemStation sells an entire system for dealing with the customer's special cleaning problems. The company's motto: "Our

Straight rebuy
A business buying situation in which the buyer routinely reorders something without any modifications.

Modified rebuy
A business buying situation in which the buyer wants to modify product specifications, prices, terms, or suppliers.

New task
A business buying situation in which the buyer purchases a product or service for the first time.

Systems selling
Buying a packaged solution to a problem from a single seller, thus avoiding all the separate decisions involved in a complex buying situation.

■ ChemStation does more than simply supply its customers with cleaning chemicals. "Our customers . . . think of us as more of a partner than a supplier."

system is your solution!" Partnering with an individual customer to find a full solution creates a lasting relationship that helps ChemStation to lock out the competition. As noted in the a recent issue of *Insights*, ChemStation's customer newsletter, "Our customers . . . oftentimes think of us as more of a partner than a supplier."[32]

Buying center
All the individuals and units that participate in the business buying-decision process.

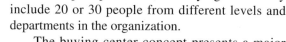

Participants in the Business Buying Process   Who does the buying of the trillions of dollars' worth of goods and services needed by business organizations? The decision-making unit of a buying organization is called its **buying center**: all the individuals and units that participate in the business decision-making process. The buying center includes all members of the organization who play a role in the purchase decision process. This group includes the actual users of the product or service, those who make the buying decision, those who influence the buying decision, those who do the actual buying, and those who control buying information.

The buying center is not a fixed and formally identified unit within the buying organization. It is a set of buying roles assumed by different people for different purchases. Within the organization, the size and makeup of the buying center will vary for different products and for different buying situations. For some routine purchases, one person—say a purchasing agent—may assume all the buying center roles and serve as the only person involved in the buying decision. For more complex purchases, the buying center may include 20 or 30 people from different levels and departments in the organization.

The buying center concept presents a major marketing challenge. The business marketer must learn who participates in the decision, each participant's relative influence, and what evaluation criteria each decision participant uses. For example, the medical products and services group of Cardinal Health sells disposable surgical gowns to hospitals. It identifies the hospital personnel involved in this buying decision as the vice president of purchasing, the operating room administrator, and the surgeons. Each participant plays a different role. The vice president of purchasing analyzes whether the hospital should buy disposable gowns or reusable gowns. If analysis favors disposable gowns, then the operating room administrator compares competing products and prices and makes a choice. This administrator considers the gown's absorbency, antiseptic quality, design, and cost, and normally buys the brand that meets requirements at the lowest cost. Finally, surgeons affect the decision later by reporting their satisfaction or dissatisfaction with the brand.

■ Buying center: Cardinal Health deals with a wide range of buying influences, from purchasing executives and hospital administrators to the surgeons who actually use its products.

The buying center usually includes some obvious participants who are involved formally in the buying decision. For example, the decision to buy a corporate jet will probably involve the company's CEO, chief pilot, a purchasing agent, some legal staff, a member of top management, and others formally charged with the buying decision. It may also involve less obvious, informal participants, some of whom may actually make or strongly affect the buying decision. Sometimes, even the people in the buying center are not aware of all the buying participants. For example, the decision about which corporate jet to buy may actually be made by a corporate board member who has an interest in flying and who knows a lot about airplanes. This board member may work behind the scenes to sway the decision. Many business buying decisions result from the complex interactions of ever-changing buying center participants.

Major Influences on Business Buyers   Business buyers are subject to many influences when they make their buying decisions. Some marketers assume that the major

■ Emotions play an important role in business buying: This Volvo truck ad mentions objective factors, such as efficiency and ease of maintenance. But it stresses more emotional factors such as the raw beauty of the truck and its comfort and roominess, features that make "drivers a lot more possessive."

influences are economic. They think buyers will favor the supplier who offers the lowest price or the best product or the most service. They concentrate on offering strong economic benefits to buyers. However, business buyers actually respond to both economic and personal factors. Far from being cold, calculating, and impersonal, business buyers are human and social as well. They react to both reason and emotion.

Today, most business-to-business marketers recognize that emotion plays an important role in business buying decisions. For example, you might expect that an advertisement promoting large trucks to corporate fleet buyers would stress objective technical, performance, and economic factors. However, a recent ad for Volvo heavy-duty trucks shows two drivers arm-wrestling and claims, "It solves all your fleet problems. Except who gets to drive." It turns out that, in the face of an industrywide driver shortage, the type of truck a fleet provides can help it to attract qualified drivers. The Volvo ad stresses the raw beauty of the truck and its comfort and roominess, features that make it more appealing to drivers. The ad concludes that Volvo trucks are "built to make fleets more profitable and drivers a lot more possessive."

Figure 5.8 lists various groups of influences on business buyers—environmental, organizational, interpersonal, and individual. *Environmental factors* play a major role. For example, buyer behavior can be heavily influenced by factors in the current and expected economic environment, such as the level of primary demand, the economic outlook, and the cost of money. Another environmental factor is shortages in key materials. Many companies now are more willing to buy and hold larger inventories of scarce materials to

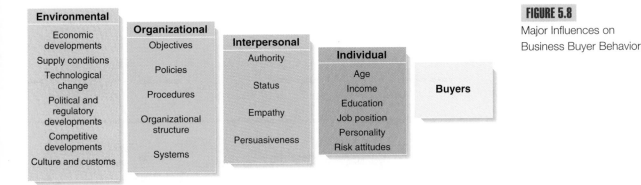

FIGURE 5.8

Major Influences on
Business Buyer Behavior

ensure an adequate supply. Business buyers also are affected by technological, political, and competitive developments in the environment. Finally, culture and customs can strongly influence business buyer reactions to the marketer's behavior and strategies, especially in the international marketing environment (see Marketing at Work 5.3).

Business buyer behavior is also influenced strongly by *organizational factors*. Each buying organization has its own objectives, policies, procedures, structure, and systems, and the business marketer must understand these factors well. Questions such as these arise: How many people are involved in the buying decision? Who are they? What are their evaluative criteria? What are the company's policies and limits on its buyers?

The buying center usually includes many participants who influence each other, so *interpersonal factors* also influence the business buying process. However, it is often difficult to assess such interpersonal factors and group dynamics. As one writer notes, "Managers do not wear tags that say 'decision maker' or 'unimportant person.' The powerful are often invisible, at least to vendor representatives."[33] Nor does the buying center participant with the highest rank always have the most influence. Participants may influence the buying decision because they control rewards and punishments, are well liked, have special expertise, or have a special relationship with other important participants. Interpersonal factors are often very subtle. Whenever possible, business marketers must try to understand these factors and design strategies that take them into account.

Finally, business buyers are influenced by *individual factors*. Each participant in the business buying decision process brings in personal motives, perceptions, and preferences. These individual factors are affected by personal characteristics such as age, income, education, professional identification, personality, and attitudes toward risk. Also, buyers have different buying styles. Some may be technical types who make in-depth analyses of competitive proposals before choosing a supplier. Other buyers may be intuitive negotiators who are adept at pitting the sellers against one another for the best deal.

The Business Buying Process Figure 5.9 lists the eight stages of the business buying process.[34] Buyers who face a new-task buying situation usually go through all stages of the buying process. Buyers making modified or straight rebuys may skip some of the stages. We will examine these steps for the typical new-task buying situation.

Problem Recognition. The buying process begins when someone in the company recognizes a problem or need that can be met by acquiring a specific product or service. Problem recognition can result from internal or external stimuli. Internally, the company may decide to launch a new product that requires new production equipment and materials. Or a machine may break down and need new parts. Perhaps a purchasing manager is unhappy with a current supplier's product quality, service, or prices. Externally, the buyer may get some new ideas at a trade show, see an ad, or receive a call from a salesperson who offers a better product or a lower price. In fact, in their advertising, business marketers often alert customers to potential problems and then show how their products provide solutions.

FIGURE 5.9

Stages of the Business Buying Process

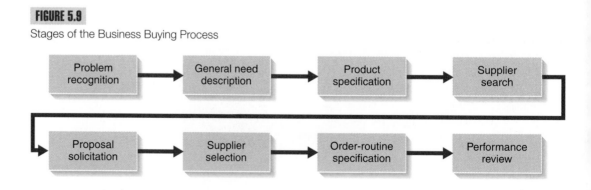

Marketing at Work | 5.3

International Marketing Manners: When in Rome, Do As the Romans Do

Picture this: Consolidated Amalgamation, Inc., thinks it's time that the rest of the world enjoyed the same fine products it has offered American consumers for two generations. It dispatches Vice President Harry E. Slicksmile to Europe, Africa, and Asia to explore the territory. Mr. Slicksmile stops first in London, where he makes short work of some bankers—he rings them up on the phone. He handles Parisians with similar ease: After securing a table at La Tour d'Argent, he greets his luncheon guest, the director of an industrial engineering firm, with the words, "Just call me Harry, Jacques."

In Germany, Mr. Slicksmile is a powerhouse. Whisking through a lavish, state-of-the-art marketing presentation, complete with flip charts and audiovisuals, he shows 'em that this Georgia boy *knows* how to make a buck. Heading on to Milan, Harry strikes up a conversation with the Japanese businessman sitting next to him on the plane. He flips his card onto the guy's tray and, when the two say good-bye, shakes hands warmly and clasps the man's right arm. Later, for his appointment with the owner of an Italian packaging design firm, our hero wears his comfy corduroy sport coat, khaki pants, and Topsiders. Everybody knows Italians are zany and laid back.

Mr. Slicksmile next swings through Saudi Arabia, where he coolly presents a potential client with a multimillion-dollar proposal in a classy pigskin binder. His final stop is Beijing, China, where he talks business over lunch with a group of Chinese executives. After completing the meal, he drops his chopsticks into his bowl of rice and presents each guest with an elegant Tiffany's clock as a reminder of his visit.

A great tour, sure to generate a pile of orders, right? Wrong. Six months

later, Consolidated Amalgamation has nothing to show for the trip but a stack of bills. Abroad, they weren't wild about Harry.

This hypothetical case has been exaggerated for emphasis. Americans are seldom such dolts. But experts say success in international business has a lot to do with knowing the territory and its people. By learning English and extending themselves in other ways, the world's business leaders have met Americans more than halfway. In contrast, Americans too often do little except assume that others will march to their music. "We want things to be 'American' when we travel. Fast. Convenient. Easy. So we become 'ugly

Americans' by demanding that others change," says one American world trade expert. "I think more business would be done if we tried harder."

Poor Harry tried, all right, but in all the wrong ways. The British do not, as a rule, make deals over the phone as much as Americans do. It's not so much a "cultural" difference as a difference in approach. A proper Frenchman neither likes instant familiarity—questions about family, church, or alma mater— nor refers to strangers by their first names. "That poor fellow, Jacques, probably wouldn't show anything, but he'd recoil. He'd *not* be pleased," explains an expert on French business practices. "It's considered poor taste,"

This HSBC ad recognizes the difficulties of doing business globally and understanding international customers needs and customs.

(continued)

he continues. "Even after months of business dealings, I'd wait for him or her to make the invitation [to use first names]. . . . You are always right, in Europe, to say 'Mister.'"

Harry's flashy presentation would likely have been a flop with the Germans, who dislike overstatement and ostentatiousness. According to one German expert, however, German businessmen have become accustomed to dealing with Americans. Although differences in body language and customs remain, the past 20 years have softened them. "I hugged an American woman at a business meeting last night," he said. "That would be normal in France, but [older] Germans still have difficulty [with the custom]." He says that calling secretaries by their first names would still be considered rude: "They have a right to be called by the surname. You'd certainly ask—and get—permission first." In Germany, people address each other formally and correctly—someone with two doctorates (which is fairly common) must be referred to as "Herr Doktor Doktor."

When Harry Slicksmile grabbed his new Japanese acquaintance by the arm, the executive probably considered him disrespectful and presumptuous. Japan, like many Asian countries, is a "no-contact culture" in which even shaking hands is a strange experience.

Harry made matters worse by tossing his business card. Japanese people revere the business card as an extension of self and as an indicator of rank. They do not *hand* it to people, they *present* it—with both hands. In addition, the Japanese are sticklers about rank. Unlike Americans, they don't heap praise on subordinates in a room; they will praise only the highest-ranking official present.

Hapless Harry also goofed when he assumed that Italians are like Hollywood's stereotypes of them. The flair for design and style that has characterized Italian culture for centuries is embodied in the businesspeople of Milan and Rome. They dress beautifully and admire flair, but they blanch at garishness or impropriety in others' attire.

To the Saudi Arabians, the pigskin binder would have been considered vile. An American salesman who really did present such a binder was unceremoniously tossed out, and his company was blacklisted from working with Saudi businesses. In China, Harry's casually dropping his chopsticks could have been misinterpreted as an act of aggression. Stabbing chopsticks into a bowl of rice and leaving them signifies death to the Chinese. The clocks Harry offered as gifts might have confirmed such dark

intentions. To "give a clock" in Chinese sounds the same as "seeing someone off to his end."

Thus, to compete successfully in global markets, or even to deal effectively with international firms in their home markets, companies must help their managers to understand the needs, customs, and cultures of international business buyers. "When doing business in a foreign country and a foreign culture—particularly a non-Western culture—assume nothing," advises an international business specialist. "Take nothing for granted. Turn every stone. Ask every question. Dig into every detail. Because cultures really are different, and those differences can have a major impact." So the old advice is still good advice: When in Rome, do as the Romans do.

Sources: Portions adapted from Susan Harte, "When in Rome, You Should Learn to Do What the Romans Do," *The Atlanta Journal-Constitution*, January 22, 1990, pp. D1, D6. Additional examples from Terri Morrison, Wayne A. Conway, and Joseph J. Douress, *Dun & Bradstreet's Guide to Doing Business Around the World* (Upper Saddle River, NJ: Prentice Hall, 2000); Craig S. Smith, "Beware of Green Hats in China and Other Cross-Cultural Faux Pas," *New York Times*, April 30, 2002, p. C11; James K. Sebenius, "The Hidden Challenge of Cross-Border Negotiations," *Harvard Business Review*, March 2002, pp. 76–85; and Daniel Joseph, "Dangerous Assumptions," *Ceramic Industry*, January 2003, p. 120.

General Need Description. Having recognized a need, the buyer next prepares a general need description that describes the characteristics and quantity of the needed item. For standard items, this process presents few problems. For complex items, however, the buyer may have to work with others—engineers, users, consultants—to define the item. The team may want to rank the importance of reliability, durability, price, and other attributes desired in the item. In this phase, the alert business marketer can help the buyers define their needs and provide information about the value of different product characteristics.

Product Specification. The buying organization next develops the item's technical product specifications, often with the help of a value analysis engineering team. **Value analysis** is an approach to cost reduction in which components are studied carefully to determine if they can be redesigned, standardized, or made by less costly methods of production. The team decides on the best product characteristics and specifies them accordingly. Sellers, too, can use value analysis as a tool to help secure a new account. By showing buyers a better way to make an object, outside sellers can turn straight rebuy situations into new-task situations that give them a chance to obtain new business.

Supplier Search. The buyer now conducts a supplier search to find the best vendors. The buyer can compile a small list of qualified suppliers by reviewing trade directories, doing a

Value analysis

An approach to cost reduction in which components are studied carefully to determine if they can be redesigned, standardized, or made by less costly methods of production.

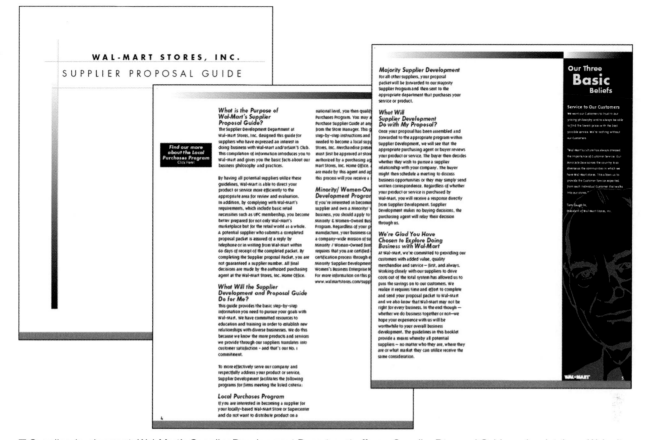

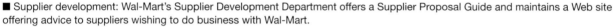

■ Supplier development: Wal-Mart's Supplier Development Department offers a Supplier Proposal Guide and maintains a Web site offering advice to suppliers wishing to do business with Wal-Mart.

computer search, or phoning other companies for recommendations. Today, more and more companies are turning to the Internet to find suppliers. For marketers, this has leveled the playing field—the Internet gives smaller suppliers many of the same advantages as larger competitors.

These days, many companies are viewing supplier search more as *supplier development*. These companies want to develop a system of supplier-partners that can help it bring more value to its customers. For example, Wal-Mart's Supplier Development Department seeks out qualified suppliers and helps them through the complex Wal-Mart buying process.

The newer the buying task, and the more complex and costly the item, the greater the amount of time the buyer will spend searching for suppliers. The supplier's task is to get listed in major directories and to build a good reputation in the marketplace. Salespeople should watch for companies in the process of searching for suppliers and make certain that their firm is considered.

Proposal Solicitation. In the proposal-solicitation stage of the business buying process, the buyer invites qualified suppliers to submit proposals. In response, some suppliers will send only a catalog or a salesperson. However, when the item is complex or expensive, the buyer will usually require detailed written proposals or formal presentations from each potential supplier.

Business marketers must be skilled in researching, writing, and presenting proposals in response to buyer proposal solicitations. Proposals should be marketing documents, not just technical documents. Presentations should inspire confidence and should make the marketer's company stand out from the competition.

Supplier Selection. The members of the buying center now review the proposals and select a supplier or suppliers. During supplier selection, the buying center often will draw up a list of the desired supplier attributes and their relative importance. In one survey, purchasing executives listed the following attributes as most important in influencing the relationship between supplier and customer: quality products and services, on-time delivery, ethical corporate behavior, honest communication, and competitive prices. Other important factors include repair and servicing capabilities, technical aid and advice, geographic location, performance history, and reputation. The members of the buying center will rate suppliers against these attributes and identify the best suppliers.

Buyers may attempt to negotiate with preferred suppliers for better prices and terms before making the final selections. In the end, they may select a single supplier or a few suppliers. Many buyers prefer multiple sources of suppliers to avoid being totally dependent on one supplier and to allow comparisons of prices and performance of several suppliers over time.

Order-Routine Specification. The buyer now prepares an order-routine specification. It includes the final order with the chosen supplier or suppliers and lists items such as technical specifications, quantity needed, expected time of delivery, return policies, and warranties. In the case of maintenance, repair, and operating items, buyers may use *blanket contracts* rather than periodic purchase orders. A blanket contract creates a long-term relationship in which the supplier promises to resupply the buyer as needed at agreed prices for a set period. A blanket order eliminates the expensive process of renegotiating a purchase each time that stock is required. It also allows buyers to write more, but smaller, purchase orders, resulting in lower inventory levels and carrying costs.

Blanket contracting leads to more single-source buying and to buying more items from that source. This practice locks the supplier in more tightly with the buyer and makes it difficult for other suppliers to break in unless the buyer becomes dissatisfied with prices or service.

Performance Review. In this stage, the buyer reviews supplier performance. The buyer may contact users and ask them to rate their satisfaction. The performance review may lead the buyer to continue, modify, or drop the arrangement. The seller's job is to monitor the same factors used by the buyer to make sure that the seller is giving the expected satisfaction.

We have described the stages that typically would occur in a new-task buying situation. The eight-stage model provides a simple view of the business buying decision process. The actual process is usually much more complex. In the modified-rebuy or straight-rebuy situation, some of these stages would be compressed or bypassed. Each organization buys in its own way, and each buying situation has unique requirements. Different buying center participants may be involved at different stages of the process. Although certain buying-process steps usually do occur, buyers do not always follow them in the same order, and they may add other steps. Often, buyers will repeat certain stages of the process. Finally, a customer relationship might involve many different types of purchases ongoing at a given time, all in different stages of the buying process. The seller must manage the total customer relationship, not just individual purchases.

Business Buying on the Internet

During the past few years, advances in information technology have changed the face of the business-to-business marketing process. Online purchasing, often called **e-procurement**, is growing rapidly. In a recent survey, almost 75 percent of business buyers indicated that they use the Internet to make at least some of their purchases. Another study found that e-procurement accounts for 14 percent of the average company's spending. One research firm estimates that the dollar value of materials purchased online swelled from $75 billion in 2000 to more than $3 trillion in 2003.[35] In addition to

e-procurement
Online purchasing.

their own Web pages on the Internet, companies are establishing extranets that link a company's communications and data with its regular suppliers and distributors.

Much online purchasing also takes place on public and private online trading exchanges, or through *reverse auctions,* in which sellers put their purchasing requests online and invite suppliers to bid for the business. For example, public trading exchanges like the auto industry's Covisint exchange offer a faster, more efficient way to communicate, collaborate, buy, sell, trade, and exchange information business to business. The exchange handled more that $50 billion in auto-parts orders last year.

E-procurement gives buyers access to new suppliers, lowers purchasing costs, and hastens order processing and delivery. In turn, business marketers can connect with customers online to share marketing information, sell products and services, provide customer support services, and maintain ongoing customer relationships.

So far, most of the products bought online are MRO materials—maintenance, repair, and operations. For instance, Los Angeles County purchases everything from chickens to light bulbs over the Internet. National Semiconductor has automated almost all of the company's 3,500 monthly requisitions to buy materials ranging from the sterile booties worn in its fabrication plants to state-of-the-art software. The actual dollar amount spent on these types of MRO materials pales in comparison with the amount spent for items such as airplane parts, computer systems, and steel tubing. Yet, MRO materials make up 80 percent of all business orders and the transaction costs for order processing are high. Thus, companies have much to gain by streamlining the MRO buying process on the Web.

General Electric, one of the world's biggest purchasers, plans to be buying *all* of its general operating and industrial supplies online within the next few years. Five years ago, GE set up its Global eXchange Services network—a central Web site through which all GE business units could make their purchases. The site was so successful that GE has now opened it up to other companies, creating a vast electronic e-purchasing clearinghouse.

Business-to-business e-procurement yields many benefits. First, it shaves transaction costs and results in more efficient purchasing for both buyers and suppliers. A Web-powered purchasing program eliminates the paperwork associated with traditional requisition and ordering procedures. On average, companies can trim the costs of purchased goods alone by 15 to 20 percent. For example, Owens Corning estimates that e-procurement has shaved 10 percent off its annual purchasing bill of $3.4 billion. And Microsoft recently reduced its purchasing costs by $700 million after implementing its MS Market e-procurement system.[36] E-procurement reduces the time between order and delivery. Time savings are particularly dramatic for companies with many overseas suppliers. Adaptec, a leading supplier of computer storage, used an extranet to tie all of its Taiwanese chip suppliers together in a kind of virtual family. Now messages from Adaptec flow in seconds from its headquarters to its Asian partners, and Adaptec has reduced the time between the order and delivery of its chips from as long as 16 weeks to just 55 days—the same turnaround time for companies that build their own chips.

Finally, beyond the cost and time savings, e-procurement frees purchasing people to focus on more-strategic issues. For many purchasing professionals, going online means reducing drudgery and paperwork and spending more time managing inventory and working creatively with suppliers.

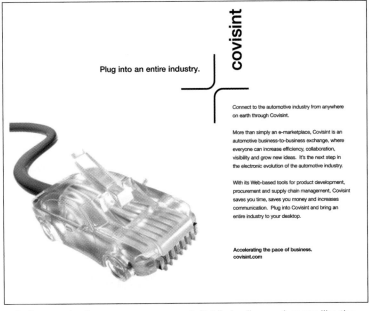

covisint

Plug into an entire industry.

Connect to the automotive industry from anywhere on earth through Covisint.

More than simply an e-marketplace, Covisint is an automotive business-to-business exchange, where everyone can increase efficiency, collaboration, visibility and grow new ideas. It's the next step in the electronic evolution of the automotive industry.

With its Web-based tools for product development, procurement and supply chain management, Covisint saves you time, saves you money and increases communication. Plug into Covisint and bring an entire industry to your desktop.

Accelerating the pace of business.
covisint.com

■ Online purchasing—or e-procurement: Public trading exchanges like the auto industry's Covisint exchange offer "a faster, more efficient way to communicate, collaborate, buy, sell, trade, and exchange information—business to business. The exchange handled more than $50 billion in auto-parts orders last year.

The rapidly expanding use of e-purchasing, however, also presents some problems. For example, at the same time that the Web makes it possible for suppliers and customers to share business data and even collaborate on product design, it can also erode decades-old customer–supplier relationships. Many firms are using the Web to search for better suppliers.

E-purchasing can also create potential security disasters. More than 80 percent of companies say security is the leading barrier to expanding electronic links with customers and partners. Although e-mail and home banking transactions can be protected through basic encryption, the secure environment that businesses need to carry out confidential interactions is still lacking. Companies are spending millions for research on defensive strategies to keep hackers at bay. Cisco Systems, for example, specifies the types of routers, firewalls, and security procedures that its partners must use to safeguard extranet connections. In fact, the company goes even further—it sends its own security engineers to examine a partner's defenses and holds the partner liable for any security breach that originates from its computer.

REST STOP:
Reviewing the Concepts

This chapter is the last of three chapters that address understanding the marketplace and consumers. Here, we've looked closely at consumers and their buying behavior. The American consumer market consists of more than 290 million people who consume many trillions of dollars' worth of goods and services each year. The business market involves far more dollars and items than the consumer market. Final consumers and business buyers vary greatly in their characteristics and circumstances. Understanding *consumer* and *business buyer behavior* is one of the biggest challenges marketers face.

1. Describe the consumer market and the major factors that influence consumer buyer behavior.

The *consumer market* consists of all the individuals and households who buy or acquire goods and services for personal consumption. A simple stimulus–response model of consumer behavior suggests that marketing stimuli and other major forces enter the consumer's "black box." This black box has two parts: buyer characteristics and the buyer's decision process. Once in the black box, the inputs result in observable buyer responses, such as product choice, brand choice, dealer choice, purchase timing, and purchase amount.

Consumer buyer behavior is influenced by four key sets of buyer characteristics: cultural, social, personal, and psychological. Understanding these factors can help marketers to identify interested buyers and to shape products and appeals to serve consumer needs better. *Culture* is the most basic determinant of a person's wants and behavior. People in different cultural, subcultural, and social class groups have different product and brand preferences. *Social factors*—such as small group and family influences—strongly affect product and brand choices, as do *personal characteristics,* such as age, life-cycle stage, occupation, economic circumstances, lifestyle, and personality. Finally, consumer buying behavior is influenced by four major

sets of *psychological factors*—motivation, perception, learning, and beliefs and attitudes. Each of these factors provides a different perspective for understanding the workings of the buyer's black box.

2. Identify and discuss the stages in the buyer decision process.

When making a purchase, the buyer goes through a decision process consisting of need recognition, information search, evaluation of alternatives, purchase decision, and postpurchase behavior. During *need recognition*, the consumer recognizes a problem or need that could be satisfied by a product or service. Once the need is recognized, the consumer moves into the *information search* stage. With information in hand, the consumer proceeds to *alternative evaluation* and assesses brands in the choice set. From there, the consumer makes a *purchase decision* and actually buys the product. In the final stage of the buyer decision process, *postpurchase behavior,* the consumer takes action based on satisfaction or dissatisfaction. The marketer's job is to understand the buyer's behavior at each stage and the influences that are operating.

3. Describe the adoption and diffusion process for new products.

The product *adoption process* is comprised of five stages: awareness, interest, evaluation, trial, and adoption. New-product marketers must think about how to help consumers move through these stages. With regard to the *diffusion process* for new products, consumers respond at different rates, depending on consumer and product characteristics. Consumers may be innovators, early adopters, early majority, late majority, or laggards. Each group may require different marketing approaches. Marketers often try to bring their new products to the attention of potential early adopters, especially those who are opinion leaders.

4. Define the business market and identify the major factors that influence business buyer behavior.

The *business market* comprises all organizations that buy goods and services for use in the production of other products and services or for the purpose of reselling or renting them to others at a profit. As compared with consumer markets, business markets usually have fewer, larger buyers who are more geographically concentrated. Business demand is derived demand, and the business buying decision usually involves more, and more professional, buyers.

Business buyers make decisions that vary with the three types of *buying situations:* straight rebuys, modified rebuys, and new tasks. The decision-making unit of a buying organization—the *buying center*—can consist of many different persons playing many different roles. The business marketer needs to know the following: Who are the major buying center participants? In what decisions do they exercise influence, and to what degree? What evaluation criteria does each decision participant use? The business marketer also needs to understand the major environmental, organizational, interpersonal, and individual influences on the buying process.

5. List and define the steps in the business buying decision process.

The *business buying decision process* itself can be quite involved, with eight basic stages: problem recognition, general need description, product specification, supplier search, proposal solicitation, supplier selection, order-routine specification, and performance review. Buyers who face a new-task buying situation usually go through all stages of the buying process. Buyers making modified or straight rebuys may skip some of the stages. Companies must manage the overall customer relationship, which often includes many different buying decisions in various stages of the buying decision process.

Recent advances in information technology have given birth to "e-purchasing," by which business buyers are purchasing all kinds of products and services electronically, either through electronic data interchange links (EDI) or on the Internet. Such cyberbuying gives buyers access to new suppliers, lowers purchasing costs, and hastens order processing and delivery. However, it can also erode customer–supplier relationships and create potential security problems. Still, business marketers are increasingly connecting with customers online to share marketing information, sell products and services, provide customer support services, and maintain ongoing customer relationships.

Navigating the Key Terms

Adoption process	Derived demand	Opinion leader
Attitude	e-procurement	Perception
Belief	Groups	Personality
Business buyer behavior	Learning	Social class
Buying center	Lifestyle	Straight rebuy
Cognitive dissonance	Modified rebuy	Subculture
Consumer buyer behavior	Motive (drive)	Systems selling
Consumer market	New product	Value analysis
Culture	New task	

Travel Log

Discussing the Issues

1. Describe how the subcultures individuals belong to and their social classes can influence their choices of an automobile. Which of these two influences is likely to have the largest influence?

2. Reference groups with which an individual desires to become associated are called aspirational groups. What is one of your aspirational groups? What types of products could marketers effectively sell using the aspirational group you selected?

3. Learning is described as changes in an individual's behavior arising from experience. In what ways do marketers attempt to get consumers to experience their products in order to influence their buying behavior?

4. Sometimes a consumer conducts an information search and other times a very minimal search. What factors might influence how much information searching a consumer does?

5. Think about a new type of product you have recently purchased. Discuss how you proceeded through the five stages of the product adoption process. Did you skip any stages?

Were any of the stages in a different order from that presented in the text?

6. Discuss how business buyer behavior is different from consumer buyer behavior. What does this mean for a company attempting to sell goods to other organizations?

Application Questions

1. Go to SRI Consulting's Web site (www.sric-bi.com/VALS/presurvey.html) and complete the VALS survey online. How accurately are you described by your primary and secondary VALS types? Do you think you will be in a different VALS category in 5 to 10 years? Discuss how Kraft food marketers might use this information to sell Velveeta cheese.

2. Examine the five adopter categories and how they differ from one another. Pick a recent technology-oriented product such as a PDA or a DVD player and discuss how such a product should be positioned differently to appeal to each of the five adopter categories. To which group do you feel would be easiest to sell? Which group might be the most profitable?

3. Relationships between the seller and buyer are often mentioned as being more critical in business-to-business transactions than in business-to-consumer transactions. Do you agree or disagree with this? What types of activities might a firm use to develop closer relations with another organization?

Under the Hood: Focus on Technology

This chapter discusses how consumer and business markets differ from one another. How do you think the company Web sites of a company selling directly to consumers will compare with one selling directly to other businesses? Visit and investigate the corporate Web sites for Dow Chemical (www.dow.com) and for Kellogg's (www.kelloggs.com).

1. How are the Web sites different?

2. Who is each Web site designed for?

3. What types of information are present on both Web sites?

4. How well does each Web site communicate with its intended audience?

Focus on Ethics

As pointed out in the chapter, mature consumers are an attractive market because of their growing ranks, financial stability, and increasing free time. Health-related products are often pitched toward these markets in an effort to help them look as young as they feel and to combat the effects of aging.

Traditionally, prescription drug advertising has been aimed directly at physicians. Recently, there has been a rise in prescription drug advertising aimed directly at the consumer, particularly the mature consumer. The goal is clear: if a patient is aware of new drugs that supposedly help combat aging, the patient will ask the physician to prescribe them. The expected result?—an increase in sales for the advertised drug.

Drug manufacturers have increased the amount of direct-to-consumer advertising, from $800 million in 1996 to $2.7 billion in 2001. While a better-educated consumer is a laudable goal, critics suggest that direct-to-consumer advertising partly fuels the escalating cost of prescription drugs, which are rising at an average of 17 percent per year. The advertising appears to be working. From 1990 to 2000, the volume prescribed of the 50 most advertised drugs increased by 24.6 percent, compared with only 4.3 percent for all other prescription drugs. Perhaps most disturbing, a study in the *Journal of Family Practice* reported that 71 percent of family physicians felt direct-to-consumer advertising pressured them to prescribe medication they wouldn't otherwise prescribe.

1. How do you feel about the rise in direct-to-consumer advertising for prescription drugs? What are some of the pros and cons of such advertising?

2. What actions, if any, should drug manufacturers take to be socially responsible in the creation of consumer advertising?

3. Does direct-to-consumer advertising in the drug industry have any negative consequences for pharmaceutical companies?

Videos

The Subaru video case that accompanies this chapter is located in Appendix 1 at the back of the book.

Student Materials

Need a tune-up? A study guide and OneKey access code are available to aid in your review of chapter material. Your instructor may choose to have these items shrink-wrapped with your text or you may purchase them separately at www.prenhall.com/marketing.

■ *After studying this chapter, you should be able to*

   1. Define the three steps of target marketing: market segmentation, market targeting, and market positioning
   2. List and discuss the major bases for segmenting consumer and business markets   *3. Explain* how companies identify attractive market segments and choose a target marketing strategy   *4. Discuss* how companies position their products for maximum competitive advantage in the marketplace

Segmentation, Targeting, and Positioning: Building the Right Relationships with the Right Customers

6

ROAD MAP | Previewing the Concepts

So far in your marketing journey, you've learned what marketing is and about the complex environments in which it operates. Marketing works with partners inside and outside the company to build profitable customer relationships in a complex and changing marketplace. With that as background, in Part 3 of the book, we'll travel more deeply into marketing strategy and tactics. The key to smart marketing is to build the *right relationships* with the *right customers*. This chapter looks further into key marketing strategy decisions—how to divide up markets into meaningful customer groups (market segmentation), choose which customer groups to serve (target marketing), and create a value proposition that best serves targeted customers (positioning). The chapters that follow explore in depth the tactical marketing tools—the *4Ps*—through which marketers bring these strategies to life.

N ext stop: Procter & Gamble, one of the world's premier consumer goods companies. Some 99 percent of all U.S. households use at least one P&G brand, and the typical household regularly buys and uses from one to two *dozen* P&G brands. How many P&G products can you name? Why does this superb marketer compete with itself on supermarket shelves by marketing eight different brands of laundry detergent? The P&G story provides a great example of how smart marketers use segmentation, targeting, and positioning.

Procter & Gamble (P&G) sells eight brands of laundry detergent in the United States (Tide, Cheer, Bold, Gain, Era, Dreft, Febreze, and Ivory Snow). It also sells six brands of hand soap (Ivory, Safeguard, Camay, Olay, Zest, and Old Spice); five brands of shampoo (Pantene, Head & Shoulders, Pert, Physique, and Vidal Sassoon); four brands of dishwashing detergent (Dawn, Ivory, Joy, and Cascade); three brands each of tissues and towels (Charmin, Bounty, Puffs), and deodorant (Secret, Sure, and Old Spice) ; and two brands each of fabric softener (Downy and Bounce), cosmetics (Cover Girl and Max Factor), skin care potions (Olay and Noxzema), and disposable diapers (Pampers and Luvs). Moreover, P&G has many additional brands in each category for different international markets. For example, it sells 16 different laundry product brands in Latin America and 19 in Europe, the Middle East, and Africa. (See Procter & Gamble's Web site at www.pg.com for a full look at the company's impressive lineup of familiar brands.)

These P&G brands compete with one another on the same supermarket shelves. But why would P&G introduce several brands in one category instead of concentrating its resources on a single leading brand? The answer lies in the fact that different people want different *mixes of benefits* from the products they buy. Take laundry detergents, for example. People use laundry detergents to get their clothes clean. But they also want other things from their detergents—such as economy, bleaching power, fabric softening, fresh smell, strength or mildness, and lots of suds or only a little. We all want *some* of every one of these benefits from our detergent, but we may have different *priorities* for each benefit. To some people, cleaning and bleaching power are most important; to others, fabric softening matters most; still others want a mild, fresh-scented detergent. Thus, there are groups—or segments—of laundry detergent buyers, and each segment seeks a special combination of benefits.

Procter & Gamble has identified at least seven important laundry detergent segments, along with numerous subsegments, and has developed a different brand designed to meet the special needs of each. The seven brands are positioned for different segments as follows:

- *Tide* provides "fabric cleaning and care at its best." It's the all-purpose family detergent that is "tough on greasy stains."
- *Cheer* is the "color expert." It helps protect against fading, color transfer, and fabric wear, with or without bleach. *Cheer Free* is "dermatologist tested . . . contains no irritating perfume or dye."
- *Bold* is the detergent with built-in fabric softener and pill/fuzz removal.
- *Gain*, originally P&G's "enzyme" detergent, was repositioned as the detergent that gives you clean, fresh-smelling clothes. It "cleans and freshens like sunshine. Great cleaning power and a smell that stays clean."
- *Era* is "the power tool for stain removal and pretreating." It contains advanced enzymes to fight a family's tough stains and help get the whole wash clean. *Era Max* has three types of active enzymes to help fight many stains that active families encounter.
- *Ivory Snow* is "Ninety-nine and forty-four one hundredths percent pure." It provides "mild cleansing benefits for a pure and simple clean."
- *Dreft* "helps remove tough baby stains . . . for a clean you can trust." It's "pediatrician recommended and the first choice of mothers." It "doesn't remove the flame resistance of children's sleepwear."

Within each segment, Procter & Gamble has identified even *narrower* niches. For example, you can buy regular Tide (in powder or liquid form) or any of several formulations:

- *Tide with Bleach* helps to "keep your whites white and your colors bright." Available in regular or "mountain spring" scents.
- *Tide Liquid with Bleach Alternative* uses active enzymes in pretreating and washing to break down and remove the toughest stains while whitening whites.
- *Tide High Efficiency* "unlocks the cleaning power of high-efficiency top-loading machines"—it prevents oversudsing.
- *Tide Clean Breeze* gives the fresh scent of laundry line-dried in a clean breeze.
- *Tide Mountain Spring* lets you "bring the fresh clean scent of the great outdoors inside—the scent of crisp mountain air and fresh wildflowers."
- *Tide Free* "provides all the stain removal benefits without any dyes or perfumes."
- *Tide Rapid Action Tablets* are portable and powerful. It's Tide "all concentrated into a little blue and white tablet that fits into your pocket."

By segmenting the market and having several detergent brands, Procter & Gamble has an attractive offering for consumers in all important preference groups. As a result, P&G is really cleaning up in the $4 billion U.S. laundry detergent market. Tide, by itself, captures a whopping 38 percent market share. All P&G brands combined take a 60 percent share of the U.S. market—more than three times that of nearest rival Unilever and much more than any single brand could obtain by itself.[1]

Companies today recognize that they cannot appeal to all buyers in the marketplace, or at least not to all buyers in the same way. Buyers are too numerous, too widely scattered, and too varied in their needs and buying practices. Moreover, the companies themselves vary widely in their abilities to serve different segments of the market. Instead, they must design strategies to build the *right* relationships with the *right* customers. Rather than trying to compete in an entire market, sometimes against superior competitors, each company must identify the parts of the market that it can serve best and most profitably.

Thus, most companies are being more choosy about the customers with whom they wish to build relationships. Most have moved away from mass marketing and toward *market segmentation and targeting*—identifying market segments, selecting one or more of them, and developing products and marketing programs tailored to each. Instead of scattering their marketing efforts (the "shotgun" approach), firms are focusing on the buyers who have greater interest in the values they create best (the "rifle" approach).

Figure 6.1 shows the three major steps in target marketing. The first is **market segmentation**—dividing a market into smaller groups of buyers with distinct needs, characteristics, or behaviors who might require separate products or marketing mixes. The company identifies different ways to segment the market and develops profiles of the resulting market segments. The second step is **target marketing**—evaluating each market segment's attractiveness and selecting one or more of the market segments to enter. The third step is **market positioning**—setting the competitive positioning for the product and creating a detailed marketing mix. We discuss each of these steps in turn.

Market segmentation
Dividing a market into distinct groups with distinct needs, characteristics, or behaviors who might require separate products or marketing mixes.

Target marketing
The process of evaluating each market segment's attractiveness and selecting one or more segments to enter.

Market positioning
Arranging for a product to occupy a clear, distinctive, and desirable place relative to competing products in the minds of target consumers.

■■ Market Segmentation

Markets consist of buyers, and buyers differ in one or more ways. They may differ in their wants, resources, locations, buying attitudes, and buying practices. Through market segmentation, companies divide large, heterogeneous markets into smaller segments that can be reached more efficiently and effectively with products and services that match their unique needs. In this section, we discuss four important segmentation topics: segmenting consumer markets, segmenting business markets, segmenting international markets, and requirements for effective segmentation.

Segmenting Consumer Markets

There is no single way to segment a market. A marketer has to try different segmentation variables, alone and in combination, to find the best way to view the market structure. Table 6.1 outlines the major variables that might be used in segmenting consumer markets. Here we look at the major *geographic*, *demographic*, *psychographic*, and *behavioral variables*.

Geographic Segmentation   **Geographic segmentation** calls for dividing the market into different geographical units such as nations, regions, states, counties, cities, or

Geographic segmentation
Dividing a market into different geographical units such as nations, states, regions, counties, cities, or neighborhoods.

Market segmentation	Target marketing	Market positioning
Identify bases for segmenting the market	Develop measure of segment attractiveness	Develop positioning for target segments
Develop segment profiles	Select target segments	Develop a marketing mix for each segment

FIGURE 6.1

Steps in Market Segmentation, Targeting, and Positioning

TABLE 6.1 Major Segmentation Variables for Consumer Markets

Geographic

World region or country	North America, Western Europe, Middle East, Pacific Rim, China, India, Canada, Mexico
Country region	Pacific, Mountain, West North Central, West South Central, East North Central, East South Central, South Atlantic, Middle Atlantic, New England
City or metro size	Under 5,000; 5,000–20,000; 20,000–50,000; 50,000–100,000; 100,000–250,000; 250,000–500,000; 500,000–1,000,000; 1,000,000–4,000,000; 4,000,000 or over
Density	Urban, suburban, rural
Climate	Northern, southern

Demographic

Age	Under 6, 6–11, 12–19, 20–34, 35–49, 50–64, 65+
Gender	Male, female
Family size	1–2, 3–4, 5+
Family life-cycle	Young, single; young, married, no children; young, married with children; older, married with children; older, married, no children under 18; older, single; other
Income	Under $10,000; $10,000–$20,000; $20,000–$30,000; $30,000–$50,000; $50,000–$100,000; $100,000 and over
Occupation	Professional and technical; managers, officials, and proprietors; clerical; sales; craftspeople; supervisors; operatives; farmers; retired; students; homemakers; unemployed
Education	Grade school or less; some high school; high school graduate; some college; college graduate
Religion	Catholic, Protestant, Jewish, Muslim, Hindu, other
Race	Asian, Hispanic, black, white
Generation	Baby boomer, Generation X, Generation Y
Nationality	North American, South American, British, French, German, Italian, Japanese

Psychographic

Social class	Lower lowers, upper lowers, working class, middle class, upper middles, lower uppers, upper uppers
Lifestyle	Achievers, strivers, strugglers
Personality	Compulsive, gregarious, authoritarian, ambitious

Behavioral

Occasions	Regular occasion; special occasion
Benefits	Quality, service, economy, convenience, speed
User status	Nonuser, ex-user, potential user, first-time user, regular user
User rates	Light user, medium user, heavy user
Loyalty status	None, medium, strong, absolute
Readiness stage	Unaware, aware, informed, interested, desirous, intending to buy
Attitude toward product	Enthusiastic, positive, indifferent, negative, hostile

even neighborhoods. A company may decide to operate in one or a few geographical areas, or to operate in all areas but pay attention to geographical differences in needs and wants.

Many companies today are localizing their products, advertising, promotion, and sales efforts to fit the needs of individual regions, cities, and even neighborhoods. For example, Campbell sells Cajun gumbo soup in Louisiana and Mississippi and makes its nacho cheese soup spicier in Texas and California. Starbucks offers more desserts and larger, more comfortable coffee shops in the South, where customers tend to arrive later in the day and to stay longer. And Parker Brothers offers localized versions of its popular Monopoly game for several major cities, including Chicago, New York, San Francisco, St. Louis, and Las Vegas. The Las Vegas version features a black board with The Strip rather than Boardwalk, hotel casinos, red Vegas dice, and custom pewter tokens including blackjack cards, a wedding chapel, and a roulette wheel.[2]

Other companies are seeking to cultivate as-yet untapped geographic territory. For example, many large companies are fleeing the fiercely competitive major cities and suburbs to set up shop in small-town America. Hampton Inns has opened a chain of smaller-format motels in towns too small for its standard-size units. For example, Townsend, Tennessee, with a population of only 329, is small even by small-town standards. But looks can be deceiving. Situated on a heavily traveled and picturesque route between Knoxville and the Smoky Mountains, the village serves both business and vacation travelers. Hampton Inns opened a unit in Townsend and plans to open 100 more in small towns. It costs less to operate in these towns, and the company builds smaller units to match lower volume. The Townsend Hampton Inn, for example, has 54 rooms instead of the usual 135.

In contrast, other retailers are developing new store concepts that will give them access to higher-density urban areas. For example, Home Depot is introducing neighborhood stores that look a lot like its traditional stores but at about two-thirds the size. It is placing these stores in high-density markets where full-size stores are impractical. Similarly, Wal-Mart is testing Neighborhood Market grocery stores to complement its supercenters.[3]

Demographic Segmentation **Demographic segmentation** divides the market into groups based on variables such as age, gender, family size, family life cycle, income, occupation, education, religion, race, generation, and nationality. Demographic factors are the most popular bases for segmenting customer groups. One reason is that consumer needs, wants, and usage rates often vary closely with demographic variables. Another is that demographic variables are easier to measure than most other types of variables. Even when market segments are first defined using other bases, such as benefits sought or behavior, their demographic characteristics must be known in order to assess the size of the target market and to reach it efficiently.

Age and Life-Cycle Stage. Consumer needs and wants change with age. Some companies use **age and life-cycle segmentation**, offering different products or using different marketing approaches for different age and life-cycle groups. For example, for kids,

Demographic segmentation
Dividing the market into groups based on demographic variables such as age, gender, family size, family life cycle, income, occupation, education, religion, race, generation, and nationality.

Age and life-cycle segmentation
Dividing a market into different age and life-cycle groups.

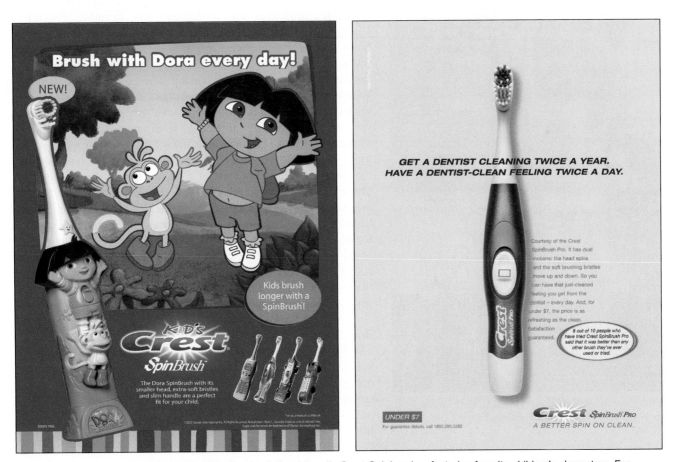

■ Age and life-cycle segmentation: For kids, Procter & Gamble sells Crest Spinbrushes featuring favorite children's characters. For adults, it sells more serious models, promising "a dentist-clean feeling twice a day."

Procter & Gamble sells Crest Spinbrushes featuring children's favorite characters and lots of fun. For adults, it sells more serious models, promising "a dentist-clean feeling twice a day."[4] Gap has branched out to target people at different life stages. In addition to its standard line of clothing, the retailer now offers baby Gap, Gap kids, and Gap Maternity. Here's another example[5]:

> In several of its stores around the country, clothing retailer Eddie Bauer places large, high-definition video screens in its storefront windows to draw in customers who might otherwise walk on by. The screens allow stores to customize in-store advertising to target different generational segments, depending on the time of day. For example, a store might post images featuring older models during the morning hours when retirees frequently shop, then change the posters to reflect the younger shopping crowd of the evening. In one initial nine-month test, sales at one location rose 56 percent from the previous nine months.

Marketers must be careful to guard against stereotypes when using age and life-cycle segmentation. For example, although some 70-year-olds require wheelchairs, others play tennis. Similarly, whereas some 40-year-old couples are sending their children off to college, others are just beginning new families. Thus, age is often a poor predictor of a person's life cycle; health, work, or family status; needs; and buying power. Companies marketing to mature consumers usually employ positive images and appeals. For example, ads for Olay ProVital—designed to improve the elasticity and appearance of the "maturing skin" of women over 50—feature attractive older spokeswomen and uplifting messages.

Gender segmentation
Dividing a market into different groups based on gender.

Gender. **Gender segmentation** has long been used in clothing, cosmetics, toiletries, and magazines. For example, Procter & Gamble was among the first with Secret, a brand specially formulated for a woman's chemistry, packaged and advertised to reinforce the female image. More recently, other marketers have noticed opportunities for targeting women. Citibank launched Women & Co. to sell financial services "designed to help women with all their personal finance and investing needs." Leatherman, which has traditionally targeted its multipurpose combination tool to men, now makes Leatherman Juice for women, hip and stylish tools offered in five vibrant colors. And after its research showed that women make 90 percent of all home improvement decisions, home improvement retailer Lowe's recently launched a family-oriented advertising campaign that reaches out to women buyers. Similarly, Owens-Corning aimed a major advertising campaign for home insulation at women after a study showed that two-thirds of all women were involved in materials installation, with 13 percent doing it themselves. Half the women surveyed compared themselves to Bob Vila, whereas less than half compared themselves to Martha Stewart.[6]

Even the National Football League and advertisers on the Super Bowl, long the holy day of testosterone, are now targeting women. The 30 million or more women who watch the average Super Bowl make up more than 36 percent of the game's audience. And advertisers know that these women influence 80 percent of all household consumer purchases. Moreover, women now account for almost half of all NFL-licensed merchandise purchases. Anheuser-Busch, the biggest advertiser in the game, actively targets its Super Bowl

■ Gender Segmentation: Leatherman targets women with its "juice" tool in five vibrant colors, with ads like this one in *Cooking Light* magazine.

advertising to both genders. Whereas its competitors are still courting men with big doses of babes and sophomoric humor, A-B is showing a more sensitive side. "Women are a huge part of this audience," says A-B's vice president of brand management. "We've been working hard for five years not to do the typical guy jokes."[7]

A growing number of Web sites also target women. For example, Oxygen Media runs a Web site "designed for women by women" (www.oxygen.com). It appeals to 18- to 34-year-old women with fresh and hip information, features, and exchanges on a wide variety of topics—from health and fitness, money and work, and style and home to relationships and self-discovery. The leading women's online community, iVillage (www.iVillage.com), offers "real solutions for real women" and entreats visitors to "join our community of smart, compassionate, real women." Various iVillage channels cover topics ranging from babies, food, fitness, pets, and relationships to careers, finance, and travel.[8]

Income. **Income segmentation** has long been used by the marketers of products and services such as automobiles, boats, clothing, cosmetics, financial services, and travel. Many companies target affluent consumers with luxury goods and convenience services. Stores such as Neiman Marcus pitch everything from expensive jewelry and fine fashions to glazed Australian apricots priced at $20 a pound. To cater to its best customers, Neiman Marcus created its InCircle Rewards program:

> InCircle members, who must spend $3,000 a year using their Neiman Marcus credit cards to be eligible, earn points with each purchase—one point for each dollar charged. They then cash in points for anything from drinks and appetizers with

Income segmentation
Dividing a market into different income groups.

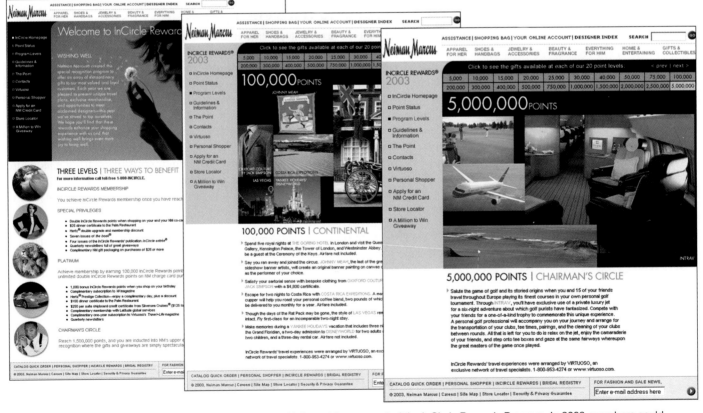

■ Income segmentation: To thank its very best customers, Neiman Marcus created the InCircle Rewards Program. In 2003, members could redeem 5 million points for a tour of Europe's finest golf courses in a private luxury jet with fifteen close friends.

friends at the St. Regis in New York (5000 points) or a one-year membership in the American Airlines Admirals club (15,000 points) to two nights at a deluxe hotel in Montréal complete with free museum admissions, a guided walking tour of the city, VIP admission to Montréal Casino, and a night as an assistant chef for the acclaimed Le Gutenberg restaurant (50,000 points). For 500,000 points, InCircle members can get an all expense paid, 10-day trip to Morocco, and for 1.5 million points, a commemorative Steinway grand piano. The top prize (for 5 million points!) is a tour of Europe's finest golf courses in a private luxury jet with 15 close friends. The trip includes a personal golf professional to arrange tee times, create the pairings for a personal tournament, and clean the member's clubs between rounds.[9]

However, not all companies that use income segmentation target the affluent. Despite their lower spending power, the nearly one-third of the nation's households that earn less than $25,000 per year offer an attractive market. For example, Greyhound Lines, with its inexpensive nationwide bus network, targets lower-income consumers. Almost half of 25 million yearly passengers have annual incomes under $15,000. Many retailers also target this lower-income group, including chains such as Dollar General and Family Dollar stores. When Family Dollar real-estate experts scout locations for new stores, they look for lower-middle-class neighborhoods where people wear less expensive shoes and drive old cars that drip a lot of oil. The typical Family Dollar customer household earns about $25,000 a year, and the average customer spends only about $8 per trip to the store. Similarly, half of Dollar General's customers earn less than $20,000 a year, and about half of its target shoppers do not work. Yet both stores' low-income strategy has put them among the fastest-growing and most-profitable discount chains in the country.[10]

Levi Strauss sells jeans to consumers spanning several income levels. It sells Levi Strauss Signature jeans in Wal-Mart at $23 a pair, Type 1 jeans at Macy's for as much as $65, and Levi Red jeans at luxury stores like Barneys for $150 or more.[11]

Psychographic segmentation

Dividing a market into different groups based on social class, lifestyle, or personality characteristics.

Psychographic Segmentation   **Psychographic segmentation** divides buyers into different groups based on social class, lifestyle, or personality characteristics. People in the same demographic group can have very different psychographic makeups.

In Chapter 5, we discussed how the products people buy reflect their *lifestyles*. As a result, marketers often segment their markets by consumer lifestyles. For example, Duck Head apparel targets a casual student lifestyle claiming "You can't get them old until you get them new." And Pottery Barn sells more than just home furnishings; it sells an entire lifestyle—all that its customers aspire to be (see Marketing at Work 6.1). One forward-looking grocery store found that segmenting its self-service meat products by lifestyle had a big payoff:

Walk by the refrigerated self-service meat cases of most grocery stores and you'll usually find the offering grouped by type of meat. Pork is in one case, lamb is another, and chicken is in a third. However, a Nashville, Tennessee, Kroger supermarket decided to experiment and offer groupings of different meats by lifestyle. For instance, the store had a section called "Meals in Minutes," one called "Cookin' Lite," another, filled with prepared products like hot dogs and ready-made hamburger patties, called "Kids Love This Stuff," and one called "I Like to Cook." By focusing on lifestyle needs and not on protein categories, Kroger's test store encouraged habitual beef and pork buyers to consider lamb and veal as well. As a result, the 16-foot service case has seen a substantial improvement in both sales and profits.[12]

Marketers also have used *personality* variables to segment markets. For example, the marketing campaign for Honda's Reflex and Elite motor scooters *appears* to target hip and trendy 22-year-olds. But it is *actually* aimed at a much broader personality group. One ad, for example, shows a delighted child bouncing up and down on his bed while the announcer says, "You've been trying to get there all your life." The ad reminds viewers of the euphoric feelings they got when they broke away from authority and did things their parents told them not to do. It suggests that they can feel that way again by riding a Honda scooter. Thus, Honda is appealing to the rebellious, independent kid in all of us. As Honda notes on its Web page, "Fresh air, freedom, and flair—on a Honda scooter, every day is independence day! When it comes to cool, this scooter is off the charts!" In fact, more than half of Honda's scooter sales are to young professionals and older buyers—15 percent are purchased by the over-50 group. Aging baby boomers, now thrill-seeking middle-agers, caused a 26 percent jump in scooter sales last year.[13]

Behavioral Segmentation **Behavioral segmentation** divides buyers into groups based on their knowledge, attitudes, uses, or responses to a product. Many marketers believe that behavior variables are the best starting point for building market segments.

Occasions. Buyers can be grouped according to occasions on which they get the idea to buy, actually make their purchase, or use the purchased item. **Occasion segmentation** can help firms build up product usage. For example, orange juice is most often consumed at breakfast, but orange growers have promoted drinking orange juice as a cool and refreshing drink at other times of the day. In contrast, Coca-Cola's "Coke in the Morning" advertising campaign attempts to increase Coke consumption by promoting the beverage as an early morning pick-me-up.

Some holidays, such as Mother's Day and Father's Day, were originally promoted partly to increase the sale of candy, flowers, cards, and other gifts. And many marketers prepare special offers and ads for holiday occasions. For example, Altoids offers a special "Love Tin," the "curiously strong valentine." Beatrice Foods runs special Thanksgiving and Christmas ads for Reddi-wip during November and December, months that account for 30 percent of all whipped cream sales. Hershey wraps its Hershey's Kisses in special

■ Psychographic Segmentation: When Honda markets its Reflex and Elite scooters, it appeals to the rebellious, independent kid in all of us.

Behavioral segmentation
Dividing a market into groups based on consumer knowledge, attitude, use, or response to a product.

Occasion segmentation
Dividing the market into groups according to occasions when buyers get the idea to buy, actually make their purchase, or use the purchased item.

■ Occasion segmentation: For Valentine's Day, Altoids created a special "Love Tin"—a "curiously strong valentine."

Marketing at Work | 6.1

Pottery Barn: Oh, What a Lifestyle!

Shortly after Hadley MacLean got married, she and her husband, Doug, agreed that their old bed had to go. It was a mattress and box spring on a cheap metal frame, a relic of Doug's Harvard days. But Hadley never anticipated how tough it would be to find a new bed. "We couldn't find anything we liked, even though we were willing to spend the money," says Hadley, a 31-year-old marketing director. It turned out to be much more than just finding a piece of furniture at the right price. It was a matter of emotion: They needed a bed that meshed with their lifestyle—with who they are and where they are going.

The couple finally ended up at the Pottery Barn on Boston's upscale Newbury Street, where Doug fell in love with a mahogany sleigh bed that Hadley had spotted in the store's catalog. The couple was so pleased with how great it looked in their Dutch Colonial home that they hurried back to the store for a set of end tables. And then they bought a quilt. And a mirror for the living room. And some stools for the dining room. "We got kind of addicted," Hadley confesses.

The MacLeans aren't alone. Pottery Barn's smart yet accessible product mix, seductive merchandising, and first-rate customer service have made it the front-runner in the fragmented home furnishings and housewares industry—not just because of the products that it sells, but also because of the connections that it makes with customers. Pottery Barn does more than just sell home furnishings. It sells an entire lifestyle.

Three thousand miles away from Hadley MacLean's home in Massachusetts, Laura Alber is obsessed with a towel. A tall, slim blond with pale-blue eyes and no makeup, Alber could be the poster child for the Pottery Barn lifestyle. The 34-year-old California mother of two says that she enjoys entertaining, describes herself as living "holistically," and has just bought the company's Westport sectional sofa, with its kid-resistant twill slipcovers. She also happens to be Pottery Barn's president.

"Feel how great this is," says Alber, pulling a large white bath towel from a stack. "It's thick, it's got a beautiful dobby [the woven band a few inches from the towel's edge], it's highly absorbent, and it's $24. I can say with great confidence that you can't top this." To some merchants, a towel is just a towel. But to Alber, the towel is a fluffy icon of the lifestyle to which Pottery Barn customers aspire: upscale but casual, active but laid back, family-

Pottery Barn sells more than just home furnishings; it sells all that its customers aspire to be. It offers idyllic scenes of the perfect childhood at Pottery Barn Kids; trendy, fashion-forward self-expression at PB Teen; and an upscale yet casual, family- and friend-focused life style at its flagship Pottery Barn stores.

and friend-focused, affluent but sensibly so.

Everyone at Pottery Barn works obsessively to understand the store's customers—who they are, how they live, and what they want out of life. They study customers first-hand and scour the marketplace for ideas. Like Alber, most staffers actually live the lifestyle themselves. They use their deep insights to develop products and store concepts that deliver the Pottery Barn lifestyle to customers.

To pass muster, a potential new Pottery Barn product needs to pass a strict five-point test. First, it has to look good, but not be too cutting edge. Second, the product has to feel good, and third, it must be of high quality. Fourth, it has to be durable—the question "Can the kids jump on it?" is a veritable mantra among Pottery Barn staffers, many of whom have children of their own to road-test the merchandise. Finally, it must pass the ultimate hurdle: "I ask my designers, 'Will you take it home or give it as a present to your best friends,'" says Celia Tejada, head of Pottery Barn's design and product development. "If they hesitate, I say, 'Throw it in the garbage.' Emotionally, it has to feel right."

It's a process that relies more on gut instinct than on rational science. At Pottery Barn, there are no panels of focus groups and no teams of market researchers. To create a powerful lifestyle brand, Tejada says, you must first have a life. So staffers are encouraged to go to restaurants and notice how the tables are set. To scavenge flea markets for interesting artifacts. To cruise real-estate open houses and model homes, looking for new architectural and design trends. To entertain friends and note what products they wish that they had: a bigger platter, a nicer serving utensil, a better bowl for salsa—anything that may be a good addition to the lifestyle line.

Individual products or lines of merchandise aren't the only things inspired by the personal lives of Pottery Barn staffers. It's no coincidence that the first Pottery Barn Kids catalog debuted simultaneously with the birth of Laura Alber's first child. The company's president was frustrated at trying to put together a good-looking nursery. She and her team developed a business plan for extending the Pottery Barn lifestyle to the bedrooms of newborns and young children. There are now 64 Pottery Barn Kids stores, with 16 more scheduled to open this year. As you might expect, Pottery Barn Kids delivers the ultimate kid lifestyle. Stores and catalogs create idyllic scenes of the perfect childhood, featuring themed bedrooms packed with accessories: fluttering curtains, cozy quilts, and stuffed animals. "My husband would tell you the furniture was for me and not the baby," says one mom. It's "a reflection of what I want her to be."

The latest Pottery Barn sibling is PBteen, which targets the lifestyles of tweens and teens. The first PBteen catalog featured furry beanbag chairs, animal-print sheets, and desks that look like lockers. The core products consist of basic things a teenager's room needs: from shag rugs and CD stands to furniture, pillows, and frames. There are some fashion-forward offerings—a skateboard headboard, for instance—but the majority have timeless designs, in keeping with Pottery Barn's other lifestyle offerings. "We've got the stuff that fits your world," says the PBteen Web site. "Go to my room?" it concludes. "Gladly."

The PBteen concept seems like a natural extension for Pottery Barn, but it was one that required significant sleuthing to divine just the right product mix. Pottery Barn staffers spent months trying to get inside the heads of their teenage customers and better under-

stand their lifestyles. "Our designers [were] going to concerts, hanging out at schools, and watching MTV," says one VP. A contest asking kids to mail in snapshots of their rooms generated photographs that gave PBteen staffers a view into the real life-spaces of teenagers. Staffers pored over them like CIA analysts. "The kids are all little pack rats," says one, "with every stuffed animal they've gotten since they were born. That's a huge opportunity for us. We hope to get parents to buy stuff that will impose some order."

Regardless of which family member it targets, Pottery Barn gives customers an attainable and inspirational vision of what a really great lifestyle might look like. That may be the reason why, when Conde Nast magazine recently asked readers to name their favorite home-decorating magazine, an overwhelming number cited the Pottery Barn catalog.

The Pottery Barn lifestyle suits the company as well as its customers. Pottery Barn sales were up almost 12 percent last year; sales at Pottery Barn Kids increased by almost half. The chain's success has helped Pottery Barn's parent company, Williams-Sonoma, to achieve a 6-fold increase in revenues during the past decade, and a 10-fold increase in earnings. Pottery Barn's allure is no mystery to Tejada. "Our brand [embraces a lifestyle]. It's a state of mind. And customers can make it their own."

Sources: Adapted from Linda Tischler, "How Pottery Barn Wins with Style," *Fast Company,* June 2003, pp. 106–113. Additional information from Amy Merrick, "Child's Play for Furniture Retailers?—Amid Signs of a Baby Boom, the Big Chains Rush to Expand Offerings to Newborns, Kids," *Wall Street Journal,* September 25, 2002, p. B1; Charlyne Varkonyi Schaub, "Pottery Barn Tailoring Itself for Teens," *Sun-Sentinel,* May 9, 2003, accessed online at www.sun-sentinel.com; "William's Sonoma, Inc.," *Hoover's Company Profiles,* Austin, May 15, 2003; and information accessed at www.pbteen.com, July 2003.

holiday colors—75 percent of the demand for Kisses is focused around Valentine's Day, Easter, and other holiday time periods. Butterball, on the other hand, advertises "Happy Thanksgrilling" during the summer to increase the demand for turkeys on non-Thanksgiving occasions.

Kodak, Konica, Fuji, and other camera makers use occasion segmentation in designing and marketing their one-time-use cameras. By mixing lenses, film speeds, and accessories, they have developed special disposable cameras for about any picture-taking occasion, from underwater photography to taking baby pictures. The Kodak Water & Sport one-time-use camera is water resistant to 50 feet deep and features a shock-proof frame, a sunscreen and scratch-resistant lens, and 800 speed film. "It survives where your regular camera won't!" claims Kodak.[14]

Benefit segmentation

Dividing the market into groups according to the different benefits that consumers seek from the product.

Benefits Sought. A powerful form of segmentation is to group buyers according to the different *benefits* that they seek from the product. **Benefit segmentation** requires finding the major benefits people look for in the product class, the kinds of people who look for each benefit, and the major brands that deliver each benefit. For example, our chapter-opening example pointed out that Procter & Gamble has identified several different laundry detergent segments. Each segment seeks a unique combination of benefits, from cleaning and bleaching to economy, fabric softening, fresh smell, strength or mildness, and lots of suds or only a little.

The Champion athletic wear division of Sara Lee Corporation segments its markets according to benefits that different consumers seek from their activewear. For example, "fit and polish" consumers seek a balance between function and style—they exercise for results but want to look good doing it. "Serious sports competitors" exercise heavily and live in and love their activewear—they seek performance and function. By contrast, "value-seeking moms" have low sports interest and low activewear involvement—they buy for the family and seek durability and value. Thus, each segment seeks a different mix of benefits. Champion must target the benefit segment or segments that it can serve best and most profitably using appeals that match each segment's benefit preferences.

User Status. Markets can be segmented into groups of nonusers, ex-users, potential users, first-time users, and regular users of a product. For example, one study found that blood donors are low in self-esteem, low risk takers, and more highly concerned about their health; nondonors tend to be the opposite on all three dimensions. This suggests that social agencies should use different marketing approaches for keeping current donors and attracting new ones.

A company's market position also influences its focus. Market share leaders focus on attracting potential users, whereas smaller firms focus on attracting current users away from the market leader.

Usage Rate. Markets can also be segmented into light, medium, and heavy product users. Heavy users are often a small percentage of the market but account for a high percentage of total consumption. Marketers usually prefer to attract one heavy user to their product or service rather than several light users.

For example, in the fast-food industry, heavy users make up only 20 percent of patrons but eat up about 60 percent of all the food served. A single heavy user, typically a single male who doesn't know how to cook, might spend as much as $40 in a day at fast-food restaurants and visit them more than 20 times a month. Heavy users "come more often, they spend more money, and that's what makes the cash registers ring," says a Burger King marketing executive. Interestingly, although fast-food companies such as Burger King, McDonald's, and KFC depend a lot on heavy users and do all they can to keep them satisfied with every visit, these companies often target light users with their ads and promotions. The heavy users "are in our restaurants already," says the Burger King marketer. The company's marketing dollars are more often spent trying to convince light users that they want a burger in the first place.[15]

Loyalty Status. A market can also be segmented by consumer loyalty. Consumers can be loyal to brands (Tide), stores (Wal-Mart), and companies (Ford). Buyers can be divided into groups according to their degree of loyalty. Some consumers are completely loyal—they buy one brand all the time. Others are somewhat loyal—they are loyal to two or three brands of a given product or favor one brand while sometimes buying others. Still other buyers show no loyalty to any brand. They either want something different each time they buy or they buy whatever's on sale.

A company can learn a lot by analyzing loyalty patterns in its market. It should start by studying its own loyal customers. For example, to better understand the needs and behavior of its core soft drink consumers, Pepsi observed them in places where its products are consumed—in homes, in stores, in movie theaters, at sporting events, and at the beach. "We learned that there's a surprising amount of loyalty and passion for Pepsi's products," says Pepsi's director of consumer insights. "One fellow had four or five cases of Pepsi in his basement and he felt he was low on Pepsi and had to go replenish." The company used these and other study findings to pinpoint the Pepsi target market and develop marketing appeals.[16]

By studying its less loyal buyers, the company can detect which brands are most competitive with its own. If many Pepsi buyers also buy Coke, Pepsi can attempt to improve its positioning against Coke, possibly by using direct-comparison advertising. By looking at customers who are shifting away from its brand, the company can learn about its marketing weaknesses. As for nonloyals, the company may attract them by putting its brand on sale.

Using Multiple Segmentation Bases Marketers rarely limit their segmentation analysis to only one or a few variables. Rather, they are increasingly using multiple segmentation bases in an effort to identify smaller, better-defined target groups. Thus, a bank may not only identify a group of wealthy retired adults but also, within that group, distinguish several segments based on their current income, assets, savings and risk preferences, and lifestyles. Companies often begin by segmenting their markets using a single base, then expand using other bases.

One good example of multivariable segmentation is "geodemographic" segmentation. Several business information services have arisen to help marketing planners link U.S. Census data with lifestyle patterns to better segment their markets down to ZIP codes, neighborhoods, and even city blocks. One of the leading lifestyle segmentation systems is PRIZM "You Are Where You Live" system by Claritas. By marrying a host of demographic factors—such as age, education, income, occupation, family life cycle, housing, ethnicity, and urbanization—with lifestyle information taken from consumer surveys, the PRIZM system classifies every one of the more than 260,000 U.S. neighborhoods into one of 62 clusters. Clusters carry such exotic names as "Kids & Cul-de-Sacs," "Blue Blood Estates," "Money & Brains," "Young Literati," "Shotguns & Pickups," "American Dreams," "New Eco-topias," "Mobility Blues," and "Gray Power."

Each cluster exhibits unique characteristics and buying behavior. For example, "Blue Blood Estates" neighborhoods are suburban areas populated by elite, super-rich families. People in this cluster are more likely to belong to health clubs, take expensive trips, buy classical music, and read *Architectural Digest*. In contrast, the "Shotguns & Pickups" cluster is populated by rural, blue-collar workers and families. People in this group are more likely to go fishing, use chain saws, own a dog, drink RC Cola, watch ESPN2, and read *Motor Trend*. People in the "Hispanic Mix" cluster are highly brand conscious, quality conscious, and brand loyal. They have a strong family and home orientation.

Such segmentation provides a powerful tool for segmenting markets, refining demand estimates, selecting target markets, and shaping promotion messages. For example, in marketing its Suave shampoo, Unilever's Helene Curtis division uses PRIZM to identify neighborhoods with high concentrations of working women. Such women respond best to advertising messages that with Suave, "looking great doesn't have to cost a fortune." Bookseller Barnes & Noble locates its stores where there are concentrations of

■ In marketing its Suave shampoo, Helene Curtis uses PRIZM to identify neighborhoods with high concentrations of working women. Such women respond best to advertising messages that with Suave, "looking great doesn't have to cost a fortune."

"Money & Brains" consumers, because they buy lots of books.[17]

Segmenting Business Markets

Consumer and business marketers use many of the same variables to segment their markets. Business buyers can be segmented geographically, demographically (industry, company size), or by benefits sought, user status, usage rate, and loyalty status. Yet, business marketers also use some additional variables, such as customer *operating characteristics*, *purchasing approaches*, *situational factors*, and *personal characteristics*.

By going after segments instead of the whole market, companies have a much better chance to deliver value to consumers and to receive maximum rewards for close attention to consumer needs. Hewlett-Packard's Computer Systems Division targets specific industries that promise the best growth prospects, such as telecommunications and financial services. Its "red team" sales force specializes in developing and serving major customers in these targeted industries.[18] Within the chosen industry, a company can further segment by *customer size* or *geographic location*. For example, Hewlett-Packard's "blue team" telemarkets to smaller accounts and to those that don't fit neatly into the strategically targeted industries on which HP focuses.

A company might also set up separate systems for dealing with larger or multiple-location customers. For example, Steelcase, a major producer of office furniture, first segments customers into 10 industries, including banking, insurance, and electronics. Next, company salespeople work with independent Steelcase dealers to handle smaller, local, or regional Steelcase customers in each segment. But many national, multiple-location customers, such as Exxon/Mobil or IBM, have special needs that may reach beyond the scope of individual dealers. So Steelcase uses national accounts managers to help its dealer networks handle its national accounts.

Within a given target industry and customer size, the company can segment by purchase approaches and criteria. As in consumer segmentation, many marketers believe that *buying behavior* and *benefits* provide the best basis for segmenting business markets.[19]

Segmenting International Markets

Few companies have either the resources or the will to operate in all, or even most, of the countries that dot the globe. Although some large companies, such as Coca-Cola or Sony, sell products in more than 200 countries, most international firms focus on a smaller set. Operating in many countries presents new challenges. Different countries, even those that are close together, can vary greatly in their economic, cultural, and political makeup. Thus, just as they do within their domestic markets, international firms need to group their world markets into segments with distinct buying needs and behaviors.

Companies can segment international markets using one or a combination of several variables. They can segment by *geographic location*, grouping countries by regions such as Western Europe, the Pacific Rim, the Middle East, or Africa. Geographic segmentation assumes that nations close to one another will have many common traits and behaviors. Although this is often the case, there are many exceptions. For example, although the United States and Canada have much in common, both differ culturally and economically from neighboring Mexico. Even within a region, consumers can differ widely. For example, many U.S. marketers think that all Central and South American countries are the same, including their 400 million inhabitants. However, the Dominican Republic is no more like Brazil than Italy is like Sweden. Many Latin Americans don't speak Spanish, including 140 million Portuguese-speaking Brazilians and the millions in other countries who speak a variety of Indian dialects.

World markets can also be segmented on the basis of *economic factors*. For example, countries might be grouped by population income levels or by their overall level of economic development. Some countries, such as the United States, Britain, France, Germany, Japan, Canada, Italy, and Russia, have established, highly industrialized economies. Other countries have newly industrialized or developing economies (Singapore, Taiwan, Korea, Brazil, Mexico). Still others are less developed (China, India). A company's economic structure shapes its population's product and service needs and, therefore, the marketing opportunities it offers.

Countries can be segmented by *political and legal factors* such as the type and stability of government, receptivity to foreign firms, monetary regulations, and the amount of bureaucracy. Such factors can play a crucial role in a company's choice of which countries to enter and how. *Cultural factors* can also be used, grouping markets according to common languages, religions, values and attitudes, customs, and behavioral patterns.

Segmenting international markets on the basis of geographic, economic, political, cultural, and other factors assumes that segments should consist of clusters of countries. However, many companies use a different approach called **intermarket segmentation**. Using this approach, they form segments of consumers who have similar needs and buying behavior even though they are located in different countries. For example, Mercedes-Benz targets the world's well-to-do, regardless of their country.

Intermarket segmentation
Forming segments of consumers who have similar needs and buying behavior even though they are located in different countries.

MTV targets the world's teenagers. The world's teens have a lot in common: They study, shop, and sleep. They are exposed to many of the same major issues: love, crime, homelessness, ecology, and working parents. In many ways, they have more in common with each other than with their parents. "Last year I was in seventeen different countries," says one expert, "and it's pretty difficult to find anything that is different, other then language, among a teenager in Japan, a teenager in the UK, and a teenager in China." Says another, "Global teens in Buenos Aires, Beijing, and Bangalore swing to the beat of MTV while sipping Coke." MTV bridges the gap between cultures, appealing to what teens around the world have in common. Sony, Reebok, Nike, Swatch, and many other firms also actively target global teens.[20]

■ Intermarket segmentation: Teens show surprising similarity no matter where in the world they live. For instance, these two teens could live almost anywhere. Thus, many companies target teenagers with worldwide marketing campaigns.

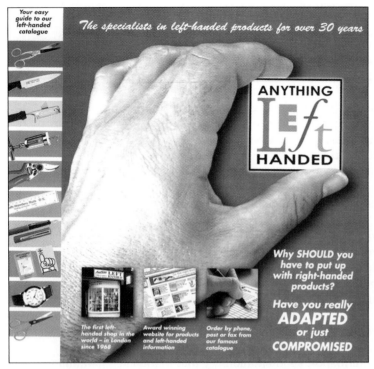

■ The "Leftie" segment can be hard to identify and measure. As a result, few companies tailor their offers to left-handers. However, some nichers such as Anything Left-Handed in the UK target this segment.

Requirements for Effective Segmentation

Clearly, there are many ways to segment a market, but not all segmentations are effective. For example, buyers of table salt could be divided into blond and brunette customers. But hair color obviously does not affect the purchase of salt. Furthermore, if all salt buyers bought the same amount of salt each month, believed that all salt is the same, and wanted to pay the same price, the company would not benefit from segmenting this market.

To be useful, market segments must be

■ *Measurable:* The size, purchasing power, and profiles of the segments can be measured. Certain segmentation variables are difficult to measure. For example, there are 32.5 million left-handed people in the United States—almost equaling the entire population of Canada. Yet few products are targeted toward this left-handed segment. The major problem may be that the segment is hard to identify and measure. There are no data on the demographics of lefties, and the U.S. Census Bureau does not keep track of left-handedness in its surveys. Private data companies keep reams of statistics on other demographic segments but not on left-handers. As a result, only market nichers like Anything Left-Handed in the UK target this segment.

■ *Accessible:* The market segments can be effectively reached and served. Suppose a fragrance company finds that heavy users of its brand are single men and women who stay out late and socialize a lot. Unless this group lives or shops at certain places and is exposed to certain media, its members will be difficult to reach.

■ *Substantial:* The market segments are large or profitable enough to serve. A segment should be the largest possible homogeneous group worth pursuing with a tailored marketing program. It would not pay, for example, for an automobile manufacturer to develop cars especially for people whose height is greater than seven feet.

■ *Differentiable:* The segments are conceptually distinguishable and respond differently to different marketing mix elements and programs. If married and unmarried women respond similarly to a sale on perfume, they do not constitute separate segments.

■ *Actionable:* Effective programs can be designed for attracting and serving the segments. For example, although one small airline identified seven market segments, its staff was too small to develop separate marketing programs for each segment.

SPEED BUMP

Linking the Concepts

Slow down a bit and smell the roses. How do the companies you do business with employ the segmentation concepts you're reading about here?

■ Can you identify specific companies, other than the examples already discussed, which practice the different types of segmentation just discussed?

■ Using the segmentation bases you've just read about, segment the U.S. footwear market. Describe each of the major segments and subsegments. Keep these segments in mind as you read the next section on target marketing.

■■ Target Marketing

Market segmentation reveals the firm's market segment opportunities. The firm now has to evaluate the various segments and decide how many and which segments it can serve best. We now look at how companies evaluate and select target segments.

Evaluating Market Segments

In evaluating different market segments, a firm must look at three factors: segment size and growth, segment structural attractiveness, and company objectives and resources.

Segment Size and Growth The company must first collect and analyze data on current segment sales, growth rates, and expected profitability for various segments. It will be interested in segments that have the right size and growth characteristics. But "right size and growth" is a relative matter. The largest, fastest-growing segments are not always the most attractive ones for every company. Smaller companies may lack the skills and resources needed to serve the larger segments. Or they may find these segments too competitive. Such companies may select segments that are smaller and less attractive, in an absolute sense, but that are potentially more profitable for them.

Segment Structural Attractiveness The company also needs to examine major structural factors that affect long-run segment attractiveness.[21] For example, a segment is less attractive if it already contains many strong and aggressive *competitors*. The existence of many actual or potential *substitute products* may limit prices and the profits that can be earned in a segment. The relative *power of buyers* also affects segment attractiveness. Buyers with strong bargaining power relative to sellers will try to force prices down, demand more services, and set competitors against one another—all at the expense of seller profitability. Finally, a segment may be less attractive if it contains *powerful suppliers* who can control prices or reduce the quality or quantity of ordered goods and services.

Company Objectives and Resources Even if a segment has the right size and growth and is structurally attractive, the company must consider its own objectives and resources in relation to that segment. Some attractive segments could be dismissed quickly because they do not mesh with the company's long-run objectives. The company must consider whether it possesses the skills and resources needed to succeed in that segment. If the company lacks the needed strengths and cannot readily obtain them, it should not enter the segment. Even if the company possesses the *required* strengths, it needs to employ skills and resources *superior* to those of the competition in order to really win in a market segment. The company should enter only segments in which it can offer superior value and gain advantages over competitors.

Selecting Target Segments

After evaluating different segments, the company must now decide which and how many segments it will target. A **target market** consists of a set of buyers who share common needs or characteristics that the company decides to serve.

Because buyers have unique needs and wants, a seller could potentially view each buyer as a separate target market. Ideally, then, a seller might design a separate marketing program for each buyer. However, although some companies do attempt to serve buyers individually, most face larger numbers of smaller buyers and do not find individual targeting worthwhile. Instead, they look for broader segments of buyers. More generally, target marketing can be carried out at several different levels. Figure 6.2 shows that companies can target very broadly (undifferentiated marketing), very narrowly (micromarketing), or somewhere in between (differentiated or concentrated marketing).

Target market
A set of buyers sharing common needs or characteristics that the company decides to serve.

FIGURE 6.2

Target Marketing Strategies

| Undifferentiated (mass) marketing | → | Differentiated (segmented) marketing | → | Concentrated (niche) marketing | → | Micromarketing (local or individual marketing) |

Targeting broadly   Targeting narrowly

FIGURE 6.2

Target Marketing Strategies

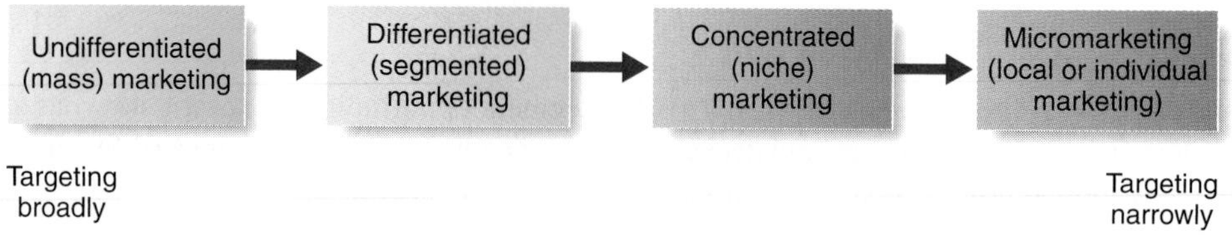

Undifferentiated (mass) marketing

A market-coverage strategy in which a firm decides to ignore market segment differences and go after the whole market with one offer.

Differentiated (segmented) marketing

A market-coverage strategy in which a firm decides to target several market segments and designs separate offers for each.

Undifferentiated Marketing Using an **undifferentiated marketing** (or **mass marketing**) strategy, a firm might decide to ignore market segment differences and target the whole market with one offer. This mass-marketing strategy focuses on what is *common* in the needs of consumers rather than on what is *different*. The company designs a product and a marketing program that will appeal to the largest number of buyers. It relies on mass distribution and mass advertising, and it aims to give the product a superior image in people's minds.

As noted earlier in the chapter, most modern marketers have strong doubts about this strategy. Difficulties arise in developing a product or brand that will satisfy all consumers. Moreover, mass marketers often have trouble competing with more focused firms that do a better job of satisfying the needs of specific segments and niches.

Differentiated Marketing Using a **differentiated marketing** (or **segmented marketing**) strategy, a firm decides to target several market segments and designs separate offers for each. General Motors tries to produce a car for every "purse, purpose, and personality." Nike offers athletic shoes for a dozen or more different sports, from running, fencing, golf, and aerobics to baseball and bicycling. Marriott markets to a variety of segments—business travelers, families, and others—with hotel formats and packages adapted to their varying needs. And American Express offers not only its traditional green cards but also gold cards, platinum cards, corporate cards, and even a black card, called the Centurian, with a $1,000 annual fee aimed at a segment of "superpremium customers."

Estée Lauder offers dozens of different products aimed at carefully defined segments:

> The four best-selling prestige perfumes in the United States belong to Estée Lauder. So do 7 of the top 10 prestige makeup products and 8 of the 10 best-selling prestige skin care products. Estée Lauder is an expert in creating differentiated brands that serve the tastes of different market segments. There's the original Estée Lauder brand, which appeals to older, Junior League types. Then there's Clinique, perfect for the middle-aged mom with a GMC Suburban and no time to waste. For the youthful hipster, there's the hip M.A.C. line. And, for the New Age type, there's upscale Aveda, with its aromatherapy line, and earthy Origins, which the company expects will become a $1 billion brand. The company even offers downscale brands, such as Jane by Sassaby, for teens at Wal-Mart and Rite Aid.[22]

By offering product and marketing variations to segments, companies hope for higher sales and a stronger position within each market segment. Developing a stronger position within several segments creates more total sales than undifferentiated marketing across all segments. Procter & Gamble gets more total market share with seven brands of laundry detergent than it could with only one. And Estée Lauder's combined brands give it a much greater market share than any single brand could. The Estée Lauder and Clinique brands alone reap a combined 40 percent share of the prestige cosmetics market.

But differentiated marketing also increases the costs of doing business. A firm usually finds it more expensive to develop and produce, say, 10 units of 10 different products than 100 units of 1 product. Developing separate marketing plans for the separate segments requires extra marketing research, forecasting, sales analysis, promotion planning, and channel management. And trying to reach different market segments with different advertising increases promotion costs. Thus, the company must weigh increased sales against increased costs when deciding on a differentiated marketing strategy.

Concentrated Marketing   A third market-coverage strategy, **concentrated marketing** (or **niche marketing**), is especially appealing when company resources are limited. Instead of going after a small share of a large market, the firm goes after a large share of one or a few segments or niches. For example, Oshkosh Truck is the world's largest producer of airport rescue trucks and front-loading concrete mixers. Tetra sells 80 percent of the world's tropical fish food, and Steiner Optical captures 80 percent of the world's military binoculars market.

Whereas segments are fairly large and normally attract several competitors, niches are smaller and may attract only one or a few competitors. Through concentrated marketing, the firm achieves a strong market position because of its greater knowledge of consumer needs in the niches it serves and the special reputation it acquires. It can market more *effectively* by fine-tuning its products, prices, and programs to the needs of carefully defined segments. It can also market more *efficiently*, targeting its products or services, channels, and communications programs toward only the consumers that it can serve best and most profitably.

> **Concentrated (niche) marketing**
> A market-coverage strategy in which a firm goes after a large share of one or a few segments, or niches.

Niching offers smaller companies an opportunity to compete by focusing their limited resources on serving niches that may be unimportant to or overlooked by larger competitors. Consider Apple Computer. Although it once enjoyed a better than 13 percent market share, Apples now a market nicher, capturing only about 3.5 percent of its market. Rather than competing head-on with other PC makers as they slash prices and focus on volume, Apple invests in research and development, making it the industry trendsetter. Such innovation has created a loyal base of consumers who are willing to pay more for Apple's cutting edge products.[23]

■ Niching: Rather than competing head-on with other PC makers, Apple has invested in research and development, creating a loyal base of consumers who are willing to pay more for Apple's cutting edge products.

Many companies start as nichers to get a foothold against larger, more resourceful competitors, then grow into broader competitors. For example, Southwest Airlines began by serving intrastate, no-frills commuters in Texas but is now one of the nation's eight largest airlines. Wal-Mart, which got its start by bringing everyday low prices to small towns and rural areas, is now the world's largest company. In contrast, as markets change, some mega-marketers are developing niche markets to create sales growth. For example, Pepsi has recently introduced several products that appeal to specific niche markets, such as Sierra Mist, Pepsi Blue, and Mountain Dew Code Red. Together, these brands account for barely 5 percent of Pepsi's overall soft-drink sales. That may not seem much, but that's the idea. Says Pepsi-Cola North America's chief marketing officer, "The era of the mass brand has been over for a long time."[24]

Today, the low cost of setting up shop on the Internet makes it even more profitable to serve seemingly minuscule niches. Small businesses, in particular, are realizing riches from serving small niches on the Web. Here is a "Webpreneur" who achieved astonishing results:

> Whereas Internet giants like Amazon.com have yet to even realize a consistent profit, Steve Warrington is earning a six-figure income selling ostriches—and every product derived from them—online (www.ostrichesonline.com). Launched for next to nothing on the Web in 1996, Ostrichesonline.com now boasts that it sends newsletters to 33,000 subscribers and sells 17,500 ostrich products to more than 18,000 satisfied clients in more than 125 countries. The site tells visitors everything they ever wanted to know about ostriches and much,

much more—it supplies ostrich facts, ostrich pictures, an ostrich farm index, and a huge ostrich database and reference index. Visitors to the site can buy ostrich meat, feathers, leather jackets, videos, eggshells, and skin care products derived from ostrich body oil.[25]

Concentrated marketing can be highly profitable. At the same time, it involves higher-than-normal risks. Companies that rely on one or a few segments for all of their business will suffer greatly if the segment turns sour. Or larger competitors may decide to enter the same segment. California Cooler's early success in the wine cooler segment attracted many large competitors, causing the original owners to sell to a larger company that had more marketing resources. For these reasons, many companies prefer to diversify in several market segments.

Micromarketing Differentiated and concentrated marketers tailor their offers and marketing programs to meet the needs of various market segments and niches. At the same time, however, they do not customize their offers to each individual customer. **Micromarketing** is the practice of tailoring products and marketing programs to suit the tastes of specific individuals and locations. Rather than seeing a customer in every individual, micromarketers see the individual in every customer. Micromarketing includes *local marketing* and *individual marketing*.

Local Marketing. **Local marketing** involves tailoring brands and promotions to the needs and wants of local customer groups—cities, neighborhoods, and even specific stores. Retailers such as Sears and Wal-Mart routinely customize each store's merchandise and promotions to match its specific clientele. Citibank provides different mixes of banking services in its branches, depending on neighborhood demographics. Kraft helps supermarket chains identify the specific cheese assortments and shelf positioning that will optimize cheese sales in low-income, middle-income, and high-income stores and in different ethnic communities.

Micromarketing

The practice of tailoring products and marketing programs to the needs and wants of specific individuals and local customer groups—includes *local marketing* and *individual marketing.*

Local marketing

Tailoring brands and promotions to the needs and wants of local customer groups—cities, neighborhoods, and even specific stores.

■ Local marketing: Some marketers tailor their offers to the needs and wants of local customers. Video screens in some Eddie Bauer storefront windows allow each store to customize in-store advertising to its specific customer mix.

Local marketing has some drawbacks. It can drive up manufacturing and marketing costs by reducing economies of scale. It can also create logistics problems, as companies try to meet the varied requirements of different regional and local markets. Furthermore, a brand's overall image might be diluted if the product and message vary too much in different localities.

Still, as companies face increasingly fragmented markets, and as new supporting technologies develop, the advantages of local marketing often outweigh the drawbacks. Local marketing helps a company to market more effectively in the face of pronounced regional and local differences in demographics and lifestyles. It also meets the needs of the company's first-line customers—retailers—who prefer more fine-tuned product assortments for their neighborhoods.

Individual marketing

Tailoring products and marketing programs to the needs and preferences of individual customers—also labeled "markets-of-one marketing," "customized marketing," and "one-to-one marketing."

Individual Marketing. In the extreme, micromarketing becomes **individual marketing**—tailoring products and marketing programs to the needs and preferences of individual customers. Individual marketing has also been labeled *one-to-one marketing, customized marketing,* and *markets-of-one marketing.*

The widespread use of mass marketing has obscured the fact that for centuries consumers were served as individuals: The tailor custom-made the suit, the cobbler designed shoes for the individual, the cabinetmaker made furniture to order. Today, however, new technologies are permitting many companies to return to customized marketing. More powerful computers, detailed databases, robotic production and flexible manufacturing, and interactive communication media such as e-mail, fax, and the Internet—all have combined to foster "mass customization." *Mass customization* is the process through which firms interact one-to-one with masses of customers to design products and services tailor-made to individual needs (see Marketing at Work 6.2).

Dell Computer delivers computers to individual customers loaded with customer-specified hardware and software. Hockey stick maker Branches Hockey lets customers choose from more than two-dozen options—including stick length, blade patterns, and blade curve—and turns out a customized stick in five days. And Ritz-Carlton Hotels creates custom-designed experiences for its delighted guests:

> Check into any Ritz-Carlton hotel around the world, and you'll be amazed at how well the hotel's employees anticipate your slightest need. Without ever asking, they seem to know that you want a nonsmoking room with a king-size bed, a nonallergenic pillow, and breakfast with decaffeinated coffee in your room. How does Ritz-Carlton work this magic? The hotel employs a system that combines information technology and flexible operations to customize the hotel experience. At the heart of the system is a huge customer database, which contains information gathered through the observations of hotel employees. Each day, hotel staffers—from those at the front desk to those in maintenance and housekeeping—discreetly record the unique habits, likes, and dislikes of each guest on small "guest preference pads." These observations are then transferred to a corporatewide "guest preference database." Every morning, a "guest historian" at each hotel reviews the files of all new arrivals who have previously stayed at a Ritz-Carlton and prepares a list of suggested extra touches that might delight each guest. Guests have responded strongly to such markets-of-one service. Since inaugurating the guest-history system, Ritz-Carlton has boosted guest retention by 23 percent. An amazing 95 percent of departing guests report that their stay has been a truly memorable experience. Business-to-business marketers are also finding new ways to customize their offerings.

For example, Becton-Dickinson, a major medical supplier, offers to customize almost anything for its hospital customers. It offers custom-designed labeling, individual packaging, customized quality control, customized computer software, and customized billing. And John Deere manufactures seeding equipment that can be configured in more than 2 million versions to individual customer specifications. The seeders are produced one at a time, in any sequence, on a single production line.[26]

The move toward individual marketing mirrors the trend in consumer *self-marketing*. Increasingly, individual customers are taking more responsibility for determining which products and brands to buy. Consider two business buyers with two different purchasing styles. The first sees several salespeople, each trying to persuade him to buy his or her product. The second sees no salespeople but rather logs on to the Internet. She searches for information on available products; interacts electronically with various suppliers, users, and product analysts; and then makes up her own mind about the best offer. The second purchasing agent has taken more responsibility for the buying process, and the marketer has had less influence over her buying decision.

As the trend toward more interactive dialogue and less advertising monologue continues, self-marketing will grow in importance. As more buyers look up consumer reports, join Internet product discussion forums, and place orders via phone or online, marketers will have to influence the buying process in new ways. Many companies now practice *customerization*.[27] They combine operationally driven mass customization with customized marketing to empower consumers to design products and services to their own preferences. They involve customers more in all phases of the product development and buying processes, increasing opportunities for buyers to practice self-marketing.

Choosing a Target Marketing Strategy Companies need to consider many factors when choosing a target-marketing strategy. Which strategy is best depends on *company resources*. When the firm's resources are limited, concentrated marketing makes

Marketing at Work | 6.2

Markets of One: Treating Customers As Individuals

Imagine walking into a booth that bathes your body in patterns of white light and, in a matter of seconds, captures your exact three-dimensional form. The digitized data are then imprinted on a credit card, which you use to order customized clothing. No, this isn't a scene from the next Star Wars sequel; it's a peek ahead at how you will be able to buy clothing in the not-so-distant future. A consortium of over 100 apparel companies, including Levi-Strauss, has banded together to develop body-scanning technology in the hope of making mass customization commonplace.

Although body-scanning technology and smart cards carrying customer measurements are still in development, many companies are now using existing technologies to tailor products to individual customers. Dell creates custom-configured computers, Reflect.com formulates customized beauty products,

Ford lets buyers "build a vehicle" from a palette of options, and Golf to Fit crafts custom clubs based on consumer measurements and preferences. Companies selling all kinds of products—from candy, clothing, and hockey sticks to fire trucks—are customizing their offerings to the needs of individual buyers.

Here are some other examples of companies in the forefront of the mass-customization economy:

Levi-Strauss. *In 1994, Levi began making measure-to-fit women's jeans under its in-store Personal Pair program. Consumer response was so positive that Levi developed an expanded in-store customization concept called Original Spin, which works a lot like the futuristic sizing scenario described above. Original Spin lets buyers create their own jeans from scratch or modify an*

existing pair. Customers—both men and women—enter a booth in which a 3-D Body Scanner creates personalized measurements against a backdrop of strobe lights and space-age music. Using the Original Spin terminals, customers can then choose from a range of cuts and styles that represent hundreds of different pairs of jeans available for purchase. Whereas a fully stocked Levi's store carries 130 pairs of ready-to-wear jeans for a given waist and inseam, with Original Spin the number jumps to 750.

Mattel. *Girls can log on to the "My Design" page of the Barbie Web site (www.barbie.com) and create their very own "friend of Barbie" doll. They choose the doll's skin tone, eye color, hairstyle and hair color, clothes, accessories, personality, and name. They even fill out a questionnaire detailing their doll's likes*

Mass customization: M&M's Colorworks site lets customers special order the tasty little candies in whatever combination of 21 colors suits their fancy.

and dislikes. When Barbie's special friend arrives in the mail, the girls find the doll's name on the packaging along with a computer-generated paragraph about her personality.

Mars M&Ms. *Looking to sweeten up a party or special celebration? Try the M&M's Colorworks site, where you can special order the tasty little candies in whatever combination of colors suits your fancy. Mix up a patriotic combo of red, white, and blue M&Ms for the chocolate lovers at your Fourth of July celebration. Or special order a blend of your school colors for the next tailgate party. Send promotional packs featuring your company colors to special customers. Don't know what colors to choose? No problem. The site is packed with suggestions for just about any occasion. Colorworks lets you pick from a palette of 21 colors and order in 8-ounce or 5-pound customized bags. It's a bit spendy— nearly three times the cost of regular M&Ms. But business is booming, with sales doubling every year. Next up? Along with the famous "m" on its candies, the company is trying out personalized messages. How about "boo" your Halloween M&Ms, or "HO HO HO" at Christmas? "Want to see your name on a batch of aqua-green M&Ms?" asks one analyst. "It could happen."*

Consumer goods marketers aren't the only ones going one-to-one. B2B marketers also provide customers with tailor-made goods, often more cheaply and quickly than it used to take to make standardized ones. Particularly for small companies, mass customization provides a way to stand out against larger competitors:

Oshkosh Truck. *Oshkosh Truck specializes in making fire, garbage,* *cement, and military trucks. Oshkosh is small—one-tenth the size of larger rivals such as Paccar and Navistar International—and the truck industry is slumping. Yet Oshkosh has more than doubled its sales and increased its earnings sixfold over the past five years. What's the secret to Oshkosh's success? Mass customization—the ability to personalize its products and services to the needs of individual customers. For example, when fire- fighters order a truck from Oshkosh, it's an event. They travel to the plant to watch the vehicle, which may cost as much as $800,000, take shape. The firefighters can choose from 19,000 options. A stripped-down fire truck costs $130,000, but 75 percent of Oshkosh's customers order lots of extras, like hideaway stairs, ladders, special doors, compartments, and firefighting foam systems for those difficult-to-extinguish fires. Some bring along paint chips so they can customize the color of their fleet. Others are content just to admire the vehicles, down to the water tanks and hideaway ladders. "Some chiefs even bring their wives; we encourage it," says the president of Oshkosh's fire- fighting unit, Pierce Manufacturing. "Buying a fire truck is a very personal thing." Indeed, Pierce customers are in town so often the Holiday Inn renamed its lounge the Hook and Ladder. Through such customization and personalization, smaller Oshkosh has gained a big edge over its lan- guishing larger rivals.*

Two trends underlie the growth in one-to-one marketing. First, today's consumers have very high expecta- tions—they expect products and ser- vices that meet their individual needs. Yet, it would be too expensive or down- right impossible to meet these individ- ual demands if it weren't for another trend: rapid advances in technology. Data warehouses now allow companies to store trillions of bytes of customer information. Computer-controlled fac- tory equipment and industrial robots can now quickly readjust assembly lines. Bar code scanners make it possi- ble to track parts and products. Most important, the Internet ties it all together and makes it easy for a company to interact with customers, learn about their preferences, and respond. Indeed, the Internet appears to be the ultimate one-to-one medium.

Unlike mass production, which elim- inates the need for human interaction, mass customization has made relation- ships with customers more important than ever. For instance, when Levi's sells made-to-order jeans, the com- pany not only captures consumer data in digitized form but also becomes the customer's "jeans adviser." And Mattel is building a database of information on all the customers of My Design dolls so it can start long-term, one-to-one rela- tionships with each customer.

Just as mass production was the marketing principle of the past century, mass customization is becoming a mar- keting principle for the twenty-first cen- tury. The world appears to be coming full circle—from the good old days when customers were treated as individuals, to mass marketing when nobody knew your name, and back again.

Sources: See James H. Gilmore and B. Joseph Pine, *Markets of One: Creating Customer-Unique Value Through Mass Customization* (Boston: Harvard Business School Press, 2001); Don Peppers and Martha Rogers, *One to One B2B: Customer Development Strategies for the Business-to- Business World* (New York, NY: Doubleday, 2001); Faith Keenan, "A Mass Market of One," *Business Week,* December 2, 2002, pp. 68–72; "Oshkosh Truck Corporation," *Hoover's Company Profiles,* Austin, May 15, 2003; and information accessed at www.us.levi.com, www.colorworks.com, www. Barbie.com/Activities/Fashion_Fun/MyDesign/look. asp, and www.oshkoshtruck.com, October 2003.

the most sense. The best strategy also depends on the degree of *product variability*. Undifferentiated marketing is more suited for uniform products such as grapefruit or steel. Products that can vary in design, such as cameras and automobiles, are more suited to differentiation or concentration.

The *product's life-cycle stage* also must be considered. When a firm introduces a new product, it may be practical to launch only one version, and undifferentiated marketing or concentrated marketing may make the most sense. In the mature stage of the product life cycle, however, differentiated marketing begins to make more sense. Another factor is *market variability*. If most buyers have the same tastes, buy the same amounts, and react the same way to marketing efforts, undifferentiated marketing is appropriate. Finally, *competitors' marketing strategies* are important. When competitors use differentiated or concentrated marketing, undifferentiated marketing can be suicidal. Conversely, when competitors use undifferentiated marketing, a firm can gain an advantage by using differentiated or concentrated marketing.

Socially Responsible Target Marketing

Smart targeting helps companies to be more efficient and effective by focusing on the segments that they can satisfy best and most profitably. Targeting also benefits consumers—companies reach specific groups of consumers with offers carefully tailored to satisfy their needs. However, target marketing sometimes generates controversy and concern. Issues usually involve the targeting of vulnerable or disadvantaged consumers with controversial or potentially harmful products.

For example, over the years, the cereal industry has been heavily criticized for its marketing efforts directed toward children. Critics worry that premium offers and high-powered advertising appeals presented through the mouths of lovable animated characters will overwhelm children's defenses. The marketers of toys and other children's products have been similarly battered, often with good justification.

Other problems arise when the marketing of adult products spills over into the kid segment—intentionally or unintentionally. For example, the Federal Trade Commission and citizen action groups have accused tobacco companies of targeting underage smokers. And a recent FTC study found that 80 percent of R-rated movies and 70 percent of video games with a mature rating were targeted to children under 17.[28] Some critics have even called for a complete ban on advertising to children. To encourage responsible advertising to children, the Children's Advertising Review Unit, the advertising industry's self-regulatory agency, has published extensive children's advertising guidelines that recognize the special needs of child audiences.

Cigarette, beer, and fast-food marketers have also generated much controversy in recent years by their attempts to target inner-city minority consumers. For example, McDonald's and other chains have drawn criticism for pitching their high-fat, salt-laden fare to low-income, inner-city residents, who are much more likely than are suburbanites to be heavy consumers. Last year, McDonald's faced lawsuits alleging that its marketing practices are responsible for teenage obesity. Similarly, R.J. Reynolds took heavy flak in the early 1990s when it announced plans to market Uptown, a menthol cigarette targeted toward low-income blacks. It quickly dropped the brand in the face of a loud public outcry and heavy pressure from black leaders.

G. Heileman Brewing made a similar mistake with PowerMaster, a potent malt liquor. Because malt liquor had become the drink of choice among many in the inner city, Heileman focused its marketing efforts for PowerMaster on inner-city consumers. However, this group suffers disproportionately from liver diseases brought on by alcohol, and the inner city is already plagued by alcohol-related problems such as crime and violence. Thus, Heileman's targeting decision drew substantial criticism.[29]

The meteoric growth of the Internet and other carefully targeted direct media has raised fresh concerns about potential targeting abuses. The Internet allows increasing refinement of audiences and, in turn, more precise targeting. This might help makers of questionable products or deceptive advertisers to more readily victimize the most vulnerable audiences.

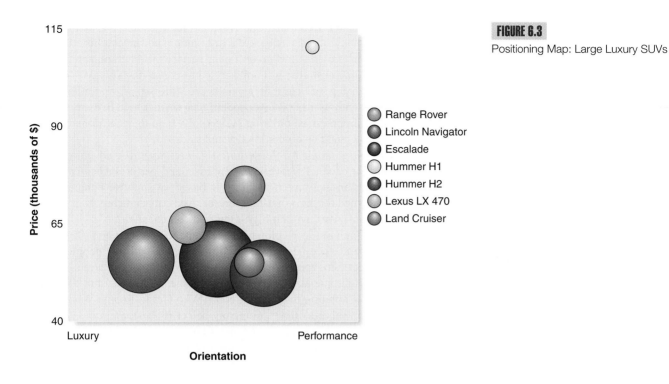

FIGURE 6.3
Positioning Map: Large Luxury SUVs

selecting an overall positioning strategy. The company must then effectively communicate and deliver the chosen position to the market.

Identifying Possible Competitive Advantages

The key to winning target customers and building profitable relationships with them is to understand their needs better than competitors do and to deliver more value. To the extent that a company can position itself as providing superior value, it gains **competitive advantage**. But solid positions cannot be built on empty promises. If a company positions its product as *offering* the best quality and service, it must then *deliver* the promised quality and service. Thus, positioning begins with actually *differentiating* the company's marketing offer so that it will give consumers more value than competitors' offers do.

To find points of differentiation, marketers must think through the customer's entire experience with the company's product or service. An alert company can find ways to differentiate itself at every point where it comes in contact with customers. In what specific ways can a company differentiate its offer from those of competitors? A company or market offer can be differentiated along the lines of *product, services, channels, people,* or *image*.

Product differentiation takes place along a continuum. At one extreme we find physical products that allow little variation: chicken, steel, aspirin. Yet even here some meaningful differentiation is possible. For example, Perdue claims that its branded chickens are better—fresher and more tender—and gets a 10 percent price premium based on this differentiation. At the other extreme are products that can be highly differentiated, such as automobiles, clothing, and furniture. Such products can be differentiated on features, performance, or style and design. Thus, Volvo provides new and better safety features; Whirlpool designs its dishwasher to run more quietly; Bose positions its speakers on their striking design characteristics. Similarly, companies can differentiate their products on attributes such as consistency, durability, reliability, or repairability.

Beyond differentiating its physical product, a firm can also differentiate the services that accompany the product. Some companies gain *services differentiation* through speedy, convenient, or careful delivery. For example, BankOne has opened full-service branches in supermarkets to provide location convenience along with Saturday, Sunday, and weekday-evening hours.

Competitive advantage
An advantage over competitors gained by offering consumers greater value, either through lower prices or by providing more benefits that justify higher prices.

Installation can also differentiate one company from another, as can repair services. Many an automobile buyer will gladly pay a little more and travel a little farther to buy a car from a dealer that provides top-notch repair services. Some companies differentiate their offers by providing customer training service or consulting services—data, information systems, and advising services that buyers need. McKesson Corporation, a major drug wholesaler, consults with its 12,000 independent pharmacists to help them set up accounting, inventory, and computerized ordering systems. By helping its customers compete better, McKesson gains greater customer loyalty and sales.

Firms that practice *channel differentiation* gain competitive advantage through the way they design their channel's coverage, expertise, and performance. Caterpillar's success in the construction-equipment industry is based on superior channels. Its dealers worldwide are renowned for their first-rate service. And Amazon.com, Dell Computer, and Avon distinguish themselves by their high-quality direct channels.

Companies can gain a strong competitive advantage through *people differentiation*—hiring and training better people than their competitors do. Disney people are known to be friendly and upbeat. Singapore Airlines enjoys an excellent reputation largely because of the grace of its flight attendants. IBM offers people who make sure that the solution customers want is the solution they get: "People Who Get It. People Who Get It Done." People differentiation requires that a company select its customer-contact people carefully and train them well. For example, Disney trains its theme park people thoroughly to ensure that they are competent, courteous, and friendly—from the hotel check-in agents, to the monorail drivers, to the ride attendants, to the people who sweep Main Street USA. Each employee is carefully trained to understand customers and to "make people happy."

Even when competing offers look the same, buyers may perceive a difference based on company or brand *image differentiation*. A company or brand image should convey the product's distinctive benefits and positioning. Developing a strong and distinctive image calls for creativity and hard work. A company cannot develop an image in the public's mind overnight using only a few advertisements. If Ritz-Carlton means quality, this image must be supported by everything the company says and does. Symbols—such as the McDonald's golden arches, the Prudential rock, the Nike swoosh, the Intel Inside logo, or the Pillsbury doughboy—can provide strong company or brand recognition and image differentiation. The company might build a brand around a famous person, as Nike did with its Air Jordan basketball shoes and Tiger Woods golfing products. Some companies even become associated with colors, such as IBM (blue), Campbell (red and white), or UPS (brown). The chosen symbols, characters, and other image elements must be communicated through advertising that conveys the company's or brand's personality.

Choosing the Right Competitive Advantages Suppose a company is fortunate enough to discover several potential competitive advantages. It now must choose the ones on which it will build its positioning strategy. It must decide *how many* differences to promote and *which ones*.

How Many Differences to Promote? Many marketers think that companies should aggressively promote only one benefit to the target market. Ad man Rosser Reeves, for example, said a company should develop a *unique selling proposition* (USP) for each brand and stick to it. Each brand should pick an attribute and tout itself as "number one" on that attribute. Buyers tend to remember number one better, especially in an overcommunicated society. Thus, Crest toothpaste consistently promotes its anticavity protection and Volvo promotes safety. A company that hammers away at one of these positions and consistently delivers on it probably will become best known and remembered for it.

Other marketers think that companies should position themselves on more than one differentiator. This may be necessary if two or more firms are claiming to be best on the same attribute. Today, in a time when the mass market is fragmenting into many small segments, companies are trying to broaden their positioning strategies to appeal to more segments. For example, Unilever introduced the first three-in-one bar soap—Lever 2000—offering cleansing, deodorizing, *and* moisturizing benefits. Clearly, many buyers want all three benefits. The challenge was to convince them that one brand can deliver all three. Judging from Lever 2000's outstanding success, Unilever easily met the challenge. However, as companies increase the number of claims for their brands, they risk disbelief and a loss of clear positioning.

In general, a company needs to avoid three major positioning errors. The first is *underpositioning*—failing ever to really position the company at all. Some companies discover that buyers have only a vague idea of the company or that they do not really know anything special about it. The second error is *overpositioning*—giving buyers too narrow a picture of the company. Thus, a consumer might think that the Steuben glass company makes only fine glass costing $1,000 and up, when in fact it makes affordable fine glass starting at around $50.

Finally, companies must avoid *confused positioning*—leaving buyers with a confused image of a company. For example, Kmart has not fared well against more strongly positioned competitors. Wal-Mart positions itself forcefully as offering "Always low prices. Always!" Target has positioned itself as the trendier "upscale discounter." But most consumers have difficulty positioning Kmart favorably on any specific differentiating attributes.

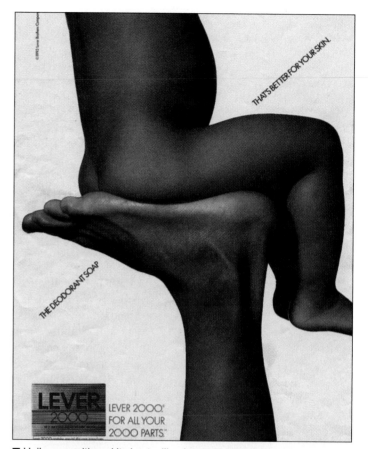

■ Unilever positioned its bestselling Lever 2000 soap on three benefits in one: cleansing, deodorizing, and moisturizing benefits. It's good "for all your 2000 parts."

Which Differences to Promote? Not all brand differences are meaningful or worthwhile; not every difference makes a good differentiator. Each difference has the potential to create company costs as well as customer benefits. Therefore, the company must carefully select the ways in which it will distinguish itself from competitors. A difference is worth establishing to the extent that it satisfies the following criteria:

- *Important:* The difference delivers a highly valued benefit to target buyers.

- *Distinctive:* Competitors do not offer the difference, or the company can offer it in a more distinctive way.

- *Superior:* The difference is superior to other ways that customers might obtain the same benefit.

- *Communicable:* The difference is communicable and visible to buyers.

- *Preemptive:* Competitors cannot easily copy the difference.

- *Affordable:* Buyers can afford to pay for the difference.

- *Profitable:* The company can introduce the difference profitably.

Many companies have introduced differentiations that failed one or more of these tests. The Westin Stamford hotel in Singapore advertises that it is the world's tallest hotel, a distinction that is not important to most tourists—in fact, it turns many off. Polaroid's Polarvision, which produced instantly developed home movies, bombed too. Although Polarvision was distinctive and even preemptive, it was inferior to another way of capturing motion, namely, camcorders. When Pepsi introduced clear Crystal Pepsi some years ago, customers were unimpressed. Although the new drink was distinctive, consumers didn't see "clarity" as an important benefit in a cola drink. Thus, choosing competitive advantages on which to position a product or service can be difficult, yet such choices may be crucial to success.

Selecting an Overall Positioning Strategy Consumers typically choose products and services that give them the greatest value. Thus, marketers want to position their brands on the key benefits that they offer relative to competing brands. The full positioning

FIGURE 6.4

Possible Value Propositions

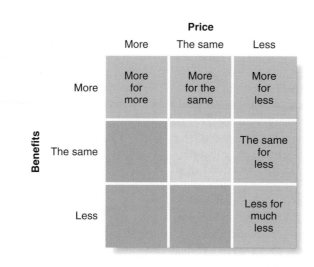

Price

	More	The same	Less
More	More for more	More for the same	More for less
The same			The same for less
Less			Less for much less

(left axis label: **Benefits**)

Value proposition

The full positioning of a brand—the full mix of benefits on which it is positioned.

■ "Much more for much more" value proposition: Häagen-Dazs offers its superpremium ice cream at a price never before charged.

of a brand is called the brand's **value proposition**—the full mix of benefits on which the brand is positioned. It is the answer to the customer's question "Why should I buy your brand?" Volvo's value proposition hinges on safety but also includes reliability, roominess, and styling, all for a price that is higher than average but seems fair for this mix of benefits.

Figure 6.4 shows possible value propositions on which a company might position its products. In the figure, the five blue cells represent winning value propositions—positioning that gives the company competitive advantage. The red cells represent losing value propositions. The center yellow cell represents at best a marginal proposition. In the following sections, we discuss the five winning value propositions on which companies can position their products: more for more, more for the same, the same for less, less for much less, and more for less.[32]

More for More. "More for more" positioning involves providing the most upscale product or service and charging a higher price to cover the higher costs. Ritz-Carlton Hotels, Mont Blanc writing instruments, Mercedes-Benz automobiles—each claims superior quality, craftsmanship, durability, performance, or style and charges a price to match. Not only is the marketing offer high in quality, it also gives prestige to the buyer. It symbolizes status and a loftier lifestyle. Often, the price difference exceeds the actual increment in quality.

Sellers offering "only the best" can be found in every product and service category, from hotels, restaurants, food, and fashion to cars and kitchen appliances. Consumers are sometimes surprised, even delighted, when a new competitor enters a category with an unusually high-priced brand. Starbucks coffee entered as a very expensive brand in a largely commodity category; Häagen-Dazs came in as a premium ice cream brand at a price never before charged.

In general, companies should be on the lookout for opportunities to introduce a "much-more-for-much-more" brand in any underdeveloped product or service category. Yet "more-for-more" brands can be vulnerable. They often invite imitators who claim the same quality but at a lower price. Luxury goods that sell well during good times may be at risk during economic downturns when buyers become more cautious in their spending.

More for the Same. Companies can attack a competitor's more-for-more positioning by introducing a brand offering comparable quality but at a lower price. For example, Toyota introduced its

Lexus line with a "more-for-the-same" value proposition. Its headline read: "Perhaps the first time in history that trading a $72,000 car for a $36,000 car could be considered trading up." It communicated the high quality of its new Lexus through rave reviews in car magazines and through a widely distributed videotape showing side-by-side comparisons of Lexus and Mercedes automobiles. It published surveys showing that Lexus dealers were providing customers with better sales and service experiences than were Mercedes dealerships. Many Mercedes owners switched to Lexus, and the Lexus repurchase rate has been 60 percent, twice the industry average.

The Same for Less.   Offering "the same for less" can be a powerful value proposition—everyone likes a good deal. For example, Dell Computer offers equivalent-quality computers at a lower "price for performance." Discounts stores such as Wal-Mart and "category killers" such as Best Buy, Circuit City, and Sportmart also use this positioning. They don't claim to offer different or better products. Instead, they offer many of the same brands as department stores and specialty stores but at deep discounts based on superior purchasing power and lower-cost operations. Other companies develop imitative but lower-priced brands in an effort to lure customers away from the market leader. For example, AMD makes less expensive versions of Intel's market-leading microprocessor chips.

Less for Much Less.   A market almost always exists for products that offer less and therefore cost less. Few people need, want, or can afford "the very best" in everything they buy. In many cases, consumers will gladly settle for less than optimal performance or give up some of the bells and whistles in exchange for a lower price. For example, many travelers seeking lodgings prefer not to pay for what they consider unnecessary extras, such as a pool, attached restaurant, or mints on the pillow. Motel chains such as Motel 6 suspend some of these amenities and charge less accordingly.

"Less for much less" positioning involves meeting consumers' lower performance or quality requirements at a much lower price. For example, Family Dollar and Dollar General stores offer more affordable goods at very low prices. Sam's Club and Costco warehouse stores offer less merchandise selection and consistency, and much lower levels of service; as a result, they charge rock-bottom prices. Southwest Airlines, the nation's most profitable air carrier, also practices less for much less positioning. It charges incredibly low prices by not serving food, not assigning seats, and not using travel agents (see Marketing at Work 6.3).

More for Less.   Of course, the winning value proposition would be to offer "more for less." Many companies claim to do this. For example, Dell Computer claims to have better products *and* lower prices for a given level of performance. Procter & Gamble claims that its laundry detergents provide the best cleaning *and* everyday low prices. In the short run, some companies can actually achieve such lofty positions. For example, when it first opened for business, Home Depot had arguably the best product selection, the best service, *and* the lowest prices compared to local hardware stores and other home improvement chains.

Yet in the long run, companies will find it very difficult to sustain such best-of-both positioning. Offering more usually costs more, making it difficult to deliver on the "for less" promise. Companies that try to deliver both may lose out to more focused competitors. For example, facing determined competition from Lowe's stores, Home Depot must now decide whether it wants to compete primarily on superior service or on lower prices.

All said, each brand must adopt a positioning strategy designed to serve the needs and wants of its target markets. "More for more" will draw one target market, "less for much less" will draw another, and so on. Thus, in any market, there is usually room for many different companies, each successfully occupying different positions.

The important thing is that each company must develop its own winning positioning strategy, one that makes it special to its target consumers. Offering only "the same for the same" provides no competitive advantage, leaving the firm in the middle of the pack. Companies offering one of the three losing value propositions—"the same for more," "less

Marketing at Work | 6.3

Southwest's Value Proposition: "Less for Much Less"

In an industry beset by hard times, Southwest Airlines flies well above its competition. In the wake of a global economic slump and the effects of September 11 and increased terrorism, most airlines are suffering huge losses, or even declaring bankruptcy. Industry leader American Airlines lost more than $3.5 billion last year. Yet even in these bleak times, Southwest has yet to suffer a loss in a single quarter. Amazingly, Southwest has experienced 30 straight years of profits. What's the secret? Southwest is the most strongly and clearly positioned airline in the world. It offers a classic "less-for-much-less" value proposition.

From the start, Southwest has positioned itself firmly as *the* no-frills, low-price airline. Its average flight time is just one hour; its average one-way fare just $86. Southwest's passengers have learned to fly without the amenities. For example, the airline provides no meals—just packaged snacks. It also offers no first-class section, only three-across seating in all of its planes. There's no such thing as a reserved seat on a Southwest flight. Passengers are assigned to one of three boarding groups when checking in and then herded onto the plane by group. "Southwest will get you and your luggage where you're going," comments an industry analyst, "but we don't call their planes cattle cars for nothing. It's a mercy that Southwest is a short-haul airline, because you can get pretzelated on their planes p.d.q."

Why, then, do so many passengers love Southwest? Perhaps most importantly, Southwest excels at the basics of getting passengers where they want to go and on time. In 1992, Southwest received the U.S. Department of

Transportation's first-ever Triple Crown Award for best on-time service, best baggage handling, *and* best customer service, a feat it repeated for the next five straight years. For more than a decade, Southwest has been among

Southwest offers a classic "less for much less" value proposition, with lots of zany fun. It all starts at the top with company founder and chairman Herb Kelleher.

for more," and "less for the same"—will inevitably fail. Customers soon realize that they've been underserved, tell others, and abandon the brand.

Positioning statement
A statement that summarizes company or brand positioning—it takes this form: *To (target segment and need) our (brand) is (concept) that (point-of-difference).*

Developing a Positioning Statement Company and brand positioning should be summed up in a **positioning statement.** The statement should follow the form: *To (target segment and need) our (brand) is (concept) that (point-of-difference).*[33] For example: "To *busy professionals who need to stay organized, Palm Pilot is an electronic organizer that*

the industry leaders in on-time performance. All this makes Southwest passengers a satisfied bunch. For the past 12 consecutive years, Southwest has ranked number one in fewest customer complaints in the Department of Transportation's Air Travel Consumer Report. And last year it rated number one in its industry in customer satisfaction on the American Customer Satisfaction Index.

Beyond the basics, however, there are two key elements to Southwest's strong positioning. The analyst sums up Southwest's positioning this way: "It is not luxurious, . . . but it's cheap and it's fun." Southwest is a model of efficiency and low-cost operations. As a result, its prices are shockingly low. When it enters a new market, Southwest proclaims: "Southwest is coming to town, and airline prices are coming down." In fact, prices are so low that when Southwest enters a market, it actually increases total air traffic by attracting customers who might otherwise travel by car or bus. For example, when Southwest began its Louisville-to-Chicago flight at a one-way rate of $49 versus competitors' $250, total weekly air passenger traffic between the two cities increased from 8,000 to 26,000.

No frills and low prices, however, don't mean drudgery. To lighten things up, Southwest adds another key positioning ingredient—lots of good, clean fun. With its happy-go-lucky Chairman and co-founder, Herb Kelleher, leading the charge, Southwest refuses to take itself seriously. Cheerful employees go out of their way to amuse, surprise, or

somehow entertain passengers. According to one account:

Southwest employees are apt to dress as leprechauns on St. Patrick's Day, rabbits on Easter, and almost anything on Halloween. I have heard flight attendants sing the safety lecture as country music, blues, and rap; I have heard them compare the pilot to Rocky Raccoon and insist that passengers introduce themselves to one another, then hug, then kiss, then propose marriage.

Kelleher himself has been known to dress up as Klinger from "MASH" at company parties and hands out snacks to passengers when flying on his airline.

During delays at the gate, ticket agents will award prizes to the passenger with the largest hole in his or her sock. Flight attendants have been known to hide in overhead luggage bins and then pop out when passengers start filing on board. Veteran Southwest fliers have learned to listen up to announcements over the intercom. On a recent flight, the pilot suggested, "Flight attendants will please prepare their hair for departure." Later in the flight, he announced, "Good morning, ladies and gentlemen. Those of you who wish to smoke will please file out to our lounge on the wing, where you can enjoy our feature film, *Gone with the Wind*." Safety instructions from the flight attendant included the advice. "In the unlikely event of a water landing, please remember to paddle, kick, kick, paddle, kick, kick, all the way back." One passenger recalls a flight on which the pilot told everyone

on the plane's left side, toward the terminal, to put their faces in the window and smile "so our competitors can see what a full flight looks like."

As a result of its strong positioning, Southwest has grown to become the nation's fourth-largest domestic carrier. The company has successfully beaten off determined challenges from several major competitors who have tried to copy its winning formula, including Continental Lite, Delta Express, and Shuttle by United. Southwest now makes 2,800 flights a day, serving 58 cities in 30 states. Its revenues have grown 250 percent during the past decade. And in the recent industry downdraft, Southwest has been the *only* major airline to turn a profit.

Simple, clear positioning has made Southwest *Fortune* magazine's most admired airline for the past seven years running. And last year, Southwest was *Fortune's* number two most admired company overall. Southwest not only promises an appealing value proposition, it delivers on the promise. It's not ritzy, but it gets you where you want to go, when you want to get there. You get low, low prices and lots of good fun. Just the ticket when you need a good lift!

Sources: Quotes from Molly Ivins, "From Texas, with Love and Peanuts," *New York Times*, March 14, 1999, p. 11; Wendy Zellner, "Southwest: After Kelleher, More Blue Skies," *Business Week*, April 2, 2001, p. 45; and Ron Suskind, "Humor Has Returned After 9/11 Hiatus," *Wall Street Journal*, January 13, 2003, p. A1. Also see Wendy Zellner, "Holding Steady," *Business Week*, February 3, 2003, pp. 66–68; "Airline of the Year: Southwest Airlines," *Air Transport World*, February 2003, pp. 26–27; and *Southwest Airlines Fact Sheet*, June 6, 2003, accessed at www.southwest.com.

allows you to backup files on your PC more easily and reliably than competitive products." Sometimes a positioning statement is more detailed:

> To young, active soft-drink consumers who have little time for sleep, Mountain Dew is the soft drink that gives you more energy than any other brand because it has the highest level of caffeine. With Mountain Dew, you can stay alert and keep going even when you haven't been able to get a good night's sleep.[34]

Note that the positioning first states the product's membership in a category (Mountain Dew is a soft drink) and then shows its point-of-difference from other members of the category (has more caffeine). Placing a brand in a specific category suggests similarities that it might share with other products in the category. But the case for the brand's superiority is made on its points of difference. Sometimes marketers put a brand in a surprisingly different category before indicating the points of difference:

> DiGiorno's is a frozen pizza whose crust rises when the pizza is heated. Instead of putting it in the frozen pizza category, the marketers positioned it in the delivered pizza category. Their ad shows party guests asking which pizza delivery service the host used. But, says the host, "It's not delivery, its DiGiorno!" This helped highlight DiGiorno's fresh quality and superior taste over the normal frozen pizza.

Communicating and Delivering the Chosen Position

Once it has chosen a position, the company must take strong steps to deliver and communicate the desired position to target consumers. All the company's marketing mix efforts must support the positioning strategy. Positioning the company calls for concrete action, not just talk. If the company decides to build a position on better quality and service, it must first *deliver* that position. Designing the marketing mix—product, price, place, and promotion—involves working out the tactical details of the positioning strategy. Thus, a firm that seizes on a more-for-more position knows that it must produce high-quality products, charge a high price, distribute through high-quality dealers, and advertise in high-quality media. It must hire and train more service people, find retailers who have a good reputation for service, and develop sales and advertising messages that broadcast its superior service. This is the only way to build a consistent and believable more-for-more position.

Companies often find it easier to come up with a good positioning strategy than to implement it. Establishing a position or changing one usually takes a long time. In contrast, positions that have taken years to build can quickly be lost. Once a company has built the desired position, it must take care to maintain the position through consistent performance and communication. It must closely monitor and adapt the position over time to match changes in consumer needs and competitors' strategies. However, the company should avoid abrupt changes that might confuse consumers. Instead, a product's position should evolve gradually as it adapts to the ever-changing marketing environment.

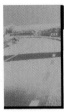

REST STOP:
Reviewing the Concepts

Time to stop and stretch your legs. In this chapter, you've learned about the major elements of marketing strategy: segmentation, targeting, and positioning. Marketers know that they cannot appeal to all buyers in their markets, or at least not to all buyers in the same way. Buyers are too numerous, too widely scattered, and too varied in their needs and buying practices. Therefore, most companies today are moving away from mass marketing. Instead, they practice *target marketing*—identifying market segments, selecting one or more of them, and developing products and marketing mixes tailored to each. In this way, sellers can develop the right product for each target market and adjust their prices, distribution channels, and advertising to reach the target market efficiently.

1. **Define the three steps of target marketing: market segmentation, target marketing, and market positioning.**

Target marketing involves designing strategies to build the *right relationships* with the *right customers.* Market segmentation is the act of dividing a market into distinct groups of buyers with different needs, characteristics, or behaviors who might require separate products or marketing mixes. Once the groups have been identified, *target marketing* evaluates each market segment's attractiveness and selects one or more segments to serve. *Market positioning* consists of deciding how to best serve target customer—setting the competitive positioning for the product and creating a detailed marketing plan.

2. List and discuss the major bases for segmenting consumer and business markets.

There is no single way to segment a market. Therefore, the marketer tries different variables to see which give the best segmentation opportunities. For consumer marketing, the major segmentation variables are geographic, demographic, psychographic, and behavioral. In *geographic segmentation,* the market is divided into different geographical units such as nations, regions, states, counties, cities, or neighborhoods. In *demographic segmentation,* the market is divided into groups based on demographic variables, including age, gender, family size, family life cycle, income, occupation, education, religion, race, generation, and nationality. In *psychographic segmentation,* the market is divided into different groups based on social class, lifestyle, or personality characteristics. In *behavioral segmentation,* the market is divided into groups based on consumers' knowledge, attitudes, uses, or responses to a product.

Business marketers use many of the same variables to segment their markets. But business markets also can be segmented by business consumer *demographics* (industry, company size), *operating characteristics, purchasing approaches, situational factors,* and *personal characteristics.* The effectiveness of segmentation analysis depends on finding segments that are *measurable, accessible, substantial, differentiable,* and *actionable.*

3. Explain how companies identify attractive market segments and choose a target marketing strategy.

To target the best market segments, the company first evaluates each segment's size and growth characteristics, structural attractiveness, and compatibility with company objectives and resources. It then chooses one of four target marketing strategies—ranging from very broad to very narrow targeting. The seller can ignore segment differences and target broadly using *undifferentiated (or mass) marketing.* This involves mass producing, mass distributing, and mass promoting about the same product in about the same way to all consumers. Or the seller can adopt *differentiated marketing*—developing different market offers for several segments. *Concentrated marketing* (or *niche marketing*) involves focusing on only one or a few market segments. Finally, *micromarketing* is the practice of tailoring products and marketing programs to suit the tastes of specific individuals and locations. Micromarketing includes *local marketing* and *individual marketing.* Which targeting strategy is best depends on company resources, product variability, product life-cycle stage, market variability, and competitive marketing strategies.

4. Discuss how companies position their products for maximum competitive advantage in the marketplace.

Once a company has decided which segments to enter, it must decide on its *market positioning* strategy—on which positions to occupy in its chosen segments. The positioning task consists of three steps: identifying a set of possible competitive advantages on which to build a position, choosing the right competitive advantages, and selecting an overall positioning strategy. The brand's full positioning is called its *value proposition*—the full mix of benefits on which the brand is positioned. In general, companies can choose from one of five winning value propositions on which to position their products: more for more, more for the same, the same for less, less for much less, or more for less. Company and brand positioning are summarized in positioning statements that state the target segment and need, positioning concept, and specific points of difference. The company must then effectively communicate and deliver the chosen position to the market.

Navigating the Key Terms

Age and life-cycle segmentation	Gender segmentation	Occasion segmentation
Behavioral segmentation	Geographic segmentation	Positioning statement
Benefit segmentation	Income segmentation	Product position
Competitive advantage	Individual marketing	Psychographic segmentation
Concentrated (niche) marketing	Intermarket segmentation	Target market
Demographic segmentation	Local marketing	Target marketing
Differentiated (segmented) marketing	Market positioning	Undifferentiated (or mass) marketing
	Market segmentation	Value proposition
	Micromarketing	

Travel Log

Discussing the Issues

1. What are the differences between mass marketing, segment marketing, niche marketing, and micro marketing? Discuss actual products that use each of these market segmentation levels.

2. For each of these three products—DVD Player, shoes, and salsa—consider each of the segmentation variables listed in Table 6.1 and assess the degree to which it is useful to segment the market for the product based on that variable.

3. Describe the student market segments for your university. To what extent are these segments measurable, accessible, substantial, differentiable, and actionable?

4. The George Foreman Grilling Machine is a compact cooking appliance with a double-sided cooking surface that is angled to allow fat to drip off the food and out of the grill. Describe a likely target market for this product. How does this target market rate with respect to size, growth, and structural attractiveness.

5. Discuss how Mountain Dew has differentiated itself from other soft drink brands on the basis of product, services, channels, people, and image differentiation.

6. Study Figure 6.4. Give examples of a hotel chain that falls into each of the five value propositions. What does each hotel you selected do on the benefits dimension to offer more, the same, or less than competitors?

Application Questions

1. One direction Levi's has gone in personalizing the shopping experience is to allow the use of a virtual model to try on clothing at the company's Web site (www.levi.com). Visitors can even customize the model to look more like themselves (or what they wish they looked like) and save this representation for future visits. Visit the company Web site and virtually try on some of the clothing in the "fitting room." What do you think of this experience? How does this feature fit with the notion of individual marketing? Do you feel that the virtual fitting room differentiates the Levi brand from other clothing companies?

2. Pick five different brands of deodorant. Based on your own perception, rate each one on the attributes of scent, price, and odor protection (use a 1 to 10 scale, with 1 being low and 10 being high). Pick two of the attributes and plot your ratings of each brand. How are the brands different and similar to each other? Are there any areas on the graph that are void of competitors? Do these represent an opportunity for a deodorant manufacturer?

3. Cable television news organizations have become more popular in recent years as consumers have started to expect and demand news coverage 24 hours a day, 7 days a week. Spend some time watching CNN, MSNBC, and Fox news. List the ways each news program tries to differentiate itself from the others. Evaluate the worthiness of their differentiation strategies using the following criteria: important, distinctive, communicable, preemptive, affordable, and profitable.

Under the Hood: Focus on Technology

Birds of a feather flock together. This is the philosophy behind Claritas's PRIZM lifestyle segmentation system. Operating under the presumption that people with similar lifestyles tend to live near each other, Claritas has classified neighborhoods into 1 of 62 categories based on census data, consumer surveys, and other public and private sources of demographic and consumer information. Companies use this geodemographic information to understand and target customers better, to develop the content for advertisements, to decide the specific media in which to place ads, to help decide where to put new stores, and to decide what kind of merchandise should go in those stores.

Claritas offers a limited version of the PRIZM segmentation online at www.yawyl.claritas.com. Visit this Web site and respond to the following questions.

1. Enter the ZIP code where you live into the PRIZM Web site and read about the descriptions of the different customer segments. Do you think it accurately describes your area?

2. What are some products that might be successfully targeted at the most popular market segment in your area?

3. How might a business selling Caribbean cruises be able to use the Claritas PRIZM segmentation tool?

Focus on Ethics

Many companies consider children an attractive market segment because of their spending power. A strategy in some middle schools and high schools is to develop exclusive "pouring rights" contracts with soft drink companies, which allow the company to be the exclusive soft drink sold on campus in exchange for payments equaling hundreds of thousands of dollars. Pepsi and Coca-Cola have led this charge in recent years, encouraged by school districts in desperate need of additional funding. However, some parents feel that soft drinks are an unhealthy beverage alternative and have lobbied to have soft drinks removed from campuses. Indeed, the nation's two largest school districts—New York and Los Angeles—have banned soft-drink sales.

1. Why would soft drink companies pay such large sums for exclusive access to middle and high school campuses? How might the controversy damage the image of the soft drink manufacturers?

2. In your mind, are there any ethical issues associated with this practice?

3. What sort of compromise might be worked out between supporters and opponents of this practice?

Videos

The Marriott video case that accompanies this chapter is located in Appendix 1 at the back of the book.

Student Materials

Need a tune-up? A study guide and OneKey access code are available to aid in your review of chapter material. Your instructor may choose to have these items shrink-wrapped with your text or you may purchase them separately at www.prenhall.com/marketing.

■ *After studying this chapter, you should be able to:*

1. Define product and the major classifications of products and services   *2. Describe* the decisions companies make regarding their individual products and services, product lines, and product mixes   *3. Discuss* branding strategy—the decisions companies make in building and managing their brands   *4. Identify* the four characteristics that affect the marketing of a service   *5. Discuss* two additional product issues

Product, Services, and Branding Strategy

7

Now that you've had a good look at marketing strategy, we'll journey on into the marketing mix—the tactical tools that marketers use to implement their strategies. In this and the next chapter, we'll study how companies develop and manage products. Then, in the chapters that follow, we'll look at pricing, distribution, and marketing communication tools. The product is usually the first and most basic marketing consideration. How well firms manage their individual brands and their overall product and service offerings has a major impact on their success in the marketplace. We'll start with a seemingly simple question: What *is* a product? As it turns out, however, the answer is not so simple.

First stop on this leg of the journey: cosmetics marketing. Remember that seemingly simple question—what is a product? The cosmetics industry example shows why there is no easy answer. What, really, *are* cosmetics? Cosmetics makers like Aveda know that when a woman buys cosmetics, she buys much, much more than scented ingredients in fancy bottles.

E ach year, cosmetics companies sell billions of dollars' worth of potions, lotions, and fragrances to consumers around the world, part of a $160 billion global beauty industry. In one sense, these products are no more than careful mixtures of oils and chemicals that have nice scents and soothing properties. But the cosmetics companies know that they sell much more than just mixtures of ingredients—they sell the promise of what these concoctions will do for the people who use them.

Of course, in the cosmetics business, like anywhere else, quality and performance contribute to success or failure. For example, perfume marketers agree, "No smell; no sell." However, $180-an-ounce perfume may cost no more than $10 to produce. Thus, to perfume consumers, many things beyond the scent and a few dollars' worth of ingredients add to a perfume's allure. Fragrance names such as Obsession, Passion, Gossip, Wildheart, Opium, Joy, White Linen, Youth Dew, Eternity, and Love suggest that the perfumes will do something more than just make you smell better.

What *is* the promise of cosmetics? The following account by a *New York Times* reporter suggests the extent to which cosmetics take on meaning far beyond their physical makeup.

Last week I bathed in purple water (*I Trust* bubble bath, made by Philosophy) and powdered up with pink powder (*Rebirth*, by 5S, "to renew the spirit and recharge the soul"). My moisturizer was *Bliss* (Chakra VII by Aveda, for "the joyful enlightenment and soaring of the spirit"); my nail polish was *Spiritual* (by Tony and Tina, "to aid connection with the higher self"). My teeth were clean, my heart was open—however, my bathroom was so crowded with bottles and brochures, the latest tools and totems from the human potential movement, that I could hardly find my third eye. Still, my "Hope in a Jar" package (from Philosophy) pretty well summed it up: "Where there is hope there can be faith. Where there is faith miracles can occur."

If you are looking for enlightenment in all the wrong places, cosmetics companies are eager to help. Because today, feeling good is the new religion. And cosmetics companies are the newest of the new prophets, turning the old notion of hope in a jar on its head.

"Cosmetics are our satellite to the divine!" This is what you'll hear from Tony and Tina, for example. Tony and Tina (Anthony Gillis and Cristina Bornstein) are nice young artists. He's from London, she grew up in New York. Chakra nail polish, which they invented for an installation at the Gershwin Gallery in Manhattan two years ago, was intended as an ironic commentary on the beauty business. But then a friend suggested they get into the beauty business, and now Tony and Tiny have a $2 million cosmetics company with a mission statement: "To aid in the evolution of human consciousness." Their products include nail polishes (Vibrational Remedies) in colors meant to do nice things to your chakras, as well as body glitter and hair mascara, lipstick and eyeshadow. You can buy them at Fred Segal, Nordstrom, and Bloomingdale's, where last month they outsold Hard Candy and Urban Decay. "We think color therapy is going to be the new medicine," said Tony.

Rainbows are proliferating as rapidly in the New Age as angels once did. Philosophy, a 3-year-old Arizona company, makes a sort of head/heart kit—"a self-help program," the company insists—called the *Rainbow Connection*. You pay $45 for seven bottles of colored bubble bath in a metal box. "Choose your colored bath according to the area of your emotional life that needs attention, i.e. self-love, self-worth," the brochure reads. "My role as I see it," said Christina Carlino, Philosophy's founder, "is to help you stay on your destiny path. It's not about what you look like. Beauty is defined by your deeds."

5S, a sprout of the Japanese cosmetics company Shiseido, offers a regimen that plays, the company says, on the "fundamental and mythical significance of 5" (Five Pillars of Islam, Five Classics of Confucianism, and so on), and which is organized into emotional rather than physical categories. At the 5S store in SoHo, you don't buy things for dry skin, you buy things that are "energizing" or "nurturing" or "adoring." The company also believes in color therapy. Hence, *Rebirth*, products tinted "nouveau pink" (the color of bubble gum). A customer can achieve rebirth with 5S pink soap, pink powder, and pink toner.

Here are products that are not intended to make you look better, but to make you act better, feel better, and be a better person. You don't need a month's visit to India to find your higher self; you need only buy this bubble bath, that lipstick, this night cream. The beauty business' old come-on (trap your man!) has been swept away in favor of a new pitch. I don't have wrinkles anymore. I've got a chakra blockage.

Of course, who knew about chakras before Aveda? In 1989, the plant-based, eco-friendly cosmetics company Aveda trademarked Chakras I through VII to use as titles for moisturizers and scents. Chakra products were perhaps a little ahead of their time back then. However, the purchase of Aveda [a while] ago by the Estée Lauder Companies, the General Motors of the cosmetics world, suggests that the pendulum of history has finally caught up. "Aveda isn't a marketing idea," says Jeanette Wagner, the vice chairman of Estée Lauder. "It is a passionately held belief. From my point of view, the appeal is first the spirituality, and then the products."

All this might sound like only so much flimflam, but the underlying point is legitimate. The success of such brands affirms that products really are more than just the physical entities. When a woman buys cosmetics, she really does buy much, much more than just oils, chemicals, and fragrances. The cosmetic's image, its promises and positioning, its ingredients, its name and package, the company that makes it, the stores that sell it—all become a part of the total cosmetic product. When Aveda, Philosophy, and 5S sell cosmetics, they sell more than just tangible goods. They sell lifestyle, self-expression, exclusivity, and spirituality; achievement, success, and status; romance, passion, and fantasy; memories, hopes, and dreams.[1]

Clearly, cosmetics are more than just cosmetics when Aveda sells them. This chapter begins with a deceptively simple question: *What is a product?* After answering this question, we look at ways to classify products in consumer and business markets. Then we discuss the important decisions that marketers make regarding individual products, product lines, and product mixes. Next, we look into the critically important issue of how marketers build and manage brands. Finally, we examine the characteristics and marketing requirements of a special form of product—services.

◼▌What Is a Product?

A Sony DVD player, a Ford Taurus, a Costa Rican vacation, a Caffé Mocha at Starbucks, Fidelity online investment services, and advice from your family doctor—all are products. We define a **product** as anything that can be offered to a market for attention, acquisition, use, or consumption and that might satisfy a want or need. Products include more than just tangible goods. Broadly defined, products include physical objects, services, events, persons, places, organizations, ideas, or mixes of these entities. Thus, throughout this book, we use the term *product* broadly to include any or all of these entities.

Because of their importance in the world economy, we give special attention to services. **Services** are a form of product that consists of activities, benefits, or satisfactions offered for sale that are essentially intangible and do not result in the ownership of anything. Examples are banking, hotel, airline, retail, tax preparation, and home repair services. We will look at services more closely later in this chapter.

Product
Anything that can be offered to a market for attention, acquisition, use, or consumption that might satisfy a want or need.

Service
Any activity or benefit that one party can offer to another that is essentially intangible and does not result in the ownership of anything.

Products, Services, and Experiences

Product is a key element in the *market offering.* Marketing-mix planning begins with formulating an offering that brings value to target customers and satisfies their needs. This offering becomes the basis on which the company builds profitable relationships with customers.

A company's market offering often includes both tangible goods and services. Each component can be a minor or a major part of the total offer. At one extreme, the offer may consist of a *pure tangible good,* such as soap, toothpaste, or salt—no services accompany the product. At the other extreme are *pure services,* for which the offer consists primarily of a service. Examples include a doctor's exam or financial services. Between these two extremes, however, many goods-and-services combinations are possible.

Today, as products and services become more and more commoditized, many companies are moving to a new level in creating value for their customers. To differentiate their offers, beyond simply making products and delivering services, companies are staging, marketing, and delivering memorable customer *experiences.* Whereas products are tangible and services are intangible, experiences are memorable. Whereas products and services are external, experiences are personal and take place in the minds of individual consumers.

Experiences have always been important in the entertainment industry—Disney has long manufactured memories through its movies and theme parks. Today, however, all kinds of firms are recasting their traditional goods and services to create experiences. For example, restaurants create value well beyond the food they serve. Starbucks patrons are paying for more than just coffee. The company treats customers to poetry on its wallpaper,

Marketing at Work | 7.1

Krispy Kreme: A Truly Sweet Experience

Want a doughnut? What's the first name that comes to mind? Five years ago, you probably would have said Dunkin' Donuts, still the world's largest coffee and doughnut chain. But today, thanks to the hot popularity of Krispy Kreme, the southern phenomenon, your answer might be different. The Krispy Kreme name and famous bowtie logo have cropped up throughout the country and around the world, bringing the company's delicious yeast-raised doughnuts to more and more satisfied customers.

Krispy Kreme is changing the way the world eats doughnuts. The company and its franchisees now make 7.5 million doughnuts each day—2.7 *billion* doughnuts each year. Larger outlets make more than 12,000 of the sweet-tasting delicacies an hour. In about 22 seconds, Krispy Kreme stores worldwide can produce enough doughnuts to make a stack as high as the empire state building. That's enough doughnuts each week to stretch from New York City to Los Angeles. In the process, they use 1.3 million pounds of sprinkles and enough chocolate to fill nearly five Olympic size swimming pools.

But to a true believer, a Krispy Kreme isn't just a doughnut. It's an *experience*. A magical moment. With every doughnut the company sells, it creates a happy customer. And each happy customer can't wait to tell others about the experience. If you haven't had a gooey, hot glazed Krispy Kreme, they'd say, you simply haven't lived.

Krispy Kreme's magical moments date all the way back to 1933, when Vernon Rudolph bought a doughnut shop in Paducah, Kentucky. The deal came with the secret recipe for the unique, yeast-raised Krispy Kreme doughnut that has become so popular today. In 1937 the Rudolph family moved the business to Winston-Salem, North Carolina. It was there that Vernon responded to customer requests by installing a retail window through which he could sell fresh, hot doughnuts directly to customers.

As the company expanded through franchises, Rudolph saw the need to

To a true believer, a Krispy Kreme isn't just a doughnut. It's a truly sweet experience. A magical moment.

apron-clad performers behind espresso machines, and a warm but modern interior ambience that leaves them feeling more affluent and fulfilled. And Krispy Kreme doesn't just sell doughnuts, it creates carefully staged "magical moments" for just about anyone within "aroma range" of a Krispy Kreme store (see Marketing at Work 7.1).

Many retailers also stage experiences. Niketown stores create "shoppertainment" by offering interactive displays, engaging activities, and promotional events in a stimulating shopping environment. At stores such as Sharper Image and Brookstone, people play with the latest gadgets, sit in massage chairs, and enjoy the experience more than the merchan-

provide a consistent Krispy Kreme experience at every outlet. So he built a mix plant and developed a distribution system that delivered the same dry mix to each store. He also began manufacturing equipment that would automate each store's doughnut-making process.

This focus on consistency continues today. The company painstakingly plans every Krispy Kreme store decision—from product placement and store design to the color of the employees' uniforms. Every poster and every sign, every piece of equipment, every light fixture, and every bag of flour, sugar, sprinkles, and icing must be purchased from Krispy Kreme. Thus, every Krispy Kreme customer experiences the same magical moment with every visit, at any Krispy Kreme store, anywhere.

The Krispy Kreme magical moment seems to appeal to everyone, regardless of age, sex, ethnicity, or socioeconomic background. And, it has built a host of fervent followers that most competitors could only dream about. Says Krispy Kreme's Senior Vice President of Store Development, "people wait in line for hours to get into a new store opening and they have fun . . . they talk to each other, share their Krispy Kreme stories . . . amazing. How many businesses could you be in where people are willing to stand in line for hours? I've never seen anything that even comes close to the passion people feel for this brand."

Krispy Kreme is so focused on the experience it creates that it actually defines its brand through the store experience. Its "Retail Environments" book, which details new store design,

states "Our brand and how our customers experience Krispy Kreme is the platform that supports us all. Nothing can be more important than the preservation and nurturing of these valuable possessions." This undying demand for perfection, unwavering consistency, and a passion for the consumer–brand relationship forms the foundation of Krispy Kreme's success.

Krispy Kreme's powerful brand experience makes it easy to attract customers in new markets. The company has an almost cult-like following. So, for many neighborhoods the arrival of a Krispy Kreme is an event to celebrate. Consumers in Clackamas, Oregon, greeted the groundbreaking for a new Krispy Kreme store with the local marching band and hordes of supporters. When a new store opened just outside of Seattle, eager customers camped out on the sidewalk overnight to be the first inside at 5:30 A.M. the next morning. When Krispy Kreme debuted in Denver, morning traffic was snarled for hours.

For those who have never heard of Krispy Kreme, word travels quickly about the chain's tasty doughnuts. But to ensure that the message gets out, local franchisees often deliver several dozen glazed doughnuts to a local radio station, or to—you guessed it—the town's fire and police stations. When a new store opened in Phoenix, Sheriff Joe Arpaio, the infamous "toughest sheriff in America"—the lawman known for making prisoners wear pink underwear—was one of the first people to try a fresh Krispy Kreme doughnut. In front of a sea of television cameras, he

uttered the perfect phrase: "These doughnuts are so good, they should be illegal." Such free promotion is the norm for Krispy Kreme. The delicious doughnuts have also played cameo roles in the movie Primary Colors and on such TV shows as Ally McBeal, NYPD Blue, and The Tonight Show with Jay Leno.

Thus, Krispy Kreme does more than sell doughnuts. It creates carefully crafted magical moments for its customers, moments that are gaining popularity with just about anyone within "aroma range" of a Krispy Kreme store. Notes marketing manager Jennifer Gardner, "I've seen a blue-collar worker, an expectant mother, a biker, a businessman, and a woman who was driven up in a Rolls Royce all standing in line inside a Krispy Kreme store, and they were talking to each other like long-lost friends." Says Krispy Kreme fan Jamie Karn, "You have to experience one. You have to eat it to understand it!" More than a doughnut, Krispy Kreme is a truly sweet customer experience. Creating magical moments for customers has also been a pretty sweet experience for Krispy Kreme. The company's sales have increased more than 73 percent in just the past two years.

Sources: Portions adapted from a case written by Peter Attwater, student at the University of North Carolina at Chapel Hill, April 2003. Other information from "It's Official: Krispy Kreme Coming to Clackamas," April 8, 2003, accessed online at www.katu.com; Sarah MacDonald, "It's a Drive-Thru or No Go," April 17, 2003, *Daily News Transcript,* accessed online at www.neponset valleydailynews.com; Christina Dyrness, "Hot Technology Now," *News & Observer,* April 23, 2003, p. 1F, 3F; and information accessed online at www.krispykreme.com/mediarelations.html, July 2003.

dise. And you don't just shop at the Toys "*R*" Us store on Times Square store in New York City, you *experience* it.

> Step into Toys "*R*" Us Times Square to enjoy three levels of incredible fun right on Broadway! Take a ride on a 60-foot-high Ferris Wheel with cool character-themed cabs. Feel like a celebrity in our amazing two-story Barbie Dollhouse. Take a stroll through our life-size Candy Land. Gaze up in wonder at our LEGO Empire State Building. And for a classic Jurassic experience, say

■ Marketing experiences: You don't just shop at the Toys "R" Us store on Times Square in New York City, you *experience* it.

hello to a larger than life, 20-foot-tall, T-Rex with realistic moves and a mighty roar. You really have to see it to believe it![2]

Companies that market experiences realize that customers are really buying much more than just products and services. They are buying what those offers will *do* for them.[3]

Levels of Product and Services Product planners need to think about products and services on three levels (see Figure 7.1). Each level adds more customer value. The most basic level is the *core benefit*, which addresses the question *What is the buyer really buying?* When designing products, marketers must first define the core, problem-solving benefits or services that consumers seek. A woman buying lipstick buys more than lip color. Charles Revson of Revlon saw this early: "In the factory, we make cosmetics; in the store, we sell hope." Charles Schwab does more than sell financial services—it promises to fulfill customers' "financial dreams."

At the second level, product planners must turn the core benefit into an *actual product*. They need to develop product and service features, design, a quality level, a brand name, and packaging. For example, a Sony camcorder is an actual product. Its name, parts, styling, features, packaging, and other attributes have all been combined carefully to

FIGURE 7.1

Three Levels of Product

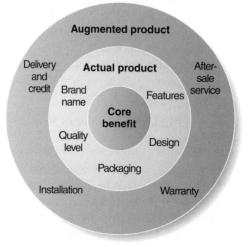

deliver the core benefit—a convenient, high-quality way to capture important moments.

Finally, product planners must build an *augmented product* around the core benefit and actual product by offering additional consumer services and benefits. Sony must offer more than just a camcorder. It must provide consumers with a complete solution to their picture-taking problems. Thus, when consumers buy a Sony camcorder, Sony and its dealers also might give buyers a warranty on parts and workmanship, instructions on how to use the camcorder, quick repair services when needed, and a toll-free telephone number to call if they have problems or questions.

Consumers see products as complex bundles of benefits that satisfy their needs. When developing products, marketers first must identify the *core* consumer needs the product will satisfy. They must then design the *actual* product and find ways to *augment* it in order to create the bundle of benefits that will provide the most satisfying customer experience.

Product and Service Classifications

Products and services fall into two broad classes based on the types of consumers that use them—*consumer products* and *industrial products*. Broadly defined, products also include other marketable entities such as experiences, organizations, persona, places, and ideas.

Consumer Products **Consumer products** are products and services bought by final consumers for personal consumption. Marketers usually classify these products and services further based on how consumers go about buying them. Consumer products include *convenience products*, *shopping products*, *specialty products*, and *unsought products*. These products differ in the ways consumers buy them and therefore in how they are marketed (see Table 7.1).

■ Core, actual, and augmented product: Consumers perceive this Sony Handycam as a complex bundle of intangible features and services that deliver a core benefit—a convenient, high-quality way to capture important moments.

TABLE 7.1   Marketing Considerations for Consumer Products

Marketing Considerations	Type of Consumer Product			
	Convenience	Shopping	Specialty	Unsought
Customer buying behavior	Frequent purchase, little planning, little comparison or shopping effort, low customer involvement	Less frequent purchase, much planning and shopping effort, comparison of brands on price, quality, style	Strong brand preference and loyalty, special purchase effort, little comparison of brands, low price sensitivity	Little product awareness, knowledge (or, if aware, little or even negative interest)
Price	Low price	Higher price	High price	Varies
Distribution	Widespread distribution, convenient locations	Selective distribution in fewer outlets	Exclusive distribution in only one or a few outlets per market area	Varies
Promotion	Mass promotion by the producer	Advertising and personal selling by both producer and resellers	More carefully targeted promotion by both producer and resellers	Aggressive advertising and personal selling by producer and resellers
Examples	Toothpaste, magazines, laundry detergent	Major appliances, televisions, furniture, clothing	Luxury goods, such as Rolex watches or fine crystal	Life insurance, Red Cross blood donations

Consumer product
Product bought by final consumer for personal consumption.

Convenience product
Consumer product that the customer usually buys frequently, immediately, and with a minimum of comparison and buying effort.

Shopping product
Consumer good that the customer, in the process of selection and purchase, characteristically compares on bases such as suitability, quality, price, and style.

Specialty product
Consumer product with unique characteristics or brand identification for which a significant group of buyers is willing to make a special purchase effort.

Unsought product
Consumer product that the consumer either does not know about or knows about but does not normally think of buying.

Industrial product
Product bought by individuals and organizations for further processing or for use in conducting a business.

Convenience products are consumer products and services that the customer usually buys frequently, immediately, and with a minimum of comparison and buying effort. Examples include soap, candy, newspapers, and fast food. Convenience products are usually low priced, and marketers place them in many locations to make them readily available when customers need them.

Shopping products are less frequently purchased consumer products and services that customers compare carefully on suitability, quality, price, and style. When buying shopping products and services, consumers spend much time and effort in gathering information and making comparisons. Examples include furniture, clothing, used cars, major appliances, and hotel and airline services. Shopping products marketers usually distribute their products through fewer outlets but provide deeper sales support to help customers in their comparison efforts.

Specialty products are consumer products and services with unique characteristics or brand identification for which a significant group of buyers is willing to make a special purchase effort. Examples include specific brands and types of cars, high-priced photographic equipment, designer clothes, and the services of medical or legal specialists. A Lamborghini automobile, for example, is a specialty product because buyers are usually willing to travel great distances to buy one. Buyers normally do not compare specialty products. They invest only the time needed to reach dealers carrying the wanted products.

Unsought products are consumer products that the consumer either does not know about or knows about but does not normally think of buying. Most major new innovations are unsought until the consumer becomes aware of them through advertising. Classic examples of known but unsought products and services are life insurance, cemetery plots, and blood donations to the Red Cross. By their very nature, unsought products require a lot of advertising, personal selling, and other marketing efforts.

Industrial Products   **Industrial products** are those purchased for further processing or for use in conducting a business. Thus, the distinction between a consumer product and an industrial product is based on the *purpose* for which the product is bought. If a consumer buys a lawn mower for use around home, the lawn mower is a consumer product. If the same consumer buys the same lawn mower for use in a landscaping business, the lawn mower is an industrial product.

The three groups of industrial products and services include materials and parts, capital items, and supplies and services. *Materials and parts* include raw materials and manufactured materials and parts. Raw materials consist of farm products (wheat, cotton, livestock, fruits, vegetables) and natural products (fish, lumber, crude petroleum, iron ore). Manufactured materials and parts consist of component materials (iron, yarn, cement, wires) and component parts (small motors, tires, castings). Most manufactured materials and parts are sold directly to industrial users. Price and service are the major marketing factors; branding and advertising tend to be less important.

Capital items are industrial products that aid in the buyer's production or operations, including installations and accessory equipment. Installations consist of major purchases such as buildings (factories, offices) and fixed equipment (generators, drill presses, large computer systems, elevators). Accessory equipment includes portable factory equipment and tools (hand tools, lift trucks) and office equipment (computers, fax machines, desks). They have a shorter life than installations and simply aid in the production process.

■ Business Services: Aramark offers everything from food, housekeeping, laundry, and office services, to equipment maintenance, to facilities and supply chain management.

The final group of business products is *supplies and services*. Supplies include operating supplies (lubricants, coal, paper, pencils) and repair and maintenance items (paint, nails, brooms). Supplies are the convenience products of the industrial field because they are usually purchased with a minimum of effort or comparison. Business services include maintenance and repair services (window cleaning, computer repair) and business advisory services (legal, management consulting, advertising). Such services are usually supplied under contract. For example, Aramark offers everything from food, housekeeping, laundry, and office services, to equipment maintenance, to facilities and supply chain management.

Organizations, Persons, Places, and Ideas In addition to tangible products and services, in recent years marketers have broadened the concept of a product to include other market offerings—organizations, persons, places, and ideas.

Organizations often carry out activities to "sell" the organization itself. *Organization marketing* consists of activities undertaken to create, maintain, or change the attitudes and behavior of target consumers toward an organization. Both profit and not-for-profit organizations practice organization marketing. Business firms sponsor public relations or corporate advertising campaigns to polish their images. *Corporate image advertising* is a major tool companies use to market themselves to various publics. For example, Lucent puts out ads with the tag line "We make the things that make communications work." IBM wants to establish itself as the company to turn to for "e-Business Solutions." And General Electric stands for "imagination at work." Similarly, nonprofit organizations, such as churches, colleges, charities, museums, and performing arts groups, market their organizations in order to raise funds and attract members or patrons.

People can also be thought of as products. *Person marketing* consists of activities undertaken to create, maintain, or change attitudes or behavior toward particular people. All kinds of people and organizations practice person marketing. Today's presidents market themselves, their parties, and their platforms to get needed votes and program support. Entertainers and sports figures use marketing to promote their careers and improve their impact and incomes. Professionals such as doctors, lawyers, accountants, and architects market themselves in order to build their reputations and increase business. Businesses, charities, sports teams, fine arts groups, religious groups, and other organizations also use person marketing. Creating or associating with well-known personalities often helps these organizations achieve their goals better. That's why more than a dozen different companies combined—including Nike, Target, Buick, American Express, Disney, and Titleist—pay more than $100 million a year to link themselves with golf superstar Tiger Woods.[4]

Place marketing involves activities undertaken to create, maintain, or change attitudes or behavior toward particular places. Cities, states, regions, and even entire nations compete to attract tourists, new residents, conventions, and company offices and factories. Texas advertises "It's Like a Whole Other Country" and New York State shouts, "I Love New York!"[5] Michigan says "Great Lakes, Great Times" to attract tourists, "Great Lakes, Great Jobs" to attract residents, and "Great Lakes, Great Location" to attract businesses. The Irish Development Agency has attracted more than 1,200 companies to locate their plants in Ireland. At the same time, the Irish

■ Organization marketing: Companies use corporate image advertising to market themselves to various publics. General Electric stands for "imagination at work."

Tourist Board has built a flourishing tourism business by advertising "Live a different life: friendly, beautiful, relaxing." And the Irish Export Board has created attractive markets for Irish exports.[6]

Ideas can also be marketed. In one sense, all marketing is the marketing of an idea, whether it be the general idea of brushing your teeth or the specific idea that Crest toothpastes "create smiles every day." Here, however, we narrow our focus to the marketing of *social ideas*. This area has been called **social marketing**, defined by the Social Marketing Institute as the use of commercial marketing concepts and tools in programs designed to influence individuals' behavior to improve their well-being and that of society.[7]

Social marketing programs include public health campaigns to reduce smoking, alcoholism, drug abuse, and overeating. Other social marketing efforts include environmental campaigns to promote wilderness protection, clean air, and conservation. Still others address issues such as family planning, human rights, and racial equality. The Ad Council of America has developed dozens of social advertising campaigns, involving issues ranging from preventive health, education, and personal safety to environmental preservation (see Marketing at Work 7.2).

But social marketing involves much more than just advertising—the Social Marketing Institute encourages the use of a broad range of marketing tools. "Social marketing goes well beyond the promotional '*P*' of the marketing mix to include every other element to achieve its social change objectives," says the SMI's executive director.[8]

Social marketing

The design, implementation, and control of programs seeking to increase the acceptability of a social idea, cause, or practice among a target group.

■▌ Product and Service Decisions

Marketers make product and services decisions at three levels: individual product decisions, product line decisions, and product mix decisions. We discuss each in turn.

Individual Product and Service Decisions

Figure 7.2 shows the important decisions in the development and marketing of individual products and services. We will focus on decisions about *product attributes*, *branding*, *packaging*, *labeling*, and *product support services*.

Product and Service Attributes Developing a product or service involves defining the benefits that it will offer. These benefits are communicated and delivered by product attributes such as *quality*, *features*, and *style and design*.

Product Quality. **Product quality** is one of the marketer's major positioning tools. Quality has a direct impact on product or service performance; thus, it is closely linked to customer value and satisfaction. In the narrowest sense, quality can be defined as "freedom from defects." But most customer-centered companies go beyond this narrow definition. Instead, they define quality in terms of customer satisfaction. The American Society for Quality defines quality as the characteristics of a product or service that bear on its ability to satisfy stated or implied customer needs. Similarly, Siemens defines quality this way: "Quality is when our customers come back and our products don't."[9] These customer-focused definitions suggest that quality begins with customer needs and ends with customer satisfaction.

Total quality management (TQM) is an approach in which all the company's people are involved in constantly improving the quality of products, services, and business

Product quality

The ability of a product to perform its functions; it includes the product's overall durability, reliability, precision, ease of operation and repair, and other valued attributes.

FIGURE 7.2
Individual Product Decisions

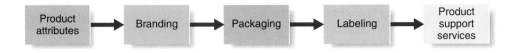

Product attributes → Branding → Packaging → Labeling → Product support services

Marketing at Work | 7.2

The Ad Council: Advertising for the Common Good

How are these for familiar phrases? "Friends don't let friends drive drunk." "Only you can prevent forest fires." "Take a bite out of crime." "A mind is a terrible thing to waste." "Loose lips sink ships." "I am an American." Or how about these familiar characters: Smokey Bear, Rosie the Riveter, the Crash Test Dummies, and McGruff the Crime Dog? What do all of these phrases and icons have in common? They were all created by the Ad Council, a private, nonprofit organization with a long history of using advertising to create positive change.

The Ad Council was formed in 1942, at a time when people were especially cynical about advertising and all the money spent on it, to show the good that advertising can do. Its mission is "to identify a select number of significant public issues and stimulate action on those issues through communications programs that make a measurable difference in our society." To that end, the Ad Council works to connect ad agencies (who donate their time), sponsors (who donate money), and media (who donate advertising time and space) with worthy nonprofit organizations and governmental agencies that need a promotional voice.

Through this joint volunteer effort, the Ad Council has created thousands of public service campaigns on issues such as improving the quality of life for children, preventive health, education, community well-being, environmental preservation, personal safety, and strengthening families. These campaigns have produced more than just catchy slogans—they've produced positive and lasting social change as well. Ad Council campaigns have achieved significant results on a wide breadth of issues:

■ *Environment:* Launched in 1944, Smokey Bear has been urging children

and adults not to play with matches, not to leave a campfire unattended, and to keep a bucket of water and a shovel nearby. Since the campaign began, the number of forest acres lost

to fires annually has decreased from 22 million to 4 million.

■ *Education:* The Ad Council teamed with Young & Rubicam advertising agency to create a campaign

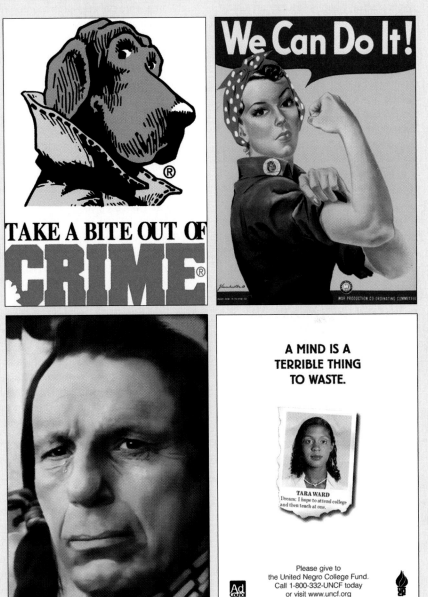

The Ad Council has created thousands of public service campaigns that have produced positive and lasting social change.

(continued)

message, "A mind is a terrible thing to waste." Now in its 30th year, the campaign has helped raise more than $1.9 billion for the United Negro College Fund and helped more than 300,000 minority students graduate college.

■ *Health:* In the 1940s, Ad Council campaigns urged Americans to get vaccinated against polio—not an easy sell at the time because the vaccination involved three sets of unpleasant shots. Today, polio is virtually unheard-of in this country.

■ *Crime awareness and prevention:* In 1978, working with the National Crime Prevention Council and the ad firm Saatchi & Saatchi, the Ad Council helped give birth to McGruff the Crime Dog. Since then, McGruff has taught both children and adults valuable crime awareness and crime prevention lessons, encouraging all of us to "Take A Bite Out Of Crime," The familiar bloodhound in a trench coat has become a popular icon. A 2000 study showed that 92 percent of American children recognize the character and believes he offers advice that helps them stay safe. In 1989 and 1990, McGruff the Crime Dog's popularity was surpassed only by that of Mickey Mouse.

■ *Seat-Belt Use:* When Vince & Larry, the crash-test dummies, first flew through a windshield on network TV in 1985, seat-belt usage was at 21 percent and most states did not mandate seat belt usage by law. Since then, most states have adopted seat-belt laws and safety-belt usage has increased from 21 percent to 73 percent, saving an estimated 85,000 lives.

■ *Drunk Driving:* Since the Ad Council began its drunk-driving prevention campaign, the old saying "One more for the road" has been replaced with "Friends Don't Let Friends Drive Drunk." Some 68 percent of Americans say they have personally stopped someone from driving drunk.

■ *Social Issues:* More than 6,000 children were paired with a mentor in just the first 18 months of the Ad Council's mentoring campaign. And public awareness about child abuse has increased from just 10 percent in the mid-1970s to more than 90 percent today. According to the CEO of Prevent Child Abuse America, "When we first started our child abuse prevention campaign, the public's understanding of the issue was very low. But our partnership with the Ad Council has brought child abuse and neglect out into the open."

The Ad Council has drawn widespread support for its social marketing mission. Some 28,000 media outlets have contributed free ad space and time, and hundreds of socially conscious corporations, foundations, and individuals have provided crucial operating funds. Big ad agencies like J. Walter Thompson, Young & Rubicam, BBDO, Doyle Dane Bernbach, and Foote, Cone & Belding, and Marstellar willingly donate their creative energies to create Ad Council campaigns. And the campaigns often turn out to be some of their very best work. For example, Marstellar's "People start pollution, people can stop it" campaign on behalf of Keep America Beautiful rates as one of the most memorable campaigns in history. The campaign ranked 50th on Advertising Age's list of top 100 ad campaigns of the century. And Foote, Cone & Belding's Smokey Bear and "Only you can prevent forest fires" campaign ranked 26th on the Ad Age top 100 list.

The Ad Council has established social marketing campaigns as an effective, admirable side of the advertising industry. It has proven that advertising can be used to do good, and its success has spawned other social marketing efforts. Nonprofit groups such as Partnership for a Drug-Free America have followed suit with additional public service announcements. And TV networks now routinely use their stars to promote worthy causes (such as NBC's "The More You Know . . . " series). "The Ad Council was a model that proved it could work," says former Ad Council president Ruth Wooden. Advertising no longer just pushes products—it improves, and even saves, human lives.

Sources: See Bob Garfield, "Inspiration and Urge-to-Serve Mark the Best of the Ad Council," *Advertising Age,* April 29, 2002, pp. c2–c20; and MEDIAWEEK Special Advertising Section, June 10, 2002. Portions adapted from "The Advertising Council," accessed at www.adcouncil.org/about/, July 2003.

processes. During the past two decades, companies large and small have credited TQM with greatly improving their market shares and profits. Recently, however, the total quality management movement has drawn criticism. Too many companies viewed TQM as a magic cure-all and created token total quality programs that applied quality principles only superficially. Still others became obsessed with narrowly defined TQM principles and lost sight of broader concerns for customer value and satisfaction. As a result, many such programs failed, causing a backlash against TQM.

When applied in the context of creating customer satisfaction, however, *total quality* principles remain a requirement for success. Although many firms don't use the TQM label anymore, for most top companies customer-driven quality has become a way of doing business. Today, companies are taking a "return on quality" approach, viewing quality as an investment and holding quality efforts accountable for bottom-line results.[10]

Product quality has two dimensions—level and consistency. In developing a product, the marketer must first choose a *quality level* that will support the product's position in the target market. Here, product quality means *performance quality*—the ability of a product to perform its functions. For example, a Rolls-Royce provides higher performance quality than a Chevrolet: It has a smoother ride, handles better, and lasts longer. Companies rarely try to offer the highest possible performance quality level—few customers want or can afford the high levels of quality offered in products such as a Rolls-Royce automobile, a Sub-Zero refrigerator, or a Rolex watch. Instead, companies choose a quality level that matches target market needs and the quality levels of competing products.

Beyond quality level, high quality also can mean high levels of quality *consistency*. Here, product quality means *conformance quality*—freedom from defects and *consistency* in delivering a targeted level of performance. All companies should strive for high levels of conformance quality. In this sense, a Chevrolet can have just as much quality as a Rolls-Royce. Although a Chevy doesn't perform as well as a Rolls, it can as consistently deliver the quality that customers pay for and expect.

Many companies today have turned customer-driven quality into a potent strategic weapon. They create customer satisfaction and value by consistently and profitably meeting customers' needs and preferences for quality.

Product Features. A product can be offered with varying features. A stripped-down model, one without any extras, is the starting point. The company can create higher-level models by adding more features. Features are a competitive tool for differentiating the company's product from competitors' products. Being the first producer to introduce a needed and valued new feature is one of the most effective ways to compete.

How can a company identify new features and decide which ones to add to its product? The company should periodically survey buyers who have used the product and ask these questions: How do you like the product? Which specific features of the product do you like most? Which features could we add to improve the product? The answers provide the company with a rich list of feature ideas. The company can then assess each feature's *value* to customers versus its *cost* to the company. Features that customers value little in relation to costs should be dropped; those that customers value highly in relation to costs should be added.

Product Style and Design. Another way to add customer value is through distinctive *product style and design*. Design is a larger concept than style. *Style* simply describes the appearance of a product. Styles can be eye-catching or yawn producing. A sensational style may grab attention and produce pleasing aesthetics, but it does not necessarily make the product *perform* better. Unlike style, *design* is more than skin deep—it goes to the very heart of a product. Good design contributes to a product's usefulness as well as to its looks.

Good style and design can attract attention, improve product performance, cut production costs, and give the product a strong competitive advantage in the target market. Here are two examples:

> Apple's original iMac—which featured a sleek, egg-shaped monitor and hard drive, all in one unit, in a futuristic translucent turquoise casing—redefined the look and feel of the personal computer. There was no clunky tower or desktop hard drive to clutter up your office area. Featuring one-button Internet access, this machine was designed specifically for cruising the Internet (that's what the "i" in "iMac" stands for). The dramatic iMac won raves for design and lured buyers in droves. Within a year, it had sold more than a million units, marking Apple's reemergence in the personal computer industry. Before it was over, Apple had sold more than 10 million of the original iMacs. "If they had not done that," says an industry insider, "they probably would have gone under. It captured the world's attention and put Apple back on the map." Four years later, Apple did it again with a stunning new iMac design—a clean, futuristic machine featuring a flat-panel display that seems to float in the air. Within only three months, Apple-lovers had snapped up nearly one-quarter million of these eye-pleasing yet functional machines.[11]

■ Product design: The design of the dramatic iMac helped reestablish Apple as a legitimate contender in the PC industry. The innovative Discover 2GO card is a gotta-have-it accessory for people who want to dash off to the gym, the mall, or a restaurant with nothing more than their keys and a credit card.

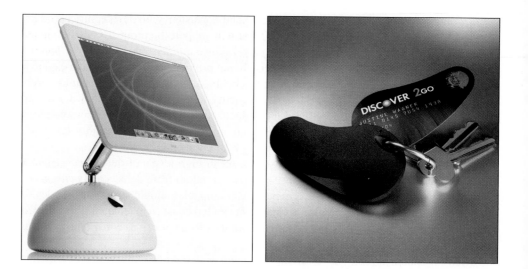

You turn the flat, kidney-shaped plastic gadget over in your hands, puzzling over what it does. Then you realize that a sliver of red plastic pivots out of the black case like a pocketknife blade. You recognize a familiar strand of embossed numbers, a magnetic stripe, and a signature bar. It's a credit card! To be precise, it's a Discover 2GO card, complete with a key chain, belt clip, and protective case. In consumer terms, the Discover 2GO card is a gotta-have-it accessory for people who want to dash off to the gym, the mall, or a restaurant with nothing more than their keys and a credit card. In industry terms, it's a big design innovation in a business that has rarely thought much outside the 2-by-3-inch box. The Discover 2GO card's design won it recognition as one of the best products of the year last year by *USA Today* and *Business Week*. It has also drawn praise from card marketing experts. "This is slick. It's different, which is good. And it's functional," says one consultant. "It's the card you'll use when you have your keys in your hand."[12]

Branding   Perhaps the most distinctive skill of professional marketers is their ability to create, maintain, protect, and enhance brands of their products and services. A **brand** is a name, term, sign, symbol, or design, or a combination of these, that identifies the maker or seller of a product or service. Consumers view a brand as an important part of a product, and branding can add value to a product. For example, most consumers would perceive a bottle of White Linen perfume as a high-quality, expensive product. But the same perfume in an unmarked bottle would likely be viewed as lower in quality, even if the fragrance were identical.

Branding has become so strong that today hardly anything goes unbranded. Salt is packaged in branded containers, common nuts and bolts are packaged with a distributor's label, and automobile parts—spark plugs, tires, filters—bear brand names that differ from those of the auto makers. Even fruits, vegetables, and poultry are branded—Sunkist oranges, Dole pineapples, Chiquita bananas, Fresh Express salad greens, and Perdue chickens.

Branding helps buyers in many ways. Brand names help consumers identify products that might benefit them. Brands also tell the buyer something about product quality. Buyers who always buy the same brand know that they will get the same features, benefits, and quality each time they buy. Branding also gives the seller several advantages. The brand name becomes the basis on which a whole story can be built about a product's special qualities. The seller's brand name and trademark provide legal protection for unique product features that otherwise might be copied by competitors. And branding helps the seller to segment markets. For example, General Mills can offer Cheerios, Wheaties, Total, Kix, Lucky Charms, Trix, and many other cereal brands, not just one general product for all consumers.

Building and managing brands is perhaps the marketer's most important task. We will discuss branding strategy in more detail later in the chapter.

Brand

A name, term, sign, symbol, or design, or a combination of these intended to identify the goods or services of one seller or group of sellers and to differentiate them from those of competitors.

Packaging **Packaging** involves designing and producing the container or wrapper for a product. The package includes a product's primary container (the tube holding Colgate Total toothpaste). It may also include a secondary package that is thrown away when the product is about to be used (the cardboard box containing the tube of Colgate). Finally, it can include a shipping package necessary to store, identify, and ship the product (a corrugated box carrying six dozen tubes of Colgate). Labeling, printed information appearing on or with the package, is also part of packaging.

Traditionally, the primary function of the package was to contain and protect the product. In recent times, however, numerous factors have made packaging an important marketing tool. Increased competition and clutter on retail store shelves means that packages must now perform many sales tasks—from attracting attention, to describing the product, to making the sale.

Companies are realizing the power of good packaging to create instant consumer recognition of the company or brand. For example, in an average supermarket, which stocks 15,000 to 17,000 items, the typical shopper passes by some 300 items per minute, and more than 60 percent of all purchases are made on impulse. In this highly competitive environment, the package may be the seller's last chance to influence buyers. "Not long ago, the package was merely the product's receptacle, and the brand message was elsewhere—usually on TV," says a packaging expert. But changes in the marketplace environment are now "making the package itself an increasingly important selling medium."[13]

Innovative packaging can give a company an advantage over competitors. Consumer packaged goods firms have recently upped their investments in packaging research to develop package designs that grab more shelf attention or make life easier for customers. Notable examples include Skippy Squeez'It peanut butter, dispensed from tubes for on-the-go families, and Coca-Cola beverage packs designed to fit neatly onto refrigerator shelves. Dutch Boy recently came up with a long overdue innovation—paint in plastic containers with twist-off caps:

> How did Dutch Boy Paint stir up the paint business? It's so simple, it's scary. Imagine a paint can that's easy to carry, doesn't take a screwdriver to pry open, doesn't dribble when pouring, and doesn't take a hammer to bang closed again. It's here—in the form of Dutch Boy's new Twist and Pour paint container. The new container is an all-plastic gallon container with a twist-off lid, side handle, and pour spout. It's lighter weight than a can and rust-proof, too. "It's so much easier to use," says Dutch Boy's marketing director. "You can hold it like a cup of coffee." It kind of makes you wonder: Why did it take so long to come up with an idea like this? The new containers cost a dollar or two more than traditional cans, but consumers don't seem to mind. More than 50 percent of Dutch Boy's customers are now buying the plastic containers, and new stores, like Wal-Mart, are now carrying it. "It's an amazing innovation. Worth noticing," says one observer. "Not only did the new packaging increase sales, but it also got them more distribution at a higher retail price!"[14]

In contrast, poorly designed packages can cause headaches for consumers and lost sales for the company (see Marketing at Work 7.3). For example, a few years ago, Planters Lifesavers Company attempted to use innovative packaging to create an association between fresh-roasted peanuts and fresh-roasted coffee. It packaged its Fresh Roast Salted Peanuts in vacuum-packed "Brik-Pacs," similar to those used for ground coffee. Unfortunately, the coffeelike

Packaging
The activities of designing and producing the container or wrapper for a product.

■ Innovative packaging: Dutch Boy recently came up with a long overdue innovation—paint in plastic containers with twist-off caps. Imagine a paint can that's easy to carry, doesn't take a screwdriver to pry open, doesn't dribble when pouring, and doesn't take a hammer to bang closed again.

Marketing at Work | 7.3

Those Frustrating, Not-So-Easy-To-Open Packages

Some things, it seems, will never change. This classic letter from an angry consumer to Robert D. Stuart, then chairman of Quaker Oats, beautifully expresses the utter frustration all of us have experienced in dealing with so-called easy-opening packages.

Dear Mr. Stuart:

I am an 86-year-old widow in fairly good health. (You may think of this as advanced age, but for me that description pertains to the years ahead. Nevertheless, if you decide to reply to this letter I wouldn't dawdle, actuarial tables being what they are.)

As I said, my health is fairly good. Feeble and elderly, as one understands these terms, I am not. My two Doberman Pinschers and I take a brisk 3-mile walk every day. They are two strong and energetic animals and it takes a bit of doing to keep "brisk" closer to a stroll than a mad dash. But I manage because as yet I don't lack the strength. You will shortly see why this fact is relevant.

I am writing to call your attention to the cruel, deceptive, and utterly [false] copy on your Aunt Jemima buttermilk complete pancake and waffle mix. The words on your package read, "to open—press here and pull back."

Mr. Stuart, though I push and press and groan and strive and writhe and curse and sweat and jab and push, poke and ram . . . whew!—I have never once been able to do what the package instructs—to "press here and pull back" the [blankety-blank]. It can't be done! Talk about failing strength! Have you ever tried and succeeded?

My late husband was a gun collector who among other lethal weapons kept a Thompson machine gun in a locked cabinet. It was a good thing that the cabinet was locked. Oh, the number of times I was tempted to give your package a few short bursts.

That lock and a sense of ladylike delicacy kept me from pursuing that vengeful fantasy. Instead, I keep a small cleaver in my pantry for those occasions when I need to open a package of your delicious Aunt Jemima pancakes.

For many years that whacking away with my cleaver served a dual purpose. Not only to open the [blankety-blank] package but also to vent my fury at your sadists who willfully and maliciously did design that torture apparatus that passes for a package.

Sometimes just for the [blank] of it I let myself get carried away. I don't stop after I've lopped off the top. I whack away until the package is utterly destroyed in an outburst of rage, frustration, and vindictiveness. I wind up with a floorful of your delicious Aunt Jemima pancake mix. But that's a small price to pay for blessed release. (Anyway, the Pinschers lap up the mess.)

So many ingenious, considerate (even compassionate) innovations in package closures have been designed since Aunt Jemima first donned her red bandana. Wouldn't you consider the introduction of a more humane package to replace the example of marketing malevolence to which you resolutely cling? Don't you care, Mr. Stuart?

I'm really writing this to be helpful and in that spirit I am sending a copy to Mr. Tucker, president of Container Corp. I'm sure their clever young designers could be of immeasurable help to you in this matter. At least I feel it's worth a try.

Really, Mr. Stuart, I hope you will not regard me as just another cranky old biddy. I am The Public, the source of your fortunes.

Ms. Roberta Pavloff
Malvern, Pa.

Source: This letter was reprinted in "Some Designs Should Just Be Torn Asunder," *Advertising Age*, January 17, 1983, p. M54.

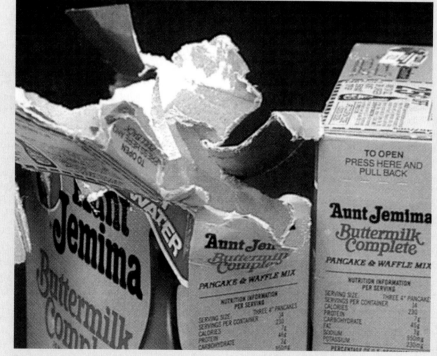

An easy to open package?

packaging worked too well: Consumers mistook the peanuts for a new brand of flavored coffee and ran them through supermarket coffee-grinding machines, creating a gooey mess, disappointed customers, and lots of irate store managers.[15]

Developing a good package for a new product requires making many decisions. First, the company must establish the *packaging concept,* which states what the package should *be* or *do* for the product. Should it mainly offer product protection, introduce a new dispensing method, suggest certain qualities about the product, or do something else? Decisions then must be made on specific elements of the package, such as size, shape, materials, color, text, and brand mark. These elements must work together to support the product's position and marketing strategy.

In recent years, product safety has also become a major packaging concern. We have all learned to deal with hard-to-open "childproof" packages. And after the rash of product tampering scares during the 1980s, most drug producers and food makers now put their products in tamper-resistant packages. In making packaging decisions, the company also must heed growing environmental concerns. Fortunately, many companies have gone "green" by reducing their packaging and using environmentally responsible packaging materials. For example, SC Johnson repackaged Agree Plus shampoo in a stand-up pouch using 80 percent less plastic. P&G eliminated outer cartons from its Secret and Sure deodorants, saving 3.4 million pounds of paperboard per year.

Labeling Labels may range from simple tags attached to products to complex graphics that are part of the package. They perform several functions. At the very least, the label *identifies* the product or brand, such as the name Sunkist stamped on oranges. The label might also *describe* several things about the product—who made it, where it was made, when it was made, its contents, how it is to be used, and how to use it safely. Finally, the label might *promote* the product through attractive graphics.

There has been a long history of legal concerns about packaging and labels. The Federal Trade Commission Act of 1914 held that false, misleading, or deceptive labels or packages constitute unfair competition. Labels can mislead customers, fail to describe important ingredients, or fail to include needed safety warnings. As a result, several federal and state laws regulate labeling. The most prominent is the Fair Packaging and Labeling Act of 1966, which set mandatory labeling requirements, encouraged voluntary industry packaging standards, and allowed federal agencies to set packaging regulations in specific industries.

Labeling has been affected in recent times by *unit pricing* (stating the price per unit of a standard measure), *open dating* (stating the expected shelf life of the product), and *nutritional labeling* (stating the nutritional values in the product). The Nutritional Labeling and Educational Act of 1990 requires sellers to provide detailed nutritional information on food products, and recent sweeping actions by the Food and Drug Administration regulate the use of health-related terms such as *low-fat, light,* and *high-fiber.* Sellers must ensure that their labels contain all the required information.

Product Support Services Customer service is another element of product strategy. A company's offer to the marketplace usually includes some support services, which can be a minor or a major part of the total offering. Later in the chapter, we will discuss services as products in themselves. Here, we discuss services that augment actual products.

The first step is to survey customers periodically to assess the value of current services and to

■ Innovative labeling can help to promote a product.

obtain ideas for new ones. For example, Cadillac holds regular focus group interviews with owners and carefully watches complaints that come into its dealerships. From this careful monitoring, Cadillac has learned that buyers are very upset by repairs that are not done correctly the first time.

Once the company has assessed the value of various support services to customers, it must next assess the costs of providing these services. It can then develop a package of services that will both delight customers and yield profits to the company. Based on its consumer interviews, Cadillac has set up a system directly linking each dealership with a group of 10 engineers who can help walk mechanics through difficult repairs. Such actions helped Cadillac jump, in one year, from 14th to 7th in independent rankings of service. For the past several years, Cadillac has rated at or near the top of its industry on the American Customer Satisfaction Index.[16]

Many companies are now using a sophisticated mix of phone, e-mail, fax, Internet, and interactive voice and data technologies to provide support services that were not possible before. Consider the following example:

> It's February 14, and you've just remembered that it's Valentine's Day. There's no time for florist shops, so you jump online to www.1800FLOWERS.com. Then you pause. Red roses? Boxed or in a vase? One dozen or two? Just as your head starts to pound, you notice a button on the Web site. Click on it, and you're connected to a customer service rep at the call center who can help sniff out your options. A chat page opens on your screen, allowing a real-time dialog with the agent. The service rep even "pushes" pages to your browser so you can see different floral arrangements and how much they cost. In minutes, you have placed your order online, with a little hand-holding. Like 1-800-Flowers, many e-marketers now offer live interaction with service reps. Some feature real-time chat sessions, others voice-over-Web capabilities. In the future, a "call cam" will even let consumers see an agent on their computer screen.[17]

Product Line Decisions

Product line

A group of products that are closely related because they function in a similar manner, are sold to the same customer groups, are marketed through the same types of outlets, or fall within given price ranges.

Beyond decisions about individual products and services, product strategy also calls for building a product line. A **product line** is a group of products that are closely related because they function in a similar manner, are sold to the same customer groups, are marketed through the same types of outlets, or fall within given price ranges. For example, Nike produces several lines of athletic shoes and apparel, Nokia produces several lines of telecommunications products, and Charles Schwab produces several lines of financial services.

The major product line decision involves *product line length*—the number of items in the product line. The line is too short if the manager can increase profits by adding items; the line is too long if the manager can increase profits by dropping items. The company should manage its product lines carefully. Product lines tend to lengthen over time, and most companies eventually need to prune unnecessary or unprofitable items from their lines to increase overall profitability.

Product line length is influenced by company objectives and resources. For example, one objective might be to allow for up-selling. Thus, BMW wants to move customers up from its 3-series models to 5- and 7-series models. Another objective might be to allow cross-selling: Hewlett-Packard sells printers as well as cartridges. Still another objective might be to protect against economic swings: Gap runs several clothing-store chains (Gap, Old Navy, Banana Republic) covering different price points.

A company can lengthen its product line in two ways: by *line stretching* or by *line filling. Product line stretching* occurs when a company lengthens its product line beyond its current range. The company can stretch its line downward, upward, or both ways.

Companies located at the upper end of the market can stretch their lines *downward*. A company may stretch downward to plug a market hole that otherwise would attract a new competitor or to respond to a competitor's attack on the upper end. Or it may add low-end products because it finds faster growth taking place in the low-end segments. DaimlerChrysler stretched its Mercedes line downward for all these reasons. Facing a slow-growth luxury car market and attacks by Japanese auto makers on its high-end positioning, it successfully introduced its Mercedes C-Class cars. These models sell at less than $30,000 without harming the firm's ability to sell other Mercedes for $100,000 or more. Similarly, Rolex launched its Rolex Tudor watch retailing for about $1,350, compared with a Rolex Submariner, usually priced at $3,875.

Companies at the lower end of a market can stretch their product lines *upward*. Sometimes, companies stretch upward in order to add prestige to their current products. Or they may be attracted by a faster growth rate or higher margins at the higher end. For example, each of the leading Japanese auto companies introduced an upmarket automobile: Toyota launched Lexus; Nissan launched Infinity; and Honda launched Acura. They used entirely new names rather than their own.

Companies in the middle range of the market may decide to stretch their lines in *both directions*. Marriott did this with its hotel product line. Along with regular Marriott hotels, it added the Renaissance Hotel line to serve the upper end of the market and the TownePlace Suites line to serve the moderate and lower ends. Each branded hotel line is aimed at a different target market. Renaissance aims to attract and please top executives; Marriotts, upper and middle managers; Courtyards, salespeople and other "road warriors"; and Fairfield Inns, vacationers and business travelers on a tight travel budget. ExecuStay by Marriott provides temporary housing for those relocating or away on long-term assignments of 30 days or longer. Marriott's Residence Inn provides a relaxed, residential atmosphere—a home away from home for people who travel for a living. Marriott TownePlace Suites provide a comfortable atmosphere at a moderate price for extended-stay travelers.[18] The major risk with this strategy is that some travelers will trade down after finding that the lower-price hotels in the Marriott chain give them pretty much everything they want. However, Marriott would rather capture its customers who move downward than lose them to competitors.

An alternative to product line stretching is *product line filling*—adding more items within the present range of the line. There are several reasons for product line filling: reaching for extra profits, satisfying dealers, using excess capacity, being the leading full-line company, and plugging holes to keep out competitors. Sony filled its Walkman line by adding solar-powered and waterproof Walkmans, an ultralight model that attaches to a sweatband for exercisers, the MiniDisc Walkman, the CD Walkman, and the Memory Stick Walkman, which enables users to download tracks straight from the Net. However, line

■ Product line stretching: Marriott offers a full line of hotel brands, each aimed at a different target market.

filling is overdone if it results in cannibalization and customer confusion. The company should ensure that new items are noticeably different from existing ones.

Product Mix Decisions

Product mix (or product assortment)

The set of all product lines and items that a particular seller offers for sale.

An organization with several product lines has a product mix. A **product mix** (or **product assortment**) consists of all the product lines and items that a particular seller offers for sale. Avon's product mix consists of five major product lines: beauty products, wellness products, jewelry and accessories, gifts, and "inspirational" products (inspiring gifts, books, music, and home accents). Each product line consists of several sublines. For example, the beauty line breaks down into makeup, skin care, bath and beauty, fragrance, and outdoor protection products. Each line and subline has many individual items. Altogether, Avon's product mix includes 1,300 items. In contrast, a typical Kmart stocks 15,000 items, 3M markets more than 60,000 products, and General Electric manufactures as many as 250,000 items.

A company's product mix has four important dimensions: width, length, depth, and consistency. Product mix *width* refers to the number of different product lines the company carries. Procter & Gamble markets a fairly wide product mix consisting of 250 brands organized into many product lines. These lines include fabric and home care; baby, feminine, and family care; beauty care; health care; and food and beverage products. Product mix *length* refers to the total number of items the company carries within its product lines. P&G typically carries many brands within each line. For example, it sells seven laundry detergents, six hand soaps, five shampoos, and four dishwashing detergents.

Product line *depth* refers to the number of versions offered of each product in the line. P&G's Crest toothpaste comes in 13 varieties, ranging from Crest Multicare, Crest Cavity Protection, and Crest Tartar Protection to Crest Sensitivity Protection, Crest Dual Action Whitening, Crest Whitening Plus Scope, Kid's Cavity Protection, and Crest Baking Soda & Peroxide Whitening formulations.[19] (Talk about niche marketing! Remember our Chapter 6 discussion?)

Finally, the *consistency* of the product mix refers to how closely related the various product lines are in end use, production requirements, distribution channels, or some other way. P&G's product lines are consistent insofar as they are consumer products that go through the same distribution channels. The lines are less consistent insofar as they perform different functions for buyers.

These product mix dimensions provide the handles for defining the company's product strategy. The company can increase its business in four ways. It can add new product lines, widening its product mix. In this way, its new lines build on the company's reputation in its other lines. The company can lengthen its existing product lines to become a more full-line company. Or it can add more versions of each product and thus deepen its product mix. Finally, the company can pursue more product line consistency—or less—depending on whether it wants to have a strong reputation in a single field or in several fields.

SPEED BUMP

Linking the Concepts

Slow down for a minute. To get a better sense of how large and complex a company's product offering can become, investigate Procter & Gamble's product mix.

- Using P&G's Web site (www.pg.com), its annual report, or other sources, develop a list of all the company's product lines and individual products. What surprises you about this list of products?
- Is P&G's product mix consistent? What overall strategy or logic appears to have guided the development of this product mix?

■■▌ Branding Strategy: Building Strong Brands

Some analysts see brands as *the* major enduring asset of a company, outlasting the company's specific products and facilities. John Stewart, co-founder of Quaker Oats, once said, "If this business were split up, I would give you the land and bricks and mortar, and I would keep the brands and trademarks, and I would fare better than you." The CEO of McDonald's agrees[20]:

> A McDonald's board member who worked at Coca-Cola once talked to us about the value of our brand. He said if every asset we own, every building, and every piece of equipment were destroyed in a terrible natural disaster, we would be able to borrow all the money to replace it very quickly because of the value of our brand. And he's right. The brand is more valuable than the totality of all these assets.

Thus, brands are powerful assets that must be carefully developed and managed. In this section, we examine the key strategies for building and managing brands.

Brand Equity

Brands are more than just names and symbols. Brands represent consumers' perceptions and feelings about a product and its performance—everything that the product or service *means* to consumers. In the final analysis, brands exist in the minds of consumers. Thus, the real value of a strong brand is its power to capture consumer preference and loyalty.

Brands vary in the amount of power and value they have in the marketplace. Some brands—such as Coca-Cola, Tide, Nike, Harley-Davidson, Volkswagen, and others—become larger-than-life icons that maintain their power in the market for years, even generations. "These brands win competitive battles not [just] because they deliver distinctive benefits, trustworthy service, or innovative technologies," notes a branding expert. "Rather, they succeed because they forge a deep connection with the culture."[21]

Brand equity

The positive differential effect that knowing the brand name has on customer response to the product or service.

A powerful brand has high *brand equity.* **Brand equity** is the positive differential effect that knowing the brand name has on customer response to the product or service. A measure of a brand's equity is the extent to which customers are willing to pay more for the brand. One study found that 72 percent of customers would pay a 20 percent premium for their brand of choice relative to the closest competing brand; 40 percent said they would pay a 50 percent premium.[22] Tide and Heinz lovers are willing to pay a 100 percent premium. Loyal Coke drinkers will pay a 50 percent premium and Volvo users a 40 percent premium.

A brand with strong brand equity is a very valuable asset. *Brand valuation* is the process of estimating the total financial value of a brand. Measuring such value is difficult. However, according to one estimate, the brand value of Coca-Cola is almost $70 billion, Microsoft is $65 billion, and IBM is $52 billion. Other brands rating among the world's most valuable include General Electric, Intel, Nokia, Disney, McDonald's, Marlboro, and Mercedes.[23]

High brand equity provides a company with many competitive advantages. A powerful brand enjoys a high level of consumer brand awareness and loyalty. Because consumers expect stores to

■ A strong brand is a valuable asset. How many familiar brands and brand symbols can you find in this picture?

carry the brand, the company has more leverage in bargaining with resellers. Because the brand name carries high credibility, the company can more easily launch line and brand extensions, as when Coca-Cola used its well-known brand to introduce Diet Coke and Vanilla Coke, and when Procter & Gamble introduced Ivory dishwashing detergent. A powerful brand offers the company some defense against fierce price competition.

Above all, a powerful brand forms the basis for building strong and profitable customer relationships. Therefore, the fundamental asset underlying brand equity is *customer equity*— the value of the customer relationships that the brand creates. A powerful brand is important, but what it really represents is a set of loyal customers. The proper focus of marketing is building customer equity, with brand management serving as a major marketing tool.[24]

Building Strong Brands

Branding poses challenging decisions to the marketer. Figure 7.3 shows that the major brand strategy decisions involve brand positioning, brand name selection, brand sponsorship, and brand development.

Brand Positioning Marketers need to position their brands clearly in target customers' minds. They can position brands at any of three levels.[25] At the lowest level, they can position the brand on *product attributes*. Thus, marketers of Dove soap can talk about the product's attribute of one-quarter cleansing cream. However, attributes are the least desirable level for brand positioning. Competitors can easily copy attributes. More important, customers are not interested in attributes as such; they are interested in what the attributes will do for them.

■ Brand positioning: The strongest brands go beyond attribute or benefit positioning. They are positioned on what the brand will *do* for those who use it. Godiva says, "let your imagination out of its shell."

A brand can be better positioned by associating its name with a desirable *benefit*. Thus, Dove marketers can go beyond the brand's cleansing cream attribute and talk about the resulting benefit of softer skin. Some successful brands positioned on benefits are Volvo (safety), Hallmark (caring), Harley-Davidson (adventure), FedEx (guaranteed overnight delivery), Nike (performance), and Lexus (quality).

The strongest brands go beyond attribute or benefit positioning. They are positioned on strong *beliefs and values*. These brands pack an emotional wallop. Thus, Dove's marketers can talk not just about cleansing cream attributes and softer skin benefits, but about how these will make you more attractive. Brand expert Marc Gobe argues that successful brands must engage customers on a deeper level, touching a universal emotion.[26] His brand design agency, which has worked on brands such as Starbucks, Victoria's Secret, Godiva, Versace, and Lancôme, relies less on a product's tangible attributes and more on creating surprise, passion, and excitement surrounding a brand.

When positioning a brand, the marketer should establish a mission for the brand and a vision of what the brand must be and do. A brand is the company's promise to deliver a specific set of features, benefits, services, and experiences consistently to the buyers. It can be thought of as a contract to the customer regarding how the product or service will deliver value and satisfaction. The brand contract must be simple and honest. Motel 6, for example, offers clean rooms, low prices, and good service but does not promise expensive furniture or large bathrooms. In contrast, Ritz-Carlton offers luxurious rooms and a truly memorable experience but does not promise low prices.

Brand Name Selection A good name can add greatly to a product's success. However, finding the best brand name is a difficult task. It begins with a careful review of the product and its benefits, the target market, and proposed marketing strategies.

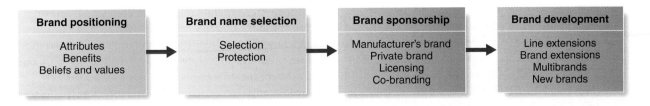

FIGURE 7.3
Major Brand Strategy Decisions

Desirable qualities for a brand name include the following: (1) It should suggest something about the product's benefits and qualities. Examples: Beautyrest, Craftsman, Snuggles, Merrie Maids, OFF! bug spray. (2) It should be easy to pronounce, recognize, and remember. Short names help. Examples: Tide, Crest, Puffs. But longer ones are sometimes effective. Examples: "Love My Carpet" carpet cleaner, "I Can't Believe It's Not Butter" margarine. (3) The brand name should be distinctive. Examples: Taurus, Kodak, Oracle. (4) It should be extendable: Amazon.com began as an online bookseller but chose a name that would allow expansion into other categories. (5) The name should translate easily into foreign languages. Before spending $100 million to change its name to Exxon, Standard Oil of New Jersey tested several names in 54 languages in more than 150 foreign markets. It found that the name Enco referred to a stalled engine when pronounced in Japanese. (6) It should be capable of registration and legal protection. A brand name cannot be registered if it infringes on existing brand names.

Once chosen, the brand name must be protected. Many firms try to build a brand name that will eventually become identified with the product category. Brand names such as Kleenex, Levi's, Jell-O, Scotch Tape, Formica, Ziploc, and Fiberglass have succeeded in this way. However, their very success may threaten the company's rights to the name. Many originally protected brand names—such as cellophane, aspirin, nylon, kerosene, linoleum, yo-yo, trampoline, escalator, thermos, and shredded wheat—are now generic names that any seller can use.

Brand Sponsorship A manufacturer has four sponsorship options. The product may be launched as a *manufacturer's brand* (or national brand), as when Kellogg and IBM sell their output under their own manufacturer's brand names. Or the manufacturer may sell to resellers who give it a *private brand* (also called a *store brand* or *distributor brand*). Although most manufacturers create their own brand names, others market *licensed brands*. Finally, two companies can join forces and *co-brand* a product.

Manufacturer's Brands Versus Private Brands. Manufacturers' brands have long dominated the retail scene. In recent times, however, an increasing number of retailers and wholesalers have created their own **private brands** (or *store brands*). For example, Sears has created several names—DieHard batteries, Craftsman tools, Kenmore appliances, and Weatherbeater paints. Wal-Mart offers Sam's Choice beverages and food products, Spring Valley nutritional products, Ol' Roy dog food (named for Sam Walton's Irish setter), and White Cloud brand toilet tissue, diapers, detergent, and fabric softener to compete against major national brands. Best Buy introduced its own brand of personal computers, VPR, which competes head to head with Dell. JCPenney has six core private label brands, including Stafford, St. John's Bay, and Arizona. In some cases, private brands even go head to head against designer brands. For example, Saks Fifth Avenue carries its own Platinum clothing line, which features $1,000 jackets and $500 cotton dress shirts. Private brands can be hard to establish and costly to stock and promote. However, they also yield higher profit margins for the reseller. And they give resellers exclusive products that cannot be bought from competitors, resulting in greater store traffic and loyalty.

In the so-called *battle of the brands* between manufacturers' and private brands, retailers have many advantages. They control what products they stock, where they go on the shelf, what prices they charge, and which ones they will feature in local circulars. Retailers

Private (or store) brand
A brand created and owned by a reseller of a product or service.

■ Store brands: Loblaw's President's Choice brand has become so popular that the company licenses it to retailers across the United States and in fifteen other countries where Loblaws has no stores of its own.

price their store brands lower than comparable manufacturers' brands, thereby appealing to budget-conscious shoppers, especially in difficult economic times. And most shoppers believe that store brands are often made by one of the larger manufacturers anyway.

Most retailers also charge manufacturers *slotting fees*—payments demanded by retailers before they will accept new products and find "slots" for them on the shelves. Slotting fees have recently received much scrutiny from the Federal Trade Commission, which worries that they might dampen competition by restricting retail shelf access for smaller manufacturers who can't afford the fees.[27]

As store brands improve in quality and as consumers gain confidence in their store chains, store brands are posing a strong challenge to manufacturers' brands. Consider the case of Loblaws, the Canadian supermarket chain.

Loblaws' President's Choice Decadent Chocolate Chip Cookies brand is now the leading cookie brand in Canada. Its private label President's Choice cola racks up 50 percent of Loblaws' canned cola sales. Based on this success, the private label powerhouse has expanded into a wide range of food and even nonfood categories. For example, it now offers more than 3,500 items under the President's Choice label, ranging from frozen desserts, paper, prepared foods, and boxed meats to pet foods, beauty care, and lawn and garden items. And the company has launched PC Financial, a Web-based bank that offers no-fee bank accounts and mortgages. The brand has become so popular that Loblaws now licenses it to retailers across the United States and fifteen other countries where Loblaws has no stores of its own. The company also offers a Web site where consumers can purchase its branded products directly.[28]

In U.S. supermarkets, taken as a single brand, private-label products are the number one, two, or three brand in over 40 percent of all grocery product categories. In all, they capture more than a 20 percent share of sales in U.S. supermarkets, drug chains, and mass merchandise stores. Private-label apparel captures a 36 percent share of all U.S. apparel sales.[29] To fend off private brands, leading brand marketers will have to invest in R&D to bring out new brands, new features, and continuous quality improvements. They must design strong advertising programs to maintain high awareness and preference. They must find ways to "partner" with major distributors in a search for distribution economies and improved joint performance.

Licensing. Most manufacturers take years and spend millions to create their own brand names. However, some companies license names or symbols previously created by other manufacturers, names of well-known celebrities, or characters from popular movies and books. For a fee, any of these can provide an instant and proven brand name.

Apparel and accessories sellers pay large royalties to adorn their products—from blouses to ties, and linens to luggage—with the names or initials of well-known fashion innovators such as Calvin Klein, Tommy Hilfiger, Gucci, or Armani. Sellers of children's products attach an almost endless list of character names to clothing, toys, school supplies, linens, dolls, lunch boxes, cereals, and other items. Licensed character names range from classics such as *Sesame Street*, Disney, Peanuts, Winnie the Pooh, the Muppets, Scooby Doo, and Dr. Seuss characters to the more recent Teletubbies, Pokemon, Powerpuff Girls, Rugrats, Blue's Clues, and Harry Potter characters. Almost half of all retail toy sales come from products based on television shows and movies such as *Scooby Doo, SpongeBob SquarePants, The Rugrats Movie, The Lion King, Batman, Star Trek, Star Wars, Spider-Man, Men in Black,* or *Harry Potter.*[30]

Name and character licensing has grown rapidly in recent years. Annual retail sales of licensed products in the United States and Canada has grown from only $4 billion in 1977 to $55 billion in 1987 and more than $71 billion today. Licensing can be a highly profitable business for many companies. For example, Warner Brothers has turned *Looney Tunes* characters into one of the world's most sought-after licenses. More than 225 licensees generate $6 billion in annual retail sales of products sporting Bugs Bunny, Daffy Duck, Foghorn Leghorn, or one of more than 100 other *Looney Tunes* characters. Warner Brothers has yet to tap the full potential of many of its secondary characters. The Tazmanian Devil, for example, initially appeared in only five cartoons. But through cross-licensing agreements with organizations such as Harley-Davidson and the NFL, Taz has become something of a pop icon. Warner Brothers sees similar potential for Michigan Frog or Speedy Gonzales for the Hispanic market.[31]

The fastest-growing licensing category is corporate brand licensing, as more and more for-profit and not-for-profit organizations are licensing their names to generate additional revenues and brand recognition. Coca-Cola, for example, has some 320 licensees in 57 countries producing more than 10,000 products, ranging from baby clothes and boxer shorts to earrings, a Coca-Cola Barbie doll, and even a fishing lure shaped like a tiny Coke can. Last year, licensees sold more than $1 billion worth of licensed Coca-Cola products.[32]

■ Character licensing: Warner Brothers has turned Looney Tunes characters into one of the world's most sought-after licenses. More than 225 licensees generate $6 billion in annual retail sales of products sporting one of more than 100 Looney Tunes characters.

Co-Branding. Although companies have been **co-branding** products for many years, there has been a recent resurgence in co-branded products. Co-branding occurs when two established brand names of different companies are used on the same product. For example, Nabisco joined forces with Pillsbury to create Pillsbury Oreo Bars baking mix, and Kellogg joined with ConAgra to co-brand Healthy Choice from Kellogg's cereals. Ford and Eddie Bauer co-branded a sport utility vehicle—the Ford Explorer, Eddie Bauer edition. General Electric worked with Culligan to develop its Water by Culligan Profile Performance refrigerator with a built-in Culligan water-filtration system. Mattel teamed with Coca-Cola to market Soda Fountain Sweetheart Barbie. In most co-branding situations, one company licenses another company's well-known brand to use in combination with its own.

Co-branding offers many advantages. Because each brand dominates in a different category, the combined brands create broader consumer appeal and greater brand equity. Co-branding also allows a company to expand its existing brand into a category it might otherwise have difficulty entering alone. For example, by licensing its Healthy Choice brand to Kellogg, ConAgra entered the breakfast segment with a solid product. In return, Kellogg could leverage the broad awareness of the Healthy Choice name in the cereal category.

Co-branding also has limitations. Such relationships usually involve complex legal contracts and licenses. Co-branding partners must carefully coordinate their advertising, sales promotion, and other marketing efforts. Finally, when co-branding, each partner must trust that the other will take good care of its brand. For example, consider the marriage between Kmart and the Martha Stewart housewares brand. When Kmart declared bankruptcy, it cast a shadow on the Martha Steward brand. In turn, when Martha Steward was accused of unethical or illegal financial dealings, it created negative associations for Kmart. As one Nabisco manager puts it, "Giving away your brand is a lot like giving away your child—you want to make sure everything is perfect."[33]

Co-branding

The practice of using the established brand names of two different companies on the same product.

FIGURE 7.4

Brand Development Strategies

PRODUCT CATEGORY

	Existing	New
Existing	Line extension	Brand extension
New	Multibrands	New brands

BRAND NAME

Brand Development A company has four choices when it comes to developing brands (see Figure 7.4). It can introduce *line extensions* (existing brand names extended to new forms, sizes, and flavors of an existing product category), *brand extensions* (existing brand names extended to new product categories), *multibrands* (new brand names introduced in the same product category), or *new brands* (new brand names in new product categories).

Line extension

Using a successful brand name to introduce additional items in a given product category under the same brand name, such as new flavors, forms, colors, added ingredients, or package sizes.

Line Extensions. **Line extensions** occur when a company introduces additional items in a given product category under the same brand name, such as new flavors, forms, colors, ingredients, or package sizes. Thus, Dannon introduced several line extensions, including seven new yogurt flavors, a fat-free yogurt, and a large, economy-size yogurt. And Morton Salt has expanded its line to include regular iodized salt plus Morton Coarse Kosher Salt, Morton Lite Salt (low in sodium), Morton Popcorn Salt, and Morton Nature's Season seasoning blend. The vast majority of all new-product activity consists of line extensions.

A company might introduce line extensions as a low-cost, low-risk way to introduce new products. Or it might want to meet consumer desires for variety, to use excess capacity, or simply to command more shelf space from resellers. However, line extensions involve some risks. An overextended brand name might lose its specific meaning, or heavily extended brands can cause consumer confusion or frustration. For example, a consumer buying cereal at the local supermarket will be confronted by more than 150 brands, up to 30 different brands, flavors, and sizes of oatmeal alone. By itself, Quaker offers its original Quaker Oats, several flavors of Quaker instant oatmeal, and several dry cereals such as Oatmeal Squares, Toasted Oatmeal, and Toasted Oatmeal-Honey Nut.

■ Line extensions: Morton sells an entire line of salts and seasonings for every occasion.

Another risk is that sales of an extension may come at the expense of other items in the line. For example, the original Nabisco Fig Newtons cookies have now morphed into a full line of Newtons Fruit Chewy Cookies, including Cranberry Newtons, Blueberry Newtons, and Apple Newtons. Although all doing well, the original Fig Newton brand now seems like just another flavor. A line extension works best when it takes sales away from competing brands, not when it "cannibalizes" the company's other items.

Brand Extensions. A **brand extension** involves the use of a successful brand name to launch new or modified products in a new category. Mattel has extended its enduring Barbie Doll brand into new categories ranging from Barbie home furnishings, Barbie cosmetics, and Barbie electronics to Barbie books, Barbie sporting goods, and even a Barbie band—Beyond Pink. Honda uses its company name to cover different products such as its automobiles, motorcycles, snowblowers, lawn mowers, marine engines, and snowmobiles. This allows Honda to advertise that it can fit "six Hondas in a two-car garage." Swiss Army brand sunglasses, Disney Cruise Lines, Cosmopolitan low-fat dairy products, Century 21 Home Improvements, and Brinks home security systems—all are brand extensions.

A brand extension gives a new product instant recognition and faster acceptance. It also saves the high advertising costs usually required to build a new brand name. At the same time, a brand extension strategy involves some risk. Brand extensions such as Bic pantyhose, Heinz pet food, LifeSavers gum, and Clorox laundry detergent met early deaths. The extension may confuse the image of the main brand. And if a brand extension fails, it may harm consumer attitudes toward the other products carrying the same brand name. Furthermore, a brand name may not be appropriate to a particular new product, even if it is well made and satisfying—would you consider buying Texaco milk or Alpo chili? A brand name may lose its special positioning in the consumer's mind through overuse. Companies that are tempted to transfer a brand name must research how well the brand's associations fit the new product.[34]

Multibrands. Companies often introduce additional brands in the same category. Thus, P&G markets many different brands in each of its product categories. *Multibranding* offers a way to establish different features and appeal to different buying motives. It also allows a company to lock up more reseller shelf space. Or the company may want to protect its major brand by setting up *flanker* or *fighter brands*. Seiko uses different brand names for its higher-priced watches (Seiko Lasalle) and lower-priced watches (Pulsar) to protect the flanks of its mainstream Seiko brand.

A major drawback of multibranding is that each brand might obtain only a small market share, and none may be very profitable. The company may end up spreading its resources over many brands instead of building a few brands to a highly profitable level. These companies should reduce the number of brands they sell in a given category and set up tighter screening procedures for new brands.

New Brands. A company might believe that the power of its existing brand name is waning and a new brand name is needed. Or a company may create a new brand name when it enters a new product category for which none of the company's current brand names is appropriate. For example, Honda created the Acura brand to differentiate its luxury car from the established Honda line. Toyota created the separate Scion automobile, now available in California, targeted toward GenY consumers. Japan's Matsushita uses separate names for its different families of products: Technics, Panasonic, National, and Quasar.

As with multibranding, offering too many new brands can result in a company spreading its resources too thin. And in some industries, such as consumer packaged goods, consumers and retailers have become concerned that there are already too many brands, with too few differences between them. Thus, Procter & Gamble, Frito-Lay, and other large consumer-product marketers are now pursuing *megabrand* strategies—weeding out weaker brands and focusing their marketing dollars only on brands that can achieve the number one or number two market share positions in their categories.

Brand extension

Using a successful brand name to launch a new or modified product in a new category.

Managing Brands

Companies must carefully manage their brands. First, the brand's positioning must be continuously communicated to consumers. Major brand marketers often spend huge amounts on advertising to create brand awareness and to build preference and loyalty. For example, AT&T spends almost a billion dollars annually to promote its brands. McDonald's spends more than $600 million.[35]

Such advertising campaigns can help to create name recognition, brand knowledge, and maybe even some brand preference. However, the fact is that brands are not maintained by advertising but by the *brand experience*. Today, customers come to know a brand through a wide range of contacts and touch points. These include advertising, but also personal experience with the brand, word of mouth, personal interactions with company people, telephone interactions, company Web pages, and many others. Any of these experiences can have a positive or negative impact on brand perceptions and feelings. The company must put as much care into managing these touch points as it does into producing its ads.

The brand's positioning will not take hold fully unless everyone in the company lives the brand. Therefore the company needs to train its people to be customer-centered. Even better, the company should build pride in its employees regarding their products and services so that their enthusiasm will spill over to customers. Companies such as Nordstrom, Lexus, Dell, and Harley-Davidson have succeeded in turning all of their employees into enthusiastic brand builders. Companies can carry on internal brand building to help employees to understand, desire, and deliver on the brand promise. Many companies go even further by training and encouraging their distributors and dealers to serve their customers well.

All of this suggests that managing a company's brand assets can no longer be left only to brand managers. Brand managers do not have enough power or scope to do all the things necessary to build and enhance their brands. Moreover, brand managers often pursue short-term results, whereas managing brands as assets calls for longer-term strategy. Thus, some companies are now setting up brand asset management teams to manage their major brands. Canada Dry and Colgate-Palmolive have appointed *brand equity managers* to maintain and protect their brands' images, associations, and quality, and to prevent short-term actions by overeager brand managers from hurting the brand. Similarly, Hewlett-Packard has appointed a senior executive in charge of the customer experience in each of its two divisions, consumer and B2B. Their job is to track, measure, and improve the customer relationship with H-P products. They report directly to the presidents of their respective divisions.

Finally, companies need to periodically audit their brands' strengths and weaknesses.[36] They should ask: Does our brand excel at delivering benefits that consumers truly value? Is the brand properly positioned? Do all of our consumer touch points support the brand's positioning? Do the brand's managers understand what the brand means to consumers? Does the brand receive proper, sustained support?

The brand audit may turn up brands that need to be repositioned because of changing customer preferences or new competitors. Some cases may call for completely *rebranding* a product, service, or company. The recent wave of corporate mergers and acquisitions has set off a flurry of corporate rebranding campaigns. A prime example is Verizon Communication, created by the merger of Bell Atlantic and GTE. The company decided that neither of the old names properly positioned the new company. "We needed a master brand to leave all our old names behind," says Verizon's senior vice president of brand management and marketing services. The old names created too much confusion, conjured up an image of old-fashioned phone companies, and "held us back from marketing in new areas of innovation—high speed Internet and wireless services." The new branding effort appears to have worked. Verizon Wireless is now the leading provider of wireless phone services, with better than a 21 percent market share. Number two is Cingular Wireless, another new brand created through a joint venture between Bell South and SBC Communications.[37]

However, building a new image and re-educating customers can be a huge undertaking. The cost of Verizon's brand overhaul included tens of millions of dollars just for a special four-week advertising campaign to announce the new name, followed by considerable ongoing advertising expenses. And that was only the beginning. The company had to repaint its fleet of 70,000 trucks, along with its garages and service centers. The campaign also required relabeling 250,000 pay phones, redesigning 91 million customer billing statements, and producing videos and other in-house employee educational materials.

Services Marketing

Services have grown dramatically in recent years. Services now account for 74 percent of U.S. gross domestic product and nearly 60 percent of personal consumption expenditures. Whereas service jobs accounted for 55 percent of all U.S. jobs in 1970, today they account for 82 percent of total employment. Services are growing even faster in the world economy, making up a quarter of the value of all international trade.[38]

Service industries vary greatly. *Governments* offer services through courts, employment services, hospitals, military services, police and fire departments, postal services, and schools. *Private not-for-profit organizations* offer services through museums, charities, churches, colleges, foundations, and hospitals. A large number of *business organizations* offer services— airlines, banks, hotels, insurance companies, consulting firms, medical and law practices, entertainment companies, real estate firms, advertising and research agencies, and retailers.

Nature and Characteristics of a Service

A company must consider four special service characteristics when designing marketing programs: *intangibility*, *inseparability*, *variability*, and *perishability* (see Figure 7.5).

Service intangibility means that services cannot be seen, tasted, felt, heard, or smelled before they are bought. For example, people undergoing cosmetic surgery cannot see the result before the purchase. Airline passengers have nothing but a ticket and the promise that they and their luggage will arrive safely at the intended destination, hopefully at the same time. To reduce uncertainty, buyers look for "signals" of service quality. They draw conclusions about quality from the place, people, price, equipment, and communications that they can see.

Therefore, the service provider's task is to make the service tangible in one or more ways and to send the right signals about quality. One analyst calls this *evidence management*, in which the service organization presents its customers with organized, honest evidence of its capabilities. The Mayo Clinic practices good evidence management[39]:

> Nobody likes going to the hospital. The experience is at best unnerving and often frightening. What's more, it's very hard for the average patient to judge the quality of the "product." You can't try it on, you can't return it if you don't like it, and you need an advanced degree to understand it. And so, when we're considering a medical facility, most of us unconsciously turn detective, looking for evidence of competence, caring, and integrity. The Mayo Clinic doesn't leave that evidence to chance. By carefully managing a set of visual and experiential clues, Mayo offers patients and their families concrete evidence of its strengths and values. For example, staff people at the clinic are trained to act in a way that clearly signals its patient-first focus. "My doctor calls me at home to check on how I am

Service intangibility
A major characteristic of services—they cannot be seen, tasted, felt, heard, or smelled before they are bought.

FIGURE 7.5
Four Service Characteristics

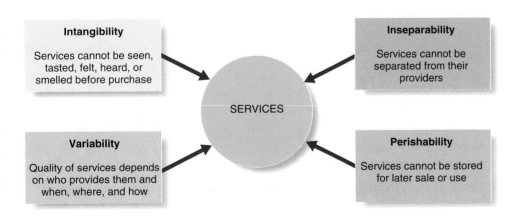

Service inseparability

A major characteristic of services—they are produced and consumed at the same time and cannot be separated from their providers, whether the providers are people or machines.

Service variability

A major characteristic of services—their quality may vary greatly, depending on who provides them and when, where, and how.

Service perishability

A major characteristic of services—they cannot be stored for later sale or use.

doing," marvels one patient. "She wants to work with what is best for my schedule." Mayo's physical facilities also send the right signals. They've been carefully designed to relieve stress, offer a place of refuge, create positive distractions, convey caring and respect, signal competence, accommodate families, and make it easy to find your way around. The result? Exceptionally positive word-of-mouth and abiding customer loyalty, which have allowed Mayo Clinic to build what is arguably the most powerful brand in health care—with very little advertising.

Physical goods are produced, then stored, later sold, and still later consumed. In contrast, services are first sold, then produced and consumed at the same time. **Service inseparability** means that services cannot be separated from their providers, whether the providers are people or machines. If a service employee provides the service, then the employee is a part of the service. Because the customer is also present as the service is produced, *provider–customer interaction* is a special feature of services marketing. Both the provider and the customer affect the service outcome.

Service variability means that the quality of services depends on who provides them as well as when, where, and how they are provided. For example, some hotels—say, Marriott—have reputations for providing better service than others. Still, within a given Marriott hotel, one registration-desk employee may be cheerful and efficient, whereas another standing just a few feet away may be unpleasant and slow. Even the quality of a single Marriott employee's service varies according to his or her energy and frame of mind at the time of each customer encounter.

Service perishability means that services cannot be stored for later sale or use. Some doctors charge patients for missed appointments because the service value existed only at that point and disappeared when the patient did not show up. The perishability of services is not a problem when demand is steady. However, when demand fluctuates, service firms often have difficult problems. For example, because of rush-hour demand, public transportation companies have to own much more equipment than they would if demand were even throughout the day. Thus, service firms often design strategies for producing a better match between demand and supply. Hotels and resorts charge lower prices in the off-season to attract more guests. And restaurants hire part-time employees to serve during peak periods.

Marketing Strategies for Service Firms

Just like manufacturing businesses, good service firms use marketing to position themselves strongly in chosen target markets. Southwest Airlines positions itself as a no-frills, short-haul airline charging very low fares. Wal-Mart promises "Always Low Prices, Always." Ritz-Carlton Hotels positions itself as offering a memorable experience that "enlivens the senses, instills well-being, and fulfills even the unexpressed wishes and needs of our guests." At the Mayo Clinic, "the needs of the patient come first." These and other service firms establish their positions through traditional marketing mix activities.

However, because services differ from tangible products, they often require additional marketing approaches. In a product business, products are fairly standardized and can sit on shelves waiting for customers. But in a service business, the customer and front-line service employee *interact* to create the service. Thus, service providers must interact effectively with customers to create superior value during service encounters. Effective interaction, in turn, depends on the skills of front-line service employees and on the support processes backing these employees.

The Service-Profit Chain   Successful service companies focus their attention on *both* their customers and their employees. They understand the **service-profit chain**, which links service firm profits with employee and customer satisfaction. This chain consists of five links[40]:

■ *Internal service quality:* superior employee selection and training, a quality work environment, and strong support for those dealing with customers, which results in . . .

■ *Satisfied and productive service employees:* more satisfied, loyal, and hardworking employees, which results in . . .

Service-profit chain

The chain that links service firm profits with employee and customer satisfaction.

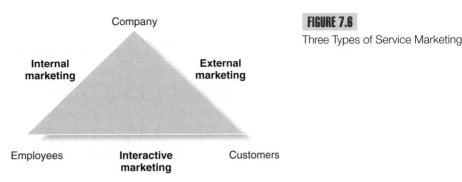

FIGURE 7.6
Three Types of Service Marketing

- *Greater service value:* more effective and efficient customer value creation and service delivery, which results in . . .

- *Satisfied and loyal customers:* satisfied customers who remain loyal, repeat purchase, and refer other customers, which results in . . .

- *Healthy service profits and growth:* superior service firm performance.

Therefore, reaching service profits and growth goals begins with taking care of those who take care of customers (see Marketing at Work 7.4).

Thus, service marketing requires more than just traditional external marketing using the four Ps. Figure 7.6 shows that service marketing also requires *internal marketing* and *interactive marketing*. **Internal marketing** means that the service firm must effectively train and motivate its customer-contact employees and supporting service people to work as a *team* to provide customer satisfaction. Marketers must get everyone in the organization to be customer-centered. In fact, internal marketing must *precede* external marketing. Ritz-Carlton orients its employees carefully, instills in them a sense of pride, and motivates them by recognizing and rewarding outstanding service deeds.

Interactive marketing means that service quality depends heavily on the quality of the buyer–seller interaction during the service encounter. In product marketing, product quality often depends little on how the product is obtained. But in services marketing, service quality depends on both the service deliverer and the quality of the delivery. Service marketers, therefore, have to master interactive marketing skills. Thus, Ritz-Carlton selects only "people who care about people" and instructs them carefully in the fine art of interacting with customers to satisfy their every need.

In today's marketplace, companies must know how to deliver interactions that are not only "high-touch" but also "high-tech." For example, customers can log on to the Charles Schwab Web site and access account information, investment research, real-time quotes, after-hours trading, and the Schwab learning center. They can also participate in live online events and chat online with customer service representatives. Customers seeking more-personal interactions can contact service reps by phone or visit a local Schwab branch office. Thus, Schwab has mastered interactive marketing at all three levels—calls, clicks, *and* visits.[41]

Today, as competition and costs increase, and as productivity and quality decrease, more service marketing sophistication is needed. Service companies face three major marketing tasks: They want to increase their *competitive differentiation*, *service quality*, and *productivity*.

Managing Service Differentiation   In these days of intense price competition, service marketers often complain about the difficulty of differentiating their services from those of competitors. To the extent that customers view the services of different providers as similar, they care less about the provider than the price.

The solution to price competition is to develop a differentiated offer, delivery, and image. The *offer* can include innovative features that set one company's offer apart from competitors' offers. Some hotels offer car rental, banking, and business center services in their lobbies. Airlines introduced innovations such as in-flight movies, advance seating,

Internal marketing
Marketing by a service firm to train and effectively motivate its customer-contact employees and all the supporting service people to work as a team to provide customer satisfaction.

Interactive marketing
Marketing by a service firm that recognizes that perceived service quality depends heavily on the quality of buyer–seller interaction.

Marketing at Work | 7.4

Ritz-Carlton: Taking Care of Those Who Take Care of Customers

Ritz-Carlton, a chain of luxury hotels renowned for outstanding service, caters to the top 5 percent of corporate and leisure travelers. The company's Credo sets lofty customer service goals: "The Ritz-Carlton Hotel is a place where the genuine care and comfort of our guests is our highest mission. We pledge to provide the finest personal service and facilities for our guests, who will always enjoy a warm, relaxed yet refined ambience. The Ritz-Carlton experience enlivens the senses, instills well-being, and fulfills even the unexpressed wishes and needs of our guests." The company's Web page concludes: "Here a calm settles over you. The world, so recently at your door, is now at your feet."

The Credo is more than just words on paper—Ritz-Carlton delivers on its promises. In surveys of departing guests, some 95 percent report that they've had a truly memorable experience. In fact, at Ritz-Carlton, exceptional service encounters have become almost commonplace. Take the experiences of Nancy and Harvey Heffner of Manhattan, who stayed at the Ritz-Carlton Naples, in Naples, Florida (recently rated the best hotel in the United States, fourth best in the world, by *Travel & Leisure* magazine). As reported in the *New York Times*:

"The hotel is elegant and beautiful," Mrs. Heffner said, "but more important is the beauty expressed by the staff. They can't do enough to please you." When the couple's son became sick last year in Naples, the hotel staff brought him hot tea with honey at all hours of the night, she said. When Mr. Heffner had to fly home on business for a day and his return flight was delayed, a driver for the hotel waited in the lobby most of the night.

Such personal, high-quality service has also made the Ritz-Carlton a favorite among conventioneers. "They not only treat us like kings when we hold our top-level meetings in their hotels, but we just never get any complaints," comments one convention planner. "Perhaps the biggest challenge a planner faces when recommending The Ritz-Carlton at Half Moon Bay to the boss, board, and attendees is convincing them that meeting there truly is work," says another. "The . . . first-rate catering and service-oriented convention services staff [and] the Ritz-Carlton's ambience and beauty—the elegant, Grand Dame-style lodge, nestled on a bluff between two championship golf courses

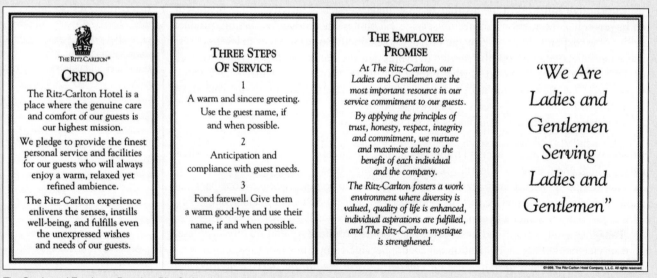

THE RITZ-CARLTON®
CREDO

The Ritz-Carlton Hotel is a place where the genuine care and comfort of our guests is our highest mission.

We pledge to provide the finest personal service and facilities for our guests who will always enjoy a warm, relaxed yet refined ambience.

The Ritz-Carlton experience enlivens the senses, instills well-being, and fulfills even the unexpressed wishes and needs of our guests.

THREE STEPS OF SERVICE

1
A warm and sincere greeting. Use the guest name, if and when possible.

2
Anticipation and compliance with guest needs.

3
Fond farewell. Give them a warm good-bye and use their name, if and when possible.

THE EMPLOYEE PROMISE

At The Ritz-Carlton, our Ladies and Gentlemen are the most important resource in our service commitment to our guests.

By applying the principles of trust, honesty, respect, integrity and commitment, we nurture and maximize talent to the benefit of each individual and the company.

The Ritz-Carlton fosters a work environment where diversity is valued, quality of life is enhanced, individual aspirations are fulfilled, and The Ritz-Carlton mystique is strengthened.

"We Are Ladies and Gentlemen Serving Ladies and Gentlemen"

The Credo and Employee Promise: Ritz-Carlton knows that to take care of customers, you must first take care of those who take care of customers.

air-to-ground telephone service, and frequent flyer award programs to differentiate their offers. British Airways even offers international travelers beds and private "demi-cabins," hot showers, and cooked-to-order breakfasts.

Service companies can differentiate their service *delivery* by having more able and reliable customer-contact people, by developing a superior physical environment in which the service product is delivered, or by designing a superior delivery process. For example,

overlooking the Pacific Ocean—makes a day's work there seem anything but."

In 1992, Ritz-Carlton became the first hotel company to win the Malcolm Baldrige National Quality Award. Since its incorporation in 1983, the company has received virtually every major award that the hospitality industry bestows. More importantly, service quality has resulted in high customer retention. More than 90 percent of Ritz-Carlton customers return. And despite its hefty room rates, the chain enjoys a 70 percent occupancy rate, almost nine points above the industry average.

Most of the responsibility for keeping guests satisfied falls to Ritz-Carlton's customer-contact employees. Thus, the hotel chain takes great care in finding just the right personnel. "We don't hire or recruit, we select," says Ritz-Carlton's director of human resources. "We want only people who care about people," notes the company's vice president of quality. Once selected, employees are given intensive training in the art of coddling customers. New employees attend a two-day orientation, in which top management drums into them the "20 Ritz-Carlton Basics." Basic number one: "The Credo will be known, owned, and energized by all employees."

Employees are taught to do everything they can never to lose a guest. "There's no negotiating at Ritz-Carlton when it comes to solving customer problems," says the quality executive. Staff learn that *anyone* who receives a customer complaint *owns* that complaint until it's resolved (Ritz-Carlton Basic number eight). They are trained to drop whatever they're doing to help a customer—no matter what they're doing or what their department. Ritz-Carlton employees are empowered to handle problems on the spot, without consulting higher-ups. Each employee can spend up to $2,000 to redress a guest grievance. And each is allowed to break from his or her routine for as long as needed to make a guest happy. "We master customer satisfaction at the individual level," adds the executive. "This is our most sensitive listening post . . . our early warning system." Thus, while competitors are still reading guest comment cards to learn about customer problems, Ritz-Carlton has already resolved them.

Ritz-Carlton instills a sense of pride in its employees. "You serve," they are told, "but you are not servants." The company motto states, "We are ladies and gentlemen serving ladies and gentlemen." Employees understand their role in Ritz-Carlton's success. "We might not be able to afford a hotel like this," says employee Tammy Patton, "but we can make it so people who can afford it will want to keep coming here."

And so they do. When it comes to customer satisfaction, no detail is too small. Customer-contact people are taught to greet guests warmly and sincerely, using guest names when possible. They learn to use the proper language with guests—phrases such as *Good morning*, *Certainly, I'll be happy to*, *Welcome back*, and *My pleasure*, never *Hi* or *How's it going*? The Ritz-Carlton Basics urge employees to escort guests to another area of the hotel rather than pointing out directions, to answer the phone within three rings and with a "smile," and to take pride and care in their personal appearance. As the general manager of the Ritz-Carlton Naples puts it, "When you invite guests to your house, you want everything to be perfect."

Ritz-Carlton recognizes and rewards employees who perform feats of outstanding service. Under its 5-Star Awards program, outstanding performers are nominated by peers and managers, and winners receive plaques at dinners celebrating their achievements. For on-the-spot recognition, managers award Gold Standard Coupons, redeemable for items in the gift shop and free weekend stays at the hotel. Ritz-Carlton further motivates its employees with events such as Super Sports Day, an employee talent show, luncheons celebrating employee anniversaries, a family picnic, and special themes in employee dining rooms. As a result, Ritz-Carlton's employees appear to be just as satisfied as its customers. Employee turnover is less than 30 percent a year, compared with 45 percent at other luxury hotels.

Ritz-Carlton's success is based on a simple philosophy: To take care of customers, you must first take care of those who take care of customers. Satisfied employees deliver high service value, which then creates satisfied customers. Satisfied customers, in turn, create sales and profits for the company.

Sources: Quotes and other information from Edwin McDowell, "Ritz-Carlton's Keys to Good Service," *New York Times*, March 31, 1993, p. D1; Howard Schlossberg, "Measuring Customer Satisfaction Is Easy to Do—Until You Try," *Marketing News*, April 26, 1993, pp. 5, 8; Ginger Conlon, "True Romance," *Sales & Marketing Management*, May 1996, pp. 85–90; "The Ritz-Carlton, Half Moon Bay," *Successful Meetings*, November 2001, p. 40; and the Ritz-Carlton Web site at www.ritzcarlton. com, August 2003. Also see Patricia Sheehan, "Back to Bed: Selling the Perfect Night's Sleep," *Lodging Hospitality*, March 15, 2001, pp. 22–24; Nicole Harris, "Can't Sleep? Try the Eye Gel in the Minibar—Hotels Roll Out Products to Help Tired Travelers Snooze," *Wall Street Journal*, June 20, 2002, p. D1; and Scott Neuman, "Relax, Put Your Feet Up," *Far Eastern Economic Review*, April 17, 2003, p. 36.

many banks offer their customers Internet banking as a better way to access banking services than having to drive, park, and wait in line.

Finally, service companies also can work on differentiating their *images* through symbols and branding. The Harris Bank of Chicago adopted the lion as its symbol on its stationery, in its advertising, and even as stuffed animals offered to new depositors. The well-known Harris lion confers an image of strength. Other well-known service symbols

■ Service differentiation: British Airways differentiates its offer by providing first-class world travelers private "demi-cabins" and other amenities.

include The Merrill Lynch's bull, MGM's lion, and Allstate's "good hands."

Managing Service Quality One of the major ways a service firm can differentiate itself is by delivering consistently higher quality than its competitors do. Like manufacturers before them, most service industries have now joined the customer-driven quality movement. And like product marketers, service providers need to identify what target customers expect concerning service quality. Unfortunately, service quality is harder to define and judge than is product quality. For instance, it is harder to agree on the quality of a haircut than on the quality of a hair dryer. Customer retention is perhaps the best measure of quality—a service firm's ability to hang onto its customers depends on how consistently it delivers value to them.[42]

Top service companies are customer obsessed and set high service quality standards. They watch service performance closely, both their own and that of competitors. They do not settle for merely good service; they aim for 100 percent defect-free service. A 98 percent performance standard may sound good, but using this standard, 64,000 FedEx packages would be lost each day, 10 words would be misspelled on each printed page, 400,000 prescriptions would be misfilled daily, and drinking water would be unsafe 8 days a year.[43]

Unlike product manufacturers, who can adjust their machinery and inputs until everything is perfect, service quality will always vary, depending on the interactions between employees and customers. As hard as they try, even the best companies will have an occasional late delivery, burned steak, or grumpy employee. However, good *service recovery* can turn angry customers into loyal ones. In fact, good recovery can win more customer purchasing and loyalty than if things had gone well in the first place. Therefore, companies should take steps not only to provide good service every time but also to recover from service mistakes when they do occur.

The first step is to *empower* front-line service employees—to give them the authority, responsibility, and incentives they need to recognize, care about, and tend to customer needs. At Marriott, for example, well-trained employees are given the authority to do whatever it takes, on the spot, to keep guests happy. They are also expected to help management ferret out the cause of guests' problems and to inform managers of ways to improve overall hotel service and guests' comfort.

Managing Service Productivity With their costs rising rapidly, service firms are under great pressure to increase service productivity. They can do so in several ways. They can train current employees better or hire new ones who will work harder or more skillfully. Or they can increase the quantity of their service by giving up some quality. The provider can "industrialize the service" by adding equipment and standardizing production, as in McDonald's assembly-line approach to fast-food retailing. Finally, the service provider can harness the power of technology. Although we often think of technology's power to save time and costs in manufacturing companies, it also has great—and often untapped—potential to make service workers more productive.

However, companies must avoid pushing productivity so hard that doing so reduces quality. Attempts to industrialize a service or to cut costs can make a service company more efficient in the short run. But they can also reduce its longer-run ability to innovate, maintain service quality, or respond to consumer needs and desires. In short, they can take the "service" out of service.

■◣ Additional Product Considerations

Here, we discuss two additional product policy considerations: social responsibility in product decisions and issues of international product and services marketing.

Product Decisions and Social Responsibility

Product decisions have attracted much public attention. Marketers should carefully consider public policy issues and regulations involving acquiring or dropping products, patent protection, product quality and safety, and product warranties.

Regarding new products, the government may prevent companies from adding products through acquisitions if the effect threatens to lessen competition. Companies dropping products must be aware that they have legal obligations, written or implied, to their suppliers, dealers, and customers who have a stake in the dropped product. Companies must also obey U.S. patent laws when developing new products. A company cannot make its product illegally similar to another company's established product.

Manufacturers must comply with specific laws regarding product quality and safety. The Federal Food, Drug, and Cosmetic Act protects consumers from unsafe and adulterated food, drugs, and cosmetics. Various acts provide for the inspection of sanitary conditions in the meat- and poultry-processing industries. Safety legislation has been passed to regulate fabrics, chemical substances, automobiles, toys, and drugs and poisons. The Consumer Product Safety Act of 1972 established a Consumer Product Safety Commission, which has the authority to ban or seize potentially harmful products and set severe penalties for violation of the law.

If consumers have been injured by a product that has been designed defectively, they can sue manufacturers or dealers. Product liability suits are now occurring in federal and state courts at the rate of almost 110,000 per year, with a median jury award of $1.8 million and individual awards often running into the tens of millions of dollars.[44] This phenomenon has resulted in huge increases in product liability insurance premiums, causing big problems in some industries. Some companies pass these higher rates along to consumers by raising prices. Others are forced to discontinue high-risk product lines. Some companies are now appointing "product stewards," whose job is to protect consumers from harm and the company from liability by proactively ferreting out potential product problems.[45]

Many manufacturers offer written product warranties to convince customers of their products' quality. To protect consumers, Congress passed the Magnuson–Moss Warranty Act in 1975. The act requires that full warranties meet certain minimum standards, including repair "within a reasonable time and without charge" or a replacement or full refund if the product does not work "after a reasonable number of attempts" at repair. Otherwise, the company must make it clear that it is offering only a limited warranty. The law has led several manufacturers to switch from full to limited warranties and others to drop warranties altogether.

International Product and Services Marketing

International product and service marketers face special challenges. First, they must figure out what products and services to introduce and in which countries. Then, they must decide how much to standardize or adapt their products and services for world markets.

On the one hand, companies would like to standardize their offerings. Standardization helps a company to develop a consistent worldwide image. It also lowers manufacturing costs and eliminates duplication of research and development, advertising, and product design efforts. On the other hand, consumers around the world differ in their cultures, attitudes, and buying behaviors. And markets vary in their economic conditions, competition, legal requirements, and physical environments. Companies must usually respond to these differences by adapting their product offerings. Something as simple as an electrical outlet can create big product problems:

> Those who have traveled across Europe know the frustration of electrical plugs, different voltages, and other annoyances of international travel. . . . Philips, the

electrical appliance manufacturer, has to produce 12 kinds of irons to serve just its European market. The problem is that Europe does not have a universal [electrical] standard. The ends of irons bristle with different plugs for different countries. Some have three prongs, others two; prongs protrude straight or angled, round or rectangular, fat, thin, and sometimes sheathed. There are circular plug faces, squares, pentagons, and hexagons. Some are perforated and some are notched. One French plug has a niche like a keyhole. Looking for a fix? One online travel service sells an elaborate 10-piece adapter plug set for international travelers for $65.00.[46]

Packaging also presents new challenges for international marketers. Packaging issues can be subtle. For example, names, labels, and colors may not translate easily from one country to another. A firm using yellow flowers in its logo might fare well in the United States but meet with disaster in Mexico, where a yellow flower symbolizes death or disrespect. Similarly, although Nature's Gift might be an appealing name for gourmet mushrooms in America, it would be deadly in Germany, where *gift* means poison. Packaging may also have to be tailored to meet the physical characteristics of consumers in various parts of the world. For instance, soft drinks are sold in smaller cans in Japan to fit the smaller Japanese hand better. Thus, although product and package standardization can produce benefits, companies must usually adapt their offerings to the unique needs of specific international markets.

Service marketers also face special challenges when going global. Some service industries have a long history of international operations. For example, the commercial banking industry was one of the first to grow internationally. Banks had to provide global services in order to meet the foreign exchange and credit needs of their home country clients wanting to sell overseas. In recent years, many banks have become truly global. Germany's Deutsche Bank, for example, serves more than 12 million customers in 75 countries. For its clients around the world who wish to grow globally, Deutsche Bank can raise money not only in Frankfurt but also in Zurich, London, Paris, and Tokyo.[47]

Professional and business services industries such as accounting, management consulting, and advertising have only recently globalized. The international growth of these firms followed the globalization of the client companies they serve. For example, as their clients began to employ worldwide marketing and advertising strategies, advertising agencies responded by globalizing their own operations. McCann-Erickson Worldwide, the largest U.S. advertising agency, operates in more than 130 countries. It serves international clients such as Coca-Cola, General Motors, ExxonMobil, Microsoft, Johnson & Johnson, and Unilever in markets ranging from the United States and Canada to Korea to Kazakhstan. Moreover, McCann-Erikson is one company in the Interpublic Group of Companies, an immense, worldwide network of advertising and marketing services companies.[48]

Retailers are among the latest service businesses to go global. As their home markets become saturated, American retailers such as Wal-Mart, Kmart, Toys 'R' Us, Office Depot, Saks Fifth Avenue, and Disney are expanding into faster-growing markets abroad. For example, every year since 1995, Wal-Mart has entered a new country; its international division's sales grew more than 10 percent last year, skyrocketing to more than $35 billion. Foreign retailers are making similar moves. The Japanese retailer Yaohan now operates the largest shopping center in Asia, the 21-story Nextage Shanghai Tower in China, and Carrefour of France is the leading retailer in Brazil and Argentina. Asian shoppers now buy American products in Dutch-owned Makro stores, now Southeast Asia's biggest store group, with sales in the region of more than $2 billion.[49]

■ Retailers are among the latest service businesses to go global. Here Asian shoppers buy American products in a Dutch-owned Makro store in Kuala Lumpur.

Service companies wanting to operate in other countries are not always welcomed with open arms. Whereas manufacturers usually face straightforward tariff, quota, or currency restrictions when attempting to sell their products in another country, service providers are likely to face more subtle barriers. In some cases, rules and regulations affecting international service firms reflect the host country's traditions. In others, they appear to protect the country's own fledgling service industries from large global competitors with greater resources. In still other cases, however, the restrictions seem to have little purpose other than to make entry difficult for foreign service firms.

Despite such difficulties, the trend toward growth of global service companies will continue, especially in banking, airlines, telecommunications, and professional services. Today service firms are no longer simply following their manufacturing customers. Instead, they are taking the lead in international expansion.

REST STOP:
Reviewing the Concepts

Time to kick back and reflect on the key concepts in this first marketing mix chapter on products and services. A product is more than a simple set of tangible features. In fact, many marketing offers consist of combinations of both tangible goods and services, ranging from *pure tangible goods* at one extreme to *pure services* at the other. Each product or service offered to customers can be viewed on three levels. The *core product* consists of the core problem-solving benefits that consumers seek when they buy a product. The *actual product* exists around the core and includes the quality level, features, design, brand name, and packaging. The *augmented product* is the actual product plus the various services and benefits offered with it, such as warranty, free delivery, installation, and maintenance.

1. Define *product* and the major classifications of products and services.

Broadly defined, a *product* is anything that can be offered to a market for attention, acquisition, use, or consumption that might satisfy a want or need. Products include physical objects but also services, events, persons, places, organizations, ideas, or mixes of these entities. *Services* are products that consist of activities, benefits, or satisfactions offered for sale that are essentially intangible, such as banking, hotel, tax preparation, and home repair services.

Products and services fall into two broad classes based on the types of consumers that use them. *Consumer products*—those bought by final consumers—are usually classified according to consumer shopping habits (convenience products, shopping products, specialty products, and unsought products). *Industrial products*—purchased for further processing or for use in conducting a business—include materials and parts, capital items, and supplies and services. Other marketable entities—such as organizations, persons, places, and ideas—can also be thought of as products.

2. Describe the decisions companies make regarding their individual products and services, product lines, and product mixes.

Individual product decisions involve product attributes, branding, packaging, labeling, and product support services. *Product attribute* decisions involve product quality, features, and style and design. *Branding* decisions include selecting a brand name and developing a brand strategy. *Packaging* provides many key benefits, such as protection, economy, convenience, and promotion. Package decisions often include designing *labels,* which identify, describe, and possibly promote the product. Companies also develop *product support services* that enhance customer service and satisfaction and safeguard against competitors.

Most companies produce a product line rather than a single product. A *product line* is a group of products that are related in function, customer-purchase needs, or distribution channels. *Line stretching* involves extending a line downward, upward, or in both directions to occupy a gap that might otherwise be filled by a competitor. In contrast, *line filling* involves adding items within the present range of the line. The set of product lines and items offered to customers by a particular seller make up the *product mix*. The mix can be described by four dimensions: width, length, depth, and consistency. These dimensions are the tools for developing the company's product strategy.

3. Discuss branding strategy—the decisions companies make in building and managing their brands.

Some analysts see brands as *the* major enduring asset of a company. Brands are more than just names and symbols—they embody everything that the product or service *means* to consumers. *Brand equity* is the positive differential effect that knowing the brand name has on customer response to the product or service. A brand with strong brand equity is a very valuable asset.

In building brands, companies need to make decisions about brand positioning, brand name selection, brand sponsorship, and brand development. The most powerful *brand positioning* builds around strong consumer beliefs and values. *Brand name selection* involves finding the best brand name based on a careful review of product benefits, the target market, and proposed marketing strategies. A manufacturer has four *brand sponsorship* options: it can launch a *manufacturer's brand* (or national brand), sell to resellers who use a *private brand*, market *licensed brands*, or join forces with another company to *co-brand* a product. A company also has four choices when it comes to developing brands. It can introduce *line extensions, brand extensions, multibrands,* or *new brands* (new brand names in new product categories).

Companies must build and manage their brands carefully. The brand's positioning must be continuously communicated to consumers. Advertising can help, but brands are not maintained by advertising but by the *brand experience*. Customers come to know a brand through a wide range of contacts and interactions. The company must put as much care into managing these touch points as it does into producing its ads. Thus, managing a company's brand assets can no longer be left only to brand managers. Some companies are now setting up brand asset management teams to manage their major brands. Finally, companies must periodically audit their brands' strengths and weaknesses. In some cases, brands may need to be repositioned because of changing customer preferences or new competitors. Other cases may call for completely *rebranding* a product, service, or company.

4. Identify the four characteristics that affect the marketing of a service and the additional marketing considerations that services require.

Services are characterized by four key characteristics; they are *intangible, inseparable, variable,* and *perishable.* Each characteristic poses problems and marketing requirements. Marketers work to find ways to make the service more tangible, to

increase the productivity of providers who are inseparable from their products, to standardize quality in the face of variability, and to improve demand movements and supply capacities in the face of service perishability.

Good service companies focus attention on *both* customers and employees. They understand the *service-profit chain,* which links service firm profits with employee and customer satisfaction. Services marketing strategy calls not only for external marketing but also for *internal marketing* to motivate employees and *interactive marketing* to create service delivery skills among service providers. To succeed, service marketers must create *competitive differentiation,* offer high *service quality,* and find ways to increase *service productivity.*

5. Discuss two additional product issues: socially responsible product decisions and international product and services marketing.

Marketers must consider two additional product issues. The first is *social responsibility.* These include public policy issues and regulations involving acquiring or dropping products, patent protection, product quality and safety, and product warranties. The second involves the special challenges facing international product and service marketers. International marketers must decide how much to standardize or adapt their offerings for world markets.

Navigating the Key Terms

Brand
Brand equity
Brand extension
Co-branding
Consumer product
Convenience product
Industrial product
Interactive marketing
Internal marketing

Line extension
Packaging
Private (or store) brand
Product
Product line
Product mix (or product assortment)
Product quality
Service

Service inseparability
Service intangibility
Service perishability
Service-profit chain
Service variability
Shopping product
Social marketing
Specialty product
Unsought product

Travel Log

Discussing the Issues

1. Brand equity is the positive differential effect that knowing the brand name has on customer response to the product or service. Name three firms that you feel have high brand equity. How does having high brand equity help them compete against rival companies?

2. Visit a grocery store and look at the packages for competing products in two or three different product categories. Which packages are the best? Why? What functions do the packages perform?

3. Visit the Kraft Foods company Web site (www.kraft.com/index.html) and examine its list of different

brands. Evaluate the company's product mix on the dimensions of width, length, depth, and consistency.

4. Consider how Cheerios cereal has been positioned in terms of product attributes, desired benefits, and strong beliefs and values.

5. What issues should a manufacturer of canned green beans consider when deciding between selling the product as a manufacturer's brand, store brand, licensed brand, or co-branded product?

6. Discuss how the services offered by a dry cleaning company are different from the products offered by an auto parts store in terms of intangibility, inseparability, variability, and perishability.

Application Questions

1. Consider the following brand extensions and evaluate how well the brand's associations fit the new product: Kodak extending from film into batteries, Winnebago motor homes extending into tents, Fisher-Price toys extending into children's eyeglass frames, Harley-Davidson motorcycles extending into cigarettes, and Dunkin' Donuts extending into cereal. What about the proposed brand extensions works or does not work for you?

2. Develop a list of five characteristics that a good brand name should possess. Based on the characteristics in your list, come up with three good brand names and three poor brand names of actual products currently sold. Imagine you are opening up a pizza restaurant. What would be a good name for the restaurant based on the characteristics in your list?

3. Describe a product you feel must be customized or adapted to sell in different markets around the world and one you feel can sell in a standardized format. Discuss what it is about the two products that requires customization in one case, but not the other. Can you articulate your reasons into general principles a company might use when considering the need to customize?

Under the Hood: Focus on Technology

The Hilton hotel's product mix is represented by nine different hotel brands located around the world. Visit the Web pages of three of Hilton's hotel brands (www.hilton.com, www.hamptoninn.com, and www.conradhotels.com) and respond to the questions below.

1. How are these three hotel brands positioned relative to each other?

2. Discuss Hilton's various hotel brands with respect to the concepts of product line stretching and product-line filling.

3. Why does Hilton use different brand names for each hotel? Do you agree or disagree with this approach?

Focus on Ethics

Companies have an interest in protecting their brand names, whether they be in the physical world or the cyberworld. The term "cybersquatting" has been used to refer to an individual registering a domain name that is identical or confusingly similar to a distinctive, famous trademark. For example, consider the Web site amazo**m**.com compared with amazo**n**.com. Cybersquaters typically did this with the goals of either using the similar Web address to bring traffic to their own Web site or with the hope of selling the domain name back to the company for a substantial profit. Cybersquatting was made illegal in the United States by the 2000 Anti-Cybersquatting Consumer Protection Act.

Under this law, individuals that are found to have registered a domain name in "bad faith" are subject to fines up to $100,000 per domain name.

1. Why should companies care about cybersquatters?

2. Some people feel that domain names should be on a "first come, first served" basis with no company or individual having a claim on unregistered domain names. How do you feel about that perspective?

3. How does protecting one's brand name in cyberspace compare with trademark protection?

Videos

The Accenture video case that accompanies this chapter is located in Appendix 1 at the back of the book.

Student Materials

Need a tune-up? A study guide and OneKey access code are available to aid in your review of chapter material. Your instructor may choose to have these items shrink-wrapped with your text or you may purchase them separately at www.prenhall.com/marketing.

■ *After studying this chapter, you should be able to*

1. *Explain* how companies find and develop new-product ideas   **2.** *List* and define the steps in the new-product development process   **3.** *Describe* the stages of the product life cycle   **4.** *Describe* how marketing strategies change during the product's life cycle

New-Product Development and Product Life-Cycle Strategies

8

ROAD MAP | Previewing the Concepts

In the previous chapter, you learned about decisions that marketers make in managing individual brands and entire product mixes. In this chapter, we'll cruise on into two additional product topics: developing new products and managing products through their life cycles. New products are the lifeblood of an organization. However, new-product development is risky, and many new products fail. So, the first part of this chapter lays out a process for finding and growing successful new products. Once introduced, marketers want their products to enjoy a long and happy life. In the second part of the chapter, you'll see that every product passes through several life-cycle stages and that each stage poses new challenges requiring different marketing strategies and tactics.

First point of interest: Microsoft. The chances are good that you use several Microsoft products and services. Microsoft's Windows software owns a mind-boggling 97 percent share of the PC operating system market and its Office software captures a 90 percent share! However, this $25 billion company doesn't rest on past performance. As you'll see, it owes much of this success to a passion for innovation, abundant new-product development, and its quest for "the Next Big Thing."

N o matter what brand of computer you're using or what you're doing on it, you're almost certain to be using some type of Microsoft product or service. In the world of computer and Internet software and technology, Microsoft dominates.

Microsoft's Windows operating system captures an astonishing 97 percent share of the PC market and a better than 40 percent share in the business server market. Microsoft Office, the company's largest moneymaker, grabs 90 percent of all office applications suite sales. The company's MSN Internet portal (www.msn.com) attracts more than 300 million unique surfers per month, second only to Yahoo!. Its MSN Internet-access service, with 9 million subscribers, trails only America Online as the most popular way for consumers to get onto the Web. Microsoft's Hotmail is the world's most used free e-mail service, hosting more than 100 million accounts, and its instant messaging service has more than 34 million users.

These and other successful products and services have made Microsoft incredibly profitable. During its first 27 years, the software giant racked up more than $50 billion in profits. An investment of $2,800 in 100 shares of Microsoft stock made back when the company went public

would by now have mushroomed into 14,400 shares worth a cool $1 million. All this has made Microsoft co-founder Bill Gates the world's richest man, worth over $43 billion.

A happy ending to a rags-to-riches fairy tale? Not quite. In Microsoft's fast-changing high-tech world, nothing lasts forever—or even for long. Beyond maintaining its core products and businesses, Microsoft knows that its future depends on its ability to conquer new markets with innovative new products.

Microsoft hasn't always been viewed as an innovator. In fact, it has long been regarded as "a big fat copycat." Gates bought the original MS/DOS operating system software upon which he built the company's initial success from a rival programmer for $50,000. Later, Microsoft was accused of copying the user-friendly Macintosh "look and feel." More recently, the company was accused of copying Netscape's Internet browser. It wasn't innovation that made Microsoft, critics claim, but rather its brute-force use of its PC operating system monopoly to crush competitors and muscle into markets. But no more. The technology giant is now innovating at a breakneck pace.

Thanks to its Windows and Office monopolies, and to Microsoft's legendary cash horde of more than $36 billion, the company has plenty of resources to pump into new products and technologies. This year alone, it will spend $5.2 billion on R&D, more than competitors America Online, Sun Microsystems, and Oracle combined. Along with the cash, Microsoft has a strong, visionary leader in its efforts to innovate—no less than Bill Gates himself. Three years ago, Gates turned the CEO-ship of the company over to longtime number two, Steve Ballmer, and named himself "Chief Software Architect." He now spends most of his time and considerable talents happily attending to the details of Microsoft's new-product and technology development.

At the heart of Gates's innovation strategy is the Internet. "Gates sees a day when Microsoft software will . . . be at nearly every point a consumer or corporation touches the Web, . . . easily connecting people to the Internet wherever they happen to be," says *Business Week* analyst Jay Greene. In this new world, any software application on your computer—or on your cell phone, handheld device, or home electronics device—will tap directly into Internet services that help you manage your work and your life. To prepare for such "anytime, anywhere" computing, Microsoft will transform itself from a software company into an Internet services company. As a part of its Web services, Microsoft will one day rent out the latest versions of its software programs via the Net. "Once that happens," says Greene, "Microsoft hopes to deliver software like a steady flow of electricity, collecting monthly or annual usage fees that will give it a lush, predictable revenue stream."

This vision drives a major new Microsoft initiative—dubbed *.NET Services*. It's all part of a strategy to connect people, information, and systems through Web services. Its initial service, called *.NET Passport*, lets registered users enter a single set of sign-in credentials—such as an e-mail address and a password—and then use this single "digital passport" to enter other Web sites without having to remember numerous passwords and user names. The idea is to make signing in to Web sites fast and easy, for anything from purchasing merchandise to scheduling airline tickets to performing transactions on eBay. Passport members can subscribe to other *.NET* services, such as notifying them of specific events or automatically updating their calendars when they make an appointment online.

Within this broad strategic framework, Microsoft is now unleashing its biggest-ever new-products assault. "We've never had a year with this many new products," crows Gates. Here are just a few of the new products and technologies that Microsoft has launched recently or will soon introduce (as described in recent *Business Week* and *Fortune* accounts):

- *.NET Services:* technology that lets unrelated Web sites talk with one another and with PC programs. One click can trigger a cascade of actions without the user having to open new programs or visit new Web sites.

- *Smartphone:* Microsoft's latest software for cell phones. It allows mobile phone users to e-mail, instant message, surf the Web, listen to music, play games, and much more.
- *Natural-language processing:* software that will let computers respond to questions or commands in everyday language, not just computerese or a long series of mouse clicks. Combine that with speech recognition—another area in which Microsoft researchers are plugging away—and one day you'll be able to talk to your computer the same way you do to another person.
- *Face mapping:* using a digital camera to scan a PC user's head into a 3D image. Software then adds a full range of emotions. The point? Microsoft thinks that gamers will want to use their own images in role-playing games.
- *Information agents:* software agents that help you sort the deluge of electronic information. One day, an agent will study what types of messages you read first and know your schedule. Then it will sort e-mail and voice mail, interrupting you with only key messages.
- *The digital home:* next-generation technologies aimed at making the PC the electronic hub of the twenty-first-century digital home. The new technologies will route music, movies, TV programming, e-mail, and news between the Web and PCs, TV set-top boxes, gadgets, and wall-size viewing screens, and sound systems that would make the neighbors call the cops. "Everything in the home will be connected," predicts Gates. And if he gets his way, most of the gizmos will use Microsoft software. The first major Microsoft connected-home product will be a gizmo code-named Mira. It's a flat-panel monitor that detaches from its stand and continues to connect wirelessly to the PC from anywhere in the house. With a stylus tapping icons or scrawling letters on a touch screen, Mom can check e-mail from the kitchen, the kids can chat with online buddies from the couch while watching MTV, and Dad can shop at Amazon.com from the back porch.
- *Smart Personal Objects Technology (SPOT):* Using chips developed in partnership with National Semiconductor, refrigerator magnets, watches, and key chains will receive FM radio waves delivering everything from traffic reports and stock quotes to movie times and sports scores. Eventually, the technology may enable alarm clocks to ring extra early when an accident is likely to lengthen your commute.

So, far from resting on its remarkable past successes, Microsoft is on a quest to discover tomorrow's exciting new technologies. "Even while its latest products are waiting on the launch-pad, it continues to pour money into R&D in search of the Next Big Thing," comments Greene. Gates is jazzed about the future. "He gets wound up like a kid over stuff like creating a computer that watches your actions with a small video camera and determines if you're too busy to be interrupted with a phone call or e-mail," says Greene. An excited Gates shares the simple but enduring principle that guides innovation at Microsoft: "The whole idea of valuing the user's time, that's the Holy Grail," he says.[1]

A company has to be good at developing and managing new products. Every product seems to go through a life cycle—it is born, goes through several phases, and eventually dies as newer products come along that better serve consumer needs. This product life cycle presents two major challenges: First, because all products eventually decline, a firm must be good at developing new products to replace aging ones (the challenge of *new-product development*). Second, the firm must be good at adapting its marketing strategies in the face of changing tastes, technologies, and competition as products pass through life-cycle stages (the challenge of *product life-cycle strategies*). We first look at the problem of finding and developing new products and then at the problem of managing them successfully over their life cycles.

■■ New-Product Development Strategy

New-product development

The development of original products, product improvements, product modifications, and new brands through the firm's own R&D efforts.

Given the rapid changes in consumer tastes, technology, and competition, companies must develop a steady stream of new products and services. A firm can obtain new products in two ways. One is through *acquisition*—by buying a whole company, a patent, or a license to produce someone else's product. The other is through **new-product development** in the company's own research-and-development department. By *new products* we mean original products, product improvements, product modifications, and new brands that the firm develops through its own research-and-development efforts. In this chapter, we concentrate on new-product development.

Innovation can be very risky. Ford lost $350 million on its Edsel automobile; RCA lost $580 million on its SelectaVision videodisk player; and Texas Instruments lost a staggering $660 million before withdrawing from the home computer business. Even these amounts pale in comparison to the failure of the $5 billion Iridium global satellite-based wireless telephone system. Other costly product failures from sophisticated companies include New Coke (Coca-Cola Company), Eagle Snacks (Anheuser-Busch), Zap Mail electronic mail (FedEx), Polarvision instant movies (Polaroid), Premier "smokeless" cigarettes (R.J. Reynolds), Clorox detergent (Clorox Company), and Arch Deluxe sandwiches (McDonald's).[2]

New products continue to fail at a disturbing rate. One source estimates that no more than 10 percent of new products are still on the market and profitable after three years. Another study suggested that of the staggering 25,000 new consumer food, beverage, beauty, and health care products to hit the market each year, only 40 percent will be around five years later. Moreover, failure rates for new industrial products may be as high as 30 percent. Still another estimates new-product failures to be as high as 95 percent.[3]

Why do so many new products fail? There are several reasons. Although an idea may be good, the market size may have been overestimated. Perhaps the actual product was not designed as well as it should have been. Or maybe it was incorrectly positioned in the market, priced too high, or advertised poorly. A high-level executive might push a favorite idea despite poor marketing research findings. Sometimes the costs of product development are higher than expected, and sometimes competitors fight back harder than expected. The reasons behind some new-product failure seem pretty obvious. Try the following on for size[4]:

Strolling the aisles at Robert McMath's New Product Showcase and Learning Center is like finding yourself in some nightmare version of a supermarket. There's Gerber food for adults (pureed sweet-and-sour pork and chicken Madeira), Hot Scoop microwaveable ice cream sundaes, Ben-Gay aspirin, Premier smokeless cigarettes, and Miller Clear Beer. How about Avert Virucidal Tissues, Dr. Care Aerosol Toothpaste, Richard Simmons Dijon Vinaigrette Salad Spray, and Look of Buttermilk shampoo? Most of the 80,000 products on display were abject flops. Behind each of them are squandered dollars and hopes.

McMath, the genial curator of this Smithsonian of consumerism, gets lots of laughs when he asks his favorite question, "What were they thinking?" For example, R.J. Reynolds's Premier smokeless cigarettes seemed like a good idea at the time—who could argue against a healthier, nonpolluting cigarette? But what is a cigarette without smoke? McMath notes, "The only people who loved the product were

■ Visiting the New Product Showcase and Learning Center is like finding yourself in some nightmare version of a supermarket. Each product failure represents squandered dollars and hopes.

nonsmokers, and they somehow aren't the market RJR was trying to reach." Looking back, what was RJR thinking?

Other companies failed because the attached trusted brand names to something totally out of character. For example, when you hear the name Ben-Gay, you immediately think of the way Ben-Gay cream sears and stimulates your skin. Can you imagine swallowing Ben-Gay aspirin? Or how would you feel about quaffing a can of Exxon fruit punch or Kodak quencher? Other misbegotten attempts to stretch a good name include Cracker Jack cereal, Smucker's premium ketchup, and Fruit of the Loom laundry detergent. "What *were* they thinking?" asks McGrath. You can tell that some innovative products were doomed as soon as you hear their names: Toaster Eggs. Cucumber antiperspirant spray. Health-Sea sea sausage. Look of Buttermilk shampoo. Dr. Care Aerosol Toothpaste (many parents questioned the wisdom of arming their kids with something like this!). Really, what were they thinking?

Because so many new products fail, companies are anxious to learn how to improve their odds of new-product success. One way is to identify successful new products and find out what they have in common. Another is to study new-product failures to see what lessons can be learned. In all, to create successful new products, a company must understand its consumers, markets, and competitors and develop products that deliver superior value to customers.

So companies face a problem—they must develop new products, but the odds weigh heavily against success. The solution lies in strong new-product planning and in setting up a systematic *new-product development process* for finding and growing new products. Figure 8.1 shows the eight major steps in this process.

Idea Generation

New-product development starts with **idea generation**—the systematic search for new-product ideas. A company typically has to generate many ideas in order to find a few good ones. According to one well-known management consultant, "For every 1,000 ideas, only 100 will have enough commercial promise to merit a small-scale experiment, only 10 of those will warrant substantial financial commitment, and of those, only a couple will turn out to be unqualified successes."[5] His conclusion? "If you want to find a few ideas with the power to enthrall customers, foil competitors, and thrill investors, you must first generate hundreds and potentially thousands of unconventional strategic ideas."

Major sources of new-product ideas include internal sources and external sources such as customers, competitors, distributors and suppliers, and others.

Idea generation
The systematic search for new-product ideas.

FIGURE 8.1

Major Stages in New-Product Development

Internal Idea Sources   Using *internal sources*, the company can find new ideas through formal research and development. It can pick the brains of its executives, scientists, engineers, manufacturing staff, and salespeople. Some companies have developed successful "intrapreneurial" programs that encourage employees to think up and develop new-product ideas. For example, 3M's well-known "15 percent rule" allows employees to spend 15 percent of their time "bootlegging"—working on projects of personal interest, whether or not those projects directly benefit the company. "For more than a century," notes one source, "3M's culture has fostered creativity and given employees the freedom to take risks and try new ideas." The spectacularly successful Post-it notes evolved out of this program. Similarly, Texas Instruments's IDEA program provides funds for employees who pursue their own ideas. Among the successful new products to come out of the IDEA program was TI's Speak 'n' Spell, the first children's toy to contain a microchip. Many other speaking toys followed, ultimately generating several hundred million dollars for TI.[6]

Companies sometimes look for creative approaches to innovation that overcome barriers to the free flow of new product ideas. For example, firms like Eureka! Ranch—a well-known "new-product hatchery"—employ both "method" and "madness" in helping companies to jumpstart their new-product idea generation process (see Marketing at Work 8.1).

External Idea Sources   Good new-product ideas also come from watching and listening to *customers*. The company can analyze customer questions and complaints to find new products that better solve consumer problems. Company engineers or salespeople can meet with and work alongside customers to get suggestions and ideas. The company can conduct surveys or focus groups to learn about consumer needs and wants.

Heinz did just that when its researchers approached children, who consume more than half of the ketchup sold, to find out what would make ketchup more appealing to them. "When we asked them what would make the product more fun," says a Heinz spokesperson, "changing the color was among the top responses." So, Heinz developed and launched EZ Squirt, green ketchup that comes in a soft, squeezable bottle targeted at kids. The new product was a smash hit, so Heinz followed up with an entire rainbow of EZ Squirt colors, including Funky Purple, Passion Pink, Awesome Orange, Totally Teal, and Stellar Blue. The EZ Squirt bottle's special nozzle also emits a thin ketchup stream, "so tykes can

■ When Heinz asked kids what would make the product more fun, they said "Change the color!" So, Heinz developed and launched EZ Squirt, now in a variety of colors targeted at kids. The EZ Squirt bottle's special nozzle also emits a thin ketchup stream, so tykes can autograph their burgers.

autograph their burgers (or squirt someone across the table, though Heinz neglects to mention that)." In all, the new line earned the company a 5 percent increase in sales in the first year after hitting the grocery shelf.[7]

Consumers often create new products and uses on their own, and companies can benefit by finding these products and putting them on the market. For example, Avon capitalized on new uses discovered by consumers for its Skin-So-Soft bath oil and moisturizer. For years, customers have been spreading the word that Skin-So-Soft bath oil is also a terrific bug repellent. Whereas some consumers were content simply to bathe in water scented with the fragrant oil, others carried it in their backpacks to mosquito-infested campsites or kept a bottle on the deck of their beach houses. Now, Avon offers a complete line of Skin-So-Soft Bug Guard products, including Bug Guard Mosquito Repellant Moisturizing Towelettes and Bug Guard Plus, a combination moisturizer, insect repellent, and sunscreen.[8]

Finally, some companies even give customers the tools and resources to design their own products.

> Many companies have abandoned their efforts to figure out exactly what products their customers want. Instead, they have equipped customers with tools that let them design their own products. The user-friendly tools employ new technologies like computer simulation and rapid prototyping to make product development faster and less expensive. For example, Bush Boake Allen (BBA), a global supplier of specialty flavors to companies like Nestle, provides a tool kit that lets its customers develop their own flavors, which BBA then manufactures. Similarly, GE Plastics gives customers access to company data sheets, engineering expertise, simulation software, and other Web-based tools for designing better plastics products. Companies like LSI Logic and VLSI Technology provide customers with do-it-yourself tools that let them design their own specialized chips and customized integrated circuits. Using customers as innovators has become a hot new way to create value.[9]

Companies must be careful not to rely too heavily on customer input when developing new products. For some products, especially highly technical ones, customers may not know what they need. In such cases, "customers should not be trusted to come up with solutions; they aren't expert or informed enough for that part of the innovation process," says the head of an innovation management consultancy. "That's what your R&D team is for. Rather, customers should be asked only for outcomes—that is, what they want a product or service to *do* for them."[10]

Competitors are another good source of new-product ideas. Companies watch competitors' ads and other communications to get clues about their new products. They buy competing new products, take them apart to see how they work, analyze their sales, and decide whether they should bring out a new product of their own. *Distributors and suppliers* can also contribute many good new-product ideas. Resellers are close to the market and can pass along information about consumer problems and new-product possibilities. Suppliers can tell the company about new concepts, techniques, and materials that can be used to develop new products. Other idea sources include trade magazines, shows, and seminars; government agencies; new-product consultants; advertising agencies; marketing research firms; university and commercial laboratories; and inventors.

The search for new-product ideas should be systematic rather than haphazard. Otherwise, few new ideas will surface and many good ideas will sputter and die. Top management can avoid these problems by installing an *idea management system* that directs the flow of new ideas to a central point where they can be collected, reviewed, and evaluated. In setting up such a system, the company can do any or all of the following[11]:

■ Appoint a respected senior person to be the company's idea manager.

■ Create a cross-functional idea management committee consisting of people from R&D, engineering, purchasing, operations, finance, and sales and marketing to meet regularly and evaluate proposed new product and service ideas.

Marketing at Work | 8.1

Eureka! Ranch: Method and Madness in Finding New-Product Ideas

Having trouble thinking up the next hot new-product idea? Try a visit to Eureka! Ranch. For $75,000 to $150,000, you can send a dozen key marketing managers to loosen up, have some fun, and get the creative juices flowing. Located on 80 acres, with a sand volleyball court, a water sports lake, and a three-hole golf course, Eureka! Ranch seems more like an executive resort than a new-product hatchery. But Eureka! Ranch isn't just about relaxing and having fun. Instead, it's all about the very serious business of creating new product ideas.

Founded by Doug Hall, a former Procter & Gamble "Master Marketing Inventor," the Ranch seems at first to be sheer madness. Consider this account:

Executives from Gardetto's, a Milwaukee-based snack foods company, stream through the doors of Eureka! Ranch. A two-man zydeco band cranks out early morning Cajun tunes. Amid the high-energy music, Doug Hall and his staff greet their visitors with laughs, handshakes, and platters of muffins, bagels, and other breakfast goodies. Hall, the opposite of Wall Street chic, in a blue Hawaiian shirt and faded jeans, soon gathers his clients in the center of the living room and welcomes everyone. A large blanket-covered mound lurks near his bare feet. After a brief introduction, in which he notes, "Today, reality isn't relevant," Hall rips the blanket off, revealing a pile of Nerf guns. With a commando yell, he grabs a foam assault rifle and starts firing away at the momentarily shocked participants. In an instant, however, they too join the battle, blasting away at one another in a frenzy of multicolored projectiles and screams. Let the games begin.

But there's method to the madness in Eureka! Ranch's intensive multi-day ses-

sions. Doug Hall, once described as "a combination of Bill Gates, Ben Franklin, and Bozo the Clown," is dedicated to helping participants throw off the self-imposed constraints that keep them from innovating. Eureka! Ranch creates a unique combination of sensory overload and a supportive environment that breaks down defensiveness and self-censorship that too often stifle creativity in a corporate conference room. The

result: breakthrough ideas and strategies for new products and services.

Gardetto's—whose main product is called Snak-ens, a mixture of seasoned pretzels, rye crisps, and breadsticks—took 15 of its people to Eureka! Ranch's standard two-and-a-half-day program. The agenda for Eureka's program was serious and simple in concept. "I'm not looking for a line extension or just a good idea," said executive vice president Nan

"When Doug meets Disney, creativity ne'er wanes; Our team explodes when he jump starts our brains!"
Ellen Guidera, Vice President
The Walt Disney Company

"A rigorous, quantifiable process for inventing breakthrough ideas for clients. Unlike many creative gurus hustling ideation wares in the corporate marketplace, Eureka! Inventing processes are quantified every step of the way."
CIO Magazine

"Eureka! has developed more new products than any other organization in America."
New York Magazine

Need Growth? We Can Help!

"Former Procter & Gamble marketing whiz Doug Hall goes to any length to encourage a fresh perspective ...clients say it works."
The Wall Street Journal

"Eureka! Ranch's unconventional approach has won raves from some of the biggest corporations in the country."
CNN

"Doug Hall is THE idea man. The former P&G marketer has guided big corporation marketing team after big corporation marketing team to stunning new product breakthroughs."
Tom Peters

JUMP START YOUR BUSINESS BRAIN

WIN MORE • LOSE LESS and MAKE MORE MONEY
with your New Products, Services, Sales & Advertising

EUREKA! RANCH®

The Eureka! Ranch delivers OUTSTANDING client satisfaction. More than 80% of Eureka! Ranch business is REPEAT from such world class companies as The Ford Motor Company, Fidelity, Tenneco, Johnson & Johnson, Walt Disney, Frito-Lay, Compaq Computer, Procter & Gamble and American Express.

Generating new product ideas: Eureka! Ranch now combines creative passion with a more systematic process and real-world data. But along with the scientific method, there's still a healthy portion of madness thrown into the brew.

Gardetto. "I'm looking for something really breakthrough." But from day one, in execution, the program was free-wheeling and action-packed. Heart-pumping Nerf bullet battles replaced mind-numbing PowerPoint bullet lectures. The majority of the first day was devoted to generating as many wild ideas as possible. Reality? Not relevant!

At Eureka! Ranch, fast-paced play and idea-generating zaniness open the flood gates for new ideas. It starts with brainstorming exercises that expand people's minds and generate new ideas around the client's problem. No idea is too far-fetched or impractical on the first day, and everything gets written down. By the time they sit down to a gourmet dinner at the ranch, clients have typically spawned some 1,500 to 2,000 ideas. Only after dinner do the participants start judging the fruits of their fun. For the Gardetto's team, ideas like Gar-Chia—a Chia-pet-like snack that expands in water—get tossed. But other ideas receive numerous votes of support. At 11 P.M., after the clients have retired for the night, Eureka! Ranch's tireless staff—its "Trained Brains"—debrief and refine the day's results.

Day 2 begins with a hearty breakfast and a stiff mug of Brain Brew coffee. Then the Gardetto's team gathers around a large board, to which Eureka! Ranch staffers have tacked the 12 most popular new product ideas and the 19 most popular new positioning ideas from the previous day. The team reviews the concepts, adds depth and refinement to the better ones, and votes again. They spend the rest of the day assessing each surviving idea in more detail. "After the previous day's anything-that-pops-up-in-your-head brainstorming," says one observer, "today is more focused; people sense that they're discussing ideas that may evolve into a completely new line of snacks."

Yet even as the group tackles the serious issues, the atmosphere remains lighthearted. "Just the fact that a Nerf ball comes whistling at your head [during an exercise] makes you think of something different. [It's] harnessed chaos," says one participant. "You'd like to have it at the office, but that's not the real world." When the day's session ends, the Gardetto's team heads out for a relaxing dinner at a local restaurant. Meanwhile, Doug Hall and his staff prepare for the final day. They whittle down the list of ideas and write concept statements for what they think are the most viable new-product options.

The final day: "Another foggy morning, another hearty breakfast, another mug of Brain Brew," notes the observer. Hall, dressed in a long purple robe and still barefoot, presents the results of the Gardetto's team's efforts—the best of the best. The team talks through each product idea. Some are sent packing—such as Saturday night Snack 'Ems (featuring Charlie's skillet corn bread) and Bistro Baguettes (sweet bread with raspberry-champagne and cream cheese). But other ideas garner enthusiastic support. Gardetto's leaves satisfied, with 16 new packaging ideas, 9 new logos, and several new snack food concepts for the R&D kitchens.

Gardetto's satisfying experience is typical. *Human Resource Executive* recently named Eureka! Ranch as one of the top 10 training programs in the country. Eighty-five percent of participants rate the program as the best training they've ever attended. And more than 80 percent of Eureka! Ranch sessions are repeat business from such world-class companies as Ford, Fidelity, Tenneco, Johnson & Johnson, Walt Disney, Nike, Frito-Lay, Procter & Gamble, and American Express. "When Doug meets Disney, creativity never wanes," says a Disney executive after a visit to Eureka! Ranch. "Our team explodes when he jumps starts our brains."

In working with more than 4,000 new products and 6,000 front-line development groups, Eureka! Ranch has learned a good many lessons on creativity itself. Interestingly, one lesson is that zany fun is only part of the process for generating creative ideas. In fact, in recent years, Eureka! Ranch sessions are becoming more serious and less chaotic. The Ranch now tackles the tough job of being creative by balancing the "madness" with a stronger mix of "method."

There's still plenty of fast-paced action and creative brainstorming (video games still line the walls), and the Ranch promises sessions that will "wake up and shake up" your thinking. But sessions are now supported by the heaps of qualitative and quantitative data gleaned from Eureka! Ranch's years of new-product development experience. Along with the brainstorming, clients now learn "the three laws of marketing physics" and the "laws of capitalist creativity." Refined product-development tools and more methodical processes now supplement the open-ended fun of previous days. For example, Eureka! Ranch has developed its Merwyn software, a scoring system for new ideas. The Merwyn software contains over one million data points that help it predict the likely market success of new products.

What has emerged is a more effective version of Eureka! Ranch. Under Hall's notions of "capitalist creativity," new-product success "is not random. . . . There are reproducible scientific lessons and laws that . . . can help you win more, lose less, and make more money." Eureka! Ranch now combines creative passion with a more systematic process and real-world data. But along with the scientific method, there's still a healthy portion of madness thrown into the brew.

Sources: Quotes and other information from Todd Datz, "Romper Ranch," *CIO*, May 15, 1999; Lori Dahm, "Pursue Passion," *Stagnito's New Products Magazine*, October 2002, p. 58; Eva Kaplan-Leiserson, "Eureka!: This little-Ranch-that-Could Teaches You to 'Win More, Lose Less, and Make More Money,'" *T&D*, December 2001, p. 50(14); Geoff Williams, "I've Got an Idea!" *Entrepreneur*, December 2001, p. 36; Monique Reece, "Expert Shares His Ideas to Jumpstart Businesses," *Denver Business Journal*, September 28, 2001, p. 33A; Doug Hall, *Jump Start Your Business Brain* (Whitehall, VA: Betterway Publications, 2002); John Eckberg, "New Radio Host takes on Small Biz," *The Cincinnati Enquirer*, January 13, 2003, p. 7B; and www.eurekaranch.com, August 2003.

- Set up a toll-free number or Web site for anyone who wants to send a new idea to the idea manager.

- Encourage all company stakeholders—employees, suppliers, distributors, dealers—to send their ideas to the idea manager.

- Set up formal recognition programs to reward those who contribute the best new ideas.

The idea manager approach yields two favorable outcomes. First, it helps create an innovation-oriented company culture. It shows that top management supports, encourages, and rewards innovation. Second, it will yield a larger number of ideas, among which will be found some especially good ones. As the system matures, ideas will flow more freely. No longer will good ideas wither for the lack of a sounding board or a senior product advocate.

Idea Screening

Idea screening
Screening new-product ideas in order to spot good ideas and drop poor ones as soon as possible.

The purpose of idea generation is to create a large number of ideas. The purpose of the succeeding stages is to *reduce* that number. The first idea-reducing stage is **idea screening**, which helps spot good ideas and drop poor ones as soon as possible. Product development costs rise greatly in later stages, so the company wants to go ahead only with the product ideas that will turn into profitable products. As one marketing executive suggests, "Three executives sitting in a room can get 40 good ideas ricocheting off the wall in minutes. The challenge is getting a steady stream of good ideas out of the labs and creativity campfires, through marketing and manufacturing, and all the way to consumers."[12]

Many companies require their executives to write up new-product ideas on a standard form that can be reviewed by a new-product committee. The write-up describes the product, the target market, and the competition. It makes some rough estimates of market size, product price, development time and costs, manufacturing costs, and rate of return. The committee then evaluates the idea against a set of general criteria. For example, at Kao Company, the large Japanese consumer-products company, the committee asks questions such as these: Is the product truly useful to consumers and society? Is it good for our particular company? Does it mesh well with the company's objectives and strategies? Do we have the people, skills, and resources to make it succeed? Does it deliver more value to customers than do competing products? Is it easy to advertise and distribute? Many companies have well-designed systems for rating and screening new-product ideas.

Concept Development and Testing

Product concept
A detailed version of the new-product idea stated in meaningful consumer terms.

An attractive idea must be developed into a **product concept**. It is important to distinguish between a product idea, a product concept, and a product image. A *product idea* is an idea for a possible product that the company can see itself offering to the market. A *product concept* is a detailed version of the idea stated in meaningful consumer terms. A *product image* is the way consumers perceive an actual or potential product.

Concept Development DaimlerChrysler is getting ready to commercialize its experimental fuel-cell-powered electric car. This car's nonpolluting fuel-cell system runs directly on methanol, which delivers hydrogen to the fuel cell with only water as a by-product. It is highly fuel efficient (75 percent more efficient than gasoline engines) and gives the new car an environmental advantage over standard internal combustion engine cars or even today's superefficient gasoline–electric hybrid cars.

- DaimlerChrysler's task is to develop its fuel-cell-powered-electric car into alternative product concepts, find out how attractive each is to customers, and choose the best one.

DaimlerChrysler is currently road-testing its NECAR 5 (New Electric Car) subcompact prototype and plans to deliver the first fuel-cell cars to customers in 2004. Based on the tiny Mercedes A-Class, the car accelerates quickly, reaches speeds of 90 miles per hour, and has a 280-mile driving range, giving it a huge edge over battery-powered electric cars that travel only about 80 miles before needing 3 to 12 hours of recharging.[13]

DaimlerChrysler's task is to develop this new product into alternative product concepts, find out how attractive each concept is to customers, and choose the best one. It might create the following product concepts for the fuel-cell electric car:

Concept 1   A moderately priced subcompact designed as a second family car to be used around town. The car is ideal for running errands and visiting friends.

Concept 2   A medium-cost sporty compact appealing to young people.

Concept 3   An inexpensive subcompact "green" car appealing to environmentally conscious people who want practical transportation and low pollution.

Concept 4   A high-end SUV appealing to those who love the space SUVs provide but lament the poor gas mileage.

Concept Testing   **Concept testing** calls for testing new-product concepts with groups of target consumers. The concepts may be presented to consumers symbolically or physically. Here, in words, is concept 3:

> An efficient, fun-to-drive, fuel-cell-powered electric subcompact car that seats four. This methanol-powered high-tech wonder provides practical and reliable transportation with virtually no pollution. It goes up to 90 miles per hour and, unlike battery-powered electric cars, it never needs recharging. It's priced, fully equipped, at $20,000.

For some concept tests, a word or picture description might be sufficient. However, a more concrete and physical presentation of the concept will increase the reliability of the concept test. Today, some marketers are finding innovative ways to make product concepts more real to consumer subjects. For example, some are using virtual reality to test product concepts. Virtual reality programs use computers and sensory devices (such as gloves or goggles) to simulate reality. A designer of kitchen cabinets can use a virtual reality program to help a customer "see" how his or her kitchen would look and work if remodeled with the company's products. Hairdressers have used virtual reality for years to show consumers how they might look with a new style. Although virtual reality is still in its infancy, its applications are increasing daily.[14]

After being exposed to the concept, consumers then may be asked to react to it by answering questions such as those in Table 8.1. The answers will help the company decide which concept has the strongest appeal. For example, the last question asks about the consumer's intention to buy. Suppose 10 percent of the consumers said they

Concept testing
Testing new-product concepts with a group of target consumers to find out if the concepts have strong consumer appeal.

TABLE 8.1   Questions for Fuel-Cell Electric Car Concept Test

1. Do you understand the concept of a fuel-cell-powered electric car?

2. Do you believe the claims about the car's performance?

3. What are the major benefits of the fuel-cell-powered electric car compared with a conventional car?

4. What are its advantages compared with a battery-powered electric car?

5. What improvements in the car's features would you suggest?

6. For what uses would you prefer a fuel-cell-powered electric car to a conventional car?

7. What would be a reasonable price to charge for the car?

8. Who would be involved in your decision to buy such a car? Who would drive it?

9. Would you buy such a car? (definitely, probably, probably not, definitely not)

"definitely" would buy and another 5 percent said "probably." The company could project these figures to the full population in this target group to estimate sales volume. Even then, the estimate is uncertain because people do not always carry out their stated intentions.

Many firms routinely test new-product concepts with consumers before attempting to turn them into actual new products. For example, each month AcuPOLL tests 40 new-product concepts in person on 100 nationally representative grocery store shoppers, rating them as "Pure Gold" or "Fool's Gold" concepts. In past polls, Nabisco's Oreo Chocolate Cones concept received a rare A+ rating, meaning that consumers think it is an outstanding concept that they would try and buy. Glad Ovenware, Reach Whitening Tape dental floss, and Lender's Bake at Home Bagels were also big hits. Other product concepts didn't fare so well. Nubrush Anti-Bacterial Toothbrush Spray disinfectant, from Applied Microdontics, received an F. Consumers found Nubrush to be overpriced, and most don't think they have a problem with "infected" toothbrushes. Nor did consumers think much of Excedrin Tension Headache Cooling Pads. Another concept that fared poorly was Chef Williams 5 Minute Marinade, which comes with a syringe customers use to inject the marinade into meats. "I can't see that on grocery shelves," comments an AcuPOLL executive. Some consumers might find the thought of injecting something into meat a bit repulsive, and "it's just so politically incorrect to have this syringe on there."[15]

Hershey does its product concept testing on the Web. It uses online test subjects to gain insight to all aspects of its product concepts. Consumers might be shown pictures of proposed candy bars or baking mixes, quizzed about flavors, and asked about potential product names. Says one Hershey researcher, "You need to test maybe 100 concepts to get one good product that might make it to market." Putting concept testing online has cut the time Hershey spends on new-product development by two-thirds.[16]

Marketing Strategy Development

Marketing strategy development
Designing an initial marketing strategy for a new product based on the product concept.

Suppose DaimlerChrysler finds that concept 3 for the fuel-cell-powered electric car tests best. The next step is **marketing strategy development**, designing an initial marketing strategy for introducing this car to the market.

The *marketing strategy statement* consists of three parts. The first part describes the target market; the planned product positioning; and the sales, market share, and profit goals for the first few years. Thus:

> The target market is younger, well-educated, moderate-to-high-income individuals, couples, or small families seeking practical, environmentally responsible transportation. The car will be positioned as more economical to operate, more fun to drive, and less polluting than today's internal combustion engine or hybrid cars. It is also less restricting than battery-powered electric cars, which must be recharged regularly. The company will aim to sell 100,000 cars in the first year, at a loss of not more than $15 million. In the second year, the company will aim for sales of 120,000 cars and a profit of $25 million.

The second part of the marketing strategy statement outlines the product's planned price, distribution, and marketing budget for the first year:

> The fuel-cell-powered electric car will be offered in three colors—red, white, and blue—and will have optional air-conditioning and power-drive features. It will sell at a retail price of $20,000—with 15 percent off the list price to dealers. Dealers who sell more than 10 cars per month will get an additional discount of 5 percent on each car sold that month. An advertising budget of $50 million will be split 50-50 between a national media campaign and local advertising. Advertising will emphasize the car's fun spirit and low emissions. During the first year, $100,000 will be spent on marketing research to find out who is buying the car and their satisfaction levels.

The third part of the marketing strategy statement describes the planned long-run sales, profit goals, and marketing mix strategy:

> DaimlerChrysler intends to capture a 3 percent long-run share of the total auto market and realize an after-tax return on investment of 15 percent. To achieve this, product quality will start high and be improved over time. Price will be raised in the second and third years if competition permits. The total advertising budget will be raised each year by about 10 percent. Marketing research will be reduced to $60,000 per year after the first year.

Business Analysis

Once management has decided on its product concept and marketing strategy, it can evaluate the business attractiveness of the proposal. **Business analysis** involves a review of the sales, costs, and profit projections for a new product to find out whether they satisfy the company's objectives. If they do, the product can move to the product development stage.

To estimate sales, the company might look at the sales history of similar products and conduct surveys of market opinion. It can then estimate minimum and maximum sales to assess the range of risk. After preparing the sales forecast, management can estimate the expected costs and profits for the product, including marketing, R&D, operations, accounting, and finance costs. The company then uses the sales and costs figures to analyze the new product's financial attractiveness.

Business analysis
A review of the sales, costs, and profit projections for a new product to find out whether these factors satisfy the company's objectives.

Product Development

So far, for many new-product concepts, the product may have existed only as a word description, a drawing, or perhaps a crude mock-up. If the product concept passes the business test, it moves into **product development**. Here, R&D or engineering develops the product concept into a physical product. The product development step, however, now calls for a large jump in investment. It will show whether the product idea can be turned into a workable product.

The R&D department will develop and test one or more physical versions of the product concept. R&D hopes to design a prototype that will satisfy and excite consumers and that can be produced quickly and at budgeted costs. Developing a successful prototype can take days, weeks, months, or even years.

Often, products undergo rigorous tests to make sure that they perform safely and effectively, or that consumers will find value in them. Here are some examples of such product tests[17]:

Product development
Developing the product concept into a physical product in order to ensure that the product idea can be turned into a workable product.

> A scuba-diving Barbie doll must swim and kick for 15 straight hours to satisfy Mattel that she will last at least one year. But because Barbie may find her feet in small owners' mouths rather than in the bathtub, Mattel has devised another, more torturous test: Barbie's feet are clamped by two steel jaws to make sure that her skin doesn't crack, and choke potential owners.

> P&G spends $150 million on 4,000 to 5,000 studies a year, testing everything from the ergonomics of picking up a shampoo bottle to how long women can keep their hands in sudsy water. On any given day, subjects meet in focus groups, sell their dirty laundry to researchers, put prototype diapers on their babies' bottoms, and rub mysterious creams on their faces. Last year, one elementary school raised $17,000 by having students and parents take part in P&G product tests. Students tested toothpaste and shampoo and ate brownies, while their mothers watched advertising for Tempo tissue, P&G's paper wipes packaged to fit in a car. This year, P&G is paying the school to have 48 students and parents wear new sneakers that they hand in every month for six months. Half the shoes return cleaned. No one knows what P&G is testing, and the company won't say.

> Taco Time International, a Canadian Mexican restaurant chain, wanted to taste test its new line of green and red hot sauces. So it decided to get input from

some real experts on hot stuff: the residents of Villa Hermosa in Mexico. Now Villa Hermosa isn't just any Mexican city, it's the capital of the state of Tabasco, which is, of course, known as the source of one of the world's most famous hot sauces. When the people of hot-sauce city reacted favorably to the firm's concoctions, Taco Time videotaped the tastings and produced the video for its franchisees. It also put shots of the tastings on its Web site and on restaurant tray liners. Straight to the source—now that's authentic!

At Gillette, almost everyone gets involved in new-product testing. Every working day at Gillette, 200 volunteers from various departments come to work unshaven, troop to the second floor of the company's gritty South Boston plant, and enter small booths with a sink and mirror. There they take instructions from technicians on the other side of a small window as to which razor, shaving cream, or aftershave to use. The volunteers evaluate razors for sharpness of blade, smoothness of glide, and ease of handling. In a nearby shower room, women perform the same ritual on their legs, underarms, and what the company delicately refers to as the "bikini area." "We bleed so you'll get a good shave at home," says one Gillette employee.

A new-product must have the required functional features and also convey the intended psychological characteristics. The fuel-cell electric car, for example, should strike consumers as being well built, comfortable, and safe. Management must learn what makes consumers decide that a car is well built. To some consumers, this means that the car has "solid-sounding" doors. To others, it means that the car is able to withstand heavy impacts in crash tests. Consumer tests are conducted, in which consumers test-drive the car and rate its attributes.

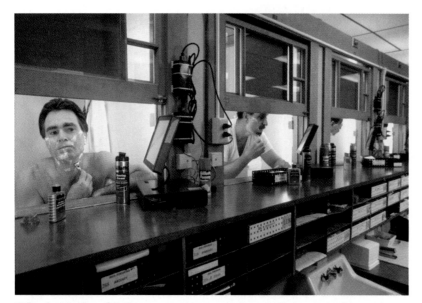

■ Product testing: Gillette uses employee-volunteers to test new shaving products—"We bleed so you'll get a good shave at home," says one Gillette employee.

Test Marketing

Test marketing
The stage of new-product development in which the product and marketing program are tested in more realistic market settings.

If the product passes functional and consumer tests, the next step is **test marketing**, the stage at which the product and marketing program are introduced into more realistic market settings. Test marketing gives the marketer experience with marketing the product before going to the great expense of full introduction. It lets the company test the product and its entire marketing program—positioning strategy, advertising, distribution, pricing, branding and packaging, and budget levels.

The amount of test marketing needed varies with each new product. Test marketing costs can be high, and it takes time that may allow competitors to gain advantages. When the costs of developing and introducing the product are low, or when management is already confident about the new product, the company may do little or no test marketing. In fact, test marketing by consumer packaged-goods firms has been declining in recent years. Companies often do not test-market simple line extensions or copies of successful competitor products. For example, Procter & Gamble introduced its Folger's decaffeinated coffee crystals without test marketing, and Pillsbury rolled out Chewy granola bars and chocolate-covered Granola Dipps with no standard test market.

However, when introducing a new product requires a big investment, or when management is not sure of the product or marketing program, a company may do a lot of test marketing. For instance, Lever USA spent two years testing its highly successful Lever 2000 bar soap in Atlanta before introducing it internationally. Frito-Lay did 18 months of testing in three markets on at least five formulations before introducing its Baked Lays line of low-fat snacks. Both Procter & Gamble and Unilever spent many months testing their new Juvian and MyHome valet laundry and home fabric care services. And Nokia test-marketed its new N-Gage cell phone/ mobile game player extensively in London before introducing it worldwide.[18]

Although test-marketing costs can be high, they are often small when compared with the costs of making a major mistake. For example, McDonald's made a costly mistake when it introduced its low-fat burger, the McLean Deluxe, nationally without the chain's normal and lengthy testing process. The new product failed after a big investment but lean results. And Nabisco's launch of one new product without testing had disastrous—and soggy—results[19]:

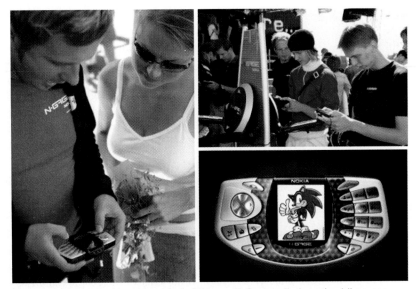

■ Test marketing: Nokia test-marketed its new N-Gage cell phone/mobile game player extensively before introducing it worldwide.

> Nabisco hit a marketing home run with its Teddy Grahams, teddy-bear-shaped graham crackers in several different flavors. So, the company decided to extend Teddy Grahams into a new area. In 1989, it introduced chocolate, cinnamon, and honey versions of Breakfast Bears Graham Cereal. When the product came out, however, consumers didn't like the taste enough, so the product developers went back to the kitchen and modified the formula. But they didn't test it. The result was a disaster. Although the cereal may have tasted better, it no longer stayed crunchy in milk, as the advertising on the box promised. Instead, it left a gooey mess of graham mush on the bottom of cereal bowls. Supermarket managers soon refused to restock the cereal, and Nabisco executives decided it was too late to reformulate the product again. So a promising new product was killed through haste to get it to market.

Still, test marketing doesn't guarantee success. For example, Procter & Gamble tested its new Fit produce rinse heavily for five years and Olay cosmetics for three years. Although market tests suggested the products would be successful, P&G had to pull the plug on both shortly after their introductions.[20]

Commercialization

Test marketing gives management the information needed to make a final decision about whether to launch the new product. If the company goes ahead with **commercialization**— introducing the new product into the market—it will face high costs. The company will have to build or rent a manufacturing facility. And it may have to spend, in the case of a new consumer packaged good, between $10 million and $200 million for advertising, sales promotion, and other marketing efforts in the first year.

The company launching a new product must first decide on introduction *timing*. If DaimlerChrysler's new fuel-cell electric car will eat into the sales of the company's other cars, its introduction may be delayed. If the car can be improved further, or if the economy is down, the company may wait until the following year to launch it.

Next, the company must decide *where* to launch the new product—in a single location, a region, the national market, or the international market. Few companies have the confidence, capital, and capacity to launch new products into full national or international distribution. They will develop a planned *market rollout* over time. In particular, small companies may enter attractive cities or regions one at a time. Larger companies, however, may quickly introduce new models into several regions or into the full national market.

Commercialization
Introducing a new product into the market.

Companies with international distribution systems may introduce new products through global rollouts. Colgate-Palmolive used to follow a "lead-country" strategy. For example, it launched its Palmolive Optima shampoo and conditioner first in Australia, the Philippines, Hong Kong, and Mexico, then rapidly rolled it out into Europe, Asia, Latin America, and Africa. However, most international companies now introduce their new products in swift global assaults. More recently, in its fastest new-product rollout ever, Colgate introduced its Actibrush battery-powered toothbrush into 50 countries in a year, generating $115 million in sales. Such rapid worldwide expansion solidified the brand's market position before foreign competitors could react.[21]

Organizing for New-Product Development

Many companies organize their new-product development process into the orderly sequence of steps shown in Figure 8.1, starting with idea generation and ending with commercialization. Under this **sequential product development** approach, one company department works individually to complete its stage of the process before passing the new product along to the next department and stage. This orderly, step-by-step process can help bring control to complex and risky projects. But it also can be dangerously slow. In fast-changing, highly competitive markets, such slow-but-sure product development can result in product failures, lost sales and profits, and crumbling market positions. "Speed to market" and reducing new-product development cycle time have become pressing concerns to companies in all industries.

In order to get their new products to market more quickly, many companies are adopting a faster, team-oriented approach called **simultaneous product development** (or team-based or collaborative product development). Under this approach, company departments work closely together through cross-functional teams, overlapping the steps in the product development process to save time and increase effectiveness. Instead of passing the new product from department to department, the company assembles a team of people from various departments that stays with the new product from start to finish. Such teams usually include people from the marketing, finance, design, manufacturing, and legal departments, and even supplier and customer companies.

Top management gives the product development team general strategic direction but no clear-cut product idea or work plan. It challenges the team with stiff and seemingly contradictory goals—"turn out carefully planned and superior new products, but do it quickly"—and then gives the team whatever freedom and resources it needs to meet the challenge. In the sequential process, a bottleneck at one phase can seriously slow the entire project. In the simultaneous approach, if one functional area hits snags, it works to resolve them while the team moves on.

The Allen-Bradley Company, a maker of industrial controls, realized tremendous benefits by using simultaneous development. Under its old sequential approach, the company's marketing department handed off a new-product idea to designers, who worked in isolation to prepare concepts that they then passed along to product engineers. The engineers, also working by themselves, developed expensive prototypes and handed them off to manufacturing, which tried to find a way to build the new product. Finally, after many years and dozens of costly design compromises and delays, marketing was asked to sell the new product, which it often found to be too high priced or sadly out of date. Now, all of Allen-Bradley's departments work together to develop new products. The results have been astonishing. For example, the company recently developed a new electrical control in just two years; under the old system, it would have taken six years.

The simultaneous team-based approach does have some limitations. Superfast product development can be riskier and more costly than the slower, more orderly sequential approach. Moreover, it often creates increased organizational tension and confusion. And the company must take care that rushing a product to market doesn't adversely affect its quality—the objective is not only to create products faster, but to create them *better* and faster.

Sequential product development
A new-product development approach in which one company department works to complete its stage of the process before passing the new product along to the next department and stage.

Simultaneous (or team-based) product development
An approach to developing new products in which various company departments work closely together, overlapping the steps in the product-development process to save time and increase effectiveness.

Despite these drawbacks, in rapidly changing industries facing increasingly shorter product life cycles, the rewards of fast and flexible product development far exceed the risks. Companies that get new and improved products to the market faster than competitors often gain a dramatic competitive edge. They can respond more quickly to emerging consumer tastes and charge higher prices for more advanced designs. As one auto industry executive states, "What we want to do is get the new car approved, built, and in the consumer's hands in the shortest time possible. . . . Whoever gets there first gets all the marbles."[22]

Thus, new-product success requires more than simply thinking up a few good ideas, turning them into products, and finding customers for them. It requires a systematic approach for finding new ways to create value for target consumers, from generating and screening new-product ideas to creating and rolling out want-satisfying products to customers. More than this, successful new-product development requires a total-company commitment. At companies known for their new-product prowess—such as 3M, Gillette, Nokia, and Intel—the entire culture encourages, supports, and rewards innovation (see Marketing at Work 8.2).

Linking the Concepts

SPEED BUMP

Take a break. Think about new products and how companies find and develop them.

■ Suppose that you're on a panel to nominate the "best new products of the year." What products would you nominate and why? See what you can learn about the new-product development process for one of these products.

■ Applying the new-product development process you've just studied, develop an idea for an innovative new snack food product and sketch out a brief plan for bringing it to market. Loosen up and have some fun with this.

■■ Product Life-Cycle Strategies

After launching the new product, management wants the product to enjoy a long and happy life. Although it does not expect the product to sell forever, the company wants to earn a decent profit to cover all the effort and risk that went into launching it. Management is aware that each product will have a life cycle, although its exact shape and length is not known in advance.

Figure 8.2 shows a typical **product life cycle (PLC)**, the course that a product's sales and profits take over its lifetime. The product life cycle has five distinct stages:

1. **Product development** begins when the company finds and develops a new-product idea. During product development, sales are zero and the company's investment costs mount.

Product life cycle (PLC)
The course of a product's sales and profits over its lifetime. It involves five distinct stages: product development, introduction, growth, maturity, and decline.

FIGURE 8.2
Sales and Profits Over the Product's Life from Inception to Decline

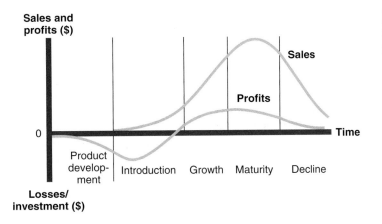

Marketing at Work | 8.2

3M: A Culture for Innovation

You see the headline in every 3M ad: "Innovation Working for You." But at 3M, innovation isn't just an advertising pitch. 3M views *innovation* as its path to growth and new products as its lifeblood. It markets more than 50,000 products. These products range from sandpaper, adhesives, and sponges to power cable splices, to optical lenses, pharmaceuticals, and futuristic synthetic ligaments; from coatings that sleeken boat hulls to hundreds of sticky tapes— Scotch Tape, masking tape, superbonding tape, acid-free photo and document tape, and even refastening-disposable-diaper tape.

3M's goal is to derive an astonishing 30 percent of each year's sales from products introduced within the previous four years. More astonishing, it usually succeeds! Each year 3M launches more than 200 new products. And last year, a full third of its $16 billion in sales came from products introduced within the past four years. This legendary emphasis on innovation has consistently made 3M one of America's most admired companies. In 2003, 3M once again placed among the leaders in *Fortune's* list of companies most admired for innovation. At 3M, new products don't just happen. The company works hard to create an environment that supports innovation. Last year, it invested more than $1 billion, or 6 percent of annual sales, in

research and development—almost twice as much as the average company.

3M encourages everyone to look for new products. The company's

renowned "15 percent rule" allows technical employees to spend up to 15 percent of their time "bootlegging"— working on projects of personal inter-

1 The world wants thinner electronics.

2 We're getting it all on tape.

3M has pioneered a whole new technology: Microflex Circuits – the world's leading mass-produced electronic circuits on tape. They're thinner, smaller, highly reliable, and allow for more connections than rigid circuit boards. They'll go anywhere a designer can dream up: phones, pagers, laptops and printers. We expand the possibilities because we make the leap *from need to...*

3M *Innovation*

For more information, call 1-800-3M-HELPS, or Internet: http://www.mmm.com

3M views innovation as its path to growth and new products as its lifeblood. Its entire culture encourages, supports, and rewards innovation.

2. **Introduction** is a period of slow sales growth as the product is introduced in the market. Profits are nonexistent in this stage because of the heavy expenses of product introduction.
3. **Growth** is a period of rapid market acceptance and increasing profits.
4. **Maturity** is a period of slowdown in sales growth because the product has achieved acceptance by most potential buyers. Profits level off or decline because of increased marketing outlays to defend the product against competition.
5. **Decline** is the period when sales fall off and profits drop.

Not all products follow this product life cycle. Some products are introduced and die quickly; others stay in the mature stage for a long, long time. Some enter the decline stage and are then cycled back into the growth stage through strong promotion or repositioning.

est. "The 15% rule is absolutely essential to 3M for generating those unique ideas and breakthrough products," says 3M's Vice President of R&D. When a promising idea comes along, 3M forms a team made up of the researcher who developed the idea and volunteers from manufacturing, sales, marketing, and legal. Team members stay with the product until it succeeds or fails. Some teams have tried three or four times before finally making a success of an idea. Each year, 3M hands out Golden Step Awards to venture teams whose new products earned more than $2 million in U.S. sales, or $4 million in worldwide sales, within three years of introduction.

3M knows that it must try thousands of new-product ideas to hit one big jackpot. One well-worn slogan at 3M is, "You have to kiss a lot of frogs to find a prince." "Kissing frogs" often means making mistakes, but 3M accepts blunders and dead ends as a normal part of creativity and innovation. In fact, its philosophy seems to be "If you aren't making mistakes, you probably aren't doing anything."

As it turns out, "blunders" have turned into some of 3M's most successful products. Old-timers at 3M love to tell the story about the early 3M scientist who had a deathly fear of shaving with a straight razor. Instead, he invented a very fine, waterproof sandpaper which he used to sand the stubble from his face each morning. Although this invention never caught on as a shaving solution, it

became one of 3M's best-selling products—wet-dry sandpaper, now used for a wide variety of commercial and industrial applications.

And then there's the one about 3M scientist Spencer Silver. Silver started out to develop a superstrong adhesive; instead he came up with one that didn't stick very well at all. He sent the apparently useless substance on to other 3M researchers to see whether they could find something to do with it. Nothing happened for several years. Then Arthur Fry, another 3M scientist, had a problem—and an idea. As a choir member in a local church, Mr. Fry was having trouble marking places in his hymnal—the little scraps of paper he used kept falling out. He tried dabbing some of Mr. Silver's weak glue on one of the scraps. It stuck nicely and later peeled off without damaging the hymnal. Thus were born 3M's Post-It Notes, a product that is now one of the top-selling office supply products in the world!

Thus, 3M could easily amend its long-running "Innovation Working for You" ad line to include "and for *3M*." Still, there are limits. Some analysts question whether such a free-wheeling, no-questions-asked creative culture is appropriate given the cost-reduction pressures of today's tougher economic times. In fact, 3M's new CEO, Jim McNerney, recently launched a "take-no-prisoners" campaign against inefficiencies. He's cutting costs and slimming down the company's workforce.

He is also overhauling the 3M R&D organization and culture, one in which even 3M old-timers agree that money hasn't always been spent wisely. According to one analyst, McNerney "vows to take an organization of myriad product and research fiefdoms—which happens to be one of the most respected manufacturing concerns in the world—and hammer it into one shared corporate culture." He is carefully examining where R&D dollars are spent and setting uniform performance standards and accountability across the company.

The risk is that the changing culture and organizational restructuring might stifle 3M's hallmark creativity. "The most important thing about 3M—the single most important thing—is you get to do things your own way," says a senior 3M executive and 33-year veteran. McNerney understands the balancing act: efficiency versus hands-off R&D spending; accountability versus individual creative freedom. "My job is to add scale in a fast-moving, entrepreneurial environment," he says. "If I end up killing that entrepreneurial spirit, I will have failed."

Sources: Quotes from Rick Mullin, "Analysts Rate 3M's New Culture," *Chemical Week,* September 26, 2001, pp. 39–40; and Michael Arndt, "3M: A Lab for Growth," *Business Week,* January 21, 2002, pp. 50–51. Also see William H. Miller, "New Leader, New Era," November 2001, accessed online at www.industryweek.com; Nicholas Stein, "America's Most Admired Companies," *Fortune,* March 3, 2003, pp. 81–87; Tim Studt, "3M—Where Innovation Rules," *R & D,* April 2003, pp. 20-24; and information accessed online at www.3m.com, July 2003.

The PLC concept can describe a *product class* (gasoline-powered automobiles), a *product form* (SUVs), or a *brand* (the Ford Explorer). The PLC concept applies differently in each case. Product classes have the longest life cycles—the sales of many product classes stay in the mature stage for a long time. Product forms, in contrast, tend to have the standard PLC shape. Product forms such as "dial telephones" and "cassette tapes" passed through a regular history of introduction, rapid growth, maturity, and decline.

A specific brand's life cycle can change quickly because of changing competitive attacks and responses. For example, although laundry soaps (product class) and powdered detergents (product form) have enjoyed fairly long life cycles, the life cycles of specific brands have tended to be much shorter. Today's leading brands of powdered laundry soap are Tide and Cheer; the leading brands 75 years ago were Fels Naptha, Octagon, and Kirkman.[23]

FIGURE 8.3

Styles, Fashions, and Fads

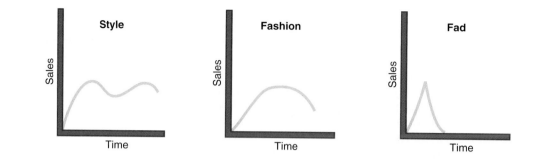

Style

A basic and distinctive mode of expression.

Fashion

A currently accepted or popular style in a given field.

Fad

A fashion that enters quickly, is adopted with great zeal, peaks early, and declines very quickly.

The PLC concept also can be applied to what are known as styles, fashions, and fads. Their special life cycles are shown in Figure 8.3. A **style** is a basic and distinctive mode of expression. For example, styles appear in homes (colonial, ranch, transitional), clothing (formal, casual), and art (realist, surrealist, abstract). Once a style is invented, it may last for generations, passing in and out of vogue. A style has a cycle showing several periods of renewed interest. A **fashion** is a currently accepted or popular style in a given field. For example, the more formal "business attire" look of corporate dress of the 1980s and early 1990s gave way to the "business casual" look of today. Fashions tend to grow slowly, remain popular for a while, and then decline slowly.

Fads are fashions that enter quickly, are adopted with great zeal, peak early, and decline very quickly. They last only a short time and tend to attract only a limited following. "Pet rocks" are a classic example of a fad. Upon hearing his friends complain about how expensive it was to care for their dogs, advertising copywriter Gary Dahl joked about his pet rock and was soon writing a spoof of a dog-training manual for it. Soon Dahl was selling some 1.5 million ordinary beach pebbles at four dollars a pop. Yet the fad, which broke in October 1975, had sunk like a stone by the next February. Dahl's advice to those who want to succeed with a fad: "Enjoy it while it lasts." Other examples of fads include Rubik's Cubes, lava lamps, CB radios, Pokemon cards, and scooters. Most fads do not survive for long because they normally do not satisfy a strong need or satisfy it well.[24]

The PLC concept can be applied by marketers as a useful framework for describing how products and markets work. But using the PLC concept for forecasting product performance or for developing marketing strategies presents some practical problems. For example, managers may have trouble identifying which stage of the PLC the product is in or pinpointing when the product moves into the next stage. They may also find it hard to determine the factors that affect the product's movement through the stages. In practice, it is difficult to forecast the sales level at each PLC stage, the length of each stage, and the shape of the PLC curve.

Using the PLC concept to develop marketing strategy also can be difficult because strategy is both a cause and a result of the product's life cycle. The product's current PLC position suggests the best marketing strategies, and the resulting marketing strategies affect product performance in later life-cycle stages. Yet, when used carefully, the PLC concept can help in developing good marketing strategies for different stages of the product life cycle.

We looked at the product development stage of the product life cycle in the first part of the chapter. We now look at strategies for each of the other life-cycle stages.

Introduction Stage

Introduction stage

The product life-cycle stage in which the new product is first distributed and made available for purchase.

The **introduction stage** starts when the new product is first launched. Introduction takes time, and sales growth is apt to be slow. Well-known products such as instant coffee, frozen orange juice, and powdered coffee creamers lingered for many years before they entered a stage of rapid growth.

In this stage, as compared to other stages, profits are negative or low because of the low sales and high distribution and promotion expenses. Much money is needed to attract distributors and build their inventories. Promotion spending is relatively high to inform consumers of the new product and get them to try it. Because the market is not generally ready for product refinements at this stage, the company and its few competitors produce basic versions of the product. These firms focus their selling on those buyers who are the most ready to buy.

A company, especially the *market pioneer*, must choose a launch strategy that is consistent with the intended product positioning. It should realize that the initial strategy is just the first step in a grander marketing plan for the product's entire life cycle. If the pioneer chooses its launch strategy to make a "killing," it will be sacrificing long-run revenue for the sake of short-run gain. As the pioneer moves through later stages of the life cycle, it will have to continuously formulate new pricing, promotion, and other marketing strategies. It has the best chance of building and retaining market leadership if it plays its cards correctly from the start.[25]

Growth Stage

If the new product satisfies the market, it will enter a **growth stage**, in which sales will start climbing quickly. The early adopters will continue to buy, and later buyers will start following their lead, especially if they hear favorable word of mouth. Attracted by the opportunities for profit, new competitors will enter the market. They will introduce new product features, and the market will expand. The increase in competitors leads to an increase in the number of distribution outlets, and sales jump just to build reseller inventories. Prices remain where they are or fall only slightly. Companies keep their promotion spending at the same or a slightly higher level. Educating the market remains a goal, but now the company must also meet the competition.

Profits increase during the growth stage, as promotion costs are spread over a large volume and as unit manufacturing costs fall. The firm uses several strategies to sustain rapid market growth as long as possible. It improves product quality and adds new product features and models. It enters new market segments and new distribution channels. It shifts some advertising from building product awareness to building product conviction and purchase, and it lowers prices at the right time to attract more buyers.

In the growth stage, the firm faces a trade-off between high market share and high current profit. By spending a lot of money on product improvement, promotion, and distribution, the company can capture a dominant position. In doing so, however, it gives up maximum current profit, which it hopes to make up in the next stage.

Maturity Stage

At some point, a product's sales growth will slow down, and the product will enter a **maturity stage**. This maturity stage normally lasts longer than the previous stages, and it poses strong challenges to marketing management. Most products are in the maturity stage of the life cycle, and therefore most of marketing management deals with the mature product.

The slowdown in sales growth results in many producers with many products to sell. In turn, this overcapacity leads to greater competition. Competitors begin marking down prices, increasing their advertising and sales promotions, and upping their R&D budgets to find better versions of the product. These steps lead to a drop in profit. Some of the weaker competitors start dropping out, and the industry eventually contains only well-established competitors.

Although many products in the mature stage appear to remain unchanged for long periods, most successful ones are actually evolving to meet changing consumer needs (see Marketing at Work 8.3). Product managers should do more than simply ride along with or defend their mature products—a good offense is the best defense. They should consider modifying the market, product, and marketing mix.

In *modifying the market*, the company tries to increase the consumption of the current product. It looks for new users and market segments, as when Johnson & Johnson targeted the adult market with its baby powder and shampoo. Or the company may want to reposition the brand to appeal to a larger or faster-growing segment, as Verizon did when it expanded into high speed Internet and wireless services. The company may also look for

Growth stage
The product life-cycle stage in which a product's sales start climbing quickly.

Maturity stage
The stage in the product life cycle in which sales growth slows or levels off.

ways to increase usage among present customers. Campbell does this by offering recipes and convincing consumers that "soup is good food." Amazon.com sends permission-based e-mails to regular customers letting them know when their favorite authors or performers publish new books or CDs. The WD-40 Company has shown a real knack for expanding the market by finding new uses for its popular substance.

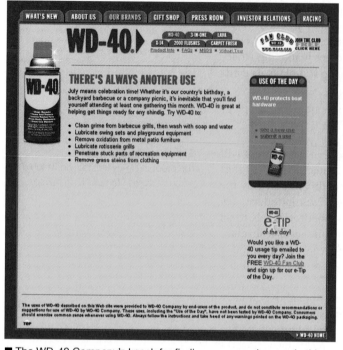

■ The WD-40 Company's knack for finding new uses has made this popular substance one of the truly essential survival items in most American homes.

In 2000, the company launched a search to uncover 2,000 unique uses for WD-40. After receiving 300,000 individual submissions, it narrowed the list to the best 2,000 and posted it on the company's Web site. Some consumers suggest simple and practical uses. One teacher uses WD-40 to clean old chalkboards in her classroom. "Amazingly, the boards started coming to life again," she reports. "Not only were they restored, but years of masking and Scotch tape residue came off as well." Others, however, report some pretty unusual applications. One man uses WD-40 to polish his glass eye; another uses it to remove a prosthetic leg. And did you hear about the nude burglary suspect who had wedged himself in a vent at a cafe in Denver? The fire department extracted him with a large dose of WD-40. Or how about the Mississippi naval officer who used WD-40 to repel an angry bear? Then there's the college student who wrote to say that a friend's nightly amorous activities in the next room were causing everyone in his dorm to lose sleep—he solved the problem by treating the squeaky bedsprings with WD-40.

The company might also try *modifying the product*—changing characteristics such as quality, features, or style to attract new users and to inspire more usage. It might improve the product's quality and performance—its durability, reliability, speed, or taste. It can improve the product's styling and attractiveness. Thus, car manufacturers restyle their cars to attract buyers who want a new look. The makers of consumer food and household products introduce new flavors, colors, ingredients, or packages to revitalize consumer buying. Heinz did this when it introduced ketchup in EZ Squirt packaging and new colors such as Blastin' Green and Awesome Orange.

Or the company might add new features that expand the product's usefulness, safety, or convenience. For example, Sony keeps adding new styles and features to its Walkman and Discman lines, and Volvo adds new safety features to its cars. Kimberly-Clark added a new twist to try to revitalize the product life cycle of an old standby, toilet tissue:

Almost without exception, every American family knows what the paper roll next to the toilet is for, knows how to use it, and purchases it faithfully. Selling an omnipresent household item requires a vital brand that stands out at the supermarket, but how do you make toilet tissue new and exciting? Kimberly-Clark, the maker of Cottonelle and Kleenex, has the answer with an unprecedented innovation: a premoistened toilet paper called Cottonelle Rollwipes, "the breakthrough product that is changing the toilet paper category." Like baby wipes on a roll, the product is designed to complement traditional toilet tissue. "In this category, your growth has to come from significant product Innovations," says a marketing director for Cottonelle. Another marketing executive agrees: "Without new products, old brands become older brands. In categories where there's basic satisfaction with the products, you still have to provide new benefits . . . to build brand share."[26]

Marketing at Work | 8.3

Age-Defying Products or Just Skillful PLC Management?

Some products are born and die quickly. Others, however, seem to defy the product life cycle, enduring for decades, or even generations, with little or no apparent change in their makeup or marketing. Look deeper, however, and you'll find that such products are far from unchanging. Rather, skillful product life-cycle management keeps them fresh, relevant, and appealing to customers. Here are examples of two products that might have been only fads but instead were turned into long-term market winners with plenty of staying power.

Barbie

Talk about age-defying products. Although Mattel's Barbie has now reached 45, Mattel has kept her both timeless and trendy. Since her creation in 1959, Barbie has mirrored girls' dreams of what they'd like to be when they grow up. As such, Barbie has changed as girls' dreams have changed. Her aspirations have evolved from jobs such as stewardess, fashion model, and nurse to astronaut, rock singer, surgeon, and presidential candidate. These days, Barbie hardly notices her age—she's too busy being a WNBA basketball player, astronaut, Olympic skater, and NASCAR race car driver.

Pursuing its mission to "engage, enchant, and empower girls," Mattel introduces new Barbie dolls every year in order to keep up with the latest definitions of achievement, glamour, romance, adventure, and nurturing. Barbie also reflects America's diverse and changing population. Mattel has produced African American Barbie dolls since 1968 and has since introduced Hispanic and Asian dolls as well. In recent years, Mattel has introduced Crystal Barbie (a gorgeous glamour doll), Puerto Rican Barbie (part of its "dolls of the world" collection), Great Shape Barbie (to tie into

the fitness craze), Flight Time Barbie (a pilot), Soccer Barbie (to tie in with the recent boom in girls' soccer), and Children's Doctor Barbie (the first in the "I Can Be" Career Series Barbies). Barbie herself has received several makeovers. The most recent one gave her a wider face, her first belly button, slightly less prominent breasts, and a more athletic body.

As a result of Mattel's adept product life-cycle handling, Barbie has kept her market allure as well as her youth. Available in 150 countries, Barbie now sells at a rate of two each second worldwide and racks up sales of more than $1.5 billion a year. If you placed head to foot every doll ever sold, Barbie and her friends would circle the globe 72 times.

Crayola Crayons

Over the past 100 years or so, Binney & Smith's Crayola crayons have become a household staple in more than 80 countries around the world. Few people can forget their first pack of "64s"—64 beau-

ties neatly arranged in the familiar green and yellow flip-top box with a sharpener on the back. The aroma of a freshly opened Crayola box still drives kids into a frenzy and takes members of the older generation back to some of their fondest childhood memories.

In some ways, Crayola crayons haven't changed much since 1903, when they were sold in an eight-pack for a nickel. But a closer look reveals that Binney & Smith has made many adjustments to keep the brand out of decline. The company has added a steady stream of new colors, shapes, sizes, and packages. It has gradually increased the number of colors from the original eight in 1903 (red, yellow, blue, green, orange, black, brown, and white) to 120 in 2003. Binney & Smith has also extended the Crayola brand to new markets such as Crayola Markers, scissors, watercolor paints, gel pens, themed stamps and stickers, and activity kits. The company has licensed the Crayola brand for use on everything from

Some products seem to defy the product life cycle: Over the years, Crayola has lived a colorful life cycle, adding a steady steam of new colors, forms, and packages.

(continued)

camera outfits, backpacks, and book-ends to cartoon cups and mousepads. Finally, the company has added several programs and services to help strengthen its relationships with Crayola customers. Its *Crayola Kids* magazine and Crayola Web site offer features for children along with interactive art and craft suggestions for parents and educators on helping develop reading skills and creativity.

Not all of Binney & Smith's life-cycle adjustments have been greeted favorably by consumers. For example, in 1990, to make room for more modern colors, it retired eight colors from the time-honored box of 64—raw umber, lemon yellow, maize, blue grey, orange yellow, orange red, green blue, and violet blue—into the Crayola Hall of Fame. The move unleashed a groundswell of

protest from loyal Crayola users, who formed such organizations as the RUMPS—the Raw Umber and Maize Preservation Society—and the National Committee to Save Lemon Yellow. Company executives were flabbergasted—"We were aware of the loyalty and nostalgia surrounding Crayola crayons," a spokesperson says, "but we didn't know we [would] hit such a nerve." The company reissued the old standards in a special collector's tin—it sold all of the 2.5 million tins made.

Thus, Crayola continues its long and colorful life cycle. Through smart product life-cycle management, Binney & Smith, now a subsidiary of Hallmark, has dominated the crayon market for almost a century. The company now makes nearly 3 billion crayons a year, enough to circle the globe six times. By the age of 10, the

average American child has worn down 730 crayons. Sixty-five percent of all American children between the ages of two and seven pick up a crayon at least once a day and color for an average of 28 minutes. Nearly 80 percent of the time, they pick up a Crayola crayon.

Sources: See "Hue and Cry over Crayola May Revive Old Colors," *Wall Street Journal*, June 14, 1991, p. B1; Margaret O. Kirk, "Coloring Our Children's World Since '03," *Chicago Tribune*, October 29, 1986, sec. 5, p. 1; "Crayola Trivia," accessed online at www.crayola.com, July 2003; Alice Cuneo and Laura Petrecca, "Barbie Has to Work Harder to Help Out Sagging Mattel," *Advertising Age*, March 6, 2000, p. 4; Christopher Palmeri, "Mattel: Up the Hill Minus Jill," *Business Week*, April 9, 2001, pp. 53–54; Alexandria Peers, "Art Journal: Goodbye Dolly!" *Wall Street Journal*, January 4, 2002, p. W1 Kate MacArthur, "Plastic Surgery: Barbie Gets a Real Makeover," *Advertising Age*, November 4, 2002, pp. 4, 53; and www.barbie.com, August 2003.

Finally, the company can try *modifying the marketing mix*—improving sales by changing one or more marketing mix elements. It can cut prices to attract new users and competitors' customers. It can launch a better advertising campaign or use aggressive sales promotions—trade deals, cents-off, premiums, and contests. Hormel Foods Corporation, maker of SPAM, recently launched a new advertising campaign and other promotions to reposition and revitalize its mature product, which has been around since the late 1930s.[27]

■ Revitalizing a mature brand: Hormel, maker of Spam, recently launched a new "crazy tasty" advertising and promotion campaign, complete with the SPAM-MOBILE, to reposition and revitalize its mature product, which has been around since the late 1930s.

Joe is the everyman that impresses crowds at barbecues, beach get-togethers, and breakfasts by offering basic-assembly SPAM recipes. . . . The pitch is that the taste of SPAM makes eggs, pizza—almost anything—better. And it's done with all the over-the-top fervor of "Monty Python's Flying Circus" famed SPAM routine. In the spots, people literally eat up the stuff, and when there's none left, Joe is able to clap his hands, yell out "More SPAM!" and call up a SPAMMOBILE that crashes the party out of the clear blue to deliver up more of the "crazy tasty" stuff. The crowd, of course, barely notices the unusual delivery, as they only have eyes for the little tins of love. The campaign tries to capture the American boldness of the brand.

In addition to pricing and promotion, the company can also move into larger market channels, using mass merchandisers, if these channels are growing. Finally, the company can offer new or improved services to buyers.

| Linking the Concepts |

Pause for a moment and think about some products that, like Crayola Crayons, have been around for a long time.

- Ask a grandparent or someone else who shaved back then to compare a 1940s or 1950s Gillette razor to the most current model. Is Gillette's latest razor really a new product or just a "retread" of the previous version? What do you conclude about product life cycles?
- The Monopoly board game has been around for decades. How has Parker Bothers protected Monopoly from old age and decline (check out www.monopoly.com)?

Decline Stage

The sales of most product forms and brands eventually dip. The decline may be slow, as in the case of oatmeal cereal, or rapid, as in the case of phonograph records. Sales may plunge to zero, or they may drop to a low level at which they continue for many years. This is the **decline stage**.

Sales decline for many reasons, including technological advances, shifts in consumer tastes, and increased competition. As sales and profits decline, some firms withdraw from the market. Those remaining may prune their product offerings. They may drop smaller market segments and marginal trade channels, or they may cut the promotion budget and reduce their prices further.

Carrying a weak product can be very costly to a firm, and not just in profit terms. There are many hidden costs. A weak product may take up too much of management's time. It often requires frequent price and inventory adjustments. It requires advertising and sales force attention that might be better used to make "healthy" products more profitable. A product's failing reputation can cause customer concerns about the company and its other products. The biggest cost may well lie in the future. Keeping weak products delays the search for replacements, creates a lopsided product mix, hurts current profits, and weakens the company's foothold on the future.

For these reasons, companies need to pay more attention to their aging products. The firm's first task is to identify those products in the decline stage by regularly reviewing sales, market shares, costs, and profit trends. Then, management must decide whether to maintain, harvest, or drop each of these declining products.

Management may decide to *maintain* its brand without change in the hope that competitors will leave the industry. For example, Procter & Gamble made good profits by remaining in the declining liquid soap business as others withdrew. Or management may decide to reposition or reformulate the brand in hopes of moving it back into the growth stage of the product life cycle. Frito-Lay did this with the classic Cracker Jack brand:

When Cracker Jack passed the 100-year-old mark, it seemed that the timeless brand was running out of time. By the time Frito-Lay acquired the classic snack-food brand from Borden Foods in 1997, sales and profits had been declining for five straight years. Frito-Lay set out to reconnect the box of candy-coated popcorn, peanuts, and a prize with a new generation of kids. "We made the popcorn bigger and fluffier with more peanuts and bigger prizes, and we put it in bags, as well as boxes," says Chris Neugent, VP-marketing for wholesome snacks for Frito-Lay. New promotional programs shared a connection with baseball and fun

Decline stage
The product life-cycle stage in which a product's sales decline.

■ Back into the growth stage: When this timeless brand was running out of time, Frito-Lay reconnected it with a new generation of kids. Sales more than doubled during the two years following the acquisition.

for kids, featuring baseball star Mark McGwire, Rawlings Sporting Goods trading cards, F.A.O. Schwartz, and Pokemon and Scooby Doo characters. The revitalized marketing pulled Cracker Jack out of decline. Sales more than doubled during the two years following the acquisition, and the brand has posted double-digit increases each year since.[28]

Management may decide to *harvest* the product, which means reducing various costs (plant and equipment, maintenance, R&D, advertising, sales force) and hoping that sales hold up. If successful, harvesting will increase the company's profits in the short run. Or management may decide to *drop* the product from the line. It can sell it to another firm or simply liquidate it at salvage value. In recent years, Procter & Gamble has sold off a number of lesser or declining brands such as Oxydol detergent and Jif peanut butter. If the company plans to find a buyer, it will not want to run down the product through harvesting.

Table 8.2 summarizes the key characteristics of each stage of the product life cycle. The table also lists the marketing objectives and strategies for each stage.[29]

TABLE 8.2 Summary of Product Life-Cycle Characteristics, Objectives, and Strategies

	Introduction	Growth	Maturity	Decline
Characteristics				
Sales	Low sales	Rapidly rising sales	Peak sales	Declining sales
Costs	High cost per customer	Average cost per customer	Low cost per customer	Low cost per customer
Profits	Negative	Rising profits	High profits	Declining profits
Customers	Innovators	Early adopters	Middle majority	Laggards
Competitors	Few	Growing number	Stable number beginning to decline	Declining number
Marketing objectives	Create product and trial	Maximize market share	Maximize profit while defending market share	Reduce expenditure and milk the brand
Strategies				
Product	Offer a basic product	Offer product extensions, service, warranty	Diversify brand and models	Phase out weak items
Price	Use cost-plus formula	Price to penetrate market	Price to match or best competitors	Cut price
Distribution	Build selective distribution	Build intensive distribution	Build more intensive distribution	Go selective: Phase out unprofitable outlets
Advertising	Build product awareness among early adopters and dealers	Build awareness and interest in the mass market	Stress brand differences and benefits	Reduce to level needed to retain hard-core loyals
Sales promotion	Use heavy sales promotion to entice trial	Reduce to take advantage of heavy consumer demand	Increase to encourage brand switching	Reduce to minimal level

Source: Philip Kotler, *Marketing Management: Analysis, Planning, Implementation, and Control,* 11th ed. (Upper Saddle River, NJ: Prentice Hall, 2003), Chapter 10.

REST STOP:
Reviewing the Concepts

Well, there's one more travel sticker on your marketing bumper. Before we move on to the next marketing mix destination, let's review the important new product and product life-cycle concepts. A company's current products face limited life spans and must be replaced by newer products. But new products can fail—the risks of innovation are as great as the rewards. The key to successful innovation lies in a total-company effort, strong planning, and a systematic *new-product development* process.

1. Explain how companies find and develop new-product ideas.

Companies find and develop new-product ideas from a variety of sources. Many new-product ideas stem from *internal sources.* Companies conduct formal research and development, pick the brains of their employees, and brainstorm at executive meetings. By conducting surveys and focus groups and analyzing *customer* questions and complaints, companies can generate new-product ideas that will meet specific consumer needs. Companies track *competitors'* offerings and inspect new products, dismantling them, analyzing their performance, and deciding whether to introduce a similar or improved product. *Distributors and suppliers* are close to the market and can pass along information about consumer problems and new-product possibilities.

2. List and define the steps in the new-product development process.

The new-product development process consists of eight sequential stages. The process starts with *idea generation.* Next comes *idea screening,* which reduces the number of ideas based on the company's own criteria. Ideas that pass the screening stage continue through *product concept development,* in which a detailed version of the new-product idea is stated in meaningful consumer terms. In the next stage, *concept testing,* new-product concepts are tested with a group of target consumers to determine whether the concepts have strong consumer appeal. Strong concepts proceed to *marketing strategy development,* in which an initial marketing strategy for the new product is developed from the product concept. In the *business analysis* stage, a review of the sales, costs, and profit projections for a new product is conducted to determine whether the new product is likely to satisfy the company's objectives. With positive results here, the ideas become more concrete through *product development* and *test marketing* and finally are launched during *commercialization.*

3. Describe the stages of the product life cycle.

Each product has a *life cycle* marked by a changing set of problems and opportunities. The sales of the typical product follow an S-shaped curve made up of five stages. The cycle begins with the *product development stage* when the company finds and develops a new-product idea. The *introduction stage* is marked by slow growth and low profits as the product is distributed to the market. If successful, the product enters a *growth stage,* which offers rapid sales growth and increasing profits. Next comes a *maturity stage,* when sales growth slows down and profits stabilize. Finally, the product enters a *decline stage,* in which sales and profits dwindle. The company's task during this stage is to recognize the decline and to decide whether it should maintain, harvest, or drop the product.

4. Describe how marketing strategies change during the product's life cycle.

In the *introduction stage*, the company must choose a launch strategy consistent with its intended product positioning. Much money is needed to attract distributors and build their inventories and to inform consumers of the new product and achieve trial. In the *growth stage,* companies continue to educate potential consumers and distributors. In addition, the company works to stay ahead of the competition and sustain rapid market growth by improving product quality, adding new product features and models, entering new market segments and distribution channels, shifting advertising from building product awareness to building product conviction and purchase, and lowering prices at the right time to attract new buyers. In the *maturity stage,* companies continue to invest in maturing products and consider modifying the market, the product, and the marketing mix. When *modifying the market,* the company attempts to increase the consumption of the current product. When *modifying the product,* the company changes some of the product's characteristics—such as quality, features, or style—to attract new users or inspire more usage. When *modifying the marketing mix,* the company works to improve sales by changing one or more of the marketing mix elements. Once the company recognizes that a product has entered the *decline stage,* management must decide whether to *maintain* the brand without change, hoping that competitors will drop out of the market; *harvest* the product, reducing costs and trying to maintain sales; or *drop* the product, selling it to another firm or liquidating it at salvage value.

Navigating the Key Terms

Business analysis
Commercialization
Concept testing
Decline stage
Fad
Fashion
Growth stage
Idea generation

Idea screening
Introduction stage
Marketing strategy
 development
Maturity stage
New-product development
Product concept
Product development

Product life cycle (PLC)
Sequential product
 development
Simultaneous (or team-based)
 product development
Style
Test marketing

Travel Log

Discussing the Issues

1. Describe some general reasons that so many new products fail. How can marketing managers use this information in the new-product development process?

2. Describe the major internal and external sources of new-product ideas. Which source do you think develops the best ideas? Which source delivers the most ideas? Explain your answer.

3. Discuss the difference between the following terms: product idea, product concept, and product image. How are they related to each other?

4. Compare sequential product development to simultaneous product development. What are the advantages and disadvantages of each approach?

5. Describe product classes that you feel represent each stage of the product life cycle. For each product class you came up with, do you think it will progress through all five stages of the product life cycle?

6. Explain the difference between maintaining, harvesting, and dropping a brand. Why would a company select one of these strategies over the other in a declining market?

Application Questions

1. Develop this new-product idea into three different product concepts: a sensor about the size of a quarter that measures ultraviolet rays from the sun and can sound an alarm when it is exposed to dangerous levels for a sustained time. Which product concept do you think is most viable? Explain your answer.

2. Take one of the product concepts you developed in the previous question and conduct a limited concept test by asking 10 people the questions in Table 8.1. The questions will have to be modified for your particular product concept. Summarize and report the results at the next class meeting.

3. Discuss a product that you feel has been modified to meet changing consumer needs and thus has been able to stay in the maturity stage of the PLC. What was modified: the market, the product, or the marketing mix? Explain your answer.

Under the Hood: Focus on Technology

Instead of trying to figure out exactly what consumers want, some firms let consumers design their own products. Nike has done just that by allowing consumers to completely design the look and performance of its Air Pegasus 2000 running shoe over the Internet. Consumers can select the outersole to best suit the type of surface they run on, the density of the midsole for their foot shape, the shoe width, the color for eight different areas of the shoe, and even a personalized name on the heel of the shoe.

Go to www.nikerunning.com and click on "create your own shoe" under the "gear" link (note that this feature requires the Macromedia Flash plug-in be installed on your computer—you will be prompted to download this if it is not currently installed). Go through the steps of creating an Air Pegasus 2000 running shoe and then respond to the following questions.

1. What do you think of the ability to create your own running shoe online? Do you think this capability provides a competitive advantage for Nike over rival running shoe manufacturers?

2. Why doesn't Nike just select several variations and sell those rather than allow consumers to customize the shoe? Describe the target market most likely to make its own shoes with this process.

3. What disadvantages might there be for Nike in allowing consumers to create their own running shoes? How can those disadvantages be minimized?

In 2004, Honda will become the first auto manufacturer to sell natural-gas-powered cars to the general public. Typically these vehicles have been sold in small fleets to entities, often governmental organizations, which use them for short trips and have the capacity to own their own natural gas refilling locations. That will change as Honda introduces a device that will allow owners to refill their vehicles in their own garages. Honda envisions eventually selling tens of thousands of these natural-gas-powered vehicles, mainly as a family's second vehicle or as a commuter car. Natural gas vehicles cost about 80 percent of what it costs to run gasoline vehicles.

1. Describe how you would construct a test market for this new product.

2. What major activities will Honda need to accomplish to make the commercialization phase of this new product launch successful?

3. How should Honda position the new natural gas powered vehicles relative to its traditional line of cars?

Focus on Ethics

Beating competitors to the marketplace with a product can result in substantial first-mover advantages for the initial market entrant. At times, this places tremendous pressure on a company's employees to speed through the product development process as fast as possible. In such cases, skipping or reducing the level of effort placed on stages in the development process (e.g., comprehensive safety testing) may become attractive alternatives for meeting tight timelines. Even the

false reporting of outcomes associated with product testing may be encountered when employees are pressured to get a product to market as soon as possible.

1. What can a company do to ensure that all the necessary product development steps are adequately followed under the pressure of being first to market? What controls might be put in place?

2. Discuss the potential negative consequences of rushing a new product to market.

Videos

The eGo Bikes video case that accompanies this chapter is located in Appendix 1 at the back of the book.

Student Materials

Need a tune-up? A study guide and OneKey access code are available to aid in your review of chapter material. Your instructor may choose to have these items shrink-wrapped with your text or you may purchase them separately at www.prenhall.com/marketing.

to stay in—from one-star ("economy hotels that provide comfort with no frills") to five-star ("the best that money can buy"). Give Priceline the usual billing information and a credit card number and decide how much you'd like to bid. Click on "Buy My Hotel Room," then sit back and wait for Priceline to broker the deal. Within 15 minutes, Priceline e-mails you with the news. If no suitable hotel is willing to accept your price, you can bid again later. If Priceline finds a taker, it immediately charges your credit card no refunds, changes, or cancellations allowed and lets you know where you'll be staying.

The concept of setting your own prices over the Internet has real appeal to consumers. It starts with a good value proposition—getting really low prices. Beyond that, "name-your-price is a great hook," say a Priceline marketing executive. "If you get it, it's like 'I won!'" As a result, Priceline is attracting more and more customers. Its customer base has grown to almost 17 million users, and as many as 9 million people visit the Priceline site monthly. Through its recent acquisition of Lowestfare.com and by forging strategic partnerships with companies such as eBay and AOL, over the past year Priceline has extended its online audience by 810 percent, now reaching more than 85 million unique Web users. Since it opened for business in 1998, Priceline has sold more than 15 million airline tickets, 7 million hotel room nights, and 6.5 million rental car days.

Despite accepting fire-sale prices, sellers also benefit from Priceline's services. It's especially attractive to those who sell products that have "time sensitivity." "If airlines or hotels don't sell seats on particular flights or rooms for certain nights, those assets become worthless," comments an analyst. "Such businesses are a natural fit for Priceline." Moreover, notes the analyst, "by requiring customers to commit to payment up front with their credit card, retailers face little risk in dumping excess inventory. It's particularly attractive in markets that have huge fixed costs from creating capacity and relatively small marginal costs, like air travel, cruise ships, and automobiles."

Priceline makes its money by buying up unsold rooms, seats, or vacation packages at heavily discounted rates, marking them up, and selling them to consumers for as much as a 12 percent return. So, on a $215 plane ticket, Priceline makes about $35, compared to the $10 gross profit made by a traditional travel agent.

Along with the successes and recent profitability, however, Priceline has encountered some formidable obstacles. For example, not all products lend themselves to Priceline's quirky business model, and the company has met with uneven success in attempts to grow beyond travel services. Although it currently takes bids in other categories, such as home financing products (home mortgages, refinancing, and home equity loans), selling products and services that aren't time sensitive has proven difficult. Priceline has tried its hand unsuccessfully at selling a variety of things, including new cars and long distance services. Last year's efforts to expand into gasoline also blew up. Priceline had no trouble lining up customers interested in buying gas over the Internet. Unfortunately, however, gas and oil companies had no incentive to dump excess inventories because gas is not a perishable good. As a result, after only eight months but millions of dollars in losses, Priceline closed its virtual gas pumps.

Moreover, not all customers are thrilled with their Priceline experiences. Forcing customers to commit to purchases before they know the details such as which hotel or airline, flight times, and hotel locations can leave some customers feeling cheated. One frustrated user recently summed up his Priceline experience this way: "You don't get what you think you're gonna get."

But for every disappointed customer, Priceline has hundreds or thousands of happy ones. Some 64 percent of those who now visit Priceline to name their own prices are repeat customers. You don't have to go far to get positive testimonials such as these:

Using Priceline.com has worked out great! I remember the first time I used it. I'm not very technically savvy, but after navigating around the site, I set what I thought was a low-ball price. It turns out that my offer was accepted and I saved more than 50 percent off the normal room rate. The hotel was great. In fact, I usually stay there when traveling, so I also knew I was getting it for a great price.

I discovered Priceline.com and decided to try it out to visit my college roommate. She's in Albuquerque, New Mexico, and I'm in Hanover, Germany. The best price from the airlines was too high. After reading about priceline.com, I decided I had nothing to lose by trying it to get a better deal. I offered a low price but was sure I wouldn't stand the slightest chance of an acceptance. To my amazement, within 20 minutes of logging in, I received a happy "congratulations" e-mail from Priceline. The visit was wonderful, my friend was amazed, and I've been telling everyone (lots of seasoned travelers who didn't believe my story at first) from Germany to the United States about this spectacular new way to travel.

More than just changing how people pay for travel services, Priceline is perhaps the best example of how the Internet is changing today's pricing practices. "Only through the Web could you match millions of bids with millions of products, all without a fixed price," says one analyst. "In the offline world, this would be a strange market indeed," says another. Try to imagine a real-world situation in which "buyers attach money to a board, along with a note stating what they want to buy for the sum. Later, sellers come along and have a look. If they like an offer, they take the money and deliver the goods." It couldn't happen anywhere but on the Web.[2]

Companies today face a fierce and fast-changing pricing environment. The recent economic downturn has put many companies in a "pricing vise." One analyst sums it up this way: "They have virtually no pricing power. It's impossible to raise prices, and often, the pressure to slash them continues unabated." It seems that almost every company is slashing prices, and that is hurting their profits.[3]

Yet, cutting prices is often not the best answer. Reducing prices unnecessarily can lead to lost profits and damaging price wars. It can signal to customers that price is more important than brand. Instead, companies should "sell value, not price."[4] They should persuade customers that paying a higher price for the company's brand is justified by the greater value it delivers. The challenge is to find the price that will let the company make a fair profit by harvesting the customer value it creates.

What Is a Price?

In the narrowest sense, **price** is the amount of money charged for a product or service. More broadly, price is the sum of all the values that consumers exchange for the benefits of having or using the product or service. Historically, price has been the major factor affecting buyer choice. However, in recent decades, nonprice factors have become more important in buyer-choice behavior.

Throughout most of history, prices were set by negotiation between buyers and sellers. *Fixed price* policies—setting one price for all buyers—is a relatively modern idea that arose with the development of large-scale retailing at the end of the nineteenth century. Now, some one hundred years later, many companies are reversing the fixed pricing trend. They are taking us back to an era of **dynamic pricing** charging different prices depending on individual customers and situations (see Marketing at Work 9.1). The Internet, corporate networks, and wireless communications are connecting sellers and buyers as never before. Web sites such as Compare.Net and PriceScan.com allow buyers to compare products and prices quickly and easily. Online auction sites such as eBay.com and Amazon.com Auctions make it easy for buyers and sellers to negotiate prices on thousands of items—from refurbished computers to antique tin trains. Sites like Priceline let customers set their own prices. At the same time, new technologies allow sellers to collect

Price

The amount of money charged for a product or service, or the sum of the values that consumers exchange for the benefits of having or using the product or service.

Dynamic pricing

Charging different prices depending on individual customers and situations.

FIGURE 9.1

Factors Affecting Pricing Decisions

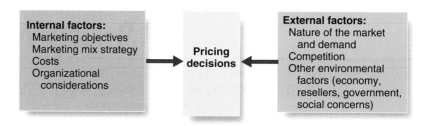

In this chapter, we focus on the process of setting prices. We look first at the factors marketers must consider when setting prices and at general pricing approaches. Then, we examine pricing strategies for new-product pricing, product mix pricing, price adjustments for buyer and situational factors, and price changes.

Factors to Consider When Setting Prices

A company's pricing decisions are affected by both internal company factors and external environmental factors (see Figure 9.1).[6]

Internal Factors Affecting Pricing Decisions

Internal factors affecting pricing include the company's marketing objectives, marketing mix strategy, costs, and organizational considerations.

Marketing Objectives   Before setting price, the company must decide on its strategy for the product. If the company has selected its target market and positioning carefully, then its marketing mix strategy, including price, will be fairly straightforward. For example, when Honda and Toyota decided to develop their Acura and Lexus brands to compete with European luxury-performance cars in the higher-income segment, this required charging a high price. In contrast, Motel 6, EconoLodge, and Red Roof Inn have positioned themselves as motels that provide economical rooms for budget-minded travelers; this position requires charging a low price. Thus, pricing strategy is largely determined by decisions on market positioning.

At the same time, the company may seek additional general or specific objectives. General objectives include survival, current profit maximization, market share leadership, and product quality leadership. At a more specific level, a company can set prices low to prevent competition from entering the market or set prices at competitors' levels to stabilize the market. Prices can be set to keep the loyalty and support of resellers or to avoid government intervention. Prices can be reduced temporarily to create excitement for a product or to draw more customers into a retail store. One product may be priced to help the sales of other products in the company's line. Thus, pricing may play an important role in helping to accomplish the company's objectives at many levels.

Marketing Mix Strategy   Price is only one of the marketing mix tools that a company uses to achieve its marketing objectives. Price decisions must be coordinated with product design, distribution, and promotion decisions to form a consistent and effective marketing program. Decisions made for other marketing mix variables may affect pricing decisions. For example, producers using many resellers who are expected to support and promote their products may have to build larger reseller margins into their prices. The

■ Product quality leadership: Four Seasons starts with very-high-quality service—"we await you with the perfect sanctuary." It then charges a price to match.

decision to position the product on high-performance quality will mean that the seller must charge a higher price to cover higher costs.

Companies often position their products on price and then tailor other marketing mix decisions to the prices they want to charge. Here, price is a crucial product-positioning factor that defines the product's market, competition, and design. Many firms support such price-positioning strategies with a technique called **target costing**, a potent strategic weapon. Target costing reverses the usual process of first designing a new product, determining its cost, and then asking, "Can we sell it for that?" Instead, it starts with an ideal selling price based on customer considerations, then targets costs that will ensure that the price is met.

P&G used target costing to price and develop its highly successful Crest SpinBrush electric toothbrush:

> P&G usually prices its goods at a premium. But with Crest SpinBrush, P&G reversed its usual thinking. It started with an attractive low market price, and then found a way to make a profit at that price. SpinBrush's inventors first came up with the idea of a low-priced electric toothbrush while walking through their local Wal-Mart, where they saw Sonicare, Interplak, and other electric toothbrushes priced at more than $50. These pricy brushes held only a fraction of the overall toothbrush market. A less expensive electric toothbrush, the designers reasoned, would have huge potential. They decided on a target price of just $5, batteries included—only $1 more than the most expensive manual brushes—and set out design a brush they could sell at that price. Every design element was carefully considered with the targeted price in mind. To meet the low price, P&G passed on the usual lavish new-product launch campaign. Instead, to give SpinBrush more point-of-sale impact, it relied on "Try Me" packaging that allowed consumers to turn the brush on in stores. Target cost pricing has made Crest SpinBrush one of P&G's most successful new products ever. It has now become the nation's best-selling toothbrush, manual or electric, with a more than 40 percent share of the electric toothbrush market. Says brand manager Darin Yates, "It's hard for P&G's business models to conceive of a business growing as quickly as SpinBrush."[7]

Other companies deemphasize price and use other marketing mix tools to create *nonprice* positions. Often, the best strategy is not to charge the lowest price, but rather to differentiate the marketing offer to make it worth a higher price. For example, Sony builds more value into its consumer electronics products and charges a higher price than many competitors. Customers recognize Sony's higher quality and are willing to pay more to get it.

Thus, marketers must consider the total marketing mix when setting prices. If the product is positioned on nonprice factors, then decisions about quality, promotion, and distribution will strongly affect price. If price is a crucial positioning factor, then price will strongly affect decisions made about the other marketing mix elements. But even when featuring price, marketers need to remember that customers rarely buy on price alone. Instead, they seek products that give them the best value in terms of benefits received for the price paid.

Costs Costs set the floor for the price that the company can charge. The company wants to charge a price that both covers all its costs for producing, distributing, and selling the product and delivers a fair rate of return for its effort and risk. A company's costs may be an important element in its pricing strategy. Many companies, such as Southwest Airlines, Wal-Mart, and Union Carbide, work to become the "low-cost producers" in their industries. Companies with lower costs can set lower prices that result in greater sales and profits.

A company's costs take two forms, fixed and variable. **Fixed costs** (also known as overhead) are costs that do not vary with production or sales level. For example, a company must pay each month's bills for rent, heat, interest, and executive salaries, whatever the company's output. **Variable costs** vary directly with the level of production. Each personal computer produced by Compaq involves a cost of computer chips, wires, plastic, packaging, and other inputs. These costs tend to be the same for each unit produced. They

Target costing

Pricing that starts with an ideal selling price, then targets costs that will ensure that the price is met.

Fixed costs

Costs that do not vary with production or sales level.

Variable costs

Costs that vary directly with the level of production.

Total costs
The sum of the fixed and variable costs for any given level of production.

are called variable because their total varies with the number of units produced. **Total costs** are the sum of the fixed and variable costs for any given level of production. Management wants to charge a price that will at least cover the total production costs at a given level of production.

The company must watch its costs carefully. If it costs the company more than it costs competitors to produce and sell its product, the company will have to charge a higher price or make less profit, putting it at a competitive disadvantage.

Organizational Considerations Management must decide who within the organization should set prices. Companies handle pricing in a variety of ways. In small companies, prices are often set by top management rather than by the marketing or sales departments. In large companies, pricing is typically handled by divisional or product-line managers. In industrial markets, salespeople may be allowed to negotiate with customers within certain price ranges. Even so, top management sets the pricing objectives and policies, and it often approves the prices proposed by lower-level management or salespeople.

In industries in which pricing is a key factor (aerospace, steel, railroads, oil companies), companies often have a pricing department to set the best prices or help others in setting them. This department reports to the marketing department or top management. Others who have an influence on pricing include sales managers, production managers, finance managers, and accountants.

External Factors Affecting Pricing Decisions

External factors that affect pricing decisions include the nature of the market and demand, competition, and other environmental elements.

The Market and Demand Whereas costs set the lower limit of prices, the market and demand set the upper limit. Both consumer and industrial buyers balance the price of a product or service against the benefits of owning it. Thus, before setting prices, the marketer must understand the relationship between price and demand for its product. In this section, we explain how the price–demand relationship varies for different types of markets and how buyer perceptions of price affect the pricing decision. We then discuss methods for measuring the price–demand relationship.

Pricing in Different Types of Markets. The seller's pricing freedom varies with different types of markets. Economists recognize four types of markets, each presenting a different pricing challenge.

Under *pure competition*, the market consists of many buyers and sellers trading in a uniform commodity such as wheat, copper, or financial securities. No single buyer or seller has much effect on the going market price. A seller cannot charge more than the going price, because buyers can obtain as much as they need at the going price. Nor would sellers charge less than the market price, because they can sell all they want at this price. If price and profits rise, new sellers can easily enter the market. In a purely competitive market, marketing research, product development, pricing, advertising, and sales promotion play little or no role. Thus, sellers in these markets do not spend much time on marketing strategy.

Under *monopolistic competition*, the market consists of many buyers and sellers who trade over a range of prices rather than a single market price. A range of prices occurs because sellers can differentiate their offers to buyers. Either the physical product can be varied in quality, features, or style, or the accompanying services can be varied. Buyers see differences in sellers' products and will pay different prices for them. Sellers try to develop differentiated offers for different customer segments and, in addition to price, freely use branding, advertising, and personal selling to set their offers apart. Thus, Kinko's differentiates its offer through strong branding and advertising, reducing the impact of price. Because there are many competitors in such markets, each firm is less affected by competitors' pricing strategies than in oligopolistic markets.

Under *oligopolistic competition*, the market consists of a few sellers who are highly sensitive to each other's pricing and marketing strategies. The product can be uniform (steel, aluminum) or nonuniform (cars, computers). There are few sellers because it is difficult for new sellers to enter the market. Each seller is alert to competitors' strategies and moves. If a steel company slashes its price by 10 percent, buyers will quickly switch to this supplier. The other steelmakers must respond by lowering their prices or increasing their services.

In a *pure monopoly*, the market consists of one seller. The seller may be a government monopoly (the U.S. Postal Service), a private regulated monopoly (a power company), or a private nonregulated monopoly (DuPont when it introduced nylon). Pricing is handled differently in each case. In a regulated monopoly, the government permits the company to set rates that will yield a "fair return," one that will let the company maintain and expand its operations as needed. Nonregulated monopolies are free to price at what the market will bear. However, they do not always charge the full price for a number of reasons: a desire not to attract competition, a desire to penetrate the market faster with a low price, or a fear of government regulation.

Consumer Perceptions of Price and Value. In the end, the consumer will decide whether a product's price is right. Pricing decisions, like other marketing mix decisions, must be buyer oriented. When consumers buy a product, they exchange something of value (the price) to get something of value (the benefits of having or using the product). Effective, buyer-oriented pricing involves understanding how much value consumers place on the benefits they receive from the product and setting a price that fits this value.

■ Monopolistic competition: Canadian pickle marketer Bick's sets its pickles apart from other brands by using both price and nonprice factors.

A company often finds it hard to measure the values customers will attach to its product. For example, calculating the cost of ingredients in a meal at a fancy restaurant is relatively easy. But assigning a value to other satisfactions such as taste, environment, relaxation, conversation, and status is very hard. And these values will vary both for different consumers and different situations. Still, consumers will use these values to evaluate a product's price. If customers perceive that the price is greater than the product's value, they will not buy the product. If consumers perceive that the price is below the product's value, they will buy it, but the seller loses profit opportunities.

Analyzing the Price–Demand Relationship. Each price the company might charge will lead to a different level of demand. The relationship between the price charged and the resulting demand level is shown in the **demand curve** in Figure 9.2. The demand curve shows the number of units the market will buy in a given time period at different prices that might be charged. In the normal case, demand and price are inversely related; that is, the higher the price, the lower the demand. Thus, the company would sell less if it raised its price from P_1 to P_2. In short, consumers with limited budgets probably will buy less of something if its price is too high.

In the case of prestige goods, the demand curve sometimes slopes upward. Consumers think that higher prices mean more quality. For example, Gibson Guitar Corporation

Demand curve

A curve that shows the number of units the market will buy in a given time period at different prices that might be charged.

The manufacturer that made the toaster probably used cost-plus pricing. If the manufacturer's standard cost of producing the toaster was $16, it might have added a 25 percent markup, setting the price to the retailers at $20. Similarly, construction companies submit job bids by estimating the total project cost and adding a standard markup for profit. Lawyers, accountants, and other professionals typically price by adding a standard markup to their costs. Some sellers tell their customers they will charge cost plus a specified markup; for example, aerospace companies price this way to the government.

Does using standard markups to set prices make sense? Generally, no. Any pricing method that ignores demand and competitor prices is not likely to lead to the best price. Still, markup pricing remains popular for many reasons. First, sellers are more certain about costs than about demand. By tying the price to cost, sellers simplify pricing—they do not have to make frequent adjustments as demand changes. Second, when all firms in the industry use this pricing method, prices tend to be similar, and price competition is thus minimized. Third, many people feel that cost-plus pricing is fairer to both buyers and sellers. Sellers earn a fair return on their investment but do not take advantage of buyers when buyers' demand becomes great.

Break-even pricing (target profit pricing)

Setting price to break even on the costs of making and marketing a product; or setting price to make a target profit.

Another cost-oriented pricing approach is **break-even pricing**, or a variation called **target profit pricing**. The firm tries to determine the price at which it will break even or make the target profit it is seeking. Target pricing uses the concept of a *break-even chart*, which shows the total cost and total revenue expected at different sales volume levels. Figure 9.4 shows a break-even chart for the toaster manufacturer discussed here. Here, fixed costs are $6 million regardless of sales volume, and variable costs are $5 per unit. Variable costs are added to fixed costs to form total costs, which rise with each unit sold. The slope of the total revenue curve reflects the price. Here, the price is $15 (for example, the company's revenue is $12 million on 800,000 units, or $15 per unit).

At the $15 price, the company must sell at least 600,000 units to *break even*—that is, at this level, total revenues will equal total costs of $9 million. If the company wants a target profit of $2 million, it must sell at least 800,000 units to obtain the $12 million of total revenue needed to cover the costs of $10 million plus the $2 million of target profits. In contrast, if the company charges a higher price, say $20 million, it will not need to sell as many units to break even or to achieve its target profit. In fact, the higher the price, the lower the company's break-even point will be.

However, as the *price* increases, *demand* decreases, and the market may not buy even the lower volume needed to break even at the higher price. Much depends on the relationship between price and demand. For example, suppose the company calculates that given its current fixed and variable costs, it must charge a price of $30 for the product in order to earn its desired target profit. But marketing research shows that few consumers will pay more than $25. In this case, the company will have to trim its costs in order to lower the break-even point so that it can charge the lower price consumers expect.

FIGURE 9.4

Break-Even Chart for Determining Target Price

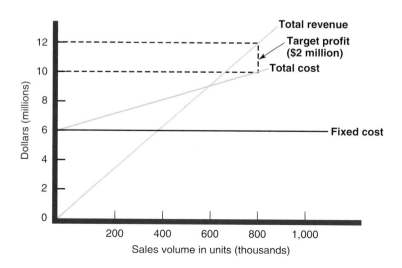

Thus, although break-even analysis and target profit pricing can help the company to determine minimum prices needed to cover expected costs and profits, they do not take the price–demand relationship into account. When using this method, the company must also consider the impact of price on sales volume needed to realize target profits and the likelihood that the needed volume will be achieved at each possible price.

Value-Based Pricing

An increasing number of companies are basing their prices on the product's perceived value. **Value-based pricing** uses buyers' perceptions of value, not the seller's cost, as the key to pricing. Value-based pricing means that the marketer cannot design a product and marketing program and then set the price. Price is considered along with the other marketing mix variables *before* the marketing program is set.

Figure 9.5 compares cost-based pricing with value-based pricing. Cost-based pricing is product driven. The company designs what it considers to be a good product, totals the costs of making the product, and sets a price that covers costs plus a target profit. Marketing must then convince buyers that the product's value at that price justifies its purchase. If the price turns out to be too high, the company must settle for lower markups or lower sales, both resulting in disappointing profits.

Value-based pricing reverses this process. The company sets its target price based on customer perceptions of the product value. The targeted value and price then drive decisions about product design and what costs can be incurred. As a result, pricing begins with analyzing consumer needs and value perceptions, and the price is set to match consumers' perceived value. It's important to remember that "good value" is not the same as "low price." For example, a Steinway piano sells at a higher price than many competing brands. But to those who buy one, it's a great value. For them, as a recent ad proclaims, "a Steinway takes you places you've never been."

A company using value-based pricing must find out what value buyers assign to different competitive offers. However, measuring perceived value can be difficult. Sometimes, companies ask consumers how much they would pay for a basic product and for each benefit added to the offer. Or a company might conduct experiments to test the perceived value of different product offers. According to an old Russian proverb, there are

A Steinway takes you places you've never been.

STEINWAY & SONS

Call 1-800-346-5086 for a complimentary color catalog and the name of your nearest Steinway dealer. Or visit us at www.steinway.com

■ Perceived value: A less expensive piano might play well, but would it take you places you've never been?

Value-based pricing

Setting price based on buyers' perceptions of value rather than on the seller's cost.

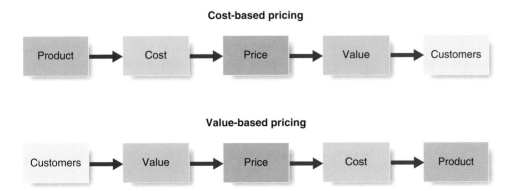

Cost-based pricing

Product → Cost → Price → Value → Customers

Value-based pricing

Customers → Value → Price → Cost → Product

FIGURE 9.5

Cost-Based Versus Value-Based Pricing

Source: Thomas T. Nagle and Reed K. Holden, *The strategy and Tactics of Pricing*, 3rd ed. (Upper Saddle River, NJ: Prentice Hall, 2002), p. 4.

two fools in every market—one who asks too much and one who asks too little. If the seller charges more than the buyers' perceived value, the company's sales will suffer. If the seller charges less, it products sell very well, but they produce less revenue than they would if they were priced at the level of perceived value.

Value Pricing During the past decade, marketers have noted a fundamental shift in consumer attitudes toward price and quality. Many companies have changed their pricing approaches to bring them into line with changing economic conditions and consumer price perceptions. More and more, marketers have adopted **value pricing** strategies—offering just the right combination of quality and good service at a fair price. In many cases, this has involved introducing less expensive versions of established, brand name products. Campbell introduced its Great Starts Budget frozen-food line, Holiday Inn opened several Holiday Express budget hotels, Revlon's Charles of the Ritz offered the Express Bar collection of affordable cosmetics, and fast-food restaurants such as Taco Bell and McDonald's offered "value menus." In other cases, value pricing has involved redesigning existing brands to offer more quality for a given price or the same quality for less.

An important type of value pricing at the retail level is *everyday low pricing (EDLP)*. EDLP involves charging a constant, everyday low price with few or no temporary price discounts. In contrast, *high-low pricing* involves charging higher prices on an everyday basis but running frequent promotions to lower prices temporarily on selected items. In recent years, high-low pricing has given way to EDLP in retail settings ranging from Saturn car dealerships to upscale department stores such as Nordstrom.

The king of EDLP is Wal-Mart, which practically defined the concept. Except for a few sale items every month, Wal-Mart promises everyday low prices on everything it sells. In contrast, Kmart's recent attempts to match Wal-Mart's EDLP strategy failed. To offer everyday low prices, a company must first have everyday low costs. However, because Kmart's costs are much higher than Wal-Mart's, it could not make money at the lower prices and quickly abandoned the attempt.[10]

Value-Added Marketing In many business-to-business marketing situations, the challenge is to build the company's *pricing power* its power to escape price competition and to justify higher prices and margins without losing market share. To do this, many companies adopt *value-added* strategies. Rather than cutting prices to match competitors, they attach value-added services to differentiate their offers and thus support higher margins.

When a company finds its major competitors offering a similar product at a lower price, the natural tendency is to try to match or beat that price. Although the idea of undercutting competitor's prices and watching customers flock in is tempting, there are dangers. Price-cutting can lead to price wars that erode the profit margins of all competitors in an industry. Or worse, discounting a product can cheapen it in the minds of customers. This greatly reduces the seller's power to maintain profitable prices in the long term. "It ends up being a losing battle," notes one marketing executive. "You focus away from quality, service, prestige—the things brands are all about."[11]

So, how can a company keep its pricing power when a competitor undercuts its price? Often, the best strategy is not to price below the competitor, but rather to price above and convince customers that the product is worth it. The company should ask, "What is the value of the product to the customer?" then stand up for what the product is worth. In this way, the company shifts the focus from price to value. Caterpillar is a master at value-added marketing[12]:

> Caterpillar charges premium prices for its heavy construction and mining equipment by convincing customers that its products and service justify every additional cent—or, rather, the extra tens of thousands of dollars. Caterpillar typically reaps a 20 to 30 percent price premium over competitors that can amount to an extra $200,000 or more on one of those huge yellow million-dollar dump trucks. When a large potential customer says, "I can get it for less from a competi-

Value pricing
Offering just the right combination of quality and good service at a fair price.

tor," rather than discounting the price, the Caterpillar dealer explains that, even at the higher price, Cat offers the best value. Caterpillar equipment is designed with modular components that can be removed and repaired quickly, minimizing machine downtime. Caterpillar dealers carry an extensive parts inventory and guarantee delivery within 48 hours anywhere in the world, again minimizing downtime. Cat's products are designed to be rebuilt, providing a "second life" that competitors cannot match. As a result, Caterpillar used-equipment prices are often 20 to 30 percent higher. In all, the dealer explains, even at the higher initial price, Caterpillar equipment delivers the lowest total cost per cubic yard of earth moved, ton of coal uncovered, or mile of road graded over the life of the product—guaranteed! Most customers seem to agree with Caterpillar's value proposition—the company dominates its markets with a more than 40 percent worldwide market share.

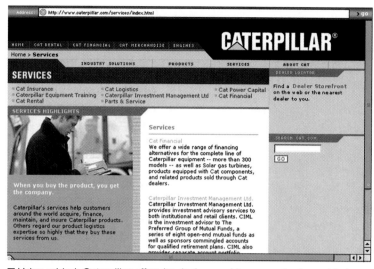

■ Value added: Caterpillar offers its dealers a wide range of value-added services—from guaranteed parts delivery to investment management advice and equipment training. Such added value supports a higher price.

Linking the Concepts

SPEED BUMP

The concept of value is critical to good pricing and to successful marketing in general. Slow down for a minute and be certain that you appreciate what value really means.

- A few years ago, Buick pitched its top-of-the-line Park Avenue model as "America's best car value." Does this fit with your idea of value?
- Pick two competing brands from a familiar product category (watches, perfume, consumer electronics, restaurants)—one low priced and the other high priced. Which, if either, offers the greatest value?
- Does "value" mean the same thing as "low price"? How do these concepts differ?

Competition-Based Pricing

Consumers will base their judgments of a product's value on the prices that competitors charge for similar products. One form of **competition-based pricing** is *going-rate pricing*, in which a firm bases its price largely on competitors' prices, with less attention paid to its own costs or to demand. The firm might charge the same as, more than, or less than its major competitors. In oligopolistic industries that sell a commodity such as steel, paper, or fertilizer, firms normally charge the same price. The smaller firms follow the leader: They change their prices when the market leader's prices change, rather than when their own demand or costs change. Some firms may charge a bit more or less, but they hold the amount of difference constant. Thus, minor gasoline retailers usually charge a few cents less than the major oil companies, without letting the difference increase or decrease.

Going-rate pricing is quite popular. When demand elasticity is hard to measure, firms feel that the going price represents the collective wisdom of the industry concerning the price that will yield a fair return. They also feel that holding to the going price will prevent harmful price wars.

Competition-based pricing is also used when firms *bid* for jobs. Using *sealed-bid pricing*, a firm bases its price on how it thinks competitors will price rather than on its own costs or on the demand. The firm wants to win a contract, and winning the contract

Competition-based pricing

Setting prices based on the prices that competitors charge for similar products.

requires pricing less than other firms. Yet the firm cannot set its price below a certain level. It cannot price below cost without harming its position. In contrast, the higher the company sets its price above its costs, the lower its chance of getting the contract.

No matter what general pricing approach the company uses, pricing decisions are subject to an incredibly complex array of environmental and competitive forces. A company sets not a single price, but rather a *pricing structure* that covers different items in its line. This pricing structure changes over time as products move through their life cycles. The company adjusts product prices to reflect changes in costs and demand and to account for variations in buyers and situations. As the competitive environment changes, the company considers when to initiate price changes and when to respond to them.

We now examine the major dynamic pricing strategies available to management. In turn, we look at *new-product pricing strategies* for products in the introductory stage of the product life cycle, *product mix pricing strategies* for related products in the product mix, *price-adjustment strategies* that account for customer differences and changing situations, and strategies for initiating and responding to *price changes*.[13]

◼◼ New-Product Pricing Strategies

Pricing strategies usually change as the product passes through its life cycle. The introductory stage is especially challenging. Companies bringing out a new product face the challenge of setting prices for the first time. They can choose between two broad strategies: *market-skimming pricing* and *market-penetration pricing*.

Market-Skimming Pricing

Market-skimming pricing

Setting a high price for a new product to skim maximum revenues layer by layer from the segments willing to pay the high price; the company makes fewer but more profitable sales.

Many companies that invent new products initially set high prices to "skim" revenues layer by layer from the market. Sony frequently uses this strategy, called **market-skimming pricing**. When Sony introduced the world's first high-definition television (HDTV) to the Japanese market in 1990, the high-tech sets cost $43,000. These televisions were purchased only by customers who could afford to pay a high price for the new technology. Sony rapidly reduced the price over the next several years to attract new buyers. By 1993, a 28-inch HDTV cost a Japanese buyer just over $6,000. In 2001, a Japanese consumer could buy a 40-inch HDTV for about $2,000, a price that many more customers could afford. An entry-level HDTV set now sells for just $1,000 in the United States. In this way, Sony skimmed the maximum amount of revenue from the various segments of the market.[14]

Market skimming makes sense only under certain conditions. First, the product's quality and image must support its higher price, and enough buyers must want the product at that price. Second, the costs of producing a smaller volume cannot be so high that they cancel the advantage of charging more. Finally, competitors should not be able to enter the market easily and undercut the high price.

Market-Penetration Pricing

Market-penetration pricing

Setting a low price for a new product in order to attract a large number of buyers and a large market share.

Rather than setting a high initial price to skim off small but profitable market segments, some companies use **market-penetration pricing**. They set a low initial price in order to *penetrate* the market quickly and deeply—to attract a large number of buyers quickly and win a large market share. The high sales volume results in falling costs, allowing the company to cut its price even further. For example, Wal-Mart and other discount retailers use penetration pricing. And Dell used penetration pricing to enter the personal computer market, selling high-quality computer products through lower-cost direct channels. Its sales soared when IBM, Apple, and other competitors selling through retail stores could not match its prices.

Several conditions must be met for this low-price strategy to work. First, the market must be highly price sensitive so that a low price produces more market growth. Second, production and distribution costs must fall as sales volume increases. Finally, the low price must help keep out the competition, and the penetration pricer must maintain its low-price position—otherwise, the price advantage may be only temporary. For example, Dell faced difficult